Oxford Beginner's German Dictionary

First edition

OXFORD
UNIVERSITY PRESS

OXFORD
UNIVERSITY PRESS

Great Clarendon Street, Oxford OX2 6DP

Oxford University Press is a department of the University of Oxford.
It furthers the University's objective of excellence in research, scholarship,
and education by publishing worldwide in

Oxford New York

Auckland Cape Town Dar es Salaam Hong Kong Karachi
Kuala Lumpur Madrid Melbourne Mexico City Nairobi
New Delhi Shanghai Taipei Toronto

With offices in

Argentina Austria Brazil Chile Czech Republic France Greece
Guatemala Hungary Italy Japan Poland Portugal Singapore
South Korea Switzerland Thailand Turkey Ukraine Vietnam

Oxford is a registered trade mark of Oxford University Press
in the UK and in certain other countries

Published in the United States
by Oxford University Press Inc., New York

© Oxford University Press 2006

British Library Cataloguing in Publication Data
Data available

Library of Congress Cataloging in Publication Data
Data available

ISBN 0-19-929857-2
ISBN 978-0-19-929857-0

10 9 8 7 6 5 4 3 2 1

Typeset in Swift and Arial
Printed in Italy by Legoprint S.p.A.

Contents

Contributors

Chief Editors
Neil and Roswitha Morris

Introduction
Graham Bishop
Mary O'Neill

Appendices
Lexus Ltd.

Proprietary terms

This dictionary includes some words which are, or are asserted to be, proprietary names or trade marks. Their inclusion does not imply that they have acquired for legal purposes a non-proprietary or general significance, nor is any other judgement implied concerning their legal status. In cases where the editor has some evidence that a word is used as a proprietary name or trade mark, this is indicated by the symbol ®, but no judgement concerning the legal status of such words is made or implied thereby.

Introduction

A fresh approach

Created to meet the specific needs of English speakers who are starting to learn German, this dictionary takes a completely fresh approach to helping you make sense of the new language. We have changed the design of the entries to make them different from entries in traditional dictionaries. What exactly is it that makes the entries so different?

- they have a new, clearer layout
- they are designed to provide the information you need in a helpful, readable way with the minimum of clutter
- since you will be using the English–German and the German–English sides of the dictionary for different tasks, each side works differently and it shows in the way the information is presented.

Because of these major changes, you will find that the dictionary is a far more efficient language-learning tool for you as a beginner. Finding the right information quickly and easily will make German more satisfying to learn.

A clearer layout

Each page of the dictionary presents the information you will need in entries which are well-spaced, easy to read, and which have a consistent layout both in English and German. The main features of the new design are:

- bullet points and numbers to indicate the various uses of each word
- different typefaces as well as the symbol = to indicate the switch from one language to the other
- use of the symbol ! to indicate important grammar points
- use of the symbol ✖ to indicate INFORMAL or colloquial words
- use of the symbol ☞ to indicate words which should be used with care.

More helpful and easy to use

The entries have been designed so that you can find the information you need quickly. Many of the conventions in traditional dictionaries which you may find confusing or off-putting have been avoided, so:

- PARTS OF SPEECH and grammatical terms are written out in full for you. A separate section explains all the terms used if you should need to find out more about them.
- Explanations of specific grammar points and notes on how a word is actually used are provided in short paragraphs at appropriate places in the dictionary text.
- Groups of words which behave in a similar way, or which present similar difficulties, are treated in a consistent manner which you will quickly come to recognize. You will also find handy language notes which deal with such concepts as colours, countries, and dates.

Words in capital letters are found in the glossary

- The language used in the examples and in the signposts to the right translation has been carefully chosen to ensure that it is clear and up to date.
- At the back of the dictionary, the basics of German grammar are explained in relation to all the important PARTS OF SPEECH that are referred to in the text.

This dictionary, with its precise and lively examples, contains all the words you will need as a beginner and includes plenty of examples of British as well as American English in both the English–German and German–English texts.

Using the two sides of the dictionary to do different things

Each side of the dictionary has been separately designed to take account of the different ways in which you will use it.

The English–German side is longer. Since you are moving from your own language into German, you will need more detailed guidance. We have provided regular reminders about essential grammar rules. The signposts which pinpoint the precise context in which a word is used are there to help you choose the right translation. These 'sense indicators' are also supported with a wide selection of useful examples.

The German–English side makes the most of what you already know about your own language. The presentation of translations from German is therefore more streamlined. There is detailed treatment of the more irregular and unpredictable features of German which you may come across in newspapers and magazines, for example. A particularly useful feature is that the variations in spelling of IRREGULAR VERBS, ADJECTIVES and PLURAL NOUNS are all listed as separate entries in the word list. These words then send you to the main dictionary form where you will find the translation you are looking for.

German spelling

In 1996 changes to the spelling of some German words were agreed by the governments of Germany, Austria, and Switzerland. The old spellings became invalid in 2005.

This dictionary uses new spellings, but German headwords also list old spellings in brackets. A special symbol ⒪ⓁⒹ is used to make this clear. Where necessary, the old spelling is cross-referred to the new spelling.

Words in capital letters are found in the glossary

How to use the dictionary

Where to look for a word

Bilingual dictionaries are divided into two sections.

- The first section gives you a list of German words followed by their English equivalents as well as information about the contexts in which they are used.
- The second section gives you a list of English words followed by the German words which match their exact meaning according to the contexts in which they are used.

  Decide first which section you need to look at.

German–English

Every dictionary entry tells you whether that particular word is a VERB, an ADJECTIVE, a PREPOSITION, or another PART OF SPEECH. If you need help to find out what any PART OF SPEECH means, look it up in the glossary of grammatical terms. NOUNS are preceded in the German wordlist by the DEFINITE ARTICLE to show their GENDER: *der* for MASCULINE, *die* for FEMININE and *das* for NEUTER nouns. This is followed by the NOUN'S PLURAL form, if it has one, and then the translation:

die **Gabel**, *plural* Gabeln
= fork

VERBS are marked if they are irregular, and you will find a list of IRREGULAR VERBS in this dictionary. A note tells you if a VERB takes *sein* in the PERFECT TENSE, and SEPARABLE VERBS are marked with a vertical bar after the PREFIX:

ab|fahren *irregular verb* (**!** *sein*)
= to leave

If there is more than one PART OF SPEECH within an entry, numbers are used to separate them. Within each PART OF SPEECH, different senses are given after bullet points (•):

sicher
1 *adjective*
= safe
= certain, = sure
2 *adverb*
= safely
= certainly, = surely
sicher! = certainly!

Cross-references are marked with a ▶. These are specially useful for VERB forms that you might not otherwise recognize:

bog ▶biegen

Words in capital letters are found in the glossary

English–German

The English–German entries tend to be longer, so it is a good idea to scan the whole entry to find the sense which is closest to the one you need. Remember, different senses are marked with a •. In examples, different words with which a PHRASE can be used are put in square brackets. This means that it is possible to substitute another word for the alternatives given in the dictionary:

> **as** [intelligent | rich | strong …] **as** = so
> [intelligent | reich | stark …] wie

On this side, you will again find additional information on points of basic German grammar such as the use of *sein* when forming the PERFECT TENSE of certain VERBS and the CASE of NOUNS following PREPOSITIONS. Additional notes in entries are there to help with special points of grammar and usage:

> **along** *preposition*
>   = entlang (+ *accusative*)
>   **!** *Note that* entlang *is usually put after the noun, which is in the accusative. When* entlang *is used with a verb, it forms a new, compound verb.*
>
>   **along the street** = die Straße entlang
>   **to run along** = entlanglaufen (**!** *sein*)

In relevant entries, a number refers you to the page with a boxed note:

> **seven** *adjective*
>   = sieben ▶ **Numbers p. 282**

Getting to know your dictionary

In the central section of this dictionary—pages 165 to 172—you will find a short section of games and exercises which will help you get to know your dictionary better and to use it more effectively. Your dictionary is a very important study aid which can greatly help you to find out how the German language works and how to expand your vocabulary.

How German–English entries work

headword ····· **ab**

numbers indicating ····· **1** *preposition* (+ *dative*) = from ······· translation clearly
different PARTS OF **2** *adverb* = off ········· indicated by =
SPEECH **ab und zu** = now and again

superior numbers ·····
show different die **Bank**¹, *plural* Banken ········· PLURAL given for
words with the ····· = bank every NOUN that has
same spelling one

die **Bank²**, *plural* Bänke
= bench

decken *verb* ········· PART OF SPEECH
bullet points ····· • = to cover
indicating separate den Tisch decken = to lay the table ····· example
senses of the • jemanden decken = to cover up for
headword someone, (*in sport*) = to mark someone

····· special meaning
GENDER ····· die **EU** indicated
(*Europäische Union*) = EU ····· ABBREVIATION
····· what ABBREVIATION
stands for
fährt ▶ fahren ········· cross-reference to
division of a ····· headword
SEPARABLE VERB **hinaus|gehen** *irregular verb* (**!** *sein*)
shown by a vertical • = to go out ····· IRREGULAR VERB
bar • das Zimmer geht nach Westen hinaus = indicated (see
the room faces west **gehen** in list of
IRREGULAR VERBS)
MASCULINE/FEMININE/ ····· **jener/jene/jenes**
NEUTER forms of a **1** *adjective* = that, (*plural*) = those
headword are given **2** *pronoun* = that one, (*plural*) = those
where necessary
····· symbol drawing
das **Klo✕** *plural* Klos attention to a
= loo German word used
only in informal
situations
los|gehen *irregular verb* (**!** *sein*) ·····
possible SUBJECTS ····· • = to set off, = to start note that this verb
used with the VERB, • = (*of a button*) = to come off takes **sein** in the
giving different • = (*of a bomb*) = to go off PERFECT TENSE
translations REFLEXIVE VERB
nähern: sich nähern *verb* shown in full
= to approach

MASCULINE and ····· der **Sänger**, *plural* Sänger
FEMININE forms of = singer
NOUNS shown as
separate headwords die **Sängerin**, *plural* Sängerinnen
= singer
····· old spelling
die **Walnuss** (**Walnuß**OLD), *plural*
Walnüsse
= walnut

Words in capital letters are found in the glossary

How English–German entries work

headword ········ **adventure** *noun*
= (das) Abenteuer
·· GENDER of German
NOUNS given in
brackets

benefit
numbers indicating ········ **1** *noun*
different PARTS OF
SPEECH
(*advantage*) = (der) Vorteil
it will be to your benefit = das wird zu
deinem Vorteil sein
2 *verb* = nützen (+ *dative*) ···························· information on the
CASE taken by a
German VERB

superior numbers ········
show different
words with the
same spelling
case¹ *noun*
= (der) Fall
in case = falls

case² *noun* ·································· PART OF SPEECH
bullet points ········ • (*suitcase*) = (der) Koffer
indicating separate
senses of the
headword
• (*for spectacles*) = (das) Etui
• (*crate*) = (die) Kiste
made clear

dentist *noun*
MASCULINE and
FEMININE forms of
NOUNS given with
GENDERS
(der) Zahnarzt / (die) Zahnärztin
▶ Professions p. 298 ·································· cross-reference to a
boxed usage note
with its page
number

kick
1 *verb*
to kick someone = jemandem einen Tritt
geben
to kick the ball = den Ball schießen ··········· translation clearly
indicated by =
2 *noun* = (der) Tritt
PHRASAL VERBS ········ **kick off**
appear separately in
blue at the end of a
VERB entry
= anstoßen
kick out
to kick someone out = jemanden
rausschmeißen* ·································· symbol drawing
attention to a
German word used
only in INFORMAL
situations

lack
1 *noun* = (der) Mangel
example showing ········ **lack of** [money|interest|tact ...] = Mangel an
alternative uses of a
PHRASE
[Geld |Interesse|Takt ...]
2 *verb* = fehlen an (+ *dative*) ···························· information on the
CASE taken by a
German PREPOSITION
he lacks confidence = ihm fehlt es an
Selbstvertrauen

melt *verb*
= schmelzen (**!** *sein*) ·································· note that this VERB
takes **sein** in the
PERFECT TENSE

such
1 *adjective* = solcher/solche/solches
information on ········
grammatical usage
! *Note that* **solcher, solche** *and* **solches**
change their endings in the same way as
der/die/das.
such a thing should not have happened =
so etwas hätte nicht passieren dürfen
2 *adverb*
example ········ **they have such a lot of money** = sie haben
so viel Geld

Words in capital letters are found in the glossary

ab
1 *preposition* (+ *dative*) = from
2 *adverb* = off
   ab und zu = now and again

die **Abbildung**, *plural* Abbildungen
   = illustration

der **Abend**, *plural* Abende
   = evening

das **Abendessen**, *plural* Abendessen
   = dinner

abends *adverb*
   = in the evening

das **Abenteuer**, *plural* Abenteuer
   = adventure

aber *conjunction*
   = but

abergläubisch *adjective*
   = superstitious

ab|fahren *irregular verb* (**!** *sein*)
   = to leave

die **Abfahrt**, *plural* Abfahrten
   • = departure
   • (*on a motorway*) = exit
   • (*ski slope*) = run

der **Abfall**, *plural* Abfälle
   = rubbish, = garbage

der **Abflug**, *plural* Abflüge
   = departure

ab|geben *irregular verb*
   • = to hand in
   • jemandem etwas abgeben = to give
     someone something

der/die **Abgeordnete**, *plural* Abgeordneten
   = member of parliament

ab|hängen *irregular verb*
   abhängen von = to depend on

ab|heben *irregular verb*
   • = to lift off
   • (*take out money*) = to withdraw

ab|holen *verb*
   = to collect

das **Abitur**
   ≈ A levels

das **Abkommen**, *plural* Abkommen
   = agreement

ab|kürzen *verb*
   = to abbreviate

die **Abkürzung**, *plural* Abkürzungen
   • = abbreviation
   • = short cut

ab|legen *verb*
   = to take off
   abgelegte Kleidung = cast-offs

ab|lehnen *verb*
   • = to refuse
   • = to reject

ab|lenken *verb*
   • = to divert
   • = to distract

ab|machen *verb*
   • (*remove*) = to take off
   • (*make arrangements*) = to fix

die **Abmachung**, *plural* Abmachungen
   = agreement

ab|melden: sich abmelden *verb*
   • (*notify authorities*) = to report that one is
     leaving
   • = to check out

ab|nehmen *irregular verb*
   • (*remove*) = to take off
     den Hörer abnehmen = to pick up the
     phone
   • = to lose weight

das **Abonnement**, *plural* Abonnements
   = subscription

ab|raten *irregular verb*
   jemandem von etwas abraten = to advise
   someone against something

ab|räumen *verb*
   = to clear away

die **Abrechnung**, *plural* Abrechnungen
   = settlement of accounts

die **Abreise**
   = departure

ab|reisen *verb* (**!** *sein*)
   = to leave

ab|reißen *irregular verb*
   • = to tear down
   • (**!** *sein*) = to break off

ab|sagen *verb*
   = to cancel

der **Absatz**, *plural* Absätze
   • (*of a shoe*) = heel
   • (*in text*) = paragraph

der **Abschied**, *plural* Abschiede
   • = farewell
   • (*separation*) = parting

ab|schließen *irregular verb*
   = to lock

ab|schneiden *irregular verb*
= to cut off
gut abschneiden = to do well

ab|schreiben *irregular verb*
= to copy

abseits *adverb*
• = far away
• (*in soccer*) = offside

der **Absender**, *plural* Absender
= sender

ab|setzen *verb*
• = to take off
• = to put down
wir setzen dich am Bahnhof ab = we'll
drop you at the station

die **Absicht**, *plural* Absichten
= intention

absichtlich *adverb*
= intentionally, = on purpose

der **Abstand**, *plural* Abstände
• = distance
• = interval

ab|stellen *verb*
• = to turn off
• (*if it's a vehicle*) = to park

die **Abstimmung**, *plural* Abstimmungen
= vote

ab|stürzen *verb* (**!** *sein*)
= to crash

das **Abteil**, *plural* Abteile
= compartment

die **Abteilung**, *plural* Abteilungen
= department

die **Abtreibung**, *plural* Abtreibungen
= abortion

ab|trocknen *verb*
= to dry up

ab|wägen *irregular verb*
= to weigh up

ab|waschen *irregular verb*
= to wash up

die **Abwechslung**, *plural* Abwechslungen
= change

abwesend *adjective*
= absent

ab|wischen *verb*
= to wipe

das **Abzeichen**, *plural* Abzeichen
= badge

ab|ziehen *irregular verb*
• = to take off
die Betten abziehen = to strip the beds

• = to take away
= to deduct
• (**!** *sein*) (*of smoke, steam*) = to escape

ab|zielen *verb*
abzielen auf = to be aimed at

ach *interjection*
= oh!

acht *adjective*
= eight

das **Achtel**, *plural* Achtel
= eighth

achten *verb*
• = to respect
• achten auf = to pay attention to
(*mind*) = to look after

achter/achte/achtes *adjective*
= eighth

die **Achterbahn**, *plural* Achterbahnen
= roller coaster

die **Achtung**
1 *noun* = respect
2 *interjection*
Achtung! = look out!

achtzehn *adjective*
= eighteen

achtzig *adjective*
= eighty

der **Acker**, *plural* Äcker
= field

die **Ader**, *plural* Adern
= vein

der **Adler**, *plural* Adler
= eagle

adoptieren *verb*
= to adopt

die **Adresse**, *plural* Adressen
= address

der **Affe**, *plural* Affen
= monkey
= ape

(das) **Afrika**
= Africa

der **Afrikaner**, *plural* Afrikaner
= African

(das) **Ägypten**
= Egypt

ähneln *verb*
= to resemble

ähnlich *adjective*
= similar
er sieht seinem Vater ähnlich = he looks
like his father

die **Ähnlichkeit**, *plural* Ähnlichkeiten
= similarity

die **Ahnung**
= idea

das **Aids**
= Aids

die **Akte**, *plural* Akten
= file

die **Aktentasche**, *plural* Aktentaschen
= briefcase

die **Aktie**, *plural* Aktien
= share

die **Aktivität**, *plural* Aktivitäten
= activity

aktuell *adjective*
= topical
= current

der **Akzent**, *plural* Akzente
= accent

alarmieren *verb*
* = to alert
* = to alarm

der **Albtraum**, *plural* Albträume ▶Alptraum

der **Alkohol**
= alcohol

alle ▶aller

allein *adverb*
* = alone
* (*automatically*) = on one's own

der/die **Alleinerziehende**, *plural*
Alleinerziehenden
= single parent

aller/alle/alles
1 *pronoun*
* = all
* = every
alle Tage = every day
* alle (*plural*) = all
alle miteinander = all together
alle beide = both
* alles = everything, = all
alles aussteigen! = all change!
alles Gute! = all the best!
vor allem = above all
2 *adjective*
alle sein✱ = to be all gone

die **Allergie**, *plural* Allergien
= allergy

allergisch *adjective*
= allergic

alles ▶aller

allgemein *adverb*
= generally
im Allgemeinen = in general

allmählich
1 *adjective* = gradual
2 *adverb* = gradually

alltäglich *adjective*
= everyday

alltags *adverb*
= on weekdays

Alpen (*plural*)
die Alpen = the Alps

das **Alphabet**, *plural* Alphabete
= alphabet

der **Alptraum**, *plural* Alpträume
= nightmare

als *conjunction*
* = when
erst als = only when
* (*as comparison*) = than
* = as
als Frau = as a woman

also
1 *adverb* = so
2 *conjunction* = so
also gut = all right then

alt *adjective*
= old

das **Alter**
= age

älter *adjective*
* = older
* = elderly

altern *verb* (**!** sein)
= to age

das **Altersheim**, *plural* Altersheime
= old people's home

ältester/älteste/ältestes
adjective
= oldest

altmodisch *adjective*
= old-fashioned

am = an dem
am Sonntag = on Sunday
am Abend = in the evening
am meisten = (the) most

die **Ameise**, *plural* Ameisen
= ant

(das) **Amerika**
= America

der **Amerikaner**, *plural* Amerikaner
= American

die **Amerikanerin**, *plural*
Amerikanerinnen
= American

amerikanisch *adjective*
= American

die **Ampel**, *plural* Ampeln
= traffic lights

amtlich *adjective*
= official

amüsant *adjective*
= amusing

an
1 *preposition* (+ *dative or accusative*)
• = at
= against
(*attached to*) = on
• = to
einen Brief an jemanden schicken = to
send a letter to someone
• (*when talking about time*) = on
2 *adverb* = on
das Licht ist an = the light is on
von heute an = from today

die **Ananas** *plural* Ananas
= pineapple

an|bieten *irregular verb*
= to offer

das **Andenken**, *plural* Andenken
= souvenir

anderer/andere/anderes
1 *adjective*
• = other
• = different
2 *pronoun*
der/die/das andere = the other one
die anderen = the others
ein anderer/eine andere/ein anderes
(*thing*) = a different one, (*person*) =
someone else
kein anderer = no one else
unter anderem = among other things

andererseits *adverb*
= on the other hand

ändern *verb*
= to change

anders *adverb*
= differently
niemand anders = no one else

anderthalb *adjective*
= one and a half

der **Anfall**, *plural* Anfälle
= fit, = attack

der **Anfang**, *plural* Anfänge
= beginning, = start

an|fangen *irregular verb*
= to begin, = to start

der **Anfänger**, *plural* Anfänger
= beginner

die **Anfängerin**, *plural* Anfängerinnen
= beginner

an|fassen *verb*
= to touch

an|geben *irregular verb*
• = to give
• = to show off

das **Angebot**, *plural* Angebote
= offer

die **Angel**, *plural* Angeln
= fishing rod

die **Angelegenheit**, *plural*
Angelegenheiten
= matter
= business

angenehm
1 *adjective* = pleasant
2 *interjection*
(*when being introduced*) = pleased to
meet you

der/die **Angestellte**, *plural* Angestellten
= employee

die **Angewohnheit**, *plural*
Angewohnheiten
= habit

an|greifen *irregular verb*
= to attack

der **Angriff**, *plural* Angriffe
= attack

die **Angst**, *plural* Ängste
= fear
Angst haben = to be afraid
jemandem Angst machen = to frighten
someone

ängstlich *adjective*
• = nervous
• = frightened
• = anxious

an|halten *irregular verb*
= to stop

der **Anhalter**, *plural* Anhalter
= hitchhiker
per Anhalter fahren = to hitchhike

die **Anhalterin**, *plural* Anhalterinnen
= hitchhiker

der **Anhang**, *plural* Anhänge
= attachment

der **Anhänger**, *plural* Anhänger
• = supporter
• = trailer
• = pendant

an|klicken *verb*
= to click on

an|kommen *irregular verb* (**!** sein)
• = to arrive
• ankommen auf = to depend on
das kommt darauf an = it depends

die **Ankunft**
= arrival

an|machen *verb*
= to turn on

an|melden *verb*
• = to register
• sich anmelden = to register, (*for an
appointment*) = to make an
appointment

die **Anmeldung**, *plural* Anmeldungen
* = registration
* = appointment

die **Annahme**, *plural* Annahmen
= assumption

an|nehmen *irregular verb*
* = to accept
* = to assume
= to suppose

an|passen: sich anpassen *verb*
= to adapt

anpassungsfähig *adjective*
= adaptable

der **Anruf**, *plural* Anrufe
= (phone) call

der **Anrufbeantworter**, *plural*
Anrufbeantworter
= answering machine

an|rufen *irregular verb*
= to ring, = to call

ans = an das
ans Telefon gehen = to answer the phone

die **Ansage**, *plural* Ansagen
= announcement

an|schlagen *irregular verb*
* = to put up
* = to knock
* = to chip, = to crack

an|schließen *irregular verb*
* = to connect
* sich einer Gruppe anschließen = to join a group

der **Anschluss** (**Anschluß** ⒪ⓛⒹ), *plural*
Anschlüsse
= connection

an|schnallen: sich anschnallen
verb
= to fasten one's seatbelt

die **Anschrift**, *plural* Anschriften
= address

die **Anschuldigung**, *plural*
Anschuldigungen
= accusation

die **Ansicht**, *plural* Ansichten
= view

der **Anspruch**, *plural* Ansprüche
= claim

anstatt
1 *preposition* (+ *genitive*) = instead of
2 *conjunction*
anstatt zu schlafen = instead of sleeping

an|stellen *verb*
* = to employ
* = to turn on

* sich anstellen = to queue, = to stand in line

die **Anstrengung**, *plural* Anstrengungen
= effort

die **Antenne**, *plural* Antennen
= aerial

das **Antibiotikum**, *plural* Antibiotika
= antibiotic

der **Antrag**, *plural* Anträge
= application

die **Antwort**, *plural* Antworten
= answer, = reply

antworten *verb*
= to answer, = to reply

anwesend *adjective*
= present

die **Anzahl**
= number

die **Anzahlung**, *plural* Anzahlungen
= deposit

die **Anzeige**, *plural* Anzeigen
* = advertisement
* (*to the police*) = report

an|zeigen *verb*
* = to report
* = to show

an|ziehen *irregular verb*
* = to attract
* (*dress*) = to put on
* sich anziehen = to get dressed

der **Anzug**, *plural* Anzüge
= suit

an|zünden *verb*
= to light

der **Apfel**, *plural* Äpfel
= apple

die **Apfelsine**, *plural* Apfelsinen
= orange

die **Apotheke**, *plural* Apotheken
= chemist's, = pharmacy

der **Apotheker**, *plural* Apotheker
= chemist, = pharmacist

die **Apothekerin**, *plural* Apothekerinnen
= chemist, = pharmacist

der **Apparat**, *plural* Apparate
* (*TV, radio*) = set
* = camera
* = telephone
am Apparat! = speaking!

das **Appartement**, *plural* Appartements
= apartment

der **Appetit**
= appetite
guten Appetit! = enjoy your meal!

die **Aprikose**, *plural* Aprikosen
= apricot

der **April**
= April

der **Äquator**
= equator

die **Arbeit**, *plural* Arbeiten
* = work
* = job
* (*at school*) = test

arbeiten *verb*
= to work

der **Arbeiter**, *plural* Arbeiter
= worker

die **Arbeiterin**, *plural* Arbeiterinnen
= worker

der **Arbeitgeber**, *plural* Arbeitgeber
= employer

arbeitslos *adjective*
= unemployed

der **Ärger**
* = annoyance
* (*problems*) = trouble

ärgerlich *adjective*
* = annoyed
* = annoying

ärgern *verb*
* = to annoy
* sich ärgern = to get annoyed

arm *adjective*
= poor

der **Arm**, *plural* Arme
= arm

das **Armband**, *plural* Armbänder
= bracelet

die **Armbanduhr**, *plural* Armbanduhren
= wrist-watch

der **Ärmel**, *plural* Ärmel
= sleeve

der **Ärmelkanal**
= (English) Channel

arrangieren *verb*
* = to arrange
* sich arrangieren = to come to an arrangement

der **Arsch**, *plural* Ärsche
= arse, = ass

die **Art**, *plural* Arten
* = way, = manner
* = kind, = sort

artig *adjective*
= good, = well-behaved

***** considered offensive

der **Arzt**, *plural* Ärzte
= doctor

die **Ärztin**, *plural* Ärztinnen
= doctor

ärztlich *adjective*
= medical

der **Aschenbecher**, *plural* Aschenbecher
= ashtray

der **Asiat**, *plural* Asiaten
= Asian

die **Asiatin**, *plural* Asiatinnen
= Asian

asiatisch *adjective*
= Asian

(das) **Asien**
= Asia

aß ▸ essen

der **Assistent**, *plural* Assistenten
= assistant

die **Assistentin**, *plural* Assistentinnen
= assistant

der **Ast**, *plural* Äste
= branch

der **Asylant**, *plural* Asylanten
= asylum-seeker

der **Atem**
= breath

atemlos *adjective*
= breathless

der **Athlet**, *plural* Athleten
= athlete

die **Athletin**, *plural* Athletinnen
= athlete

der **Atlantik**
= the Atlantic

der **Atlas**, *plural* Atlanten
= atlas

atmen *verb*
= to breathe

die **Atmosphäre**, *plural* Atmosphären
= atmosphere

attraktiv *adjective*
= attractive

das **At-Zeichen**, *plural* At-Zeichen
= at (@ in email addresses)

auch *adverb*
= also, = too
nicht nur . . . sondern auch . . . = not only . . . but also . . .
auch wenn = even if
wann|was|wer|wo auch = whenever | whatever | whoever | wherever

auf
1 *preposition*
- (+ *dative*) (*indicating position*) = on
  auf der Party = at the party
- (+ *accusative*) (*moving in the direction of*) = on, = onto
- auf Deutsch = in German
- (*indicating time*) = for
  etwas auf morgen verschieben = to put something off until tomorrow
  auf Wiedersehen! = goodbye!
2 *adverb* = open
  auf und ab = up and down

aufeinander *adverb*
- = one on top of the other
- = one after the other
- aufeinander warten = to wait for each other

der **Aufenthalt**, *plural* Aufenthalte
- = stay
- (*pause in a journey*) = stop

die **Aufgabe**, *plural* Aufgaben
- = task
- (*at school*) = exercise, = assignment
  Aufgaben = homework

auf|geben *irregular verb*
- = to give up
- = to post
- Hausaufgaben aufgeben = to set homework

auf|halten *irregular verb*
- = to hold
- = to hold open
- sich aufhalten = to stay

auf|heben *irregular verb*
- (*from the ground*) = to pick up
- (*preserve*) = to keep

auf|hören *verb*
= to stop

der **Aufkleber**, *plural* Aufkleber
= sticker

auf|laden *irregular verb*
= to recharge

auf|legen *verb*
- = to put on
- = to publish
- (*when phoning*) = to hang up

auf|machen *verb*
= to open

aufmerksam *adjective*
= attentive
er machte sie auf einen Fehler aufmerksam = he drew her attention to a mistake

die **Aufnahme**, *plural* Aufnahmen
- = photograph, = shot
- = recording
- (*to hospital, club*) = admission

auf|nehmen *irregular verb*
- = to receive
  (*into hospital, club*) = to admit
- = to record
- (*with a camera*) = to film
  = to photograph

auf|passen *verb*
= to pay attention
aufpassen auf = to look after, = to look out for

auf|räumen *verb*
= to tidy up

auf|regen *verb*
- = to excite
- = to annoy
- sich aufregen = to get worked up

die **Aufregung**, *plural* Aufregungen
= excitement

aufrichtig *adjective*
= sincere

der **Aufsatz**, *plural* Aufsätze
= essay

auf|schließen *irregular verb*
= to unlock

der **Aufschnitt**
= sliced cold meat and cheese

auf|schreiben *irregular verb*
= to write down

die **Aufsicht**
- = supervision
- (*person*) = supervisor

auf|stehen *irregular verb* (**!** *sein*)
= to get up

der **Auftrag**, *plural* Aufträge
- = job
- (*in business*) = order

auf|wachen *verb* (**!** *sein*)
= to wake up

auf|wachsen *irregular verb* (**!** *sein*)
= to grow up

auf|wecken *verb*
= to wake up

auf|ziehen *irregular verb*
= to wind up

der **Aufzug**, *plural* Aufzüge
= lift, = elevator

das **Auge**, *plural* Augen
= eye
unter vier Augen = in private

der **Augenblick**, *plural* Augenblicke
= moment

die **Augenbraue**, *plural* Augenbrauen
= eyebrow

das **Augenlid**, *plural* Augenlider
= eyelid

der **August**
= August

aus
1 *preposition* (+ *dative*)
* (*indicating direction*) = out of
* (*originating from*) = from
  aus welchem Grund? = for what reason?
* (*consisting of*) = made of
  aus Spaß = for fun
2 *adverb* = out
  das Licht ist aus = the light is off
  von mir aus = as far as I'm concerned

aus|beuten *verb*
= to exploit

die **Ausbildung**
= education
= training

der **Ausdruck**, *plural* Ausdrücke
= expression

aus|drücken *verb*
* = to squeeze
* = to express
* sich ausdrücken = to express oneself

auseinander *adverb*
= apart

die **Ausfahrt**, *plural* Ausfahrten
= exit
'Ausfahrt freihalten' = 'keep clear'

der **Ausflug**, *plural* Ausflüge
= trip

aus|füllen *verb*
= to fill in

die **Ausgabe**, *plural* Ausgaben
* = edition
* Ausgaben = expenditure

der **Ausgang**, *plural* Ausgänge
= exit, = way out

aus|geben *irregular verb*
= to spend

aus|gehen *irregular verb* (**!** *sein*)
= to go out
gut ausgehen = to end well

ausgezeichnet *adjective*
= excellent

aus|halten *irregular verb*
= to stand

die **Aushilfe**, *plural* Aushilfen
= temporary assistant, = temp

die **Auskunft**, *plural* Auskünfte
= information
(*when telephoning*) = inquiries

das **Ausland**
im Ausland = abroad
ins Ausland reisen = to travel abroad

ⓄⓁⒹ = old spelling

der **Ausländer**, *plural* Ausländer
= foreigner

die **Ausländerin**, *plural* Ausländerinnen
= foreigner

aus|machen *verb*
* = to put out
* = to turn off
* = to arrange
  das macht mir nichts aus = I don't mind

die **Ausnahme**, *plural* Ausnahmen
= exception

aus|nutzen *verb*
= to use
= to take advantage of

aus|packen *verb*
= to unpack

der **Auspuff**, *plural* Auspuffe
= exhaust

die **Ausrede**, *plural* Ausreden
= excuse

das **Ausrufezeichen**, *plural*
Ausrufezeichen
= exclamation mark

aus|ruhen: sich ausruhen *verb*
= to have a rest

die **Ausrüstung**
= equipment

aus|schalten *verb*
* = to switch off
* = to eliminate

aus|schneiden *irregular verb*
= to cut out

der **Ausschuss** (**Ausschuß**ⓄⓁⒹ), *plural*
Ausschüsse
= committee
= board

aus|sehen *irregular verb*
= to look

außen *adverb*
= outside
nach außen = outwards

der **Außenminister**, *plural* Außenminister
= Foreign Secretary, = Foreign Minister

außer
1 *preposition* (+ *dative*) = except (for)
= apart from
alle außer ihr = everyone except (for) her
2 *conjunction* = except
außer wenn = unless

außerdem *adverb*
* = as well
* = moreover

äußerer/äußere/äußeres *adjective*
= external

außerhalb *preposition* (+ *genitive*)
= outside

äußerlich *adjective*
= external

außerordentlich *adjective*
= extraordinary

äußerst *adverb*
= extremely

die **Aussicht**, *plural* Aussichten
• (*from a window*) = view
• = prospect

die **Aussprache**, *plural* Aussprachen
= pronunciation

aus|sprechen *irregular verb*
• = to pronounce
• = to express

aus|steigen *irregular verb* (**!** *sein*)
= to get out

aus|stellen *verb*
• (*in a shop, museum*) = to display
= to exhibit
• (*write*) = to make out
= to issue

die **Ausstellung**, *plural* Ausstellungen
= exhibition

aus|suchen *verb*
• = to choose
• sich etwas aussuchen = to choose
something

der **Austausch**
= exchange

(das) **Australien**
= Australia

der **Australier**, *plural* Australier
= Australian

die **Australierin**, *plural* Australierinnen
= Australian

australisch *adjective*
= Australian

aus|trinken *irregular verb*
= to drink up

der **Ausverkauf**
= sale

die **Auswahl**, *plural* Auswahlen
= choice

aus|wandern *verb* (**!** *sein*)
= to emigrate

der **Ausweis**, *plural* Ausweise
= identity card

auswendig *adverb*
= by heart

aus|wirken: sich auswirken *verb*
sich auf etwas auswirken = to affect
something

aus|ziehen *irregular verb*
• = to take off
= to undress
• sich ausziehen = to get undressed
• (**!** *sein*) (*move house*) = to move out

das **Auto**, *plural* Autos
= car

die **Autobahn**, *plural* Autobahnen
= motorway, = freeway

der **Autobus**, *plural* Autobusse
= bus

das **Autogramm**, *plural* Autogramme
= autograph

der **Automat**, *plural* Automaten
= machine

die **Autonummer**, *plural* Autonummern
= registration number

der **Autor**, *plural* Autoren
= author

die **Autorin**, *plural* Autorinnen
= authoress

die **Autorität**
= authority

die **Axt**, *plural* Äxte
= axe, = ax

Bb

der **Bach**, *plural* Bäche
= stream

die **Backe**, *plural* Backen
= cheek

backen *irregular verb*
= to bake

der **Bäcker**, *plural* Bäcker
= baker

die **Bäckerei**, *plural* Bäckereien
= baker's (shop), = bakery

die **Backpflaume**, *plural* Backpflaumen
= prune

das **Bad**, *plural* Bäder
• = bath
• = bathroom
• (*for swimming*) = pool

der **Badeanzug** *plural* Badeanzüge
= bathing costume, = swimsuit

die **Badehose**, *plural* Badehosen
= swimming trunks

baden *verb*
- = to have a bath
= to bathe
- (*wash someone*) = to bath

die **Badewanne**, *plural* Badewannen
= bath-tub
= bath

das **Badezimmer**, *plural* Badezimmer
= bathroom

die **Bahn**, *plural* Bahnen
- = train
= tram, = streetcar
- (*in sport*) = track
(*single*) = lane

der **Bahnhof**, *plural* Bahnhöfe
= (railway) station

der **Bahnsteig**, *plural* Bahnsteige
= platform

der **Bahnübergang**, *plural*
Bahnübergänge
= level crossing, = grade crossing

bald *adverb*
= soon

der **Balkon**, *plural* Balkons
= balcony

der **Ball**, *plural* Bälle
= ball

das **Ballett**, *plural* Ballette
= ballet

die **Banane**, *plural* Bananen
= banana

das **Band¹** *plural* Bänder
- = ribbon
- (*for recording*) = tape
- am laufenden Band = non-stop

der **Band²** *plural* Bände
= volume

die **Band³** *plural* Bands
(*group*) = band

die **Bande**, *plural* Banden
= gang

die **Bank¹** *plural* Banken
= bank

die **Bank²** *plural* Bänke
= bench

bankrott *adjective*
= bankrupt

bar *adverb*
= (in) cash

der **Bär**, *plural* Bären
= bear

barfuß *adverb*
= barefoot

das **Bargeld**
= cash

der **Barren**, *plural* Barren
- = bar
- (*in gymnastics*) = parallel bars

der **Bart**, *plural* Bärte
= beard

bärtig *adjective*
= bearded

basta *interjection*
= and that's that!

basteln *verb*
= to make
sie bastelt gerne = she likes making
things

bat ▶bitten

der **Bauch**, *plural* Bäuche
= stomach

Bauchschmerzen (*plural*)
= stomach-ache

bauen *verb*
= to build

der **Bauer**, *plural* Bauern
= farmer

die **Bäuerin**, *plural* Bäuerinnen
= farmer's wife

der **Bauernhof**, *plural* Bauernhöfe
= farm

der **Baum**, *plural* Bäume
= tree

die **Baumwolle**
= cotton

die **Bausparkasse**, *plural* Bausparkassen
= building society

die **Baustelle**, *plural* Baustellen
= building site

(das) **Bayern**
= Bavaria

beabsichtigen *verb*
= to intend

beachten *verb*
- = to take notice of
- = to observe
= to follow

der **Beamte**, *plural* Beamten
= civil servant
= official

die **Beamtin**, *plural* Beamtinnen
= civil servant
= official

die **Beanstandung**, *plural*
Beanstandungen
= complaint

beantragen *verb*
= to apply for

beantworten *verb*
= to answer

beaufsichtigen *verb*
= to supervise

beauftragen *verb*
= to instruct
= to commission

der **Becher**, *plural* Becher
= beaker, = mug
= pot, = carton

das **Becken**, *plural* Becken
• (*for washing*) = basin
• (*for swimming*) = pool
• (*part of the body*) = pelvis

bedanken: sich bedanken *verb*
= to say thank you
ich habe mich bei ihm bedankt = I
thanked him

der **Bedarf**
= need
bei Bedarf = if required

bedauerlicherweise *adverb*
= unfortunately

bedauern *verb*
• = to regret
• jemanden bedauern = to feel sorry for
someone

bedecken *verb*
= to cover

bedeckt *adjective*
= overcast

bedenken *irregular verb*
= to consider

das **Bedenken**, *plural* Bedenken
= reservation
ohne Bedenken = without hesitation

bedenklich *adjective*
• (*serious*) = worrying
• = dubious

bedeuten *verb*
= to mean

die **Bedeutung**, *plural* Bedeutungen
• = meaning
• = importance

bedienen *verb*
• (*help*) = to serve
• = to operate
• sich bedienen = to help oneself

die **Bedienung**, *plural* Bedienungen
• = service
Bedienung inbegriffen = service included
• (*person*) = waiter/waitress
• (*of a machine*) = operation

die **Bedingung**, *plural* Bedingungen
= condition

bedingungslos *adjective*
= unconditional

die **Bedrohung** *plural* Bedrohungen
= threat

bedürftig *adjective*
= needy

beeilen: sich beeilen *verb*
= to hurry (up)

beeindrucken *verb*
= to impress

die **Beerdigung**, *plural* Beerdigungen
= funeral

die **Beere**, *plural* Beeren
= berry

das **Beet**, *plural* Beete
(*of flowers*) = bed
(*of vegetables*) = patch

befahl ▶befehlen

der **Befehl**, *plural* Befehle
= order

befehlen *irregular verb*
jemandem etwas befehlen = to order
someone to do something

befestigen *verb*
= to fasten, = to attach

befinden: sich befinden *irregular*
verb
= to be

befördern *verb*
• (*by lorry, train*) = to transport
• (*in a job*) = to promote

die **Befreiung**
= liberation

befreunden: sich befreunden
verb
= to make friends
befreundet sein = to be friends

befriedigen *verb*
= to satisfy

die **Befugnis**, *plural* Befugnisse
= authority

begabt *adjective*
= gifted

die **Begabung**
= gift, = talent

begann ▶beginnen

begegnen *verb* (**I** sein)
• jemandem begegnen = to meet someone
• sich begegnen = to meet (each other)

begehen *irregular verb*
= to commit

B

begeistert *adjective*
= enthusiastic

die **Begeisterung**
= enthusiasm

der **Beginn**
= beginning

beginnen *irregular verb*
= to begin, = to start

begleiten *verb*
= to accompany

beglückwünschen *verb*
= to congratulate

begnadigen *verb*
= to pardon

begraben *irregular verb*
= to bury

begreifen *irregular verb*
= to understand

der **Begriff**, *plural* Begriffe
• = concept
• (*expression*) = term

die **Begründung**, *plural* Begründungen
= reason

begrüßen *verb*
= to greet
= to welcome

begünstigen *verb*
= to favour

behalten *irregular verb*
• = to keep
• = to remember

der **Behälter**, *plural* Behälter
= container

die **Behandlung**, *plural* Behandlungen
= treatment

behaupten *verb*
• = to claim
• sich behaupten = to assert oneself

die **Behauptung**, *plural* Behauptungen
= claim, = assertion

beherrschen *verb*
• = to rule over
• = to know
• sich berherrschen = to control oneself

behilflich *adjective*
jemandem behilflich sein = to help
someone

behindern *verb*
= to obstruct

behindert *adjective*
= disabled, = handicapped

der/die **Behinderte**, *plural* Behinderten
= disabled person, = handicapped person

die **Behörde**, *plural* Behörden
= authority

behüten *verb*
= to protect

bei *preposition* (+ *dative*)
• = near, = by
nimm ihn bei der Hand = take him by the
hand
• (*indicating a place, time*) = at
bei mir = at my place
bei uns in der Firma = in our company
bei Schmidt = c/o Schmidt
bei Regen = when *or* if it rains
• (*indicating cause*) = with
bei der hohen Miete = (what) with the
high rent

bei‖bringen *irregular verb*
jemandem etwas beibringen = to teach
someone something

beide
1 *adjective* = both
die beiden Schwestern = the two sisters
2 *pronoun* = both
ihr beide = both of you, = you two
(*in tennis*) dreißig beide = thirty all

der **Beifall**
= applause

beiläufig *adjective*
= casual

beim = bei dem
beim Lesen sein = to be reading

das **Bein**, *plural* Beine
= leg

beinah(e) *adverb*
= almost

beiseite *adverb*
= aside

das **Beispiel**, *plural* Beispiele
= example
zum Beispiel = for example

beißen *irregular verb*
= to bite

der **Beitrag**, *plural* Beiträge
• = contribution
• (*in a newspaper*) = article
• (*members'*) = subscription

bekam ▶bekommen

bekämpfen *verb*
= to fight, = to combat

bekannt *adjective*
• = well-known
• = familiar
• etwas bekannt machen = to announce
something
• jemanden bekannt machen = to
introduce someone

der/die **Bekannte**, *plural* Bekannten
= acquaintance

die **Bekanntschaft**, *plural*
Bekanntschaften
= acquaintance
(*group of people*) = acquaintances

beklagen: sich beklagen *verb*
= to complain

die **Bekleidung**
= clothes

bekommen *irregular verb*
• = to get
• = to catch
• es bekommt mir gut (**!** *sein*) (*of the
climate*) = it is good for me, (*of food*) =
it agrees with me

der **Belag**, *plural* Beläge
= covering, = coating

belästigen *verb*
• = to bother
• (*sexually*) = to harass

belegt *adjective*
• = occupied
• ein belegtes Brot = an open sandwich

beleidigen *verb*
= to insult

die **Beleidigung**, *plural* Beleidigungen
= insult

die **Beleuchtung**
= lighting

(das) **Belgien**
= Belgium

der **Belgier**, *plural* Belgier
= Belgian

die **Belgierin**, *plural* Belgierinnen
= Belgian

belgisch *adjective*
= Belgian

belichten *verb*
(*in photography*) = to expose

beliebig
1 *adjective* = any
2 *adverb*
beliebig [oft | lange | viele ...] = as [often |
long | many ...] as one likes

beliebt *adjective*
= popular

bellen *verb*
= to bark

belohnen *verb*
= to reward

bemerkbar *adjective*
sich bemerkbar machen (*of a person*) =
to attract attention, (*of a thing*) = to
become noticeable

bemerken *verb*
• = to notice
• (*utter*) = to remark
nebenbei bemerkt = by the way

die **Bemerkung**, *plural* Bemerkungen
= remark

bemühen: sich bemühen *verb*
= to try
sich um eine Stelle bemühen = to try to
get a job

die **Bemühung**, *plural* Bemühungen
= effort

benachrichtigen *verb*
= to inform
(*officially*) = to notify

benehmen: sich benehmen
irregular verb
= to behave

das **Benehmen**
= behaviour, behavior

beneiden *verb*
= to envy

benutzen, benützen *verb*
= to use

das **Benzin**
= petrol, = gas

beobachten *verb*
= to observe, = to watch

bequem *adjective*
• = comfortable
• = lazy

beraten *irregular verb*
• = to advise
• = to discuss
• sich über etwas beraten = to discuss
something

der **Berater**, *plural* Berater
= adviser

die **Beratung**, *plural* Beratungen
• = advice
• = discussion
• (*with a doctor*) = consultation

der **Bereich**, *plural* Bereiche
= area

bereit *adjective*
= ready

bereits *adverb*
= already

bereuen *verb*
= to regret

der **Berg**, *plural* Berge
= mountain

bergab *adverb*
= downhill

der **Bergarbeiter**, *plural* Bergarbeiter
= miner

bergauf *adverb*
= uphill

bergen *irregular verb*
= to rescue

der **Bergsteiger**, *plural* Bergsteiger
= climber, = mountaineer

die **Bergwacht**
= mountain rescue (service)

das **Bergwerk**, *plural* Bergwerke
= mine

der **Bericht**, *plural* Berichte
= report

berichten *verb*
= to report

berücksichtigen *verb*
= to take into account

der **Beruf**, *plural* Berufe
= occupation
= profession
= trade
was sind Sie von Beruf? = what do you
do for a living?

beruflich
1 *adjective* = professional
= vocational
2 *adverb* = professionally

die **Berufsberatung**
= careers advice

berufstätig *adjective*
= working

beruhigen *verb*
= to calm (down)

berühmt *adjective*
= famous

berühren *verb*
* = to touch
• sich berühren = to touch

besaß ▶ besitzen

beschädigen *verb*
= to damage

beschäftigen *verb*
• (*keep busy*) = to occupy
beschäftigt sein = to be busy
• (*in a job*) = to employ
• sich beschäftigen = to occupy oneself

die **Beschäftigung**, *plural*
Beschäftigungen
• (*work*) = occupation
• (*hobby*) = activity

der **Bescheid**
= information
jemandem Bescheid sagen = to let
someone know

bescheiden *adjective*
= modest

die **Bescheinigung**, *plural*
Bescheinigungen
* = (written) confirmation
* = certificate

die **Bescherung**, *plural* Bescherungen
= giving out of Christmas presents

beschimpfen *verb*
= to abuse

beschlagnahmen *verb*
= to confiscate

beschleunigen *verb*
= to speed up
= to accelerate

beschließen *irregular verb*
= to decide

beschreiben *irregular verb*
= to describe

die **Beschreibung**, *plural* Beschreibungen
= description

beschuldigen *verb*
= to accuse

beschützen *verb*
= to protect

die **Beschwerde**, *plural* Beschwerden
= complaint

beschweren: sich beschweren
verb
= to complain

beschwipst✗ *adjective*
= tipsy

beseitigen *verb*
= to remove

der **Besen**, *plural* Besen
= broom

besetzt *adjective*
= occupied
besetzt sein (*of a phone, toilet*) = to be
engaged, (*of a seat*) = to be taken, (*of a
train, bus*) = to be full (up)

besichtigen *verb*
= to look round
= to see

die **Besichtigung**, *plural* Besichtigungen
= visit

besinnungslos *adjective*
= unconscious

der **Besitz**
= property

✗ in informal situations

besitzen *irregular verb*
= to own

der **Besitzer**, *plural* Besitzer
= owner

die **Besitzerin**, *plural* Besitzerinnen
= owner

**besonderer/besondere/
besonderes** *adjective*
* = special
* = particular

besonders *adverb*
= particularly

besorgen *verb*
= to get

besorgt *adjective*
= worried

besprechen *irregular verb*
* = to discuss
* (*write article on*) = to review

die **Besprechung**, *plural* Besprechungen
* = discussion
* (*of a film, play*) = review
* (*conference*) = meeting

besser
1 *adjective* = better
2 *adverb* = better
alles besser wissen = to know better

die **Besserung**
= improvement
gute Besserung! = get well soon!

beständig *adjective*
* = constant
* (*of the weather*) = settled

bestätigen *verb*
= to confirm

die **Bestätigung**, *plural* Bestätigungen
= confirmation

beste ▶ bester

die **Bestechung**, *plural* Bestechungen
= bribery

das **Besteck**, *plural* Bestecke
= (set of) cutlery

bestehen *irregular verb*
* = to exist
es besteht die Gefahr, dass . . . = there is
a danger that . . .
* eine Prüfung bestehen = to pass an exam
* auf etwas bestehen = to insist on
something
* aus etwas bestehen = to consist of
something, = to be made of something

bestellen *verb*
* (*in a restaurant, factory*) = to order
* (*reserve*) = to book

* = to tell
bestell ihr schöne Grüße = give her my
regards

die **Bestellung**, *plural* Bestellungen
(*for goods*) = order
(*of tickets*) = reservation

bester/beste/bestes
1 *adjective* = best
besten Dank = many thanks
2 *adverb*
am besten = best

bestimmen *verb*
* (*arrange*) = to fix
etwas allein bestimmen = to decide (on)
something on one's own
* für jemanden bestimmt sein = to be
meant for someone
* = to be in charge

bestimmt
1 *adjective* = definite, = certain
2 *adverb* = definitely, = certainly

die **Bestimmung**, *plural* Bestimmungen
= regulation

bestrafen *verb*
= to punish

bestreiten *irregular verb*
* = to deny
* = to dispute
* = to pay for

bestürzt *adjective*
= dismayed

der **Besuch**, *plural* Besuche
= visit

besuchen *verb*
= to visit
= to go to, = to attend

der **Besucher**, *plural* Besucher
= visitor

die **Besucherin**, *plural* Besucherinnen
= visitor

die **Betäubung**
= anaesthesia
örtliche Betäubung = local anaesthetic

beteiligen *verb*
* = to give a share to
* sich an etwas beteiligen = to take part in
something

beten *verb*
= to pray

der **Beton**
= concrete

betonen *verb*
= to stress

der **Betrag**, *plural* Beträge
= amount

betragen *irregular verb*
* = to amount to
* sich betragen = to behave

betreffen *irregular verb*
= to concern
was mich betrifft = as far as I'm concerned

betreten *irregular verb*
* = to step on
* (*go into*) = to enter

der **Betrieb**, *plural* Betriebe
* = business
* = activity
außer Betrieb = not in use, (*broken*) = out of order

betrinken: sich betrinken
irregular verb
= to get drunk

betrog ▶betrügen

der **Betrug**
= deception, = fraud

betrügen *irregular verb*
= to cheat
= to be unfaithful to

betrunken *adjective*
= drunk

das **Bett**, *plural* Betten
= bed

betteln *verb*
= to beg

der **Bettler**, *plural* Bettler
= beggar

die **Bettlerin**, *plural* Bettlerinnen
= beggar

die **Bettwäsche**
= bed linen

beugen *verb*
* = to bend
* (*in grammar*) = to decline
= to conjugate

die **Beule**, *plural* Beulen
* = bump
= lump
* = dent

beurteilen *verb*
= to judge

der **Beutel**, *plural* Beutel
= bag

die **Bevölkerung**, *plural* Bevölkerungen
= population

bevor *conjunction*
= before
bevor nicht = until

bevorzugen *verb*
= to prefer

bewachen *verb*
= to guard

bewährt *adjective*
= reliable

bewegen *verb*
* = to move
* sich bewegen = to move

die **Bewegung**, *plural* Bewegungen
= movement
körperliche Bewegung = physical exercise

der **Beweis**, *plural* Beweise
= proof
= evidence

beweisen *irregular verb*
* = to prove
* = to show

bewerben: sich bewerben
irregular verb
= to apply
sich um einen Job bewerben = to apply for a job

die **Bewerbung**, *plural* Bewerbungen
= application

bewilligen *verb*
= to grant

der **Bewohner**, *plural* Bewohner
* (*of a house*) = resident, = occupant
* (*of a region*) = inhabitant

die **Bewohnerin**, *plural* Bewohnerinnen
* (*of a house*) = resident, = occupant
* (*of a region*) = inhabitant

bewundern *verb*
= to admire

bewusst (**bewußt**ⓄⓁⒹ) *adjective*
* = conscious
* = deliberate

bewusstlos (**bewußtlos**ⓄⓁⒹ)
adjective
= unconscious

das **Bewusstsein** (**Bewußtsein**ⓄⓁⒹ)
= consciousness
bei vollem Bewusstsein sein = to be fully conscious

bezahlen *verb*
= to pay
= to pay for

die **Bezahlung**
= payment

beziehen *irregular verb*
* = to cover
* ein Haus beziehen = to move into a house
* (*receive goods*) = to get
* sich auf jemanden beziehen = to refer to someone

B

die **Beziehung**, *plural* Beziehungen
- = connection
- = relationship

beziehungsweise *conjunction*
- = or rather
- = respectively

der **Bezirk**, *plural* Bezirke
= district

bezweifeln *verb*
= to doubt

der **BH**, *plural* BHs
= bra

die **Bibel**, *plural* Bibeln
= Bible

die **Bibliothek**, *plural* Bibliotheken
= library

biegen *irregular verb*
- = to bend
- (**!** *sein*) = to turn
- sich biegen = to bend

die **Biene**, *plural* Bienen
= bee

das **Bier**, *plural* Biere
= beer

bieten *irregular verb*
- = to offer
- (*at auction*) = to bid

das **Bild**, *plural* Bilder
= picture

bilden *verb*
- = to form
- sich bilden = to form
  (*gain knowledge*) = to educate oneself

der **Bildschirm**, *plural* Bildschirme
= screen

die **Bildung**
- = formation
- (*knowledge*) = education

billig *adjective*
= cheap

die **Billion**, *plural* Billionen
(*million million*) = billion

bin ▶sein

die **Binde**, *plural* Binden
- = bandage
- = sanitary towel

binden *irregular verb*
- = to tie
- = to bind
- (*in cooking*) = to thicken
- sich binden = to commit oneself

der **Bindestrich**, *plural* Bindestriche
= hyphen

der **Bindfaden**, *plural* Bindfäden
= (piece of) string

die **Bindung**, *plural* Bindungen
- = tie
- = relationship
- (*on a ski*) = binding

die **Biokost**
= health food

die **Biologie**
= biology

die **Birne**, *plural* Birnen
- = pear
- = (light) bulb

bis
1 *preposition* (+ *accusative*)
- (*with a place*) = as far as, = to
- (*indicating limit*) = up to
  bis auf = except for, (*including*) = down to
- (*with time*) = until, = till
  bis bald! = see you soon!
- (*at the latest*) = by
- = to
  drei bis vier Tage = three to four days
2 *conjunction* = until

der **Bischof**, *plural* Bischöfe
= bishop

bisher *adverb*
= so far

biss (**biß**ⓄⓁⒹ) ▶beißen

bisschen (**bißchen**ⓄⓁⒹ) *pronoun*
ein bisschen = a bit, = a little
kein bisschen = not a bit

bist ▶sein

bitte *adverb*
- = please
- (*in reply to thanks*) = you're welcome
  (*in response to a knock at the door*) =
  come in
- (*in a shop*) bitte? = yes, please?
  wie bitte? = sorry?

die **Bitte**, *plural* Bitten
= request

bitten *irregular verb*
= to ask

bitter *adjective*
= bitter

blamieren *verb*
= to disgrace

die **Blase**, *plural* Blasen
- = bubble
- = blister
- (*part of the body*) = bladder

blasen *irregular verb*
= to blow

blass (**blaß**ⓄⓁⒹ) *adjective*
= pale

das **Blatt**, *plural* Blätter
- = leaf

- (*piece of paper*) = sheet
  (*in a book*) = page
- = (news)paper

blau *adjective*
- = blue
  ein blaues Auge = a black eye
- blau sein✱ (*be drunk*) = to be tight

das **Blech**, *plural* Bleche
- = tin
- = baking tray
- (*in music*) = brass

das **Blei**
= lead

bleiben *irregular verb* (❗ *sein*)
- = to stay, = to remain
  bleiben Sie am Apparat = hold the line
- (*of remains*) = to be left

bleifrei *adjective*
= unleaded

der **Bleistift**, *plural* Bleistifte
= pencil

der **Bleistiftspitzer**, *plural* Bleistiftspitzer
= pencil sharpener

blenden *verb*
- = to dazzle
- = to blind

der **Blick**, *plural* Blicke
- = look
- = view

blieb ▶ bleiben

blies ▶ blasen

blind *adjective*
= blind

der **Blinddarm**, *plural* Blinddärme
= appendix

der/die **Blinde**, *plural* Blinden
= blind person, = blind man/woman

blinken *verb*
- = to flash
- (*of a car*) = to indicate

der **Blinker**, *plural* Blinker
(*on a car*) = indicator

der **Blitz**, *plural* Blitze
- (flash of) lightning
- flash

blitzen *verb*
= to flash
es hat geblitzt = there was a flash of
lightning

der **Block**, *plural* Blocks or Blöcke
- (*for writing*) = pad
- (*of apartments*) = block

die **Blockflöte**, *plural* Blockflöten
= recorder

blöd *adjective*
= stupid, = silly

der **Blödsinn**
= nonsense

die **Blondine**, *plural* Blondinen
= blonde

bloß *adverb*
= only, = just

blühen *verb*
- (*of a plant*) = to blossom, = to flower
- (*of a business*) = to flourish

die **Blume**, *plural* Blumen
= flower

der **Blumenkohl**
= cauliflower

die **Bluse**, *plural* Blusen
= blouse

das **Blut**
= blood

bluten *verb*
= to bleed

der **Bock**, *plural* Böcke
(*deer, rabbit*) = buck
(*goat*) = billy-goat
(*sheep*) = ram

der **Boden**, *plural* Böden
- = ground
  (*in a room*) = floor
  (*of a container*) = bottom
- = loft, = attic

der **Bodensee**
= Lake Constance

bog ▶ biegen

der **Bogen**, *plural* Bögen
- = curve
  = arch
- (*in skiing*) = turn

die **Bohne**, *plural* Bohnen
= bean

bohren *verb*
= to drill

der **Bohrer**, *plural* Bohrer
= drill

der **Bolzen**, *plural* Bolzen
= bolt

der or das **Bonbon**, *plural* Bonbons
= sweet

das **Boot**, *plural* Boote
= boat

die **Bordkarte**, *plural* Bordkarten
= boarding pass

borgen *verb*
- = to borrow

* sich etwas borgen = to borrow something
* jemandem etwas borgen = to lend someone something

die **Börse**, *plural* Börsen
= stock exchange

böse *adjective*
* = bad
= evil
* (*of a child*) = naughty
* = angry
ich bin ihm böse = I am angry with him

boshaft *adjective*
= malicious

bot ▶ bieten

der **Bote**, *plural* Boten
= messenger

die **Botin**, *plural* Botinnen
= messenger

die **Botschaft**, *plural* Botschaften
* = message
* = embassy

der **Botschafter**, *plural* Botschafter
= ambassador

die **Botschafterin**, *plural* Botschafterinnen
= ambassador

die **Bowle**, *plural* Bowlen
(*drink*) = punch

boxen *verb*
* = to box
* = to punch

brach ▶ brechen

brachte ▶ bringen

die **Branche**, *plural* Branchen
= (line of) business

das **Branchenverzeichnis**, *plural* Branchenverzeichnisse
= classified directory

die **Brandung**
= surf

brannte ▶ brennen

(das) **Brasilien**
= Brazil

braten *irregular verb*
* = to fry
* = to roast

die **Bratpfanne**, *plural* Bratpfannen
= frying pan

der **Brauch**, *plural* Bräuche
= custom

brauchen *verb*
= to need

die **Brauerei**, *plural* Brauereien
= brewery

braun *adjective*
= brown

die **Bräune**
= tan

die **Brause**, *plural* Brausen
= fizzy drink

die **Braut**, *plural* Bräute
= bride

der **Bräutigam**, *plural* Bräutigame
= bridegroom

brav *adjective*
= good

die **BRD**
(*Bundesrepublik Deutschland*) = FRG

brechen *irregular verb*
* = to break
er hat sich den Arm gebrochen = he broke his arm
* = to vomit

breit *adjective*
= wide, = broad

das **Breitband**
= broadband

die **Breite**, *plural* Breiten
= width

die **Bremse**, *plural* Bremsen
* (*of a car, bike*) = brake
* = horsefly

bremsen *verb*
= to brake
= to slow down

brennen *irregular verb*
* = to burn
* (*of a light*) = to be on

der **Brenner**, *plural* Brenner
= burner

der **Brennpunkt**, *plural* Brennpunkte
= focus

das **Brett**, *plural* Bretter
* = board
* = plank
* = shelf

bricht ▶ brechen

der **Brief**, *plural* Briefe
= letter

der **Brieffreund**, *plural* Brieffreunde
= pen friend

die **Brieffreundin**, *plural* Brieffreundinnen
= pen friend

der **Briefkasten**, *plural* Briefkästen
* = letterbox
* = postbox, = mailbox

die **Briefmarke**, plural Briefmarken
= stamp

die **Brieftasche**, plural Brieftaschen
= wallet

der **Briefträger**, plural Briefträger
= postman, = mailman

der **Briefumschlag**, plural
Briefumschläge
= envelope

brief ▶braten

der **Brillant**, plural Brillanten
= diamond

die **Brille**, plural Brillen
= glasses, = spectacles

bringen irregular verb
• = to bring
(bring away) = to take
ich bringe dich nach Hause = I'll take you
home
• (in a cinema) = to show

die **Brise**, plural Brisen
= breeze

der **Brite**, plural Briten
= Briton
die Briten = the British

die **Britin**, plural Britinnen
= Briton

britisch adjective
= British

die **Brombeere**, plural Brombeeren
= blackberry

die **Brosche**, plural Broschen
= brooch

die **Broschüre**, plural Broschüren
= brochure

das **Brot**, plural Brote
= bread
ein Brot = a loaf of bread or a slice of
bread

das **Brötchen**, plural Brötchen
= roll

der **Bruch**, plural Brüche
• = break
(of a bone) = fracture
• (in maths) = fraction

der **Bruchteil**, plural Bruchteile
= fraction

die **Brücke**, plural Brücken
= bridge

der **Bruder**, plural Brüder
= brother

die **Brühe**, plural Brühen
= broth
(for cooking) = stock

brüllen verb
= to roar

brummen verb
= to buzz
(of an animal) = to growl
(of an engine) = to hum

der **Brunnen**, plural Brunnen
• = well
• = fountain

die **Brust**, plural Brüste
= chest
= breast

brutto adverb
= gross

das **Buch**, plural Bücher
= book

buchen verb
= to book

die **Bücherei**, plural Büchereien
= library

der **Buchhalter**, plural Buchhalter
= accountant, = bookkeeper

die **Buchhalterin**, plural Buchhalterinnen
= accountant, = bookkeeper

die **Buchhandlung**, plural
Buchhandlungen
= bookshop

die **Büchse**, plural Büchsen
= tin, = can

der **Buchstabe**, plural Buchstaben
= letter
ein großer Buchstabe = a capital letter
ein kleiner Buchstabe = a small letter

buchstabieren verb
= to spell

die **Bucht**, plural Buchten
= bay

bücken: sich bücken verb
= to bend down

die **Bude**, plural Buden
• = hut
• (in a market) = stall
• seine Bude ✗= his room

das **Bügeleisen**, plural Bügeleisen
= iron

bügeln verb
= to iron

die **Bühne**, plural Bühnen
= stage

der **Bulle**, plural Bullen
= bull

✗ in informal situations

bummeln *verb*
- (**!** *sein*) (*around town*) = to stroll
- (*be slow*) = to dawdle

der **Bundesrat**
= Upper House (*of the German Parliament*)

die **Bundesrepublik**
= federal republic

der **Bundestag**
= Lower House (*of the German Parliament*)

die **Bundeswehr**
= army

bunt *adjective*
= colourful, = colorful

der **Buntstift**, *plural* Buntstifte
= coloured pencil, = crayon

die **Burg**, *plural* Burgen
= castle

bürgen *verb*
bürgen für = to vouch for

der **Bürger**, *plural* Bürger
= citizen

die **Bürgerin**, *plural* Bürgerinnen
= citizen

bürgerlich *adjective*
- = civil
- = middle-class

der **Bürgermeister**, *plural* Bürgermeister
= mayor

der **Bürgersteig**, *plural* Bürgersteige
= pavement, = sidewalk

das **Büro**, *plural* Büros
= office

die **Büroklammer**, *plural* Büroklammern
= paper clip

die **Bürste**, *plural* Bürsten
= brush

bürsten *verb*
= to brush

der **Bus**, *plural* Busse
= bus

der **Busch**, *plural* Büsche
= bush

der **Busen**, *plural* Busen
= bosom

der **Büstenhalter**, *plural* Büstenhalter
= bra

das **Butterbrot**, *plural* Butterbrote
= sandwich

bzw. ▶beziehungsweise

Cc

ca. *abbreviation*
(*circa*) = approx.

der **Callcenter**, *plural* Callcenters
= call centre

der **Campingplatz**, *plural* Campingplätze
= campsite

die **CD**, *plural* CDs
= CD

der **CD-Spieler**, *plural* CD-Spieler
= CD player

Celsius *adjective*
= Celsius, = centigrade

der **Cent**, *plural* Cents
= cent

der **Champignon**, *plural* Champignons
= mushroom

die **Chance**, *plural* Chancen
= chance

der **Charakter**, *plural* Charaktere
= character

charakteristisch *adjective*
= characteristic

charmant *adjective*
= charming

der **Chef**, *plural* Chefs
= boss

die **Chefin**, *plural* Chefinnen
= boss

die **Chemie**
= chemistry

der **Chemiker**, *plural* Chemiker
= chemist

die **Chemikerin**, *plural* Chemikerinnen
= chemist

chemisch *adjective*
= chemical
chemische Reinigung = dry-cleaning

chinesisch *adjective*
= Chinese

Chips (*plural*)
= crisps, = chips

der **Chirurg**, *plural* Chirurgen
= surgeon

die **Chirurgin**, *plural* Chirurginnen
= surgeon

der **Chor**, *plural* Chöre
= choir

der **Christ**, *plural* Christen
= Christian

die **Christin**, *plural* Christinnen
= Christian

der **Christus**
= Christ

circa *adverb*
= approximately

der **Clown**, *plural* Clowns
= clown

der **Club**, *plural* Clubs
= club

die or das **Cola**®, *plural* Colas *or* Cola
= Coke®

der **Comic**, *plural* Comics
= cartoon

das **Comicheft**, *plural* Comichefte
= comic

der **Computer**, *plural* Computer
= computer

der **Container**, *plural* Container
• = container
• = skip

der **Cordsamt**
= corduroy

die **Couch**, *plural* Couchs
= sofa

die **Creme**, *plural* Cremes
= cream

D d

da
1 *adverb*
• = there
  da unten = down there
• (*indicating time*) = then
  von da an = from then on
• (*for that reason*) = so
  der Zug war weg, da habe ich den Bus genommen = the train had gone, so I took the bus
• da sein = to be there/here
  sind alle da? = is everyone here?
  ich bin gleich wieder da = I'll be right back
  ist noch Brot da? = is there any bread left?
2 *conjunction*
  = as, = since

dabei *adverb*
• (*next to, included*) = with it
  dicht dabei = close by
• (*referring to something previously mentioned*) = about it
  wichtig dabei ist, dass ... = the important thing about it is that ...
  da ist doch nichts dabei = there's nothing to it
• = at the same time
  = during this
• (*although*) = and yet
• dabei sein (*be present*) = to be there
• dabei sein (*take part*) = to be involved
  dabei sein, etwas zu tun = to be just doing something

das **Dach**, *plural* Dächer
= roof

der **Dachboden**, *plural* Dachböden
= loft, = attic

dachte ▶denken

der **Dackel**, *plural* Dackel
= dachshund

dadurch *adverb*
• = through it/them
• (*for that reason*) = because of that
• dadurch, dass = because

dafür *adverb*
• = for it/them
  dafür kriegst du nicht viel = you won't get much for it/them
• = instead
• (*to even things out*) = but then
• dafür, dass = considering (that)

dagegen *adverb*
• = against it/them
• (*when swapping*) = for it/them
• (*showing the opposite*) = by comparison

daheim *adverb*
= at home

daher *adverb*
• = from there
• (*for that reason*) = that's why

dahin *adverb*
= there
bis dahin = until then, (*in the future*) = by then

dahinter *adverb*
• = behind it/them
• dahinter kommen = to find out

da|lassen *irregular verb*
= to leave there

damals *adverb*
= at that time

die **Dame**, *plural* Damen
• = lady
• (*in chess, cards*) = queen
• (*game*) = draughts, = checkers

OLD = old spelling

damit
1 *adverb*
* = with it/them
hör auf damit = stop it
* (*thus*) = therefore
2 *conjunction* = so that
schreib es auf, damit du es nicht vergisst
= write it down so that you don't forget

der **Damm**, *plural* Dämme
* = dam
* = embankment

dämmern *verb*
es dämmert (*in the morning*) = it is getting light, (*in the evening*) = it is getting dark

die **Dämmerung**
* = dawn
* = dusk

der **Dampf**, *plural* Dämpfe
= steam

dampfen *verb*
= to steam

dämpfen *verb*
* (*in cooking*) = to steam
* = to muffle
* (*reduce*) = to dampen

danach *adverb*
* = after it/them
danach suchen = to search for it/them
danach riechen = to smell of it/them
es sieht danach aus = it looks like it
* = according to it/them
* = afterwards

daneben *adverb*
* = next to it/them
* = in addition
* = by comparison

(das) **Dänemark**
= Denmark

der **Dank**
= thanks
vielen Dank = thank you very much

dankbar *adjective*
= grateful

danke *interjection*
= thank you, = thanks
danke schön = thank you very much

danken *verb*
= to thank
nichts zu danken = don't mention it

dann *adverb*
= then

daran *adverb*
* = on it/them, = at it/them
* daran denken = to think of it/them
* nahe daran sein, etwas zu tun = to be on the point of doing something

darauf *adverb*
* = on it/them
* darauf warten = to wait for it
* darauf antworten = to reply to it
* = after that

daraufhin *adverb*
= as a result

daraus *adverb*
* (*from a container*) = out of it/them
* (*from material*) = from it/them
* was ist daraus geworden? = what has become of it?

darf, darfst ▶ dürfen

das **Darlehen**, *plural* Darlehen
= loan

der **Darm**, *plural* Därme
= intestine(s)

dar|stellen *verb*
* = to represent
* = to portray
* = to describe
* (*in the theatre*) = to play

der **Darsteller**, *plural* Darsteller
= actor

die **Darstellerin**, *plural* Darstellerinnen
= actress

die **Darstellung**, *plural* Darstellungen
* = representation
* = portrayal
* = description
* = interpretation

darüber *adverb*
* = over it/them
* (*higher up*) = above it/them
* darüber lachen = to laugh about it

darum *adverb*
* = round it/them
* darum kämpfen = to fight for it
* (*for that reason*) = that's why
* darum, weil = because

darunter *adverb*
* = under it/them
(*lower*) = below it/them
* = less
fünfzig Mark oder sogar darunter = 50 marks or even less

das
1 *article* (*neuter*) = the
2 *pronoun*
* (*object*) = which
(*person*) = who
das Kind, das weint = the child who is crying
* that
das da = that one
das geht = that's all right

da sein = dasein ▶ da

das **Dasein**
= existence

dass (**daß**ⓄⓁⒹ) *conjunction*
= that
ich bin froh, dass ... = I'm glad that ...

dasselbe *pronoun*
= the same, = the same one

die **Datei**, *plural* Dateien
= (data) file

Daten (*plural*)
= data

die **Datenverarbeitung**
= data processing

datieren *verb*
= to date

das **Datum**, *plural* Daten
= date

die **Dauer**
= duration, = length
auf die Dauer = in the long run

der **Dauerauftrag**, *plural* Daueraufträge
= standing order

die **Dauerkarte**, *plural* Dauerkarten
= season ticket

dauern *verb*
= to last

dauernd *adjective*
= constant

die **Dauerwelle**, *plural* Dauerwellen
= perm

der **Daumen**, *plural* Daumen
= thumb

die **Daunendecke**, *plural* Daunendecken
= duvet, = continental quilt

davon *adverb*
• = from it/them
• = about it/them
• die Hälfte davon = half of of it/them

davor *adverb*
• = in front of it/them
• Angst davor haben = to be frightened of it
• = beforehand

dazu *adverb*
• = to it/them
• = in addition, = with it/them
  noch dazu = in addition to it
• = for it
  ich habe keine Lust dazu = I don't feel like it
• jemanden dazu bringen, etwas zu tun = to get someone to do something
  er kam nicht dazu = he didn't get round to it

dazu|geben *irregular verb*
= to add

dazu|gehören *verb*
• = to belong to it/them
• (*of accessories*) = to go with it/them

dazu|kommen *irregular verb* (**!** *sein*)
• = to arrive
• = to be added
  kommt noch etwas dazu? = would you like anything else?

dazwischen *adverb*
= in between

dazwischen|kommen *irregular verb* (**!** *sein*)
= to crop up

die **Debatte**, *plural* Debatten
= debate

die **Decke**, *plural* Decken
• (*on a bed*) = blanket, = cover
• (*on a table*) = cloth
• = ceiling

der **Deckel**, *plural* Deckel
= lid
(*on a bottle*) = top

decken *verb*
• = to cover
  den Tisch decken = to lay the table
• jemanden decken = to cover up for someone, (*in sport*) = to mark someone

die **Deckung**
• = cover
  in Deckung gehen = to take cover
• (*in sport*) = marking, = defence

das **Defizit**, *plural* Defizite
= deficit

der **Degen**, *plural* Degen
= sword
(*in fencing*) = épée

dehnbar *adjective*
= elastic

dehnen *verb*
= to stretch

der **Deich**, *plural* Deiche
= dike

dein *adjective*
= your

deiner/deine/deins *pronoun*
= yours

der **Delfin**, *plural* Delfine ▶Delphin
= dent

die **Delle**, *plural* Dellen
= dent

der **Delphin**, *plural* Delphine
= dolphin

dem
1 *article* = (to) the
2 *pronoun*
• (*person*) = to him
  (*object*) = to it, = to that one
• (*person*) = to whom

(*object*) = to which
der Junge, dem der Ball gehört = the boy
to whom the ball belongs

demnächst *adverb*
= shortly

die **Demokratie**, *plural* Demokratien
= democracy

demokratisch *adjective*
= democratic

der **Demonstrant**, *plural* Demonstranten
= demonstrator
= protester

den
1 *article* = the
2 *pronoun*
• (*person*) = him
(*object*) = it, = that one
• (*person*) = whom
(*object*) = which
der Rock, den ich gekauft habe = the
skirt I bought

denen *pronoun*
• = (to) them
• (*person*) = to whom
(*object*) = to which
die Zuschauer, denen der Film gezeigt
wurde = the audience to whom the
film was shown

denken *irregular verb*
= to think
das kann ich mir denken = I can imagine

das **Denkmal**, *plural* Denkmäler
= monument

denn
1 *conjunction* = for
2 *adverb*
warum denn nicht? = why ever not?
es sei denn = unless

dennoch *adverb*
= nevertheless

deprimieren *verb*
= to depress

der
1 *article*
• (*masculine*) = the
• (*genitive of die*) = of the
das Kleid der Frau = the woman's dress
(*dative of die*) = (to) the
sie gab es der Frau = she gave it to the
woman
2 *pronoun*
• (*person*) = who
(*object*) = which
der Arzt, der mir geholfen hat = the
doctor who helped me
• (*person*) = he, = him
(*object*) = that (one)

deren *pronoun*
• = their

• (*person*) = whose
(*object*) = of which

derselbe *pronoun*
= the same, = the same one

des *article*
= of the
die Mütze des Jungen = the boy's cap

deshalb *adverb*
= therefore

desinfizieren *verb*
= to disinfect

dessen *pronoun*
• (*person*) = his
(*object*) = its
• (*person*) = whose
(*object*) = of which
der Junge, dessen Hund bellt = the boy
whose dog is barking

desto *adverb*
= the
je mehr, desto besser = the more the
better

deswegen *adverb*
= therefore

der **Detektiv**, *plural* Detektive
= detective

deutlich *adjective*
= clear

deutsch *adjective*
= German
auf Deutsch = in German

das **Deutsch**
= German

der/die **Deutsche**, *plural* Deutschen
= German

(das) **Deutschland**
= Germany

Devisen (*plural*)
= foreign currency

der **Dezember**
= December

d.h. *abbreviation*
(*das heißt*) = i.e.

das **Dia**, *plural* Dias
= slide

der **Dialekt**, *plural* Dialekte
= dialect

der **Diamant**, *plural* Diamanten
= diamond

die **Diät**, *plural* Diäten
= diet

dich *pronoun*
• = you
• (*reflexive*) = yourself

dicht *adjective*
* = thick, = dense
* = airtight
* = watertight

der **Dichter**, *plural* Dichter
= poet

die **Dichterin**, *plural* Dichterinnen
= poetess

die **Dichtung**, *plural* Dichtungen
* = poetry
* = seal, = washer

dick *adjective*
* = thick
= swollen
* (*of person*) = fat

die
1 *article*
* (*feminine singular*) = the
* (*plural of the articles der, die and das*) = the
2 *pronoun*
* (*person*) = who
(*object*) = which
die Frau, die ich gesehen habe = the woman I saw
* (*plural of the pronouns der, die and das*) die [Kinder | Sachen | Städte ...], die ich gesehen habe = the [children | things | towns ...] I saw
* (*person*) = she, = her, (*plural*) = them (*object*) = that (one), (*plural*) = those

der **Dieb**, *plural* Diebe
= thief

die **Diebin**, *plural* Diebinnen
= thief

der **Diebstahl**, *plural* Diebstähle
= theft

die **Diele**, *plural* Dielen
* = hall
* = floorboard

dienen *verb*
= to serve

der **Dienst**, *plural* Dienste
= service
Dienst haben = to work, (*of a soldier or doctor*) = to be on duty

der **Dienstag**
= Tuesday

dienstags *adverb*
= on Tuesdays

dienstfrei *adjective*
= free
ein dienstfreier Tag = a day off

dienstlich *adverb*
= on business

---

die **Dienstreise**, *plural* Dienstreisen
= business trip

dies *pronoun*
= this

dieselbe *pronoun*
= the same, = the same one

dieser/diese/dieses
1 *adjective* = this, (*plural*) = these
2 *pronoun* = this one, (*plural*) = these

diesmal *adverb*
= this time

die **Digitaluhr**, *plural* Digitaluhren
= digital watch
= digital clock

das **Diktat**, *plural* Diktate
= dictation

die **Diktatur**, *plural* Diktaturen
= dictatorship

das **Ding**, *plural* Dinge
= thing

der/die/das **Dings**
= thingamy

das **Diplom**, *plural* Diplome
= diploma, = degree

dir *pronoun*
* = (to) you
* (*reflexive*) = yourself

direkt *adjective*
= direct

der **Direktor**, *plural* Direktoren
= director
(*of a bank*) = manager
(*of a school*) = headmaster, = principal
(*of a prison*) = governor

die **Direktorin**, *plural* Direktorinnen
= director
(*of a bank*) = manager
(*of a school*) = headmistress, = principal
(*of a prison*) = governor

der **Dirigent**, *plural* Dirigenten
= conductor

die **Diskette**, *plural* Disketten
= (floppy) disk

die **Diskussion**, *plural* Diskussionen
= discussion

diskutieren *verb*
= to discuss

die **Disziplin**, *plural* Disziplinen
= discipline

DM *abbreviation*
(*Deutsche Mark*) = DM, = Deutschmark

die **D-Mark**, *plural* D-Mark
= German mark, = Deutschmark

doch
1 *adverb*
• = yes
 das stimmt nicht—doch! = that's not
 right—yes it is!
• = after all
2 *conjunction* = but

der **Doktor**, *plural* Doktoren
 = doctor

das **Dokument**, *plural* Dokumente
 = document

der **Dokumentarfilm**, *plural*
 Dokumentarfilme
 = documentary (film)

dolmetschen *verb*
 = to interpret

der **Dolmetscher**, *plural* Dolmetscher
 = interpreter

die **Dolmetscherin**, *plural*
 Dolmetscherinnen
 = interpreter

der **Dom**, *plural* Dome
 = cathedral

die **Donau**
 = Danube

der **Donner**
 = thunder

donnern *verb*
 = to thunder

der **Donnerstag**
 = Thursday

donnerstags *adverb*
 = on Thursdays

doof✶ *adjective*
 = stupid

das **Doppel**, *plural* Doppel
• = duplicate
• (*in sport*) = doubles

der **Doppelpunkt**, *plural* Doppelpunkte
 = colon

doppelt
1 *adjective* = double
2 *adverb* = twice
 doppelt so viel = twice as much

das **Dorf**, *plural* Dörfer
 = village

der **Dorn**, *plural* Dornen
 = thorn

dort *adverb*
 = there

die **Dose**, *plural* Dosen
 = tin, = can

der **Dosenöffner**, *plural* Dosenöffner
 = tin opener, = can opener

die **Dosis**, *plural* Dosen
 = dose

der **Dozent**, *plural* Dozenten
 = lecturer

die **Dozentin**, *plural* Dozentinnen
 = lecturer

der **Drache**, *plural* Drachen
 = dragon

der **Drachen**, *plural* Drachen
 = kite

das **Drachenfliegen**
 = hang-gliding

der **Draht**, *plural* Drähte
 = wire

drahtlos *adjective*
 = wireless

dran✶ ▶daran
 ich bin dran = it's my turn

drängen *verb*
• = to push
• (*persuade*) = to press

dran|kommen✶ *irregular verb* (**!** *sein*)
 = to have one's turn
 wer kommt dran? = whose turn is it?

draußen *adverb*
 = outside

der **Dreck**
 = dirt

dreckig *adjective*
 = dirty
 = filthy

das **Drehbuch**, *plural* Drehbücher
 = screenplay
 = script

drehen *verb*
• = to turn
• (*make a film*) = to shoot
• sich drehen = to turn
 es dreht sich um unsere Ferien = it is
 about our holidays

drei *adjective*
 = three

das **Dreieck**, *plural* Dreiecke
 = triangle

dreifach *adjective*
 = triple

dreißig *adjective*
 = thirty

drei viertel (**dreiviertel**⃝ᴼᴸᴰ) *adverb*
 = three-quarters

die **Dreiviertelstunde**, *plural*
 Dreiviertelstunden
 = three-quarters of an hour

D

dreizehn *adjective*
= thirteen

dressieren *verb*
= to train

dringend *adjective*
= urgent

drinnen *adverb*
= inside
= indoors

dritt *adverb*
wir sind zu dritt = there are three of us

dritte ▶dritter

das **Drittel**, *plural* Drittel
= third

drittens *adverb*
= thirdly

dritter/dritte/drittes *adjective*
= third

die **Droge**, *plural* Drogen
= drug

drogensüchtig *adjective*
= addicted to drugs

der/die **Drogensüchtige**, *plural* Drogensüchtigen
= drug addict

die **Drogerie**, *plural* Drogerien
= chemist's, = drugstore

drohen *verb*
= to threaten

die **Drohung**, *plural* Drohungen
= threat

drüben *adverb*
= over there

der **Druck¹**
= pressure

der **Druck²** *plural* Drucke
= print

drucken *verb*
= to print

drücken *verb*
• = to press
= to push
= to hug
• (*of shoes*) = to pinch

der **Drucker**, *plural* Drucker
= printer

die **Drucksache**, *plural* Drucksachen
= printed matter

die **Druckschrift**, *plural* Druckschriften
• = type
• = block letters
• = pamphlet

der **Dschungel**, *plural* Dschungel
= jungle

du *pronoun*
= you

der **Duft**, *plural* Düfte
= fragrance, = scent

duften *verb*
nach etwas duften = to smell of
something

dumm *adjective*
= stupid

dunkel *adjective*
• = dark
im Dunkeln = in the dark
• eine dunkle Stimme = a deep voice

die **Dunkelheit**
= darkness

dünn *adjective*
= thin
(*watery*) = weak

das **Duo**, *plural* Duos
= duet

durch
1 *preposition* (+ *accusative*)
• = through
• (*with the help of*) = by
• (*because of*) = as a result of
2 *adverb* = through
die Nacht durch = throughout the night

durchaus *adverb*
= absolutely

durch|brechen *irregular verb*
• = to snap
• (**!** *sein*) das Brett ist durchgebrochen =
the board has snapped

durcheinander *adverb*
durcheinander sein (*of a room*) = to be in
a mess, (*of a person*) = to be confused

das **Durcheinander**
= muddle, = chaos

der **Durchfall**
= diarrhoea

durch|fallen *irregular verb* (**!** *sein*)
• = to fall through
• (*in an exam*) = to fail

durch|führen *verb*
= to carry out

der **Durchgang**, *plural* Durchgänge
• = passage
• (*in sport*) = round

der **Durchgangsverkehr**
= through traffic

durch|gehen *irregular verb* (**!** *sein*)
• = to go through
• (*escape*) = to run away

durch|halten *irregular verb*
* (*in a battle*) = to hold out
* = to keep up, = to stand

durch|kommen *irregular verb* (**!** *sein*)
* = to come through
* (*on the phone, in an exam*) = to get through
* (*beat illness*) = to pull through

durch|lassen *irregular verb*
* = to let through
* = to let in

der **Durchmesser**, *plural* Durchmesser
= diameter

die **Durchsage**, *plural* Durchsagen
= announcement

der **Durchschnitt**, *plural* Durchschnitte
= average

durchschnittlich
1 *adjective* = average
2 *adverb* = on average

durch|setzen *verb*
* = to carry through
* sich durchsetzen (*of a person*) = to assert oneself, (*of an idea*) = to catch on

durchsichtig *adjective*
= transparent

durch|streichen *irregular verb*
= to cross out

durch|wählen *verb*
= to dial direct

der **Durchzug**
= draught

dürfen *irregular verb*
* = to be allowed
  er darf nicht auf der Straße spielen = he is not allowed to play in the street
* (*in questions*) darf ich? = may I?
* das darf er nicht sehen = he must not see it
* das dürfte genügen = that should be enough

durfte, durften. durftest, durftet ▶ dürfen

die **Dürre**, *plural* Dürren
= drought

der **Durst**
= thirst

durstig *adjective*
= thirsty

die **Dusche**, *plural* Duschen
= shower

duschen *verb*
* = to have a shower
* sich duschen = to have a shower

das **Düsenflugzeug**, *plural* Düsenflugzeuge
= jet (aircraft)

düster *adjective*
= gloomy

das **Dutzend**, *plural* Dutzende
= dozen

duzen *verb*
jemanden duzen (*use the familiar form of 'you'*) = to call someone 'du'

der **D-Zug**, *plural* D-Züge
= fast train, = express

Ee

die **Ebbe**, *plural* Ebben
= low tide

eben
1 *adjective* = level, = flat
2 *adverb*
* = just
  er war eben hier = he was just here
* eben! = exactly!

die **Ebene**, *plural* Ebenen
* (*in geography*) = plain
* (*in geometry*) = plane
* = level

ebenso *adverb*
= just as

echt *adjective*
= genuine, = real

der **Eckball**, *plural* Eckbälle
= corner (kick)

die **Ecke**, *plural* Ecken
= corner

eckig *adjective*
= square
= angular

der **Edelstein**, *plural* Edelsteine
= precious stone

der **Efeu**, *plural* Efeus
= ivy

die **EG**
(*Europäische Gemeinschaft*) = EC

egal *adjective*
das ist mir egal = it's all the same to me, = I don't care
egal, wie groß = no matter how big

egoistisch *adjective*
= selfish

ehe conjunction
= before

die **Ehe**, plural Ehen
= marriage

die **Ehefrau**, plural Ehefrauen
= wife

ehemalig adjective
= former

der **Ehemann**, plural Ehemänner
= husband

das **Ehepaar**, plural Ehepaare
= married couple

eher adverb
• = earlier, = sooner
• = rather
er ist eher faul als dumm = he's lazy
rather than stupid

die **Ehre**, plural Ehren
= honour

der **Ehrgeiz**
= ambition

ehrgeizig adjective
= ambitious

ehrlich adjective
= honest
ehrlich gesagt = to be honest

das **Ei**, plural Eier
= egg

die **Eiche**, plural Eichen
= oak

das **Eichhörnchen**, plural Eichhörnchen
= squirrel

der **Eid**, plural Eide
= oath

die **Eidechse**, plural Eidechsen
= lizard

der **Eifer**
= eagerness

eifersüchtig adjective
= jealous

eigen adjective
= own

eigenartig adjective
= peculiar

die **Eigenschaft**, plural Eigenschaften
• = quality
• = characteristic

eigentlich
1 adjective = actual
2 adverb = actually

das **Eigentum**
= property

der **Eigentümer**, plural Eigentümer
= owner

eignen: sich eignen verb
= to be suitable

die **Eile**
= hurry

eilen verb (**!** sein)
= to hurry

eilig
1 adjective
• = urgent
• = hurried
2 adverb
= hurriedly
es eilig haben = to be in a hurry

der **Eimer**, plural Eimer
= bucket

ein
1 article = a, = an
2 adjective = one
eines Tages = one day
einer Meinung sein = to be of the same
opinion
3 adverb
(on appliances) ein-aus = on-off
ein und aus gehen = to come and go

einander pronoun
= each other, = one another

die **Einbahnstraße**, plural
Einbahnstraßen
= one-way street

der **Einband**, plural Einbände
= cover

ein|bauen verb
= to fit
= to install

die **Einbauküche**, plural Einbauküchen
= fitted kitchen

ein|biegen irregular verb (**!** sein)
= to turn

ein|bilden: sich einbilden verb
= to imagine

ein|brechen irregular verb (**!** sein)
= to break in

der **Einbrecher**, plural Einbrecher
= burglar

eindeutig adjective
= clear
= obvious
= definite

der **Eindruck**, plural Eindrücke
= impression

---

eine ▶ einer

eineinhalb *adjective*
= one and a half

einer/eine/eins *pronoun*
* = one
* = someone
  kaum einer = hardly anyone
* das macht einen müde = it makes you
  tired

einerseits *adverb*
= on the one hand

einfach
1 *adjective*
* = simple, = easy
* (*of a ticket*) = single
2 *adverb* = simply

die **Einfahrt**, *plural* Einfahrten
* = entrance
* (*of a train*) = arrival
* (*on a motorway*) = slip road

der **Einfall**, *plural* Einfälle
= idea

ein|fallen *irregular verb* (**!** *sein*)
jemandem einfallen = to occur to
someone
sein Name fällt mir nicht ein = I can't
think of his name

der **Einfluss** (**Einfluß**ⓄⓁⒹ), *plural* Einflüsse
= influence

ein|frieren *irregular verb* (**!** *sein*)
= to freeze

die **Einfuhr**, *plural* Einfuhren
= import

ein|führen *verb*
* = to introduce
* = to import

die **Einführung**, *plural* Einführungen
= introduction

der **Eingang**, *plural* Eingänge
= entrance, = way in
kein Eingang = no entry

ein|geben *irregular verb*
* = to hand in
* (*in computing*) = to input

eingebildet *adjective*
* = imaginary
* = conceited

der/die **Eingeborene**, *plural* Eingeborenen
= native

ein|gehen *irregular verb* (**!** *sein*)
* (*arrive*) = to come in
* (*of clothes*) = to shrink
* (*of plants*) = to die
* auf einen Plan eingehen = to agree to a
  plan
  ein Risiko eingehen = to take a risk

ein|gießen *irregular verb*
= to pour

der **Eingriff**, *plural* Eingriffe
* = intervention
* (*medical*) = operation

einheimisch *adjective*
* = native
* = local

die **Einheit**, *plural* Einheiten
* = unity
* (*measure*) = unit

einheitlich *adjective*
= uniform

der **Einheitspreis**, *plural* Einheitspreise
* = standard price
* = flat fare

einhundert *adjective*
= one hundred

einige ▶ einiger

einigen *verb*
* = to unite
* sich einigen = to come to an agreement

einiger/einige/einiges
1 *adjective*
= some
= quite a lot of
vor einiger Zeit = some time ago
2 *pronoun*
* einige (*plural*) = some
  (*more*) = several
  (*even more*) = quite a lot
  nur einige waren noch da = there were
  only a few left
* einiges = some things

einigermaßen *adverb*
= fairly
= fairly well

einiges ▶ einiger

der **Einkauf**, *plural* Einkäufe
* = shopping
* (*single item*) = purchase
  Einkäufe machen = to do some shopping

ein|kaufen *verb*
* = to buy
* = to shop
  einkaufen gehen = to go shopping

das **Einkaufszentrum**, *plural*
Einkaufszentren
= shopping centre, = shopping mall

das **Einkommen**, *plural* Einkommen
= income

die **Einkommenssteuer**, *plural*
Einkommenssteuern
= income tax

ein|laden *irregular verb*
* = to invite
* = to load

E

die **Einladung**, *plural* Einladungen
= invitation

die **Einleitung**, *plural* Einleitungen
= introduction

ein|lösen *verb*
= to cash

einmal *adverb*
* (*in the past*) = once
(*in the future*) = one day
* (*other uses*)
auf einmal = suddenly, (*at once*) = at the same time
nicht einmal = not even

einmalig *adjective*
* = unique
* einmalig!�れ = fantastic!

ein|mischen: sich einmischen
verb
= to interfere

ein|ordnen *verb*
* = to put in order
* sich einordnen (*when driving*) = to get in lane

ein|packen *verb*
* = to pack
* = to wrap

ein|reichen *verb*
= to hand in

die **Einreise**
= entry

ein|richten *verb*
* = to furnish
* sich einrichten = to furnish one's home

die **Einrichtung**, *plural* Einrichtungen
* = furnishing
(*furniture*) = furnishings
* = institution

eins
1 *adjective* = one
2 *pronoun* ▶einer

einsam *adjective*
= lonely

der **Einsatz**, *plural* Einsätze
* = use
* (*bet*) = stake

ein|schalten *verb*
* = to switch on
* sich einschalten = to intervene

ein|schicken *verb*
= to send in

ein|schlafen *irregular verb* (! *sein*)
= to go to sleep

ein|schließen *irregular verb*
* = to lock in

* = to include
Bedienung eingeschlossen = service included

einschließlich
1 *preposition* (+ *genitive*) = including
2 *adverb* = inclusive

ein|schränken *verb*
* = to restrict
* = to cut back
* sich einschränken = to economize

das **Einschreiben**, *plural* Einschreiben
= registered letter *or* parcel
per Einschreiben = by registered post, = registered

ein|sehen *irregular verb*
= to realize

einseitig
1 *adjective* = one-sided
2 *adverb* = on one side

ein|senden *irregular verb*
= to send in

ein|setzen *verb*
* = to use
* (*when betting*) = to stake
* = to insert
* sich für jemanden einsetzen = to support someone

die **Einsicht**
* = insight
* = sense

ein|sperren *verb*
= to lock up

der **Einspruch**, *plural* Einsprüche
= objection

einspurig *adjective*
= single-lane

einst *adverb*
* = once
* (*in the future*) = one day

ein|steigen *irregular verb* (! *sein*)
= to get in
(*if it's a bus, train*) = to get on

ein|stellen *verb*
* (*in a job*) = to employ
* (*if it's a machine*) = to adjust
(*if it's a programme, station*) = to tune into
* = to stop
(*if it's a strike, search*) = to call off

die **Einstellung**, *plural* Einstellungen
* (*of workers*) = employment
* (*of machines*) = adjustment
* (*of a station*) = tuning
* = stopping
(*of strike, search*) = calling off
* = attitude, = view

einstöckig *adjective*
= single-storey

ein|stürzen *verb* (**!** *sein*)
= to collapse

einstweilen *adverb*
• = for the time being
• = meanwhile

eintausend *adjective*
= one thousand

ein|teilen *verb*
• = to divide up
• = to organize

der **Eintopf**, *plural* Eintöpfe
= stew

der **Eintrag**, *plural* Einträge
= entry

ein|tragen *irregular verb*
• (*in a list*) = to enter
• sich eintragen = to register, = to put your name down

ein|treten *irregular verb* (**!** *sein*)
= to enter
in einen Klub eintreten = to join a club

der **Eintritt**
= entrance, = entry
= admission

die **Eintrittskarte**, *plural* Eintrittskarten
= (admission) ticket

der **Eintrittspreis**, *plural* Eintrittspreise
= admission charge

einverstanden *adjective*
einverstanden sein = to agree
mit jemandem einverstanden sein = to approve of someone

der **Einwand**, *plural* Einwände
= objection

der **Einwanderer**, *plural* Einwanderer
= immigrant

die **Einwanderin**, *plural* Einwanderinnen
= immigrant

einwandfrei *adjective*
= perfect

die **Einwegflasche**, *plural* Einwegflaschen
= non-returnable bottle

ein|weichen *verb*
= to soak

ein|weisen *irregular verb*
(*to hospital*) = to admit

ein|werfen *irregular verb*
• = to post, = to mail
(*if it's a coin*) = to put in
• (*in soccer*) = to throw in

ein|wickeln *verb*
= to wrap (up)

ein|willigen *verb*
= to agree

der **Einwohner**, *plural* Einwohner
= inhabitant

der **Einwurf**, *plural* Einwürfe
• (*for coins*) = slot
• (*comment*) = objection
• (*in soccer*) = throw-in

die **Einzahl**
= singular

ein|zahlen *verb*
= to pay in

das **Einzel**, *plural* Einzel
(*in sport*) = singles

der **Einzelhandel**
= retail trade

die **Einzelheit**, *plural* Einzelheiten
= detail

das **Einzelkind**, *plural* Einzelkinder
= only child

einzeln
1 *adjective*
• = single
• = individual
• (*not matching*) = odd
2 *adverb*
• = individually
• (*one after another*) = separately

der/die/das **Einzelne**, *plural* Einzelnen
• der/die Einzelne = the individual
• ein Einzelner/eine Einzelne/ein Einzelnes = a single one
jeder/jede Einzelne = every single one
Einzelne (*plural*) = some
• ins Einzelne gehen = to go into detail

das **Einzelzimmer**, *plural* Einzelzimmer
= single room

ein|ziehen *irregular verb*
• (*if it's a payment*) = to collect
• (*if it's feelers, claws*) = to draw in
den Kopf einziehen = to duck
• = to breathe in
• (**!** *sein*) (*into a house*) = to move in
(*be absorbed*) = to soak in

einzig *adjective*
= only
ein einziges Mal = only once

der/die/das **Einzige**, *plural* Einzigen
• = the only one
kein Einziger/keine Einzige/kein Einziges = not a single one
• das Einzige, was mich stört = the only thing that bothers me

das **Eis**
• = ice
• = ice cream

die **Eisbahn**, *plural* Eisbahnen
= skating rink

das **Eisen**, *plural* Eisen
= iron

die **Eisenbahn**, *plural* Eisenbahnen
= railway, = railroad

eisig *adjective*
= icy, = freezing

das **Eislaufen**
= ice-skating

der **Eiszapfen**, *plural* Eiszapfen
= icicle

die **Eiszeit**, *plural* Eiszeiten
= ice age

eitel *adjective*
= vain

der **Eiter**
= pus

der **Ekel**
= disgust

ekeln: sich ekeln *verb*
sich vor etwas ekeln = to find something
disgusting

eklig *adjective*
= disgusting

der **Elefant**, *plural* Elefanten
= elephant

der **Elektriker**, *plural* Elektriker
= electrician

elektrisch *adjective*
= electrical

die **Elektrizität**
= electricity

die **Elektronik**
= electronics

elektronisch *adjective*
= electronic

das **Elend**
= misery

elf *adjective*
= eleven

die **Elfe**, *plural* Elfen
= fairy

der **Elfmeter**, *plural* Elfmeter
(*in soccer*) = penalty

der **Ellbogen**, *plural* Ellbogen
= elbow

Eltern (*plural*)
= parents

die **E-Mail**, *plural* E-Mails
= email

die **E-Mail-Adresse**, *plural* E-Mail-
Adressen
= email address

das **Email**, *plural* Emails
= enamel

empfahl ▶ empfehlen

der **Empfang**, *plural* Empfänge
• (*party*) = reception
• = receipt

empfangen *irregular verb*
= to receive

der **Empfänger**, *plural* Empfänger
• = recipient
(*of a letter*) = addressee
• (*TV, radio*) = receiver

die **Empfängnisverhütung**
= contraception

der **Empfangs-/Sendebereich**
= coverage (*mobile phones*)

empfehlen *irregular verb*
= to recommend

empfindlich *adjective*
• = delicate
• = sensitive

empfing ▶ empfangen

empört *adjective*
= indignant

das **Ende**, *plural* Enden
= end
(*of a film, novel*) = ending
zu Ende sein = to be finished

enden *verb*
= to end

endgültig
1 *adjective* = final
2 *adverb* = finally
sich endgültig trennen = to separate for
good

endlich *adverb*
= at last, = finally

die **Endstation**, *plural* Endstationen
= terminus

die **Energie**
= energy

energisch *adjective*
= energetic

eng *adjective*
• = narrow
= tight
• (*of friendship*) = close
eng befreundet sein = to be close friends

der **Engel**, *plural* Engel
= angel

---

der **Engländer**, *plural* Engländer
= Englishman

die **Engländerin**, *plural* Engländerinnen
= Englishwoman

englisch *adjective*
= English
auf Englisch = in English

der **Enkel**, *plural* Enkel
= grandson

die **Enkelin**, *plural* Enkelinnen
= granddaughter

das **Enkelkind**, *plural* Enkelkinder
= grandchild

entdecken *verb*
= to discover

die **Entdeckung**, *plural* Entdeckungen
= discovery

die **Ente**, *plural* Enten
= duck

entfernen *verb*
= to remove

entfernt
1 *adjective* = distant
fünf Kilometer entfernt = 5 kilometres away
2 *adverb*
entfernt verwandt = distantly related

die **Entfernung**, *plural* Entfernungen
• = distance
• (*of stains*) = removal

entführen *verb*
• = to kidnap
• = to hijack

entgegengesetzt *adjective*
• = opposite
• (*of views*) = opposing

entgegenkommend *adjective*
• = obliging
• (*of traffic*) = oncoming

das **Entgelt**
= payment

das **Enthaarungsmittel**, *plural* Enthaarungsmittel
= hair remover

enthalten *irregular verb*
• = to contain
im Preis enthalten = included in the price
• sich der Stimme enthalten = to abstain

entkommen *irregular verb* (**!** *sein*)
= to escape

entlang *preposition* (+ *accusative*)
= along
die Straße entlang = along the road

entlang|gehen *irregular verb* (**!** *sein*)
= to walk along

entlang|laufen *irregular verb* (**!** *sein*)
= to run along

entlassen *irregular verb*
• (*from a job*) = to dismiss
• (*from hospital*) = to discharge
(*from prison*) = to release

die **Entlassung**, *plural* Entlassungen
• = dismissal
• = discharge
• = release

die **Entschädigung**, *plural* Entschädigungen
= compensation

entscheiden *irregular verb*
• = to decide (on)
• sich entscheiden = to decide

die **Entscheidung**, *plural* Entscheidungen
= decision

entschließen: sich entschließen *irregular verb*
= to decide
sich anders entschließen = to change one's mind

entschlossen *adjective*
= determined

der **Entschluss** (**Entschluß**ⓞⓛⓓ), *plural* Entschlüsse
= decision

entschuldigen *verb*
• = to excuse
entschuldigen Sie bitte – excuse me
• sich bei jemandem entschuldigen = to apologize to someone

die **Entschuldigung**, *plural* Entschuldigungen
• = apology
Entschuldigung! = sorry!, (*following a question*) = excuse me?
• = excuse

das **Entsetzen**
= horror

entsetzlich *adjective*
= horrible
= terrible

entspannen: sich entspannen *verb*
= to relax

die **Entspannung**
= relaxation

entsprechend
1 *adjective*
• = corresponding
• = appropriate
2 *preposition* (+ *dative*) = in accordance with

entstehen *irregular verb* (**!** *sein*)
• = to develop
• (*of a building*) = to be built
• (*of damage*) = to result

enttäuschen *verb*
= to disappoint

die **Enttäuschung**, *plural* Enttäuschungen
= disappointment

entweder *conjunction*
= either

entwerten *verb*
• = to devalue
• (*in a ticket machine*) = to cancel

der **Entwerter**, *plural* Entwerter
= ticket-cancelling machine

entwickeln *verb*
• = to develop
• sich entwickeln = to develop

die **Entwicklung**, *plural* Entwicklungen
= development
= developing

das **Entwicklungsland**, *plural*
Entwicklungsländer
= developing country

der **Entwurf**, *plural* Entwürfe
• = design
• = draft

entzünden *verb*
• = to light
• sich entzünden = to ignite, (*of a wound*)
= to become inflamed

die **Entzündung**, *plural* Entzündungen
= inflammation

der **Enzian**, *plural* Enziane
= gentian

er *pronoun*
= he, (*thing*) = it

der **Erbe**¹ *plural* Erben
= heir

das **Erbe**²
= inheritance, = heritage

erben *verb*
= to inherit

die **Erbin**, *plural* Erbinnen
= heiress

erblich *adjective*
= hereditary

die **Erbschaftssteuer**,
plural Erbschaftssteuern
= inheritance tax

die **Erbse**, *plural* Erbsen
= pea

das **Erdbeben**, *plural* Erdbeben
= earthquake

die **Erdbeere**, *plural* Erdbeeren
= strawberry

die **Erde**, *plural* Erden
• = earth, = soil
• = ground
• (*planet*) = Earth
• (*for electrical circuit*) = earth, = ground

das **Erdgeschoss** (**Erdgeschoß**⊙ᴸᴰ),
plural Erdgeschosse
= ground floor, (*US*) = first floor

die **Erdkunde**
= geography

die **Erdnuss** (**Erdnuß**⊙ᴸᴰ), *plural*
Erdnüsse
= peanut

ereignen: sich ereignen *verb*
= to happen

das **Ereignis**, *plural* Ereignisse
= event

erfahren
1 *irregular verb* = to learn
2 *adjective* = experienced

die **Erfahrung**, *plural* Erfahrungen
= experience

erfinden *irregular verb*
= to invent

die **Erfindung**, *plural* Erfindungen
= invention

der **Erfolg**, *plural* Erfolge
= success
= hit
viel Erfolg! = good luck!

erfolglos *adjective*
= unsuccessful

erfolgreich *adjective*
= successful

erforderlich *adjective*
= necessary

erforschen *verb*
= to explore
= to investigate

die **Erfrischung**, *plural* Erfrischungen
= refreshment

erfüllen *verb*
• = to fulfil
• sich erfüllen = to come true

das **Ergebnis**, *plural* Ergebnisse
= result

erhalten *irregular verb*
• = to receive
• = to preserve

erhältlich *adjective*
= obtainable, = available

erheben *irregular verb*
• = to raise
• eine Gebühr erheben = to charge a fee
• sich erheben = to rise (up)

✕ in informal situations   ⊙ᴸᴰ = old spelling

erheblich *adjective*
= considerable

erhöhen *verb*
- = to increase
- sich erhöhen = to rise

die **Erhöhung**, *plural* Erhöhungen
= increase

erholen: sich erholen *verb*
- = to rest
- sich von einer Krankheit erholen = to recover from an illness

erholsam *adjective*
= restful

die **Erholung**
- = rest
- = recovery

erinnern *verb*
- = to remind
- sich erinnern = to remember

die **Erinnerung**, *plural* Erinnerungen
- = memory
- = souvenir

erkälten: sich erkälten *verb*
= to catch a cold
erkältet sein = to have a cold

die **Erkältung**, *plural* Erkältungen
= cold

erkennen *irregular verb*
- = to recognize
- = to realize

erklären *verb*
- = to explain
- = to declare

die **Erklärung**, *plural* Erklärungen
- = explanation
- = declaration

erkundigen: sich erkundigen *verb*
= to inquire, = to ask about

die **Erkundigung**, *plural* Erkundigungen
= inquiry

erlauben *verb*
= to allow

die **Erlaubnis**, *plural* Erlaubnisse
= permission

erleben *verb*
= to experience
eine Überraschung erleben = to have a surprise

das **Erlebnis**, *plural* Erlebnisse
= experience

erledigen *verb*
= to deal with
= to settle

erledigt *adjective*
(*of a matter*) = settled
ich bin erledigt✱ = I'm worn out

der **Erlös**
= proceeds

die **Ermäßigung**, *plural* Ermäßigungen
= reduction

ermorden *verb*
= to murder
= to assassinate

ermutigen *verb*
= to encourage

ernähren *verb*
- = to feed
- sich von Bananen ernähren = to live on bananas

die **Ernährung**
= nutrition
= diet

erneut
1 *adjective* = renewed
2 *adverb* = once again

ernst *adjective*
= serious

der **Ernst**
= seriousness

ernstlich *adjective*
= serious

die **Ernte**, *plural* Ernten
= harvest

ernten *verb*
= to harvest

erobern *verb*
= to conquer

die **Eroberung**, *plural* Eroberungen
= conquest

eröffnen *verb*
= to open

die **Eröffnung**, *plural* Eröffnungen
= opening

erpressen *verb*
= to blackmail

der **Erreger**, *plural* Erreger
= germ

erreichbar *adjective*
= reachable

erreichen *verb*
- = to reach
- (*be in time for*) = to catch
- = to achieve

erröten *verb* (**!** sein)
= to blush

der **Ersatz**
= replacement, = substitute

E

das **Ersatzteil**, *plural* Ersatzteile
= spare part

erscheinen *irregular verb* (**!** *sein*)
= to appear
(*of a book*) = to be published

erschöpft *adjective*
= exhausted

erschrecken *verb*
• = to scare
• *irregular* (**!** *sein*) = to get a fright

ersetzen *verb*
= to replace
einen Schaden ersetzen = to compensate
for damages

erst *adverb*
• = first
• = only
eben erst = only just
erst nächste Woche = not until next
week

erstaunlich *adjective*
= astonishing

erste ▶erster

der/die/das **Erste**
• der/die Erste = the first one
das Erste = the first thing
der Erste, der gekommen ist = the first
one who came
als Erstes = first of all
• fürs Erste = for the time being
• = the best
sie war die Erste in Latein = she was top
in Latin

erstens *adverb*
= firstly

erster/erste/erstes *adjective*
= first
der erste April = the first of April
das erste Mal = the first time
erste Hilfe = first aid

erteilen *verb*
= to give

der **Ertrag**, *plural* Erträge
= yield

ertragen *irregular verb*
= to bear, = to endure

ertrinken *irregular verb* (**!** *sein*)
= to drown

erwachsen *adjective*
= grown-up

der/die **Erwachsene**, *plural* Erwachsenen
= adult, = grown-up

erwähnen *verb*
= to mention

erwarten *verb*
= to expect

die **Erwartung**, *plural* Erwartungen
= expectation

erzählen *verb*
= to tell

die **Erzählung**, *plural* Erzählungen
= story

das **Erzeugnis**, *plural* Erzeugnisse
= product

erziehen *irregular verb*
• = to bring up
• = to educate

die **Erziehung**
• = upbringing
• = education

erzogen *adjective*
gut erzogen = well brought up

es *pronoun*
= it
(*female person*) = she, (*accusative*) = her
(*male person*) = he, (*accusative*) = him
es gibt = there is/there are
ich hoffe es = I hope so

der **Esel**, *plural* Esel
= donkey

essbar (**eßbar** ⓄⓁⒹ) *adjective*
= edible

essen *irregular verb*
= to eat

das **Essen**, *plural* Essen
• = meal
• = food

der **Essig**, *plural* Essige
= vinegar

das **Esszimmer** (**Eßzimmer** ⓄⓁⒹ), *plural*
Esszimmer
= dining room

die **Etage**, *plural* Etagen
= floor, = storey

das **Etikett**, *plural* Etikette
= label

das **Etui**, *plural* Etuis
= case

etwa *adverb*
• = about
etwa so = roughly like this
• = for example

etwas *pronoun*
• = something
(*in questions and with negatives*) =
anything
• = some
(*in questions and with negatives*) = any
• = a little

ⓄⓁⒹ = old spelling

die **EU**
(*Europäische Union*) = EU

euch *pronoun*
= (to) you
(*reflexive*) = yourselves

euer *adjective*
= your

die **Eule**, *plural* Eulen
= owl

eurer/eure/eures *pronoun*
= yours

der **Euro**, *plural* Euro(s)
= euro
20 Euro kosten = to cost 20 euros

(das) **Europa**
= Europe

der **Europäer**, *plural* Europäer,
die **Europäerin**, *plural* Europäerinnen
= European

europäisch *adjective*
= European

die **Eurozone**
= eurozone

eventuell
1 *adjective* = possible
2 *adverb* = possibly

ewig
1 *adjectivo* = eternal
2 *adverb* = forever

das **Examen**, *plural* Examen
= examination

das **Exemplar**, *plural* Exemplare
= copy
= specimen

existieren *verb*
= to exist

explodieren *verb* (**!** *sein*)
= to explode

extra *adverb*
• = separately
• = extra
• = specially

F f

die **Fabel**, *plural* Fabeln
= fable

fabelhaft *adjective*
= fantastic

die **Fabrik**, *plural* Fabriken
= factory

das **Fach**, *plural* Fächer
• = compartment
• (*at school*) = subject

der **Fächer**, *plural* Fächer
= fan

der **Fachmann**, *plural* Fachleute
= expert

die **Fachschule**, *plural* Fachschulen
= technical college

der **Faden**, *plural* Fäden
= thread

fähig *adjective*
• = able
• = capable

die **Fahndung**, *plural* Fahndungen
= search

die **Fahne**, *plural* Fahnen
= flag

die **Fahrbahn**, *plural* Fahrbahnen
= road

die **Fähre**, *plural* Fähren
= ferry

fahren *irregular verb* (**!** *sein*)
(*in a vehicle*) = to go
(*of a motorist*) = to drive
(*of a cyclist*) = to ride
(*of a train*) = to run
mit dem [Auto | Zug | Bus ...] fahren = to go
by [car | train | bus ...]
wann fahrt ihr? = when are you leaving?

der **Fahrer**, *plural* Fahrer
= driver

die **Fahrerin**, *plural* Fahrerinnen
= (woman) driver

der **Fahrgast**, *plural* Fahrgäste
= passenger

das **Fahrgeld**, *plural* Fahrgelder
= fare

die **Fahrkarte**, *plural* Fahrkarten
= ticket

der **Fahrplan**, *plural* Fahrpläne
= timetable

fahrplanmäßig *adjective*
= scheduled

der **Fahrpreis**, *plural* Fahrpreise
= fare

die **Fahrprüfung**, *plural* Fahrprüfungen
= driving test

das **Fahrrad**, *plural* Fahrräder
= bicycle

die **Fahrradspur**, *plural* Fahrradspuren
= cycle lane

der **Fahrschein**, *plural* Fahrscheine
= ticket

die **Fahrschule**, *plural* Fahrschulen
= driving school

der **Fahrstuhl**, *plural* Fahrstühle
= lift, = elevator

die **Fahrt**, *plural* Fahrten
* = journey
  (*in a car*) = drive
* in voller Fahrt = at full speed

fährt ▶fahren

das **Fahrzeug**, *plural* Fahrzeuge
= vehicle

der **Fall**, *plural* Fälle
* = fall
* = case
  auf jeden Fall = in any case
  auf keinen Fall = on no account

die **Falle**, *plural* Fallen
= trap

fallen *irregular verb* (**!** *sein*)
* = to fall
* etwas fallen lassen = to drop something
  sie haben den Plan fallen lassen = they
    dropped the idea
* im Krieg fallen = to die in the war

fällig *adjective*
= due

falls *conjunction*
* = if
* = in case

der **Fallschirm**, *plural* Fallschirme
= parachute

falsch *adjective*
* = wrong
* = false
* = forged

fälschen *verb*
= to forge

die **Fälschung**, *plural* Fälschungen
= fake
= forgery

die **Falte**, *plural* Falten
* = crease
  = fold
  = pleat
* = line, = wrinkle

falten *verb*
= to fold

die **Familie**, *plural* Familien
= family

der **Familienname**, *plural* Familiennamen
= surname

---

fand ▶finden

fangen *irregular verb*
* = to catch
* sich fangen = to get caught

die **Fantasie**, *plural* Fantasien
▶Phantasie

fantastisch ▶phantastisch

die **Farbe**, *plural* Farben
* = colour, = color
* = paint
  = dye
* (*playing cards*) = suit

farbecht *adjective*
= colour-fast, = color-fast

färben *verb*
= to colour, = to color
sich die Haare färben = to dye one's hair

der **Farbfilm**, *plural* Farbfilme
= colour film, = color film

farbig *adjective*
= coloured, = colored

der **Farbstoff**, *plural* Farbstoffe
* = dye
* (*for food*) = colouring, = coloring

der **Fasching**, *plural* Faschinge
= carnival

die **Faser**, *plural* Fasern
= fibre, = fiber

das **Fass** (**Faß**⟨OLD⟩), *plural* Fässer
= barrel
Bier vom Fass = draught beer

fassen *verb*
* (*with one's hands, understand*) = to
    grasp
  einen Dieb fassen = to catch a thief
  nicht zu fassen = unbelievable
* (*of a container*) = to hold
* sich fassen = to compose oneself

die **Fassung**, *plural* Fassungen
* = version
* = composure
  jemanden aus der Fassung bringen = to
    upset someone
* (*for gems*) = setting

fast *adverb*
= almost, = nearly
fast nie = hardly ever

die **Fastnacht**, *plural* Fastnächte
= carnival

faszinieren *verb*
= to fascinate

faul *adjective*
* = lazy
* (*of fruit*) = bad, = rotten

faulenzen *verb*
= to laze about

die **Faust**, *plural* Fäuste
= fist
auf eigene Faust = off one's own bat

das **Fax**, *plural* Fax *or* Faxe
= fax

faxen *verb*
= to fax

der **Februar**
= February

fechten *irregular verb*
= to fence

die **Feder**, *plural* Federn
* = feather
* (*on a pen*) = nib
* = spring

der **Federball**
= badminton

das **Federmäppchen**, *plural*
Federmäppchen
= pencil case

die **Federung**, *plural* Federungen
= suspension

die **Fee**, *plural* Feen
= fairy

fegen *verb*
= to sweep (up)

fehl *adverb*
fehl am Platz = out of place

fehlen *verb*
* = to be missing
* = to be lacking
es fehlt an Lehrern = there is a shortage
of teachers
was fehlt dir? = what's the matter?
sie fehlt mir sehr = I miss her very much

der **Fehler**, *plural* Fehler
* = mistake, = error
* = fault

fehl|schlagen *irregular verb* (**!** *sein*)
= to fail

die **Feier**, *plural* Feiern
= party
= celebration

der **Feierabend**
= finishing time
nach Feierabend = after work

feierlich *adjective*
= ceremonial
= formal

feiern *verb*
= to celebrate

der **Feiertag**, *plural* Feiertage
= holiday
= festival
ein gesetzlicher Feiertag = a public
holiday, = a bank holiday

feiertags *adverb*
= on public holidays

feige *adjective*
= cowardly
feige sein = to be a coward

die **Feige**, *plural* Feigen
= fig

der **Feigling**, *plural* Feiglinge
= coward

die **Feile**, *plural* Feilen
= file

fein *adjective*
* = fine, = delicate
sich fein machen = to dress up
* = great

der **Feind**, *plural* Feinde
= enemy

die **Feindin**, *plural* Feindinnen
= enemy

feindlich *adjective*
= hostile

das **Feinkostgeschäft**, *plural*
Feinkostgeschäfte
= delicatessen

das **Feld**, *plural* Felder
* = field
= pitch
* (*on a form*) = box
(*on a board game*) = space, = square

das **Fell**, *plural* Felle
= fur
= skin

der **Fels**, *plural* Felsen
= rock

der **Felsen**, *plural* Felsen
= rock
= cliff

feministisch *adjective*
= feminist

das **Fenster**, *plural* Fenster
= window

Ferien (*plural*)
= holidays, = vacation

fern
1 *adjective* = distant
2 *adverb* = far away

die **Fernbedienung**
= remote control

die **Ferne**
= distance
in weiter Ferne = far away

das **Ferngespräch**, *plural* Ferngespräche
= long-distance call

ferngesteuert *adjective*
= remote-controlled

das **Fernglas**, *plural* Ferngläser
= binoculars

das **Fernrohr**, *plural* Fernrohre
= telescope

das **Fernschreiben**, *plural* Fernschreiben
= telex

der **Fernsehapparat**, *plural*
Fernsehapparate
= television set

fern|sehen *irregular verb*
= to watch television

das **Fernsehen**
= television

der **Fernseher**, *plural* Fernseher
= television

der **Fernsprecher**, *plural* Fernsprecher
= telephone

die **Ferse**, *plural* Fersen
= heel

fertig
adjective
• = finished
fertig sein✱ = to be worn out
• = ready
• etwas fertig machen = to finish
something
fertig essen = to finish eating
• etwas fertig machen = to get something
ready
• sich fertig machen = to get ready
• jemanden fertig machen✱ = to wear
someone out

fesseln *verb*
• = to tie up
• = to fascinate

fest
1 *adjective*
• = solid
• = firm, = tight
• (*of a salary, address*) = fixed
• (*of a job*) = permanent
2 *adverb*
fest schlafen = to be fast asleep

das **Fest**, *plural* Feste
• = party
= celebration
• = festival

fest|binden *irregular verb*
= to tie (up)

fest|halten *irregular verb*
• = to hold on to
• sich an etwas festhalten = to hold on to
something

fest|legen *verb*
• = to fix

✱ in informal situations

• sich auf etwas festlegen = to commit
oneself to something

fest|machen *verb*
= to fix
= to fasten

fest|nehmen *irregular verb*
= to arrest

die **Festplatte**, *plural* Festplatten
= hard disk

fest|stehen *irregular verb*
= to be certain

fest|stellen *verb*
= to establish

die **Festung**, *plural* Festungen
= fortress

das **Fett**, *plural* Fette
= fat
= grease

fett *adjective*
= fatty
fette Haare = greasy hair

fettarm *adjective*
= low-fat

fettig *adjective*
= greasy

feucht *adjective*
= damp

die **Feuchtigkeit**
= damp

das **Feuer**, *plural* Feuer
= fire
jemandem Feuer geben = to give
someone a light

feuergefährlich *adjective*
= flammable, = inflammable

der **Feuerlöscher**, *plural* Feuerlöscher
= fire extinguisher

die **Feuerwache**, *plural* Feuerwachen
= fire station

die **Feuerwehr**, *plural* Feuerwehren
= fire brigade

das **Feuerwerk**
= fireworks

das **Feuerzeug**, *plural* Feuerzeuge
= lighter

das **Fieber**
= (high) temperature, = fever
Fieber haben = to have a temperature

fiel ▶ fallen

die **Figur**, *plural* Figuren
• = figure
• = character

die **Filiale**, *plural* Filialen
= branch

der **Film**, *plural* Filme
= film, = movie

der **Filzstift**, *plural* Filzstifte
= felt pen

finanziell *adjective*
= financial

finanzieren *verb*
= to finance

finden *irregular verb*
• = to find
• = to think
findest du? = do you think so?

der **Finderlohn**, *plural* Finderlöhne
= reward

fing ▶ fangen

der **Finger**, *plural* Finger
= finger

(das) **Finnland**
= Finland

finster *adjective*
• = dark
im Finstern = in the dark
• = sinister

die **Firma**, *plural* Firmen
= firm, = company

das **Firmenzeichen**, *plural* Firmenzeichen
= trade mark

der **Fisch**, *plural* Fische
• = fish
• Fische = Pisces

der **Fischer**, *plural* Fischer
= fisherman

fix *adjective*
= quick
eine fixe Idee = an obsession
fix und fertig✶ = all finished

flach *adjective*
• = flat, = level
• = low
• = shallow

der **Flachbildschirm**, *plural*
Flachbildschirme
= flat screen

die **Fläche**, *plural* Flächen
• = surface
• = area

flackern *verb*
= to flicker

die **Flagge**, *plural* Flaggen
= flag

die **Flamme**, *plural* Flammen
= flame

die **Flasche**, *plural* Flaschen
= bottle

flechten *irregular verb*
= to weave
= to plait

der **Fleck**, *plural* Flecke
= stain, = spot
ein blauer Fleck = a bruise

die **Fledermaus**, *plural* Fledermäuse
= bat

das **Fleisch**
• = flesh
• = meat

der **Fleischer**, *plural* Fleischer
= butcher

fleißig *adjective*
= hard-working

flicken *verb*
= to mend

die **Fliege**, *plural* Fliegen
• = fly
• = bow tie

fliegen *irregular verb* (**!** *sein*)
• = to fly
• er ist geflogen✶ = he's been fired

fliehen *irregular verb* (**!** *sein*)
= to flee, = to escape

die **Fliese**, *plural* Fliesen
= tile

das **Fließband**, *plural* Fließbänder
= conveyor belt

fließen *irregular verb* (**!** *sein*)
= to flow

fließend *adjective*
• = running
(of traffic) = moving
• fließendes Deutsch = fluent German

flirten *verb*
= to flirt

Flitterwochen (*plural*)
= honeymoon

die **Flocke**, *plural* Flocken
= flake

flog ▶ fliegen

der **Floh**, *plural* Flöhe
= flea

die **Flosse**, *plural* Flossen
• = fin
• = flipper

die **Flöte**, *plural* Flöten
= flute

die **Flotte**, *plural* Flotten
= fleet

der **Fluch**, *plural* Flüche
= curse

fluchen verb
= to curse, = to swear

flüchten verb (! sein)
* to flee
* sich flüchten (! haben) = to take refuge

der **Flüchtling**, plural Flüchtlinge
= refugee

der **Flug**, plural Flüge
= flight

der **Flügel**, plural Flügel
* = wing
* = grand piano

der **Fluggast**, plural Fluggäste
= (air) passenger

der **Flughafen**, plural Flughäfen
= airport

der **Flugplatz**, plural Flugplätze
= airport, = airfield

der **Flugschein**, plural Flugscheine
= (air) ticket

der **Flugsteig**, plural Flugsteige
= gate

das **Flugzeug**, plural Flugzeuge
= aeroplane, = airplane

der **Flur**, plural Flure
= hall

der **Fluss (Fluß**ⓄⓁⒹ**)**, plural Flüsse
= river

flüssig adjective
= liquid

die **Flüssigkeit**, plural Flüssigkeiten
= liquid

flüstern verb
= to whisper

die **Flut**, plural Fluten
= high tide

der **Föhn**, plural Föhne
= hair-dryer

föhnen verb
= to (blow-) dry

die **Folge**, plural Folgen
* = consequence
* = episode

folgen verb (! sein)
= to follow

folgend adjective
= following
Folgendes = the following

folglich adverb
= consequently

die **Folie**, plural Folien
= foil
= film

der **Fön**ⓄⓁⒹ® plural Föne
▶Föhn

fönen ⓄⓁⒹ ▶föhnen

fordern verb
= to demand

fördern verb
* = to promote
* (financially) = to support
* Kohle fördern = to mine coal

die **Forderung**, plural Forderungen
* = demand
* = claim

die **Forelle**, plural Forellen
= trout

die **Form**, plural Formen
* = form
in Form sein = to be in good form
* = shape
* (for baking) = tin

formen verb
* = to form
= to shape
* sich formen = to take shape

förmlich adjective
= formal

das **Formular**, plural Formulare
= form

der **Forscher**, plural Forscher
* = researcher
* = explorer

die **Forschung**, plural Forschungen
= research

der **Förster**, plural Förster
= forester

fort adverb
= away
und so fort = and so on

fort|bewegen verb
* = to move
* sich fortbewegen = to move

die **Fortbildung**
= further education

fortgeschritten adjective
= advanced

der/die **Fortgeschrittene**, plural
Fortgeschrittenen
= advanced student

die **Fortpflanzung**
= reproduction

der **Fortschritt**, plural Fortschritte
= progress

fort|setzen *verb*
- = to continue
- sich fortsetzen = to continue

die **Fortsetzung**, *plural* Fortsetzungen
- = continuation
- = instalment

das **Foto**, *plural* Fotos
= photo

der **Fotoapparat**, *plural* Fotoapparate
= camera

der **Fotograf**, *plural* Fotografen
= photographer

die **Fotografie**, *plural* Fotografien
- = photography
- = photograph

fotografieren *verb*
= to photograph
= to take photographs

die **Fotografin**, *plural* Fotografinnen
= photographer

die **Fracht**, *plural* Frachten
= freight
= cargo

der **Frack**, *plural* Fräcke
(*evening dress*) = tails

die **Frage**, *plural* Fragen
= question

der **Fragebogen**, *plural* Fragebogen
= questionnaire

fragen *verb*
- = to ask
- sich fragen = to wonder

das **Fragezeichen**, *plural* Fragezeichen
= question mark

(das) **Frankreich**
= France

der **Franzose**, *plural* Franzosen
= Frenchman

die **Französin**, *plural* Französinnen
= Frenchwoman

französisch *adjective*
= French

die **Frau**, *plural* Frauen
- = woman
- = wife
- (*with a name*) = Mrs, = Ms

das **Frauenhaus**, *plural* Frauenhäuser
= women's refuge

das **Fräulein**, *plural* Fräulein
- = single woman
- = young lady
- (*with a name*) = Miss

frech *adjective*
= cheeky

die **Frechheit**, *plural* Frechheiten
- = cheek
- = cheeky remark

frei *adjective*
- = free
  sich frei nehmen = to take time off
- = freelance
- = vacant
  ist dieser Platz frei? = is this seat taken?
  'Zimmer frei' = 'vacancies'

das **Freibad**, *plural* Freibäder
= open-air swimming pool

das **Freie**
im Freien = in the open air

frei|haben *irregular verb*
= to have time off
eine Stunde freihaben (*at school*) = to
have a free period

die **Freiheit**, *plural* Freiheiten
= freedom, = liberty

frei|machen *verb*
- = to take time off
- = to frank
- sich freimachen = to take time off

frei|sprechen *irregular verb*
= to acquit

der **Freispruch**, *plural* Freisprüche
= acquittal

der **Freistoß**, *plural* Freistöße
= free kick

der **Freitag**
= Friday

freitags *adverb*
= on Fridays

freiwillig *adjective*
= voluntary

die **Freizeit**
= spare time
= leisure

fremd *adjective*
- = foreign
- = strange
  fremde Leute = strangers
  ich bin hier fremd = I'm a stranger here

der/die **Fremde**, *plural* Fremden
- = foreigner
- = stranger

der **Fremdenführer**, *plural* Fremdenführer
= tourist guide

der **Fremdenverkehr**
= tourism

das **Fremdenverkehrsbüro**, *plural*
Fremdenverkehrsbüros
= tourist office

die **Fremdsprache**, *plural*
Fremdsprachen
= foreign language

fressen *irregular verb*
• (*of an animal*) = to eat
• fressen✗ (*of a person*) = to guzzle

die **Freude**, *plural* Freuden
= joy, = pleasure

freuen *verb*
• = to please
es freut mich = I'm pleased
• sich über etwas freuen = to be pleased
about something
sich auf etwas freuen = to look forward
to something

der **Freund**, *plural* Freunde
= friend
= boyfriend

die **Freundin**, *plural* Freundinnen
= friend
= girlfriend

freundlich *adjective*
= friendly
= kind

die **Freundschaft**, *plural* Freundschaften
= friendship
mit jemandem Freundschaft schließen =
to make friends with someone

der **Frieden**
= peace

der **Friedhof**, *plural* Friedhöfe
= cemetery

frieren *irregular verb*
• = to be cold
• (**!** *sein*) = to freeze

frisch
1 *adjective* = fresh
sich frisch machen = to freshen up
2 *adverb* = freshly
'frisch gestrichen' = 'wet paint'

der **Friseur**, *plural* Friseure
= hairdresser

die **Friseuse**, *plural* Friseusen
= hairdresser

frisieren *verb*
• jemanden frisieren = to do someone's hair
• sich frisieren = to do one's hair

die **Frisur**, *plural* Frisuren
= hairstyle

froh *adjective*
• = happy
• über etwas froh sein = to be pleased
about something

fröhlich *adjective*
= cheerful

fromm *adjective*
= devout

fror ▶ frieren

der **Frosch**, *plural* Frösche
= frog

das **Frottee**, *plural* Frottees
= towelling

die **Frucht**, *plural* Früchte
= fruit

fruchtbar *adjective*
= fertile

früh
1 *adjective* = early
2 *adverb* = early
heute früh = this morning

die **Frühe**
in aller Frühe = at the crack of dawn

früher
1 *adjective*
• = earlier
• = former
2 *adverb* = formerly
ich wohnte früher in München = I used to
live in Munich
früher oder später = sooner or later

frühestens *adverb*
= at the earliest

der **Frühling**, *plural* Frühlinge
= spring

das **Frühstück**, *plural* Frühstücke
= breakfast

frühstücken *verb*
= to have breakfast

der **Fuchs**, *plural* Füchse
= fox

fühlen *verb*
• = to feel
• sich krank fühlen = to feel ill

fuhr ▶ fahren

führen *verb*
• = to lead
• = to show round
• (*be in charge of*) = to run
• ein Tagebuch führen = to keep a diary

der **Führer**, *plural* Führer
• = leader
• = guide

der **Führerschein**, *plural* Führerscheine
= driving licence, = driver's license
den Führerschein machen = to take one's
driving test

die **Führung**, *plural* Führungen
• = leadership
• = guided tour
• in Führung = in the lead

✗ in informal situations ✒ considered offensive

füllen verb
- = to fill
 (*in cooking*) = to stuff
- sich füllen = to fill (up)

der **Füller**, *plural* Füller
 = fountain pen

das **Fundament**, *plural* Fundamente
 = foundations

das **Fundbüro**, *plural* Fundbüros
 = lost property office

fünf adjective
 = five

das **Fünftel**, *plural* Fünftel
 = fifth

fünfter/fünfte/fünftes adjective
 = fifth

fünfzehn adjective
 = fifteen

fünfzig adjective
 = fifty

der **Funk**
 = radio

der **Funke**, *plural* Funken
 = spark

funkeln verb
 = to sparkle
 (*of a star*) = to twinkle

die **Funkstreife**, *plural* Funkstreifen
 = radio patrol

funktionieren verb
 = to work

für preposition (+ *accusative*)
 = for
 für sich = by oneself/itself

die **Furcht**
 = fear

furchtbar adjective
 = terrible

fürchten verb
- = to fear
- sich vor jemandem fürchten = to be afraid
 of someone

fürchterlich adjective
 = dreadful

die **Fürsorge**
- = care
- = welfare
- = social security

furzen verb
 = to fart

der **Fuß**, *plural* Füße
 = foot

der **Fußball**, *plural* Fußbälle
 = football

der **Fußboden**, *plural* Fußböden
 = floor

der **Fußgänger**, *plural* Fußgänger
 = pedestrian

die **Fußgängerzone**, *plural* Fußgängerzonen
 = pedestrian precinct

der **Fußweg**, *plural* Fußwege
 = footpath

das **Futter**
- = feed
- = lining

füttern verb
- = to feed
- = to line

Gg

gab ▶geben

die **Gabel**, *plural* Gabeln
 = fork

gähnen verb
 = to yawn

die **Galerie**, *plural* Galerien
 = gallery

der **Galgen**, *plural* Galgen
 = gallows

galoppieren verb (**!** *sein*)
 = to gallop

der **Gammler**, *plural* Gammler
 = drop-out

die **Gammlerin**, *plural* Gammlerinnen
 = drop-out

der **Gang**, *plural* Gänge
- = walk
 in Gang setzen = to get going
 im Gange = in progress
- = errand
- = corridor
- (*part of a meal*) = course
- (*of a car*) = gear

gängig adjective
- = common
- = popular

die **Gangschaltung**, *plural* Gangschaltungen
 = gear change

die **Gans**, *plural* Gänse
 = goose

das **Gänseblümchen**, *plural*
Gänseblümchen
= daisy

ganz
1 *adjective*
• = whole
eine ganze Menge = quite a lot
ganz Deutschland = the whole of
Germany
im Großen und Ganzen = on the whole
• = all
die ganzen Leute = all the people
• = intact
etwas wieder ganz machen = to mend
something
2 *adverb* = quite
ganz und gar = completely

ganztägig *adjective*
= all-day, = full-time

ganztags *adverb*
= all day, = full time

gar
1 *adjective* = done, = cooked
2 *adverb*
gar [nichts | keiner | nicht…] = [nothing | no
one | not…] at all

die **Garantie**, *plural* Garantien
= guarantee

garantieren *verb*
= to guarantee

garantiert *adverb*
er kommt garantiert zu spät✱ = he's bound
or sure to be late

die **Garderobe**, *plural* Garderoben
= cloakroom, = checkroom

die **Gardine**, *plural* Gardinen
= curtain, = drape

das **Garn**, *plural* Garne
= thread

die **Garnele**, *plural* Garnelen
= shrimp
= prawn

der **Garten**, *plural* Gärten
= garden

der **Gärtner**, *plural* Gärtner
= gardener

die **Gärtnerei**, *plural* Gärtnereien
= nursery

die **Gärtnerin**, *plural* Gärtnerinnen
= gardener

das **Gas**, *plural* Gase
• = gas
• = petrol, = gas
Gas geben = to accelerate

die **Gasse**, *plural* Gassen
= lane

der **Gast**, *plural* Gäste
= guest
= visitor

der **Gastarbeiter**, *plural* Gastarbeiter
= foreign worker, = guest worker

das **Gästezimmer**, *plural* Gästezimmer
• (*in a hotel*) = room
• (*in a house*) = spare room

gastfreundlich *adjective*
= hospitable

die **Gastfreundschaft**
= hospitality

der **Gastgeber**, *plural* Gastgeber
= host

die **Gastgeberin**, *plural* Gastgeberinnen
= hostess

das **Gasthaus**, *plural* Gasthäuser
= inn

der **Gasthof**, *plural* Gasthöfe
= inn

die **Gaststätte**, *plural* Gaststätten
= restaurant

der **Gastwirt**, *plural* Gastwirte
= landlord

die **Gastwirtin**, *plural* Gastwirtinnen
= landlady

der **Gaumen**, *plural* Gaumen
= palate

der **Gauner**, *plural* Gauner
= crook

das **Gebäck**
= pastries
= biscuits

das **Gebäude**, *plural* Gebäude
= building

geben *irregular verb*
• = to give
(*on the phono*) geben Sie mir bitte Herrn
Braun = please put me through to Mr
Braun
etwas in die Reinigung geben = to have
something cleaned
• (*when playing cards*) = to deal
• (*at school*) = to teach
• sich geben = to wear off, = to get better
sich natürlich geben = to act naturally
• es gibt = there is/there are
was gibt es im Kino? = what's on at the
cinema?

das **Gebet**, *plural* Gebete
= prayer

gebeten ▶bitten

das **Gebiet**, *plural* Gebiete
* = area
* (*subject*) = field

gebildet *adjective*
= educated

das **Gebirge**, *plural* Gebirge
= mountain range
im Gebirge = in the mountains

gebirgig *adjective*
= mountainous

das **Gebiss** (**Gebiß**ⓞⓛⓓ), *plural* Gebisse
* = teeth
* = false teeth, = dentures
* (*for a horse*) = bit

geboren *adjective*
= born
Frau Petra Schmidt geborene Meyer =
Mrs Petra Schmidt née Meyer

der **Gebrauch**, *plural* Gebräuche
* = use
* = custom

gebrauchen *verb*
= to use

die **Gebrauchsanweisung**, *plural*
Gebrauchsanweisungen
= instructions (for use)

gebraucht *adjective*
= used, = second-hand

gebrochen
1 *adjective* = broken
2 *adverb*
gebrochen Deutsch sprechen = to speak
broken German

die **Gebühr**, *plural* Gebühren
= charge, = fee

gebührenfrei *adjective*
= free (of charge)

gebührenpflichtig *adjective*
= subject to a charge
eine gebührenpflichtige Straße = a toll
road

die **Geburt**, *plural* Geburten
= birth

die **Geburtenregelung**
= birth control

das **Geburtsdatum**, *plural* Geburtsdaten
= date of birth

der **Geburtsort**
= place of birth

der **Geburtstag**, *plural* Geburtstage
= birthday

die **Geburtsurkunde**, *plural*
Geburtsurkunden
= birth certificate

das **Gedächtnis**, *plural* Gedächtnisse
= memory

der **Gedanke**, *plural* Gedanken
= thought
sich über jemanden Gedanken machen =
to worry about someone

gedankenlos
1 *adjective* = thoughtless
2 *adverb* = without thinking

das **Gedeck**, *plural* Gedecke
* = place setting
* = set meal

das **Gedicht**, *plural* Gedichte
= poem

die **Geduld**
= patience

geduldig *adjective*
= patient

gedurft ▶dürfen

geehrt *adjective*
= honoured, = honored
Sehr geehrter Herr Roth = Dear Mr Roth

geeignet *adjective*
= suitable
= right

die **Gefahr**, *plural* Gefahren
= danger
= risk

gefährlich *adjective*
= dangerous

gefallen *irregular verb*
* = to please
es gefällt mir = I like it
* sich etwas gefallen lassen = to put up
with something

der **Gefallen**[1] *plural* Gefallen
= favour, = favor

das **Gefallen**[2]
= pleasure
dir zu Gefallen = to please you

der/die **Gefangene**, *plural* Gefangenen
= prisoner

das **Gefängnis**, *plural* Gefängnisse
= prison, = jail

das **Gefäß**, *plural* Gefäße
= container

gefasst (**gefaßt**ⓞⓛⓓ) *adjective*
* = calm, = composed
* auf etwas gefasst sein = to be prepared
for something

gefiel ▶gefallen

das **Geflügel**
= poultry

gefrieren *irregular verb* (❗ *sein*)
= to freeze

G

das **Gefrierfach**, plural Gefrierfächer
= freezer (compartment)

der **Gefrierschrank**, plural
Gefrierschränke
= freezer

das **Gefühl**, plural Gefühle
= feeling
= emotion

gefüllt adjective
* = filled, = full
* (in cooking) = stuffed

gefunden ▶finden

gefüttert adjective
= lined

gegangen ▶gehen

gegebenenfalls adverb
= if need be

gegen
1 preposition (+ accusative)
* = against
ein Mittel gegen Kopfschmerzen = a
remedy for headaches
* (in direction) = towards
* (in time) = around
gegen Abend = towards evening
* (in sport) = versus
* = compared with
2 adverb
gegen fünfzig Leute = about 50 people

die **Gegend**, plural Gegenden
* = area
* = district

gegeneinander adverb
= against each other, = against one
another

die **Gegenfahrbahn**, plural
Gegenfahrbahnen
= opposite carriageway

das **Gegenmittel**, plural Gegenmittel
* = remedy
* = antidote

die **Gegenrichtung**, plural
Gegenrichtungen
= opposite direction

der **Gegensatz**, plural Gegensätze
* = contrast
* = opposite

gegenseitig
1 adjective = mutual
2 adverb
sich gegenseitig helfen = to help each
other or one another

der **Gegenstand**, plural Gegenstände
* = object
* (theme) = subject

---

das **Gegenteil**
= opposite
im Gegenteil = on the contrary

gegenüber
1 preposition (+ dative)
* = opposite
* = compared with
* jemandem gegenüber freundlich sein = to
be kind to or friendly towards someone
2 adverb = opposite

der **Gegenverkehr**
= oncoming traffic

die **Gegenwart**
* = present
* = presence

gegessen ▶essen

der **Gegner**, plural Gegner
= opponent

gehabt ▶haben

das **Gehalt**, plural Gehälter
= salary

geheim adjective
= secret

das **Geheimnis**, plural Geheimnisse
= secret

geheimnisvoll adjective
= mysterious

gehen irregular verb (! sein)
* = to go
* = to walk
über die Straße gehen = to cross the road
* = to work
meine Uhr geht falsch = my watch is
wrong
* (other uses)
es geht = it's not too bad
das geht nicht = that's impossible
wie geht es dir? = how are you?
worum geht es hier? = what is all this
about?

das **Gehirn**, plural Gehirne
= brain

die **Gehirnerschütterung**, plural
Gehirnerschütterungen
= concussion

geholfen ▶helfen

das **Gehör**
= hearing

gehorchen verb
= to obey

gehören verb
* = to belong
dazu gehört Mut = that takes courage
zu den Besten gehören = to be one of the
best
* sich gehören = to be fitting
es gehört sich nicht = it isn't done

---

gehorsam *adjective*
= obedient

die **Geige**, *plural* Geigen
= violin

die **Geisel**, *plural* Geiseln
= hostage

der **Geist**, *plural* Geister
* = mind
* = wit
* = ghost

die **Geisteskrankheit**, *plural* Geisteskrankheiten
= mental illness

Geisteswissenschaften (*plural*)
= arts, = humanities

geistig *adjective*
= mental

der **Geistliche**, *plural* Geistlichen
= clergyman

geizig *adjective*
= mean

gekonnt ▶ können

das **Gelächter**, *plural* Gelächter
= laughter

gelähmt *adjective*
= paralysed

das **Geländer**, *plural* Geländer
* = banisters
* = railings
* = parapet

gelassen *adjective*
= calm, = composed

gelaunt *adjective*
gut gelaunt sein = to be in a good mood

gelb *adjective*
= yellow

das **Geld**, *plural* Gelder
= money

der **Geldautomat**, *plural* Geldautomaten
= cash dispenser

die **Geldbörse**, *plural* Geldbörsen
= purse

der **Geldschein**, *plural* Geldscheine
= banknote, = bill

die **Geldstrafe**, *plural* Geldstrafen
= fine

die **Gelegenheit**, *plural* Gelegenheiten
* = opportunity
* = occasion

gelegentlich *adverb*
= occasionally

das **Gelenk**, *plural* Gelenke
= joint

der/die **Geliebte**, *plural* Geliebten
= lover

gelingen *irregular verb* (**!** *sein*)
= to succeed
es ist mir gelungen = I succeeded

gelten *irregular verb*
* = to be valid
das gilt nicht = that doesn't count
* (*of a rule*) = to apply
* als etwas gelten = to be regarded as something
[viel | wenig | mehr ...] gelten = to be worth
[a lot | little | more ...]

das **Gemälde**, *plural* Gemälde
= painting

gemäß *preposition* (+ *dative*)
= in accordance with

gemein *adjective*
= mean

die **Gemeinde**, *plural* Gemeinden
* = community
* = parish
* (*in a church*) = congregation

gemeinsam
1 *adjective* = common
2 *adverb* = together

die **Gemeinschaft**, *plural* Gemeinschaften
= community

gemocht ▶ mögen

das **Gemüse**, *plural* Gemüse
= vegetables

der **Gemüsehändler**, *plural* Gemüsehändler
= greengrocer

gemusst (**gemußt**ⓞⓛⓓ) ▶ müssen

gemustert *adjective*
= patterned

gemütlich *adjective*
= cosy
es sich gemütlich machen = to make oneself comfortable

genau
1 *adjective*
* = exact, = precise
* = meticulous
2 *adverb* = exactly

genauso *adverb*
= just the same
genauso viel = just as much, = just as many

die **Genehmigung**, *plural* Genehmigungen
* = permission
* = permit
= licence, = license

G

die **Generation**, *plural* Generationen
= generation

generell *adjective*
= general

(das) **Genf**
= Geneva

der **Genfer See**
= Lake Geneva

genial *adjective*
= brilliant

das **Genick**, *plural* Genicke
= (back of the) neck

das **Genie**, *plural* Genies
= genius

genießen *irregular verb*
= to enjoy

genommen ▶nehmen

genug *adverb*
= enough

genügend *adjective*
= enough

der **Genuss** (**Genuß** ⓞⓛⓓ), *plural* Genüsse
• = enjoyment
• = consumption

geöffnet *adjective*
= open

das **Gepäck**
= luggage, = baggage

die **Gepäckaufbewahrung**, *plural*
Gepäckaufbewahrungen
= left-luggage office, = check room

der **Gepäckschein**, *plural* Gepäckscheine
= luggage ticket, = baggage check

der **Gepäckträger**, *plural* Gepäckträger
• = porter
• (*on a car*) = roof rack
• (*on a bike*) = carrier

gerade
1 *adjective*
• = straight
• = upright
• eine gerade Zahl = an even number
2 *adverb*
• = just
gerade erst = only just
• = directly
gerade an dem Tag = on that very day
nicht gerade billig = not exactly cheap

geradeaus *adverb*
= straight ahead

das **Gerät**, *plural* Geräte
= appliance, = piece of equipment
(*TV, radio*) = set

─────────
ⓞⓛⓓ = old spelling

(*for gardening*) = tool
(*for cooking*) = utensil

geraten *irregular verb* (**!** *sein*)
= to get
schlecht geraten = to turn out badly
nach jemandem geraten = to take after
someone

geräumig *adjective*
= spacious

das **Geräusch**, *plural* Geräusche
= noise

gerecht *adjective*
= just, = fair

die **Gerechtigkeit**
= justice

das **Gericht**, *plural* Gerichte
• = court
• = dish

gering *adjective*
• = small
• = low
• = slight

das **Gerippe**, *plural* Gerippe
= skeleton

gerissen *adjective*
= crafty

gern(**e**) *adverb*
= gladly
etwas gern(e) tun = to like doing
something
jemanden gern(e) haben = to like
someone
das glaube ich gern(e) = I can well
believe that

der **Geruch**, *plural* Gerüche
= smell

das **Gerücht**, *plural* Gerüchte
= rumour, = rumor

das **Gerüst**, *plural* Gerüste
= scaffolding

gesamt *adjective*
= whole, = entire

die **Gesamtschule**, *plural*
Gesamtschulen
= comprehensive school

das **Geschäft**, *plural* Geschäfte
• = business
• = deal
• = shop, = store

der **Geschäftsführer**, *plural*
Geschäftsführer
= manager

Geschäftszeiten (*plural*)
= business hours

geschehen *irregular verb* (**!** *sein*)
= to happen

gescheit *adjective*
= clever

das **Geschenk**, *plural* Geschenke
= present, = gift

die **Geschichte**, *plural* Geschichten
• = history, = story

das **Geschick**
• = skill, = fate

geschickt *adjective*
• = skilful
• = clever

geschieden *adjective*
= divorced

das **Geschirr**, *plural* Geschirre
• = crockery
= dishes
• = harness

die **Geschirrspülmaschine**, *plural*
Geschirrspülmaschinen
= dishwasher

das **Geschirrtuch**, *plural* Geschirrtücher
= tea towel, = dish towel

das **Geschlecht**, *plural* Geschlechter
• = sex, = gender

geschlossen ▶schließen

der **Geschmack**, *plural* Geschmäcke
= taste

geschrieben ▶schreiben

die **Geschwindigkeit**, *plural*
Geschwindigkeiten
= speed

die **Geschwindigkeitsbeschränkung**, *plural*
Geschwindigkeitsbeschränkungen
= speed limit

die **Geschwindigkeitsüberwach-
ungskamera**
= speed camera

Geschwister (*plural*)
= brother(s) and sister(s), = siblings

geschwommen ▶schwimmen

der/die **Geschworene**, *plural*
Geschworenen
= juror

gesellig *adjective*
= sociable

die **Gesellschaft**, *plural* Gesellschaften
• = society
• = party
• = company
jemandem Gesellschaft leisten = to keep
someone company

gesessen ▶sitzen

das **Gesetz**, *plural* Gesetze
= law

gesetzlich *adjective*
= legal, = lawful

das **Gesicht**, *plural* Gesichter
= face

gesollt ▶sollen

gespannt *adjective*
• = eager
auf etwas gespannt sein = to look
forward eagerly to something
ich bin gespannt, ob . . . = I am keen to
know whether . . .
• = tense

das **Gespenst**, *plural* Gespenster
= ghost

das **Gespräch**, *plural* Gespräche
= conversation
(*on the phone*) = call

gesprochen ▶sprechen

die **Gestalt**, *plural* Gestalten
• = figure, = character
• = form

gestanden ▶stehen

gestatten *verb*
= to permit, = to allow
gestatten Sie? = may I?
nicht gestattet = prohibited

gestern *adverb*
= yesterday

gestorben ▶sterben

gestreift *adjective*
= striped

gesund *adjective*
= healthy
Obst ist gesund = fruit is good for you

die **Gesundheit**
= health
(*said after a sneeze*) Gesundheit! = bless
you!

gesungen ▶singen

getan ▶tun

das **Getränk**, *plural* Getränke
= drink

die **Getränkekarte**, *plural*
Getränkekarten
= wine list

das **Getreide**
= grain

das **Getriebe**, *plural* Getriebe
= gearbox

getroffen ▶treffen

getrunken ▶trinken

das **Getue**
= fuss

G

die **Gewalt**, plural Gewalten
- * = power
- * = force
- * = violence

gewalttätig adjective
= violent

gewann ▶ gewinnen

das **Gewehr**, plural Gewehre
= rifle, = gun

die **Gewerkschaft**, plural
Gewerkschaften
= trade union

gewesen ▶ sein

das **Gewicht**, plural Gewichte
= weight

der **Gewinn**, plural Gewinne
- * = profit
- * = prize, = winnings
- * = win

gewinnen irregular verb
= to win
Zeit gewinnen = to gain time

gewiss (**gewiß** ⓞⓛⓓ)
1 adjective = certain
2 adverb = certainly

das **Gewissen**, plural Gewissen
= conscience

gewissenhaft adjective
= conscientious

das **Gewitter**, plural Gewitter
= thunderstorm

gewöhnen verb
- * jemanden an etwas gewöhnen = to get someone used to something
- * sich an etwas gewöhnen = to get used to something

die **Gewohnheit**, plural Gewohnheiten
= habit

gewöhnlich
1 adjective
- * = ordinary
- * = usual
- * = common
2 adverb = usually
wie gewöhnlich = as usual

gewohnt adjective
= usual
etwas gewohnt sein = to be used to something

⎯⎯⎯⎯⎯
ⓞⓛⓓ = old spelling

gewollt ▶ wollen

gewonnen ▶ gewinnen

geworden ▶ werden

geworfen ▶ werfen

das **Gewürz**, plural Gewürze
= spice

Gezeiten (plural)
= tides

gezwungen ▶ zwingen

gibt ▶ geben

gierig adjective
= greedy

gießen irregular verb
- * = to pour
- * = to water

das **Gift**, plural Gifte
= poison

giftig adjective
= poisonous
= toxic

ging ▶ gehen

der **Gipfel**, plural Gipfel
= peak, = summit

der **Gips**, plural Gipse
= plaster

das **Girokonto**, plural Girokonten
= current account

die **Gitarre**, plural Gitarren
= guitar

das **Gitter**, plural Gitter
= bars

der **Glanz**
- * = shine
  (on paper, colour) = gloss
- * = splendour, = splendor

glänzen verb
= to shine

glänzend adjective
- * = shining, = shiny
- * = brilliant

das **Glas**, plural Gläser
- * = glass
- * = jar

die **Glasscheibe**, plural Glasscheiben
= pane (of glass)

glatt
1 adjective
- * = smooth
  = slippery
- * eine glatte Absage = a flat refusal
2 adverb
- * = smoothly

- das ist glatt gelogen = that's a downright lie
- das habe ich glatt vergessen = it completely slipped my mind

das **Glatteis**
= (black) ice

die **Glatze**, *plural* Glatzen
= bald patch
eine Glatze haben = to be bald

der **Glaube**
= belief, = faith

glauben *verb*
= to believe, = to think
das ist nicht zu glauben = that's incredible

gleich
1 *adjective*
= same
das ist mir gleich = it's all the same to me
ganz gleich, wer = no matter who
2 *adverb*
- = the same
- = equally
- = immediately

gleichberechtigt *adjective*
= equal

die **Gleichberechtigung**
= equality
= equal rights

gleichen *irregular verb*
- = to be like
- sich gleichen = to be alike

gleichfalls *adverb*
= also, = likewise
danke gleichfalls! = (thanks and) the same to you!

das **Gleichgewicht**
= balance

gleichgültig *adjective*
= indifferent

gleichmäßig *adjective*
= regular, = even

die **Gleichung**, *plural* Gleichungen
= equation

gleichzeitig
1 *adjective* = simultaneous
2 *adverb* = at the same time

das **Gleis**, *plural* Gleise
- = track
- = platform

das **Glied**, *plural* Glieder
- = limb
- = link

die **Glocke**, *plural* Glocken
= bell

das **Glück**

- = luck
zum Glück = luckily
- = happiness

glücklich *adjective*
- = lucky
- = happy

glücklicherweise *adverb*
= luckily, = fortunately

der **Glückwunsch**, *plural* Glückwünsche
= congratulations
herzlichen Glückwunsch zum Geburtstag! = happy birthday!

die **Glühbirne**, *plural* Glühbirnen
= light bulb

glühen *verb*
= to glow

die **Glut**
- = embers
- = passion

die **Gnade**
- = mercy
- (*in religion*) = grace

das **Gold**
= gold

der **Golf**[1] *plural* Golfe
= gulf

das **Golf**[2]
= golf

goss (**goß** OLD) ▶gießen

der **Gott**, *plural* Götter
= god

der **Gottesdienst**, *plural* Gottesdienste
= service

die **Göttin**, *plural* Göttinnen
= goddess

das **Grab**, *plural* Gräber
= grave

graben *irregular verb*
= to dig

der **Grad**, *plural* Grade
= degree

der **Graf**, *plural* Grafen
= count
= earl

die **Gräfin**, *plural* Gräfinnen
= countess

das **Gramm**, *plural* Gramme
= gram

die **Grammatik**, *plural* Grammatiken
= grammar

grantig *adjective*
= grumpy

G

das **Gras**, *plural* Gräser
= grass

grässlich (**gräßlich**⊙ᴸᴰ) *adjective*
= horrible

die **Gräte**, *plural* Gräten
= (fish)bone

die **Gratifikation**, *plural* Gratifikationen
= bonus

gratis *adverb*
= free (of charge)

gratulieren *verb*
= to congratulate
ich gratuliere! = congratulations!

grau *adjective*
= grey, = gray

grausam *adjective*
= cruel

greifen *irregular verb*
* = to take hold of, = to grasp
* = to catch
* = to reach

grell *adjective*
* = glaring
* = garish
* = shrill

die **Grenze**, *plural* Grenzen
* = border
= frontier
* = limit

grenzen *verb*
an etwas grenzen = to border on
something

der **Grieche**, *plural* Griechen
= Greek

(das) **Griechenland**
= Greece

die **Griechin**, *plural* Griechinnen
= Greek

griechisch *adjective*
= Greek

griff ▶ greifen

der **Griff**, *plural* Griffe
* = grasp, = hold
* = handle

griffbereit *adjective*
= handy

der **Grill**, *plural* Grills
= grill
= barbecue

die **Grille**, *plural* Grillen
* = cricket
* (*idea*) = whim

grillen *verb*
* = to grill
* = to barbecue, = to have a barbecue

das **Grillfest**, *plural* Grillfeste
= barbecue

grinsen *verb*
= to grin

die **Grippe**, *plural* Grippen
= flu

grob *adjective*
* = coarse
* = rough
* = rude
* ein grober Fehler = a bad mistake

groß *adjective*
* = big, = large
im Großen und Ganzen = on the whole
groß werden = to grow up
* = great
* = tall
* ein großer Buchstabe = a capital letter

großartig *adjective*
= great, = magnificent

(das) **Großbritannien**
= Great Britain

die **Größe**, *plural* Größen
* = size
* = height
* = greatness

Großeltern (*plural*)
= grandparents

der **Großmarkt**, *plural* Großmärkte
= hypermarket

die **Großmutter**, *plural* Großmütter
= grandmother

groß|schreiben *irregular verb*
ein Wort großschreiben = to write a word
with a capital

die **Großstadt**, *plural* Großstädte
= city

der **Großvater**, *plural* Großväter
= grandfather

großzügig *adjective*
= generous

grün *adjective*
= green

der **Grund**, *plural* Gründe
* = ground
* = bottom
im Grunde genommen = basically
* = reason

gründen *verb*
* = to found, = to set up
* = to base
* sich auf etwas gründen = to be based on
something

die **Grundlage**, *plural* Grundlagen
= basis, = foundation

gründlich *adjective*
= thorough

grundsätzlich *adjective*
= fundamental, = basic

die **Grundschule**, *plural* Grundschulen
= primary school, = grade school

das **Grundstück**, *plural* Grundstücke
= plot (of land)

die **Gruppe**, *plural* Gruppen
= group

der **Gruß**, *plural* Grüße
• = greeting
einen schönen Gruß an Emma = give my
regards to Emma
mit herzlichen Grüßen = with best wishes
• = salute

grüßen *verb*
• = to greet
grüße deine Eltern von mir = give your
parents my regards
• = to say hello
grüß Gott! = hello
• = to salute

gucken *verb*
= to look

gültig *adjective*
= valid

der **Gummi**, *plural* Gummis
= rubber

das **Gummiband**, *plural* Gummibänder
= rubber band

der **Gummistiefel**, *plural* Gummistiefel
= rubber boot, = wellington

günstig *adjective*
= favourable, = favorable
= convenient

die **Gurke**, *plural* Gurken
• = cucumber
• = gherkin

der **Gurt**, *plural* Gurte
• = strap
• = belt

der **Gürtel**, *plural* Gürtel
= belt

die **Gürteltasche**, *plural* Gürteltaschen
= bum bag, = fanny pack

gut
1 *adjective* = good
2 *adverb* = well
• es gut haben = to be well off, = to be
lucky
• der Laden geht gut = the shop is doing
well
es geht mir gut = I am well

die **Güte**
= goodness
= quality

der **Güterzug**, *plural* Güterzüge
= goods train, = freight train

gutgehen OLD ▶gut

der **Gutschein**, *plural* Gutscheine
= voucher
= coupon

das **Gymnasium**, *plural* Gymnasien
= grammar school

die **Gymnastik**
= gymnastics
= exercises

H

Hh

das **Haar**, *plural* Haare
= hair

der **Haarschnitt**, *plural* Haarschnitte
= haircut

haben *irregular verb*
• = to have
[Angst | Hunger | Durst…] haben = to be
[frightened | hungry | thirsty…]
heute haben wir Montag = it's Monday
today
was hat er? = what's the matter with
him?
• (*forming the perfect tense*)
er hat es gewusst = he knew it
• sich haben✱ = to make a fuss

hacken *verb*
• = to chop
• = to peck
• (*in computing*) = to hack

das **Hackfleisch**
= minced meat, = ground meat

der **Hafen**, *plural* Häfen
= harbour, = port

Haferflocken (*plural*)
= (porridge) oats

haften *verb*
• = to stick, = to cling
• für etwas haften = to be responsible for
something

die **Haftung**
= liability

der **Hagel**
= hail

hageln verb
= to hail

der **Hahn**, plural Hähne
* = cock
* = tap, = faucet

der **Hai**, plural Haie
= shark

häkeln verb
= to crochet

der **Haken**, plural Haken
* = hook
* (mark) = tick
* der Haken dran* = the catch, = the snag

halb
1 adjective = half
halb eins = half past twelve
2 adverb = half

halbfett adjective
= low-fat, = semi-skimmed

halbieren verb
= to halve

die **Halbinsel**, plural Halbinseln
= peninsula

der **Halbkreis**, plural Halbkreise
= semicircle

halbtags adverb
= part-time

halbwegs adverb
* = half-way
* = more or less

die **Halbzeit**, plural Halbzeiten
* = half
* = half-time

half ▶helfen

die **Hälfte**, plural Hälften
= half

die **Halle**, plural Hallen
* = hall
* = foyer

das **Hallenbad**, plural Hallenbäder
= indoor swimming pool

hallo interjection
* = hey!
* = hello!

der **Hals**, plural Hälse
= neck
= throat

das **Halsband**, plural Halsbänder
= collar

Halsschmerzen (plural)
= sore throat

⏻OLD = old spelling

halt interjection
= stop!

der **Halt**
* = hold
* = stop
Halt machen = to stop

haltbar adjective
* = hard-wearing
* mindestens haltbar bis ... = best before ...

halten irregular verb
* = to hold
* = to keep
zu jemandem halten = to be loyal to someone
viel von jemandem halten = to think a lot of someone
* = to stop
* (in soccer) = to save
* (subscribe to) = to take
* eine Rede halten = to give a talk
* sich halten = to keep, = to last
sich gut halten = to do well

die **Haltestelle**, plural Haltestellen
= stop

das **Halteverbot**
'Halteverbot' = 'no stopping'

haltmachen⏻OLD ▶Halt

die **Haltung**, plural Haltungen
* = posture
* = attitude
* = composure

das **Hammelfleisch**
= mutton

der **Hammer**, plural Hämmer
= hammer

hämmern verb
= to hammer

die **Hand**, plural Hände
= hand

die **Handarbeit**, plural Handarbeiten
* = handicraft
* = hand-made article

der **Handel**
= trade

handeln verb
* = to trade, = to deal
= to haggle
* = to act
* es handelt sich um ... = it's about ...
von etwas handeln = to be about something

die **Handelsschule**, plural Handelsschulen
= business school, = vocational college

die **Handfläche**, plural Handflächen
= palm

das **Handgelenk**, *plural* Handgelenke
= wrist

das **Handgepäck**
= hand luggage

handhaben *verb*
= to handle

der **Händler**, *plural* Händler
= trader, = dealer

die **Handlung**, *plural* Handlungen
* = act
* = action
* = plot

die **Handschrift**, *plural* Handschriften
= handwriting

der **Handschuh**, *plural* Handschuhe
= glove

die **Handtasche**, *plural* Handtaschen
= handbag, = pocketbook

das **Handtuch**, *plural* Handtücher
= towel

der **Handwerker**, *plural* Handwerker
= craftsman

das **Handwerkszeug**
= tools

das **Handy**, *plural* Handys
= mobile (phone), cell phone

die **Hängematte**, *plural* Hängematten
= hammock

hängen *irregular verb*
= to hang

der **Happen**, *plural* Happen
= mouthful

die **Harfe**, *plural* Harfen
= harp

die **Harke**, *plural* Harken
= rake

harmlos *adjective*
* = harmless
* = innocent

hart *adjective*
* = hard
* = harsh

die **Härte**, *plural* Härten
* = hardness
* = harshness

der **Hase**, *plural* Hasen
= hare

die **Haselnuss (Haselnuß**⊙ᴸᴰ**)**, *plural*
Haselnüsse
= hazelnut

der **Hass (Haß**⊙ᴸᴰ**)**
= hatred

hassen *verb*
= to hate

hässlich (häßlich⊙ᴸᴰ**)** *adjective*
* = ugly
* = nasty

hast ▶ haben

hastig *adjective*
= hasty, = hurried

**hat, hatte, hatten, hattest,
hattet** ▶ haben

die **Haube**, *plural* Hauben
* = bonnet
= cap
* (*of a car*) = bonnet, = hood

hauen *verb*
* = to beat
* = to thump, = to bang
* sich hauen = to fight, = to have a punch-up

der **Haufen**, *plural* Haufen
* = heap, = pile
* (*of people*) = crowd

häufig *adjective*
= frequent

der **Hauptbahnhof**, *plural* Hauptbahnhöfe
= main station

die **Hauptrolle**, *plural* Hauptrollen
(*in a film*) = lead

die **Hauptsache**, *plural* Hauptsachen
= main thing

hauptsächlich
1 *adjective* = main
2 *adverb* = mainly

die **Hauptstadt**, *plural* Hauptstädte
= capital

die **Hauptstraße**, *plural* Hauptstraßen
= main road

das **Haus**, *plural* Häuser
= house
nach Hause = home
zu Hause = at home

die **Hausarbeit**, *plural* Hausarbeiten
* = housework
* = homework

Hausaufgaben (*plural*)
= homework

der **Haushalt**, *plural* Haushalte
* = household
den Haushalt machen = to do the housework
* = budget

H

das **Haushaltswarengeschäft**, *plural*
Haushaltswarengeschäfte
= hardware shop *or* store

der **Hausmeister**, *plural* Hausmeister
= caretaker, = porter

der **Hausschlüssel**, *plural* Hausschlüssel
= front-door key

der **Hausschuh**, *plural* Hausschuhe
= slipper

das **Haustier**, *plural* Haustiere
= pet

die **Haustür**, *plural* Haustüren
= front door

die **Haut**, *plural* Häute
= skin
aus der Haut fahren✱ = to go up the wall

die **Hebamme**, *plural* Hebammen
= midwife

der **Hebel**, *plural* Hebel
= lever

heben *irregular verb*
• = to lift, = to raise
• sich heben = to rise

die **Hecke**, *plural* Hecken
= hedge

das **Heer**, *plural* Heere
= army

die **Hefe**, *plural* Hefen
= yeast

das **Heft**, *plural* Hefte
• = exercise book
• (*magazine*) = issue

heften *verb*
• = to pin, = to clip
• = to staple
• = to stick
• (*in sewing*) = to tack

heftig *adjective*
• = violent
• = heavy

die **Heftklammer**, *plural* Heftklammern
= staple

die **Heftzwecke**, *plural* Heftzwecken
= drawing pin, = thumbtack

heil *adjective*
• = intact
• = unhurt

heilen *verb*
• = to cure
• = to heal

heilig *adjective*
= holy
= sacred

der **Heiligabend**
= Christmas Eve

der/die **Heilige**, *plural* Heiligen
= saint

das **Heim**, *plural* Heime
= home

die **Heimat**, *plural* Heimaten
• = home
• = native land

die **Heimfahrt**, *plural* Heimfahrten
= journey home
= drive home

heimlich *adjective*
= secret

der **Heimweg**, *plural* Heimwege
= way home

das **Heimweh**
= homesickness
Heimweh haben = to be homesick

die **Heirat**, *plural* Heiraten
= marriage

heiraten *verb*
= to marry
= to get married

heiser *adjective*
= hoarse

heiß *adjective*
= hot

heißen *irregular verb*
• = to be called
ich heiße Emma = my name is Emma
• = to mean
das heißt = that is

heiter *adjective*
• = bright
• = cheerful

heizen *verb*
• = to heat
• = to have the heating on

die **Heizung**, *plural* Heizungen
• = heating
• = radiator

der **Held**, *plural* Helden
= hero

helfen *irregular verb*
• = to help
es hilft nichts = it's no good
• sich zu helfen wissen = to know what
to do

der **Helfer**, *plural* Helfer
= helper, = assistant

die **Helferin**, *plural* Helferinnen
= helper, = assistant

hell *adjective*
• = light

✱ in informal situations

- = bright
- eine helle Stimme = a clear voice
- heller Wahnsinn✶ = sheer madness

hellwach *adjective*
= wide awake

der **Helm**, *plural* Helme
= helmet

das **Hemd**, *plural* Hemden
- = shirt
- = vest, = undershirt

der **Hengst**, *plural* Hengste
= stallion

der **Henkel**, *plural* Henkel
= handle

die **Henne**, *plural* Hennen
= hen

her *adverb*
- = here
  komm her = come here
  her mit dem Geld✶ = give me the money
  von der Farbe her = as far as the colour is concerned
- = ago
  von ihrer Kindheit her = since childhood

herab *adverb*
= down (here)

herab|setzen *verb*
- = to reduce, = to cut
- = to belittle

heran
= near
bis an die Wand heran = up to the wall

heran|kommen *irregular verb* (**!** *sein*)
= to come near, = to approach

herauf *adverb*
= up (here)

herauf|kommen *irregular verb* (**!** *sein*)
= to come up

heraus *adverb*
= out

heraus|finden *irregular verb*
- = to find out
- = to find one's way out

heraus|geben *irregular verb*
- = to hand over, = to give
- = to bring out

heraus|kommen *irregular verb* (**!** *sein*)
= to come out

heraus|stellen *verb*
- = to put out
- sich herausstellen = to turn out

die **Herberge**, *plural* Herbergen
= hostel

her|bringen *irregular verb*
= to bring (here)

der **Herbst**, *plural* Herbste
= autumn, = fall

der **Herd**, *plural* Herde
= cooker

die **Herde**, *plural* Herden
= herd
= flock

herein *adverb*
= in (here)
herein! = come in!

herein|fallen *irregular verb* (**!** *sein*)
= to be taken in

herein|kommen *irregular verb* (**!** *sein*)
= to come in

herein|lassen *irregular verb*
= to let in

die **Herfahrt**
= journey here
= drive here

her|geben *irregular verb*
- = to hand over
- = to give away

her|kommen *irregular verb* (**!** *sein*)
= to come here

die **Herkunft**, *plural* Herkünfte
= origin
(*of a person*) = background

der **Herr**, *plural* Herren
- = gentleman
- = master
- (*with a name*) = Mr
  Sehr geehrte Herren = Dear Sirs

her|richten *verb*
= to get ready, = to prepare

herrlich *adjective*
= marvellous

herrschen *verb*
= to rule
es herrschte Stille = there was silence

her|stellen *verb*
= to produce, = to manufacture
in Deutschland hergestellt = made in Germany

die **Herstellung**, *plural* Herstellungen
= production, = manufacture

herüber *adverb*
= over (here)

herum|drehen *verb*
- = to turn (over)
- sich herumdrehen = to turn round

herum|gehen *irregular verb* (**!** *sein*)
- = to go round
- (*of time*) = to pass

H

herunter adverb
= down (here)

herunter|fallen irregular verb (**!** sein)
= to fall down, = to fall off

herunter|kommen irregular verb
(**!** sein)
= to come down

herunter|lassen irregular verb
= to let down, = to lower

hervor adverb
= out

hervorragend
1 adjective = outstanding
2 adverb = outstandingly well

das **Herz**, plural Herzen
* = heart
* (playing cards) = hearts

der **Herzanfall**, plural Herzanfälle
= heart attack

herzlich adjective
* = warm
* = kind
* = sincere
herzlichen Dank = many thanks

herzlos adjective
= heartless

der **Herzog**, plural Herzöge
= duke

die **Herzogin**, plural Herzoginnen
= duchess

der **Herzschlag**, plural Herzschläge
* = heartbeat
* = heart failure

hetzen verb
* = to rush
* sich hetzen = to rush

das **Heu**
= hay

heulen verb
= to howl

die **Heuschrecke**, plural Heuschrecken
= grasshopper

heute adverb
= today

heutig adjective
= today's
in der heutigen Zeit = nowadays

heutzutage adverb
= nowadays

die **Hexe**, plural Hexen
= witch

✕ in informal situations

hielt ▶ halten

hier adverb
= here

hierher adverb
= here

hierhin adverb
= here

hieß ▶ heißen

die **Hilfe**, plural Hilfen
= help, = aid

hilflos adjective
= helpless

hilfsbereit adjective
= helpful

hilft ▶ helfen

die **Himbeere**, plural Himbeeren
= raspberry

der **Himmel**, plural Himmel
* = sky
* = heaven

hin adverb
* = there
einmal Köln hin und zurück = a return to
Cologne
hin und her = back and forth
* hin und wieder = now and again

hinauf adverb
= up (there)

hinaus adverb
= out (there)
zur Tür hinaus = out of the door

hinaus|gehen irregular verb (**!** sein)
* = to go out
* das Zimmer geht nach Westen hinaus =
the room faces west

hindern verb
* = to stop, = to prevent
* = to hinder

das **Hindernis**, plural Hindernisse
= obstacle

hindurch adverb
= through it/them
das ganze Jahr hindurch = throughout
the year

hinein adverb
= in (there)
in etwas hinein = into something

hinein|gehen irregular verb (**!** sein)
= to go in
in etwas hineingehen = to go into
something

hin|fahren irregular verb (**!** sein)
= to go there, = to drive there

die **Hinfahrt**
= journey there
= drive there

hin|fallen *irregular verb* (**!** *sein*)
= to fall over

hing ▶ hängen

hin|gehen *irregular verb* (**!** *sein*)
• = to go (there)
• (*of time*) = to go by

hinken *verb*
= to limp

hin|kommen *irregular verb* (**!** *sein*)
• = to get there
• (*belong somewhere*) = to go
• mit etwas hinkommen✗ = to manage (with something)

hin|legen *verb*
• = to put down
• sich hinlegen = to lie down

die **Hinreise**, *plural* Hinreisen
= journey there

hin|setzen *verb*
• = to put down
• sich hinsetzen = to sit down

hinten *adverb*
= at the back
von hinten = from behind

hinter *preposition* (+ *dative or accusative*)
= behind
hinter jemandem herlaufen = to run after someone
etwas hinter sich bringen = to get something over with

hintere ▶ hinterer

hintereinander *adverb*
• = one behind the other
• = one after another
dreimal hintereinander = three times in a row

hinterer/hintere/hinteres
adjective
= back, = rear

der **Hintergrund**, *plural* Hintergründe
= background

hinterlistig *adjective*
= deceitful

der **Hintern✗**, *plural* Hintern
= bottom

hinüber *adverb*
= over (there), = across (there)

hinunter *adverb*
= down (there)

der **Hinweg**, *plural* Hinwege
= way there

der **Hinweis**, *plural* Hinweise
• = hint
• unter Hinweis auf = with reference to

hin|weisen *irregular verb*
= to point
jemanden auf etwas hinweisen = to point something out to someone

hinzu *adverb*
= in addition

hinzu|kommen *irregular verb* (**!** *sein*)
• = to come along, = to arrive
• = to be added

das **Hirn**, *plural* Hirne
= brain

der **Hirsch**, *plural* Hirsche
• = deer
• (*male*) = stag
• (*as food*) = venison

die **Hitze**
= heat

hoch
1 *adjective*
• = high
• (*of a tree*) = tall
• (*of snow*) = deep
• (*of age, weight*) = great
• (*of damage*) = severe
2 *adverb*
• = high
= highly
• die Treppe hoch = up the stairs

das **Hoch**, *plural* Hochs
• = cheer
• (*weather system*) = high

hochachtungsvoll *adverb*
(*ending a letter*) = yours faithfully

das **Hochhaus**, *plural* Hochhäuser
= high-rise building
= tower block

hoch|heben *irregular verb*
= to lift up, = to raise

die **Hochschule**, *plural* Hochschulen
= college
= university

hoch|scrollen *verb*
= to scroll up

höchst *adverb*
= extremely, = most

höchster/höchste/höchstes
adjective
= highest
es ist höchste Zeit = it is high time

die **Hochzeit**, *plural* Hochzeiten
= wedding

der **Hochzeitstag**, *plural* Hochzeitstage
• = wedding day
• = wedding anniversary

H

hocken *verb*
= to squat

der **Hocker**, *plural* Hocker
= stool

der **Hof**, *plural* Höfe
- = courtyard
- (*at school*) = playground
- = court
- = farm

hoffen *verb*
= to hope

hoffentlich *adverb*
= hopefully
= I hope so
hoffentlich nicht = I hope not

die **Hoffnung**, *plural* Hoffnungen
= hope

hoffnungslos *adjective*
= hopeless

höflich *adjective*
= polite

die **Höflichkeit**, *plural* Höflichkeiten
= politeness, = courtesy

die **Höhe**, *plural* Höhen
= height
= altitude
das ist die Höhe!✖ = that's the limit!

hoher/hohe/hohes ▶hoch

hohl *adjective*
= hollow

die **Höhle**, *plural* Höhlen
- = cave
- = den

holen *verb*
- = to fetch, = to get
- sich etwas holen = to get *or* catch
  something

der **Holländer**, *plural* Holländer
= Dutchman

die **Holländerin**, *plural* Holländerinnen
= Dutchwoman

holländisch *adjective*
= Dutch

die **Hölle**, die, *plural* Höllen
= hell

das **Holz**, *plural* Hölzer
= wood

der **Honig**, *plural* Honige
= honey

das **Honorar**, *plural* Honorare
= fee

horchen *verb*
- = to listen
- = to eavesdrop

hören *verb*
= to hear
= to listen (to)

der **Hörer**, *plural* Hörer
- = listener
- (*of phone*) = receiver

die **Hörerin**, *plural* Hörerinnen
= listener

der **Horizont**, *plural* Horizonte
= horizon

die **Hose**, *plural* Hosen
= trousers, = pants

das **Hotel**, *plural* Hotels
= hotel

hübsch *adjective*
= pretty
= nice

der **Hubschrauber**, *plural* Hubschrauber
= helicopter

der **Huf**, *plural* Hufe
= hoof

das **Hufeisen**, *plural* Hufeisen
= horseshoe

die **Hüfte**, *plural* Hüften
= hip

der **Hügel**, *plural* Hügel
= hill

das **Huhn**, *plural* Hühner
= chicken
= hen

die **Hülle**, *plural* Hüllen
= cover
= wrapping

die **Hummel**, *plural* Hummeln
= bumble-bee

der **Hummer**, *plural* Hummer
= lobster

der **Humor**
= humour, = humor
Humor haben = to have a sense of
humour

humpeln *verb* (**!** *sein*)
= to hobble

der **Hund**, *plural* Hunde
= dog

die **Hundehütte**, *plural* Hundehütten
= kennel, = doghouse

hundert *adjective*
= a hundred, = one hundred

der **Hunger**
= hunger

---

die **Hungersnot**, *plural* Hungersnöte
= famine

hungrig *adjective*
= hungry

die **Hupe**, *plural* Hupen
= horn

hupen *verb*
= to beep

hüpfen *verb* (**!** *sein*)
= to hop

hurra *interjection*
= hurray!

husten *verb*
= to cough

der **Husten**, *plural* Husten
= cough

der **Hut**, *plural* Hüte
= hat

hüten *verb*
• = to look after
• sich hüten = to be on one's guard

die **Hütte**, *plural* Hütten
• = hut
• = iron and steel works

die **Hyäne**, *plural* Hyänen
= hyena

hypnotisieren *verb*
= to hypnotize

die **Hypothek**, *plural* Hypotheken
= mortgage

hysterisch *adjective*
= hysterical

I i

---

ich *pronoun*
= I

der **IC-Zug**, *plural* IC-Zuge
(*Intercity-Zug*) = intercity train

die **Idee**, *plural* Ideen
= idea

identifizieren *verb*
= to identify

identisch *adjective*
= identical

der **Idiot**, *plural* Idioten
= idiot

idiotisch *adjective*
= idiotic

der **Igel**, *plural* Igel
= hedgehog

ihm *pronoun*
= (to) him
(*thing*) = (to) it

ihn *pronoun*
= him
(*thing*) = it

ihnen *pronoun*
= (to) them

Ihnen *pronoun*
= (to) you

ihr
1 *pronoun*
• (*plural*) = you
• = (to) her
(*thing*) = (to) it
2 *adjective* = her
(*thing*) = its
(*plural*) = their

Ihr *adjective*
= your

ihrer/ihre/ihrs *pronoun*
= hers
(*plural*) = theirs

Ihrer/Ihre/Ihrs *pronoun*
= yours

die **Illustrierte**, *plural* Illustrierten
= magazine

im = in dem
im Juni = in June
im Kino = at the cinema

der **Imbiss** (**Imbiß**ᴼᴸᴰ), *plural* Imbisse
• = snack
• = snack bar

imitieren *verb*
= to imitate

immer *adverb*
= always
immer wieder = again and again
für immer = for ever
immer noch = still
wo/wer/wann immer =
wherever/whoever/whenever

immerzu *adverb*
= all the time, = the whole time

impfen *verb*
= to vaccinate, = to inoculate

imprägniert *adjective*
= waterproof

imstande *adverb*
= able

in *preposition*
* (+ *dative*) = in
  in diesem Monat = this month
* (+ *accusative*) = into, = in
  in die Stadt gehen = to go to town

inbegriffen *adjective*
= included
Essen ist inbegriffen = food is included

indem *conjunction*
* = while
* indem man etwas tut = by doing
  something

der **Inder**, *plural* Inder
= Indian

die **Inderin**, *plural* Inderinnen
= Indian

der **Indianer**, *plural* Indianer
= (American) Indian

die **Indianerin**, *plural* Indianerinnen
= (American) Indian

(das) **Indien**
= India

indisch *adjective*
= Indian

die **Industrie**, *plural* Industrien
= industry

die **Infektion**, *plural* Infektionen
= infection

infizieren *verb*
* = to infect
* sich bei jemandem infizieren = to be
  infected by someone

infolge *preposition* (+ *genitive*)
= as a result of

die **Informatik**
= information technology
= computer studies

die **Information**, *plural* Informationen
= (piece of) information

informieren *verb*
* = to inform
  informiert sein = to be aware
* sich über etwas informieren = to find out
  about something

der **Ingenieur**, *plural* Ingenieure
= engineer

der **Ingwer**
= ginger

der **Inhaber**, *plural* Inhaber
* (*of an office*) = holder
* (*of a shop*) = owner

die **Inhaberin**, *plural* Inhaberinnen
* (*of an office*) = holder

* (*of a shop*) = owner

der **Inhalt**, *plural* Inhalte
* = contents
* (*of a story*) = content
* (*of a rectangle*) = area
* (*of a cylinder*) = volume

das **Inhaltsverzeichnis**, *plural*
Inhaltsverzeichnisse
= contents list

innen *adverb*
= inside
nach innen = inwards

die **Innenstadt**, *plural* Innenstädte
* = inner city
* = city centre, = town centre

das **Innere**
= inside
= interior

innerer/innere/inneres *adjective*
* = inner
* = inside
* (*in medicine*) = internal

innerhalb
1 *preposition* (+ *genitive*) = within
2 *adverb*
innerhalb von = within

innerlich
1 *adjective* = inner
2 *adverb* = inwardly

ins = in das
ins Kino gehen = to go to the cinema

das **Insekt**, *plural* Insekten
= insect

die **Insel**, *plural* Inseln
= island

das **Inserat**, *plural* Inserate
= advertisement

inserieren *verb*
= to advertise

insgesamt *adverb*
= in all, = all in all

der **Installateur**, *plural* Installateure
* = fitter
* = plumber

der **Instinkt**, *plural* Instinkte
= instinct

die **Intelligenz**
= intelligence

interessant *adjective*
= interesting

das **Interesse**, *plural* Interessen
= interest

interessieren *verb*
* = to interest

✗ in informal situations ⓞⓛⓓ = old spelling

- sich für etwas interessieren = to be interested in something

das **Internat**, *plural* Internate
= boarding school

das **Internet**
= Internet

das **Interview**, *plural* Interviews
= interview

die **Investion**, *plural* Investionen
= investment

inzwischen *adverb*
= in the meantime
= meanwhile

der **Ire**, *plural* Iren
= Irishman
die Iren = the Irish

irgend *adverb*
= at all
wenn irgend möglich = if at all possible

irgendein *article*
= some, = any
irgendein anderer = someone *or* anyone else

irgendeiner/irgendeine/ irgendeins *pronoun*
= someone, = somebody
(*in questions and negatives*) = anyone, = anybody

irgendetwas *pronoun*
= something
(*in questions and negatives*)
= anything

irgendjemand *pronoun*
= someone, = somebody
(*in questions and negatives*) = anyone, = anybody

irgendwann *adverb*
= (at) some time, = (at) any time

irgendwie *adverb*
= somehow

irgendwo *adverb*
= somewhere, = anywhere

die **Irin**, *plural* Irinnen
= Irishwoman

irisch *adjective*
= Irish

(das) **Irland**
= Ireland

ironisch *adjective*
= ironic

irre
1 *adjective*
= mad, = crazy
2 *adverb*
irre gut✲ = incredibly good

irren *verb*
- = to be wrong, = to be mistaken
- (**!** *sein*) (*when lost*) = to wander
- sich irren = to be wrong, = to be mistaken

der **Irrtum**, *plural* Irrtümer
= mistake

isolieren *verb*
- = to isolate
- = to insulate

isst (**ißt** OLD) ▶essen

ist ▶sein

(das) **Italien**
= Italy

der **Italiener**, *plural* Italiener
= Italian

die **Italienerin**, *plural* Italienerinnen
= Italian

italienisch *adjective*
= Italian

Jj

ja *adverb*
= yes
ich glaube ja = I think so

die **Jacht**, *plural* Jachten
= yacht

die **Jacke**, *plural* Jacken
- = jacket
- = cardigan

das **Jackett**, *plural* Jacketts
= jacket

die **Jagd**, *plural* Jagden
= hunt
auf die Jagd gehen = to go hunting

jagen *verb*
- = to hunt
- = to chase

der **Jäger**, *plural* Jäger
- = hunter
- (*plane*) = fighter

das **Jahr**, *plural* Jahre
= year

der **Jahrestag**, *plural* Jahrestage
= anniversary

die **Jahreszeit**, *plural* Jahreszeiten
= season

der **Jahrgang**, *plural* Jahrgänge
= year
= vintage

das **Jahrhundert**, *plural* Jahrhunderte
= century

die **Jahrhundertwende**
= turn of the century

jährlich
1 *adjective*
= annual, = yearly
2 *adverb*
= annually, = yearly
zweimal jährlich = twice a year

der **Jahrmarkt**, *plural* Jahrmärkte
= fair

das **Jahrtausend**, *plural* Jahrtausende
= millennium

das **Jahrzehnt**, *plural* Jahrzehnte
= decade

jähzornig *adjective*
= hot-tempered

jammern *verb*
= to moan

der **Januar**
= January

der **Japaner**, *plural* Japaner
= Japanese

die **Japanerin**, *plural* Japanerinnen
= Japanese

japanisch *adjective*
= Japanese

jawohl *adverb*
= yes
= certainly

je
1 *adverb*
• = ever
• = each
2 *preposition* (+ *accusative*) = per
3 *conjunction*
je mehr, desto besser = the more the
better

jede ▶jeder

jedenfalls *adverb*
= in any case

jeder/jede/jedes
1 *adjective*
• = every
jedes Mal = every time
jedes Mal wenn = whenever
• = each
• = any
2 *pronoun*
• = everyone
• = each one
• = anyone

jederzeit *adverb*
= (at) any time

jedes ▶jeder

jedesmal(OLD) ▶jeder

jedoch *adverb*
= however

jemand *pronoun*
= someone, = somebody
(*in questions and negatives*) = anyone, =
anybody

jener/jene/jenes
1 *adjective* = that, (*plural*) = those
2 *pronoun* = that one, (*plural*) = those

jenseits
1 *preposition* (+ *genitive*)
= (on) the other side of
= beyond
2 *adverb* = (on) the other side

jetzt *adverb*
= now

jobben✗ *verb*
= to work

joggen *verb* (**!** *sein*)
= to jog

der or das **Joghurt**, *plural* Joghurts
= yoghurt

die **Johannisbeere**, *plural*
Johannisbeeren
rote Johannisbeeren = redcurrants
schwarze Johannisbeeren =
blackcurrants

der **Journalist**, *plural* Journalisten
= journalist

die **Journalistin**, *plural* Journalistinnen
= journalist

jubeln *verb*
= to cheer

das **Jubiläum**, *plural* Jubiläen
• = jubilee
• = anniversary

jucken *verb*
• = to itch
• sich jucken = to scratch

der **Jude**, *plural* Juden
= Jew

die **Jüdin**, *plural* Jüdinnen
= Jewess

jüdisch *adjective*
= Jewish

die **Jugend**
= youth

die **Jugendherberge**, *plural*
Jugendherbergen
= youth hostel

✗ in informal situations   (OLD) = old spelling

der/die **Jugendliche**, *plural* Jugendlichen
= young person
= youth

(das) **Jugoslawien**
= Yugoslavia

der **Juli**
= July

jung *adjective*
= young

der **Junge**, *plural* Jungen
= boy

die **Jungfrau**, *plural* Jungfrauen
• = virgin
• = Virgo

der **Junggeselle**, *plural* Junggesellen
= bachelor

jüngster/jüngste/jüngstes
adjective
= youngest
in jüngster Zeit = recently

der **Juni**
= June

Jura (*plural*)
= law

die **Jury**, *plural* Jurys
• = jury
• (*in sport*) = judges

Kk

das **Kabarett**, *plural* Kabaretts
= cabaret

das **Kabel**, *plural* Kabel
= cable

der **Kabeljau**, *plural* Kabeljaus
= cod

die **Kabine**, *plural* Kabinen
• = cabin
• (*for changing*) = cubicle
• (*of cable car*) = car

das **Kabrio**, *plural* Kabrios
= convertible

die **Kachel**, *plural* Kacheln
= tile

der **Käfer**, *plural* Käfer
= beetle

der **Kaffee**, *plural* Kaffees
= coffee

der **Käfig**, *plural* Käfige
= cage

kahl *adjective*
• = bald
• = bare

der **Kai**, *plural* Kais
= quay

der **Kaiser**, *plural* Kaiser
= emperor

die **Kaiserin**, *plural* Kaiserinnen
= empress

die **Kajüte**, *plural* Kajüten
= cabin

der **Kakao**, *plural* Kakaos
= cocoa

der **Kakerlak**, *plural* Kakerlaken
= cockroach

der **Kaktus**, *plural* Kakteen
= cactus

das **Kalb**, *plural* Kälber
= calf

das **Kalbfleisch**
= veal

der **Kalender**, *plural* Kalender
• = calendar
• = diary

der **Kalk**, *plural* Kalke
• = lime
• = limescale
• = calcium

die **Kalorie**, *plural* Kalorien
= calorie

kalorienarm *adjective*
= low-calorie

kalt *adjective*
= cold

die **Kälte**
• = cold
zehn Grad Kälte = 10 degrees below zero
• (*emotional*) = coldness

kam ▶kommen

das **Kamel**, *plural* Kamele
= camel

die **Kamera**, *plural* Kameras
= camera

der **Kamin**, *plural* Kamine
= fireplace

der **Kamm**, *plural* Kämme
• = comb
• = ridge

kämmen *verb*
• = to comb
• sich die Haare kämmen = to comb one's
hair

K

die **Kammer**, *plural* Kammern
- • = store room
- • = chamber

der **Kampf**, *plural* Kämpfe
- • = battle
- • = fight
- • (*in sport*) = contest

kämpfen *verb*
= to fight

der **Kämpfer**, *plural* Kämpfer
= fighter

die **Kämpferin**, *plural* Kämpferinnen
= fighter

(das) **Kanada**
= Canada

der **Kanadier**, *plural* Kanadier
= Canadian

die **Kanadierin**, *plural* Kanadierinnen
= Canadian

kanadisch *adjective*
= Canadian

der **Kanal**, *plural* Kanäle
- • = canal
- • = channel
  - der Kanal = the (English) Channel
- • = sewer

die **Kanalisation**
= sewers
= drains

der **Kandidat**, *plural* Kandidaten
= candidate

das **Känguru** (**Känguruh**ᴼᴸᴰ), *plural* Kängurus
= kangaroo

das **Kaninchen**, *plural* Kaninchen
= rabbit

kann ▶können

das **Kännchen**, *plural* Kännchen
- • = pot
  - ein Kännchen Kaffee bitte = a pot of coffee please
- • = jug

die **Kanne**, *plural* Kannen
- • (*for water*) = jug
- • (*for coffee, tea*) = pot
- • (*for oil*) = can
- • (*for milk*) = churn

kannst ▶können

kannte ▶kennen

die **Kante**, *plural* Kanten
= edge

die **Kantine**, *plural* Kantinen
= canteen

das **Kanu**, *plural* Kanus
= canoe

der **Kanzler**, *plural* Kanzler
= chancellor

die **Kapelle**, *plural* Kapellen
- • = chapel
- • = band

kapieren✱ *verb*
= to understand, = to get

das **Kapital**
= capital

der **Kapitän**, *plural* Kapitäne
= captain

das **Kapitel**, *plural* Kapitel
= chapter

die **Kappe**, *plural* Kappen
= cap

kaputt *adjective*
= broken
ich bin kaputt✱ = I'm shattered

kaputt|gehen✱ *irregular verb* (**!** sein)
= to break, = to pack up

kaputt|machen✱ *verb*
- • = to break
- • sich kaputtmachen = to wear oneself out

die **Kapuze**, *plural* Kapuzen
= hood

der **Karfreitag**
= Good Friday

kariert *adjective*
- • = check
- • (*of paper*) = squared

der **Karneval**, *plural* Karnevale
= carnival

das **Karo**
(*playing cards*) = diamonds

die **Karotte**, *plural* Karotten
= carrot

die **Karte**, *plural* Karten
- • = card
- • = ticket
- • = menu
- • = map

die **Kartoffel**, *plural* Kartoffeln
= potato

der **Kartoffelbrei**
= mashed potatoes

der **Karton**, *plural* Kartons
- • = cardboard
- • = cardboard box, = carton

das **Karussell**, *plural* Karussells
= merry-go-round

✱ in informal situations   ᴼᴸᴰ = old spelling

der **Käse**
= cheese

die **Kasse**, *plural* Kassen
- = till
- (*in a supermarket*) = checkout
- (*in a bank*) = cash desk
- (*in a theatre*) = box-office
- knapp bei Kasse sein = to be short of money

die **Kassette**, *plural* Kassetten
- = cassette
- = box

kassieren *verb*
- = to collect
- = to collect the money
  darf ich bei Ihnen kassieren? = would you like your bill?

die **Kastanie**, *plural* Kastanien
= chestnut

der **Kasten**, *plural* Kästen
- = box
- (*for bottles*) = crate
- (*for bread*) = bin

der **Katalog**, *plural* Kataloge
= catalogue

der **Katalysator**, *plural* Katalysatoren
- = catalyst
- = catalytic converter

die **Katastrophe**, *plural* Katastrophen
= catastrophe

der **Kater**, *plural* Kater
- = tom-cat
- einen Kater haben✱ = to have a hangover

die **Kathedrale**, *plural* Kathedralen
= cathedral

katholisch *adjective*
= Catholic

die **Katze**, *plural* Katzen
= cat

kauen *verb*
= to chew

der **Kauf**, *plural* Käufe
- = purchase
- etwas in Kauf nehmen = to put up with something

kaufen *verb*
= to buy

der **Käufer**, *plural* Käufer
= buyer

die **Käuferin**, *plural* Käuferinnen
= buyer

die **Kauffrau**, *plural* Kauffrauen
= businesswoman

das **Kaufhaus**, *plural* Kaufhäuser
= department store

der **Kaufmann**, *plural* Kaufleute
= businessman

der **Kaugummi**, *plural* Kaugummis
= chewing gum

kaum *adverb*
= hardly, = scarcely

die **Kaution**, *plural* Kautionen
- = deposit
- = bail

der **Kegel**, *plural* Kegel
- = cone
- = skittle

kehren *verb*
- = to turn
- = to sweep

kein *adjective*
= no
keine fünf Minuten = less than five minutes

keiner/keine/keins *pronoun*
= no one, = nobody
(*thing*) = none, = not one

keinmal *adverb*
= not once

keins ▶ keiner

der **Keks**, *plural* Kekse
= biscuit, = cookie

der **Keller**, *plural* Keller
= cellar

das **Kellergeschoss**
(**Kellergeschoß**ⓄⒺⒹ), *plural*
Kellergeschosse
= basement

der **Kellner**, *plural* Kellner
= waiter

die **Kellnerin**, *plural* Kellnerinnen
= waitress

kennen *irregular verb*
- = to know
  kennen lernen = to get to know, = to meet
  ich habe sie in London kennen gelernt = I met her in London
- sich kennen lernen = to get to know each other, = to meet

Kenntnisse (*plural*)
= knowledge

das **Kennzeichen**, *plural* Kennzeichen
- = distinguishing mark
- = characteristic
- (*of a vehicle*) = registration number

der **Kerl**, *plural* Kerle
= fellow, = bloke

der **Kern**, *plural* Kerne
- = pip

K

(*in an apricot, peach*) = stone
(*in a nut*) = kernel
- = core
- der Kern der Sache = the heart of the matter

die **Kernenergie**
= nuclear power

das **Kernkraftwerk**, *plural* Kernkraftwerke
= nuclear power station

die **Kerze**, *plural* Kerzen
= candle

der **Kessel**, *plural* Kessel
= kettle

die **Kette**, *plural* Ketten
- = chain
- = necklace

keuchen *verb*
= to pant

der **Keuchhusten**
= whooping cough

kichern *verb*
= to giggle

der **Kiefer**¹ *plural* Kiefer
= jaw

die **Kiefer**² *plural* Kiefern
= pine (tree)

der **Kieselstein**, *plural* Kieselsteine
= pebble

das **Kilo**, *plural* Kilo or Kilos
= kilo

der **Kilometer**, *plural* Kilometer
= kilometre, = kilometer

das **Kind**, *plural* Kinder
= child

der **Kindergarten**, *plural* Kindergärten
= nursery school

die **Kindertagesstätte**, *plural* Kindertagesstätten
= day nursery

der **Kinderwagen**, *plural* Kinderwagen
= pram, = baby carriage

die **Kindheit**, *plural* Kindheiten
= childhood

kindisch *adjective*
= childish

das **Kinn**, *plural* Kinne
= chin

das **Kino**, *plural* Kinos
= cinema, = movie theater

kippen *verb*
= to tip (up)

---

die **Kirche**, *plural* Kirchen
= church

die **Kirsche**, *plural* Kirschen
= cherry

das **Kissen**, *plural* Kissen
- = cushion
- = pillow

die **Kiste**, *plural* Kisten
= box, = crate

kitschig *adjective*
= kitsch

das **Kitz**, *plural* Kitze
(*goat*) = kid
(*deer*) = fawn

kitzeln *verb*
= to tickle

die **Klage**, *plural* Klagen
= complaint

klagen *verb*
= to complain

die **Klammer**, *plural* Klammern
- (*for washing*) = peg
- (*for hair*) = grip
- (*in text*) = bracket

der **Klang**, *plural* Klänge
- = sound
- = tone

die **Klappe**, *plural* Klappen
- = flap
- = clapperboard
- halt die Klappe!✘ = shut up!

klappen *verb*
- nach vorne klappen = to tilt forward
  nach oben/unten klappen = to lift up/put down
- klappen✘ = to work out

klar
1 *adjective*
- = clear
- = definite
- sich über etwas im Klaren sein = to realize something
- klar werden = to become clear
  sich über etwas klar werden = to realize something
2 *adverb*
- = clearly
- = of course

klären *verb*
- = to clarify
  = to sort out
- sich klären = to clear

die **Klarinette**, *plural* Klarinetten
= clarinet

klarwerden ⓄⓁⒹ ▶klar

die **Klasse**, *plural* Klassen
= class

---

die **Klassenarbeit**, *plural* Klassenarbeiten
= (written) test

das **Klassenzimmer**, *plural*
Klassenzimmer
= classroom

klassisch *adjective*
= classical

der **Klatsch**
= gossip

klatschen *verb*
* = to clap
* = to splash
* = to gossip

klauen× *verb*
= to pinch

das **Klavier**, *plural* Klaviere
= piano

kleben *verb*
= to stick
= to glue

klebrig *adjective*
= sticky

der **Klebstoff**, *plural* Klebstoffe
= adhesive, = glue

der **Klebstreifen**, *plural* Klebstreifen
= sticky tape

der **Klecks**, *plural* Kleckse
= stain
= spot

das **Kleid**, *plural* Kleider
* = dress
* Kleider (*plural*) = clothes

der **Kleiderbügel**, *plural* Kleiderbügel
= clothes-hanger

der **Kleiderschrank**, *plural*
Kleiderschränke
= wardrobe

die **Kleidung**
= clothes, = clothing

klein *adjective*
* = small, = little
* = short

das **Kleingeld**
= change

die **Kleinigkeit**, *plural* Kleinigkeiten
= trifle, = small thing
eine Kleinigkeit essen = to have a bite to
eat

kleinlich *adjective*
= petty

klemmen *verb*
* = to stick, = to jam
* sich den Finger klemmen = to get one's
finger caught

klettern *verb* (**!** *sein*)
= to climb

das **Klima**, *plural* Klimas
= climate

die **Klimaanlage**, *plural* Klimaanlagen
= air-conditioning

der **Klimawechsel**
= climate change

die **Klinge**, *plural* Klingen
= blade

die **Klingel**, *plural* Klingeln
= bell

klingeln *verb*
= to ring
es klingelt = there's a ring at the door

klingen *irregular verb*
= to sound

die **Klinik**, *plural* Kliniken
= clinic

die **Klinke**, *plural* Klinken
= handle

die **Klippe**, *plural* Klippen
= rock

das **Klo×**, *plural* Klos
= loo

klopfen *verb*
* = to knock
* = to beat

das **Klosett**, *plural* Klosetts
= lavatory

das **Kloster**, *plural* Klöster
* = monastery
* = convent

der **Klotz**, *plural* Klötze
= block
= log

der **Klub**, *plural* Klubs
= club

klug *adjective*
= clever
aus etwas nicht klug werden = to not
understand something

der **Klumpen**, *plural* Klumpen
= lump

der **Knall**, *plural* Knalle
= bang

knallen *verb*
= to go bang
* (of a whip) = to crack
* (of a cork) = to pop
* (of a door) = to slam

K

knapp adjective
* = scarce
  mit etwas knapp sein = to be short of
    something
  mit knapper Mehrheit = by a narrow
    majority
* = tight
  eine knappe Stunde = just under an hour
  das war knapp✶ = that was a close shave

knarren verb
  = to creak

knautschen verb
* = to crease
* = to crumple

kneifen irregular verb
* = to pinch
* kneifen✶ = to chicken out

die **Kneipe✶**, plural Kneipen
  = pub, = bar

kneten verb
* (in baking) = to knead
* (in pottery) = to mould

knicken verb
* = to bend
* = to fold

das **Knie**, plural Knie
  = knee

knien verb
* = to kneel
* sich knien = to kneel (down)

knipsen verb
* (photograph) = to snap
* (make a hole in) = to punch

der **Knoblauch**
  = garlic

der **Knöchel**, plural Knöchel
* = ankle
* = knuckle

der **Knochen**, plural Knochen
  = bone

der **Knopf**, plural Knöpfe
* = button
* = knob

die **Knospe**, plural Knospen
  = bud

der **Knoten**, plural Knoten
* = knot
* (hairstyle) = bun

knurren verb
* = to growl
* = to rumble
* = to grumble

knusprig adjective
  = crisp, = crunchy

OLD = old spelling

der **Koch**, plural Köche
  = cook
  = chef

kochen verb
* = to cook
* (of water) = to boil
* Kaffee kochen = to make coffee

die **Köchin**, plural Köchinnen
  = cook

der **Kochtopf**, plural Kochtöpfe
  = saucepan

der **Koffer**, plural Koffer
  = (suit)case

der **Kofferkuli**, plural Kofferkulis
  = luggage trolley

der **Kofferraum**, plural Kofferräume
  = boot, = trunk

der **Kohl**
  = cabbage

die **Koje**, plural Kojen
* = berth
* = bunk

die **Kokosnuss** (**Kokosnuß**OLD), plural
  Kokosnüsse
  = coconut

der **Kollege**, plural Kollegen
  = colleague

die **Kollegin**, plural Kolleginnen
  = colleague

(das) **Köln**
  = Cologne

die **Kombination**, plural Kombinationen
* = combination
* (clothing) = suit

komisch adjective
  = funny

das **Komma**, plural Kommas
* = comma
* = decimal point
  eins Komma fünf = one point five

kommen irregular verb (! sein)
  = to come
  etwas kommen lassen = to send for
    something
  hinter etwas kommen = to find out about
    something
  wie kommt das? = why is that?
  wer kommt zuerst? = who's first?

der **Kommissar**, plural Kommissare
  = superintendent

die **Kommode**, plural Kommoden
  = chest of drawers

die **Komödie**, plural Komödien
  = comedy

der **Kompass** (**Kompaß**ⓈⓄ), *plural*
Kompasse
= compass

komplett *adjective*
= complete

das **Kompliment**, *plural* Komplimente
= compliment

kompliziert *adjective*
= complicated

der **Komponist**, *plural* Komponisten
= composer

das **Kompott**, *plural* Kompotte
= stewed fruit

die **Konditorei**, *plural* Konditoreien
= patisserie, = cake shop

das **Kondom**, *plural* Kondome
= condom

das **Konfekt**
= confectionery

die **Konferenz**, *plural* Konferenzen
= conference

der **Konflikt**, *plural* Konflikte
= conflict

der **König**, *plural* Könige
= king

die **Königin**, *plural* Königinnen
= queen

das **Königreich**, *plural* Königreiche
= kingdom

die **Konkurrenz**, *plural* Konkurrenzen
= competition

konkurrenzfähig *adjective*
= competitive

können *irregular verb*
= to be able to
das kann ich nicht = I can't do that
können Sie Deutsch? = can you speak
German?
das kann gut sein = that may well be

der **Könner**, *plural* Könner
= expert

könnt ▶ können

**konnte, konnten, konntest,
konntet** ▶ können

das **Konsulat**, *plural* Konsulate
= consulate

der **Konsum**
= consumption

der **Kontakt**, *plural* Kontakte
= contact

die **Kontaktlinse**, *plural* Kontaktlinsen
= contact lens

der **Kontinent**, *plural* Kontinente
= continent

das **Konto**, *plural* Konten
= account

der **Kontoauszug**, *plural* Kontoauszüge
= bank statement

die **Kontrolle**, *plural* Kontrollen
• = check, = inspection
• = control

der **Kontrolleur**, *plural* Kontrolleure
= inspector

kontrollieren *verb*
• = to check, = to inspect
• = to control

konzentrieren *verb*
• = to concentrate
• sich auf etwas konzentrieren = to
concentrate on something

das **Konzert**, *plural* Konzerte
= concert

der **Kopf**, *plural* Köpfe
• = head
sich den Kopf zerbrechen = to rack one's
brains
seinen Kopf durchsetzen = to get one's
own way
• ein Kopf Kohl/Salat = a cabbage/a lettuce

köpfen *verb*
• = to behead
• (*in soccer*) = to head

der **Kopfhörer**, *plural* Kopfhörer
= headphones

das **Kopfkissen**, *plural* Kopfkissen
= pillow

Kopfschmerzen (*plural*)
= headache

die **Kopie**, *plural* Kopien
= copy

der **Korb**, *plural* Körbe
= basket
jemandem einen Korb geben = to turn
someone down

der **Kork**, *plural* Korke
= cork

der **Korken**, *plural* Korken
= cork

der **Korkenzieher**, *plural* Korkenzieher
= corkscrew

das **Korn**, *plural* Körner
= grain
= corn

der **Körper**, *plural* Körper
= body

der **Körperbau**
= build, = physique

K

körperlich *adjective*
= physical

der **Korridor**, *plural* Korridore
= corridor

korrigieren *verb*
= to correct

korrupt *adjective*
= corrupt

die **Kosmetik**
= beauty care

die **Kost**
= food

kostbar *adjective*
= valuable, = precious

kosten *verb*
• = to cost
• = to taste

Kosten (*plural*)
• = cost
• = expenses

kostenlos *adjective*
= free (of charge)

der **Kostenvoranschlag**, *plural*
Kostenvoranschläge
= estimate

köstlich *adjective*
• = delicious
• = funny

das **Kostüm**, *plural* Kostüme
• = suit
• (*fancy dress*) = costume

das **Kotelett**, *plural* Koteletts
= chop, = cutlet

die **Krabbe**, *plural* Krabben
• = crab
• = shrimp

der **Krach**, *plural* Kräche
= row

krachen *verb*
• = to crash
• = to crack

krächzen *verb*
= to croak

die **Kraft**, *plural* Kräfte
• = strength
= force
= power
• = worker

kräftig *adjective*
• = strong, = powerful
• = nourishing

der **Kraftstoff**, *plural* Kraftstoffe
= fuel

der **Kraftwagen**, *plural* Kraftwagen
= motor car

das **Kraftwerk**, *plural* Kraftwerke
= power station

der **Kragen**, *plural* Kragen
= collar

die **Krähe**, *plural* Krähen
= crow

die **Kralle**, *plural* Krallen
= claw

der **Kram**
• = stuff
• = affair

kramen *verb*
= to rummage about

der **Krampf**, *plural* Krämpfe
= cramp

der **Kran**, *plural* Kräne
= crane

der **Kranich**, *plural* Kraniche
= crane

krank *adjective*
= sick, = ill
krank werden = to fall ill

der/die **Kranke**, *plural* Kranken
= sick man/woman
(*in hospital*) = patient

kränken *verb*
= to hurt

das **Krankenhaus**, *plural* Krankenhäuser
= hospital

die **Krankenkasse**, *plural* Krankenkassen
= health insurance

die **Krankenschwester**, *plural*
Krankenschwestern
= nurse

der **Krankenwagen**, *plural*
Krankenwagen
= ambulance

die **Krankheit**, *plural* Krankheiten
= illness, = disease

kratzen *verb*
= to scratch

der **Kratzer**, *plural* Kratzer
= scratch

kraulen *verb*
• = to do the crawl
• = to tickle

das **Kraut**, *plural* Kräuter
• = herb
• = cabbage

✱ in informal situations

der **Krawall**, plural Krawalle
• = riot
• = row

die **Krawatte**, plural Krawatten
= tie

der **Krebs**, plural Krebse
• = crab
• (illness) = cancer
• = Cancer

der **Kredit**, plural Kredite
• = credit
• = loan

die **Kreide**, plural Kreiden
= chalk

kreieren verb
= to create

der **Kreis**, plural Kreise
• = circle
• = district

der **Kreislauf**
• = cycle
• = circulation

das **Kreuz**, plural Kreuze
• = cross
• (of a motorway) = intersection
• = small of the back
• (playing cards) = clubs

kreuzen verb
• = to cross
• sich kreuzen = to cross

die **Kreuzfahrt**, plural Kreuzfahrten
= cruise

die **Kreuzung**, plural Kreuzungen
• = crossroads
• (plant, animal) = cross

das **Kreuzworträtsel**, plural Kreuzworträtsel
= crossword (puzzle)

kriechen irregular verb (I sein)
= to crawl

der **Krieg**, plural Kriege
= war

kriegen✷ verb
= to get

der **Krimi**, plural Krimis
= crime story
= thriller

kriminell adjective
= criminal

die **Krippe**, plural Krippen
• = manger
• = crib
• = crèche

die **Krise**, plural Krisen
= crisis

die **Kritik**, plural Kritiken
• = criticism
• = review

kritisch adjective
= critical

kritisieren verb
• = to criticize
• = to review

das **Krokodil**, plural Krokodile
= crocodile

die **Krone**, plural Kronen
= crown

krönen verb
= to crown

die **Krücke**, plural Krücken
= crutch

der **Krug**, plural Krüge
• = jug
• = mug

der **Krümel**, plural Krümel
= crumb

krümelig adjective
= crumbly

krumm adjective
= bent
= crooked

krümmen verb
• = to bend
• sich krümmen = to bend, (with laughter) = to double up

der **Krüppel**, plural Krüppel
= cripple

die **Kruste**, plural Krusten
= crust

die **Küche**, plural Küchen
• = kitchen
• = cooking
kalte Küche = cold food
warme Küche = hot food

der **Kuchen**, plural Kuchen
= cake

die **Küchenschabe**, plural Küchenschaben
= cockroach

der **Kuckuck**, plural Kuckucke
= cuckoo

die **Kugel**, plural Kugeln
• = ball
• = sphere
• = bullet

der **Kugelschreiber**, plural Kugelschreiber
= ballpoint (pen)

die **Kuh**, plural Kühe
= cow

K

kühl *adjective*
= cool

kühlen *verb*
• = to cool, = to chill
• = to refrigerate

der **Kühler**, *plural* Kühler
= radiator

die **Kühlerhaube**, *plural* Kühlerhauben
= bonnet, = hood

der **Kühlschrank**, *plural* Kühlschränke
= refrigerator, = fridge

die **Kultur**, *plural* Kulturen
= culture

der **Kulturbeutel**, *plural* Kulturbeutel
= toilet bag

kulturell *adjective*
= cultural

die **Kulturturismus**
= heritage tourism

der **Kummer**
• = sorrow, = grief
• = worry
• = trouble

kümmern *verb*
= to concern
sich um jemanden kümmern = to take
care of someone
kümmere dich um deine eigenen
Angelegenheiten = mind your own
business

der **Kunde**, *plural* Kunden
= customer, = client

der **Kundendienst**
= customer service

kündigen *verb*
• = to cancel
• = to give notice

die **Kundin**, *plural* Kundinnen
= customer, = client

die **Kundschaft**
= customers, = clientele

die **Kunst**, *plural* Künste
• = art
• = skill

der **Künstler**, *plural* Künstler
= artist

die **Künstlerin**, *plural* Künstlerinnen
= artist

künstlerisch *adjective*
= artistic

künstlich *adjective*
= artificial

der **Kunststoff**, *plural* Kunststoffe
= plastic

das **Kunststück**, *plural* Kunststücke
• = trick
• = feat

das **Kunstwerk**, *plural* Kunstwerke
= work of art

das **Kupfer**
= copper

die **Kupplung**, *plural* Kupplungen
• (*of a car*) = clutch
• = coupling

der **Kurs**, *plural* Kurse
• = course
• = price
= exchange rate

die **Kurve**, *plural* Kurven
• = curve
• = bend, = corner

kurz
1 *adjective*
= short
= brief
vor kurzem = a short time ago
2 *adverb* = shortly, = briefly
kurz gesagt = in a word

kurzärmelig *adjective*
= short-sleeved

kürzen *verb*
= to shorten

kurzfristig
1 *adjective* = short-term
2 *adverb*
• = at short notice
• = for a short time

kürzlich *adverb*
= recently

der **Kurzschluss** (**Kurzschluß**ⓄⓁⒹ),
plural Kurzschlüsse
= short circuit

kurzsichtig *adjective*
= short-sighted

Kurzwaren (*plural*)
= haberdashery, = notions

die **Kusine**, *plural* Kusinen
= cousin

der **Kuss** (**Kuß**ⓄⓁⒹ), *plural* Küsse
= kiss

küssen *verb*
= to kiss

die **Küste**, *plural* Küsten
= coast

die **Kutsche**, *plural* Kutschen
= coach, = carriage

das **Kuvert**, *plural* Kuverts
= envelope

---

das **Labor**, *plural* Labors
= laboratory

die **Lache**, *plural* Lachen
= pool

lächeln *verb*
= to smile

lachen *verb*
= to laugh

lächerlich *adjective*
= ridiculous

der **Lachs**, *plural* Lachse
= salmon

der **Lack**, *plural* Lacke
• = varnish
• (*on a car*) = paint

lackieren *verb*
• = to varnish
• (*with paint*) = to spray

der **Laden**, *plural* Läden
• = shop, = store
• = shutter

die **Ladung**, *plural* Ladungen
• = cargo
• (*electrical*) = charge
• = summons

lag ▶ liegen

die **Lage**, *plural* Lagen
= situation

das **Lager**, *plural* Lager
• = camp
• = warehouse
• = stock
• (*in a machine*) = bearing

lagern *verb*
= to store

die **Lähmung**, *plural* Lähmungen
= paralysis

das **Laken**, *plural* Laken
= sheet

das **Lamm**, *plural* Lämmer
= lamb

die **Lampe**, *plural* Lampen
= lamp

das **Land**, *plural* Länder
• = country
• = land
• (*in Germany*) = state

die **Landebahn**, *plural* Landebahnen
= runway

landen *verb* (**!** *sein*)
• = to land
• im Krankenhaus landen✖ = to end up in hospital

die **Landkarte**, *plural* Landkarten
= map

ländlich *adjective*
= rural, = country

die **Landschaft**, *plural* Landschaften
= countryside, = landscape

der **Landtag**
= state parliament

die **Landwirtschaft**
= agriculture, = farming

lang
1 *adjective*
• = long
• = tall
2 *adverb*
eine Stunde lang = for an hour

langärmelig *adjective*
= long-sleeved

lange *adverb*
• = a long time
• hier ist es lange nicht so schön = it's not nearly as nice here

die **Länge**, *plural* Längen
• = length
• = longitude

die **Langeweile**
= boredom

langsam *adjective*
= slow

längst *adverb*
• = a long time ago
• = for a long time
• hier ist es längst nicht so schön = it's not nearly as nice here

langweilen *verb*
• = to bore
• sich langweilen = to be bored

langweilig *adjective*
= boring

der **Laptop**, *plural* Laptops
= laptop (computer)

der **Lärm**
= noise

der **Laser**, *plural* Laser
= laser

lassen *irregular verb*
• = to let
etwas machen lassen = to have something done *or* made
jemanden warten lassen = to keep someone waiting

L

* to leave
lass das! = stop it!
* die Tür lässt sich leicht öffnen = the door opens easily

lässig *adjective*
= casual

die **Last**, *plural* Lasten
* = load
* = burden

lästig *adjective*
= troublesome

der **Lastwagen**, *plural* Lastwagen
= lorry, = truck

das **Latein**
= Latin

das **Laub**
= leaves

der **Lauf**, *plural* Läufe
* = run
* = course
im Laufe des Abends = during the course of the evening
* = race
* (*of a gun*) = barrel

die **Laufbahn**, *plural* Laufbahnen
= career

laufen *irregular verb* (**!** *sein*)
* = to run
* = to walk
* (*of a machine*) = to be running, = to be on

laufend
1 *adjective*
* = running
* = current
auf dem Laufenden sein = to be up to date
* = regular
2 *adverb* = constantly
= continually

der **Läufer**, *plural* Läufer
* = runner
* = rug

die **Laufmasche**, *plural* Laufmaschen
= ladder (*in tights*)

die **Laune**, *plural* Launen
= mood

launisch *adjective*
= moody

die **Laus**, *plural* Läuse
= louse

lauschen *verb*
= to listen

laut *adjective*
= loud, = noisy
lauter stellen = to turn up

läuten *verb*
= to ring

lauter *adjective*
= nothing but

der **Lautsprecher**, *plural* Lautsprecher
= loudspeaker

die **Lautstärke**
= volume

lauwarm *adjective*
= lukewarm

die **Lawine**, *plural* Lawinen
= avalanche

leben *verb*
= to live
= to be alive
leb wohl! = farewell!

das **Leben**, *plural* Leben
= life

lebendig *adjective*
* = living
* = lively

die **Lebensgefahr**
= mortal danger
der Patient war in Lebensgefahr = the patient was critically ill

lebensgefährlich
1 *adjective*
* = extremely dangerous
* (*of an injury*) = critical
2 *adverb* = critically

Lebenshaltungskosten (*plural*)
= cost of living

lebenslänglich
1 *adjective* = life
2 *adverb* = for life

der **Lebenslauf**, *plural* Lebensläufe
= CV, = résumé

Lebensmittel (*plural*)
= food, = groceries

das **Lebensmittelgeschäft**, *plural* Lebensmittelgeschäfte
= grocer's (shop), = food shop

der **Lebensmittelhändler**, *plural* Lebensmittelhändler
= grocer

der **Lebensunterhalt**
= livelihood, = living

die **Lebensversicherung**, *plural* Lebensversicherungen
= life insurance

die **Leber**, *plural* Lebern
= liver

OLD = old spelling

das **Lebewesen**, *plural* Lebewesen
  = living being, = living thing

lebhaft *adjective*
* = lively
* = vivid

leblos *adjective*
  = lifeless

das **Leck**, *plural* Lecks
  = leak

lecken *verb*
* = to lick
* = to leak

lecker *adjective*
  = delicious

ledig *adjective*
  = single

lediglich *adverb*
  = merely

leer *adjective*
  = empty

leeren *verb*
* = to empty
* sich leeren = to empty

der **Leerlauf**
  = neutral

die **Leerung**, *plural* Leerungen
  = collection

legen *verb*
* = to lay, = to put
* sich legen = to lie down, (*of a storm*) = to die down

die **Legende**, *plural* Legenden
  = legend

leger *adjective*
  = casual

der **Lehm**
  = clay

die **Lehne**, *plural* Lehnen
* = back
* = arm

lehnen *verb*
* = to lean
* sich an etwas lehnen = to lean against something

das **Lehrbuch**, *plural* Lehrbücher
  = textbook

der **Lehrer**, *plural* Lehrer
  = teacher
  = instructor

die **Lehrerin**, *plural* Lehrerinnen
  = teacher
  = instructor

der **Lehrling**, *plural* Lehrlinge
  = apprentice
  = trainee

der **Leibwächter**, *plural* Leibwächter
  = bodyguard

die **Leiche**, *plural* Leichen
  = (dead) body, = corpse

leicht *adjective*
* = light
* ein leichter Akzent = a slight accent
* = easy
  jemandem leicht fallen = to be easy for somebody
  es ist ihnen nicht leicht gefallen = it wasn't easy for them

die **Leichtathletik**
  = athletics, = track and field

leichtfallen ⓞⅬⒹ ▸leicht

leichtsinnig *adjective*
  = careless
  = reckless

leid *adjective*
  jemanden leid sein = to be fed up with somebody
  etwas leid werden = to get fed up with something

das **Leid**
* = sorrow, = grief
* = harm
* es tut mir Leid = I'm sorry
  er tut mir Leid = I feel sorry for him

leiden *irregular verb*
  = to suffer
  jemanden gut leiden können = to like someone

die **Leidenschaft**, *plural* Leidenschaften
  = passion

leidenschaftlich *adjective*
  = passionate

leider *adverb*
  = unfortunately
  leider ja = I'm afraid so

leihen *irregular verb*
* = to lend
* sich etwas leihen = to borrow something

die **Leihgebür**, *plural* Leihgebühren
* = rental
* = borrowing fee

der **Leihwagen**, *plural* Leihwagen
  = hire car

leihweise *adverb*
  = on loan

der **Leim**, *plural* Leime
  = glue

die **Leine**, *plural* Leinen
* = rope
* (*for washing*) = line
* (*for a dog*) = lead

L

das **Leinen**
= linen

die **Leinwand**, plural Leinwände
- = screen
- = canvas

leise
1 adjective = quiet
2 adverb = quietly
die Musik leiser stellen = to turn the music down

leisten verb
- = to achieve
jemandem Hilfe leisten = to help someone
- sich etwas leisten = to treat oneself to something
sich etwas nicht leisten können = to not be able to afford something

die **Leistung**, plural Leistungen
- = achievement
- = performance
- = payment

leiten verb
- = to lead
- (if it's a business) = to manage
- = to conduct
- (if it's traffic) = to direct

die **Leiter**1 plural Leitern
= ladder

der **Leiter**2 plural Leiter
- = leader
- = manager
- = director
- (of a school) = headmaster

die **Leiterin**, plural Leiterinnen
- = leader
- = manageress
- = director
- (of a school) = headmistress

die **Leitplanke**, plural Leitplanken
= crash barrier

die **Leitung**, plural Leitungen
- = direction
- = management
- (phone) = line
- = pipe
(electric) = lead, = cable
- unter der Leitung von (of an orchestra) = conducted by

das **Leitungswasser**
= tap water

lenken verb
- = to steer
- = to guide

das **Lenkrad**, plural Lenkräder
= steering wheel

die **Lenkstange**, plural Lenkstangen
= handlebars

die **Lenkung**
= steering

lernen verb
- = to learn
- = to study

lesen irregular verb
= to read

das **Lesezeichen**, plural Lesezeichen
= bookmark

(das) **Lettland**
= Latvia

letzte ▶ letzter

der/die/das **Letzte**, plural Letzten
der/die Letzte = the last (one)
das Letzte =the last (thing)
sie kam als Letzte = she arrived last

letztens adverb
- = lastly
- = recently

letzter/letzte/letztes adjective
- = last
zum letzten Mal = for the last time.
in letzter Zeit = recently
- = latest

leuchten verb
= to shine

der **Leuchter**, plural Leuchter
= candlestick

der **Leuchtturm**, plural Leuchttürme
= lighthouse

leugnen verb
= to deny

Leute (plural)
= people

das **Lexikon**, plural Lexika
- = encyclopaedia
- = dictionary

das **Licht**, plural Lichter
= light

das **Lichtbild**, plural Lichtbilder
= photograph

die **Lichtung**, plural Lichtungen
= clearing

das **Lid**, plural Lider
= (eye)lid

der **Lidschatten**, plural Lidschatten
= eye shadow

lieb adjective
- = dear
sein liebstes Spielzeug = his favourite toy
es wäre mir lieber = I should prefer it
- = nice, = good

- jemanden lieb haben = to be fond of somebody

die **Liebe**, *plural* Lieben
= love

lieben *verb*
= to love

lieber *adverb*
- = rather
- = better

liebevoll *adjective*
= loving

der **Liebling**, *plural* Lieblinge
- = darling
- = favourite, = favorite

Lieblings- *prefix*
= favourite, = favorite

liebste ▶liebster

liebsten *adverb*
am liebsten = best (of all)

liebster/liebste/liebstes *adjective*
- = dearest
- = favourite, = favorite

das **Lied**, *plural* Lieder
= song

lief ▶laufen

liefern *verb*
- = to deliver
- = to supply

die **Lieferung**, *plural* Lieferungen
= delivery

der **Lieferwagen**, *plural* Lieferwagen
= (delivery) van

liegen *irregular verb*
- = to lie
- = to be situated, = to be
- liegen bleiben = to stay, = to be left
  (*forgotten*) = to be left behind
  die Arbeit ist liegen geblieben =the job
  was left undone
- liegen lassen = to leave
  alles stehen und liegen lassen = to drop
  everything
- es liegt mir nicht = it doesn't suit me
- an etwas liegen = to be due to something
  das liegt an ihm = it's up to him

der **Liegestuhl**, *plural* Liegestühle
= deckchair

ließ ▶lassen

liest ▶lesen

der **Lift**, *plural* Lifte *or* Lifts
= lift, = elevator

lila *adjective*
= mauve
(*darker*) = purple

die **Limo**, *plural* Limos *or* Limo
▶Limonade

die **Limonade**, *plural* Limonaden
- = lemonade
- = fizzy drink

lindern *verb*
= to relieve
= to calm

das **Lineal**, *plural* Lineale
= ruler

die **Linie**, *plural* Linien
- = line
- (*of a bus*) = route
  Linie 7 = number 7

linker/linke/linkes *adjective*
- = left
- = left-wing

links *adverb*
- = on the left
  nach links = left
- = inside out

linksklicken *verb*
= to left-click

die **Linse**, *plural* Linsen
- = lens
- = lentil

die **Lippe**, *plural* Lippen
= lip

der **Lippenstift**, *plural* Lippenstifte
= lipstick

die **List**, *plural* Listen
- = cunning
- = trick

die **Liste**, *plural* Listen
= list

listig *adjective*
= cunning

(das) **Litauen**
= Lithuania

der **Liter**, *plural* Liter
= litre, = liter

die **Literatur**, *plural* Literaturen
= literature

der **Lkw**, *plural* Lkws
(*Lastkraftwagen*) = lorry, = truck

loben *verb*
= to praise

das **Loch**, *plural* Löcher
= hole

die **Locke**, *plural* Locken
= curl

locken *verb*
- = to tempt
- = to curl

L

locker *adjective*
- = loose
- (*of a rope*) = slack

lockig *adjective*
= curly

der **Löffel**, *plural* Löffel
- = spoon
- = spoonful

logisch *adjective*
= logical

der **Lohn**, *plural* Löhne
- = wages, = pay
- = reward

lohnen: sich lohnen *verb*
= to be worth it

das **Lokal**, *plural* Lokale
= bar
= restaurant

die **Lokomotive**, *plural* Lokomotiven
= locomotive, = engine

los
1 *adjective*
- es ist viel los = there is a lot going on
  was ist mit ihm los? = what's up with
  him?
- etwas los sein = to be rid of something
2 *adverb*
  los! = go on!
  Achtung, fertig, los! = ready, steady, go!

das **Los**, *plural* Lose
- = lot
- (*in a lottery*) = ticket
  das große Los ziehen = to hit the jackpot

löschen *verb*
- = to put out, = to extinguish
- seinen Durst löschen = to quench one's
  thirst
- = to cancel, = to delete

lose *adjective*
= loose

lösen *verb*
- = to undo
- = to solve
- eine Fahrkarte lösen = to buy a ticket
- sich lösen = to come undone, (*of a puzzle
  or mystery*) = to be solved

los|fahren *irregular verb* (**!** *sein*)
- = to set off
- = to drive off

los|gehen *irregular verb* (**!** *sein*)
- = to set off, = to start
- (*of a button*) = to come off
- (*of a bomb*) = to go off

los|lassen *irregular verb*
- = to let go of, = to release

- = to let go

die **Lösung**, *plural* Lösungen
= solution

los|werden *irregular verb* (**!** *sein*)
= to get rid of

die **Lotterie**, *plural* Lotterien
= lottery

das **Lotto**, *plural* Lottos
= (national) lottery

der **Löwe**, *plural* Löwen
- = lion
- = Leo

die **Löwin**, *plural* Löwinnen
= lioness

die **Lücke**, *plural* Lücken
= gap

die **Luft**, *plural* Lüfte
= air
in die Luft gehen✱ = to blow one's top

der **Luftballon**, *plural* Luftballons
= balloon

luftdicht *adjective*
= airtight

lüften *verb*
- = to air
- ein Geheimnis lüften = to reveal a secret

die **Luftmatratze**, *plural* Luftmatratzen
= air-bed

die **Luftpost**
= airmail

die **Lüftung**
= ventilation

die **Luftwaffe**
= air force

die **Lüge**, *plural* Lügen
= lie

lügen *irregular verb*
= to lie

der **Lügner**, *plural* Lügner
= liar

die **Lügnerin**, *plural* Lügnerinnen
= liar

die **Lunge**, *plural* Lungen
= lungs

die **Lungenentzündung**
= pneumonia

die **Lupe**, *plural* Lupen
= magnifying glass

die **Lust**
- = pleasure
- = desire
  Lust haben, etwas zu tun = to feel like
  doing something

lustig *adjective*
- = jolly, = funny
- sich über jemanden lustig machen = to make fun of someone

lutschen *verb*
= to suck

der **Lutscher**, *plural* Lutscher
= lollipop

der **Luxus**
= luxury

Mm

machen *verb*
- = to make
- = to do
  was macht die Arbeit? = how is work?
  das macht nichts = it doesn't matter
- sich an die Arbeit machen = to get down to work

die **Macht**, *plural* Mächte
= power

das **Mädchen**, *plural* Mädchen
- = girl
- = maid

der **Mädchenname**
= maiden name

die **Made**, *plural* Maden
= maggot

mag ▶mögen

das **Magazin**, *plural* Magazine
= magazine

der **Magen**, *plural* Mägen
= stomach

mager *adjective*
- = thin
- = lean
- = low-fat

die **Magie**
= magic

die **Magnetkarte**, *plural* Magnetkarten
= swipe card

magst ▶mögen

mähen *verb*
= to mow

mahlen *irregular verb*
= to grind

die **Mahlzeit**, *plural* Mahlzeiten
= meal
Mahlzeit! = enjoy your meal!

die **Mahnung**, *plural* Mahnungen
- = reminder
- = admonition

der **Mai**
= May

der **Mais**
= maize, = corn

der **Major**, *plural* Majore
= major

der **Makler**, *plural* Makler
= estate agent

mal *adverb*
- (*in maths*) = times
- (*with measurements*) = by
- (*in the future*) = sometime
- schon mal = once before
- nicht mal = not even
- hört mal! = listen!

das **Mal**, *plural* Male
- = time
  nächstes Mal = next time
- = mark
- = mole

malen *verb*
= to paint

der **Maler**, *plural* Maler
= painter

die **Malerei**
= painting

die **Malerin**, *plural* Malerinnen
= painter

man *pronoun*
- = one, = you
- = they, = people
  man hat mir gesagt = I was told

mancher/manche/manches
1 *adjective* = many a, (*plural*) = some
2 *pronoun* = many a person, (*plural*) = some (people)

manchmal *adverb*
= sometimes

die **Mandel**, *plural* Mandeln
- = almond
- = tonsil

der **Mangel**, *plural* Mängel
- = lack, = shortage
- = defect

mangelhaft *adjective*
- = faulty, = defective
- (*school mark*) = unsatisfactory

Manieren (*plural*)
= manners

der **Mann**, *plural* Männer
- = man
- = husband

M

das **Männchen**, *plural* Männchen
= male

das **Mannequin**, *plural* Mannequins
= model

männlich *adjective*
• = male
• = manly
• (*in grammar*) = masculine

die **Mannschaft**, *plural* Mannschaften
• = team
• = crew

die **Manschette**, *plural* Manschetten
= cuff

der **Mantel**, *plural* Mäntel
= coat

die **Mappe**, *plural* Mappen
• = folder
• = briefcase
• (*satchel*) = bag

das **Märchen**, *plural* Märchen
= fairy tale

der **Marienkäfer**, *plural* Marienkäfer
= ladybird

die **Marine**, *plural* Marinen
= navy

die **Mark**, *plural* Mark
= mark

die **Marke**, *plural* Marken
• = make, = brand
• = tag
• = stamp
• = coupon

das **Markenzeichen**, *plural* Markenzeichen
= trade mark

markieren *verb*
• = to mark
• = to fake

der **Markt**, *plural* Märkte
= market

die **Marmelade**, *plural* Marmeladen
= jam

der **Marmor**
= marble

der **Marsch**, *plural* Märsche
= march

der **März**
= March

die **Masche**, *plural* Maschen
= stitch

die **Maschine**, *plural* Maschinen
• = machine

• = plane

Masern (*plural*)
= measles

die **Maske**, *plural* Masken
= mask

das **Maß**, *plural* Maße
• = measure
• = degree

die **Masse**, *plural* Massen
• = mass
(*of people*) = crowd
• (*in cooking*) = mixture

massenhaft *adverb*
= in huge quantities

massieren *verb*
= to massage

mäßig *adjective*
= moderate

die **Maßnahme**, *plural* Maßnahmen
= measure

der **Maßstab**, *plural* Maßstäbe
• = standard
• = scale

der **Mast**, *plural* Masten
• = mast
• = pole
= pylon

das **Material**, *plural* Materialien
= material
= materials

die **Mathe✘**
= maths, = math

die **Mathematik**
= mathematics

die **Matratze**, *plural* Matratzen
= mattress

der **Matrose**, *plural* Matrosen
= sailor

matt *adjective*
• = weak
• = matt
• (*in chess*) matt! = checkmate!

die **Matte**, *plural* Matten
= mat

die **Mauer**, *plural* Mauern
= wall

das **Maul**, *plural* Mäuler
= mouth

der **Maulkorb**, *plural* Maulkörbe
= muzzle

das **Maultier**, *plural* Maultiere
= mule

der **Maulwurf**, *plural* Maulwürfe
= mole

✘ in informal situations

der **Maurer**, *plural* Maurer
= bricklayer

die **Maus**, *plural* Mäuse
= mouse

mechanisch *adjective*
= mechanical

meckern *verb*
• = to bleat
• = to grumble

die **Medaille**, *plural* Medaillen
= medal

Medien (*plural*)
= media

das **Medikament**, *plural* Medikamente
= medicine

die **Medizin**, *plural* Medizinen
= medicine

medizinisch *adjective*
• = medical
• = medicinal

das **Meer**, *plural* Meere
= sea

Meeresfrüchte (*plural*)
= seafood

das **Mehl**
= flour

mehr *adverb*
= more
nie mehr = never again

mehrere *pronoun*
= several

mehrfach
1 *adjective*
• = multiple
• = repeated
2 *adverb* = several times

die **Mehrheit**, *plural* Mehrheiten
= majority

mehrmals *adverb*
= several times

die **Mehrwertsteuer**
= value added tax

die **Mehrzahl**, *plural* Mehrzahlen
• = majority
• = plural

meiden *irregular verb*
= to avoid

die **Meile**, *plural* Meilen
= mile

mein *adjective*
= my

meine ▶ meiner

meinen *verb*
• = to think

• = to mean
• = to say

meiner/meine/meins *pronoun*
= mine

meinetwegen *adverb*
• = for my sake
• = because of me
• = as far as I'm concerned

meins ▶ meiner

die **Meinung**, *plural* Meinungen
= opinion

meist *adverb*
= mostly

der/die/das **meiste**
= most

meistens *adverb*
= mostly

der **Meister**, *plural* Meister
• = master
• = champion

die **Meisterin**, *plural* Meisterinnen
= champion

die **Meisterschaft**, *plural* Meisterschaften
• = championship
• = mastery

melden *verb*
• = to report
• = to register
• = to announce
• sich melden = to report, (*on the phone*) =
  to answer
  sich bei jemandem melden = to get in
  touch with someone

die **Melodie**, *plural* Melodien
= melody, = tune

die **Melone**, *plural* Melonen
• = melon
• (*hat*) = bowler

die **Menge**, *plural* Mengen
• = quantity, = amount
• = crowd
• (*in maths*) = set

der **Mensch**, *plural* Menschen
= human being
= person
kein Mensch = nobody
die Menschen = people

menschenleer *adjective*
= deserted

die **Menschheit**
= mankind

menschlich *adjective*
• = human
• = humane

die **Mentalität**, *plural* Mentalitäten
= mentality

M

das **Menü**, *plural* Menüs
* = menu
* = set meal

merken *verb*
* = to notice
* sich etwas merken = to remember something

das **Merkmal**, *plural* Merkmale
= feature

merkwürdig *adjective*
= strange, = odd

die **Messe**, *plural* Messen
* = mass
* = trade fair

messen *irregular verb*
* = to measure
  Fieber messen = to take someone's temperature
* sich mit jemandem messen können = to be as good as someone

das **Messer**, *plural* Messer
= knife

das **Messing**
= brass

das **Metall**, *plural* Metalle
= metal

der **Meter**, *plural* Meter
= metre, = meter

das **Metermaß**, *plural* Metermaße
= tape measure
= metre rule, = meter rule

die **Methode**, *plural* Methoden
= method

der **Metzger**, *plural* Metzger
= butcher

die **Metzgerei**, *plural* Metzgereien
= butcher's (shop)

meutern *verb*
* = to mutiny
* = to grumble

miauen *verb*
= to miaow, = to mew

mich *pronoun*
* = me
* (*reflexive*) = myself

mies✗ *adjective*
= lousy

die **Miete**, *plural* Mieten
* = rent
  zur Miete wohnen = to live in rented accommodation
* = hire charge

mieten *verb*
* = to rent
* = to hire

der **Mietwagen**, *plural* Mietwagen
= hire car

das **Mikrofon**, *plural* Mikrofone
= microphone

das **Mikroskop**, *plural* Mikroskope
= microscope

der **Mikrowellenherd**, *plural* Mikrowellenherde
= microwave oven

die **Milch**
= milk

mild *adjective*
= mild

das **Militär**
= army

die **Milliarde**, *plural* Milliarden
(*thousand million*) = billion

die **Million**, *plural* Millionen
= million

der **Millionär**, *plural* Millionäre
= millionaire

die **Minderheit**, *plural* Minderheiten
= minority

minderjährig *adjective*
= under age

mindestens *adverb*
= at least

mindester/mindeste/mindestes *adjective*
= least

die **Mine**, *plural* Minen
* = mine
* (*in a pencil*) = lead
  (*for a ballpoint*) = refill

der **Minister**, *plural* Minister
= minister

die **Ministerin**, *plural* Ministerinnen
= minister

das **Ministerium**, *plural* Ministerien
= ministry, = department

die **Minute**, *plural* Minuten
= minute

mir *pronoun*
* = (to) me
* (*reflexive*) = myself

mischen *verb*
* = to mix
* (*when playing cards*) = to shuffle
* sich mischen = to mix

✗ in informal situations ⓄLD = old spelling

die **Mischung**, *plural* Mischungen
= mixture
= blend

miserabel✕ *adjective*
= hopeless, = dreadful

**missbrauchen
(mißbrauchen**ⓞⓛⓓ**)** *verb*
= to abuse

der **Misserfolg (Mißerfolg**ⓞⓛⓓ**)**, *plural*
Misserfolge
= failure

missglücken (mißglückenⓞⓛⓓ**)**
verb (**!** *sein*)
= to fail

misshandeln (mißhandelnⓞⓛⓓ**)**
verb
= to ill-treat

misslingen (mißlingenⓞⓛⓓ**)**
irregular verb (**!** *sein*)
= to fail
es misslang ihm = he failed

misstrauen (mißtrauenⓞⓛⓓ**)** *verb*
= to mistrust, = to distrust

das **Missverständnis
(Mißverständnis**ⓞⓛⓓ**)**, *plural*
Missverständnisse
= misunderstanding

der **Mist**
• ⁻ manure, ⁻ dung
• so ein Mist!✕ = rubbish!

mit
1 *preposition* (+ *dative*) = with
mit fünf Jahren = at the age of five
mit der Bahn fahren = to go by train
mit lauter Stimme = in a loud voice
2 *adverb* = too, = as well
er war nicht mit dabei = he wasn't there

der **Mitarbeiter**, *plural* Mitarbeiter
• = colleague
• = employee

die **Mitarbeiterin**, *plural* Mitarbeiterinnen
• = colleague
• = employee

mit|bringen *irregular verb*
= to bring (along)

miteinander *adverb*
= with each other, = with one another

mit|fahren *irregular verb* (**!** *sein*)
= to go along
mit jemandem mitfahren = to go with
someone, = to get a lift with someone

mit|gehen *irregular verb* (**!** *sein*)
mit jemandem mitgehen = to go with
someone

das **Mitglied**, *plural* Mitglieder
= member

mit|halten *irregular verb*
= to keep up

mit|kommen *irregular verb* (**!** *sein*)
• = to come too
• = to keep up

das **Mitleid**
= pity

mit|machen *verb*
• = to join in
• = to take part in
(*experience*) = to go through

mit|nehmen *irregular verb*
= to take (along)
zum Mitnehmen = to take away, = to go

der **Mitschüler**, *plural* Mitschüler
= fellow pupil

die **Mitschülerin**, *plural* Mitschülerinnen
= fellow pupil

der **Mittag**, *plural* Mittage
• = midday
• = lunch(-break)

das **Mittagessen**, *plural* Mittagessen
= lunch

mittags *adverb*
= at midday

die **Mitte**, *plural* Mitten
= middle
= centre

die **Mitteilung**, *plural* Mitteilungen
= announcement

das **Mittel**, *plural* Mittel
• = means
• ein Mittel gegen Husten = a cough
remedy

das **Mittelalter**
= Middle Ages

mittelmäßig *adjective*
= mediocre

das **Mittelmeer**
= Mediterranean (Sea)

der **Mittelpunkt**, *plural* Mittelpunkte
= centre, = center
im Mittelpunkt stehen = to be the centre
of attention

der **Mittelstand**
= middle class

mitten *adverb*
= in the middle of
mitten durch = right through

die **Mitternacht**
= midnight

mittlerer/mittlere/mittleres
adjective
• = middle

M

- (*in quality, size*) = medium
- = average

mittlerweile *adverb*
- = meanwhile
- = by now

der **Mittwoch**
= Wednesday

mittwochs *adverb*
= on Wednesdays

Möbel (*plural*)
= furniture

der **Möbelwagen**, *plural* Möbelwagen
= removal van

das **Mobiltelefon**, *plural* Mobiltelefone
= mobile phone, cell phone

möbliert *adjective*
= furnished

mochte, mochten, mochtest, mochtet ▶ mögen

möchte ▶ mögen

die **Mode**, *plural* Moden
= fashion

der **Moderator**, *plural* Moderatoren
(*TV*) = presenter

modisch *adjective*
= fashionable

mogeln *verb*
= to cheat

mögen *irregular verb*
- = to like
ich möchte lieber Tee = I would prefer tea
ich möchte gern wissen = I would like to know
möchtest du nach Hause? = do you want to go home?
ich mag nicht mehr = I've had enough
- das mag sein = maybe
wer mag das sein? = whoever can it be?

möglich *adjective*
= possible
alles Mögliche = all sorts of things

die **Möglichkeit**, *plural* Möglichkeiten
= possibility

möglichst *adverb*
= if possible
möglichst früh = as early as possible

die **Möhre**, *plural* Möhren
= carrot

der **Monat**, *plural* Monate
= month

monatlich
1 *adjective* = monthly

2 *adverb* = monthly, = every month

der **Mond**, *plural* Monde
= moon

der **Montag**
= Monday

montags *adverb*
= on Mondays

das **Moos**, *plural* Moose
= moss

die **Moral**
- = moral
- = morals

moralisch *adjective*
= moral

der **Mord**, *plural* Morde
= murder

der **Mörder**, *plural* Mörder
= murderer

die **Mörderin**, *plural* Mörderinnen
= murderess

morgen *adverb*
= tomorrow
morgen in einer Woche = a week tomorrow
bis morgen! = see you tomorrow!

der **Morgen**, *plural* Morgen
= morning
heute Morgen = this morning

morgens *adverb*
= in the morning

die **Mosel**
= Moselle

der **Moslem**, *plural* Moslems
= Muslim

moslemisch *adjective*
= Muslim

die **Moslime**, *plural* Moslimen
= Muslim

das **Motiv**, *plural* Motive
- = motive
- = motif

der **Motor**, *plural* Motoren
= engine, = motor

das **Motorrad**, *plural* Motorräder
= motorcycle, = motorbike

die **Motte**, *plural* Motten
= moth

die **Möwe**, *plural* Möwen
= seagull

die **Mücke**, *plural* Mücken
- = gnat, = midge
- = mosquito

müde *adjective*
= tired

die **Müdigkeit**
= tiredness

die **Mühe**, *plural* Mühen
= effort
= trouble

die **Mühle**, *plural* Mühlen
= mill
(*for coffee*) = grinder

mühsam *adjective*
= laborious

der **Müll**
= rubbish, = garbage

die **Mülltonne**, *plural* Mülltonnen
= dustbin, = garbage can

die **Mumie**, *plural* Mumien
= mummy

(das) **München**
= Munich

der **Mund**, *plural* Münder
= mouth
halt den Mund!✶ = shut up!

die **Mundharmonika**, *plural*
Mundharmonikas
= mouth organ

mündlich *adjective*
= oral

die **Mündung**, *plural* Mündungen
= mouth

die **Münze**, *plural* Münzen
= coin

murmeln *verb*
• = to mumble
• = to murmur

murren *verb*
= to grumble

mürrisch *adjective*
= grumpy

die **Muschel**, *plural* Muscheln
• = mussel
• = (sea) shell

das **Museum**, *plural* Museen
= museum

die **Musik**
= music

der **Musiker**, *plural* Musiker
= musician

die **Musikerin**, *plural* Musikerinnen
= musician

der **Muskel**, *plural* Muskeln
= muscle

muss (muß⊙ᴸᴰ**)** ▶ müssen

müssen *irregular verb*
= to have to
er muss es tun = he has (got) to do it,
= he must do it
muss das sein? = is that necessary?
sie muss gleich hier sein = she will be
here at any moment

das **Muster**, *plural* Muster
• = pattern
• = sample
• = model

der **Mut**
= courage
jemandem Mut machen = to encourage
someone

mutig *adjective*
= courageous, = brave

die **Mutter**[1] *plural* Mütter
= mother

die **Mutter**[2] *plural* Muttern
= nut

die **Muttersprache**, *plural*
Muttersprachen
= mother tongue, = native language

der **Muttertag**, *plural* Muttertage
= Mother's Day

die **Mutti**, *plural* Muttis
= mum, = mom

die **Mütze**, *plural* Mützen
= cap

der **Mythos**, *plural* Mythen
= myth

Nn

na *interjection*
= well
na und? = so what?

der **Nabel**, *plural* Nabel
= navel

nach
1 *preposition* (+ *dative*)
• = to
nach Hause gehen = to go home
nach oben = upwards, (*indoors*) =
upstairs
nach rechts abbiegen = to turn right
• = after
zehn nach zwei = ten past two
• = according to
meiner Meinung nach = in my opinion

2 *adverb*
nach und nach = bit by bit, = gradually

nach|ahmen *verb*
= to imitate, = to copy

der **Nachbar**, *plural* Nachbarn
= neighbour, = neighbor

die **Nachbarin**, *plural* Nachbarinnen
= neighbour, = neighbor

nachdem *conjunction*
= after
je nachdem = it depends, = depending on

nach|denken *irregular verb*
= to think

nachdenklich *adjective*
= thoughtful

nacheinander *adverb*
= one after the other

die **Nachfrage**, *plural* Nachfragen
= demand

nach|geben *irregular verb*
= to give in

nach|gehen *irregular verb* (**!** *sein*)
• = to follow
einer Sache nachgehen = to look into a
matter
• (*lose time*) = to be slow

nachher *adverb*
= afterwards, = later
bis nachher! = see you later!

nach|kommen *irregular verb* (**!** *sein*)
• = to follow, = to come later
• einem Versprechen nachkommen = to
carry out a promise

nach|lassen *irregular verb*
• = to let up, = to ease
• (*of health*) = to deteriorate
• etwas vom Preis nachlassen = to take
something off the price

nachlässig *adjective*
= careless

nach|machen *verb*
= to copy, = to imitate

der **Nachmittag**, *plural* Nachmittage
= afternoon

nachmittags *adverb*
= in the afternoon

die **Nachnahme**
per Nachnahme = cash on delivery

der **Nachname**, *plural* Nachnamen
= surname

nach|prüfen *verb*
= to check

die **Nachricht**, *plural* Nachrichten
= news, text (message)
eine Nachricht hinterlassen = to leave a
message
jemandem eine Nachricht schicken
= to text someone

der **Nachrichtensprecher**
= newsreader

nach|schlagen *irregular verb*
= to look up

nach|sehen *irregular verb*
• = to check
• = to look up

nach|sitzen *irregular verb*
= to be in detention
nachsitzen müssen = to have detention

nächste ▶nächster

der/die/das **Nächste**, *plural* Nächsten
= the next one
der Nächste, bitte! = next please
als Nächstes = next

nächstens *adverb*
= shortly

nächster/nächste/nächstes
adjective
• = next
• = nearest
in nächster Nähe = close by

die **Nacht**, *plural* Nächte
= night

der **Nachteil**, *plural* Nachteile
= disadvantage

der **Nachtfalter**, *plural* Nachtfalter
= moth

das **Nachthemd**, *plural* Nachthemden
= nightdress, = nightshirt

die **Nachtigall**, *plural* Nachtigallen
= nightingale

der **Nachtisch**, *plural* Nachtische
= dessert, = sweet

nachträglich
1 *adjective*
• = subsequent
• = belated
2 *adverb*
• = later, = afterwards
• = belatedly

nachts *adverb*
= at night
um drei Uhr nachts = at 3 o'clock in the
morning

der **Nacken**, *plural* Nacken
= neck

nackt *adjective*
= naked
= bare

✗ in informal situations   ⌗⌗⌗ = old spelling

die **Nadel**, plural Nadeln
* = needle
* = pin

der **Nagel**, plural Nägel
= nail

nageln verb
= to nail

nah✶ ▶nahe

nahe
1 adjective
* = near, = nearby
* = close
  der Nahe Osten = the Middle East
2 adverb = closely
  nahe bei = close to
  nahe gelegen = close by
3 preposition (+ dative)
= near, = close to

die **Nähe**
= closeness, = proximity
in der Nähe = nearby

nähen verb
* = to sew
* (when closing a wound) = to stitch

näher
1 adjective
* = closer
* (in distance) = shorter
* nähere Einzelheiten = further details
2 adverb
= closer, = more closely

nähern: sich nähern verb
= to approach

das **Nähgarn**
= cotton

nahm ▶nehmen

die **Nahrung**
= food

die **Naht**, plural Nähte
= seam

der **Name**, plural Namen
= name

nämlich adverb
* = namely
* = because

nannte ▶nennen

die **Narbe**, plural Narben
= scar

die **Nase**, plural Nasen
= nose
die Nase voll haben✶ = to have had
enough

das **Nasenloch**, plural Nasenlöcher
= nostril

das **Nashorn**, plural Nashörner
= rhinoceros

nass (naß ⒪⒧⒟**)** adjective
= wet

die **Nation**, plural Nationen
= nation

die **Nationalhymne**, plural
Nationalhymnen
= national anthem

die **Nationalität**, plural Nationalitäten
= nationality

die **Natur**, plural Naturen
= nature

natürlich
1 adjective = natural
2 adverb = naturally, = of course

das **Naturschutzgebiet**, plural
Naturschutzgebiete
= nature reserve

die **Naturwissenschaft**, plural
Naturwissenschaften
= natural science

der **Nebel**, plural Nebel
= fog, = mist

neben preposition (+ dative or
accusative)
* = next to, = beside
* = apart from

nebenan adverb
= next door

nebenbei adverb
* = in addition
* = by the way, = in passing

nebensächlich
= trivial, = unimportant

neblig adjective
= foggy, = misty

necken verb
= to tease

der **Neffe**, plural Neffen
= nephew

negativ adjective
= negative

nehmen irregular verb
* = to take
* sich etwas nehmen = to take something,
(take food) = to help oneself to
something

der **Neid**
= envy, = jealousy

neidisch adjective
= envious, = jealous

nein adverb
= no

die **Nelke**, plural Nelken
= carnation

N

nennen *irregular verb*
- = to call
- sein Name wurde nicht genannt = his name was not mentioned
- sich nennen = to be called, = to call oneself

der **Nerv**, *plural* Nerven
    = nerve
    er geht mir auf die Nerven = he gets on my nerves

nervös *adjective*
    = nervous

die **Nessel**, *plural* Nesseln
    = nettle

das **Nest**, *plural* Nester
- = nest
- (*village*) = little place

nett *adjective*
    = nice

netto *adverb*
    = net

das **Netz**, *plural* Netze
- = net
- = network
- (*of a spider*) = web

neu
    1 *adjective* = new
    die neueste Mode = the latest fashion
    das ist mir neu = that's news to me
    2 *adverb* = newly
    es ist neu eingetroffen = it has just come in
    etwas neu schreiben = to rewrite something

neuerdings *adverb*
    = recently

die **Neugier**
    = curiosity

neugierig *adjective*
    = curious, = inquisitive

die **Neuigkeit**, *plural* Neuigkeiten
    = piece of news
    Neuigkeiten = news

das **Neujahr**
    = New Year, = New Year's Day

neulich *adverb*
    = recently, = the other day

neun *adjective*
    = nine

neunter/neunte/neuntes *adjective*
    = ninth

neunzehn *adjective*
    = nineteen

neunzig *adjective*
    = ninety

(das) **Neuseeland**
    = New Zealand

nicht *adverb*
    = not
    nicht wahr? = isn't he/she/it?
    du magst das, nicht (wahr)? = you like that, don't you?
    gar nicht = not at all
    nicht mehr = no more
    bitte nicht = please don't

die **Nichte**, *plural* Nichten
    = niece

nichts *pronoun*
    = nothing

nicken *verb*
    = to nod

nie *adverb*
    = never

nieder
    1 *adjective* = low
    2 *adverb* = down

die **Niederlage**, *plural* Niederlagen
    = defeat

die **Niederlande** (*plural*)
    = the Netherlands

niedlich *adjective*
    = sweet, = cute

niedrig *adjective*
    = low

niemals *adverb*
    = never

niemand *pronoun*
    = no one, = nobody

die **Niere**, *plural* Nieren
    = kidney

niesen *verb*
    = to sneeze

das **Nilpferd**, *plural* Nilpferde
    = hippopotamus

nimmt ▶ nehmen

nirgends *adverb*
    = nowhere

noch
    1 *adverb*
- = still
    noch nicht = not yet
- = just
    gerade noch = only just
- = else
    wer war noch da? = who else was there?
- = even
    noch größer = even bigger

- (*other uses*)
noch einmal = again
noch ein Bier = another beer
2 *conjunction* = nor
weder . . . noch = neither . . . nor

nochmals *adverb*
= again

die **Nonne**, *plural* Nonnen
= nun

der **Norden**
= north

nördlich *adjective*
- = northern
- = northerly

nörgeln *verb*
= to grumble

normalerweise *adverb*
= normally

(das) **Norwegen**
= Norway

norwegisch *adjective*
= Norwegian

die **Not**, *plural* Nöte
- = need
zur Not = if need be
- = distress, = hardship

der **Notausgang**, *plural* Notausgänge
= emergency exit

der **Notdienst**
Notdienst haben = to be on call

die **Note**, *plural* Noten
- = note
Noten lesen = to read music
- = mark, = grade

der **Notfall**, *plural* Notfälle
= emergency

notfalls *adverb*
= if need be

die **Notfallstation**, *plural* Notfallstationen
= accident and emergency department

notieren *verb*
- = to note down
- sich etwas notieren = to make a note of
something

nötig
1 *adjective* = necessary
2 *adverb* = urgently

die **Notiz**, *plural* Notizen
- = note
keine Notiz von etwas nehmen = to take
no notice of something
- (*in a newspaper*) = report, = item

die **Notlage**, *plural* Notlagen
= crisis

der **Notruf**, *plural* Notrufe

- = emergency call
- = emergency number

notwendig *adjective*
= necessary

die **Notwendigkeit**, *plural*
Notwendigkeiten
= necessity

der **November**
= November

nüchtern *adjective*
- = sober
- auf nüchternen Magen = on an empty
stomach

Nudeln (*plural*)
- = noodles
- = pasta

null *adjective*
- = nought, = zero
- (*in sport*) = nil
(*in tennis*) = love

die **Null**, *plural* Nullen
- = nought, = zero
- (*person*) = failure

die **Nummer**, *plural* Nummern
- = number
- (*periodical*) = issue
- (*in a circus*) = act
- (*of clothing*) = size

nummerieren *verb*
= to number

das **Nummernschild**, *plural*
Nummernschilder
= number plate, = license plate

nun *adverb*
= now

nur *adverb*
= only
er soll es nur versuchen! = just let him
try!

(das) **Nürnberg**
= Nuremberg

die **Nuss** (**Nuß**ᴼᴸᴰ), *plural* Nüsse
= nut

nutzen *verb*
- = to use
- = to be useful

der **Nutzen**
- = benefit
- = profit

nützen *verb*
- = to be useful
nichts nützen = to be no use
- = to use

nützlich *adjective*
= useful

N

Oo

nutzlos *adjective*
= useless

ob *conjunction*
= whether
ob sie wohl krank ist? = I wonder if she is ill
und ob! = you bet!

der/die **Obdachlose**, *plural* Obdachlosen
= homeless person

oben *adverb*
• = up
nach oben = up
von oben = from above, (*indoors*) = from upstairs
• = on top
oben auf = on top of
• = at the top
• = upstairs
• (*in text*) = above
oben genannt = above-mentioned

der **Ober**, *plural* Ober
= waiter

oberer/obere/oberes *adjective*
= upper, = top

die **Oberfläche**, *plural* Oberflächen
= surface

oberflächlich *adjective*
= superficial

das **Oberhaupt**, *plural* Oberhäupter
= head

das **Oberhemd**, *plural* Oberhemden
= shirt

der **Oberschenkel**, *plural* Oberschenkel
= thigh

die **Oberschule**, *plural* Oberschulen
= secondary school

das **Objektiv**, *plural* Objektive
= lens

das **Obst**
= fruit

obszön *adjective*
= obscene

obwohl *conjunction*
= although, = though

der **Ochse**, *plural* Ochsen
= ox

öde *adjective*
• = desolate
• = dreary

oder *conjunction*
= or
sie ist doch hier, oder? = she is here, isn't she?

der **Ofen**, *plural* Öfen
• = oven
• = stove
• = heater

offen
1 *adjective*
• = open
ein Tag der offenen Tür = an open day
offen haben = to be open
offen bleiben = to stay open, = to be left open
• = vacant
• = frank
• (*of a bill*) = outstanding
2 *adverb*
• = openly
• = frankly
offen gesagt = frankly

offenbar *adjective*
= obvious

offenbleiben⊙ᴸᴰ ▶offen

offensichtlich *adjective*
= obvious

öffentlich *adjective*
= public
der öffentliche Dienst = the civil service

die **Öffentlichkeit**
= public
in aller Öffentlichkeit = in public

offiziell *adjective*
= official

der **Offizier**, *plural* Offiziere
= officer

öffnen *verb*
• = to open
• sich öffnen = to open

die **Öffnung**, *plural* Öffnungen
= opening

oft *adverb*
= often

öfter *adverb*
= quite often

öfters* *adverb*
= quite often

✗ in informal situations   ⊙ᴸᴰ = old spelling

ohne
1 *preposition* (+ *accusative*) = without
ohne weiteres = easily, = readily
ohne mich! = count me out!
2 *conjunction* = without

die **Ohnmacht**, *plural* Ohnmachten
• = faint
in Ohnmacht fallen = to faint
• = powerlessness

ohnmächtig *adjective*
• = unconscious
ohnmächtig werden = to faint
• = powerless

das **Ohr**, *plural* Ohren
= ear

der **Ohrring**, *plural* Ohrringe
= earring

oje *interjection*
= oh dear!

der **Ökoladen**, *plural* Ökoläden
= health-food shop, = health-food store

die **Ökologie**
= ecology

der **Oktober**
= October

das **Öl**, *plural* Öle
= oil

die **Olympiade**, *plural* Olympiaden
= Olympic Games, = Olympics

die **Oma**, *plural* Omas
= granny

der **Omnibus**, *plural* Omnibusse
= bus, = coach

der **Onkel**, *plural* Onkel
= uncle

der **Opa**, *plural* Opas
= grandad

die **Oper**, *plural* Opern
= opera

die **Operation**, *plural* Operationen
= operation

operieren *verb*
• = to operate
• = to operate on

das **Opfer**, *plural* Opfer
• = sacrifice
• = victim

der **Optiker**, *plural* Optiker
= optician

die **Orange**, *plural* Orangen
= orange

das **Orchester**, *plural* Orchester
= orchestra

ordentlich *adjective*
• = tidy
• = respectable
(*of a meal, job*) = proper

ordinär *adjective*
= vulgar, = crude

ordnen *verb*
• = to arrange
• = to put in order

die **Ordnung**
= order

das **Organ**, *plural* Organe
• = organ
• = voice

organisieren *verb*
• = to organize

die **Orgel**, *plural* Orgeln
= organ

orientieren: sich orientieren
verb
= to get one's bearings
sich über etwas orientieren = to inform
oneself about something

die **Orientierung**
• = orientation
• die Orientierung verlieren = to lose one's
bearings
• zu Ihrer Orientierung = for your
information

der **Orientierungspunkt**
= landmark

der **Orientierungssinn**
= sense of direction

originell *adjective*
= original

der **Orkan**, *plural* Orkane
= hurricane

der **Ort**, *plural* Orte
• = place
an Ort und Stelle = in the right place,
(*immediately*) = on the spot
• = (small) town

örtlich *adjective*
= local

die **Ortschaft**, *plural* Ortschaften
= village

die **Öse**, *plural* Ösen
= eye

der **Ossi***, *plural* Ossis
= East German

der **Osten**
= east

die **Osterglocke** *plural* Osterglocken
= daffodil

das **Ostern**, *plural* Ostern
= Easter

O

(das) **Österreich**
= Austria

der **Österreicher**, *plural* Österreicher
= Austrian

die **Österreicherin**, *plural*
Österreicherinnen
= Austrian

österreichisch *adjective*
= Austrian

östlich *adjective*
• = eastern
• = easterly

die **Ostsee**
= Baltic (Sea)

der **Ozean**, *plural* Ozeane
= ocean

der *or* das **Ozon**
= ozone

Pp

paar *pronoun*
ein paar = a few

das **Paar**, *plural* Paare
• = pair
• = couple

das **Päckchen**, *plural* Päckchen
= package, = small packet

die **Packung**, *plural* Packungen
= packet, = pack

der **Pädagoge**, *plural* Pädagogen
• = educationalist
• = teacher

paddeln *verb* (**!** *sein*)
= to paddle

das **Paket**, *plural* Pakete
• = parcel, = package
• = packet

der **Palast**, *plural* Paläste
= palace

die **Palme**, *plural* Palmen
= palm (tree)

die **Pampelmuse**, *plural* Pampelmusen
= grapefruit

die **Panik**, *plural* Paniken
= panic
in Panik geraten = to panic

(OLD) = old spelling

die **Panne**, *plural* Pannen
• = breakdown, = mishap

der **Papagei**, *plural* Papageien
= parrot

das **Papier**, *plural* Papiere
= paper

der **Papierkorb**, *plural* Papierkörbe
= waste-paper basket

die **Pappe**, *plural* Pappen
= cardboard

der **Pappkarton**, *plural* Pappkartons
= cardboard box

der **Papst**, *plural* Päpste
= pope

die **Parabolantenne**, *plural*
Parabolantennen
= satellite dish

der **Paragraph**, *plural* Paragraphen
• = section
• = clause

das **Parfüm**, *plural* Parfüms
= perfume

der **Park**, *plural* Parks
= park

parken *verb*
= to park

der **Park-and-ride-Parkplatz**
= park and ride

das **Parkhaus**, *plural* Parkhäuser
= multi-storey car park

der **Parkplatz**, *plural* Parkplätze
• = car park, = parking lot
• = parking space

die **Parkuhr**, *plural* Parkuhren
= parking meter

das **Parkverbot**
'Parkverbot' = 'no parking'

das **Parlament**, *plural* Parlamente
= parliament

die **Partei**, *plural* Parteien
= party
für jemanden Partei ergreifen = to side
with someone

das **Parterre**, *plural* Parterres
= ground floor, (*US*) = first floor

die **Partie**, *plural* Partien
• = part, = game

der **Partner**, *plural* Partner
= partner

die **Partnerin**, *plural* Partnerinnen
= partner

die **Party**, *plural* Partys
= party

der **Pass** (**Paß**ⓄⓁⒹ), *plural* Pässe
* = passport, = pass

der **Passagier**, *plural* Passagiere
= passenger

passen *verb*
* = to fit
* = to be suitable
jemandem passen = to suit someone
zu etwas passen = to go well with
   something
* (*in sport*) = to pass

passend *adjective*
* = suitable, = matching

passieren *verb* (**!** *sein*)
= to happen

der **Pate**, *plural* Paten
= godfather

das **Patenkind**, *plural* Patenkinder
= godchild

patent *adjective*
= capable, = clever

der **Patient**, *plural* Patienten
= patient

die **Patientin**, *plural* Patientinnen
= patient

die **Patin**, *plural* Patinnen
= godmother

die **Pause**, *plural* Pausen
* = break
* = pause
* = interval, = intermission

pausenlos *adjective*
= continuous, = nonstop

der **Pazifik**
= the Pacific

der **PC**, *plural* PCs
= PC, personal computer

das **Pech**
* = bad luck
* = pitch

das **Pedal**, *plural* Pedale
= pedal

peinlich *adjective*
* = embarrassing
* = meticulous

die **Peitsche**, *plural* Peitschen
= whip

peitschen *verb*
* = to whip
* = to lash

der **Pelz**, *plural* Pelze
= fur

der **Pendler**, *plural* Pendler
= commuter

die **Pension**, *plural* Pensionen
* = pension
in Pension gehen = to retire
* = guesthouse
bei voller Pension = with full board

das **Pensum**
= quota

per *preposition* (+ *accusative*)
* = by
* = per

perfekt *adjective*
= perfect

die **Perle**, *plural* Perlen
* = pearl
* = bead

die **Person**, *plural* Personen
* = person
* = character

das **Personal**
= personnel, = staff

der **Personalausweis**, *plural*
Personalausweise
= identity card

persönlich *adjective*
= personal

die **Perücke**, *plural* Perücken
= wig

pessimistisch *adjective*
= pessimistic

die **Pest**
= plague

der **Pfad**, *plural* Pfade
= path

der **Pfadfinder**, *plural* Pfadfinder
= (Boy) Scout

die **Pfadfinderin**, *plural* Pfadfinderinnen
= (Girl) Guide

das **Pfand**, *plural* Pfänder
* = pledge
* = forfeit
* (*on a bottle*) = deposit

die **Pfanne**, *plural* Pfannen
= (frying) pan

der **Pfannkuchen**, *plural* Pfannkuchen
= pancake

der **Pfarrer**, *plural* Pfarrer
* = vicar
* = priest

der **Pfau**, *plural* Pfauen
= peacock

der **Pfeffer**, *plural* Pfeffer
= pepper

der **Pfefferkuchen**
= gingerbread

P

die **Pfeife**, *plural* Pfeifen
* • = whistle
* • = pipe

pfeifen *irregular verb*
= to whistle

der **Pfeil**, *plural* Pfeile
= arrow

der **Pfeiler**, *plural* Pfeiler
* • = pillar
* • = pier

der **Pfennig**, *plural* Pfennige
= pfennig

das **Pferd**, *plural* Pferde
* • = horse
* • (*in chess*) = knight

der **Pferdeschwanz**, *plural*
Pferdeschwänze
= ponytail

pfiff ▶pfeifen

das **Pfingsten**, *plural* Pfingsten
= Whitsun

der **Pfirsich**, *plural* Pfirsiche
= peach

die **Pflanze**, *plural* Pflanzen
= plant

pflanzen *verb*
= to plant

das **Pflaster**, *plural* Pflaster
* • = pavement, = surface
* • = plaster

die **Pflaume**, *plural* Pflaumen
= plum

die **Pflege**
= care
(*in hospital*) = nursing

Pflegeeltern (*plural*)
= foster parents

das **Pflegeheim**, *plural* Pflegeheime
= nursing home

pflegeleicht *adjective*
= easy-care

pflegen *verb*
= to care for, = to look after
(*in hospital*) = to nurse

der **Pfleger**, *plural* Pfleger
= nurse

die **Pflicht**, *plural* Pflichten
= duty
Pflicht sein = to be compulsory

pflichtbewusst
(**pflichtbewußt** ⓞⓛⓓ) *adjective*
= conscientious

pflücken *verb*
= to pick

pflügen *verb*
= to plough, = to plow

der **Pförtner**, *plural* Pförtner
= porter

die **Pfote**, *plural* Pfoten
= paw

pfui *interjection*
= ugh!

das **Pfund**, *plural* Pfunde
= pound

die **Pfütze**, *plural* Pfützen
= puddle

die **Phantasie**, *plural* Phantasien
= imagination
Phantasien = fantasies

phantastisch *adjective*
= fantastic

der **Philosoph**, *plural* Philosophen
= philosopher

die **Philosophie**, *plural* Philosophien
= philosophy

die **Physik**
= physics

der **Pickel**, *plural* Pickel
= spot, = pimple

das **Picknick**, *plural* Picknicks
= picnic

das **Pik**
(*playing cards*) = spades

die **Pille**, *plural* Pillen
= pill

der **Pilz**, *plural* Pilze
* • = mushroom
* • = fungus

der **Pinguin**, *plural* Pinguine
= penguin

der **Pinsel**, *plural* Pinsel
= brush

die **Pistole**, *plural* Pistolen
= pistol

der **Pkw**, *plural* Pkws
(*Personenkraftwagen*) = car

die **Plage**, *plural* Plagen
= nuisance

plagen *verb*
* • = to torment
* • = to pester

das **Plakat**, *plural* Plakate
= poster

✖ in informal situations   ⓞⓛⓓ = old spelling

der **Plan**, *plural* Pläne
- = plan
- = map

planen *verb*
= to plan

das **Plastik**[1]
= plastic

die **Plastik**[2] *plural* Plastiken
= sculpture

die **Platte**, *plural* Platten
- (*wooden*) = board
  (*of a table*) = top
- (*stone*) = slab
- (*metal, glass*) = sheet
- = hotplate
- = plate
  (*for serving*) = dish
  kalte Platte = cold meats and cheeses
- = record, = disc

der **Plattenspieler**, *plural* Plattenspieler
= record player

der **Platz**, *plural* Plätze
- = square
- (*for sport*) = ground, = pitch
  (*for tennis*) = court
  (*for golf*) = course
- = place
  viel Platz haben = to have a lot of room
- = seat
  Platz nehmen = to take a seat, = to sit
  down

platzen *verb* (**!** *sein*)
- = to burst
- der Plan ist geplatzt✱ = the plan fell
  through

plaudern *verb*
= to chat

pleite✱ *adjective*
= broke

plötzlich
1 *adjective* = sudden
2 *adverb* = suddenly

plump *adjective*
- = plump
- = clumsy

der **Po✱**, *plural* Pos
= bottom

die **Poesie**
= poetry

der **Pokal**, *plural* Pokale
- = goblet
- = cup

der **Pole**, *plural* Polen
= Pole

(das) **Polen**
= Poland

die **Police**, *plural* Policen
= policy

polieren *verb*
= to polish

die **Polin**, *plural* Polinnen
= Pole

die **Politik**
- = politics
- = policy

der **Politiker**, *plural* Politiker
= politician

die **Politikerin**, *plural* Politikerinnen
= politician

politisch *adjective*
= political

die **Polizei**
= police

polizeilich
1 *adjective* = police
2 *adverb* = by the police

die **Polizeiwache**, *plural* Polizeiwachen
= police station

der **Polizist**, *plural* Polizisten
= policeman

die **Polizistin**, *plural* Polizistinnen
= policewoman

polnisch *adjective*
= Polish

das **Polster**, *plural* Polster
- = upholstery
- = pad

Pommes frites (*plural*)
= chips, = French fries

das **Pony**[1] *plural* Ponys
= pony

der **Pony**[2] *plural* Ponys
= fringe

das **Portemonnaie**, *plural* Portemonnaies
= purse

der **Portier**, *plural* Portiers
= porter

das **Portmonee**, *plural* Portmonees
= purse

das **Porto**
= postage

das **Porzellan**
= porcelain, = china

die **Post**
- = post, = mail
- = post office

das **Postamt**, *plural* Postämter
= post office

P

der **Postbote**, plural Postboten
= postman, = mailman

das **Postfach**, plural Postfächer
= PO box

die **Postkarte**, plural Postkarten
= postcard

die **Postleitzahl**, plural Postleitzahlen
= postcode, = Zip code

prächtig adjective
= splendid

prahlen verb
= to boast

praktisch
1 adjective = practical
ein praktischer Arzt = a general
practitioner
2 adverb
• = practically
• = in practice

die **Praline**, plural Pralinen
= chocolate

das **Präservativ**, plural Präservative
= condom

der **Präsident**, plural Präsidenten
= president

die **Präsidentin**, plural Präsidentinnen
= president

die **Praxis**, plural Praxen
• = practice
• (doctor's) = surgery

predigen verb
= to preach

der **Preis**, plural Preise
• = price
• = prize, = award

das **Preisausschreiben**, plural
Preisausschreiben
= competition

preiswert adjective
= reasonable, = cheap

die **Prellung**, plural Prellungen
= bruise

der **Premierminister**, plural
Premierminister
= prime minister

prima adjective
= brilliant

der **Prinz**, plural Prinzen
= prince

die **Prinzessin**, plural Prinzessinnen
= princess

privat adjective
= private

pro preposition (+ accusative)
= per

die **Probe**, plural Proben
• = test
• = sample
• = rehearsal

probeweise adverb
= on a trial basis

probieren verb
= to try, = to taste

der **Profi**, plural Profis
= professional

das **Programm**, plural Programme
• = programme, = program
• (on TV) = channel

programmieren verb
= to program

der **Programmierer**, plural
Programmierer
= programmer

das **Promille**
= alcohol level
zu viel Promille haben = to be over the
limit

die **Prosa**
= prose

der **Prospekt**, plural Prospekte
= brochure

prost interjection
= cheers!

das **Protokoll**, plural Protokolle
• = protocol
• = minutes

protzen verb
= to show off

der **Proviant**
= provisions

das **Prozent**, plural Prozente
= per cent
auf etwas Prozente bekommen = to get a
discount on something

der **Prozentsatz**, plural Prozentsätze
= percentage

der **Prozess** (**Prozeß**(OLD)), plural
Prozesse
• = court case, = trial
• = process

prüfen verb
• = to test, = to check
• = to examine

die **Prüfung**, plural Prüfungen
• = examination, = exam
• = test

× in informal situations   (OLD) = old spelling

die **Prügelei**, *plural* Prügeleien
= fight

prügeln *verb*
• = to beat
• sich prügeln = to fight

der **Psychiater**, *plural* Psychiater
= psychiatrist

die **Psychiaterin**, *plural* Psychiaterinnen
= psychiatrist

psychisch *adjective*
= psychological

die **Psychologie**
= psychology

das **Publikum**
• = public
• = audience, = spectators

der **Pudding**, *plural* Puddings
= blancmange
= pudding

der **Puder**, *plural* Puder
= powder

der **Pulli***, *plural* Pullis
= sweater, = jumper

der **Pullover**, *plural* Pullover
= sweater, = jumper

der **Puls**, *plural* Pulse
= pulse

das **Pult**, *plural* Pulte
= desk

das **Pulver**, *plural* Pulver
= powder

der **Pulverkaffee**
= instant coffee

die **Pumpe**, *plural* Pumpen
= pump

pumpen *verb*
• = to pump
• jemandem Geld pumpen* = to lend someone money
• sich etwas pumpen* = to borrow something

der **Punker**, *plural* Punker
= punk

die **Punkerin**, *plural* Punkerinnen
= punk

der **Punkt**, *plural* Punkte
• = dot, = spot
Punkt vier Uhr = at 4 o'clock on the dot
• = full stop, = period
• = point

pünktlich *adjective*
= punctual

die **Puppe**, *plural* Puppen
• = doll
• = puppet

der **Purzelbaum**, *plural* Purzelbäume
= somersault

pusten* *verb*
= to blow

die **Pute**, *plural* Puten
= turkey

der **Putz**
= plaster

putzen *verb*
• = to clean
• sich (+ *dative*) die Nase putzen = to blow one's nose

putzig* *adjective*
= cute

das **Puzzle**, *plural* Puzzles
= jigsaw (puzzle)

die **Pyramide**, *plural* Pyramiden
= pyramid

Qq

das **Quadrat**, *plural* Quadrate
= square

der **Quadratmeter**, *plural* Quadratmeter
= square metre, = square meter

quaken *verb*
• (*of a duck*) = to quack
• (*of a frog*) = to croak

die **Qual**, *plural* Qualen
• = torment
• = agony

quälen *verb*
• = to torment
• = to torture
• = to pester
• sich quälen = to suffer, = to struggle

der **Quälgeist***, *plural* Quälgeister
= pest

die **Qualität**, *plural* Qualitäten
= quality

die **Qualle**, *plural* Quallen
= jellyfish

das **Quartett**, *plural* Quartette
= quartet

das **Quartier**, *plural* Quartiere
• = accommodation
• = quarters

der **Quatsch×**
= rubbish, = nonsense

quatschen× verb
= to chat

die **Quelle**, plural Quellen
* = source
* = spring

quellen irregular verb (! sein)
* = to pour
* = to swell

quer adverb
* = across
= crosswise
= diagonally
* quer durch = straight through

die **Querstraße**, plural Querstraßen
= side street, = side road

quetschen verb
= to crush, = to squash

quietschen verb
= to squeak

quitt× adjective
= quits

die **Quittung**, plural Quittungen
= receipt

Rr

der **Rabatt**, plural Rabatte
= discount

die **Rache**
= revenge

rächen verb
* = to avenge
* sich an jemandem rächen = to take revenge on someone

das **Rad**, plural Räder
* = wheel
* = bike
* Rad fahren = to cycle, = to ride a bike
er fährt gern Rad = he likes cycling

der **Radfahrer**, plural Radfahrer
= cyclist

die **Radfahrerin**, plural Radfahrerinnen
= cyclist

der **Radfahrweg**, plural Radfahrwege
= cycle lane

× in informal situations   ⓪ⓛⓓ = old spelling

der **Radiergummi**, plural Radiergummis
= rubber, = eraser

das **Radieschen**, plural Radieschen
= radish

das **Radio**, plural Radios
= radio

der **Radler**, plural Radler
= cyclist

die **Radlerin**, plural Radlerinnen
= cyclist

raffiniert adjective
= crafty, = cunning

der **Rahmen**, plural Rahmen
* = frame
* = framework

die **Rakete**, plural Raketen
= rocket

ran× ▶heran

der **Rand**, plural Ränder
= edge
= rim
(of a page) = margin
etwas am Rande erwähnen = to mention something in passing
mit etwas nicht zu Rande kommen = not be able to cope with something

der **Randstreifen**, plural Randstreifen
= hard shoulder

der **Rang**, plural Ränge
* = rank
* (in a theatre) = circle

rangieren verb
* = to rank
* = to shunt, = to switch

rannte ▶rennen

rasch adjective
= quick

rascheln verb
= to rustle

rasen verb (! sein)
= to tear along

der **Rasen**, plural Rasen
= lawn, = grass

der **Rasierapparat**, plural Rasierapparate
= razor
= shaver

rasieren verb
* = to shave
* sich rasieren = to shave

das **Rasierwasser**
= aftershave

die **Rasse**, plural Rassen
= race

rassisch *adjective*
= racial

rassistisch *adjective*
= racist

rasten *verb*
= to rest

der **Rastplatz**, *plural* Rastplätze
= picnic area (*on a motorway*)

die **Raststätte**, *plural* Raststätten
= services (*on a motorway*)

der **Rat**, *plural* Räte
• = (piece of) advice
• = council

raten *irregular verb*
• = to advise
• = to guess

das **Rathaus**, *plural* Rathäuser
= town hall

rationell *adjective*
= efficient

ratlos *adjective*
= helpless

ratsam *adjective*
= advisable

der **Ratschlag**, *plural* Ratschläge
= (piece of) advice

das **Rätsel**, *plural* Rätsel
= puzzle
= mystery

rätselhaft *adjective*
= mysterious

die **Ratte**, *plural* Ratten
= rat

rau *adjective*
• = rough
• = harsh
• einen rauen Hals haben = to have a sore
throat

der **Raub**
• = robbery
• = loot

rauben *verb*
= to steal, = to rob

das **Raubtier**, *plural* Raubtiere
= predator

der **Rauch**
= smoke

rauchen *verb*
= to smoke

der **Raucher**, *plural* Raucher
= smoker

die **Raucherin**, *plural* Raucherinnen
= smoker

rauf× ▶herauf, hinauf

rauh⃝ᴸᴰ ▶rau

der **Raum**, *plural* Räume
• = room
• = space
• = area

räumen *verb*
• = to clear
• = to vacate

die **Raumfahrt**
= space travel

der **Raumschiff**, *plural* Raumschiffe
= space ship

Raupe, die, *plural* Raupen
= caterpillar

raus× ▶heraus, hinaus

das **Rauschgift**, *plural* Rauschgifte
= drug
Rauschgift nehmen = to take drugs

rauschgiftsüchtig *adjective*
= addicted (to drugs)

der/die **Rauschgiftsüchtige**, *plural*
Rauschgiftsüchtigen
= drug addict

raus|kriegen× *verb*
= to get out
ein Geheimnis rauskriegen = to find out
a secret
er hat die Aufgabe nicht rausgekriegt = he
couldn't do the exercise

räuspern: sich räuspern *verb*
= to clear one's throat

die **Razzia**, *plural* Razzien
= raid

reagieren *verb*
= to react

rebellieren *verb*
= to rebel

rechnen *verb*
• = to count, = to calculate
gut rechnen können = to be good at
figures
• = to reckon
mit etwas rechnen = to expect
something, (*rely on*) = to count on
something
• = to work out

das **Rechnen**
= arithmetic

der **Rechner**, *plural* Rechner
• = calculator
• = computer

die **Rechnung**, *plural* Rechnungen
• = bill, = check
= invoice
• = calculation

R

recht
1 *adjective*
- = right
  jemandem recht sein = to be all right
  with someone
- = real
  ich habe keine rechte Lust = I don't really
  feel like it
2 *adverb*
- = correctly
- = very
- = quite
  recht vielen Dank = many thanks

das **Recht**, *plural* Rechte
- = law
- = right
  mit Recht = rightly
  Recht haben = to be right
- jemandem Recht geben = to agree with
  someone

rechte ▶ rechter

das **Rechteck**, *plural* Rechtecke
= rectangle

rechteckig *adjective*
= rectangular

rechter, rechte, rechtes *adjective*
- = right, = right-wing

rechtfertigen *verb*
= to justify

rechtlich *adjective*
= legal

rechts *adverb*
= on the right
von rechts = from the right
rechts sein = to be right-wing

der **Rechtsanwalt**, *plural* Rechtsanwälte
= lawyer, = solicitor
= barrister

die **Rechtsanwältin**, *plural*
Rechtsanwältinnen
= lawyer, = solicitor, = barrister

die **Rechtschreibung**
= spelling

rechtsklicken *verb*
= to right-click

rechtzeitig
1 *adjective* = timely
2 *adverb* = in time

der **Redakteur**, *plural* Redakteure
= editor

die **Redakteurin**, *plural* Redakteurinnen
= editor

die **Rede**, *plural* Reden
= speech
nicht der Rede wert = not worth
mentioning

reden *verb*
= to speak, = to talk

reduzieren *verb*
- = to reduce
- sich reduzieren = to decrease

das **Reformhaus**, *plural* Reformhäuser
= health-food shop, = health-food store

das **Regal**, *plural* Regale
= shelf
= shelves

die **Regel**, *plural* Regeln
- = rule
  in der Regel = as a rule
- (*menstruation*) = period

regelmäßig *adjective*
= regular

regeln *verb*
- = to regulate
  den Verkehr regeln = to direct the traffic
- (*sort out*) = to settle

die **Regelung**, *plural* Regelungen
- = regulation
- = settlement

der **Regen**
= rain

der **Regenbogen**, *plural* Regenbogen
= rainbow

der **Regenschirm**, *plural* Regenschirme
= umbrella

der **Regenwurm**, *plural* Regenwürmer
= earthworm

die **Regie**
= direction
Regie führen = to direct

regieren *verb*
- = to govern
- = to rule

die **Regierung**, *plural* Regierungen
- = government
- (*of a monarch*) = reign

der **Regisseur**, *plural* Regisseure
= director

die **Regisseurin**, *plural* Regisseurinnen
= director

regnen *verb*
= to rain

reiben *irregular verb*
- = to rub
- = to grate

reibungslos *adjective*
= smooth

reich *adjective*
= rich

das **Reich**, *plural* Reiche
= empire

✗ in informal situations ⓄⓁⒹ = old spelling

reichen verb
* = to hand, = to pass
* = to be enough
mit dem Geld reichen = to have enough money
mir reichts!✶ = I've had enough!
* bis zu etwas reichen = to reach (up to) something

reichlich
1 adjective = ample, = large
2 adverb = plenty of

der **Reichtum**, plural Reichtümer
= wealth

reif adjective
* = ripe
* = mature

der **Reifen**, plural Reifen
* = tyre, = tire
* = hoop

die **Reifenpanne**, plural Reifenpannen
= puncture

die **Reihe**, plural Reihen
* = row
* = series
du bist an der Reihe = it's your turn

die **Reihenfolge**, plural Reihenfolgen
= order

das **Reihenhaus**, plural Reihenhäuser
= terraced house

reimen verb
* = to rhyme
* sich reimen = to rhyme

rein¹ adjective
= pure
= clean
etwas ins Reine schreiben = to make a fair copy of something
etwas ins Reine bringen = to clear something up

rein² adverb
rein✶ ▶ herein, hinein

reinigen verb
= to clean

die **Reinigung**, plural Reinigungen
* = cleaning
* = cleaner's

der **Reis**
= rice

die **Reise**, plural Reisen
= journey, = trip
(by boat) = voyage

das **Reisebüro**, plural Reisebüros
= travel agency

der **Reisebus**, plural Reisebusse
= coach

der **Reiseführer**, plural Reiseführer
* = guidebook
* = courier

reisen verb (**!** sein)
= to travel

der/die **Reisende**, plural Reisenden
= traveller, = traveler

der **Reisepass** (**Reisepaß**ⓞⓛⓓ), plural Reisepässe
= passport

der **Reisescheck**, plural Reiseschecks
= traveller's cheque, = traveler's check

reißen irregular verb
* = to tear
* = to pull
* sich um etwas reißen = to fight for something
* (**!** sein) = to tear, = to break

der **Reißverschluss** (**Reißverschluß**ⓞⓛⓓ), plural Reißverschlüsse
= zip, = zipper

die **Reißzwecke**, plural Reißzwecken
= drawing pin, = thumbtack

reiten irregular verb (**!** sein)
= to ride

der **Reiter**, plural Reiter
= rider

die **Reiterin**, plural Reiterinnen
= rider

der **Reitweg**, plural Reitwege
= bridle path

der **Reiz**, plural Reize
* = stimulus
* = attraction

reizen verb
* = to provoke
* = to attract, = to tempt
* (when playing cards) = to bid

reizend adjective
= charming, = delightful

reizvoll adjective
= attractive

die **Reklame**, plural Reklamen
= advertisement
(on TV) = commercial
für etwas Reklame machen = to advertise something

der **Rektor**, plural Rektoren
* (of a school) = head, = principal
* (of a university) = vice-chancellor

die **Religion**, plural Religionen
= religion

rennen irregular verb (**!** sein)
= to run

das **Rennen**, plural Rennen
= race

R

renovieren *verb*
= to renovate, = to redecorate

die **Renovierung**, *plural* Renovierungen
= renovation, = redecoration

die **Rente**, *plural* Renten
= pension
in Rente gehen = to retire

der **Rentner**, *plural* Rentner
= pensioner

die **Rentnerin**, *plural* Rentnerinnen
= pensioner

die **Reparatur**, *plural* Reparaturen
= repair

reparieren *verb*
= to repair

reservieren *verb*
= to reserve

respektieren *verb*
= to respect

der **Rest**, *plural* Reste
= rest, = remainder
die Reste = the remains, (*of food*) = the
leftovers

das **Restaurant**, *plural* Restaurants
= restaurant

restlich *adjective*
= remaining

restlos *adjective*
= complete

das **Resultat**, *plural* Resultate
= result

retten *verb*
• = to save, = to rescue
• sich retten = to escape

die **Rettung**
= rescue

der **Rettungsring**, *plural* Rettungsringe
= lifebelt

der **Rettungswagen**, *plural*
Rettungswagen
= ambulance

das **Rezept**, *plural* Rezepte
• = prescription
• = recipe

das **R-Gespräch**, *plural* R-Gespräche
= reverse-charge call, = collect call

der **Rhein**
= Rhine

das **Rheuma**
= rheumatism

der **Rhythmus**, *plural* Rhythmen
= rhythm

richten *verb*
• = to direct
• = to aim
• eine Frage an jemanden richten = to put
a question to someone
• = to judge
• sich richten = to be directed
sich nach jemandes Wünschen richten =
to fit in with someone's wishes

der **Richter**, *plural* Richter
= judge

richtig *adjective*
• = right, = correct
• = real

die **Richtlinie**, *plural* Richtlinien
= guideline

die **Richtung**, *plural* Richtungen
• = direction
• = trend

riechen *irregular verb*
= to smell

rief ▶rufen

der **Riegel**, *plural* Riegel
= bolt
ein Riegel Schokolade = a bar of
chocolate

der **Riemen**, *plural* Riemen
• = strap
• = oar

der **Riese**, *plural* Riesen
= giant

riesig *adjective*
= huge, = enormous

das **Riff**, *plural* Riffe
= reef

die **Rille**, *plural* Rillen
= groove

das **Rindfleisch**
= beef

der **Ring**, *plural* Ringe
= ring

das **Ringen**
= wrestling

ringsherum *adverb*
= all around

der **Rinnstein**, *plural* Rinnsteine
= gutter

die **Rippe**, *plural* Rippen
= rib

das **Risiko**, *plural* Risiken
= risk

riskant *adjective*
= risky

riskieren *verb*
= to risk

riss (**riß**⑩), ▶reißen

der **Riss** (**Riß**⑩), *plural* Risse
• = tear
• = crack

ritt ▶reiten

der **Ritter**, *plural* Ritter
= knight

der **Roboter**, *plural* Roboter
= robot

der **Rock**, *plural* Röcke
= skirt

der **Roggen**
= rye

roh *adjective*
• = raw
• = rough
• = brutal

das **Rohr**, *plural* Rohre
• = pipe
• = reed

die **Röhre**, *plural* Röhren
• = tube
• = valve, = tube

die **Rolle**, *plural* Rollen
• = roll
= reel
• = role, = part
es spielt keine Rolle = it doesn't matter

rollen *verb*
= to roll

der **Roller**, *plural* Roller
= scooter

das **Rollo**, *plural* Rollos
= roller blind

der **Rollschuh**, *plural* Rollschuhe
= roller-skate

das **Rollschuhlaufen**
= roller-skating

der **Rollstuhl**, *plural* Rollstühle
= wheelchair

die **Rolltreppe**, *plural* Rolltreppen
= escalator

(das) **Rom**
= Rome

der **Roman**, *plural* Romane
= novel

romantisch *adjective*
= romantic

röntgen *verb*
= to X-ray

rosa *adjective*
= pink

der **Rosenkohl**
= (Brussels) sprouts

der **Rost**, *plural* Roste
• = grate, = grill
• = rust

rösten *verb*
• = to roast
• = to toast

rostig *adjective*
= rusty

rot *adjective*
= red

das **Rotkehlchen**, *plural* Rotkehlchen
= robin

rüber× ▶herüber, hinüber

der **Rücken**, *plural* Rücken
• = back
• (*of a book*) = spine

die **Rückenlehne**, *plural* Rückenlehnen
= back (of a chair)

die **Rückfahrkarte**, *plural* Rückfahrkarten
= return ticket

die **Rückgabe**, *plural* Rückgaben
= return

rückgängig *adjective*
etwas rückgängig machen = to cancel
something

die **Rückhand**
= backhand

das **Rücklicht**, *plural* Rücklichter
= rear light

die **Rückseite**, *plural* Rückseiten
= back, = reverse

die **Rücksicht**
= consideration

rücksichtslos *adjective*
• = inconsiderate
• = ruthless

rücksichtsvoll *adjective*
= considerate

der **Rückstand**
= residue
im Rückstand sein = to be behind

rückwärts *adverb*
= backwards

der **Rückweg**, *plural* Rückwege
= way back, = return journey

die **Rückzahlung**, *plural* Rückzahlungen
= repayment

das **Ruder**, *plural* Ruder
• = oar
• = rudder

R

das **Ruderboot**, *plural* Ruderboote
  = rowing boat, = rowboat

rudern *verb* (**!** *sein*)
  = to row

der **Ruf**, *plural* Rufe
  • = call
  • = telephone number
  • = reputation

rufen *irregular verb*
  = to call

die **Rufnummer**, *plural* Rufnummern
  = telephone number

die **Ruhe**
  • = silence, = quiet
  • = peace
  • = rest

ruhen *verb*
  = to rest

der **Ruhetag**, *plural* Ruhetage
  = closing day
  'Montag Ruhetag' = 'closed on Mondays'

ruhig *adjective*
  • = quiet
  • = peaceful
  • = calm

der **Ruhm**
  = fame

das **Rührei**
  = scrambled eggs

rühren *verb*
  • = to move
  • = to stir
  • sich rühren = to move

die **Ruine**, *plural* Ruinen
  = ruin

ruinieren *verb*
  = to ruin

rülpsen *verb*
  = to belch, = to burp

(das) **Rumänien**
  = Romania

der **Rumpf**, *plural* Rümpfe
  • = trunk
  • (*of a ship*) = hull
  (*of a plane*) = fuselage

rund *adjective*
  = round

die **Runde**, *plural* Runden
  • = round
  • = lap
  • = circle

die **Rundfahrt**, *plural* Rundfahrten
  = tour

die **Rundfrage**, *plural* Rundfragen
  = poll

der **Rundfunk**
  = radio

rundherum *adverb*
  = all around

das **Rundschreiben**, *plural*
  Rundschreiben
  = circular

runterscrollen *verb*
  = to scroll down

runzlig *adjective*
  = wrinkled

die **Rüsche**, *plural* Rüschen
  = frill

der **Ruß**
  = soot

der **Russe**, *plural* Russen
  = Russian

der **Rüssel**, *plural* Rüssel
  = trunk

die **Russin**, *plural* Russinnen
  = Russian

russisch *adjective*
  = Russian

(das) **Russland** (**Rußland**ᴼᴸᴰ)
  = Russia

die **Rüstung**, *plural* Rüstungen
  • = arms, = armour

die **Rutschbahn**, *plural* Rutschbahnen
  = slide

rutschen *verb* (**!** *sein*)
  = to slide, = to slip

rutschig *adjective*
  = slippery

rütteln *verb*
  = to shake

Ss

der **Saal**, *plural* Säle
  = hall

die **Sache**, *plural* Sachen
  • = matter, = business
  zur Sache kommen = to get to the point
  • = thing
  meine Sachen (*clothing*) = my things

✗ in informal situations   ᴼᴸᴰ = old spelling

das **Sachgebiet**, *plural* Sachgebiete
= field, = area

sachlich *adjective*
* = objective
* = factual

sächlich *adjective*
= neuter

(das) **Sachsen**
= Saxony

der **Sack**, *plural* Säcke
* = sack
* = bag

die **Sackgasse**, *plural* Sackgassen
= cul-de-sac

der **Saft**, *plural* Säfte
* = juice
* = sap

saftig *adjective*
= juicy

die **Sage**, *plural* Sagen
= legend, = saga

die **Säge**, *plural* Sägen
= saw

sagen *verb*
* = to say
was ich noch sagen wollte = by the way
* = to tell
jemandem etwas sagen = to tell
  someone something
sag mal = tell me
* = to mean
das hat nichts zu sagen = that doesn't
  mean anything

sägen *verb*
= to saw

sah ▶ sehen

die **Sahne**
= cream

die **Saison**, *plural* Saisons
= season

die **Saite**, *plural* Saiten
= string

das **Sakko**, *plural* Sakkos
= jacket

der **Salat**, *plural* Salate
* = lettuce
* = salad

die **Salbe**, *plural* Salben
= ointment

salopp *adjective*
= casual, = informal

das **Salz**, *plural* Salze
= salt

salzig *adjective*
= salty

der **Samen**, *plural* Samen
* = seed
* = semen, = sperm

sammeln *verb*
* = to collect, = to gather
* sich sammeln = to gather

die **Sammlung**, *plural* Sammlungen
= collection

der **Samstag**
= Saturday

samstags *adverb*
= on Saturdays

samt *preposition* (+ *dative*)
= together with

der **Samt**, *plural* Samte
= velvet

**sämtlicher/sämtliche/
sämtliches** *pronoun*
= all (the)
meine sämtlichen Bücher = all my books

die **Sandale**, *plural* Sandalen
= sandal

sandig *adjective*
= sandy

sanft *adjective*
= gentle
= soft

sang ▶ singen

der **Sänger**, *plural* Sänger
= singer

die **Sängerin**, *plural* Sängerinnen
= singer

der **Sanitäter**, *plural* Sanitäter
= paramedic

der **Sarg**, *plural* Särge
= coffin

saß ▶ sitzen

der **Satellit**, *plural* Satelliten
= satellite

das **Satellitenfernsehen**
= satellite television

satt *adjective*
* = full (up)
* jemanden satt haben✗ = to be fed up
  with someone

der **Sattel**, *plural* Sättel
= saddle

der **Satz**, *plural* Sätze
* = sentence
* = leap
* (*in tennis*) = set
* (*in music*) = movement
* (*of tax, interest*) = rate

S

sauber *adjective*
- = clean
- = neat
- sauber machen = to clean (up)

sauer *adjective*
- = sour
  = pickled
  saurer Regen = acid rain
- er ist sauer✘ = he's annoyed

der **Sauerstoff**
= oxygen

saufen✘ *irregular verb*
= to drink, = to booze

saugen *verb*
- = to suck
- = to vacuum, = to hoover

das **Säugetier**, *plural* Säugetiere
= mammal

der **Säugling**, *plural* Säuglinge
= baby

die **Säule**, *plural* Säulen
= column

der **Saum**, *plural* Säume
= hem

die **Säure**, *plural* Säuren
= acid

die **S-Bahn**, *plural* S-Bahnen
= city and suburban railway

das **Schach**, *plural* Schachs
= chess
Schach! = check!

die **Schachtel**, *plural* Schachteln
= box

schade *adjective*
schade sein = to be a pity
schade! = pity!, = (what a) shame!
zu schade für jemanden sein = to be too good for someone

schaden *verb*
= to damage, = to harm

der **Schaden**, *plural* Schäden
- = damage
- = disadvantage

schädlich *adjective*
= harmful

das **Schaf**, *plural* Schafe
= sheep

der **Schäfer**, *plural* Schäfer
= shepherd

der **Schäferhund**, *plural* Schäferhunde
= sheepdog

schaffen *verb*
- = to manage
  eine Prüfung schaffen = to pass an exam
- jemandem zu schaffen machen = to trouble someone
  geschafft sein✘ = to be worn out
- (*irregular*) = to create

der **Schaffner**, *plural* Schaffner
= conductor

die **Schaffnerin**, *plural* Schaffnerinnen
= conductress

der **Schal**, *plural* Schals
= scarf

die **Schale**, *plural* Schalen
- = skin, = peel
- = shell
- = dish, = bowl

schälen *verb*
- = to peel
- sich schälen = to peel

die **Schallplatte**, *plural* Schallplatten
= record

schalten *verb*
- = to switch, = to turn
- = to change gear
- schnell schalten✘ = to catch on quickly

der **Schalter**, *plural* Schalter
- = switch
- = counter

die **Schaltung**, *plural* Schaltungen
- = gear change
- = circuit

schämen: sich schämen *verb*
= to be ashamed

die **Schande**
= disgrace
= shame

scharf *adjective*
- = sharp
  scharf sein (*in photography*) = to be in focus
- (*of food*) = hot
  scharf auf etwas sein✘ = to be really keen on something
- = hard
- = fierce

der **Schatten**, *plural* Schatten
- = shadow
- = shade

schattig *adjective*
= shady

der **Schatz**, *plural* Schätze
- = treasure
- mein Schatz✘ = my darling

schätzen *verb*
- = to estimate

- = to reckon
- = to value

die **Schau**, *plural* Schauen
= show

schauen *verb*
= to look

der **Schauer**, *plural* Schauer
= shower

die **Schauergeschichte**, *plural*
Schauergeschichten
= horror story

die **Schaufel**, *plural* Schaufeln
- = shovel
- = dustpan

das **Schaufenster**, *plural* Schaufenster
= shop window

die **Schaukel**, *plural* Schaukeln
= swing

der **Schaukelstuhl**, *plural* Schaukelstühle
= rocking chair

der **Schaum**
= foam, = froth
= lather

schäumen *verb*
= to foam, = to froth
= to lather

das **Schauspiel**, *plural* Schauspiele
- = play
- = spectacle

der **Schauspieler**, *plural* Schauspieler
= actor

die **Schauspielerin**, *plural*
Schauspielerinnen
= actress

der **Scheck**, *plural* Schecks
= cheque, = check

das **Scheckbuch**, *plural* Scheckbücher
= chequebook, = checkbook

die **Scheibe**, *plural* Scheiben
- = disc
- = pane
- = slice

der **Scheibenwischer**, *plural*
Scheibenwischer
= windscreen wiper

scheiden *irregular verb*
- = to separate
- sich scheiden = to differ
- sich scheiden lassen = to get divorced

die **Scheidung**, *plural* Scheidungen
= divorce

der **Schein**, *plural* Scheine
- = light

- = appearance, = pretence
etwas nur zum Schein machen = to only
pretend to do something
- = certificate
- (*money*) = note

scheinbar *adjective*
= apparent

scheinen *irregular verb*
- = to shine
- = to seem

der **Scheinwerfer**, *plural* Scheinwerfer
= headlamp, = headlight

die **Scheiße** = shit

scheitern *verb* (**!** *sein*)
= to fail

der **Schelm**, *plural* Schelme
= rogue

der **Schenkel**, *plural* Schenkel
= thigh

schenken *verb*
= to give

die **Schere**, *plural* Scheren
- = (pair of) scissors
- (*of a crab*) = claw

der **Scherz**, *plural* Scherze
= joke

scheu *adjective*
= shy

scheuern *verb*
- = to scrub
- = to rub

die **Scheune**, *plural* Scheunen
= barn

der **Schi**, *plural* Schier
▶Ski

die **Schicht**, *plural* Schichten
- = layer
- = class
- = shift

schick *adjective*
- = chic, = stylish
- ein schickes Auto✱ = a great car

schicken *verb*
= to send

das **Schicksal**, *plural* Schicksale
= fate

das **Schiebedach**, *plural* Schiebedächer
= sun-roof

schieben *irregular verb*
- = to push
etwas auf jemanden schieben = to blame
somebody for something
- schieben✱ = to deal in

der **Schiedsrichter**, *plural* Schiedsrichter
= referee, = umpire

S

schief
1 *adjective*
= crooked
2 *adverb*
das Bild hängt schief = the picture is not straight

schielen *verb*
= to squint

schien ▶ scheinen

das **Schienbein**, *plural* Schienbeine
= shin

die **Schiene**, *plural* Schienen
* = rail
 = runner
* = splint

schießen *irregular verb*
* = to shoot
* ein Tor schießen = to score a goal
* schießen✗ (**!** *sein*) (*rush*) = to shoot

das **Schiff**, *plural* Schiffe
* = ship
* (*in a church*) = nave

schikanieren *verb*
= to bully

das **Schild**, *plural* Schilder
* = sign
* = badge
* = label

die **Schildkröte**, *plural* Schildkröten
= tortoise
= turtle

der **Schimmel**, *plural* Schimmel
* = mould, = mold
* = white horse

der **Schimpanse**, *plural* Schimpansen
= chimpanzee

schimpfen *verb*
* = to grumble
* = to tell off

der **Schinken**, *plural* Schinken
= ham

der **Schirm**, *plural* Schirme
= umbrella
= shade
= sunshade

der **Schlaf**
= sleep

der **Schlafanzug**, *plural* Schlafanzüge
= pyjamas, = pajamas

schlafen *irregular verb*
= to sleep
= to be asleep
schlafen gehen = to go to bed

der **Schlafsaal**, *plural* Schlafsäle
= dormitory

der **Schlafsack**, *plural* Schlafsäcke
= sleeping bag

das **Schlafzimmer**, *plural* Schlafzimmer
= bedroom

der **Schlag**, *plural* Schläge
* = blow
 Schläge kriegen = to get a beating
 Schlag auf Schlag = all at once
* (*in sport*) = shot, = stroke
* (*of the heart*) = beat
* (*electric*) = shock

schlagen *irregular verb*
* = to hit
* = to beat
* = to bang
* (*of a clock*) = to strike
* sich schlagen = to fight

der **Schlager**, *plural* Schlager
= hit

der **Schläger**, *plural* Schläger
(*in tennis*) = racket
(*in baseball*) = bat
(*in golf*) = club
(*in hockey*) = stick

die **Schlagsahne**
= whipping cream
= whipped cream

die **Schlagzeile**, *plural* Schlagzeilen
= headline

der **Schlamm**
= mud

schlampig *adjective*
= sloppy

die **Schlange**, *plural* Schlangen
* = snake
* = queue, = line
 Schlange stehen = to queue, = to stand in line

schlank *adjective*
= slim

schlau *adjective*
* = crafty
* = clever

der **Schlauch**, *plural* Schläuche
= hose, = tube

schlecht *adjective*
* = bad
* mir ist schlecht = I feel sick
* es geht ihr schlecht = she's not well

schleichen *irregular verb* (**!** *sein*)
* = to creep
 = to crawl
* sich schleichen = to creep

✗ in informal situations   ⃝LD = old spelling

die **Schleife**, *plural* Schleifen
- = bow
- = loop

schleifen¹ *verb*
= to drag

schleifen² *irregular verb*
= to sharpen

schleimig *adjective*
= slimy

schleppen *verb*
= to drag
= to tow

der **Schlepplift**, *plural* Schlepplifte
= T-bar lift

schleudern *verb*
- = to hurl
- (*of a washing machine*) = to spin
- (**!** *sein*) = to skid

schlicht *adjective*
= plain, = simple

schlief ▶ schlafen

schließen *irregular verb*
- = to close (down)
- = to lock
- = to conclude
  einen Vertrag schließen = to enter into a
  contract
- sich schließen = to close

das **Schließfach**, *plural* Schließfächer
= locker

schließlich *adverb*
- = finally
- = after all

schlimm *adjective*
= bad

der **Schlips**, *plural* Schlipse
= tie

der **Schlitten**, *plural* Schlitten
= sledge, = toboggan

der **Schlittschuh**, *plural* Schlittschuhe
= [ice-]skate
Schlittschuh laufen = to [ice-]skate

das **Schlittschuhlaufen**
= ice-skating

der **Schlitz**, *plural* Schlitze
- = slit, = slot
- (*in trousers*) = flies

schloss (**schloß**⟨OLD⟩) ▶ schließen

das **Schloss** (**Schloß**⟨OLD⟩), *plural*
Schlösser
- = lock
- = castle

der **Schluck**, *plural* Schlucke
- = mouthful
- = gulp

der **Schluckauf**
= hiccups

schlucken *verb*
= to swallow

schlug ▶ schlagen

der **Schlüpfer**, *plural* Schlüpfer
= knickers

der **Schluss** (**Schluß**⟨OLD⟩), *plural* Schlüsse
- = end, = ending
- = conclusion

der **Schlüssel**, *plural* Schlüssel
- = key
- = spanner

schmal *adjective*
- = narrow
- = thin

schmecken *verb*
= to taste

schmeicheln *verb*
= to flatter

schmeißen* *irregular verb*
= to chuck
mit etwas schmeißen = to chuck
something

schmelzen *irregular verb*
= to melt

der **Schmerz**, *plural* Schmerzen
- = pain
- = grief

schmerzen *verb*
= to hurt

schmerzhaft *adjective*
= painful

das **Schmerzmittel**, *plural* Schmerzmittel
= painkiller

der **Schmetterling**, *plural* Schmetterlinge
= butterfly

schmieren *verb*
- = to lubricate
- (*with butter*) = to spread
- = to scrawl
- = to smudge

die **Schminke**, *plural* Schminken
= make-up

schmiss (**schmiß**⟨OLD⟩) ▶ schmeißen

der **Schmuck**
- = jewellery, = jewelry
- = decoration

schmücken *verb*
= to decorate

schmuggeln *verb*
= to smuggle

schmusen *verb*
= to cuddle

S

der **Schmutz**
= dirt

schmutzig adjective
= dirty

der **Schnabel**, plural Schnäbel
= beak

die **Schnalle**, plural Schnallen
= buckle

schnarchen verb
= to snore

die **Schnauze**, plural Schnauzen
• = snout, = muzzle
• die Schnauze halten✱ = to keep one's
  mouth shut

die **Schnecke**, plural Schnecken
= snail

der **Schnee**
= snow

schneiden irregular verb
= to cut
= to slice
Gesichter schneiden = to pull faces

der **Schneider**, plural Schneider
= tailor

die **Schneiderin**, plural Schneiderinnen
= dressmaker

schneien verb
= to snow

schnell adjective
= quick, = fast

der **Schnellzug**, plural Schnellzüge
= express (train)

schnitt ▶schneiden

das **Schnitzel**, plural Schnitzel
• = escalope
• = scrap

schnitzen verb
= to carve

der **Schnorchel**, plural Schnorchel
= snorkel

der **Schnuller**, plural Schnuller
= dummy, = pacifier

der **Schnupfen**, plural Schnupfen
= cold

die **Schnur**, plural Schnüre
• = (piece of) string
• = cord
• = flex

der **Schnurrbart**, plural Schnurrbärte
= moustache, = mustache

der **Schnürsenkel**, plural Schnürsenkel
= (shoe)lace

die **Schokolade**, plural Schokoladen
= chocolate

schon adverb
• = already
  komm schon! = come on!
• = even
  das ist schon möglich = that's quite
  possible
• = just
  schon deshalb = for that reason alone

schön adjective
• = beautiful
• = nice
• = good
  na schön = all right then

schonen verb
• = to look after
• sich schonen = to take things easy

die **Schönheit**, plural Schönheiten
= beauty

der **Schornstein**, plural Schornsteine
= chimney, = funnel

schoss (schoß OLD**)** ▶schießen

der **Schoß**, plural Schöße
= lap

der **Schotte**, plural Schotten
= Scot, = Scotsman

die **Schottin**, plural Schottinnen
= Scot, = Scotswoman

schottisch adjective
= Scottish

(das) **Schottland**
= Scotland

schräg adjective
= diagonal
= sloping

der **Schrank**, plural Schränke
= cupboard, = wardrobe

die **Schraube**, plural Schrauben
= screw

schrauben verb
= to screw

der **Schraubenzieher**, plural
Schraubenzieher
= screwdriver

der **Schreck**, plural Schrecke
= fright

schrecklich adjective
= terrible

der **Schrei**, plural Schreie
= cry, = shout
der letzte Schrei✱ = the latest thing

✱ in informal situations   OLD = old spelling

schreiben *irregular verb*
* = to write
wie schreibt man das? = how is it spelt?
* = to type

die **Schreibkraft**, *plural* Schreibkräfte
= typist

die **Schreibmaschine**, *plural*
Schreibmaschinen
= typewriter

der **Schreibtisch**, *plural* Schreibtische
= desk

Schreibwaren (*plural*)
= stationery

schreien *irregular verb*
= to cry, = to shout

schrieb ▶ schreiben

die **Schrift**, *plural* Schriften
* = writing
= script
* = type

schriftlich
1 *adjective* = written
2 *adverb* = in writing

der **Schriftsteller**, *plural* Schriftsteller
= writer

die **Schriftstellerin**, *plural*
Schriftstellerinnen
= writer

der **Schritt**, *plural* Schritte
= step

der **Schrott**
= scrap (metal)

die **Schublade**, *plural* Schubladen
= drawer

schubsen *verb*
= to shove

schüchtern *adjective*
= shy

der **Schuh**, *plural* Schuhe
= shoe

das **Schuhwerk**
= shoes

die **Schuld**, *plural* Schulden
* = blame
es ist nicht seine Schuld = it is not his
fault
* = guilt
* = debt
Schulden haben = to be in debt

schulden *verb*
= to owe

schuldig *adjective*
* = guilty
* jemandem etwas schuldig sein = to owe
someone something

die **Schule**, *plural* Schulen
= school

schulen *verb*
= to train

der **Schüler**, *plural* Schüler
= pupil
= student
= schoolboy

die **Schülerin**, *plural* Schülerinnen
= pupil
= student
= schoolgirl

schulfrei *adjective*
ein schulfreier Tag = a day off school

der **Schulhof**, *plural* Schulhöfe
= playground

die **Schulter**, *plural* Schultern
= shoulder

schummeln* *verb*
= to cheat

die **Schuppe**, *plural* Schuppen
= scale
Schuppen = dandruff

die **Schürze**, *plural* Schürzen
= apron

der **Schuss** (**Schuß**ⓞⓛⓓ), *plural* Schüsse
* = shot
* (*small amount*) = dash
* (*in skiing*) = schuss

die **Schüssel**, *plural* Schüsseln
= bowl, = dish

der **Schuster**, *plural* Schuster
= shoemaker

schütteln *verb*
= to shake

schütten *verb*
* = to pour
= to tip
* es schüttet = it is pouring (with rain)

der **Schutz**
= protection
= shelter

der **Schütze**, *plural* Schützen
* = marksman
* = Sagittarius

schützen *verb*
= to protect

schwach *adjective*
* = weak
* = poor

die **Schwäche**, *plural* Schwächen
= weakness

der **Schwager**, *plural* Schwäger
= brother-in-law

S

die **Schwägerin**, plural Schwägerinnen
= sister-in-law

die **Schwalbe**, plural Schwalben
= swallow

der **Schwamm**, plural Schwämme
= sponge

der **Schwan**, plural Schwäne
= swan

schwanger adjective
= pregnant

die **Schwangerschaft**, plural
Schwangerschaften
= pregnancy

schwanken verb
• = to sway
• = to fluctuate
• = to waver
• (! sein) = to stagger

der **Schwanz**, plural Schwänze
= tail

schwänzen✷ verb
= to skip
die Schule schwänzen = to play truant or
hookey

der **Schwarm**, plural Schwärme
= swarm

schwarz
1 adjective
= black
ins Schwarze treffen = to hit the nail on
the head
2 adverb = illegally

schweben verb
• in Gefahr schweben = to be in danger
• (! sein) = to float

(das) **Schweden**
= Sweden

schwedisch adjective
= Swedish

schweigen irregular verb
= to be silent, = to say nothing

das **Schwein**, plural Schweine
• = pig
(meat) = pork
• du Schwein!✷ = you swine!
• Schwein haben✷ = to be lucky

das **Schweinefleisch**
= pork

der **Schweiß**
= sweat

die **Schweiz**
= Switzerland

der **Schweizer**, plural Schweizer
= Swiss

die **Schweizerin**, plural Schweizerinnen
= Swiss

schweizerisch adjective
= Swiss

schwer adjective
• = heavy
zwei Kilo schwer sein = to weigh 2 kilos
• = difficult
• (of an injury) = serious
• schwer arbeiten = to work hard
• jemandem schwer fallen = to be hard for
someone

schwerhörig adjective
= hard of hearing

das **Schwert**, plural Schwerter
= sword

die **Schwester**, plural Schwestern
• = sister
• = nurse

Schwiegereltern (plural)
= parents-in-law

die **Schwiegermutter**, plural
Schwiegermütter
= mother-in-law

der **Schwiegervater**, plural
Schwiegerväter
= father-in-law

schwierig adjective
= difficult

die **Schwierigkeit**, plural Schwierigkeiten
= difficulty

das **Schwimmbad**, plural Schwimmbäder
= swimming baths

das **Schwimmbecken**, plural
Schwimmbecken
= swimming pool

schwimmen irregular verb (! sein)
• = to swim
• = to float

die **Schwimmweste**, plural
Schwimmwesten
= life-jacket

schwindlig adjective
= dizzy

schwitzen verb
= to sweat

schwören irregular verb
= to swear

schwul✷ adjective
(homosexual) = gay

schwül adjective
= close

✷ in informal situations

der **Schwung**, *plural* Schwünge
• = swing
• *(of a person)* = drive

scrollen *verb*
= to scroll

sechs *adjective*
= six

sechseckig *adjective*
= hexagonal

sechster/sechste/sechstes
adjective
= sixth

sechzehn *adjective*
= sixteen

sechzig *adjective*
= sixty

der **See¹** *plural* Seen
= lake

die **See²**
= sea

die **Seele**, *plural* Seelen
= soul

der **Seemann**, *plural* Seeleute
= seaman, = sailor

das **Segel**, *plural* Segel
= sail

das **Segelboot**, *plural* Segelboote
– sailing boat, – sailboat

segeln *verb* (**!** *sein*)
= to sail

segnen *verb*
= to bless

sehen *irregular verb*
= to see, = to look
nach jemandem sehen = to look after
someone

die **Sehenswürdigkeit**, *plural*
Sehenswürdigkeiten
= sight

die **Sehnsucht**
= longing

sehr *adverb*
= very
danke sehr = thank you very much

seid ▶ sein

die **Seide**, *plural* Seiden
= silk

die **Seife**, *plural* Seifen
= soap

das **Seil**, *plural* Seile
= rope, = cable

die **Seilbahn**, *plural* Seilbahnen
= cable railway

sein¹ *irregular verb* (**!** *sein*)
• = to be
wie dem auch sei = be that as it may
aus Wolle sein = to be made of wool
mir ist schlecht = I feel sick
• sein lassen = to stop
lass das sein! = stop it!
• *(forming the perfect tense)*
sie ist angekommen = she (has) arrived
wir sind gerettet worden = we were saved

sein² *adjective*
= his
(of a thing) = its
(referring to the German pronoun 'man')
= one's

seiner/seine/seins *pronoun*
= his
(referring to the German pronoun 'man')
= one's own

seinlassen ▶ sein¹

seins ▶ seiner

seit
1 *preposition* (+ *dative*) = since
ich bin seit zwei Wochen hier = I've been
here for two weeks
2 *conjunction* = since

seitdem
1 *conjunction* = since
2 *adverb* = since then

die **Seite**, *plural* Seiten
• = side
auf der einen Seite = on the one hand
• = page

seither *adverb*
= since then

die **Sekretärin**, *plural* Sekretärinnen
= secretary

die **Sekunde**, *plural* Sekunden
= second

selbst
1 *pronoun*
ich/du/er/sie/es selbst = I myself/you
yourself/he himself/she herself/it itself
wir/ihr/sie selbst = we ourselves/you
yourselves/they themselves
Sie selbst = you yourself/you yourselves
von selbst = automatically, = by itself
2 *adverb* = even

selbständig *adjective*
• = independent
• = self-employed
sich selbständig machen = to set up on
one's own

die **Selbstbedienung**
= self-service

S

selbstbewusst
(**selbstbewußt**ⓞⓛⒹ) *adjective*
= self-confident

der **Selbstmord**, *plural* Selbstmorde
= suicide

selbstständig *adjective* ▶selbständig

selbstverständlich
1 *adjective* = natural
2 *adverb* = naturally, = of course

das **Selbstvertrauen**
= self-confidence

selten
1 *adjective* = rare
2 *adverb* = rarely

seltsam *adjective*
= strange, = odd

das **Semester**, *plural* Semester
= semester, = term

die **Semmel**, *plural* Semmeln
= roll

senden *verb*
• = to send
• = to broadcast, = to transmit

die **Sendung**, *plural* Sendungen
• = programme
• = consignment

der **Senf**, *plural* Senfe
= mustard

der **Senior**, *plural* Senioren
• = senior
• = senior citizen

senken *verb*
• = to lower
• sich senken = to come down

senkrecht *adjective*
= vertical

der **September**
= September

die **Serie**, *plural* Serien
= series, = serial

der **Server**, *plural* Server
= server

servieren *verb*
= to serve

die **Serviette**, *plural* Servietten
= napkin, = serviette

der **Sessel**, *plural* Sessel
= armchair

der **Sessellift**, *plural* Sessellifte
= chair-lift

setzen *verb*
• = to put , = to set down

• (*in games*) = to move
• = to bet
• sich setzen = to sit (down)

seufzen *verb*
= to sigh

sexuell *adjective*
= sexual

sich *pronoun*
• (*as part of a reflexive verb*)
(*with er|sie|es*) = himself|herself|itself
(*with plural sie*) = themselves
(*with Sie*) = yourself, (*plural*) = yourselves
(*referring to one*) = oneself
sich freuen = to be pleased
sich die Haare kämmen = to comb one's
hair
• = each other, = one another

sicher
1 *adjective*
• = safe
• = certain, = sure
2 *adverb*
• = safely
• = certainly, = surely
sicher! = certainly!

die **Sicherheit**
• = safety
• = security
• = certainty

der **Sicherheitsgurt**, *plural*
Sicherheitsgurte
= seatbelt

die **Sicherheitsnadel**, *plural*
Sicherheitsnadeln
= safety-pin

sicherlich *adverb*
= certainly

die **Sicherung**, *plural* Sicherungen
• = safeguard
• = safety catch
• = fuse

die **Sicht**
• = view
auf lange Sicht = in the long term
• = visibility

sichtbar *adjective*
= visible

sie *pronoun*
(*singular*) = she, (*accusative*) = her
(*thing*) = it
(*plural*) = they, (*accusative*) = them

Sie *pronoun*
= you
warten Sie! = wait!

das **Sieb**, *plural* Siebe
= sieve, = strainer

sieben *adjective*
= seven

siebter/siebte/siebtes *adjective*
= seventh

siebzehn *adjective*
= seventeen

siebzig *adjective*
= seventy

die **Siedlung**, *plural* Siedlungen
• = (housing) estate
• = settlement

der **Sieg**, *plural* Siege
= victory, = win

das **Siegel**, *plural* Siegel
= seal

der **Sieger**, *plural* Sieger
= winner

die **Siegerin**, *plural* Siegerinnen
= winner

sieht ▶sehen

die **Silbe**, *plural* Silben
= syllable

das **Silber**
= silver

silbern *adjective*
= silver

das **Silvester**
= New Year's Eve

die **Sim-Karte**, *plural* Sim-Karten
= SIM-card

sind ▶sein

singen *irregular verb*
= to sing

sinken *irregular verb* (**!** *sein*)
• = to sink, = to go down

der **Sinn**, *plural* Sinne
• = sense, = meaning
• = point
es hat keinen Sinn = there's no point

sinnlos *adjective*
= pointless

sinnvoll *adjective*
• = sensible
• = meaningful

die **Sitte**, *plural* Sitten
• = custom
• Sitten = manners

die **Situation**, *plural* Situationen
= situation

der **Sitz**, *plural* Sitze
• = seat
• (*of clothes*) = fit

sitzen *irregular verb*
• = to sit
• = to fit

der **Sitzplatz**, *plural* Sitzplätze
= seat

die **Sitzung**, *plural* Sitzungen
• = meeting
• = session

das **Skelett**, *plural* Skelette
= skeleton

der **Ski**, *plural* Skier *or* Ski
= ski
Ski fahren *or* laufen = to ski

das **Skifahren**, das **Skilaufen**
= skiing

der **Skiläufer**, *plural* Skiläufer
= skier

die **Skiläuferin**, *plural* Skiläuferinnen
= skier

die **Skizze**, *plural* Skizzen
= sketch

der **Skorpion**, *plural* Skorpione
• = scorpion
• = Scorpio

der **Slip**, *plural* Slips
= briefs

die **Slowakei**
= Slovakia

der **Smaragd**, *plural* Smaragde
= emerald

der **Smoking**, *plural* Smokings
= dinner jacket, = tuxedo

so
1 *adverb*
• = so
• = like this, = like that
gut so = that's fine
• = as
so gut ich konnte = as best I could
• so = such
so ein Zufall! = what a coincidence!
2 *conjunction*
so dass = so that

sobald *conjunction*
= as soon as

die **Socke**, *plural* Socken
= sock

sodass *conjunction*
= so that

sofort *adverb*
• = immediately
• = in a moment

die **Sohle**, *plural* Sohlen
= sole

der **Sohn**, *plural* Söhne
= son

solange *conjunction*
= as long as

S

solch *pronoun*
= such

solcher/solche/solches
1 *adjective* = such
eine solche Frau = a woman like that
2 *pronoun*
solche wie die = people like that

der **Soldat**, *plural* Soldaten
= soldier

sollen *irregular verb*
* = should
* = be supposed to
was soll das heißen? = what is that
supposed to mean?
* (*other uses*)
er soll warten = let him wait
sagen Sie ihm, er soll hereinkommen =
tell him to come in

sollte, sollten, solltest, solltet
▶ sollen

der **Sommer**, *plural* Sommer
= summer

sommerlich *adjective*
= summery, = summer

die **Sommersprosse**, *plural*
Sommersprossen
= freckle

das **Sonderangebot**, *plural*
Sonderangebote
= special offer

sonderbar *adjective*
= odd, = strange

sondern *conjunction*
= but

der **Sonnabend**
= Saturday

sonnabends *adverb*
= on Saturdays

die **Sonne**, *plural* Sonnen
= sun

der **Sonnenaufgang**
= sunrise

der **Sonnenbrand**
= sunburn

die **Sonnenbrille**, *plural* Sonnenbrillen
= sunglasses

der **Sonnenschein**
= sunshine

der **Sonnenschirm**, *plural* Sonnenschirme
= sunshade

der **Sonnenstich**
= sunstroke

der **Sonnenuntergang**
= sunset

sonnig *adjective*
= sunny

der **Sonntag**
= Sunday

sonntags *adverb*
= on Sundays

sonst *adverb*
* = usually
* = else
sonst noch was? = anything else?
sonst niemand = no one else
* = otherwise

sooft *conjunction*
= whenever

die **Sorge**, *plural* Sorgen
= worry
sich Sorgen machen = to worry

sorgen *verb*
* für etwas sorgen = to take care of
something
dafür sorgen, dass = to make sure that
* sich sorgen = to worry

sorgfältig *adjective*
= careful

die **Sorte**, *plural* Sorten
= sort, = kind

die **Soße**, *plural* Soßen
= sauce, = gravy
= dressing

soviel
1 *conjunction* = as far as
2 *adverb* ⃝ᴸᴰ ▶ viel

sowenig ⃝ᴸᴰ ▶ wenig

sowie *conjunction*
* = as well as
* = as soon as

sowieso *adverb*
= anyway

sowohl *adverb*
sowohl er wie auch sie = both he and she

der **Sozialarbeiter**, *plural* Sozialarbeiter
= social worker

sozialistisch *adjective*
= socialist

die **Sozialwohnung**, *plural*
Sozialwohnungen
= council flat

die **Soziologie**
= sociology

die **Spalte**, *plural* Spalten
* = crack
* (*in text*) = column

(das) **Spanien**
= Spain

spanisch *adjective*
= Spanish

spannend *adjective*
= exciting

die **Spannung**, *plural* Spannungen
• = tension, = voltage

sparen *verb*
= to save
auf etwas sparen = to save up for
something

sparsam *adjective*
• = economical, = thrifty

der **Spaß**, *plural* Späße
• = fun
es macht mir Spaß = I enjoy it
viel Spaß! = have a good time!
• = joke

spät *adjective*
= late
wie spät ist es? = what time is it?

der **Spaten**, *plural* Spaten
= spade

später *adjective*
= later

spätestens *adverb*
= at the latest

der **Spatz**, *plural* Spatzen
= sparrow

spazieren *verb* (**!** *sein*)
• to stroll
• spazieren gehen = to go for a walk

der **Spaziergang**, *plural* Spaziergänge
= walk

der **Speck**
= bacon

der **Speicher**, *plural* Speicher
• = loft, = attic
• (*of a computer*) = memory

speichern *verb*
• = to store
• (*computing*) = to save

der **Speicherstab**, *plural* Speicherstäbe
= memory stick

die **Speise**, *plural* Speisen
• = food
• = dish

die **Speisekarte**, *plural* Speisekarten
= menu

die **Spende**, *plural* Spenden
= donation

spenden *verb*
= to donate
= to give, = to contribute

sperren
= to close
= to block
den Strom sperren = to cut off the
electricity
einen Scheck sperren = to stop a cheque

Spesen (*plural*)
= expenses

der **Spiegel**, *plural* Spiegel
= mirror

das **Spiegelbild**, *plural* Spiegelbilder
= reflection

spiegeln *verb*
• = to reflect
• sich spiegeln = to be reflected

das **Spiel**, *plural* Spiele
= game
auf dem Spiel stehen = to be at stake
ein Spiel Karten = a pack of cards

spielen *verb*
• = to play
• = to gamble
• = to act
der Film spielt in Berlin = the film is set
in Berlin

die **Spielhalle**, *plural* Spielhallen
= amusement arcade

der **Spielplatz**, *plural* Spielplätze
= playground

das **Spielzeug**
• = toy
• = toys

der **Spinat**
= spinach

die **Spinne**, *plural* Spinnen
= spider

spinnen *irregular verb*
• = to spin
• sie spinnt✖ = she's crazy

das **Spinnennetz**, *plural* Spinnennetze
= spider's web, = cobweb

der **Spion**, *plural* Spione
= spy

spitz *adjective*
= pointed

die **Spitze**, *plural* Spitzen
• = point, = tip
• = top, = peak
Spitze sein✖ = to be great
• = front
an der Spitze liegen = to be in the lead
• = lace

der **Spitzname**, *plural* Spitznamen
= nickname

der **Splitter**, *plural* Splitter
= splinter

S

der **Sportler**, *plural* Sportler
= sportsman

die **Sportlerin**, *plural* Sportlerinnen
= sportswoman

sportlich *adjective*
= sporting
= sporty

der **Sportwagen**, *plural* Sportwagen
* = sports car
* = pushchair, = stroller

spotten *verb*
= to mock

sprach ▶sprechen

die **Sprache**, *plural* Sprachen
* = language
* = speech
etwas zur Sprache bringen = to bring
something up

sprang ▶springen

sprechen *irregular verb*
= to speak, = to talk

die **Sprechstunde**, *plural* Sprechstunden
= surgery

der **Sprengstoff**, *plural* Sprengstoffe
= explosive

spricht ▶sprechen

das **Sprichwort**, *plural* Sprichwörter
= proverb

springen *irregular verb* (**!** *sein*)
* = to jump, = to bounce
* = to dive

die **Spritze**, *plural* Spritzen
* = syringe
* = injection
* = hose

spritzen *verb*
* = to inject
* = to spray
= to splash
(*of fat*) = to spit

der **Spruch**, *plural* Sprüche
= saying

der **Sprudel**, *plural* Sprudel
= sparkling mineral water

sprühen *verb*
* = to spray
* (*of eyes*) = to sparkle
* (*of sparks*) = to fly

der **Sprung**, *plural* Sprünge
* = jump, = leap
* = dive
* (*in china*) = crack

das **Sprungbrett**, *plural* Sprungbretter
= diving board

spucken *verb*
= to spit

das **Spülbecken**, *plural* Spülbecken
= sink

spülen *verb*
* = to rinse
* = to wash up
* = to flush

die **Spur**, *plural* Spuren
* = track
* = lane
* = trail

spüren *verb*
= to sense, = to feel

der **Staat**, *plural* Staaten
= state

staatlich
1 *adjective* = state
2 *adverb* = by the state

die **Staatsangehörigkeit**
= nationality

stabil *adjective*
= stable
= sturdy

der **Stachel**, *plural* Stacheln
* = spine
* = spike
* = sting

die **Stachelbeere**, *plural* Stachelbeeren
= gooseberry

das **Stadion**, *plural* Stadien
= stadium

das **Stadium**, *plural* Stadien
= stage

die **Stadt**, *plural* Städte
= town, = city

städtisch *adjective*
= urban, = municipal

die **Stadtmitte**
= town centre, = downtown area

der **Stadtplan**, *plural* Stadtpläne
= street map

stahl ▶stehlen

der **Stahl**
= steel

der **Stall**, *plural* Ställe
= stable
(*for cows*) = shed
(*for pigs*) = sty
(*for sheep*) = pen
(*for hens*) = coop
(*for rabbits*) = hutch

✗ in informal situations   ⃝ᴸᴰ = old spelling

der **Stamm**, plural Stämme
- = trunk
- = tribe

stand ▶stehen

ständig adjective
= constant

die **Stange**, plural Stangen
= bar
= pole

starb ▶sterben

stark adjective
- = strong
- = severe, = heavy
- das ist stark✶ = that's great

die **Stärke**, plural Stärken
- = strength, = power
- = starch

starrsinnig adjective
= obstinate

der **Start**, plural Starts
- = start
- = take-off

die **Startbahn**, plural Startbahnen
= runway

die **Station**, plural Stationen
- = station
- = stop
  Station machen = to stop over
- (in a hospital) = ward

statt
1 preposition (+ genitive) = instead of
2 conjunction
  statt zu arbeiten = instead of working

stattdessen adverb
= instead

statt|finden irregular verb
= to take place

der **Stau**, plural Staus
- = congestion
- = traffic jam, = tailback

der **Staub**
= dust

der **Staubsauger**, plural Staubsauger
= vacuum cleaner, = Hoover®

staunen verb
= to be amazed

stechen irregular verb
- = to prick
- = to stab
- (of an insect) = to sting, = to bite

die **Steckdose**, plural Steckdosen
= socket

stecken verb
= to put

der **Stecker**, plural Stecker
= plug

die **Stecknadel**, plural Stecknadeln
= pin

stehen irregular verb
- = to stand
- = to be
  es steht schlecht um ihn = he is in a bad
  way
- (! sein) stehen bleiben = to stop
  das Spiel steht eins zu eins = the score is
  one all
  in der Zeitung steht = it says in the paper
- die Uhr steht = the clock has stopped
- jemandem (gut) stehen = to suit someone
- zu jemandem stehen = to stand by
  someone

stehen bleiben ⓞⓛⓓ▶stehen

stehlen irregular verb
= to steal

steif adjective
= stiff

steigen irregular verb (! sein)
= to climb
in den Bus steigen = to get on the bus

steigern verb
- = to raise, = to boost
- sich steigern = to increase

steil adjective
= steep

der **Stein**, plural Steine
= stone

der **Steinbock**, plural Steinböcke
- = ibex
- = Capricorn

die **Stelle**, plural Stellen
- = place
  an Stelle = instead of
  auf der Stelle = immediately
- = job, = post

stellen verb
- = to put, = to place
  etwas zur Verfügung stellen = to provide
  something
- eine Uhr stellen = to set a clock
  die Heizung höher stellen = to turn the
  heating up
- sich krank stellen = to pretend to be ill

die **Stellenanzeige**, plural
  Stellenanzeigen
= job advertisement

die **Stellung**, plural Stellungen
= position

der **Stellvertreter**, plural Stellvertreter
= deputy

der **Stempel**, plural Stempel
- = stamp
- = postmark
- = hallmark

S

stempeln *verb*
- = to stamp
- = to postmark

die **Steppdecke**, *plural* Steppdecken
= quilt

sterben *irregular verb* (**!** *sein*)
= to die

die **Stereoanlage**, *plural* Stereoanlagen
= stereo (system)

der **Stern**, *plural* Sterne
= star

die **Sternwarte**, *plural* Sternwarten
= observatory

das **Steuer¹** *plural* Steuer
- = steering wheel
- = helm

die **Steuer²** *plural* Steuern
= tax

die **Steuererklärung**, *plural*
Steuererklärungen
= tax return

steuerfrei *adjective*
= tax-free

steuern *verb*
- = to steer
- (*in an aircraft*) = to fly

steuerpflichtig *adjective*
= taxable

die **Steuerung**, *plural* Steuerungen
- = steering
- = controls

die **Stewardess** (**Stewardeß**Ⓞ),
plural Stewardessen
= stewardess, = air hostess

der **Stich**, *plural* Stiche
- (*with a needle*) = prick
- (*with a knife*) = stab
- (*of an insect*) = sting, = bite
- (*when sewing*) = stitch
- (*when playing cards*) = trick
- jemanden im Stich lassen = to leave someone in the lurch

sticken *verb*
= to embroider

der **Stiefbruder**, *plural* Stiefbrüder
= stepbrother

der **Stiefel**, *plural* Stiefel
= boot

das **Stiefkind**, *plural* Stiefkinder
= stepchild

die **Stiefmutter**, *plural* Stiefmütter
= stepmother

das **Stiefmütterchen**, *plural*
Stiefmütterchen
= pansy

die **Stiefschwester**, *plural*
Stiefschwestern
= stepsister

der **Stiefvater**, *plural* Stiefväter
= stepfather

stiehlt ▶ stehlen

der **Stiel**, *plural* Stiele
- = handle
- = stem

der **Stier**, *plural* Stiere
- = bull
- = Taurus

der **Stift**, *plural* Stifte
- (*nail*) = tack
- = pencil

der **Stil**, *plural* Stile
= style

still *adjective*
= quiet
= still

stillen *verb*
- = to satisfy
- = to quench
- = to breast-feed

die **Stimme**, *plural* Stimmen
- = voice
- = vote

stimmen *verb*
- = to be right
- stimmt das? = is that right?
- = to vote
- = to tune

die **Stimmung**, *plural* Stimmungen
= mood
= atmosphere

stinken *irregular verb*
= to smell, = to stink

stirbt ▶ sterben

die **Stirn**, *plural* Stirnen
= forehead

der **Stock¹** *plural* Stöcke
= stick

der **Stock²** *plural* Stock
= floor, = storey

das **Stockwerk**, *plural* Stockwerke
= floor, = storey

der **Stoff**, *plural* Stoffe
- = material
- = substance

stöhnen *verb*
= to groan, = to moan

stolpern verb
= to stumble, = to trip

stolz adjective
= proud

stopfen verb
• = to stuff
• = to darn

stoppen verb
= to stop

die **Stoppuhr**, plural Stoppuhren
= stopwatch

der **Stöpsel**, plural Stöpsel
• = plug
• = stopper

der **Storch**, plural Störche
= stork

stören verb
= to disturb, = to bother

die **Störung**, plural Störungen
= disturbance
eine technische Störung = a technical
fault
entschuldigen Sie die Störung = I'm sorry
to bother you

der **Stoß**, plural Stöße
• = push, = knock
• = pile, = stack

stoßen irregular verb
• = to push, = to knock
(with one's foot) = to kick
• (**!** sein) gegen etwas stoßen = to bump
into something
auf etwas stoßen = to come across
something
• sich stoßen = to knock oneself
sich an etwas stoßen = to object to
something

die **Stoßstange**, plural Stoßstangen
= bumper

die **Stoßzeit**, plural Stoßzeiten
= rush hour

stottern verb
= to stutter, = to stammer

die **Strafe**, plural Strafen
= punishment
= penalty, = fine
= sentence

der **Strahl**, plural Strahlen
• = ray, = beam
• (of water) = jet

strahlen verb
= to shine
= to beam

der **Strand**, plural Strände
= beach

die **Straße**, plural Straßen
= street, = road

die **Straßenbahn**, plural Straßenbahnen
= tram, = streetcar

der **Strauch**, plural Sträucher
= bush

der **Strauß**[1] plural Sträuße
= bunch of flowers, = bouquet

der **Strauß**[2] plural Strauße
= ostrich

die **Strecke**, plural Strecken
• = distance
• = route, = line

strecken verb
• = to stretch (out)
• sich strecken = to stretch

streicheln verb
= to stroke

streichen irregular verb
• = to paint
'frisch gestrichen' = 'wet paint'
• (with butter) = to spread
• = to delete, = to cross off
• jemandem über den Kopf streichen = to
stroke someone's head

das **Streichholz**, plural Streichhölzer
= match

die **Streife**, plural Streifen
= patrol

der **Streifen**, plural Streifen
• = stripe
• = strip

die **Streifenkarte**, plural Streifenkarten
= multiple ticket (for economy travel)

der **Streifenwagen**, plural Streifenwagen
= patrol car

der **Streik**, plural Streiks
= strike

streiken verb
= to strike

der **Streit**, plural Streite
= quarrel, = argument

streiten irregular verb
• = to quarrel, = to argue
• sich streiten = to quarrel, = to argue

Streitkräfte (plural)
= armed forces

streng adjective
= strict

der **Stress (Streß**ⓞⓛⒹ**)**
= stress

stressigˣ adjective
= stressful

S

streuen *verb*
= to spread
= to sprinkle

stricken *verb*
= to knit

die **Strickjacke**, *plural* Strickjacken
= cardigan

das **Stroh**
= straw

der **Strohhalm**, *plural* Strohhalme
= straw

der **Strom**, *plural* Ströme
* = river
* = stream
  es regnet in Strömen = it's pouring with
  rain
* = electricity

strömen *verb* (**!** *sein*)
= to stream

die **Strömung**, *plural* Strömungen
= current

der **Strumpf**, *plural* Strümpfe
* = stocking
* = sock

die **Strumpfhose**, *plural* Strumpfhosen
= tights, = pantyhose

die **Stube**, *plural* Stuben
= room

das **Stück**, *plural* Stücke
* = piece, = bit
* = item
  zwei Euro das Stück = two euros each
* = play

der **Student**, *plural* Studenten
= student

die **Studentin**, *plural* Studentinnen
= student

studieren *verb*
= to study

das **Studium**, *plural* Studien
= study
= studies

die **Stufe**, *plural* Stufen
= step

der **Stuhl**, *plural* Stühle
= chair

stumm *adjective*
* = dumb
* = silent

stumpf *adjective*
* = blunt
* = dull

✕ in informal situations

die **Stunde**, *plural* Stunden
* = hour
* = lesson

stundenlang *adverb*
= for hours

der **Stundenplan**, *plural* Stundenpläne
= timetable

stündlich *adjective*
= hourly

stur✕ *adjective*
= stubborn

der **Sturm**, *plural* Stürme
= storm

der **Stürmer**, *plural* Stürmer
= forward

stürmisch *adjective*
* = stormy
* = tumultuous

der **Sturz**, *plural* Stürze
= fall

stürzen *verb*
* (**!** *sein*) = to fall
* (**!** *sein*) = to rush
* = to overthrow
* sich in etwas stürzen = to throw oneself
  into something
  sich auf jemanden stürzen = to pounce
  on someone

der **Sturzhelm**, *plural* Sturzhelme
= crash helmet

stützen *verb*
= to support
sich auf jemanden stützen = to lean on
someone

suchen *verb*
* = to search
* = to look for
  'Zimmer gesucht' = 'room wanted'

süchtig *adjective*
= addicted

(das) **Südafrika**
= South Africa

der **Süden**
= south

südlich *adjective*
* = southern
* = southerly

der **Südosten**
= southeast

der **Südwesten**
= southwest

die **Summe**, *plural* Summen
= sum

summen *verb*
= to hum
= to buzz

super* adjective
= great

der **Supermarkt**, plural Supermärkte
= supermarket

die **Suppe**, plural Suppen
= soup

surfen verb
= to surf

süß adjective
= sweet

die **Süßigkeit**, plural Süßigkeiten
= sweet, = candy

Süßwaren (plural)
= confectionery
= sweets, = candy

sympathisch adjective
= likeable

die **Szene**, plural Szenen
= scene

Tt

der **Tabak**, plural Tabake
= tobacco

die **Tabelle**, plural Tabellen
= table

das **Tablett**, plural Tabletts
= tray

die **Tablette**, plural Tabletten
= tablet

die **Tafel**, plural Tafeln
• = board, = blackboard
• eine Tafel Schokolade = a bar of
  chocolate

der **Tag**, plural Tage
= day
guten Tag = good morning/afternoon

das **Tagebuch**, plural Tagebücher
= diary

tagelang adverb
= for days

die **Tageskarte**, plural Tageskarten
• = today's menu
• = day ticket

die **Tagesmutter**, plural Tagesmütter
= childminder

die **Tagesschau**
= news

täglich
1 adjective = daily
2 adverb
zweimal täglich = twice a day

tagsüber adverb
= during the day

die **Taille**, plural Taillen
= waist

der **Takt**, plural Takte
• = tact
• = time, = rhythm

taktlos adjective
= tactless

taktvoll adjective
= tactful

das **Tal**, plural Täler
= valley

tanken verb
= to fill up (with petrol)

die **Tankstelle**, plural Tankstellen
= petrol station, = gas station

die **Tanne**, plural Tannen
= fir

der **Tannenbaum**, plural Tannenbäume
= fir tree

die **Tante**, plural Tanten
= aunt

der **Tanz**, plural Tänze
= dance

tanzen verb
= to dance

der **Tänzer**, plural Tänzer
= dancer

die **Tänzerin**, plural Tänzerinnen
= dancer

die **Tapete**, plural Tapeten
= wallpaper

tapfer adjective
= brave

die **Tasche**, plural Taschen
• = bag
• = pocket

das **Taschenbuch**, plural Taschenbücher
= paperback

das **Taschengeld**
= pocket money

die **Taschenlampe**, plural
Taschenlampen
= torch, = flashlight

das **Taschenmesser**, plural
Taschenmesser
= penknife

T

das **Taschentuch**, *plural* Taschentücher
= handkerchief

die **Tasse**, *plural* Tassen
= cup

die **Taste**, *plural* Tasten
• = key
• (*on a phone*) = button

tasten *verb*
• = to feel
• sich tasten = to feel one's way

das **Tastentelefon**, *plural* Tastentelefone
= push-button phone

tat ▶ tun

die **Tat**, *plural* Taten
• = action
in der Tat = indeed
• crime

der **Täter**, *plural* Täter
= culprit
= offender

die **Tätigkeit**, *plural* Tätigkeiten
= activity
= job

die **Tatsache**, *plural* Tatsachen
= fact

tatsächlich
1 *adjective* = actual
2 *adverb* = actually

der **Tau**¹
= dew

das **Tau**² *plural* Taue
= rope

taub *adjective*
= deaf

die **Taube**, *plural* Tauben
= dove, = pigeon

tauchen *verb*
• = to dive
• = to dip

der **Taucher**, *plural* Taucher
= diver

die **Taucherin**, *plural* Taucherinnen
= diver

tauen *verb*
= to melt, = to thaw

die **Taufe**, *plural* Taufen
= christening
= baptism

taufen *verb*
= to christen
= to baptize

tauschen *verb*
= to exchange, = to swap

täuschen *verb*
• = to deceive
• sich täuschen = to be mistaken

tausend *adjective*
= a thousand, = one thousand

das **Taxi**, *plural* Taxis
= taxi

der **Taxistand**, *plural* Taxistände
= taxi rank, = taxi stand

die **Technik**, *plural* Techniken
• = technology
• = technique

der **Techniker**, *plural* Techniker
= technician

technisch *adjective*
= technical
= technological

der **Tee**, *plural* Tees
= tea

der **Teich**, *plural* Teiche
= pond

der **Teig**, *plural* Teige
= dough
= pastry
(*for baking*) = mixture

der **Teil**¹ *plural* Teile
• = part
zum Teil = partly
• = share

das **Teil**² *plural* Teile
• = part
• = spare part
• = share

teilen *verb*
• = to divide
• = to share
• sich etwas mit jemandem teilen = to
share something with someone

teil|nehmen *irregular verb*
an etwas teilnehmen = to take part in
something

der **Teilnehmer**, *plural* Teilnehmer,
die **Teilnehmerin**, *plural* Teilnehmerinnen
• = participant
• = competitor

teils *adverb*
= partly

die **Teilung**, *plural* Teilungen
= division

die **Teilzeitarbeit**
= part-time work

das **Telefax**, *plural* Telefax *or* Telefaxe
= fax

das **Telefon**, *plural* Telefone
= telephone

das **Telefonbuch**, *plural* Telefonbücher
= telephone directory, = phone book

telefonieren *verb*
= to telephone, = to make a phone call

telefonisch
1 *adjective* = telephone
2 *adverb* = by telephone

die **Telefonkarte**, *plural* Telefonkarten
= phone card

die **Telefonzelle**, *plural* Telefonzellen
= telephone box, = telephone booth

telegrafieren *verb*
= to send a telegram

der **Teller**, *plural* Teller
= plate

der **Tempel**, *plural* Tempel
= temple

die **Temperatur**, *plural* Temperaturen
= temperature

das **Tempo**, *plural* Tempos
= speed

das **Tennis**
= tennis

der **Tennisschläger**, *plural*
Tennisschläger
= tennis racket

der **Teppich**, *plural* Teppiche
= carpet, = rug

der **Termin**, *plural* Termine
= date
= appointment

der **Terminplaner**, *plural* Terminpläne
= personal organizer

der **Tesafilm**®
= Sellotape®

teuer *adjective*
= expensive

der **Teufel**, *plural* Teufel
= devil

der **Text**, *plural* Texte

die **Textnachricht**, *plural*
Textnachrichten
= text message

die **Textverarbeitung**
= word processing

das **Textverarbeitungssystem**,
plural Textverarbeitungssysteme
= word processor

das **Theater**, *plural* Theater
• = theatre

das **Theaterstück**, *plural* Theaterstücke
= play

das **Thema**, *plural* Themen
= theme, = subject

der **Themenpark**, *plural* Themenparks
= theme park

der **Thron**, *plural* Throne
= throne

der **Thunfisch**, *plural* Thunfische
= tuna

tief *adjective*
= deep
= low

die **Tiefe**, *plural* Tiefen
= depth

die **Tiefgarage**, *plural* Tiefgaragen
= underground car park

das **Tiefkühlfach**, *plural* Tiefkühlfächer
= freezer compartment

die **Tiefkühlkost**
= frozen food

das **Tier**, *plural* Tiere
= animal

der **Tierarzt**, *plural* Tierärzte
= vet, = veterinarian

der **Tierkreis**
= zodiac

der **Tierpark**, *plural* Tierparks
= zoo

die **Tinte**, *plural* Tinten
= ink

der **Tintenfisch**, *plural* Tintenfische
= octopus
= squid

tippen *verb*
• = to type
• = to tap
• auf etwas tippen = to bet on something
im Lotto tippen = to do the lottery

der **Tisch**, *plural* Tische
= table

der **Tischler**, *plural* Tischler
= joiner, = carpenter

das **Tischtuch**, *plural* Tischtücher
= tablecloth

toben *verb*
• = to rage
(*play boisterously*) = to go wild
• (*! sein*) = to rush

die **Tochter**, *plural* Töchter
= daughter

der **Tod**, *plural* Tode
= death

T

tödlich adjective
- = fatal
- = deadly

die **Toilette**, plural Toiletten
= toilet

toll✗ adjective
= brilliant, = fantastic

die **Tollwut**
= rabies

die **Tomate**, plural Tomaten
= tomato

der **Ton¹** plural Töne
- = tone, = note
- = sound
- (of colour) = shade

der **Ton²**
= clay

das **Tonband**, plural Tonbänder
= tape

das **Tonbandgerät**, plural Tonbandgeräte
= tape recorder

die **Tonne**, plural Tonnen
- = barrel
- (for rubbish) = bin
- = tonne

der **Topf**, plural Töpfe
- = pot, = jar
- = pan

die **Töpferei**, plural Töpfereien
= pottery

das **Tor**, plural Tore
- = gate
- = goal

die **Torte**, plural Torten
= gateau, = cake

der **Torwart**, plural Torwarte
= goalkeeper

tot adjective
= dead

der/die **Tote**, plural Toten
= dead man/woman, = fatality
die Toten = the dead

die **Tour**, plural Touren
- = tour, = trip
- auf diese Tour✗ = in this way

der **Tourismus**
= tourism

der **Tourist**, plural Touristen
= tourist

die **Touristin**, plural Touristinnen
= tourist

die **Tournee**, plural Tournees
= tour

die **Tracht**, plural Trachten
- = (national) costume
- eine Tracht Prügel = a good hiding

traditionell adjective
= traditional

traf ▸treffen

tragen irregular verb
- = to carry
- = to wear
- = to support
- = to bear

der **Träger**, plural Träger
- = porter
- (holder) = bearer
- (on a dress) = strap
- = girder

der **Trainer**, plural Trainer
= trainer, = coach
(of a soccer team) = manager

trainieren verb
= to train, = to coach

der **Trainingsanzug**, plural
Trainingsanzüge
= tracksuit

der **Traktor**, plural Traktoren
= tractor

die **Träne**, plural Tränen
= tear

trank ▸trinken

der **Transport**, plural Transporte
- = transport
- = consignment

transportieren verb
= to transport

trat ▸treten

die **Traube**, plural Trauben
= grape

trauen verb
- = to trust
- = to marry
- sich trauen = to dare

die **Trauer**
- = grief
- = mourning

der **Traum**, plural Träume
= dream

träumen verb
= to dream

traurig adjective
= sad

die **Trauung**, plural Trauungen
= wedding

treffen *irregular verb*
- = to hit, = to strike
- = to meet
- (*if it's an arrangement, a choice, a decision*) = to make
- sich treffen = to meet
  sich gut treffen = to be convenient

das **Treffen**, *plural* Treffen
= meeting

der **Treffpunkt**, *plural* Treffpunkte
= meeting place

treiben *irregular verb*
- = to drive
- = to do
  Handel treiben = to trade
- (**!** *sein*) = to drift

der **Treibhauseffekt**
= greenhouse effect

der **Treibstoff**
= fuel

trennen *verb*
- = to separate
- = to divide, = to split
- sich trennen = to separate, = to split up
  sich von etwas trennen = to part with something

die **Trennung**, *plural* Trennungen
- = separation
- = division

die **Treppe**, *plural* Treppen
= stairs, = steps
eine Treppe = a flight of stairs

treten *irregular verb*
- (**!** *sein*) = to step
- = to tread
- = to kick

treu *adjective*
= faithful, = loyal

die **Treukarte**, *plural* Treukarten
= loyalty card

der **Trickfilm**, *plural* Trickfilme
= cartoon

trifft ▶treffen

trinken *irregular verb*
= to drink

das **Trinkgeld**, *plural* Trinkgelder
= tip

das **Trinkwasser**
= drinking water

tritt ▶treten

der **Tritt**, *plural* Tritte
- = step, = kick

triumphieren *verb*
- = to rejoice, = to be triumphant

trocken *adjective*
= dry

trocknen *verb*
= to dry

der **Trockner**, *plural* Trockner
= drier

die **Trommel**, *plural* Trommeln
= drum

trommeln *verb*
= to drum
= to play the drums

die **Trompete**, *plural* Trompeten
= trumpet

Tropen (*plural*)
= tropics

tropfen *verb*
= to drip

der **Tropfen**, *plural* Tropfen
= drop

trösten *verb*
= to comfort, = to console

trotz *preposition* (+ *genitive*)
= despite, = in spite of

trotzdem *adverb*
= nevertheless
trotzdem danke = thanks anyway

trüb(e) *adjective*
= dull

trug ▶tragen

die **Truhe**, *plural* Truhen
= chest, = trunk

Trümmer (*plural*)
= ruins

der **Trumpf**, *plural* Trümpfe
= trump (card)
= trumps

die **Trunkenheit**
= drunkenness
Trunkenheit am Steuer = drink-driving

tschechisch *adjective*
= Czech

tschüs ▶tschüss

tschüss *interjection*
= bye!

das **Tuch**, *plural* Tücher
- = cloth
- = scarf

tüchtig *adjective*
- = competent
- = big

die **Tulpe**, *plural* Tulpen
= tulip

tun *irregular verb*
- = to do
  das tut man nicht = it isn't done

T

- • = to put
- • das Radio tuts noch✗ = the radio is still working
- • er tut nur so = he's just pretending
  freundlich tun = to act friendly
- • es hat sich einiges getan = quite a lot has happened

der **Tunnel**, *plural* Tunnel
= tunnel

tupfen *verb*
- • = to dab
- • = to touch

die **Tür**, *plural* Türen
= door

die **Türkei**
= Turkey

der **Turm**, *plural* Türme
- • = tower
- • (*in chess*) = rook, = castle

das **Turnen**
= gymnastics
= physical education, = PE

die **Turnhalle**, *plural* Turnhallen
= gymnasium

das **Turnier**, *plural* Tourniere
= tournament

tuscheln *verb*
= to whisper

die **Tüte**, *plural* Tüten
= bag

der **Typ**, *plural* Typen
- • = type
- • ein netter Typ✗ = a nice bloke

typisch *adjective*
= typical

Uu

die **U-Bahn**, *plural* U-Bahnen
= underground, = subway

übel *adjective*
= bad
mir ist übel = I feel sick

die **Übelkeit**
= nausea

üben *verb*
= to practise

✗ in informal situations

über
1 *preposition*
- • (+ *dative*)
  (*indicating position*) = over, = above
  (*more than*) = above
  über jemandem wohnen = to live above someone
- • (+ *accusative*)
  (*indicating direction*) = over
  (*concerning*) = about, = on
  (*indicating an amount*) = for
  (*more than, during*) = over
  über die Straße gehen = to go across the street
  über München fahren = to go via Munich
  heute über eine Woche = a week today
2 *adverb*
über und über = all over

überall *adverb*
= everywhere

der **Überblick**, *plural* Überblicke
- • = overall view
- • = summary

überblicken *verb*
- • = to overlook
- • = to assess

übereinander *adverb*
= one on top of the other
übereinander sprechen = to talk about each other

überein|stimmen *verb*
= to agree

überfahren *irregular verb*
= to run over

die **Überfahrt**, *plural* Überfahrten
= crossing

der **Überfall**, *plural* Überfälle
= attack
(*on a bank*) = raid

überfallen *irregular verb*
= to attack, = to mug
= to raid

überflüssig *adjective*
= superfluous

die **Überführung**, *plural* Überführungen
- • = transfer
- • (*road*) = flyover
  (*for pedestrians*) = footbridge

überfüllt *adjective*
= crowded

der **Übergang**, *plural* Übergänge
- • = crossing
- • = transition

übergeben *irregular verb*
- • = to hand over
- • sich übergeben = to be sick, = to vomit

überhaupt adverb
• = altogether
überhaupt nicht = not at all
überhaupt nichts = nothing at all
• = anyway

überholen verb
= to overtake

überlassen irregular verb
jemandem etwas überlassen = to leave
someone something, = to give someone
something

über|laufen irregular verb (**!** sein)
= to overflow

überleben verb
= to survive

überlegen verb
• = to think
• sich etwas überlegen = to think
something over
es sich anders überlegen = to change
one's mind

übermorgen adverb
= the day after tomorrow

**übernächster/übernächste/
übernächstes** adjective
= next but one
übernächstes Jahr = the year after next

übernachten verb
= to stay the night

übernehmen irregular verb
• = to take over
• = to take on

überraschen verb
= to surprise

die **Überraschung**, plural
Überraschungen
= surprise

übers = über das

die **Überschrift**, plural Überschriften
= heading

die **Überschwemmung**, plural
Überschwemmungen
= flood

übersehen irregular verb
= to overlook

übersetzen verb
= to translate

der **Übersetzer**, plural Übersetzer
= translator

die **Übersetzerin**, plural Übersetzerinnen
= translator

die **Übersetzung**, plural Übersetzungen
= translation

die **Überstunde**, plural Überstunden
Überstunden machen = to work overtime

übertragen irregular verb
• = to transfer
• = to communicate
• (on TV) = to broadcast

die **Übertragung**, plural Übertragungen
• (on TV) = broadcast
• (of an illness) = communication

übertreiben irregular verb
• = to exaggerate
• = to overdo

die **Übertreibung**, plural Übertreibungen
= exaggeration

überweisen irregular verb
• = to transfer
• = to refer

überzeugen verb
• = to convince, = to persuade
• sich überzeugen = to satisfy oneself

die **Überzeugung**, plural Überzeugungen
= conviction

überziehen[1] irregular verb
• = to cover
• = to overdraw

über|ziehen[2] irregular verb
(if it's clothes) = to put on

üblich adjective
= usual

übrig adjective
= remaining, = spare
übrig sein = to be left over

übrigens adverb
= by the way

die **Übung**, plural Übungen
= exercise
außer Übung sein = to be out of practice

das **Ufer**, plural Ufer
(of a river) = bank
(of the sea) = shore

die **Uhr**, plural Uhren
= clock
= watch
es ist zwei Uhr = it is 2 o'clock
wie viel Uhr ist es? = what time is it?

die **Uhrzeit**, plural Uhrzeiten
= time

die **UKW**
(Ultrakurzwelle) = VHF

ulkig adjective
= funny

um
1 preposition (+ accusative)
• around
• (indicating time) = at
(approximately) = around, = about
um zwei Uhr = at 2 o'clock

U

• = for
um etwas bitten = to ask for something
sich um etwas streiten = to quarrel over
something
sich um jemanden sorgen = to worry
about someone
• (*indicating difference*) = by
2 *adverb* = around, = about
3 *conjunction*
um zu = (in order) to

umarmen *verb*
= to hug

der **Umbau**, *plural* Umbauten
= renovation
= conversion

um|binden *irregular verb*
= to put on

um|blättern *verb*
= to turn over

um|bringen *irregular verb*
= to kill

um|drehen *verb*
• to turn
• sich umdrehen = to turn round, (*when
lying down*) = to turn over

um|fallen *irregular verb* (**!** *sein*)
= to fall down

die **Umfrage**, *plural* Umfragen
= survey

die **Umgangssprache**
= slang

umgeben *irregular verb*
= to surround

die **Umgebung**, *plural* Umgebungen
= surroundings
= neighbourhood

umgekehrt *adjective*
= opposite
es war umgekehrt = it was the other way
round

der **Umhang**, *plural* Umhänge
= cloak

um|kehren *verb* (**!** *sein*)
= to turn back

der **Umkleideraum**, *plural*
Umkleideräume
= changing room

der **Umlaut**, *plural* Umlaute
= umlaut

die **Umleitung**, *plural* Umleitungen
= diversion

um|rechnen *verb*
= to convert

---

um|rühren *verb*
= to stir

ums = um das

der **Umsatz**, *plural* Umsätze
= turnover

um|schalten *verb*
= to turn over
auf Rot umschalten = to change to red

der **Umschlag**, *plural* Umschläge
• = envelope
• = cover

um|sehen: sich umsehen *irregular
verb*
= to look round

umso *conjunction*
umso besser = all the better
umso mehr = all the more

umsonst *adverb*
• = in vain
• = free, = for nothing

umständlich *adjective*
= laborious

um|steigen *irregular verb* (**!** *sein*)
= to change

der **Umtausch**
= exchange

um|tauschen *verb*
= to change, = to exchange

die **Umwelt**
= environment

umweltfreundlich *adjective*
= environmentally friendly

die **Umweltverschmutzung**
= pollution

um|ziehen *irregular verb*
• (**!** *sein*) = to move
• = to change
• sich umziehen = to get changed

der **Umzug**, *plural* Umzüge
= move

unabhängig *adjective*
= independent

die **Unabhängigkeit**
= independence

unangenehm *adjective*
• = unpleasant
• = embarrassing

unanständig *adjective*
= indecent, = vulgar

unartig *adjective*
= naughty

unbehaglich *adjective*
= uncomfortable, = uneasy

unbekannt *adjective*
= unknown

unbequem *adjective*
= uncomfortable

und *conjunction*
= and

undankbar *adjective*
= ungrateful

undeutlich *adjective*
= unclear

undicht *adjective*
= leaking, = leaky
eine undichte Stelle = a leak

unentbehrlich *adjective*
= indispensable

unentschieden *adjective*
= undecided
unentschieden spielen = to draw

unerträglich *adjective*
= unbearable

unerwartet *adjective*
= unexpected

unfähig *adjective*
= incompetent

der **Unfall**, *plural* Unfälle
= accident

unfreundlich *adjective*
= unfriendly

der **Unfug**
= nonsense

(das) **Ungarn**
= Hungary

ungeduldig *adjective*
= impatient

ungefähr
1 *adjective* = approximate
2 *adverb* = approximately, = about

ungefährlich *adjective*
= safe

das **Ungeheuer**, *plural* Ungeheuer
= monster

ungemütlich *adjective*
= uncomfortable

ungenügend *adjective*
• = insufficient
• (*mark at school*) = unsatisfactory

ungerade *adjective*
eine ungerade Zahl = an odd number

ungerecht *adjective*
= unjust

ungern *adverb*
= reluctantly

ungesund *adjective*
= unhealthy

ungewöhnlich *adjective*
= unusual

das **Ungeziefer**
= vermin

unglaublich *adjective*
= incredible, = unbelievable

das **Unglück**, *plural* Unglücke
• = accident
• = misfortune
• = bad luck

unglücklich *adjective*
• = unhappy
• = unfortunate

unheimlich *adjective*
• = eerie
• unheimlich viel✘ = a terrific amount

unhöflich *adjective*
= impolite

die **Universität**, *plural* Universitäten
= university

Unkosten (*plural*)
= expenses

das **Unkraut**
= weed

unmodern *adjective*
= old-fashioned

unmöglich *adjective*
= impossible

unnötig *adjective*
= unnecessary

unordentlich *adjective*
= untidy

die **Unordnung**
= disorder
= mess

unpraktisch *adjective*
= impractical

unpünktlich *adjective*
= unpunctual
unpünktlich sein = to be late

das **Unrecht**
= wrong
zu Unrecht = wrongly

unregelmäßig *adjective*
= irregular

die **Unruhe**, *plural* Unruhen
= restlessness
= agitation
Unruhen = unrest

uns *pronoun*
• = us

U

- (*reflexive*) = ourselves
  wir waschen uns die Hände = we are
  washing our hands

unschuldig *adjective*
= innocent

unser *adjective*
= our

unserer/unsere/unsers *pronoun*
= ours

der **Unsinn**
= nonsense

unten *adverb*
= at the bottom
(*indoors*) = downstairs
nach unten = down

unter
1 *preposition* (+ *dative or accusative*)
- = under
  (*lower than*) = below
- = among
  unter anderem = among other things
  unter sich = by themselves
2 *adjective* = lower
die untere Etage = the bottom floor

das **Unterbewusstsein**
(**Unterbewußtsein** ⓄⓁⒹ)
= subconscious

unterbrechen *irregular verb*
= to interrupt

die **Unterbrechung**, *plural*
Unterbrechungen
= interruption

unter|bringen *irregular verb*
- = to put
- (*as a guest*) = to put up

die **Unterdrückung**
= suppression

untere ▶ unterer

untereinander *adverb*
- among ourselves/yourselves/themselves
- one below the other

unterer/untere/unteres *adjective*
= lower

die **Unterführung**, *plural* Unterführungen
= subway, = underpass

unter|gehen *irregular verb* (**!** *sein*)
- (*of the sun*) = to set
- (*of a ship*) = to sink
- (*of the world*) = to come to an end

die **Untergrundbahn**, *plural*
Untergrundbahnen
= underground, = subway

unterhalten *irregular verb*
- = to entertain

- (*feed*) = to support
- sich unterhalten = to talk, (*have fun*) = to
  enjoy oneself

die **Unterhaltung**, *plural* Unterhaltungen
- = conversation
- = entertainment

das **Unterhemd**, *plural* Unterhemden
= vest

die **Unterhose**, *plural* Unterhosen
= underpants

unterirdisch *adjective*
= underground

die **Unterkunft**, *plural* Unterkünfte
= accommodation, = accommodations

Unterlagen (*plural*)
= documents, = papers

unternehmen *irregular verb*
= to undertake
etwas unternehmen = to do something

der **Unterricht**
= lessons
jemandem Unterricht geben = to teach
someone

unterrichten *verb*
- = to teach
- = to inform
- sich unterrichten = to inform oneself

der **Unterrock**, *plural* Unterröcke
= slip

untersagt *adjective*
= prohibited

unterscheiden *irregular verb*
- = to distinguish
- = to tell apart
- sich unterscheiden = to differ, = to be
  different

der **Unterschied**, *plural* Unterschiede
= difference

unterschreiben *irregular verb*
= to sign

die **Unterschrift**, *plural* Unterschriften
= signature

unterstreichen *irregular verb*
= to underline

unterstützen *verb*
= to support

untersuchen *verb*
- = to examine
- = to investigate

die **Untersuchung**, *plural*
Untersuchungen
- = examination, = check-up
- = investigation

die **Untertasse**, *plural* Untertassen
= saucer

✱ in informal situations   ⓄⓁⒹ = old spelling

die **Unterwäsche**
= underwear

unterwegs
1 *adverb* = on the way
2 *adjective*
unterwegs sein = to be on the way
den ganzen Tag unterwegs sein = to be
out all day

untreu *adjective*
= disloyal
(*in marriage*) = unfaithful

ununterbrochen *adjective*
= uninterrupted

unvergleichlich *adjective*
= incomparable

unverheiratet *adjective*
= unmarried

unverkäuflich *adjective*
= not for sale
ein unverkäufliches Muster = a free
sample

unverschämt *adjective*
= impertinent

unverständlich *adjective*
= incomprehensible

unwahrscheinlich *adjective*
• = unlikely, = improbable
• das ist unwahrscheinlich!✖ = that's
incredible!

das **Unwetter**, *plural* Unwetter
= storm

unwichtig *adjective*
= unimportant

unzerbrechlich *adjective*
= unbreakable

unzufrieden *adjective*
= dissatisfied

üppig *adjective*
= lavish

uralt *adjective*
= ancient

der **Urenkel**, *plural* Urenkel
= great-grandson
die Urenkel = the great-grandchildren

die **Urenkelin**, *plural* Urenkelinnen
= great-granddaughter

Urgroßeltern (*plural*)
= great-grandparents

die **Urkunde**, *plural* Urkunden
= certificate, = deed

der **Urlaub**, *plural* Urlaube
= holiday, = vacation
Urlaub haben = to be on holiday *or*
vacation

der **Urlauber**, *plural* Urlauber
= holidaymaker, = vacationer

die **Ursache**, *plural* Ursachen
= cause
keine Ursache! = don't mention it!

der **Ursprung**, *plural* Ursprünge
= origin

ursprünglich *adjective*
= original

das **Urteil**, *plural* Urteile
• = judgement, = verdict, = opinion

der **Urwald**, *plural* Urwälder
= jungle

der **USB-Anschluss**, *plural* USB-Anschlusse
= USB-port

usw. *abbreviation*
(*und so weiter*) = etc.

Vv

---

die **Vanille**
= vanilla

der **Vater**, *plural* Väter
= father

der **Vati**, *plural* Vatis
= dad

der **Vegetarier**, *plural* Vegetarier
= vegetarian

die **Vegetarierin**, *plural* Vegetarierinnen
= vegetarian

vegetarisch *adjective*
= vegetarian

das **Veilchen**, *plural* Veilchen
= violet

die **Vene**, *plural* Venen
= vein

das **Ventil**, *plural* Ventile
= valve

verabreden *verb*
• to arrange
• sich mit jemandem verabreden = to
arrange to meet someone

die **Verabredung**, *plural* Verabredungen
• = appointment
• = date
• = arrangement

verabschieden *verb*
• = to say goodbye to
• sich verabschieden = to say goodbye

die **Verachtung**
= contempt

verändern verb
* to change
* sich verändern = to change

die **Veränderung**, plural Veränderungen
= change

veranstalten verb
= to organize

die **Veranstaltung**, plural
Veranstaltungen
= event
Veranstaltungen = activities

verantwortlich adjective
= responsible

die **Verantwortung**
= responsibility

verarbeiten verb
= to process

der **Verband**, plural Verbände
* = association
* = bandage

verbessern verb
* = to improve
* = to correct

die **Verbesserung**, plural Verbesserungen
* = improvement
* = correction

verbeugen: sich verbeugen verb
= to bow

verbieten irregular verb
= to forbid
= to ban

verbilligt adjective
= reduced

verbinden irregular verb
* = to connect
* = to join
* = to combine
* (with a dressing) = to bandage
* (on the phone) = to put through
falsch verbunden sein = to have got the
wrong number

die **Verbindung**, plural Verbindungen
* = connection
sich in Verbindung setzen = to get in
touch
* = combination
* (in chemistry) = compound

verblühen verb (**!** sein)
= to fade

verbot ▶verbieten

das **Verbot**, plural Verbote
= ban

──────────
⊙⊡⊙ = old spelling

verboten adjective
= forbidden

der **Verbrauch**
= consumption

verbrauchen verb
= to consume, = to use

der **Verbraucher**, plural Verbraucher
= consumer

das **Verbrechen**, plural Verbrechen
= crime

der **Verbrecher**, plural Verbrecher
= criminal

verbreitet adjective
= widespread

verbrennen irregular verb
* (**!** sein) = to burn
* sich verbrennen = to burn oneself
sich den Finger verbrennen = to burn
one's finger

verbringen irregular verb
= to spend

der **Verdacht**
= suspicion

verdächtig adjective
= suspicious

der/die **Verdächtige**, plural Verdächtigen
= suspect

die **Verdauung**
= digestion

verderben irregular verb
* = to spoil
ich habe mir den Magen verdorben =
I have an upset stomach
* (**!** sein) = to go off

verdienen verb
= to earn

der **Verdienst**, plural Verdienste
* = salary
* = achievement

verdoppeln verb
* to double
* sich verdoppeln = to double

verdünnen verb
= to dilute

verdursten verb (**!** sein)
= to die of thirst

verehren verb
= to worship

der **Verehrer**, plural Verehrer
= admirer

die **Verehrerin**, plural Verehrerinnen
= admirer

der **Verein**, *plural* Vereine
= society
= organization
(*sports*) = club

vereinbaren *verb*
= to arrange

die **Vereinbarung**, *plural* Vereinbarungen
= agreement
= arrangement

Vereinigte Staaten (*plural*)
= United States

die **Vereinigung**, *plural* Vereinigungen
= organization

verfahren *irregular verb*
• (**!** *sein*) = to proceed
• sich verfahren = to lose one's way

verfallen *irregular verb* (**!** *sein*)
• = to decay
• (*run out*) = to expire

die **Verfassung**, *plural* Verfassungen
• = constitution
• (*of a person*) = state

verfaulen *verb* (**!** *sein*)
= to rot

verfolgen *verb*
• = to follow
• = to persecute

verführen *verb*
• = to tempt
• = to seduce

die **Verführung**, *plural* Verführungen
• = temptation
• = seduction

vergangen *adjective*
= last

die **Vergangenheit**
• = past
• (*in grammar*) = past tense

der **Vergaser**, *plural* Vergaser
= carburettor

vergaß ▶vergessen

vergeben *irregular verb*
• = to forgive
• = to award

vergeblich
1 *adjective* = futile
2 *adverb* = in vain

vergessen *irregular verb*
= to forget

vergesslich (**vergeßlich**⊙ᴸᴰ)
adjective
= forgetful

die **Vergewaltigung**, *plural*
Vergewaltigungen
= rape

vergiften *verb*
= to poison

vergisst (**vergißt**⊙ᴸᴰ) ▶vergessen

der **Vergleich**, *plural* Vergleiche
= comparison

vergleichen *irregular verb*
= to compare

das **Vergnügen**, *plural* Vergnügen
= pleasure
viel Vergnügen! = have fun!

vergnügt *adjective*
= cheerful

vergrößern *verb*
• = to enlarge
= to increase
• = to magnify
• = to extend
• sich vergrößern = to expand, (*in amount*)
= to increase

die **Vergrößerung**, *plural* Vergrößerungen
• = expansion
• (*in photography*) = enlargement

verhaften *verb*
= to arrest

verhalten: sich verhalten
irregular verb
= to behave

das **Verhältnis**, *plural* Verhältnisse
• = relationship
• (*in maths*) = ratio

verhältnismäßig *adverb*
= relatively

verhandeln *verb*
= to negotiate
über etwas verhandeln = to negotiate
something

die **Verhandlung**, *plural* Verhandlungen
• = negotiation
• = hearing

verheimlichen *verb*
= to keep secret

verheiratet *adjective*
= married

verhindern *verb*
= to prevent

verhungern *verb* (**!** *sein*)
= to starve

verirren: sich verirren *verb*
= to get lost

der **Verkauf**, *plural* Verkäufe
= sale
zum Verkauf = for sale

verkaufen *verb*
= to sell
zu verkaufen = for sale

V

der **Verkäufer**, *plural* Verkäufer
- • = seller
- • = sales assistant

die **Verkäuferin**, *plural* Verkäuferinnen
- • = seller
- • = sales assistant

der **Verkehr**
= traffic

die **Verkehrsampel**, *plural*
Verkehrsampeln
= traffic lights

verkehrt *adjective*
= wrong
verkehrt herum = inside out, = upside
down

verklagen *verb*
= to sue

die **Verkleidung**, *plural* Verkleidungen
= disguise
(*at a party*) = fancy dress

verkommen *irregular verb* (**!** sein)
- • (*of food*) = to go off
- • (*of a house*) = to become dilapidated

verkratzt *adjective*
= scratched

der **Verlag**, *plural* Verlage
= publishing house, = publisher's

verlangen *verb*
= to demand
= to require
du wirst am Telefon verlangt = you're
wanted on the phone

verlängern *verb*
= to extend
= to lengthen
einen Pass verlängern = to renew a
passport

die **Verlängerung**, *plural* Verlängerungen
- • = extension
- = renewal
- • (*in sport*) = extra time

verlassen *irregular verb*
- • = to leave
- • sich auf etwas verlassen = to rely on
something

verlaufen *irregular verb*
- • (**!** sein) = to go
- • sich verlaufen = to lose one's way

verlegen[1] *verb*
- • = to mislay
- • = to postpone
- • = to publish
- • (*if it's a cable, pipe, carpet*) = to lay

verlegen[2] *adjective*
= embarrassed

OLD = old spelling

die **Verlegenheit**
= embarrassment

der **Verleih**, *plural* Verleihe
- • = renting out, = hiring out
- • = rental firm, = hire shop

verleihen *irregular verb*
- • = to hire out, = to rent out
- • = to lend
- • = to award

verlernen *verb*
= to forget

verletzen *verb*
- • = to injure
- = to hurt
- • sich verletzen = to hurt oneself

der/die **Verletzte**, *plural* Verletzten
= injured person
= casualty

die **Verletzung**, *plural* Verletzungen
= injury

verlieben: sich verlieben *verb*
= to fall in love

verlieren *irregular verb*
= to lose

verloben: sich verloben *verb*
= to get engaged

die **Verlobung**, *plural* Verlobungen
= engagement

verlor ▶ verlieren

die **Verlosung**, *plural* Verlosungen
= prize draw

der **Verlust**, *plural* Verluste
= loss

vermeiden *irregular verb*
= to avoid

vermieten *verb*
= to rent out, = to hire out
ein Zimmer vermieten = to let a room

der **Vermieter**, *plural* Vermieter
= landlord

die **Vermieterin**, *plural* Vermieterinnen
= landlady

vermissen *verb*
= to miss

die **Vermittlung**, *plural* Vermittlungen
- • = arrangement
- • (*office*) = agency
- • = switchboard
- = telephone exchange
- • = mediation

das **Vermögen**, *plural* Vermögen
= fortune

vermuten *verb*
= to suspect

vermutlich adverb
= probably

vernichten verb
= to destroy

die **Vernunft**
= reason

vernünftig adjective
= sensible

verpacken verb
= to pack
= to wrap up

die **Verpackung**, plural Verpackungen
= packaging

verpassen verb
= to miss

die **Verpflegung**
= food
Unterkunft und Verpflegung = board and
lodging

verpflichten: sich verpflichten
verb
• = to promise
• = to sign a contract

die **Verpflichtung**, plural Verpflichtungen
= obligation
= commitment

verprügeln verb
= to beat up

der **Verrat**
= betrayal

verraten irregular verb
• = to betray
= to give away
• = to tell
• sich verraten = to give oneself away

verrechnen: sich verrechnen
verb
= to make a mistake
= to miscalculate

verreisen verb (! sein)
= to go away

verrosten verb (! sein)
= to rust

verrostet adjective
= rusty

verrückt adjective
= mad, = crazy

versagen verb
= to fail

versammeln verb
• = to assemble
• sich versammeln = to assemble

die **Versammlung**, plural Versammlungen
= meeting

verschenken verb
= to give away

verschieben irregular verb
• = to postpone
• = to move

verschieden adjective
= different
= various

verschlafen irregular verb
= to oversleep

der **Verschluss** (**Verschluß**⟨OLD⟩), plural
Verschlüsse
= fastener
(on a bottle) = top

die **Verschmutzung**, plural
Verschmutzungen
= pollution

verschreiben irregular verb
• = to prescribe
• sich verschreiben = to make a mistake

verschwenden verb
= to waste

verschwinden irregular verb (! sein)
= to disappear

das **Versehen**, plural Versehen
= oversight
aus Versehen = by mistake

versichern verb
• = to insure
• = to assert
jemandem versichern = to assure
someone

die **Versicherung**, plural Versicherungen
• = insurance
• = assurance

versöhnen: sich versöhnen verb
= to become reconciled
sich mit jemandem versöhnen = to make
it up with someone

versorgen verb
• = to supply
• = to provide for
• = to look after

verspäten: sich verspäten verb
= to be late

die **Verspätung**, plural Verspätungen
= lateness
mit Verspätung = late
zehn Minuten Verspätung haben = to be
ten minutes late

versprechen irregular verb
• = to promise
• sich versprechen = to make a slip of the
tongue

das **Versprechen**, plural Versprechen
= promise

V

verstaatlichen *verb*
= to nationalize

verstand ▶verstehen

der **Verstand**
= mind
= reason

verständigen *verb*
• = to notify
• sich verständigen = to communicate, =
   to make oneself understood

die **Verständigung**, *plural*
Verständigungen
• = communication
• = notification

verständlich *adjective*
• = comprehensible
   jemandem etwas verständlich machen =
   to make something clear to someone
• = understandable

das **Verständnis**
= understanding

der **Verstärker**, *plural* Verstärker
= amplifier

verstauchen: sich verstauchen
verb
sich den Fuß verstauchen = to sprain
one's ankle

das **Versteck**, *plural* Verstecke
= hiding place

verstecken *verb*
• = to hide
• sich verstecken = to hide

verstehen *irregular verb*
• = to understand
   etwas falsch verstehen = to
   misunderstand something
• sich verstehen = to get on

verstellen *verb*
• = to adjust
• = to block
• = to disguise
• sich verstellen = to pretend

der **Versuch**, *plural* Versuche
• = attempt
• = experiment

versuchen *verb*
= to try, = to attempt

verteidigen *verb*
= to defend

die **Verteidigung**, *plural* Verteidigungen
= defence

verteilen *verb*
= to distribute

der **Vertrag**, *plural* Verträge
= contract

vertragen *irregular verb*
• = to stand, = to take
• sich vertragen = to get on

vertrauen *verb*
= to trust

das **Vertrauen**
= trust, = confidence

vertraulich *adjective*
= confidential

vertreten *irregular verb*
• = to stand in for
• = to represent

der **Vertreter**, *plural* Vertreter
• = representative
• = deputy

die **Vertreterin**, *plural* Vertreterinnen
• = representative
• = deputy

die **Vertretung**, *plural* Vertretungen
• = representative
• = deputy
• = supply teacher

verunglücken *verb* (**!** *sein*)
= to have an accident

verursachen *verb*
= to cause

verurteilen *verb*
• = to sentence
• = to condemn

die **Verwaltung**, *plural* Verwaltungen
= administration

verwandeln *verb*
= to change

verwandt *adjective*
= related

der/die **Verwandte**, *plural* Verwandten
= relative

die **Verwandtschaft**, *plural*
Verwandtschaften
• (*family*) = relatives
• = relationship

verwechseln *verb*
= to mix up
jemanden mit jemandem verwechseln =
   to mistake someone for someone

verwenden *verb*
= to use

die **Verwendung**
= use

verwirrt *adjective*
= confused

verwöhnen *verb*
= to spoil

der/die **Verwundete**, *plural* Verwundeten
= casualty
die Verwundeten = the wounded

verzählen: sich verzählen *verb*
= to miscount

verzeihen *irregular verb*
= to forgive
verzeihen Sie! = excuse me!

die **Verzeihung**
= forgiveness
jemanden um Verzeihung bitten = to
apologize to someone
Verzeihung! = sorry!

verzichten *verb*
= to do without

verzögern *verb*
• = to delay
• sich verzögern = to be delayed

die **Verzögerung**, *plural* Verzögerungen
= delay

verzweifelt *adjective*
= desperate

die **Verzweiflung**
= despair

der **Vetter**, *plural* Vettern
= cousin

das **Video**, *plural* Videos
= video

die **Videokamera**, *plural* Videokameras
= video camera

der **Videorekorder**, *plural* Videorekorder
= video recorder

die **Videothek**, *plural* Videotheken
= video shop, = video store

das **Vieh**
= cattle

viel
1 *pronoun*
• = a great deal of, = a lot of
(*plural*) = many, = a lot of
• = much, = a lot, (*plural*) = too many
zu viel = too much
vielen Dank = thank you very much
viel Spaß! = have fun!
2 *adverb* = much, = a lot
viel weniger = much less
das dauert viel zu lange = it will take far
too long
so viel wie möglich = as much as possible

vielleicht *adverb*
= perhaps

vier *adjective*
= four

viereckig *adjective*
= rectangular

das **Viertel**, *plural* Viertel
= quarter

die **Viertelstunde**, *plural* Viertelstunden
= quarter of an hour

vierter/vierte/viertes *adjective*
= fourth

vierzehn *adjective*
= fourteen

vierzig *adjective*
= forty

die **Villa**, *plural* Villen
= villa

der **Virus**, *plural* Viren
= virus

der **Vogel**, *plural* Vögel
= bird

das **Volk**, *plural* Völker
= people

das **Volkslied**, *plural* Volkslieder
= folk song

voll
1 *adjective* = full
die volle Wahrheit = the whole truth
2 *adverb*
= fully, = completely
voll tanken! = fill her up! *(car)*

völlig
1 *adjective* = complete
2 *adverb* = completely

vollkommen
1 *adjective*
• = perfect
• = complete
2 *adverb*
• = perfectly
• = completely

die **Vollpension**
= full board

vollständig *adjective*
= complete

vom = von dem

von *preposition* (+ *dative*)
• = from
von jetzt an = from now on
• (*instead of the genitive*) = of
ein Vetter von mir = a cousin of mine
• = by
er ist Lehrer von Beruf = he is a teacher
by profession
• = about
von etwas sprechen = to talk about
something

voneinander *adverb*
= from each other, = from one another

vor *preposition*
• (+ *dative or accusative*) = in front of

V

- (+ *dative*) (*indicating time, succession*)
  = before
  sie kamen vor uns an = they arrived
  before us
  vor drei Tagen = three days ago
  vor kurzem = recently
  zehn vor eins = ten to one
- (+ *dative*) (*because of*) = with
  vor Kälte zittern = to tremble with cold
  vor jemandem Angst haben = to be
  frightened of someone

voraus *adverb*
jemandem voraus sein = to be ahead of
someone
im Voraus = in advance

voraus|gehen *irregular verb* (**!** *sein*)
= to go on ahead

voraus|setzen *verb*
= to take for granted
vorausgesetzt, dass = provided that

die **Voraussetzung**, *plural*
Voraussetzungen
- = condition
- = assumption

vorbei *adverb*
- = past
- (*finished*) = over

vorbei|fahren *irregular verb* (**!** *sein*)
= to drive past, = to pass

vorbei|gehen *irregular verb* (**!** *sein*)
- = to pass
- (*visit*) = to drop in

vorbei|kommen *irregular verb* (**!** *sein*)
- = to pass
- = to get past
- (*visit*) = to drop in

vor|bereiten *verb*
- = to prepare
- sich vorbereiten = to prepare

die **Vorbereitung**, *plural* Vorbereitungen
= preparation

vor|beugen *verb*
- = to prevent
- sich vorbeugen = to lean forward

das **Vorbild**, *plural* Vorbilder
= example

vorderer/vordere/vorderes
adjective
= front

der **Vordergrund**
= foreground

vor|drängen: sich vordrängen
verb
= to push forward

die **Vorfahrt**
= right of way
'Vorfahrt beachten' = 'give way'

die **Vorfahrtsstraße**, *plural*
Vorfahrtsstraßen
= major road

der **Vorfall**, *plural* Vorfälle
= incident

die **Vorführung**, *plural* Vorführungen
- = performance
- (*of a machine*) = demonstration

der **Vorgänger**, *plural* Vorgänger
= predecessor

die **Vorgängerin**, *plural* Vorgängerinnen
= predecessor

vor|gehen *irregular verb* (**!** *sein*)
- = to go on ahead
- = to go forward
- = to proceed
- (*of a clock*) = to be fast
- = to happen, = to go on

vorgestern *adverb*
= the day before yesterday

vor|haben *irregular verb*
= to intend
etwas vorhaben = to have something
planned

die **Vorhand**
= forehand

der **Vorhang**, *plural* Vorhänge
= curtain, = drape

vorher *adverb*
= beforehand, = before

die **Vorhersage**, *plural* Vorhersagen
- = forecast
- = prediction

vorhin *adverb*
= just now

voriger/vorige/voriges *adjective*
= last

vor|kommen *irregular verb* (**!** *sein*)
- = to occur, = to happen
- = to exist
- = to seem
  jemandem verdächtig vorkommen = to
  seem suspicious to someone
- = to come forward

vor|lassen *irregular verb*
jemanden vorlassen = to let someone go
first

vorläufig
1 *adjective* = provisional
2 *adverb* = provisionally

vor|lesen *irregular verb*
= to read (out)
= to read aloud

OLD = old spelling

die **Vorlesung**, *plural* Vorlesungen
= lecture

vorletzter/vorletzte/vorletztes
adjective
= last ... but one
vorletztes Jahr = the year before last

der **Vormittag**, *plural* Vormittage
= morning

vormittags *adverb*
= in the morning

vorn *adverb*
= at the front
nach vorn = to the front
von vorn = from the beginning
da vorn = over there

der **Vorname**, *plural* Vornamen
= first name

vorne ▶ vorn

vornehm *adjective*
= elegant

vor|nehmen *irregular verb*
* = to carry out
* sich vornehmen, etwas zu tun = to plan
to do something

der **Vorort**, *plural* Vororte
= suburb

der **Vorrat**, *plural* Vorräte
= supply, = stock

die **Vorschau**, *plural* Vorschauen
= preview
(*of a film*) = trailer

der **Vorschlag**, *plural* Vorschläge
= suggestion

vor|schlagen *irregular verb*
= to suggest

die **Vorschrift**, *plural* Vorschriften
= regulation

die **Vorschule**, *plural* Vorschulen
= infant school

der **Vorschuss** (**Vorschuß**⊙ᴸᴰ), *plural*
Vorschüsse
= advance

vor|sehen: sich vorsehen *verb*
= to be careful

die **Vorsicht**
= care
Vorsicht! = careful!, (*on a sign*) = caution!

vorsichtig *adjective*
= careful

die **Vorsichtsmaßnahme**, *plural*
Vorsichtsmaßnahmen
= precaution

die **Vorspeise**, *plural* Vorspeisen
= starter

der **Vorsprung**, *plural* Vorsprünge
(*advantage*) = lead

vor|stellen *verb*
* = to introduce
* (*turn on*) = to put forward
* sich vorstellen = to introduce oneself,
(*when applying for a job*) = to go for an
interview
* sich etwas vorstellen = to imagine
something
stell dir vor! = can you imagine?

die **Vorstellung**, *plural* Vorstellungen
* = performance
* = introduction
(*for a job*) = interview
* = idea
* = imagination

der **Vorteil**, *plural* Vorteile
= advantage

der **Vortrag**, *plural* Vorträge
= talk

vorübergehend
1 *adjective* = temporary
2 *adverb* = temporarily

das **Vorurteil**, *plural* Vorurteile
= prejudice

die **Vorwahl**, *plural* Vorwahlen
= dialling code, = area code

vorwärts *adverb*
= forward(s)
vorwärts kommen = to make progress

vorwiegend *adverb*
= predominantly

der **Vorwurf**, *plural* Vorwürfe
= reproach
jemandem Vorwürfe machen = to
reproach someone

vor|zeigen *verb*
= to show

vor|ziehen *irregular verb*
* = to prefer
* = to pull up
den Vorhang vorziehen = to draw the
curtain

vorzüglich *adjective*
= excellent

vulgär *adjective*
= vulgar

der **Vulkan** *plural* Vulkane
= volcano

V

Ww

die **Waage**, *plural* Waagen
- scales
- Libra

waagerecht *adjective*
= horizontal

wach *adjective*
= awake
wach werden = to wake up

die **Wache**, *plural* Wachen
- = guard
- = (police) station

der **Wachhund**, *plural* Wachhunde
= guard dog

das **Wachs**, *plural* Wachse
= wax

wachsen¹ *irregular verb* (**!** *sein*)
= to grow

wachsen² *verb*
= to wax

das **Wachstum**
= growth

der **Wächter**, *plural* Wächter
= guard

wackelig *adjective*
= wobbly

wackeln *verb*
= to wobble

die **Wade**, *plural* Waden
= calf

die **Waffe**, *plural* Waffen
= weapon

wagen *verb*
= to risk
es wagen, etwas zu tun = to dare to do
something

der **Wagen**, *plural* Wagen
- = car
- (*of a train*) = carriage
- = cart

der **Wagenheber**, *plural* Wagenheber
= jack

die **Wahl**, *plural* Wahlen
- = choice
- = election

wählen *verb*
- = to choose
- = to elect

- = to vote
- (*when phoning*) = to dial

das **Wahlfach**, *plural* Wahlfächer
= optional subject

der **Wahnsinn**
= madness

wahnsinnig *adjective*
- = mad
- wahnsinnigen Durst haben**✶** = to be
terribly thirsty

wahr *adjective*
= true

während
1 *conjunction* = while
2 *preposition* (+ *genitive*) = during

die **Wahrheit**, *plural* Wahrheiten
= truth

die **Wahrsagerin**, *plural* Wahrsagerinnen
= fortune-teller

wahrscheinlich
1 *adjective* = probable
2 *adverb* = probably

die **Währung**, *plural* Währungen
= currency

die **Waise**, *plural* Waisen
= orphan

der **Wal**, *plural* Wale
= whale

der **Wald**, *plural* Wälder
= wood, = forest

der **Waliser**, *plural* Waliser
= Welshman

die **Waliserin**, *plural* Waliserinnen
= Welshwoman

walisisch *adjective*
= Welsh

die **Wallfahrt**, *plural* Wallfahrten
= pilgrimage

die **Walnuss** (**Walnuß** ⓄⓁⒹ), *plural*
Walnüsse
= walnut

die **Wand**, *plural* Wände
= wall

wandern *verb* (**!** *sein*)
= to hike, = to ramble
= to go walking

die **Wanderung**, *plural* Wanderungen
= hike, = ramble

wann *adverb*
= when
seit wann wohnst du hier? = how long
have you been living here?

die **Wanne**, *plural* Wannen
= tub
= bath

✶ in informal situations   ⓄⓁⒹ = old spelling

war ▶sein

die **Ware**, *plural* Waren
- = article, = product
- Waren = goods

waren ▶sein

das **Warenhaus**, *plural* Warenhäuser
= department store

das **Warenzeichen**, *plural* Warenzeichen
= trademark

warf ▶werfen

warm *adjective*
= warm
eine warme Mahlzeit = a hot meal

die **Wärme**
= warmth
wir haben zwanzig Grad Wärme = the
temperature is 20 degrees

wärmen *verb*
= to warm

warnen *verb*
= to warn

die **Warnung**, *plural* Warnungen
= warning

warst, wart ▶sein

warten *verb*
= to wait

der **Wärter**, *plural* Wärter
= keeper, = attendant
= warder, = guard

die **Wärterin**, *plural* Wärterinnen
= keeper, = attendant
= warder, = guard

das **Wartezimmer**, *plural* Wartezimmer
= waiting room

die **Wartung**, *plural* Wartungen
= service

warum *adverb*
= why

die **Warze**, *plural* Warzen
= wart

was *pronoun*
- what
was kostet das? = how much is it?
was für? = what kind of?
was für ein Glück! = what luck!
- = that
vieles, was er sagt = a lot that he says
- (*short for etwas*) = something
(*in questions and negatives*) = anything
hier ist was zu essen = here's something
to eat
hast du was zu lesen? = have you got
anything to read?

das **Waschbecken**, *plural* Waschbecken
= washbasin

die **Wäsche**
- = washing
- = underwear

waschen *irregular verb*
- to wash
- sich waschen = to have a wash
sich die Hände waschen = to wash one's
hands

die **Wäscherei**, *plural* Wäschereien
= laundry

der **Waschlappen**, *plural* Waschlappen
= flannel

die **Waschmaschine**, *plural*
Waschmaschinen
= washing machine

der **Waschsalon**, *plural* Waschsalons
= launderette

die **Waschstraße**, *plural* Waschstraßen
= car wash

das **Wasser**
= water

der **Wasserball**, *plural* Wasserbälle
- = beach ball
- = water polo

wasserdicht *adjective*
= waterproof
= watertight

der **Wasserfall**, *plural* Wasserfälle
= waterfall

der **Wasserhahn**, *plural* Wasserhähne
= tap, = faucet

der **Wassermann**
= Aquarius

das **Wasserskilaufen**
= water-skiing

wässrig (**wäßrig**ᴼᴸᴰ) *adjective*
= watery

die **Watte**
= cotton wool

wattiert *adjective*
= padded

das **Web**
= the Web

weben *verb*
= to weave

die **Website**, *plural* Websites
= website

der **Wechsel**, *plural* Wechsel
- = change
- (*of foreign currency*) = exchange

das **Wechselgeld**
= change

W

der **Wechselkurs**, *plural* Wechselkurse
= exchange rate

wechseln *verb*
= to change

wecken *verb*
= to wake (up)

der **Wecker**, *plural* Wecker
= alarm clock

weder *conjunction*
weder . . . noch = neither . . . nor

weg *adverb*
= away
sie ist schon weg = she's already gone
Hände weg! = hands off!

der **Weg**, *plural* Wege
= way
= path
sich auf den Weg machen = to set off

wegen *preposition* (+ *genitive*)
= because of

weg|fahren *irregular verb* (! *sein*)
= to leave

weg|gehen *irregular verb* (! *sein*)
* = to go away
= to leave
* (*for entertainment*) = to go out
* (*of a stain*) = to come out

weg|lassen *irregular verb*
* = to let go
* = to leave out

weg|laufen *irregular verb* (! *sein*)
= to run away

weg|legen *verb*
= to put down
= to put away

weg|räumen *verb*
= to clear away

weg|schicken *verb*
= to send off
= to send away

weg|tun *irregular verb*
= to put away

der **Wegweiser**, *plural* Wegweiser
= signpost

weg|werfen *irregular verb*
= to throw away

weh *adjective*
= sore
weh tun⊙ᴸᴰ ▸ wehtun
o weh! = oh dear!

wehen *verb*
= to blow

der **Wehrdienst**
= military service

---

wehren: sich wehren *verb*
= to defend oneself

wehrlos *adjective*
= defenceless

wehtun *irregular verb* = to hurt

das **Weibchen**, *plural* Weibchen
= female

weiblich *adjective*
* = female
* (*in grammar*) = feminine

weich *adjective*
= soft

die **Weiche**, *plural* Weichen
= points

die **Weide**, *plural* Weiden
* = willow
* = pasture

weigern: sich weigern *verb*
= to refuse

das **Weihnachten**, *plural* Weihnachten
= Christmas

der **Weihnachtsmann**, *plural* Weihnachtsmänner
= Father Christmas

weil *conjunction*
= because

der **Wein**, *plural* Weine
* = vine
* = wine

der **Weinberg**, *plural* Weinberge
= vineyard

weinen *verb*
= to cry

die **Weintraube**, *plural* Weintrauben
= grape

weise *adjective*
= wise

die **Weisheit**, *plural* Weisheiten
= wisdom

weiß¹ *adjective*
= white

weiß² ▸ wissen

weit
1 *adjective*
* = wide
* = long
eine weite Reise = a long journey
2 *adverb*
* = wide, = widely
* = far
von weitem = from a distance
bei weitem = by far
ich bin so weit = I'm ready

weiten: sich weiten *verb*
= to widen
= to stretch

weiter *adverb*
- = further
  etwas weiter tun = to go on doing
    something
  und so weiter = and so on
- = in addition
  ich brauche nichts weiter = I don't need
    anything else
  weiter niemand = no one else

weiterer/weitere/weiteres
  adjective
  = further
  ohne weiteres = just like that
  bis auf weiteres = for the time being

weiter|fahren *irregular verb* (**!** *sein*)
  = to go on

weiter|gehen *irregular verb* (**!** *sein*)
  = to go on

weiterhin *adverb*
- = still
  etwas weiterhin tun = to go on doing
    something
- = in future

weiter|machen *verb*
  = to carry on

der **Weitsprung**
  = long jump

der **Weizen**
  = wheat

welcher/welche/welches
  1 *adjective* = which
  um welche Zeit? = at what time?
  2 *pronoun*
- = which one
  welcher von euch? = which (one) of you?
- = some
  (*in questions*) = any
  ich möchte welches = I'd like some
  hast du welche? = have you got any?

die **Welle**, *plural* Wellen
  = wave

der **Wellensittich**, *plural* Wellensittiche
  = budgerigar

wellig *adjective*
  = wavy

die **Welt**, *plural* Welten
  = world
  zur Welt kommen = to be born

das **Weltall**
  = universe

der **Weltmeister**, *plural* Weltmeister
  = world champion

die **Weltmeisterin**, *plural*
  Weltmeisterinnen
  = world champion

die **Weltmeisterschaft**, *plural*
  Weltmeisterschaften
  = world championship

der **Weltraum**
  = space

wem *pronoun*
  = to whom

wen *pronoun*
  = whom, = who

die **Wende**
- = change
- = reunification (of Germany)

wenden: sich wenden *irregular
  verb*
  = to turn
  sich an jemanden wenden = to consult
    someone

wenig
  1 *pronoun* = little
  (*plural*) wenige = few
  in wenigen Tagen = in a few days
  2 *adverb* = little
  wenig bekannt = little known
  so wenig wie möglich = as little as
    possible
  zu wenig = too little, (*plural*) = too few

weniger
  1 *pronoun* = less
  (*plural*) = fewer
  immer weniger = less and less, = fewer
    and fewer
  2 *conjunction* = less
  fünf weniger zwei = five minus two
  3 *adverb* = less

wenigste ▶wenigster

wenigstens *adverb*
  = at least

wenigster/wenigste/wenigstes
  pronoun
  = least
  am wenigsten = least

wenn *conjunction*
- = when
  immer wenn = whenever
- (*conditional*) = if
  außer wenn = unless

wer *pronoun*
- = who
- (*informal for* jemand) = someone
  (*in questions*) = anyone

werben *irregular verb*
- = to advertise
- = to recruit

der **Werbespot**, *plural* Werbespots
  = advert, = commercial

die **Werbung**
  = advertising

werden *irregular verb* (**!** *sein*)
- = to become
  müde werden = to get tired
  wach werden = to wake up
  mir wurde schlecht = I felt sick

W

- *(forming the future tense)* = shall, = will
  er wird es kaufen = he'll buy it
- *(forming the passive tense)*
  unsere Wohnung wird gestrichen = our
  flat is being painted
- *(in the conditional)*
  wir würden kommen = we would come

werfen *irregular verb*
= to throw

das **Werk**, *plural* Werke
- = work
- *(factory)* = works

die **Werkstatt**, *plural* Werkstätten
= workshop

der **Werktag**, *plural* Werktage
= working day

das **Werkzeug**, *plural* Werkzeuge
= tool

wert *adjective*
wert sein = to be worth
nichts wert sein = to be worthless

der **Wert**, *plural* Werte
= value
im Wert von … = worth …

wertlos *adjective*
= worthless

wertvoll *adjective*
= valuable

das **Wesen**, *plural* Wesen
- *(character)* = nature
- = creature

wesentlich
1 *adjective* = essential
im Wesentlichen = essentially
2 *adverb* = considerably

weshalb *adverb*
= why

die **Wespe**, *plural* Wespen
= wasp

wessen *pronoun*
= whose

der **Wessi**ˣ, *plural* Wessis
= West German

die **Weste**, *plural* Westen
= waistcoat, = vest

der **Westen**
= west

westlich *adjective*
- = western
- = westerly

weswegen *adverb*
= why

der **Wettbewerb**, *plural* Wettbewerbe
= competition, = contest

die **Wette**, *plural* Wetten
= bet
um die Wette laufen = to race

wetten *verb*
= to bet
mit jemandem um etwas wetten = to bet
someone something

das **Wetter**
= weather

der **Wettkampf**, *plural* Wettkämpfe
= contest

das **Wettrennen**, *plural* Wettrennen
= race

wichtig *adjective*
= important

wickeln *verb*
= to wind
ein Kind wickeln = to change a baby

der **Widder**, *plural* Widder
- = ram
- = Aries

widerlich *adjective*
= disgusting

widersprechen *irregular verb*
= to contradict

der **Widerspruch**, *plural* Widersprüche
= contradiction

der **Widerstand**
- = resistance
- = opposition

widerstandsfähig *adjective*
= resistant

widerstehen *irregular verb*
= to resist

die **Widmung**, *plural* Widmungen
= dedication

wie
1 *adverb*
- = how
  wie ist das Wetter? = what is the weather
  like?
  wie bitte? = sorry?
  wie spät ist es? = what is the time?
- wie viel = how much, *(plural)* = how
  many
  um wie viel Uhr? = at what time?
2 *conjunction*
- = as
  so schnell wie möglich = as quickly as
  possible
  nichts wie = nothing but
- = like
  genau wie du = just like you

wieder *adverb*
= again
etwas wieder finden = to find something (again)

wieder|bekommen *irregular verb*
= to get back

wiederfinden ⓞⓛⓓ ▶wieder

wieder|geben *irregular verb*
• = to give back
• = to portray

wiederholen *verb*
• = to repeat
• (*learn*) = to revise
• sich wiederholen (*happen again*) = to recur, (*say again*) = to repeat oneself

die **Wiederholung**, *plural* Wiederholungen
• = repetition
• (*at school*) = revision

das **Wiederhören**
(*on the phone*) auf Wiederhören! = goodbye!

wieder|kommen *irregular verb*
(**!** *sein*)
= to come back
= to come again

das **Wiedersehen**, *plural* Wiedersehen
= reunion
auf Wiedersehen! = goodbye!

die **Wiedervereinigung**, *plural* Wiedervereinigungen
= reunification

die **Wiege**, *plural* Wiegen
= cradle

wiegen *irregular verb*
= to weigh

wiehern *verb*
= to neigh

(das) **Wien**
= Vienna

die **Wiese**, *plural* Wiesen
= meadow

wieso *adverb*
= why

wieviel ⓞⓛⓓ ▶wie

wievielter/wievielte/wievieltes *adjective*
= which
zum wievielten Mal? = how many times?

das **Wildleder**
= suede

will ▶wollen

der **Wille**
= will
seinen Willen durchsetzen = to get one's way

willkommen *adjective*
= welcome

willst ▶wollen

die **Wimper**, *plural* Wimpern
= eyelash

die **Wimperntusche**, *plural* Wimperntuschen
= mascara

der **Wind**, *plural* Winde
= wind

die **Windel**, *plural* Windeln
= nappy, = diaper

der **Windhund**, *plural* Windhunde
= greyhound

windig *adjective*
= windy

die **Windmühle**, *plural* Windmühlen
= windmill

Windpocken (*plural*)
= chickenpox

die **Windschutzscheibe**, *plural* Windschutzscheiben
= windscreen, = windshield

der **Winkel**, *plural* Winkel
• = angle
• = corner

winken *verb*
= to wave

der **Winter**, *plural* Winter
= winter

der **Winterschlaf**
= hibernation

winzig *adjective*
= tiny

wir *pronoun*
= we
wir sind es = it's us

die **Wirbelsäule**, *plural* Wirbelsäulen
= spine

wird ▶werden

wirft ▶werfen

wirken *verb*
• = to have an effect
gegen etwas wirken = to be effective against something
• (*appear*) = to seem

wirklich
1 *adjective* = real
2 *adverb* = really

die **Wirklichkeit**
= reality

wirksam *adjective*
= effective

W

die **Wirkung**, *plural* Wirkungen
= effect

wirst ▶werden

der **Wirt**, *plural* Wirte
= landlord

die **Wirtin**, *plural* Wirtinnen
= landlady

die **Wirtschaft**, *plural* Wirtschaften
* = economy
* = pub

wirtschaftlich *adjective*
= economic

das **Wirtshaus**, *plural* Wirtshäuser
= pub

wischen
= to wipe
Staub wischen = to dust

wissen *irregular verb*
= to know

das **Wissen**
= knowledge

die **Wissenschaft**, *plural* Wissenschaften
= science

der **Wissenschaftler**, *plural*
Wissenschaftler
= scientist

die **Wissenschaftlerin**, *plural*
Wissenschaftlerinnen
= scientist

die **Witwe**, *plural* Witwen
= widow

der **Witwer**, *plural* Witwer
= widower

der **Witz**, *plural* Witze
= joke

witzig *adjective*
= funny

wo
1 *adverb* = where
2 *conjunction*
* (*because*) = seeing that
* = although
= when

woanders *adverb*
= elsewhere, = somewhere else

die **Woche**, *plural* Wochen
= week

das **Wochenende**, *plural* Wochenenden
= weekend

wochenlang *adverb*
= for weeks

der **Wochentag**, *plural* Wochentage
= weekday

wochentags *adverb*
= on weekdays

wöchentlich *adjective*
= weekly

wofür *adverb*
= for what
wofür brauchst du das Geld? = what do
you need the money for?

woher *adverb*
= where . . . from
woher weißt du das? = how do you know
that?

wohin *adverb*
= where (. . . to)

wohl *adverb*
* = well
sich wohl fühlen = to feel well, (*be
comfortable*) = to feel happy
* = probably
du bist wohl verrückt = you must be mad

das **Wohl**
= welfare
= well-being
zum Wohl! = cheers!

der **Wohlstand**
= prosperity

wohltätig *adjective*
= charitable

wohnen *verb*
= to live
(*for a short time*) = to stay

wohnhaft *adjective*
= resident

das **Wohnheim**, *plural* Wohnheime
= hostel
(*for old people*) = home

der **Wohnort**, *plural* Wohnorte
= place of residence

der **Wohnsitz**, *plural* Wohnsitze
= place of residence

die **Wohnung**, *plural* Wohnungen
= flat, = apartment

der **Wohnwagen**, *plural* Wohnwagen
= caravan

das **Wohnzimmer**, *plural* Wohnzimmer
= living room

der **Wolf**, *plural* Wölfe
= wolf

die **Wolke**, *plural* Wolken
= cloud

der **Wolkenkratzer**, *plural* Wolkenkratzer
= skyscraper

wolkig *adjective*
= cloudy

die **Wolldecke**, *plural* Wolldecken
= blanket

die **Wolle**
= wool

wollen *irregular verb*
= to want
er wollte gerade gehen = he was just
about to go

womit *adverb*
• (*in questions*) = what ... with
womit schreibt er? = what is he writing
with?
• = with which
womit er schreibt = with which he is
writing

wonach *adverb*
• (*in questions*) = after what
wonach suchst du? = what are you
looking for?
• = after which

woran *adverb*
• (*in questions*) = what ... of
= on what
woran hast du ihn erkannt? = how did
you recognize him?
• = of which

woraus *adverb*
• (*in questions*) = what ... from
woraus ist das? = what is it made of?
• = from which

worin *adverb*
• (*in questions*) = in what, = what ... in
• in which

das **Wort**, *plural* Worte *or* Wörter
= word

das **Wörterbuch**, *plural* Wörterbücher
= dictionary

wörtlich *adjective*
= word for word

der **Wortschatz**
= vocabulary

worüber *adverb*
• (*in questions*) = what ... over
= about what
worüber lachst du? = what are you
laughing about?
• = over which
= about which

worum *adverb*
• (*in questions*) = about what
worum geht es? = what's it about?
• = for which

wovon *adverb*
• (*in questions*) = what ... from
= about what
• = from which
= about which

wovor *adverb*
• (*in questions*) = what ... of
wovor hast du Angst? = what are you
afraid of?
• = of which

wozu *adverb*
= why, = what for

das **Wrack**, *plural* Wracks
= wreck

wuchs ▶ wachsen

der **Wuchs**
= growth

wund *adjective*
= sore

die **Wunde**, *plural* Wunden
= wound

das **Wunder**, *plural* Wunder
• = miracle
• = wonder

wunderbar *adjective*
= wonderful

wundern: sich wundern *verb*
= to be surprised

der **Wunsch**, *plural* Wünsche
= wish
auf Wunsch = on request

wünschen *verb*
• = to wish
was wünschen Sie? = can I help you?
• sich etwas wünschen = to want
something

wurde ▶ werden
er wurde gerufen = he was called

würde ▶ werden
er würde kommen = he would come

wurden, würden ▶ werden

wurdest, würdest ▶ werden

wurdet, würdet ▶ werden

der **Wurf**, *plural* Würfe
= throw

der **Würfel**, *plural* Würfel
= cube
(*in games*) = dice

würfeln *verb*
= to throw the dice

der **Wurm**, *plural* Würmer
= worm

die **Wurst**, *plural* Würste
= sausage

die **Wurzel**, *plural* Wurzeln
= root

würzen *verb*
= to season

W

würzig *adjective*
= spicy

wusch ▶waschen

wusste (**wußte** ⓞⓛⓓ) ▶wissen

die **Wüste**, *plural* Wüsten
= desert

die **Wut**
= rage

wütend *adjective*
= furious

Xx

x-beliebig✗ *adjective*
= any

x-mal✗ *adverb*
= umpteen times

Yy

die **Yacht**, *plural* Yachten
= yacht

das **Yoga**
= yoga

das **Ypsilon**, *plural* Ypsilons
= Y

Zz

zäh *adjective*
= tough

die **Zahl**, *plural* Zahlen
= number
= figure

zahlen *verb*
= to pay
= to pay for
bitte zahlen! = the bill please!

zählen *verb*
= to count
zählen zu = to be among

der **Zähler**, *plural* Zähler
= meter

zahlreich *adjective*
= numerous

die **Zahlung**, *plural* Zahlungen
= payment

die **Zählung**, *plural* Zählungen
• = count
• = census

zahm *adjective*
= tame

zähmen *verb*
= to tame

der **Zahn**, *plural* Zähne
= tooth

der **Zahnarzt**, *plural* Zahnärzte
= dentist

die **Zahnärztin**, *plural* Zahnärztinnen
= dentist

das **Zahnfleisch**
= gum
= gums

die **Zahnpasta**, *plural* Zahnpasten
= toothpaste

Zahnschmerzen (*plural*)
= toothache

die **Zange**, *plural* Zangen
= pliers

zanken: sich zanken *verb*
= to squabble

zappeln *verb*
= to wriggle

zart *adjective*
= delicate
= tender

zärtlich *adjective*
= affectionate

der **Zauber**
= magic
= spell

der **Zauberer**, *plural* Zauberer
= magician, = conjurer

zauberhaft *adjective*
= enchanting

zaubern *verb*
= to do magic

der **Zaun**, *plural* Zäune
= fence

z.B. *abbreviation*
(*zum Beispiel*) = e.g.

✗ in informal situations   ⓞⓛⓓ = old spelling

der **Zebrastreifen**, *plural* Zebrastreifen
= zebra-crossing, = crosswalk

der **Zeh**, *plural* Zehen
= toe

die **Zehe**, *plural* Zehen
• = toe
• (*of garlic*) = clove

zehn *adjective*
= ten

das **Zehntel**, *plural* Zehntel
= tenth

zehnter/zehnte/zehntes *adjective*
= tenth

das **Zeichen**, *plural* Zeichen
• = sign
• = signal

zeichnen *verb*
= to draw

die **Zeichnung**, *plural* Zeichnungen
= drawing

der **Zeigefinger**, *plural* Zeigefinger
= index finger

zeigen *verb*
• to show
• auf jemanden zeigen = to point at
someone
• sich zeigen = to appear, (*emerge*) = to
become clear

der **Zeiger**, *plural* Zeiger
= hand

die **Zeile**, *plural* Zeilen
= line

die **Zeit**, *plural* Zeiten
= time
sich Zeit lassen = to take one's time

das **Zeitalter**, *plural* Zeitalter
= age

zeitlich *adverb*
= chronologically
zeitlich begrenzt = for a limited time

die **Zeitlupe**
= slow motion

der **Zeitraum**, *plural* Zeiträume
= period

die **Zeitschrift**, *plural* Zeitschriften
= magazine

die **Zeitung**, *plural* Zeitungen
= newspaper

zeitweise *adverb*
= at times

die **Zelle**, *plural* Zellen
• = cell
• = booth

das **Zelt**, *plural* Zelte
= tent

der **Zement**
= cement

der **Zentimeter**, *plural* Zentimeter
= centimetre, = centimeter

das **Zentimetermaß**, *plural*
Zentimetermaße
= tape measure

zentral *adjective*
= central

die **Zentrale**, *plural* Zentralen
• = central office
• = headquarters
• = (telephone) exchange

die **Zentralheizung**, *plural*
Zentralheizungen
= central heating

das **Zentrum**, *plural* Zentren
= centre

zerbrechen *irregular verb*
• = to break
• (**!** *sein*) = to break
die Tasse ist zerbrochen = the cup has
broken

zerbrechlich *adjective*
= fragile

die **Zeremonie**, *plural* Zeremonien
= ceremony

zerreißen *irregular verb*
• = to tear
= to tear up
• (**!** *sein*) = to tear

zerschneiden *irregular verb*
= to cut (up)

zerstören *verb*
= to destroy

die **Zerstörung**
= destruction

zerstreut *adjective*
= absent-minded

der **Zettel**, *plural* Zettel
• = piece of paper
• **✱**= note

das **Zeug✱**
= stuff

der **Zeuge**, *plural* Zeugen
= witness

die **Zeugin**, *plural* Zeuginnen
= witness

das **Zeugnis**, *plural* Zeugnisse
• = certificate
• (*at school*) = report

die **Ziege**, *plural* Ziegen
= goat

Z

der **Ziegel**, *plural* Ziegel
* = tile, = brick

ziehen *irregular verb*
* = to pull
  = to pull out
  (*gently*) = to draw
  einen Strich ziehen = to draw a line
* (*in a lottery*) = to draw
* sich ziehen (*of a path, road*) = to run
* (*cultivate*) = to grow
* es zieht = there is a draught
* (**!** *sein*) = to move
  wir ziehen nach London = we are moving
  to London

das **Ziel**, *plural* Ziele
* = destination
* = goal, = aim
* (*in sport*) = finish

zielen *verb*
= to aim

die **Zielscheibe**, *plural* Zielscheiben
= target

ziemlich *adverb*
= quite

zierlich *adjective*
= dainty

die **Ziffer**, *plural* Ziffern
= figure

das **Zifferblatt**, *plural* Zifferblätter
= face, = dial

die **Zigarette**, *plural* Zigaretten
= cigarette

die **Zigarre**, *plural* Zigarren
= cigar

der **Zigeuner**, *plural* Zigeuner
= gypsy

die **Zigeunerin**, *plural* Zigeunerinnen
= gypsy

das **Zimmer**, *plural* Zimmer
= room
Zimmer frei = vacancies
Zimmer mit Frühstück = bed and
breakfast

das **Zinn**
= zinc

Zinsen (*plural*)
= interest

der **Zinssatz**, *plural* Zinssätze
= interest rate

zirka *adverb*
= about

der **Zirkel**, *plural* Zirkel
= pair of compasses

✗ in informal situations

der **Zirkus**, *plural* Zirkusse
= circus

zischen *verb*
= to hiss

zitieren *verb*
= to quote

die **Zitrone**, *plural* Zitronen
= lemon

zittern *verb*
= to tremble, = to shake
(*with cold*) = to shiver

der **Zivildienst**
= community service

die **Zivilisation**, *plural* Zivilisationen
= civilization

zog ▶ ziehen

zögern *verb*
= to hesitate

der **Zoll**, *plural* Zölle
* = customs
* = duty

zollfrei *adjective*
= duty-free

der **Zopf**, *plural* Zöpfe
= plait, = braid

der **Zorn**
= anger

zornig *adjective*
= angry

zu
1 *preposition* (+ *dative*)
* = to
  zu . . . hin = towards
  zu Hause = at home
* = with
  die Jacke passt nicht zu dem Rock = the
  jacket doesn't go with that skirt
* (*with time, price*) = at
  das Stück zu fünf Euro = at 5 euros each
* (*showing purpose*) = for
  zum Spaß = for fun
* (*indicating change, a result*) = into
  zu etwas werden = to turn into
  something
* (*towards*)
  nett zu jemandem sein = to be nice to
  someone
* zu Fuß = on foot
* (*with numbers and quantities*)
  wir waren zu zweit = there were two of us
  das Ergebnis war zwei zu eins = the
  result was 2–1
* (*on the occasion of*)
  was schenkst du ihm zum Geburtstag? =
  what are you giving him for his
  birthday?
  jemandem zu etwas gratulieren = to
  congratulate someone on something

2 *adverb*
* = too
zu sehr = too much
* (*indicating direction*) = towards
* Tür zu!✖ = shut the door!
3 *conjunction* = to
nichts zu trinken = nothing to drink
zu verkaufen = for sale

das **Zubehör**
= accessories

zu|bereiten *verb*
= to prepare

zu|binden *irregular verb*
= to tie (up)

züchten *verb*
= to breed

zucken *verb*
= to twitch

der **Zucker**
= sugar

der **Zuckerguß**
= icing

zuckern *verb*
= to sweeten

zu|decken *verb*
= to cover (up)

zueinander *adverb*
= to one another
sie passen gut zueinander = they go well
together

zuerst *adverb*
* = first
* = at first

der **Zufall**, *plural* Zufälle
= chance
= coincidence

zufällig
1 *adjective* = chance
2 *adverb* = by chance

zufrieden *adjective*
= content
mit etwas zufrieden sein = to be satisfied
with something

der **Zug**, *plural* Züge
* = train
* = procession
* = draught
* (*of a person*) = characteristic
* (*in board games*) = move
* (*when drinking*) = swig
* (*when smoking*) = drag

die **Zugabe**, *plural* Zugaben
* = free gift
* (*at a concert*) = encore

der **Zugang**, *plural* Zugänge
= access

die **Zugbrücke**, *plural* Zugbrücken
= drawbridge

zu|geben *irregular verb*
* = to add
* = to admit

der **Zügel**, *plural* Zügel
= rein

zügig *adjective*
= quick

zu|greifen *irregular verb*
* to grab it/them
* (*at table*) = to help oneself
* = to lend a hand

zugunsten *preposition* (+ *genitive*)
= in favour of

zu|haben *irregular verb*
= to be closed

das **Zuhause**
= home

zu|hören *verb*
= to listen

der **Zuhörer**, *plural* Zuhörer
= listener
die Zuhörer = the audience

die **Zuhörerin**, *plural* Zuhörerinnen
= listener

zu|kleben *verb*
* = to seal
* = to glue

zu|knöpfen *verb*
= to button up

die **Zukunft**
= future

zukünftig *adjective*
= future

zu|lassen *irregular verb*
* = to allow
ein Auto zulassen = to register a car
* = to leave closed

die **Zulassung**, *plural* Zulassungen
* = registration
* = admission

zuletzt *adverb*
* = last
nicht zuletzt = not least
* = in the end

zum = zu dem

zu|machen *verb*
= to close
= to fasten

zunächst *adverb*
* = first
* = at first

der **Zuname**, *plural* Zunamen
= surname

Z

das **Zündholz**, *plural* Zündhölzer
= match

die **Zündung**, *plural* Zündungen
= ignition

zu|nehmen *irregular verb*
• = to increase
• = to put on weight

die **Zunge**, *plural* Zungen
= tongue

zur = zu der
zur Schule = to school

zurecht|kommen *irregular verb*
(**!** *sein*)
= to cope, = to manage

zurück *adverb*
= back
Berlin, hin und zurück = return to Berlin

zurück|bekommen *irregular verb*
= to get back

zurück|bringen *irregular verb*
• = to bring back
• = to take back

zurück|fahren *irregular verb*
• = to drive back
• (**!** *sein*) = to go back, (*by car*) = to drive back

zurück|führen *verb*
• = to lead back
• = to attribute

zurück|geben *irregular verb*
= to give back

zurück|gehen *irregular verb* (**!** *sein*)
• = to go back
• = to go down, = to decrease

zurück|halten *irregular verb*
• = to hold back
• sich zurückhalten = to restrain oneself

zurück|kommen *irregular verb*
(**!** *sein*)
= to come back
(*arrive*) = to get back

zurück|lassen *irregular verb*
= to leave behind

zurück|legen *verb*
• = to put back
• = to keep, = to put aside
• (*when walking*) = to cover
• sich zurücklegen = to lie back

zurück|lehnen: sich zurücklehnen *verb*
= to lean back

zurück|nehmen *irregular verb*
= to take back

zurück|rufen *irregular verb*
= to call back

zurück|treten *irregular verb* (**!** *sein*)
• = to step back
• = to resign

zurück|zahlen *verb*
= to pay back

zurück|ziehen *irregular verb*
• = to draw back
• sich zurückziehen = to withdraw, = to retire

zurzeit *adverb*
= at the moment

die **Zusage**, *plural* Zusagen
= acceptance

zusammen *adverb*
• = together
• = altogether

die **Zusammenarbeit**
= co-operation

zusammen|arbeiten *verb*
= to co-operate

zusammen|bauen *verb*
= to assemble

zusammen|brechen *irregular verb*
(**!** *sein*)
= to collapse

zusammen|fassen *verb*
= to summarize

die **Zusammenfassung**, *plural*
Zusammenfassungen
= summary

zusammen|halten *irregular verb*
= to hold together
= to keep together
wir halten zusammen = we'll stick together

der **Zusammenhang**, *plural*
Zusammenhänge
• = context
• = connection

zusammen|kommen *irregular verb*
(**!** *sein*)
= to meet

zusammen|legen *irregular verb*
• = to put together
• = to fold up
• (*pool money*) = to club together

zusammen|nehmen: sich zusammennehmen *irregular verb*
= to pull oneself together

zusammen|passen *verb*
= to match
(*of people*) = to be well matched
(*of parts*) = to fit together

der **Zusammenstoß**, *plural*
Zusammenstöße
= collision, = crash

zusammen|stoßen *irregular verb*
(**!** *sein*)
= to collide, = to crash

zusammen|zählen *verb*
= to add up

zusätzlich
1 *adjective* = additional, = extra
2 *adverb* = in addition, = extra

zu|schauen *verb*
= to watch

der **Zuschauer**, *plural* Zuschauer
= spectator
(*TV*) = viewer
die Zuschauer = the audience

die **Zuschauerin**, *plural* Zuschauerinnen
= spectator
(*TV*) = viewer

der **Zuschlag**, *plural* Zuschläge
= surcharge
(*on a train*) = supplement

zu|schließen *irregular verb*
= to lock (up)

der **Zuschuss** (**Zuschuß**ᴼᴸᴰ), *plural*
Zuschüsse
= contribution
= grant

zu|sehen *irregular verb*
= to watch
zusehen, dass = to see to it that

der **Zustand**, *plural* Zustände
= condition
= state

zuständig *adjective*
= responsible

die **Zustellung**, *plural* Zustellungen
= delivery

zu|stimmen *verb*
= to agree

die **Zustimmung**, *plural* Zustimmungen
= agreement

zu|stoßen *irregular verb* (**!** *sein*)
= to happen

die **Zutat**, *plural* Zutaten
= ingredient

zu|trauen *verb*
jemandem etwas zutrauen = to
think someone capable of
something

zu|treffen *irregular verb*
auf etwas zutreffen = to apply to
something

der **Zutritt**
= entry
Zutritt haben = to have access

zuverlässig *adjective*
= reliable

zuviel ᴼᴸᴰ▶viel

zuwenig ᴼᴸᴰ▶wenig

zu|zahlen *verb*
= to pay extra

zu|ziehen *irregular verb*
• = to pull tight
die Vorhänge zuziehen = to draw the
curtains
• sich eine Verletzung zuziehen = to
sustain an injury

zuzüglich *preposition* (+ *genitive*)
= plus

der **Zwang**, *plural* Zwänge
• = force
• = obligation

zwängen *verb*
= to squeeze

zwanglos *adjective*
= casual, = informal

zwanzig *adjective*
= twenty

zwar *adverb*
= admittedly
und zwar = to be exact

der **Zweck**, *plural* Zwecke
= purpose
es hat keinen Zweck = there's no point

zwei *adjective*
= two

zweideutig *adjective*
= ambiguous

zweifach *adjective*
= twice

der **Zweifel**, *plural* Zweifel
= doubt

zweifellos *adverb*
= undoubtedly

zweifeln *verb*
= to doubt
an etwas zweifeln = to doubt something

der **Zweig**, *plural* Zweige
= branch

zweimal *adverb*
= twice

zweisprachig *adjective*
= bilingual

zweit *adverb*
zu zweit = in twos
wir waren zu zweit = there were two of us

Z

zweite ▶zweiter

zweiteilig *adjective*
= two-piece
= two-part

zweitens *adverb*
= secondly

zweiter/zweite/zweites *adjective*
= second

der **Zwerg**, *plural* Zwerge
= dwarf

die **Zwiebel**, *plural* Zwiebeln
• = onion
• = bulb

der **Zwilling**, *plural* Zwillinge
• = twin
• Zwillinge = Gemini

zwingen *irregular verb*
• to force
• sich zwingen = to force oneself

zwischen *preposition* (+ *dative or accusative*)
= between
(*in a crowd*) = among

zwischendurch *adverb*
= in between
= now and again

der **Zwischenfall**, *plural* Zwischenfälle
= incident

der **Zwischenraum**, *plural* Zwischenräume
= gap, = space

die **Zwischenzeit**
in der Zwischenzeit = in the meantime

zwo✕ *adjective*
= two

zwölf *adjective*
= twelve

zwoter/zwote/zwotes✕ *adjective*
= second

zynisch *adjective*
= cynical

✕ in informal situations

Dictionary know-how

Dictionary know-how

This section contains a number of short exercises which will help you to use your dictionary more effectively. You will find answers to all of the exercises at the end of the section.

1 Which is which?

Here is an extract from a German holiday advertisement. Find fifteen nouns and underline them, and eight adjectives and circle them — or make two lists. If you are not sure of some words, look them up in the German–English part of the dictionary and see if the term 'noun' or 'adjective' is used to describe them.

> ### URLAUB AUF DEM BAUERNHOF
>
> Besonders geeignet für Familien mit kleinen Kindern, Hunde erlaubt.
> Gemütliche Zimmer mit Dusche und Balkon. Gute, österreichische
> Küche. Wir haben eigene Ponys und Fahrräder und einen großen
> Spielplatz. Kinder fünfzig Prozent Ermäßigung.

2 Der, die, or das?

Here are some English nouns which appear in the English–German part of the dictionary. Find out their German equivalents and make a list with three columns: *der* for masculine nouns, *die* for feminine nouns and *das* for neuter nouns. If there is more than one German equivalent, put each one in the right gender column.

bag	cake	door	child
penguin	library	raincoat	thunderstorm
shirt	underpants	house	sun
moon	glasses	book	snow
plane	tyre	ear	adventure

3 Jumbled-up buildings

Each of these German words is a building, but the letters have been jumbled up. Put them in the right order and look up the word on the German–English side of the dictionary to find the right article for each building.

TOPS	RICHEK	LEUSCH	HABFOHN
HUSTARA	HUFAUSAK	KUSEPRARMT	AHSU

4 **Nouns and pronouns**

The following example shows how pronouns can replace nouns:

Emma erklärt Peter die Regeln

sie erklärt Peter die Regeln

sie erklärt ihm die Regeln

sie erklärt sie ihm *(note the change of order)*

Underline the pronouns in the example sentences above, and change the next two sentences in the same way.

Gabi zeigt Fritz das Bild

der Mann gibt der Frau die Tasche

5 **Verbspotting**

Rearrange the following groups of words to form correct sentences. Then list the infinitive of the verb in each sentence—as it appears on the German–English side of the dictionary.

fährt nach Berlin er heute

Dienstag jeden ihr Fußball spielt?

Postkarte was nach kostet eine England?

zeigt uns er neue die Wohnung

wie Film der hieß?

6 **Where does the verb go?**

German verbs often consist of more than one word. This happens when they combine with another word or with an auxiliary verb to form the perfect or future tense. Place the two missing German words in the correct position in the following sentences. For example:

Er (*can tell*) gute Geschichten. **(kann erzählen)**
= Er kann gute Geschichten erzählen.

Der kleine Junge (*can walk*) noch nicht. **(kann laufen)**

Meine Schwester (*has bought*) ein neues Kleid für die Party. **(hat gekauft)**

Er (*will go*) mit dem Zug nach Frankfurt. **(wird fahren)**

Seine Mutter (*would like to visit*) uns in Italien. **(möchte besuchen)**

Ich (*must sign*) den Brief noch. **(muss unterschreiben)**

7 Separable or inseparable?

Here is a list of German verbs. Some have prefixes which are always separable, and others have prefixes which are never separable. Sort the separable from the inseparable verbs in two lists. If you are not sure of some of them, look them up on the German–English side of the dictionary. Separable verbs are marked in the dictionary with a vertical bar after the prefix.

verstehen	**ausgehen**	**zerstören**	**losfahren**
ankommen	**beginnen**	**einsteigen**	**verlaufen**
festhalten	**aufhören**	**mitmachen**	**erfinden**

8 Splitting verbs

Put the separable verbs in the right place in the following sentences. Be careful with the ending of the first part of each verb.

Die Kinder . . . nach Weihnachten . . . . **(wiederkommen)**

Heute . . . wir ein Picknick . . . . **(mitnehmen)**

Ich . . . morgens um sieben Uhr . . . . **(aufstehen)**

Er . . . erst nach Weihnachten . . . . . **(zurückfahren)**

9 Subject or object?

Subjects and objects have been left out of sentences in this German newspaper report. Choose suitable words from the the list below to fill in the gaps. Look up the words on the German–English side of the dictionary and add the right article to the nouns.

FRANZ KATER VERHAFTET

Die .... verhaftete einen gefährlichen .... am Dienstag Abend. Franz Kater stahl letzte Woche ein wertvolles .... aus einer Galerie. Obwohl es dunkel war, erkannten zwei .... den Einbrecher sofort. Kater trug einen braunen .... und eine schwarze .... Er zog eine .... aus der Tasche. "Hände hoch, oder .... schieße", schrie der .... Nach genauer Untersuchung stellte die .... fest, dass .... nur eine .... hatte.

Einbrecher	Spielzeugpistole	Polizei	Bild	Mantel	Polizei
Polizisten	ich	Mütze	er	Pistole	Einbrecher

10 **Finding separable verbs**

Find the separable verb(s) in each sentence and write them down in the infinitive — as they appear on the German–English side of the dictionary. Leave out the vertical bar, which is only there in the dictionary to show you that the verb is separable.

Um wie viel Uhr kommt ihr an?

Der Vater holt die Kinder von der Schule ab.

Wann findet das Konzert statt?

Die Kinder sehen viel fern.

11 **Word search**

Fourteen German words are hidden in this grid. They are listed below on the right. Most read across, but some read down. When you have found them, ring them, list them by part of speech (noun, adjective, etc.), and add the right article to nouns.

G	P	A	L	A	S	T	X	G	E
F	A	H	R	E	R	I	N	A	J
K	Q	M	J	U	N	G	I	S	L
Ä	Q	U	A	D	R	A	T	E	P
L	A	B	B	A	D	E	N	G	F
T	L	T	X	Y	F	A	C	H	A
E	T	D	E	R	Z	W	T	O	H
Z	E	I	C	H	N	U	N	G	R
U	L	C	H	O	R	W	A	Y	E
L	Ä	C	H	E	L	N	K	S	R

alt	Gas
baden	jung
Chor	Kälte
der	lächeln
Fach	Palast
Fahrer	Quadrat
Fahrerin	Zeichnung

12 **Find the plural**

Use your dictionary to find the plural of the following nouns.

der Mantel	**die** ....
ein Mädchen	**zwei** ....
ein Korb	**zehn** ....
eine Möglichkeit	**viele** ....
das Buch	**die** ....
ein Radio	**drei** ....
eine Verkäuferin	**zwei** ....
eine Kette	**viele** ....
das Auto	**die** ....
ein Tischtuch	**zwei** ....

13 **Building a sentence**

In a German main clause the subject usually comes before the verb. If there are two objects, the indirect object comes before the direct object. For example:

● | ■ | ▶ | ▲
Der Lehrer | gibt | dem Mädchen | das Buch

Make ten sentences using the following words. You don't always have to use both direct and indirect object in your sentences.

- ● **subjects:**   der Junge, das Mädchen
- ■ **verbs:**   kauft, schreibt, singt, spielt, gibt
- ▲ **direct objects:**   Klavier, eine CD, einen Brief, ein Lied
- ▶ **indirect objects:**   dem Lehrer, seiner Mutter, ihr

14 **Time—manner—place**

A useful rule for word order when speaking or writing German is TIME–MANNER–PLACE. For example:

Ich fahre morgen mit dem Zug nach Frankfurt
(*time* = morgen), (*manner* = mit dem Zug), (*place* = nach Frankfurt).

Practise the TIME–MANNER–PLACE sequence by inserting the words in the brackets in the right place in each of the following sentences.

Emma fährt jeden Morgen zur Universität. (mit dem Rad)

Wir sind mit dem Auto nach Italien gefahren. (letzten Sommer)

Wir fahren dieses Jahr zu Weihnachten. (nach München)

15 **Find the meaning**

Some words have more than one meaning, and it's important to check that you have chosen the right one. In this dictionary different meanings of a word are marked by a bullet point (•).

We have given you one meaning of the German words below. Use your dictionary to find another one.

die Dame	• lady	• ....
die Decke	• blanket	• ....
aufheben	• to pick up	• ....
dick	• thick	• ....
der Zug	• train	• ....
der Hahn	• tap	• ....
der Satz	• set	• ....

16 **Asking questions**

In German questions are often introduced by a pronoun such as *wer* or an adverb such as *wann*. In these cases the verb is the second element. For example:

statement   Emma wohnt in London

question   Wer wohnt in London?

Look up the bracketed words on the English-German side of the dictionary and use them to turn these statements into questions.

Das Buch liegt auf dem Tisch.   (*what*)

Peter wohnt in dieser Wohnung.   (*who*)

Wir fahren morgen nach Oxford.   (*when*)

Die Großeltern wohnen in Spanien. (*where*)

17 **Umlauts**

The double dots of all the umlauts (ä, ö, ü) have been left out in this letter. Use your dictionary to help put the dots over the right vowels.

Liebe Gabi,

danke fur die Einladung zu deiner Party. Ich wurde gern kommen, aber mochte nicht alleine zuruckfahren. Ist es moglich, zwei Nachte bei dir zu bleiben? Mein Vater kann mich dann nach funf abholen. Ruf mich bald an, damit wir uns uber alles unterhalten konnen.

Herzliche Gruße

deine Karin

18 **Find the word**

German nouns are often made up of two or more separate words. Ten such compound nouns have been split in two and put in separate lists. Choosing the first part of the word from list 1 and the second from list 2 , use your dictionary to help you find out what they are. Sometimes different word combinations make different nouns.

(list 1)

DAUER, AUTO, BAHN, OHR, SCHLAF, SEIL, FLUG, ZAHN, TELEFON, BRIEF

(list 2)

BUCH, BAHN, ZIMMER, MARKE, WELLE, RING, HAFEN, ZEIT, HOF, ARZT

19 **Which preposition?**

Look up the preposition 'to' and choose the right German word for the preposition gaps in the following sentences.

Nächste Woche fahren wir . . . Deutschland.

Ich muss . . . die Toilette gehen.

Peter schreibt einen Brief . . . seine Schwester.

Es ist jetzt zehn Minuten . . . fünf.

Wie komme ich . . . Bahnhof?

20 **Find the verb**

Some words in English can be both nouns and verbs, for example, **race**. For this exercise, look up the following English words on the English–German side of the dictionary and then give the German for the verb only.

insult   kiss   dance   measure   rain

Answers

1

Nouns: Urlaub, Bauernhof, Familien, Kindern, Hunde, Zimmer, Dusche, Balkon, Küche, Ponys, Fahrräder, Spielplatz, Kinder, Prozent, Ermäßigung.

Adjectives: geeignet, kleinen, gemütliche, gute, österreichische, eigene, großen, fünfzig

2

Masculine nouns: der Kuchen, der Pinguin, der Regenmantel, der Mond, der Schnee, der Reifen.

Feminine nouns: die Tasche/die Tüte, die Tür, die Bibliothek, die Unterhose, die Sonne, die Brille.

Neuter nouns: das Kind, das Gewitter, das Hemd, das Haus, das Buch, das Flugzeug, das Ohr, das Abenteuer.

3

die Post, die Kirche, die Schule, der Bahnhof, das Rathaus, das Kaufhaus, der Supermarkt, das Haus.

4

Emma erklärt Peter die Regeln, **sie** erklärt Peter die Regeln, **sie** erklärt **ihm** die Regeln, **sie** erklärt **sie ihm**;

Gabi zeigt Fritz das Bild, **sie** zeigt Fritz das Bild, **sie** zeigt **ihm** das Bild, **sie** zeigt **es ihm**;

der Mann gibt der Frau die Tasche, **er** gibt der Frau die Tasche, **er** gibt **ihr** die Tasche, **er** gibt **sie ihr**.

5

er fährt heute nach Berlin (fahren); spielt ihr jeden Dienstag Fußball? (spielen); was kostet eine Postkarte nach England? (kosten); er zeigt uns die neue Wohnung (zeigen); wie hieß der Film? (heißen).

6

Der kleine Junge kann noch nicht laufen.

Meine Schwester hat ein neues Kleid für die Party gekauft.

Er wird mit dem Zug nach Frankfurt fahren.

Seine Mutter möchte uns in Italien besuchen.

Ich muss den Brief noch unterschreiben.

7

Separable verbs: ausgehen, losfahren, ankommen, einsteigen, festhalten, aufhören, mitmachen.

Inseparable verbs: verstehen, zerstören, beginnen, verlaufen, erfinden.

8

Die Kinder kommen nach Weihnachten wieder.

Heute nehmen wir ein Picknick mit.

Ich stehe morgens um sieben Uhr auf.

Er fährt erst nach Weihnachten zurück.

9

Die **Polizei** verhaftete einen gefährlichen **Einbrecher** am Dienstag Abend. Franz Kater stahl letzte Woche ein wertvolles **Bild** aus einer Galerie. Obwohl es dunkel war, erkannten zwei **Polizisten** den Einbrecher sofort. Kater trug einen braunen **Mantel** und eine schwarze **Mütze**. Er zog eine **Pistole** aus der Tasche. "Hände hoch, oder **ich** schieße", schrie der **Einbrecher**. Nach genauer Untersuchung stellte die **Polizei** fest, dass **er** nur eine **Spielzeugpistole** hatte.

Subjects: die Polizei, die Polizisten, ich, der Einbrecher, die Polizei, er.

Objects: der Einbrecher, das Bild, der Mantel, die Mütze, die Pistole, die Spielzeugpistole.

10

ankommen; abholen; stattfinden; fernsehen.

11

Masculine nouns: der Palast, der Fahrer, der Chor; **feminine nouns:** die Fahrerin, die Kälte, die Zeichnung; **neuter nouns:** das Gas, das Quadrat, das Fach; **adjectives:** alt, jung; **verbs:** lächeln, baden; **article:** der.

12

der Mantel, die Mäntel; ein Mädchen, zwei Mädchen; ein Korb, zehn Körbe; eine Möglichkeit, viele Möglichkeiten; das Buch, die Bücher; ein Radio, drei Radios; eine Verkäuferin, zwei Verkäuferinnen; eine Kette, viele Ketten; das Auto, die Autos; ein Tischtuch, zwei Tischtücher.

13

der Junge kauft (dem Lehrer/seiner Mutter/ihr) eine CD

der Junge schreibt (dem Lehrer/seiner Mutter/ihr) einen Brief

der Junge singt (dem Lehrer/seiner Mutter/ihr) ein Lied

der Junge spielt Klavier/eine CD

der Junge gibt (dem Lehrer/seiner Mutter/ihr) eine CD

das Mädchen kauft (dem Lehrer/ihr) eine CD

das Mädchen schreibt (dem Lehrer/ihr) einen Brief

das Mädchen singt (dem Lehrer/ihr) ein Lied

das Mädchen spielt Klavier/eine CD

das Mädchen gibt (dem Lehrer/ihr) eine CD

14

Emma fährt jeden Morgen mit dem Rad zur Universität.

Wir sind letzten Sommer mit dem Auto nach Italien gefahren.

Wir fahren dieses Jahr zu Weihnachten nach München.

15

Possible answers:

die Dame	• queen
	• draughts, checkers
die Decke	• cloth
	• ceiling
aufheben	• to keep
dick	• fat
der Zug	• procession
	• draught
	• characteristic
	• move
	• swig
	• drag
der Hahn	• cock
der Satz	• sentence
	• leap
	• movement
	• rate

16

Was liegt auf dem Tisch?

Wer wohnt in dieser Wohnung?

Wann fahren wir nach Oxford?

Wo wohnen die Großeltern?

17

Liebe Gabi,

danke für die Einladung zu deiner Party. Ich würde gern kommen, aber möchte nicht alleine zurückfahren. Ist es möglich, zwei Nächte bei dir zu bleiben? Mein Vater kann mich dann nach fünf abholen. Ruf mich bald an, damit wir uns über alles unterhalten können.

Herzliche Grüße

deine Karin

18

Dauerwelle, Autobahn, Bahnhof, Ohrring, Schlafzimmer, Seilbahn, Flughafen, Zahnarzt, Telefonbuch, Briefmarke; **extra nouns:** Flugbahn, Flugzeit, Automarke.

19

Nächste Woche fahren wir **nach** Deutschland.

Ich muss **auf** die Toilette gehen.

Peter schreibt einen Brief **an** seine Schwester.

Es ist jetzt zehn Minuten **vor** fünf.

Wie komme ich **zum** Bahnhof?

20

beleidigen, küssen, tanzen, messen, regnen.

English–German

Aa

a *article*
= ein/eine/ein

> ! Note that the article changes according to the gender of the noun it goes with: a table = ein Tisch (*masculine*); a flower = eine Blume (*feminine*); a house = ein Haus (*neuter*).

not a = kein/keine/kein

ability *noun*
(*talent*) = (die) Begabung

able *adjective*
(*competent*) = fähig
to be able to do something = etwas tun können

about
1 *preposition*
(*on the subject of*) = über (+ *accusative*)
a programme about life in Germany = eine Sendung über das Leben in Deutschland
2 *adverb*
(*approximately*) = ungefähr
in about three weeks = in ungefähr drei Wochen
she is about to [cry | sneeze | go …] = sie [weint | niest | geht …] gleich

above
1 *preposition* = über (+ *dative*)
their flat is above the shop = ihre Wohnung ist über dem Geschäft
the shelf above it = das Regal darüber
2 *adverb* = oben
above all = vor allem

abroad *adverb*
= im Ausland
to travel abroad = ins Ausland reisen

absent *adjective*
= abwesend
to be absent from school = in der Schule fehlen

accent *noun*
= (der) Akzent
to speak with a German accent = mit deutschem Akzent sprechen

accept *verb*
(*receive*) = annehmen

access *noun*
• = (der) Zugang
access to the internet = Zugang zum Internet
• (*road*) = (die) Zufahrt

accident *noun*
• (*causing injury or damage*) = (der) Unfall
the accident and emergency department = die Notfallstation

• (*chance*) = (der) Zufall
by accident = zufällig

accommodation (*British*), **accommodations** (*US*) *noun*
= (die) Unterkunft
accommodation is very expensive in London = Wohnungen *or* Zimmer sind in London sehr teuer

accompany *verb*
= begleiten

account *noun*
• (*in a bank*) = (das) Konto
there's money in my account = ich habe Geld auf meinem Konto
• you have to take expenses into account = man muß die Unkosten berücksichtigen

accountant *noun*
= (der) Buchhalter/(die) Buchhalterin

accurate *adjective*
• (*correct*) = richtig
• (*precise*) = genau
an accurate description = eine genaue Beschreibung

accuse *verb*
= beschuldigen
he accused them of stealing his bike = er beschuldigte sie, sein Rad gestohlen zu haben

across *preposition*
• = über (+ *accusative*)
to go across the street = über die Straße gehen (! *sein*)
• (*on the other side of*) = auf der anderen Seite (+ *genitive*)
across the river = auf der anderen Seite des Flusses
he lives across the street = er wohnt gegenüber

act *verb*
• (*take action*) = handeln
• (*perform as an actor*) = spielen

activity *noun*
= (die) Aktivität
activities = Veranstaltungen

actor *noun*
= (der) Schauspieler

actress *noun*
= (die) Schauspielerin

actually *adverb*
• (*in fact*) = eigentlich
I haven't actually seen the film yet = ich habe den Film eigentlich noch nicht gesehen

* (really) = wirklich
did he actually say that? = hat er das
wirklich gesagt?
* (by the way) = übrigens

adapt verb
(get used to) = sich anpassen
to adapt to = sich anpassen (+ dative)
**she quickly adapted to her new
environment** = sie hat sich schnell der
neuen Umgebung angepasst

add verb
* = hinzufügen
to add a spoonful of lemon juice = einen
Löffel Zitronensaft dazugeben
* (in maths) = addieren

addicted adjective
= süchtig
to become addicted to drugs =
drogensüchtig werden (**!** sein)

address noun
= (die) Adresse, = (die) Anschrift
what's his address? = wo wohnt er?

adhesive noun
= (der) Klebstoff

adjust verb
* (get used to) = sich gewöhnen
to adjust to something = sich an etwas
(accusative) gewöhnen
* (alter setting) = einstellen

administration noun
= (die) Verwaltung

admire verb
= bewundern

admit verb
* (own up) = zugeben
he won't admit to being jealous = er will
nicht zugeben, dass er eifersüchtig ist
* (allow in) = hereinlassen
he was admitted to hospital = er wurde im
Krankenhaus aufgenommen

adolescent noun
= (der/die) Jugendliche

adopt verb
= adoptieren

adore verb
= lieben
she adores strawberries = sie mag
Erdbeeren wahnsinnig gern

adult noun
= (der/die) Erwachsene

advance noun
in advance = im Voraus
here's £30 in advance = hier sind dreißig
Pfund als Vorschuss

advantage noun
* (positive point) = (der) Vorteil
to have an advantage over someone =
jemandem gegenüber im Vorteil sein

* **to take advantage of a situation** = eine
Situation ausnutzen

adventure noun
= (das) Abenteuer

advert, advertisement noun
* (on TV) = (der) Werbespot
* (in a newspaper) = (die) Anzeige
to answer a job advertisement = sich auf
eine Stellenanzeige melden

advertising noun
= (die) Werbung

advice noun
= (der) Rat
to ask someone's advice = jemanden um
Rat fragen
a piece of advice = ein Ratschlag

advise verb
= raten (+ dative)
to advise someone to rest = jemandem
raten, sich auszuruhen
to advise against it = davon abraten

aerial noun
= (die) Antenne

aerobics noun
= (das) Aerobic
to do aerobics = Aerobic machen

aeroplane noun
= (das) Flugzeug

affect verb
* (have an effect on) = sich auswirken auf
(+ accusative)
* (distress) = treffen
they were badly affected by the loss = der
Verlust traf sie hart

afford verb
to be able to afford a car = sich (dative) ein
Auto leisten können
he can't afford to move = er kann es sich
(dative) nicht leisten umzuziehen

afraid adjective
* (scared)
to be afraid = Angst haben
to be afraid of spiders = Angst vor Spinnen
haben
* (expressing regret)
I'm afraid not = leider nicht
I'm afraid I can't come = ich kann leider
nicht kommen

Africa noun
= (das) Afrika ▶ **Countries p. 208**

African
1 noun = (der) Afrikaner/(die) Afrikanerin
2 adjective = afrikanisch ▶ **Countries p. 208**

after
1 preposition = nach (+ dative)
we'll leave after breakfast = wir fahren
nach dem Frühstück ab
the day after tomorrow = übermorgen
after that = danach

2 *conjunction* = nachdem
after brushing her teeth, she went to bed =
nachdem sie sich die Zähne geputzt
hatte, ging sie ins Bett
after all = schließlich

afternoon *noun*
= (der) Nachmittag
in the afternoon = am Nachmittag
this afternoon = heute Nachmittag
on Monday afternoon =
am Montagnachmittag

aftershave *noun*
= (das) Rasierwasser

afterward (*US*), **afterwards** (*British*)
adverb
• (*later*) = nachher
• (*after a particular event*) = danach
he died soon afterwards = er starb kurz
danach

again *adverb*
= wieder
are you going to Germany again this year?
= fahrt ihr dieses Jahr wieder nach
Deutschland?
let's try again = versuchen wir es noch
einmal
again and again = immer wieder

against *preposition*
• (*close to*) = gegen (+ *accusative*)
he leaned against the wall = er lehnte sich
gegen die Wand
• (*not in favour of*) = gegen (+ *accusative*)
to be against violence = gegen Gewalt sein

age
1 *noun* = (das) Alter
under age = minderjährig
2 *verb* = altern
he has aged = er ist alt geworden

aged *adjective*
= im Alter von
a boy aged 10 = ein zehnjähriger Junge

ago *adverb*
= vor (+ *dative*)
two weeks ago = vor zwei Wochen

agree *verb*
• (*have the same opinion*) = einer Meinung
sein
I don't agree with you = ich bin anderer
Meinung
• (*give one's consent*) = einwilligen
to agree to a plan = mit einem Plan
einverstanden sein
• (*reach a decision*) = sich einigen
to agree on a price = sich auf einen Preis
einigen

agreement *noun*
• (*settlement*) = (die) Abmachung
• (*contract*) = (das) Abkommen
• (*when sharing an opinion*) = (die)
Übereinstimmung

to be in agreement with someone = mit
jemandem einer Meinung sein

agriculture *noun*
= (die) Landwirtschaft

ahead *adverb*
• **we went on ahead** = wir sind vorgegangen
I would like to send my baggage on ahead
= ich möchte mein Gepäck
vorausschicken
• **ahead of** = vor (+ *dative*)
the people ahead of us = die Leute vor uns

Aids *noun*
= (das) Aids

aim
1 *noun*
= (das) Ziel
2 *verb*
• (*try*) = versuchen
• (*direct*)
to be aimed at someone = auf jemanden
abgezielt sein
(*when using a weapon*)
to aim a rifle at someone = ein Gewehr auf
jemanden richten

air
1 *noun* = (die) Luft
2 *verb*
to air a room = ein Zimmer lüften

air-conditioning *noun*
= (die) Klimaanlage

aircraft *noun*
= (das) Flugzeug

air hostess *noun*
= (die) Stewardess

airline *noun*
= (die) Fluggesellschaft

airmail *noun*
= (die) Luftpost
to send a letter by airmail = einen Brief mit
or per Luftpost schicken

airplane (*US*) ▶aeroplane

airport *noun*
= (der) Flughafen

alarm clock *noun*
= (der) Wecker

alcohol *noun*
= (der) Alkohol

A levels *noun*
≈ (das) Abitur

alive *adjective*
= lebendig
to be alive = leben

all
1 *adjective*
• (*with a singular noun*) = ganz
all the time = die ganze Zeit
• (*with a plural noun*) = alle
all trains stop here = alle Züge halten hier

2 *pronoun*
- (*everybody*) = alle
  all of them = sie alle
- (*everything*) = alles
  that's all = das ist alles
  all of the town = die ganze Stadt
3 *adverb*
- = ganz
  to be all alone = ganz allein sein
  all at once = auf einmal
- (*score in sport*) **two all** = zwei zu zwei

allergy *noun*
= (die) Allergie

allow *verb*
to allow someone to leave = jemandem
  erlauben zu gehen
to be allowed to take a week off = eine
  Woche Urlaub nehmen dürfen
she's not allowed to hitchhike = sie darf
  nicht per Anhalter fahren
smoking is not allowed = Rauchen ist nicht
  gestattet

all right *adjective*
- (*when giving an opinion*) = ganz gut
  the film was all right = der Film war ganz
  gut
- (*when talking about health*)
  I'm all right = mir gehts ganz gut

  > ! Note that gehts, *written as one word, is*
  > *short for* geht es.

- (*when giving an opinion*) = in Ordnung, =
  okay✗

almond *noun*
= (die) Mandel

almost *adverb*
= fast
I almost forgot = ich hätte es fast vergessen

alone
1 *adjective* = allein
  leave me alone! = lass mich in Ruhe!
2 *adverb* = allein
  she doesn't like living alone = sie lebt
  nicht gern allein

along *preposition*
= entlang (+ *accusative*)

  > ! Note that entlang *is usually put after the*
  > *noun, which is in the accusative. When*
  > entlang *is used with a verb, it forms a*
  > *new, compound verb.*

along the street = die Straße entlang
to run along = entlanglaufen (! *sein*)

aloud *adverb*
= laut
to read aloud = vorlesen

already *adverb*
= schon
have you finished already? = bist du schon
  fertig?

also *adverb*
= auch

alternative *noun*
= (die) Alternative
you have no alternative = du hast keine
  andere Wahl

although *conjunction*
= obwohl
**although it was cold, he didn't have a coat
  on** = obwohl es kalt war, hatte er keinen
  Mantel an

altogether *adverb*
= insgesamt
how much is that altogether? = wie viel
  macht das insgesamt?

always *adverb*
= immer

amazing *adjective*
= erstaunlich

ambassador *noun*
= (der) Botschafter/ (die) Botschafterin

ambition *noun*
= (der) Ehrgeiz

ambitious *adjective*
= ehrgeizig

ambulance *noun*
= (der) Krankenwagen

America *noun*
= (das) Amerika ▶Countries p. 208

American
1 *noun* = (der) Amerikaner/ (die) Amerikanerin
2 *adjective* = amerikanisch ▶Countries p. 208

among, amongst *preposition*
- = unter (+ *dative*)
  among other things = unter anderem
- (*one of*)
  **Japan is among the world's richest
  countries** = Japan gehört zu den
  reichsten Ländern der Welt

amount *noun*
- (*quantity*) = (die) Menge
  I've got a huge amount of work = ich habe
  eine Menge Arbeit
- (*sum of money*) = (der) Betrag

amusement arcade *noun*
= (die) Spielhalle

amusing *adjective*
= amüsant

an ▶a

ancestor *noun*
= (der) Vorfahre

anchor *noun*
= (der) Anker

and *conjunction*
- = und

A

and so on = und so weiter
try and come = versuche zu kommen
faster and faster = immer schneller
for weeks and weeks = wochenlang
it's nice and warm today = heute ist es
  schön warm
* (*in numbers*)
  three hundred and fifty =
    dreihundertfünfzig ▶**Numbers p. 282**

anger *noun*
= (der) Zorn

angry *adjective*
= zornig
to be angry with someone = auf jemanden
  böse sein
you'll make her angry = du verärgerst sie
to get angry with someone = sich über
  jemanden ärgern

animal *noun*
= (das) Tier

ankle *noun*
= (der) Knöchel

anniversary *noun*
= (der) Jahrestag
my parents' wedding anniversary = der
  Hochzeitstag meiner Eltern

announcement *noun*
(*public statement*) = (die) Bekanntmachung

annoy *verb*
= ärgern
to be annoyed with someone = sich über
  jemanden ärgern
he's starting to annoy me = er regt mich
  langsam auf

annoyed *adjective*
= ärgerlich
she's annoyed with me = sie ist ärgerlich
  auf mich
he got very annoyed = er hat sich darüber
  sehr geärgert

annoying *adjective*
= ärgerlich
he is very annoying = er geht mir auf die
  Nerven

annual
1 *noun* = (das) Jahresalbum
2 *adjective* = jährlich
  the annual meeting = die
    Jahresversammlung

another
1 *adjective*
* (*additional*) = noch ein
  I'll buy another ticket = ich kaufe noch eine
    Karte
  it will take another three weeks = es wird
    noch drei Wochen dauern
* (*different*) = ein anderer/eine andere/ein
    anderes
  we can visit him another time = wir
    können ihn ein anderes Mal besuchen

2 *pronoun*
* (*one more*) = noch einer/noch eine/noch
    eins
* (*different one*) = ein anderer/eine
    andere/ein anderes
  one after another = einer nach dem
    anderen/eine nach der anderen/eins nach
    dem anderen

answer
1 *noun*
* (*reply*) = (die) Antwort
  to give the right answer = die richtige
    Antwort geben
  there's no answer (*at the door*) = niemand
    macht die Tür auf, (*on the phone*) =
    niemand meldet sich
* (*solution*) = (die) Lösung
2 *verb* = antworten (+ *dative*)
  he wouldn't answer me = er wollte mir
    nicht antworten
  to answer a question = eine Frage
    beantworten
  to answer the door = an die Tür gehen
  to answer the phone (*on one occasion*) =
    ans Telefon gehen, (*speak*) = sich melden
  to answer back = eine freche Antwort
    geben

answering machine *noun*
= (der) Anrufbeantworter

ant *noun*
= (die) Ameise

antibiotic *noun*
= (das) Antibiotikum
to be on antibiotics = Antibiotika nehmen

antique shop *noun*
= (das) Antiquitätengeschäft

anxious *adjective*
* (*worried*) = besorgt
  she was anxious about the children = sie
    war um die Kinder besorgt
* (*keen*)
  she was anxious to talk to him = sie wollte
    unbedingt mit ihm sprechen

any
1 *adjective*
* (*some*) = irgendein, (*plural*) =
    irgendwelche
  (*every*) = jeder/jede/jedes, (*plural*) = alle
  if you have any difficulties = wenn du
    irgendwelche Schwierigkeiten hast
  have you got any vegetables? = haben Sie
    Gemüse?
* (*with the negative*) = kein
  he didn't have any friends = er hatte keine
    Freunde
* (*whatever*) = jeder beliebige/jede
    beliebige/jedes beliebige
  choose any two numbers = nimm zwei
    beliebige Zahlen
2 *pronoun*
* (*in questions*) = welcher/welche/welches
  I need some pins—have you got any? =
    ich brauche Stecknadeln—hast du
    welche?

- (*in negatives*) = keiner/keine/keins
  there aren't any = es gibt keine
- (*no matter which one*) = jeder/jede/jedes,
  (*plural*) = alle
3 *adverb* = noch
  would you like any more? = möchtest du
  noch etwas?

anyone *pronoun*
- (*in questions*) = irgendjemand
- (*in negatives*) = niemand
  there isn't anyone in = niemand ist zu
  Hause
- (*everyone*) = jeder
  anyone can do it = das kann jeder

anything *pronoun*
- (*in questions*) = irgendetwas
  do you have anything for the children? =
  habt ihr irgendetwas für die Kinder?
- (*in negatives*) = nichts
  she didn't say anything = sie hat nichts
  gesagt
- (*everything*) = alles
  I eat anything = ich esse alles

anyway *adverb*
- (*besides*) = sowieso
  I didn't want to go there anyway = ich
  wollte da sowieso nicht hingehen
- (*all the same*) = trotzdem
  thanks anyway = trotzdem danke
- (*in conversation*) = jedenfalls

anywhere *adverb*
- (*in questions*) = irgendwo
  can you see a phone booth anywhere? =
  kannst du irgendwo eine Telefonzelle
  sehen?
- (*in negatives*) = nirgends
  we couldn't find him anywhere = er war
  nirgends zu finden
- (*in any place*) = überall
  anywhere but London = überall, außer
  London
- (*to any place*)
  to go anywhere (*wherever*) = überallhin
  gehen, (*somewhere*) = irgendwohin
  gehen

apart *adverb*
= auseinander
to live apart = getrennt leben
apart from = außer (+ *dative*)

apartment *noun*
= (die) Wohnung

apologize *verb*
= sich entschuldigen
to apologize to someone = sich bei
jemandem entschuldigen

apology *noun*
= (die) Entschuldigung

appear *verb*
- (*seem*) = scheinen

─────────────
✴ considered offensive

he appears to be happy = er scheint
glücklich zu sein
- (*come into view*) = erscheinen (**!** *sein*)
- (*be on TV*) = auftreten (**!** *sein*)

appendix *noun*
- (*of a book*) = (der) Anhang
- (*in anatomy*) = (der) Blinddarm

appetite *noun*
= (der) Appetit

applause *noun*
= (der) Beifall

apple *noun*
= (der) Apfel

application *noun*
- (*for a job*) = (die) Bewerbung
- (*for membership*) = (der) Antrag

apply *verb*
- = sich bewerben
  I've applied for the job = ich habe mich um
  die Stellung beworben
- (*make a formal request*) = beantragen
  to apply for a passport = einen Pass
  beantragen

appointment *noun*
= (der) Termin

appreciate *verb*
- (*be grateful*) = dankbar sein für
  (+ *accusative*)
  I appreciate your help = ich bin dir für
  deine Hilfe dankbar
- (*enjoy*) = schätzen
  she appreciates good wine = sie schätzt
  guten Wein

approach *verb*
= sich nähern (+ *dative*)
to approach someone = sich jemandem
nähern

approve *verb*
to approve of someone = mit jemandem
einverstanden sein

approximately *adverb*
= ungefähr
approximately 200 kilometres = ungefähr
zweihundert Kilometer
at approximately 8 o'clock = gegen acht Uhr

apricot *noun*
= (die) Aprikose

April *noun*
= (der) April ▶Dates p. 213
April fool! = April, April!

apron *noun*
= (die) Schürze

Aquarius *noun*
= (der) Wassermann

arch *noun*
= (der) Bogen

architect *noun*
= (der) Architekt/(die) Architektin

area *noun*
• (*region*) = (die) Gegend
• (*part of a building*) = (der) Bereich
• a picnic area = ein Picknickplatz

argue *verb*
(*quarrel*) = sich streiten
to argue about something = sich über
etwas (*accusative*) streiten

argument *noun*
• (*quarrel*) = (der) Streit
to have an argument with someone = sich
mit jemandem streiten
• (*reasons for or against*) = (das) Argument

Aries *noun*
= (der) Widder

arithmetic *noun*
= (das) Rechnen

arm *noun*
= (der) Arm

armchair *noun*
= (der) Sessel

armed *adjective*
= bewaffnet

arms *noun*
= Waffen (*plural*)

army *noun*
• (*force*) = (das) Heer
• (*profession*) = (das) Militär
to join the army = zum Militär gehen

around
1 *preposition* = um (+ *accusative*) ... herum
the people around me = die Leute um mich
herum
all around = ringsherum
2 *adverb*
• = herum

> **!** Note that around *is often used with*
> verbs—look around, turn around, *etc. You*
> will find translations for these under the
> entries look, turn, *etc.*

• (*approximately*) = ungefähr
• (*in the area*)
he's not around = er ist nicht da
around here = hier in der Gegend

arrange *verb*
(*organize*) = arrangieren
to arrange an appointment = einen Termin
vereinbaren
to arrange to go to the cinema =
vereinbaren, ins Kino zu gehen

arrest *verb*
= verhaften
to be arrested by the police = von der
Polizei verhaftet werden (**!** *sein*)

arrival *noun*
= (die) Ankunft
on arrival = bei der Ankunft

arrive *verb*
= ankommen (**!** *sein*)
I arrive at midday = ich komme mittags an

arrow *noun*
= (der) Pfeil

arse *noun* (*British*)
= (der) Arsch◆*

art *noun*
• = (die) Kunst
a work of art = ein Kunstwerk
• (*school subject*) = (die) Kunsterziehung

artificial *adjective*
= künstlich

artist *noun*
= (der) Künstler/(die) Künstlerin

artistic *adjective*
= künstlerisch
to be artistic = künstlerisch begabt sein

arts *noun*
the arts (*fine arts*) = die schönen Künste,
(*humanities*) = die Geisteswissenschaften

arts and crafts *noun*
• (*at school*) = (das) Werken
• (*for sale*) = (das) Kunstgewerbe

art school *noun*
= (die) Kunsthochschule

as
1 *conjunction*
• (*when*) = als
I used to live there as a child = als Kind
habe ich dort gewohnt
• (*while*) = während
the phone rang as I was opening the door
= während ich die Tür aufmachte,
klingelte das Telefon
• (*introducing a statement*) = wie
as you know, we moved to Berlin in June =
wie du weißt, sind wir im Juni nach
Berlin gezogen
• (*since*) = da
as you were out, I left a message = da du
nicht zu Hause warst, habe ich eine
Nachricht hinterlassen
• (*when used with* the same)
they have the same car as us = sie haben
das gleiche Auto wie wir
2 *preposition* = als
to work as a doctor = als Arzt tätig sein
3 *adverb*
• (*in comparisons*)
as [intelligent | rich | strong ...] as = so
[intelligent | reich | stark ...] wie
I have as much work as you = ich habe so
viel Arbeit wie du

- (*expressing degree*)
  as fast as you can = so schnell du kannst
  to pay as little as possible = so wenig wie
  möglich zahlen
  as far as I'm concerned = was mich betrifft
  as well = auch
  as for us = was uns betrifft
  as soon as = sobald
  as long as (*for the duration*) = solange,
  (*provided that*) = vorausgesetzt
  I'll go with you as long as it's free = ich
  komme mit, vorausgesetzt, dass es
  umsonst ist

ash *noun*
- (die) Asche
- (*tree*) = (die) Esche

ashamed *adjective*
  to be ashamed = sich schämen
  **you should be ashamed of yourself for
  telling lies** = du solltest dich schämen zu
  lügen

ashes *noun*
  = (die) Asche

ashtray *noun*
  = (der) Aschenbecher

Asia *noun*
  = (das) Asien ▶Countries p. 208

Asian
1 *noun* = (der) Asiat/(die) Asiatin
2 *adjective* = asiatisch ▶Countries p. 208

ask *verb*
- = fragen
  he asked her the way = er fragte sie nach
  dem Weg
  to ask someone's advice = jemanden um
  Rat fragen
  to ask someone to call = jemanden bitten
  anzurufen
  to ask someone a favour = jemanden um
  einen Gefallen bitten
  to ask a question = eine Frage stellen
- (*invite*) = einladen
  to ask some friends for dinner = Freunde
  zum Essen einladen
  he asked her out = er hat sie eingeladen
- (*make inquiries*) = sich erkundigen
  did you ask about the plane tickets? = hast
  du dich nach den Flugkarten erkundigt?
- **ask for** = verlangen
  to ask for money = Geld verlangen

asleep *adjective*
  to be asleep = schlafen
  to fall asleep = einschlafen

ass *noun* (*US: backside*) = (der) Arsch♠*

assassinate *verb*
  = ermorden

assemble *verb*
- (*come together*) = sich versammeln
- (*put together*) zusammenbauen

assignment *noun*
  (*for school*) = (die) Aufgabe

assistance *noun*
  = (die) Hilfe

assistant *noun*
- = (der) Helfer/(die) Helferin
- (*in school*) = (der) Assistent/(die) Assistentin

association *noun*
  = (der) Verband

assume *verb*
  = annehmen

assure *verb*
  = versichern
  he assured her it was not true = er
  versicherte ihr, dass es nicht stimmte

astronaut *noun*
  = (der) Astronaut/(die) Astronautin

at *preposition*

> **!** *The German preposition and the
> following article are often shortened to
> form one word: an dem becomes* am, *in
> dem:* im, *bei dem:* beim.

- (*when talking about a position*) = an
  (+ *dative*)
  at the station = am Bahnhof
  he's not at his desk = er ist nicht an
  seinem Schreibtisch
- (*when talking about a place*) = in
  (+ *dative*)
  at [school | a hotel | the chemist's …] = in [der
  Schule | einem Hotel | der Drogerie …]
  at home = zu Hause

> **!** *You will find translations for phrases like*
> **at the back of, at the front of,** *etc., under
> the entries* **back, front,** *etc.*

- (*at the house, shop of*) = bei (+ *dative*)
  let's meet at my mother's = treffen wir uns
  bei meiner Mutter
  at the supermarket = im Supermarkt
- (*when talking about time*) = um
  (+ *accusative*)
  the film starts at 9 o'clock = der Film fängt
  um neun Uhr an
  at [Christmas | Easter | Whitsun …] = zu
  [Weihnachten | Ostern | Pfingsten …]
- (*when talking about age*)
  at your age = in deinem Alter
  she could read at four = sie konnte schon
  mit vier lesen
- (*in email addresses*) (das) At-zeichen

athlete *noun*
  = (der) Athlet/(die) Athletin

athletics *noun*
(*British*) = (die) Leichtathletik
(*US*) = (der) Sport

Atlantic *noun*
the Atlantic, the Atlantic Ocean = der
Atlantik

atlas *noun*
= (der) Atlas

atmosphere *noun*
= (die) Atmosphäre

attach *verb*
= befestigen
to be attached to the wall = an der Wand
befestigt sein
to attach a letter to an application = einen
Brief einer Bewerbung beiheften

attachment *noun*
= (der) Anhang

attack
1 *verb* = angreifen
to attack a town = eine Stadt angreifen
to attack someone in the street =
jemanden auf der Straße überfallen
2 *noun* = (der) Angriff

attempt
1 *verb* = versuchen
2 *noun* = (der) Versuch

attend *verb*
to attend a wedding = bei einer Hochzeit
anwesend sein
to attend a meeting = an einer
Besprechung teilnehmen
to attend a comprehensive school = eine
Gesamtschule besuchen

attention *noun*
= (die) Aufmerksamkeit
to catch someone's attention = jemandes
Aufmerksamkeit erregen
he drew her attention to a mistake = er
machte sie auf einen Fehler aufmerksam
to pay attention = aufpassen
to pay attention to something = etwas
beachten

attic *noun*
= (der) Dachboden

attitude *noun*
• (*way of acting*) = (die) Haltung
• (*way of thinking*) = (die) Einstellung

attract *verb*
= anziehen
the exhibition has attracted more visitors
than expected = die Ausstellung hat
mehr Besucher als erwartet angezogen

attractive *adjective*
to be attractive = attraktiv sein
an attractive offer = ein reizvolles Angebot

audience *noun*
• (*in a theatre*) = (das) Publikum

• (*for TV*) = Zuschauer (*plural*)
• (*for radio*) = Zuhörer (*plural*)

August *noun*
= (der) August ▶ Dates p. 213

aunt *noun*
= (die) Tante

au pair *noun*
= (das) Au-pair-Mädchen

Australia *noun*
= (das) Australien ▶ Countries p. 208

Australian
1 *noun* = (der) Australier/(die) Australierin
2 *adjective* = australisch ▶ Countries p. 208

Austria *noun*
= (das) Österreich ▶ Countries p. 208

Austrian
1 *noun* = (der) Österreicher/
(die) Österreicherin
2 *adjective* = österreichisch ▶ Countries p. 208

author *noun*
= (der) Autor/(die) Autorin

authority *noun*
• (*power*) = (die) Autorität
• (*organization*) = (die) Behörde
the school authorities = die Schulleitung

authorize *verb*
to authorize someone to [sell | pay | sign ...] =
jemanden ermächtigen zu [verkaufen |
zahlen | unterschreiben ...]

autograph *noun*
= (das) Autogramm

automatic *adjective*
= automatisch

autumn *noun*
= (der) Herbst
in the autumn = im Herbst

available *adjective*
• (*on sale*) = erhältlich
• (*free*)
to be available = zur Verfügung stehen, (*of
a person*) = frei sein
are you available this afternoon? = sind
Sie heute Nachmittag frei?

avalanche *noun*
= (die) Lawine

average
1 *noun* = (der) Durchschnitt
to be above average = über dem
Durchschnitt liegen
2 *adjective* = durchschnittlich

avoid *verb*
• (*prevent*) = vermeiden
I had to brake hard to avoid an accident =
ich musste scharf bremsen, um einen
Unfall zu vermeiden
to avoid spending money = vermeiden,
Geld auszugeben

- (*keep away from*) = meiden
  to avoid someone = jemanden meiden
- (*if it's a car, cyclist*) ausweichen (+ *dative*)
  to avoid a car = einem Auto ausweichen

awake *adjective*
  to be awake = wach sein
  I'm wide awake now = ich bin jetzt
    hellwach

award
  1 *noun* = (der) Preis
  2 *verb*
  to award a prize to someone = jemandem
    einen Preis verleihen

aware *adjective*
- (*conscious*)
  to be aware of [a problem | danger | the risk ...]
    = sich (*dative*) [eines Problems | einer
    Gefahr | des Risikos ...] bewusst sein
- (*up to date*) = informiert
  to be aware of what's happening =
    informiert sein, was vor sich geht

away *adverb*
- (*absent*)
  to be away = nicht da sein
  to be away on business = geschäftlich
    unterwegs sein
- (*when talking about distance*)
  to be far away = weit weg sein
  London is 40 kilometres away = London
    liegt vierzig Kilometer entfernt

awful *adjective*
  = furchtbar

awkward *adjective*
  it's an awkward situation = das ist eine
    schwierige Situation
  to ring at an awkward time = zu einem
    ungünstigen Zeitpunkt anrufen

ax (*US*), **axe** (*British*) *noun*
  = (die) Axt

Bb

baby *noun*
  = (das) Baby
  to have a baby = ein Kind bekommen

babysitter *noun*
  = (der) Babysitter

back
  1 *noun*
- (*part of the body*) = (der) Rücken
- (*rear*) = (der) hintere Teil
  at the back of the room = hinten im
    Zimmer
  the back of a chair = die Rückenlehne

- (*reverse side*) = (die) Rückseite
  2 *adverb*
- (*returning to original position*) = zurück
  I'll be back in five minutes = ich bin in fünf
    Minuten wieder zurück
  back to front = verkehrt herum
- (*before in time*) = zurück
  a month back = vor einem Monat

  > **!** Note that **back** *is often used with*
  > *verbs*—**come back, get back,** *etc. You will*
  > *find translations for these under the*
  > *entries* **come, get,** *etc.*

back down
  = klein beigeben

back up
- (*support*) = unterstützen
- (*confirm*) = bestätigen

back door *noun*
  = (die) Hintertür

background *noun*
- (*of a picture*) = (der) Hintergrund
- (*of a person*) = (die) Herkunft
  family background = Familienverhältnisse
    (*plural*)

backward (*US*), **backwards** (*British*)
  adverb
  = rückwärts
  to lean backwards = sich nach hinten
    lehnen

bacon *noun*
  = (der) Speck
  bacon and eggs = Eier mit Speck

bad *adjective*
- (*not good*) = schlecht
- (*serious*) = schlimm
  a bad mistake = ein schlimmer Fehler
  a bad accident = ein schwerer Unfall
- (*naughty*) = unartig
- (*weak*) = schwach
  to have a bad heart = ein schwaches Herz
    haben

badly *adverb*
- (*not well*) = schlecht
  he did badly in his exams = er hat in der
    Prüfung schlecht abgeschnitten
- (*seriously*) = schwer
  he was badly injured = er war schwer
    verletzt
- (*very much*) = dringend
  to want something badly = sich (*dative*)
    etwas sehr wünschen

badminton *noun*
  = (der) Federball, = (das) Badminton

bad-tempered *adjective*
  = schlecht gelaunt

bag *noun*
- (*handbag, luggage*) = (die) Tasche
  he packed his bags = er hat sein Gepäck
    gepackt
- (*made of paper, plastic*) (die) Tüte
  a bag of cement = ein Sack Zement

baggage *noun*
= (das) Gepäck

bake *verb*
= backen

baker *noun*
= (der) Bäcker ▶ **Professions p. 298**

bakery *noun*
= (die) Bäckerei

balance
1 *noun*
- (*equilibrium*) = (das) Gleichgewicht
  to lose one's balance = das Gleichgewicht
  verlieren
- (*of a bank account*) = (der) Kontostand
- (*remainder*) = (der) Rest
2 *verb*
- (*keep steady*) = balancieren
- (*weigh up*) = abwägen

balcony *noun*
= (der) Balkon

bald *adjective*
= kahl
(*of a person*) = kahlköpfig
to go bald = eine Glatze bekommen

ball *noun*
- (*in football, tennis, golf*) = (der) Ball
- (*in billiards, croquet*) = (die) Kugel
- (*dance*) = (der) Ball
  I'm going to the ball = ich gehe auf den Ball

ballet *noun*
= (das) Ballett

balloon *noun*
= (der) Luftballon

ballpoint (pen) *noun*
= (der) Kugelschreiber

ban *verb*
= verbieten
to ban someone from doing something =
  jemandem verbieten, etwas zu tun
he was banned from driving = er erhielt
  Fahrverbot

banana *noun*
= (die) Banane

band *noun*
(*musical group*) = (die) Band

bandage *noun*
= (der) Verband

bang
1 *noun*
(*noise*) = (der) Knall
2 *verb*
- (*hit*)
  I banged my head on the ceiling = ich habe
    mir den Kopf an der Decke gestoßen
  he banged his fist on the table = er hat mit
    der Faust auf den Tisch geschlagen
- (*shut loudly*) = zuknallen

bank *noun*
= (die) Bank

bank account *noun*
= (das) Bankkonto

bank holiday *noun*
= (der) gesetzliche Feiertag

banknote *noun*
= (der) Geldschein

bankrupt *adjective*
= bankrott
to go bankrupt = Bankrott machen

bank statement *noun*
= (der) Kontoauszug

bar *noun*
- (*place*) = (die) Bar
- (*counter*) = (die) Theke
- (*piece of metal*) = (die) Stange
  behind bars = hinter Gittern
- (*block*)
  a bar of soap = ein Stück Seife
  a bar of chocolate = eine Tafel Schokolade

barbecue *noun*
- (*apparatus*) = (der) Grill
- (*party*) = (das) Grillfest

bare *adjective*
- (*uncovered*) = nackt
  to have bare feet = barfuß sein
- (*empty*) = leer
  bare walls = kahle Wände

barely *adverb*
= kaum

bargain *noun*
- (*cheap buy*) = (der) gute Kauf
- (*agreement*) = (das) Geschäft

bark *verb*
= bellen

barn *noun*
= (die) Scheune

barrel *noun*
= (das) Fass

barrier *noun*
- (*fence*) = (die) Absperrung
- (*problem*) = (die) Barriere

barrister *noun*
= (der) Rechtsanwalt/(die) Rechtsanwältin
  ▶ **Professions p. 298**

base
1 *noun*
- (*bottom part*) = (der) Fuß
- (*place*) = (der) Sitz
  military base = (der) Stützpunkt
2 *verb*
  to be based in London = in London
    wohnen
  to be based on a true story = auf einer
    wahren Geschichte basieren

basement *noun*
= (das) Kellergeschoss

basic *adjective*
• grundlegend
the basic problem = das Hauptproblem
• (*simple*) = einfach

basically *adverb*
= grundsätzlich

basin *noun*
= (das) Becken

basis *noun*
= (die) Grundlage
on a weekly basis = wöchentlich

basket *noun*
= (der) Korb

basketball
= (der) Basketball

bat *noun*
• (*animal*) = (die) Fledermaus
• (*in games*) = (der) Schläger

bath *noun*
• = (das) Bad
to have a bath = baden
• (*tub*) = (die) Badewanne

bathroom *noun*
= (das) Badezimmer

battery *noun*
= (die) Batterie

battle *noun*
• (*in war*) = (die) Schlacht
• (*contest*) = (der) Kampf

bay *noun*
= (die) Bucht

be *verb*
• = sein (**!** *sein*)
we are [rich | happy | lazy …] = wir sind [reich |
glücklich | faul …]
it is getting late = es wird spät
she'll be 18 next week = sie wird nächste
Woche achtzehn
• (*exist*) = sein (**!** *sein*)
there is/are = da ist/da sind, = es gibt
• (*describing a job*) = sein (**!** *sein*)
I am a doctor = ich bin Arzt ▶ **Professions
p. 298**
• (*describing health, the weather*) = sein
(**!** *sein*)
to be ill = krank sein
how are you? = wie geht es dir?
she is hot = ihr ist heiß
• (*describing a visit or travelling*) = sein
(**!** *sein*)
I've never been to Spain = ich bin noch nie
in Spanien gewesen
• (*referring to cost*) = kosten
how much is it? = wie viel kostet es?
• (*referring to time, measurements*) = sein
(**!** *sein*)
what time is it? = wie viel Uhr ist es?

• (*in the continuous tense*)
I am going = ich gehe
it's raining = es regnet
• (*at the end of sentences*)
it's cold, isn't it? = es ist kalt, nicht wahr?
• (*when giving orders*)
you are to do it at once = du musst es
sofort machen
• (*expressing the future*)
the president is to arrive at noon = der
Präsident soll um zwölf Uhr eintreffen
• (*forming the passive*) = werden (**!** *sein*)
to be attacked = überfallen werden

beach *noun*
= (der) Strand

bead *noun*
= (die) Perle

beak *noun*
= (der) Schnabel

beam *noun*
• (*made of wood*) = (der) Balken
• (*of light*) = (der) Strahl

bean *noun*
= (die) Bohne

bear
1 *noun* = (der) Bär
2 *verb*
• (*tolerate*) = ertragen

beard *noun*
= (der) Bart

beat *verb*
= schlagen
beat up
= verprügeln

beautiful *adjective*
= schön

beauty *noun*
= (die) Schönheit

because
1 *conjunction* = weil
I'm shivering because I'm cold = ich
zittere, weil mir kalt ist
2 *adverb*
because of = wegen (+ *genitive*)
because of the rain = wegen des Regens
because of me = meinetwegen

become *verb*
= werden (**!** *sein*)
to become king = König werden
what became of him? = was ist aus ihm
geworden?

bed *noun*
= (das) Bett
to go to bed = ins *or* zu Bett gehen (**!** *sein*)
bed and breakfast = Zimmer mit Frühstück

bedroom *noun*
= (das) Schlafzimmer

bee *noun*
= (die) Biene

beef *noun*
= (das) Rindfleisch

beer *noun*
= (das) Bier
two beers please = zwei Bier bitte

beetle *noun*
= (der) Käfer

before
1 *preposition*
• (*of time*) = vor (+ *dative*)
before the holidays = vor den Ferien
• (*in front of*) = vor (+ *dative*)
before my eyes = vor meinen Augen
2 *adverb*
• (*of time*) = vorher
long before = lange vorher
• (*already*) = schon einmal
I've seen that film before = ich habe den
Film schon einmal gesehen
3 *conjunction* = bevor
before the train leaves = bevor der Zug
abfährt

beg *verb*
• = betteln
to beg for money = um Geld betteln
• (*ask*) = bitten
to beg someone to do something =
jemanden bitten, etwas zu tun
I beg your pardon = entschuldigen Sie bitte

begin *verb*
= anfangen, = beginnen
it began to rain = es fing an zu regnen
to begin with = zunächst

beginner *noun*
= (der) Anfänger/ (die) Anfängerin

beginning *noun*
= (der) Anfang
in the beginning = am Anfang
at the beginning of May = Anfang Mai

behalf *noun*
on behalf of (*British*), **in behalf of** (*US*) = für
(+ *accusative*)

behave *verb*
• = sich verhalten
to behave well = sich gut benehmen
they behaved badly towards him = sie
haben ihn schlecht behandelt
• **to behave oneself** = sich benehmen

behavior (*US*), **behaviour** (*British*)
noun
• = (das) Verhalten
• (*manners*) **good/bad behaviour** =
gutes/schlechtes Benehmen

behind
1 *preposition* = hinter (+ *dative or
accusative*)

! *Note that* hinter *is followed by a noun in
the dative when position is described.
The accusative follows when there is
movement towards something.*
he stood behind the fence = er stand
hinter dem Zaun
she put it behind the sofa = sie hat es
hinter das Sofa gestellt
2 *adverb*
• = hinten
to look behind = nach hinten sehen
to stay behind = dableiben (**!** *sein*)
to leave something behind = etwas
zurücklassen
• (*late*) = im Rückstand

Belgian
1 *noun* = (der) Belgier/(die) Belgierin
2 *adjective* = belgisch ▶**Countries p. 208**

Belgium *noun*
= (das) Belgien ▶**Countries p. 208**

belief *noun*
= (der) Glaube

believe *verb*
= glauben
I don't believe you = das glaube ich dir
nicht
to believe in God = an Gott glauben

bell *noun*
• = (die) Glocke
• (*on a door or bike*) = (die) Klingel

belong *verb*
• (*be the property of*)
to belong to = gehören (+ *dative*)
it belongs to me = es gehört mir
• (*be a member of*)
to belong to = angehören (+ *dative*)
• (*be kept or stored*) = gehören
the cutlery belongs in this drawer = das
Besteck gehört in diese Schublade

belongings *noun*
= Sachen (*plural*)

below
1 *preposition*
• (*showing position*) = unter (+ *dative*)
the kitchen is below my bedroom = die
Küche ist unter meinem Schlafzimmer
• (*with movement to a different place*) =
unter (+ *accusative*)
he went below deck = er ging unter Deck
2 *adverb* = unten
the flat below = die Wohnung darunter

belt *noun*
= (der) Gürtel

bench *noun*
= (die) Bank

bend
1 *noun*
• (*in a road*) = (die) Kurve
• (*in a river, pipe*) = (die) Biegung

2 *verb*
• (*bow*) = beugen
  bend your knees = beuge die Knie
• (*make crooked*) = biegen
• (*make a bend*)
  the trees bend in the wind = die Bäume
  biegen sich im Wind
  the road bends = die Straße macht eine
  Kurve
• **to bend down** = sich bücken

beneath
1 *preposition* = unter (+ *dative or
  accusative*)

> ! *Note that* **unter** *is followed by a noun in
> the dative when position is described.
> The accusative follows when there is
> movement towards something.*

  the dog lay beneath the table = der Hund
  lag unter dem Tisch
  the baby crawled beneath the chair =das
  Baby kroch unter den Stuhl
2 *adverb* = unten

benefit
1 *noun*
  (*advantage*) = (der) Vorteil
  it will be to your benefit = das wird zu
  deinem Vorteil sein
2 *verb* = nützen (+ *dative*)

berry *noun*
  = (die) Beere

beside *preposition*
  = neben (+ *dative or accusative*)

> ! *Note that* **neben** *is followed by a noun in
> the dative when position is described.
> The accusative follows when there is
> movement towards something.*

  he stood beside me = er stand neben mir
  she sat down beside me = sie hat sich
  neben mich gesetzt

besides *adverb*
  = außerdem
  besides, it's too late = außerdem ist es zu
  spät

best
1 *noun*
  the best = der/die/das Beste
  to do one's best = sein Bestes tun
  to make the best of it = das Beste daraus
  machen
  all the best! = alles Gute!
2 *adjective* = bester/beste/bestes
  the best hotel = das beste Hotel
3 *adverb* = am besten
  blue suits you best = Blau steht dir am
  besten
  I like oranges best = ich mag Orangen am
  liebsten
  (*on food*) **best before . . .** = mindestens
  haltbar bis . . .

bet
1 *noun* = (die) Wette

2 *verb* = wetten
  I bet you he'll win = ich wette mit dir, dass
  er gewinnt
  to bet on a horse = auf ein Pferd setzen

betray *verb*
  = verraten

better
1 *adjective* = besser
  he was ill but now he is better = er war
  krank, aber jetzt geht es ihm besser
2 *adverb* = besser
  we'd better go now = wir gehen jetzt besser

between
1 *preposition* = zwischen (+ *dative or
  accusative*)

> ! *Note that* **zwischen** *is followed by a
> noun in the dative when position is
> described. The accusative follows when
> there is movement towards something.*

  I stood between them = ich stand zwischen
  ihnen
  he ran between them = er lief zwischen sie
  between 8 and 11 o'clock = zwischen acht
  und elf Uhr
  between now and next year = bis nächstes
  Jahr
2 *adverb*
  in between = dazwischen

beyond *preposition*
• (*at the other side of*) = jenseits (+ *genitive*)
• (*later than*) = nach (+ *dative*)
  beyond midnight = nach Mitternacht
• (*out of reach*) = außer (+ *dative*)
  it's beyond me = das ist mir
  unverständlich

bicycle *noun*
  = (das) Fahrrad
  to ride a bicycle = Rad fahren (! *sein*)
  he rides a bicycle = er fährt Rad

big
1 *adjective* = groß
  a big book = ein großes Buch, (*thick*) = ein
  dickes Buch
2 *adverb*
  to talk big = angeben

bike *noun*
  = (das) Rad

bikini *noun*
  = (der) Bikini

bilingual *adjective*
  = zweisprachig

bill *noun*
  = (die) Rechnung
  may we have the bill? = die Rechnung bitte

billion *noun*
• (*thousand million*) = (die) Milliarde
• (*million million*) = (die) Billion

bin *noun*
  = (der) Mülleimer

binoculars *noun*
= (das) Fernglas

biology *noun*
= (die) Biologie

bird *noun*
= (der) Vogel

biro ® *noun* (*British*)
= (der) Kugelschreiber

birth *noun*
= (die) Geburt
place of birth = (der) Geburtsort

birth certificate *noun*
= (die) Geburtsurkunde

birth control *noun*
= (die) Geburtenregelung

birthday *noun*
= (der) Geburtstag
happy birthday! = herzlichen Glückwunsch
zum Geburtstag!

biscuit *noun*
= (der) Keks

bishop *noun*
= (der) Bischof

bit *noun*
a bit = ein bisschen
not a bit = überhaupt nicht

bite
1 *noun* = (der) Biss
(*by an insect*) = (der) Stich
2 *verb* = beißen
(*of an insect*) = stechen
he bites his nails = er kaut an den Nägeln

bitter *adjective*
= bitter

black *adjective*
= schwarz ▶**Colours p. 204**

blackberry *noun*
= (die) Brombeere

blackboard *noun*
= (die) Tafel

blackcurrant *noun*
= (die) schwarze Johannisbeere

blackmail
1 *noun* = (die) Erpressung
2 *verb*
to blackmail someone = jemanden
erpressen

bladder *noun*
= (die) Blase

blade *noun*
• (*of a knife or sword*) = (die) Klinge
• **a blade of grass** = ein Grashalm

blame
1 *noun* = (die) Schuld
to put the blame on someone = die Schuld
auf jemanden schieben

2 *verb*
to blame someone for something =
jemandem die Schuld an etwas (*dative*)
geben
no one is to blame = keiner ist schuld
daran

blank *adjective*
= leer
a blank tape = eine unbespielte Kassette

blanket *noun*
= (die) Decke

blast *noun*
= (die) Explosion

blaze
1 *noun* = (das) Feuer
2 *verb* = brennen

bleach
1 *noun* = (das) Bleichmittel
2 *verb* = bleichen

bleed *verb*
= bluten

bless *verb*
= segnen
(*said after a sneeze*) **bless you!** =
Gesundheit!

blind
1 *adjective* = blind
to go blind = blind werden (**!** *sein*)
2 *verb* = blenden
the sun blinded them = die Sonne blendete
sie
3 *noun*
(*on a window*) = (das) Rollo

blink *verb*
• (*of a person*) = blinzeln
• (*of light*) = blinken

blister *noun*
= (die) Blase

blizzard *noun*
= (der) Schneesturm

block
1 *noun*
• (*large piece*) = (der) Block
(*wood*) = (der) Klotz
a block of ice = ein Eisblock
• (*building*) = (der) Block
a block of flats = ein Wohnblock
2 *verb*
(*obstruct*) = blockieren
block off
to block off a road = eine Straße sperren
block out
to block out the light = das Licht
wegnehmen
block up
to block up a hole = ein Loch zustopfen
the pipe is blocked up = das Rohr ist
verstopft

B

blonde
1 *adjective* = blond
2 *noun* = (die) Blondine

blood *noun*
= (das) Blut

bloom
1 *noun* = (die) Blüte
to be in full bloom = in voller Blüte stehen
2 *verb* = blühen

blossom *verb*
= blühen

blouse *noun*
= (die) Bluse

blow
1 *verb*
• = blasen
to blow bubbles = Blasen machen
blow your nose! = putz dir die Nase!
• (*of wind*) = wehen
the flag is blowing in the wind = die Fahne
weht im Wind
• (*of a referee*) = pfeifen
he blew his whistle = er hat gepfiffen
• (*of a fuse or bulb*) = durchbrennen (**!** *sein*)
2 *noun* = (der) Schlag

blow down
= umwehen

blow off
= wegblasen

blow out
= ausblasen

blow up
• (*in an explosion*)
the building blew up = das Gebäude ist
explodiert
• (*inflate*) = aufblasen

blue *adjective*
= blau ▶Colours p. 204

blunt *adjective*
• = stumpf
• a blunt question = eine direkte Frage

blur *verb*
= verwischen

blush *verb*
= erröten (**!** *sein*)

board
1 *noun*
• (*piece of wood, game*) = (das) Brett
• (*committee*) = (der) Ausschuss
the board of directors = der Vorstand
• (*accommodation*)
board and lodging = Unterkunft und
Verpflegung
full board = Vollpension
2 *verb*
to board a train = in einen Zug einsteigen
(**!** *sein*)

boarding card *noun*
= (die) Bordkarte

─────────────
✗ in informal situations

boarding school *noun*
= (das) Internat

boast *verb*
= prahlen
he boasts about his car = er prahlt mit
seinem Auto

boat *noun*
= (das) Boot

body *noun*
= (der) Körper
a dead body = eine Leiche

bodyguard *noun*
= (der) Leibwächter

bog *noun*
= (der) Sumpf

boil *verb*
= kochen
the kettle is boiling = das Wasser kocht
to boil the kettle = Wasser aufsetzen
you must boil the water = das Wasser muss
abgekocht werden
boiled potatoes = Salzkartoffeln

boil over
= überkochen (**!** *sein*)

bolt
1 *noun*
• (*lock*) = (der) Riegel
• (*screw*) = (der) Bolzen
2 *verb*
(*lock*) = verriegeln

bomb
1 *noun* = (die) Bombe
2 *verb* = bombardieren

bond *noun*
= (die) Verbindung

bone *noun*
• = (der) Knochen
• (*of fish*) = (die) Gräte

bonnet *noun*
• (*hat*) = (die) Haube
• (*of a car*) = (die) Motorhaube

book
1 *noun* = (das) Buch
2 *verb* = buchen
to book a flight = einen Flug buchen
this performance is fully booked = diese
Vorstellung ist ausverkauft

bookcase *noun*
= (das) Bücherregal

booking *noun*
= (die) Buchung

bookshop *noun*
= (die) Buchhandlung

boom
1 *noun*
(*in the economy*) = (der) Boom
2 *verb* = dröhnen

boost verb
= steigern
to boost profits = den Gewinn steigern

boot noun
• (footwear) = (der) Stiefel
• (of a car) = (der) Kofferraum

border
1 noun
• (frontier) = (die) Grenze
• (edge) = (der) Rand
• (in a garden) = (die) Rabatte
• (of a picture or dress) = (die) Bordüre
2 verb
(of countries) = grenzen an (+ accusative)

bore verb
= langweilen

bored adjective
to be bored = sich langweilen

boredom noun
= (die) Langeweile

boring adjective
= langweilig

born adjective
to be born = geboren werden (! sein)
I was born in Italy = ich bin in Italien
geboren

borrow verb
= sich (dative) borgen, = sich (dative)
leihen
to borrow money from someone = sich
Geld von jemandem borgen

boss noun
= (der) Chef/(die) Chefin

boss about
= herumkommandieren

bossy adjective
= herrisch

both
1 adjective = beide
both my sons = meine beiden Söhne
2 pronoun = beide
they are both red = sie sind beide rot
3 adverb
both boys and girls = sowohl Jungen als
auch Mädchen
both of us = wir beide

bother verb
• (inconvenience) = stören
I'm sorry to bother you = es tut mir Leid,
dich zu stören
• (take trouble) = sich kümmern
to bother about something = sich um
etwas (accusative) kümmern
• (trouble oneself)
you needn't bother to wait = du brauchst
nicht zu warten
he didn't even bother to say goodbye = er
hat sich nicht einmal verabschiedet
I can't be bothered = ich habe keine Lust

bottle noun
= (die) Flasche

bottle bank noun
= (der) Altglascontainer

bottom
1 noun
• (lowest part) = (der) Boden
the bottom of the mountain = der Fuß des
Berges
at the bottom of the sea = auf dem
Meeresgrund
at the bottom of the page = unten auf der
Seite
at the bottom of the bag = unten in der
Tasche
• (part of the body) = (der) Hintern✱
2 adjective
• (lowest) = unterster/unterste/unterstes
in the bottom drawer = in der untersten
Schublade
• (last, worst) = schlechtester/schlechteste/
schlechtestes

bounce verb
• (jump) = springen (! sein)
• (of a cheque) = nicht gedeckt sein

bound adjective
• to be bound to do something = etwas ganz
bestimmt tun
she's bound to be late = sie kommt ganz
bestimmt zu spät
• (heading in the direction of)
to be bound for London = nach London
unterwegs sein

boundary noun
= (die) Grenze

bow1 noun
• (knot) = (die) Schleife
• (weapon) = (der) Bogen

bow2
1 noun = (die) Verbeugung
2 verb
(as a formal greeting) = sich verbeugen

bowl noun
= (die) Schüssel
(shallower) = (die) Schale
(for soup) = (der) Teller

bowling noun
= (das) Kegeln

bow tie noun
= (die) Fliege

box noun
= (die) Schachtel
a box of chocolates = eine Schachtel
Pralinen
(wooden) = (die) Kiste
a cardboard box = ein Karton

boxer noun
(person) = (der) Boxer ▶Professions p. 298

boxing *noun*
= (das) Boxen

Boxing Day *noun*
= (der) zweite Weihnachtstag

boy *noun*
= (der) Junge

boyfriend *noun*
= (der) Freund

bra *noun*
= (der) BH

bracelet *noun*
= (das) Armband

brain *noun*
= (das) Gehirn

brake
1 *noun* = (die) Bremse
2 *verb* = bremsen

branch *noun*
• (*of a tree*) = (der) Ast
• (*of a shop*) = (die) Filiale

brand *noun*
(*name*) = (die) Marke

brand-new *adjective*
= nagelneu

brass *noun*
= (das) Messing

brave *adjective*
= tapfer

Brazil *noun*
= (das) Brasilien ▶Countries p. 208

bread *noun*
= (das) Brot
a piece of bread and butter = ein
Butterbrot

break
1 *noun*
• (*pause*) = (die) Pause
to take a break = Pause machen
• (*interruption*) = (die) Unterbrechung
• the summer break = die Sommerferien
2 *verb*
• (*get damaged*) = zerbrechen (**!** *sein*), =
kaputtgehen✱ (**!** *sein*)
the rope broke = das Seil ist zerrissen
• (*crack, smash*) = zerbrechen
• (*damage*) = kaputtmachen✱
• (*injure*)

> **!** When you break a bone in your body,
> you don't use the possessive in German.
> See the following two examples.
>
> I broke my arm = ich habe mir den Arm
> gebrochen
> she broke her leg = sie hat sich (*dative*) das
> Bein gebrochen

✱ in informal situations

• (*not keep*) = brechen
to break a promise = ein Versprechen
brechen
• (*tell*) to break the news that . . . = melden,
dass . . .

break down
(*of a car*) = eine Panne haben
(*of a machine*) = versagen

break in
= einbrechen (**!** *sein*)

break into
= einbrechen in (+ *accusative*) (**!** *sein*)
our house was broken into = bei uns
wurde eingebrochen

break out
= ausbrechen (**!** *sein*)
the fire broke out in the cellar = das Feuer
brach im Keller aus
he broke out of prison = er ist aus dem
Gefängnis ausgebrochen

break up
• (*of a couple*) = sich trennen
• (*bring to an end*) = abbrechen

breakfast *noun*
= (das) Frühstück
to have breakfast = frühstücken

breast *noun*
= (die) Brust

breath *noun*
= (der) Atem
to be out of breath = außer Atem sein
to hold one's breath = den Atem anhalten

breathe *verb*
= atmen

breed
1 *noun* = (die) Rasse
2 *verb*
• (*rear animals*) = züchten
• (*reproduce*) = sich vermehren

breeze *noun*
= (die) Brise

brew *verb*
• to brew beer = Bier brauen
• the tea is brewing = der Tee zieht noch

bribe *verb*
= bestechen

brick *noun*
= (der) Ziegelstein
made of brick = aus Ziegel

bride *noun*
= (die) Braut

bridge *noun*
= (die) Brücke

brief *adjective*
= kurz

bright *adjective*
• (*vivid*) = leuchtend
bright blue = leuchtend blau
the light was too bright = das Licht war zu
grell

- (*luminous, sunny*) = hell
  a bright light = ein helles Licht
  cloudy with bright spells = bewölkt mit
  Aufheiterungen
- (*shiny*) = glänzend

brilliant *adjective*
- (*very clever*) = genial
- (*wonderful*) = toll

bring *verb*
- (*take along*) = mitbringen
  he brought me some flowers = er hat mir
  Blumen mitgebracht
- (*transport, result in*) = bringen
  to bring someone home = jemanden nach
  Hause bringen
- (*lead*) = führen
  the path brings you to the village = der
  Weg führt ins Dorf
bring back
- (*return*) = zurückbringen
- (*get shopping, gift*) = mitbringen
bring down
  to bring prices down = die Preise senken
bring in
  to bring in lots of money = viel Geld
  einbringen
bring up
  (*educate*) = erziehen

bristle *noun*
- (*of a brush*) = (die) Borste
- (*on chin*) = (die) Bartstoppel

Britain *noun*
= (das) Großbritannien ▶Countries p. 208

British
1 *noun*
  the British = die Briten
2 *adjective* = britisch ▶Countries p. 208

broad *adjective*
- (*wide*) = breit
- (*wide-ranging*) = weit
  a broad range of programmes = ein
  umfassendes Programmangebot
- in broad daylight = am helllichten Tag

broadband *noun*
= (das) Breitband

broadcast *noun*
= (die) Sendung

brochure *noun*
= (die) Broschüre

broke *adjective*
= pleite✗

broken *adjective*
= zerbrochen, = kaputt✗
  to have a broken leg = ein gebrochenes
  Bein haben
  in broken German = in gebrochenem
  Deutsch

bronze
1 *noun* = (die) Bronze
2 *adjective* = Bronze-
  a bronze statue = eine Bronzestatue

broom *noun*
= (der) Besen

brother *noun*
= (der) Bruder

brother-in-law *noun*
= (der) Schwager

brown *adjective*
= braun ▶Colours p. 204

bruise
1 *noun*
- (*on a person*) = (der) blaue Fleck
- (*on fruit*) = (die) Druckstelle
2 *verb*
  I bruised my knee = ich habe einen blauen
  Fleck am Knie bekommen

brush
1 *noun*
- (*for hair, teeth, shoes*) = (die) Bürste
- (*broom*) = (der) Besen
- (*for use with a dustpan*) = (der) Handfeger
- (*for painting*) = (der) Pinsel
2 *verb* = bürsten
  he brushed the children's hair = er
  bürstete den Kindern die Haare
  I brushed my teeth = ich putzte mir die
  Zähne

bubble *noun*
= (die) Blase

bucket *noun*
= (der) Eimer

bud *noun*
= (die) Knospe

budgerigar *noun*
= (der) Wellensittich

buggy *noun* (*British*)
= (der) Sportwagen

build *verb*
- = bauen
- (*establish*) = aufbauen

builder *noun*
- (*workman*) = (der) Bauarbeiter
- (*contractor*) = (der) Bauunternehmer
  ▶Professions p. 298

building *noun*
= (das) Gebäude

built-in *adjective*
= eingebaut
  a built-in wardrobe = ein Einbauschrank

built-up *adjective*
  (*of an area*) = bebaut

bulb *noun*
- (*light bulb*) = (die) Birne
- (*of a plant*) = (die) Zwiebel

Bulgaria *noun*
= (das) Bulgarien ▶Countries p. 208

bulge *verb*
- (*swell out*) = sich wölben
- (*be full*) = voll gestopft sein
  a bulging suitcase = ein prall gefüllter
  Koffer

bull *noun*
= (der) Bulle

bullet *noun*
= (die) Kugel

bulletin *noun*
- (*on TV, radio*) = (die) Kurzmeldung
- (*publication*) = (das) Bulletin

bully
1 *noun*
- (*in school*) = Schüler, der Schwächere
  schikaniert
- (*adult*) = (der) Tyrann
2 *verb* = schikanieren

bump
1 *noun*
- (*on a surface*) = (die) Unebenheit
- (*swelling on the body*) = (die) Beule
- (*sound*) = (der) Bums
- (*jolt*) = (der) Stoß
2 *verb* = stoßen
  he bumped his head = er hat sich (*dative*)
  den Kopf gestoßen
  to bump into someone (*meet*) = jemanden
  zufällig treffen

bumper *noun*
= (die) Stoßstange

bun *noun*
- (*bread roll*) = (das) Brötchen, = (die) Semmel
- (*hairstyle*) = (der) Knoten

bunch *noun*
- (*of flowers*) = (der) Strauß
- (*of keys*) = (das) Bund
  a bunch of grapes = eine ganze
  Weintraube

bundle *noun*
= (das) Bündel

bunk *noun*
= (die) Koje

bunk beds *noun*
= (das) Etagenbett

burden *noun*
= (die) Last

bureaucracy *noun*
= (die) Bürokratie

burger *noun*
= (der) Hamburger

burglar *noun*
= (der) Einbrecher

burglar alarm *noun*
= (die) Alarmanlage

burglary *noun*
= (der) Einbruch

burn
1 *noun*
- (*on the skin*) = (die) Verbrennung
- (*on material*) = (die) Brandstelle
2 *verb*
- = verbrennen
  the candle is burning = die Kerze brennt
- (*injure oneself*)
  to burn one's finger = sich (*dative*) den
  Finger verbrennen
- (*when cooking*) = anbrennen
- (*in the sun*)
  he burns easily = er bekommt leicht einen
  Sonnenbrand

burner *noun*
= (der) Brenner

burst *verb*
- = platzen (**!** *sein*)
  the tyre has burst = der Reifen ist geplatzt
- you burst my balloon = du hast meinen
  Luftballon platzen lassen
burst into
  to burst into the room = ins Zimmer
  stürzen (**!** *sein*)
  to burst into tears = in Tränen ausbrechen
  (**!** *sein*)
burst out
  to burst out laughing = in Lachen
  ausbrechen (**!** *sein*)

bury *verb*
- (*dead person*) = begraben
- (*hide underground*) = vergraben

bus *noun*
= (der) Bus

bush *noun*
= (der) Busch

business *noun*
- (*commercial activities*) = Geschäfte (*plural*)
  business is good at the moment =
  momentan gehen die Geschäfte gut
- (*company*) = (der) Betrieb
- (*trade, profession*) = (die) Branche
  he works in the hotel business = er ist in
  der Hotelbranche
- (*matters that concern a person*) =
  (die) Angelegenheit
  mind your own business = kümmere dich
  um deine eigenen Angelegenheiten
  it's none of your business = das geht dich
  nichts an

businessman/businesswoman
noun
= (der) Geschäftsmann/(die) Geschäftsfrau

bus stop *noun*
= (die) Bushaltestelle

busy *adjective*
- (*occupied*) = beschäftigt
  she was busy packing = sie war mit
  Packen beschäftigt
  he is very busy = er hat sehr viel zu tun

- (*full of people*) = belebt
  it's always very busy before Christmas = vor Weihnachten ist es immer sehr voll
- (*full of traffic*) = verkehrsreich

but
1 *conjunction* = aber
  it was sunny but cold = es war sonnig aber kalt

> **!** *After a negative, especially when contradicting the previous statement,* sondern *is used.*

  he is not rich, but poor = er ist nicht reich, sondern arm
  not only ... but also ... = nicht nur ..., sondern auch ...
2 *preposition*
- (*except*) = außer (+ *dative*)
  we have nothing but water to drink = wir haben nichts außer Wasser zu trinken
  the last but one = der/die/das Vorletzte
- **but for** (*without*) = ohne (+ *accusative*)

butcher *noun*
= (der) Fleischer, = (der) Metzger
▶Professions p. 298

butter *noun*
= (die) Butter

butterfly *noun*
= (der) Schmetterling

button *noun*
= (der) Knopf

buy *verb*
= kaufen
  to buy a present for someone = jemandem ein Geschenk kaufen

buyer *noun*
= (der) Käufer/(die) Käuferin

buzz *verb*
= summen

by
1 *preposition*
- (*close to*) = an (+ *dative*)
  by the sea = am Meer
- (*expressing cause*) = von (+ *dative*)
  he was bitten by a dog = er wurde von einem Hund gebissen
- (*by means of*) = durch (+ *accusative*)
  we escaped by the back door = wir flüchteten durch die Hintertür
- (*travelling by means of*) = mit (+ *dative*)
  by bus = mit dem Bus
- (*indicating the author, painter*) = von (+ *dative*)
- (*during*) = bei (+ *dative*)
  by day/night = bei Tag/Nacht
- (*not later than*) = bis (+ *accusative*)
  by next Thursday = bis nächsten Donnerstag
  by now = inzwischen
- (*indicating an amount*)
  to increase by 20% = um zwanzig Prozent erhöhen

- (*indicating a rate*) = pro (+ *accusative*)
  to be paid by the hour = pro Stunde bezahlt werden (**!** *sein*)
- (*in measurements*)
  2 metres by 4 = zwei mal vier Meter
  10 divided by 2 = zehn geteilt durch zwei
- (*in other phrases*)
  by mistake = versehentlich
  little by little = nach und nach
  one by one = einzeln
2 *adverb*
  (*past*) = vorbei
  to go by (*walk*) = vorbeigehen (**!** *sein*), (*drive*) = vorbeifahren (**!** *sein*)
  as time goes by = mit der Zeit

Cc

cab *noun*
= (das) Taxi

cabbage *noun*
= (der) Kohl

cabin *noun*
- (*on a ship or plane*) = (die) Kabine
- (*for a ship's crew*) = (die) Kajüte
- (*wooden house*) = (die) Hütte

cable car *noun*
= (die) Seilbahn

cable TV *noun*
= (das) Kabelfernsehen

café *noun*
= (das) Café

cage
1 *noun* = (der) Käfig
2 *verb* = einsperren

cake *noun*
= (der) Kuchen

calculator *noun*
= (der) Taschenrechner

calendar *noun*
= (der) Kalender

calf *noun*
- (*young cow*) = (das) Kalb
- (*part of the leg*) = (die) Wade

call
1 *verb*
- (*name, describe*) = nennen
  they called the baby Sam = sie haben das Baby Sam genannt
  she's called Emma = sie heißt Emma
  what is it called in German? = wie heißt das auf Deutsch?

- (*summon*) = rufen
  he is calling us = er ruft uns
  to call a taxi = ein Taxi rufen
  to call a flight = einen Flug aufrufen
- (*phone*) = anrufen
  who's calling? = wer spricht da, bitte?
- (*arrange*)
  to call a meeting = eine Versammlung
  einberufen
- (*wake*) = wecken
- (*pay a visit*) = vorbeikommen (**!** sein)
  they called yesterday = sie kamen gestern
  vorbei
- (*stop en route*)
  the train calls at Reading = der Zug hält in
  Reading ·
2 *noun*
- (*phone call*) = (der) Anruf
  to return someone's call = jemanden
  zurückrufen
- (*visit*) = (der) Besuch
- (*shout*) = (der) Ruf
  a call for help = ein Hilferuf
  to be on call = Bereitschaftsdienst haben
call back
- (*return*) = zurückkommen (**!** sein)
- (*phone back*) = zurückrufen
call off
= absagen
call on
- (*visit*) = besuchen
- (*urge*)
  to call on someone to do something =
  jemanden auffordern, etwas zu tun
call out
= rufen
call up
(*phone*) = anrufen

call box *noun*
= (die) Telefonzelle

call centre *noun*
= (das) Callcenter

calm
1 *adjective* = ruhig
2 *noun* = (die) Ruhe
3 *verb*
- = beruhigen
- (*ease, relieve*) = lindern
calm down
= sich beruhigen

camcorder *noun*
= (der) Camcorder

camel *noun*
= (das) Kamel

camera *noun*
- (*for taking photos*) = (der) Fotoapparat
- (*film, video*) = (die) Kamera

camp
1 *noun* = (das) Lager
2 *verb* = zelten

camping *noun*
= (das) Camping

campsite *noun*
= (der) Campingplatz

can¹ *verb*
- = können
  I can't see it = ich kann es nicht sehen
  I can speak German = ich spreche Deutsch
- (*be allowed to*) = dürfen, = können

  ! Note that dürfen *is usually used to*
  translate can *in the sense of* may.
  can I smoke? = darf ich rauchen?

can² *noun*
= (die) Dose

Canada *noun*
= (das) Kanada ▶ **Countries p. 208**

Canadian
1 *noun* = (der) Kanadier/(die) Kanadierin
2 *adjective* = kanadisch ▶ **Countries p. 208**

canal *noun*
= (der) Kanal

cancel *verb*
- (*call off*) = absagen
- (*change plan*) = rückgängig machen
  you must cancel the booking = du musst
  die Buchung rückgängig machen
  to cancel a newspaper = eine Zeitung
  abbestellen

cancer *noun*
- = (der) Krebs
- **Cancer** = (der) Krebs

candle *noun*
= (die) Kerze

candy *noun* (*US*)
- (*confectionery*) = Süßigkeiten (*plural*)
- (*sweet*) = (der) *or* (das) Bonbon

canoe *noun*
= (das) Kanu

can opener *noun*
= (der) Dosenöffner

canteen *noun*
= (die) Kantine

cap *noun*
= (die) Kappe

capable *adjective*
= fähig
to be capable of doing something = fähig
sein, etwas zu tun
to be capable of anything = zu allem fähig
sein

capital
1 *noun*
- (*money*) = (das) Kapital
- (*city*) = (die) Hauptstadt
- (*letter*) = (der) Großbuchstabe
2 *adjective* = groß
  a capital P = ein großes P

Capricorn *noun*
= (der) Steinbock

captain
1 *noun* = (der) Kapitän
2 *verb*
  to captain a team = Mannschaftskapitän
    sein

capture *verb*
  to capture an animal = ein Tier fangen
  to capture a city = eine Stadt einnehmen

car *noun*
  = (das) Auto, = (der) Wagen
  we went there by car = wir sind mit dem
    Auto hingefahren

caravan *noun*
  = (der) Wohnwagen

card *noun*
• = (die) Karte
• (*cardboard*) = (die) Pappe

care
1 *noun*
• (*caution*) = (die) Vorsicht
  to take care crossing the street =
    vorsichtig beim Überqueren der Straße
    sein
  to take care not to make mistakes =
    aufpassen, dass man keine Fehler macht
• (*attention*)
  medical care = ärztliche Betreuung
  to take care of the children = sich um die
    Kinder kümmern
2 *verb*
  to care about something = etwas wichtig
    finden
  to care about someone = jemanden mögen
  I don't care = das ist mir egal

career *noun*
• (*job*) = (der) Beruf
• (*progress in professional life*) =
    (die) Laufbahn

careful *adjective*
• (*cautious*) = vorsichtig
  be careful! = Vorsicht!
• (*thorough*) = sorgfältig

careless *adjective*
  = nachlässig

carnival *noun*
• (*British: festival*) = (der) Karneval
• (*US: funfair*) = (der) Jahrmarkt

carousel *noun*
• (*merry-go-round*) = (das) Karussell
• (*for baggage*) = (das) Gepäckförderband

car park *noun*
  = (der) Parkplatz
  (*multi-storey*) = (das) Parkhaus

carpenter *noun*
  = (der) Tischler

carpet *noun*
  = (der) Teppich

carriage *noun*
• (*British: of a train*) = (das) Abteil
• (*horse-drawn*) = (die) Kutsche

carry *verb*
  = tragen
  I can carry the case = ich kann den Koffer
    tragen
  to carry the baggage upstairs = das Gepäck
    herauftragen

> **!** *When the sentence emphasizes the*
> *destination of the carrying,* bringen *is*
> *used.*

  he carried the case to her room = er hat
    den Koffer auf ihr Zimmer gebracht

carry on
  (*continue*) = weitermachen
  carry on with your work = mach deine
    Arbeit weiter

cartoon *noun*
• (*film*) = (der) Zeichentrickfilm
• (*drawing*) = (der) Cartoon

case¹ *noun*
  = (der) Fall
  in case = falls

case² *noun*
• (*suitcase*) = (der) Koffer
• (*for spectacles*) = (das) Etui
• (*crate*) = (die) Kiste

cash
1 *noun*
  = (das) Bargeld
  to pay cash = bar zahlen
2 *verb* = einlösen
  to cash a cheque = einen Scheck einlösen

cash card *noun*
  = (die) Bankkarte

cash desk *noun*
  = (die) Kasse

cash dispenser *noun*
  = (der) Geldautomat

cashier *noun*
  = (der) Kassierer/(die) Kassiererin

cassette *noun*
  = (die) Kassette

cassette recorder *noun*
  = (der) Kassettenrekorder

cast *noun*
  (*of a play*) = (die) Besetzung

castle *noun*
• = (das) Schloss
• (*fortified*) = (die) Burg
• (*in chess*) = (der) Turm

casual *adjective*
• (*relaxed*) = zwanglos
• (*offhand*) = lässig
• (*informal*) = leger

casualty *noun*
• (*injured person*) = (der/die) Verletzte
• (*hospital department*) = (die) Unfallstation

cat *noun*
= (die) Katze

catalog (*US*), **catalogue** (*British*) *noun*
• (der) Katalog

catch *verb*
• = fangen
the cat caught a bird = die Katze hat einen
Vogel gefangen
to catch a thief = einen Dieb fassen
• (*trap, become hooked*)
he caught his finger in the door = er hat
sich (*dative*) den Finger in der Tür
geklemmt
to get caught on something = an etwas
(*dative*) hängen bleiben (**!** *sein*)
• (*get or take*) = nehmen
to catch a [bus | plane | train …] = [einen Bus |
ein Flugzeug | einen Zug …] nehmen
• (*be in time*) = erreichen
he ran to catch his train = er rannte, um
seinen Zug zu erreichen
• (*take by surprise*) = erwischen
to catch someone stealing = jemanden
beim Stehlen erwischen
to get caught = erwischt werden (**!** *sein*)
• (*hear*) = verstehen
• (*become ill with*) = bekommen
to catch flu = die Grippe bekommen
to catch a cold = sich erkälten

catch up
• (*reach*) = einholen
I'll catch up with you = ich hole euch ein
• = aufholen
to have a lot to catch up on = viel
aufzuholen haben

caterpillar *noun*
= (die) Raupe

cathedral *noun*
= (die) Kathedrale

cattle *noun*
= (das) Vieh

cauliflower *noun*
= (der) Blumenkohl

cause *verb*
= verursachen

cautious *adjective*
= vorsichtig

cave *noun*
= (die) Höhle

CD *noun*
= (die) CD

CD player *noun*
= (der) CD-Player

ceiling *noun*
= (die) Decke

celebrate *verb*
= feiern

✗ in informal situations

celery *noun*
= (der) Sellerie

cell *noun*
(*in prison*) = (die) Zelle

cellar *noun*
= (der) Keller

cell phone *noun*
= (das) Handy

cement *noun*
= (der) Zement

cemetery *noun*
= (der) Friedhof

cent *noun*
= (der) Cent

center (*US*) ▶ centre

centimeter (*US*), **centimetre**
(*British*) *noun*
= (der) Zentimeter

central heating *noun*
= (die) Zentralheizung

centre *noun* (*British*)
= (das) Zentrum
(*middle*) = (die) Mitte

century *noun*
= (das) Jahrhundert

certain *adjective*
• (*sure*) = sicher
I'm absolutely certain = ich bin mir ganz
sicher
• (*particular*) = bestimmt
• (*not named*) = gewiss

certainly *adverb*
= bestimmt
(*of course*) = sicher

certificate *noun*
• (*for performance*) = (die) Bescheinigung
a birth certificate = eine Geburtsurkunde
• (*at school*) = (das) Zeugnis

chain *noun*
= (die) Kette

chair *noun*
= (der) Stuhl

chair lift *noun*
= (der) Sessellift

champagne *noun*
= (der) Champagner

champion *noun*
= (der) Meister/(die) Meisterin

championship *noun*
= (die) Meisterschaft

chance *noun*
* (*likely event*) = (die) Aussicht

> **!** *Note that* **chance** *in this sense is often translated by the plural,* **Aussichten.**

  will she win?—she has a good chance = gewinnt sie?—sie hat gute Aussichten
* (*opportunity*) = (die) Gelegenheit
  to have the chance to [travel | work abroad ...] = die Gelegenheit haben [zu reisen | , im Ausland zu arbeiten ...]
* (*luck*) = (das) Glück
  by chance = zufällig
  on the off chance = auf gut Glück

change
1 *noun*
* = (die) Veränderung
  (*alteration*) = (die) Änderung
  I haven't got a change of clothes with me = ich habe nichts anderes zum Anziehen dabei
* (*different experience*) = (die) Abwechslung
  we could go to the cinema for a change = wir könnten zur Abwechslung mal ins Kino gehen
* (*money back*) = (das) Wechselgeld
  (*coins*) = (das) Kleingeld
2 *verb*
* (*become different*) = sich verändern
  the town has changed a lot = die Stadt hat sich sehr verändert
* (*make different*) = ändern
  to change one's address = seine Anschrift ändern
* (*replace*) = auswechseln
  to change a light bulb = eine Glühbirne auswechseln
* (*exchange in a shop*) = umtauschen
  to change a shirt for a smaller size = ein Hemd gegen eine kleinere Größe umtauschen
* (*switch*) = wechseln
  I'd like to change jobs = ich würde gerne meine Stellung wechseln
* (*exchange*) = tauschen
  to change places with someone = mit jemandem den Platz tauschen
* (*put on other clothes*) = sich umziehen
* (*when using transport*) = umsteigen (**!** *sein*)
* (*get foreign currency*) = wechseln

changing room *noun*
= (der) Umkleideraum

channel *noun*
* (*TV station*) = (der) Kanal
  to change channels = auf einen anderen Kanal schalten
* = (der) Kanal
  the English Channel = der Ärmelkanal

Channel Islands *noun*
the Channel Islands = die Kanalinseln

Channel Tunnel *noun*
the Channel Tunnel = der Eurotunnel

chapter *noun*
= (das) Kapitel

character *noun*
* = (der) Charakter
* (*in a play or film*) = (die) Rolle

charge
1 *verb*
* (*ask for payment*) = berechnen
  to charge someone for [delivery | the damage | packing ...] = jemandem [die Lieferung | den Schaden | die Verpackung ...] berechnen
* (*run*) = stürmen (**!** *sein*)
2 *noun*
* (*price*) = (die) Gebühr
  free of charge = kostenlos
* (*care*) = (die) Verantwortung
  to be in charge = die Verantwortung haben

charming *adjective*
= reizend

charter flight *noun* (*British*)
= (der) Charterflug

chase
1 *verb* = jagen
2 *noun* = (die) Verfolgungsjagd
chase away
= wegjagen

chat
1 *verb* = plaudern
2 *noun* = (die) Plauderei
  to have a chat with someone = mit jemandem plaudern
chat up
= anmachen✳

cheap *adjective*
= billig

cheat
1 *verb* = betrügen
  they cheated him out of all his money = sie haben ihn um sein ganzes Geld betrogen
  (*in games*) = mogeln
  to cheat at cards = beim Kartenspielen mogeln
2 *noun* = (der) Betrüger/(die) Betrügerin
  (*in games*) = (der) Mogler/(die) Moglerin

check
1 *verb*
* (*examine accuracy*) = nachprüfen
* (*inspect*) = kontrollieren
  they checked our passports = sie haben unsere Pässe kontrolliert
* (*test*) = überprüfen
  to check on something = etwas überprüfen
  to check with someone = bei jemandem nachfragen
2 *noun*
* (*inspection for quality*) = (die) Kontrolle
* (*US: bill*) = (die) Rechnung
  to pick up the check = zahlen
* (*US: cheque*) = (der) Scheck
check in
(*at an airport*) = einchecken
check out
= abreisen (**!** *sein*)

checkbook noun (*US*)
= (das) Scheckbuch

checkers noun (*US*)
= (das) Damespiel

check-in noun
(*at an airport*) = (der) Abfertigungsschalter
(*at a hotel*) = (die) Rezeption

checkout noun
= (die) Kasse

check-up noun
= (die) Untersuchung

cheek noun
(*part of the face*) = (die) Backe

cheeky adjective
= frech

cheerful adjective
= fröhlich

cheers interjection
(*when drinking*) = prost!

cheese noun
= (der) Käse

chef noun
= (der) Koch

chemist noun
• (*in a pharmacy*) = (der) Apotheker/(die)
  Apothekerin ▶ **Professions p. 298**
• (*in a laboratory*) = (der) Chemiker/(die)
  Chemikerin
• (*dispensing*) = (die) Apotheke
  (*shop*) = (die) Drogerie

chemistry noun
= (die) Chemie

cheque noun (*British*)
= (der) Scheck
to pay by cheque = mit Scheck bezahlen

chequebook noun (*British*)
= (das) Scheckbuch

cherry noun
= (die) Kirsche

chess noun
= (das) Schach

chest noun
• (*part of the body*) = (die) Brust
• (*piece of furniture*) = (die) Truhe

chestnut
1 noun = (die) Kastanie
2 adjective = kastanienbraun ▶ **Colours p. 204**

chest of drawers noun
= (die) Kommode

chew verb
= kauen

✱ in informal situations

chewing gum noun
= (der) Kaugummi

chicken noun
= (das) Huhn

child noun
= (das) Kind
when I was a child = als ich klein war

childminder noun (*British*)
= (die) Tagesmutter

chilly adjective
= kühl

chimney noun
= (der) Schornstein

chimpanzee noun
= (der) Schimpanse

chin noun
= (das) Kinn

China noun
= (das) China ▶ **Countries p. 208**

Chinese
1 noun
• (*people*) **the Chinese** = die Chinesen
• (*language*) = (das) Chinesisch
2 adjective = chinesisch ▶ **Countries p. 208**
a Chinese restaurant = ein China-
Restaurant

chips noun
• (*British: fried potatoes*) = Pommes frites
  (*plural*)
• (*US: crisps*) = Chips (*plural*)

chocolate noun
• = (die) Schokolade
• (*sweet*) = (die) Praline

choice noun
• = (die) Wahl
  we had no choice = wir hatten keine
  andere Wahl
• (*variety*) = (die) Auswahl
  you have a choice of three = du hast drei
  zur Auswahl

choir noun
= (der) Chor

choke
1 verb = sich verschlucken
to choke to death = ersticken (**!** *sein*)
2 noun = (der) Choke

choose verb
• (*select*) = wählen
• (*select from a group*) = sich (*dative*)
  aussuchen
  choose something from the menu = suche
  dir etwas auf der Karte aus

christening noun
= (die) Taufe

Christian name noun
= (der) Vorname

Christmas *noun*
= (das) Weihnachten
Happy Christmas! = Frohe Weihnachten!

Christmas Day *noun*
= (der) erste Weihnachtstag

Christmas Eve *noun*
= (der) Heiligabend

church *noun*
= (die) Kirche

cider *noun*
≈ (der) Apfelwein

cigar *noun*
= (die) Zigarre

cigarette *noun*
= (die) Zigarette

cinema *noun*
= (das) Kino

circle *noun*
• (*shape*) = (der) Kreis
• (*in a theatre*) = (der) Rang

circumstances *noun*
= Umstände (*plural*)
under no circumstances = unter gar
keinen Umständen

circus *noun*
= (der) Zirkus

citizen *noun*
= (der) Bürger/(die) Bürgerin

city *noun*
= (die) Großstadt
the City = die City

city center (*US*), **city centre** (*British*)
noun
= (das) Stadtzentrum

civilized *adjective*
= zivilisiert

civil servant *noun*
= (der) Beamte/(die) Beamtin

clap
1 *verb* = klatschen
2 *noun*
• (*applause*)
to give someone a clap = jemandem
Beifall klatschen
• **a clap of thunder** = ein Donnerschlag

clarinet *noun*
= (die) Klarinette

class *noun*
• = (die) Klasse
to travel first class = erster Klasse reisen
• (*lesson*) = (die) Stunde
we talked about it in class = wir haben es
im Unterricht besprochen
to take a history class (*British: to give one*)
= Geschichte unterrichten, (*US: to attend
one*) = Geschichte haben
• (*style*) = (der) Stil

classical *adjective*
= klassisch

classroom *noun*
= (das) Klassenzimmer

claw *noun*
• (*of a cat*) = (die) Kralle
• (*of a crab*) = (die) Schere

clay *noun*
= (der) Lehm
(*in pottery*) = (der) Ton

clean
1 *adjective* = sauber
are your hands clean? = hast du saubere
Hände?
2 *verb* = putzen
to clean the windows = die Fenster putzen
to have a jacket cleaned = eine Jacke
reinigen lassen

clean up
= sauber machen

clear
1 *adjective*
• = klar
the instructions are not very clear = die
Gebrauchsanweisung ist nicht ganz klar
is that clear? = ist das klar?✱
he has a clear advantage = er ist eindeutig
im Vorteil
on a clear day = bei klarem Wetter
your writing must be clear = du musst
deutlich schreiben
• (*free from spots*) = rein
to have clear skin = reine Haut haben
• (*not blocked*) = frei
2 *verb*
• (*empty*) = räumen
to clear the building = das Gebäude
räumen
to clear the table = den Tisch abräumen
• (*disappear*) = sich auflösen
the fog cleared after an hour = der Nebel
hat sich nach einer Stunde aufgelöst
• (*go through*)
to clear customs = vom Zoll abgefertigt
werden (**!** *sein*)

clear away
= wegräumen

clear up
• **to clear up the living room** = das
Wohnzimmer aufräumen
• (*clouds, weather*) aufklären

clever *adjective*
• (*intelligent*) = klug
to be clever at chess = gut im
Schachspielen sein
• (*smart*) = clever
• (*skilful*) = geschickt

click *verb*
= anklicken

client *noun*
= (der) Kunde/(die) Kundin

climate *noun*
= (das) Klima
climate change = (der) Klimawechsel

climb *verb*
• = hinaufsteigen (**!** *sein*)
to climb over a wall = über eine Mauer
klettern (**!** *sein*)
• (*rise higher*) = steigen (**!** *sein*)
the aircraft is still climbing = das Flugzeug
steigt noch immer

cloakroom *noun*
• (*for coats*) = (die) Garderobe
• (*British: toilets*) = (die) Toilette

clock *noun*
= (die) Uhr

close¹
1 *adjective*
• (*near*) = nahe, = nah

> **!** *In everyday speech,* nah *is used more
> often than* nahe.

the station is quite close to the hotel = der
Bahnhof ist ganz nah am Hotel
• (*of a friend*) = eng
• (*of a relative, an acquaintance*) = nahe
• (*other uses*)
a close contest = ein harter Wettkampf
it's very close today = heute ist es sehr
schwül
2 *adverb* = nah(e)
to come closer = näher kommen (**!** *sein*)
to live close (by) = in der Nähe wohnen
close to
• (*when talking about location*) = nah(e) an
(+ *dative or accusative*)

> **!** *Note that* an *is followed by a noun in the
> dative when position is described. The
> accusative follows when there is
> movement towards something.*

• (*when talking about a situation*) = nah(e)
to be close to tears = den Tränen nahe sein
to come close to leaving = nahe daran sein
wegzugehen

close² *verb*
• = zumachen, = schließen
the shop closes at midday = das Geschäft
macht mittags zu
the door closed suddenly = die Tür schloss
sich plötzlich
• to close a road = eine Straße sperren
close down
= schließen
close off
= sperren
close up
= zumachen

closed *adjective*
= geschlossen

---

cloth *noun*
• (*material*) = (der) Stoff
• (*for household use*) = (das) Tuch

clothes *noun*
= Kleider (*plural*)
to put on one's clothes = sich anziehen
to take off one's clothes = sich ausziehen

cloud *noun*
= (die) Wolke

cloudy *adjective*
= bewölkt

club *noun*
• (*association, nightclub*) = (der) Klub
• (*for playing golf*) = (der) Schläger
• (*playing cards*) **clubs** = (das) Kreuz

clue *noun*
• (*in an investigation*) = (der) Anhaltspunkt
• (*in a crossword*) = (die) Frage

clumsy *adjective*
= ungeschickt

coach
1 *noun*
• (*bus*) = (der) Bus
• (*trainer*) = (der) Trainer
• (*British: of a train*) = (der) Wagen
2 *verb* = trainieren

coal *noun*
= (die) Kohle

coast *noun*
= (die) Küste

coastguard *noun*
= (die) Küstenwache

coat *noun*
• (*garment*) = (der) Mantel
• (*of an animal*) = (das) Fell

coat-hanger *noun*
= (der) Kleiderbügel

cobweb *noun*
= (das) Spinnennetz

cock *noun*
(*British: rooster*) = (der) Hahn

cockroach *noun*
= (die) Küchenschabe

cocoa *noun*
= (der) Kakao

coconut *noun*
= (die) Kokosnuss

cod *noun*
= (der) Kabeljau

coffee *noun*
= (der) Kaffee
two white coffees = zwei Kaffee mit Milch

coffin *noun*
= (der) Sarg

coin *noun*
= (die) Münze

coincidence *noun*
= (der) Zufall

Coke® *noun*
= (die) *or* (das) Cola®

cold
1 *adjective* = kalt
I'm cold = mir ist kalt
2 *noun*
• (*illness*) = (die) Erkältung, = (der) Schnupfen
to catch a cold = sich erkälten
• (*temperature*) = (die) Kälte

collapse *verb*
• (*of a building*) = einstürzen (**!** *sein*)
• (*of a person*) = zusammenbrechen (**!** *sein*)
• (*fail*) = scheitern (**!** *sein*)

collar *noun*
• (*on a shirt*) = (der) Kragen
• (*for a pet*) = (das) Halsband

colleague *noun*
= (der) Kollege/(die) Kollegin

collect
1 *verb*
• = sammeln
to collect wood = Holz sammeln
to collect the exercise books = die Hefte
einsammeln
he collects stamps = er sammelt
Briefmarken
• (*fetch*) = abholen
to collect the children from school = die
Kinder von der Schule abholen
2 *adverb* (*US*)
to call someone collect = ein R-Gespräch
mit jemandem führen

collection *noun*
• (*collected objects, money for charity*) = (die)
Sammlung
• (*in church*) = (die) Kollekte
• (*from a letterbox*) = (die) Leerung
• (*designer's new fashion*) = (die) Kollektion

collision *noun*
= (der) Zusammenstoß

color (*US*), **colour** (*British*)
1 *noun*
• = (die) Farbe
• (*of a person's skin*) = (die) Hautfarbe
2 *verb*
• (*paint*) = malen
to colour the picture (in) = das Bild
ausmalen
• (*dye*) = färben

color film (*US*), **colour film** (*British*)
noun
= (der) Farbfilm

colorful (*US*), **colourful** (*British*)
adjective
= bunt

comb
1 *noun* = (der) Kamm
2 *verb*
to comb one's hair = sich (*dative*) die Haare
kämmen

come *verb*
• = kommen (**!** *sein*)
is the bus coming? = kommt der Bus?
he'll be coming around 10 o'clock = er
kommt gegen zehn Uhr
Christmas is coming = bald ist
Weihnachten
turn left when you come to the traffic lights
= wenn du an der Ampel bist, bieg
links ab
• (*be a native or product of*) = kommen
(**!** *sein*)
she comes from Italy = sie ist Italienerin
• (*be available*) = erhältlich sein
the dress comes in four colours = das
Kleid ist in vier Farben erhältlich
• (*referring to position in a contest*)
to come first = Erster/Erste werden (**!** *sein*)
come back
= zurückkommen (**!** *sein*)
when are you coming back from holiday?
= wann kommst du aus dem Urlaub
zurück?
come down
(*be reduced*) = fallen (**!** *sein*)
come in
• (*enter*) = hereinkommen (**!** *sein*)
• (*arrive*) = ankommen (**!** *sein*)
the train comes in at 5 o'clock = der Zug
kommt um fünf Uhr an
come off
• (*become detached*) = abgehen (**!** *sein*)
the button has come off = der Knopf ist
abgegangen
• (*succeed*) = klappen
come on
• (*start to work*) = angehen (**!** *sein*)
the light comes on when you open the
door = wenn man die Tür aufmacht, geht
das Licht an
• (*encouraging someone*)
come on! = komm!
come out
• (*emerge*) = herauskommen (**!** *sein*)
when he came out of the shop = als er aus
dem Laden herauskam
• (*become available*) = herauskommen
(**!** *sein*)
the magazine comes out every month =
die Zeitschrift kommt monatlich heraus
• (*wash out*) = herausgehen (**!** *sein*)
• (*describing a photograph*) =
herauskommen (**!** *sein*)
the photo didn't come out = das Foto ist
nichts geworden
• (*be revealed*) = herauskommen (**!** *sein*)
the truth will come out = die Wahrheit
kommt bestimmt heraus
the exam results are coming out today =
die Prüfungsergebnisse werden heute
bekannt gegeben

Colours

Adjectives

Most colours take adjectival endings:

a blue shirt	= ein blaues Hemd
the brown jacket	= die braune Jacke
the dress is red	= das Kleid ist rot

But some, such as **lila** (= purple), **orange** (= orange) and **rosa** (= pink), never change:

a purple dress	= ein lila Kleid
pink carnations	= rosa Nelken

When two adjectives are put together, they form a new adjective spelt as one word:

a light-blue suit	= ein hellblauer Anzug
the curtains are dark green	= die Vorhänge sind dunkelgrün
black and white stripes	= schwarzweiße Streifen
navy blue	= marineblau

For adjectives with the ending *-ish*, to show that something is approximately a certain colour, the German equivalent is **-lich**. Note that certain colours add an umlaut:

yellowish	= gelblich
greenish	= grünlich
bluish	= bläulich
reddish	= rötlich

Nouns

All colours are neuter nouns, written with a capital letter:

green	= das Grün
the blue of the sky	= das Blau des Himmels
my favourite colour is red	= meine Lieblingsfarbe ist Rot

Some colour phrases

to paint something green	= etwas grün anmalen
dressed in green	= in Grün, = grün gekleidet
blue suits her	= Blau steht ihr gut
the traffic lights are red	= die Ampel steht auf Rot

---

come round
- (*visit*) = vorbeikommen (**!** sein)
- (*regain consciousness*) = wieder zu sich (*dative*) kommen (**!** sein)

come to
- (*amount to*) = sich belaufen auf (+ *accusative*)
  that comes to £20 = das macht zwanzig Pfund

come up
- (*be discussed*) = erwähnt werden (**!** sein)
  his name came up = sein Name wurde erwähnt
- (*occur*) = passieren (**!** sein)
- (*rise*) = aufgehen (**!** sein)

comfortable *adjective*
- = bequem
  the sofa is very comfortable = das Sofa ist sehr bequem
- (*relaxed*)
  to feel comfortable = sich wohl fühlen

comic strip *noun*
= (der) Comic

commercial
1 *adjective* = kommerziell
2 *noun* = (der) Werbespot

commit *verb*
- (*carry out*) = begehen
  to commit suicide = Selbstmord begehen
- (*make a promise*)
  to commit oneself to doing something = sich verpflichten, etwas zu tun

common *adjective*
- (*frequent*) = häufig
  it's a common mistake = das ist ein häufiger Fehler
- (*usual*) = normal
- (*shared*) = gemeinsam
  in common = gemeinsam

communicate *verb*
  to communicate with someone = sich mit jemandem verständigen

community *noun*
= (die) Gemeinschaft

company noun
- (business) = (die) Gesellschaft, = (die) Firma
- (group of actors) = (die) Truppe
- (presence of other people) =
  (die) Gesellschaft
  to keep someone company = jemandem
  Gesellschaft leisten
  to expect company = Besuch erwarten

compare verb
= vergleichen
compared with or **to** = verglichen mit

compartment noun
- (of a train) = (das) Abteil
- (section) = (das) Fach

compass noun
= (der) Kompass
a pair of compasses = ein Zirkel

competent adjective
= fähig

competition noun
- (rivalry or rivals) = (die) Konkurrenz
- (contest) = (der) Wettbewerb
  (in a newspaper) = (das) Preisausschreiben

competitive adjective
= konkurrenzfähig

complain verb
= sich beschweren
to complain about the noise = sich über
den Krach beschweren
she complained to the headmistress = sie
hat sich bei der Direktorin beschwert

complete
1 adjective
- (total) = völlig
  this is a complete waste of time = das ist
  völlige Zeitvergeudung
- (finished) = fertig
2 verb
- (finish) = beenden
- (fill in) = ausfüllen

completely adverb
= völlig

complicated adjective
= kompliziert

compliment noun
= (das) Kompliment

comprehensive school noun (British)
= (die) Gesamtschule

compulsory adjective
= obligatorisch
a compulsory subject = ein Pflichtfach
to be compulsory = Pflicht sein

computer noun
= (der) Computer

computer game noun
= (das) Computerspiel

computer programmer noun
= (der) Programmierer/(die)
Programmiererin

computer studies noun
= (die) Informatik

computing noun
= (die) Computertechnik

concentrate verb
= sich konzentrieren

concerned adjective
to be concerned about someone = um
jemanden besorgt sein

concert noun
= (das) Konzert

concrete
1 noun = (der) Beton
2 adjective = Beton-
a concrete floor = ein Betonboden

condemn verb
(sentence) = verurteilen

condition noun
- (physical state) = (der) Zustand
- (proviso) = (die) Bedingung
  on condition that . . . = unter der
  Bedingung, dass . . .

condom noun
= (das) Kondom

conductor noun
- (of an orchestra or choir) =
  (der) Dirigent/(die) Dirigentin
- (of a bus or tram) = (der) Schaffner/
  (die) Schaffnerin

cone noun
- = (der) Kegel
- (ice cream) = (die) Eistüte

confectionery noun
= Süßigkeiten (plural)

conference noun
= (die) Konferenz

confidence noun
- (trust) = (das) Vertrauen
  to have confidence in someone = zu
  jemandem Vertrauen haben
- (self-confidence) = (das) Selbstvertrauen
  to lack confidence = kein Selbstvertrauen
  haben

confident adjective
(self-confident) = selbstbewusst
I am confident that . . . = ich bin mir sicher,
dass . . .

confidential adjective
= vertraulich

confiscate verb
= beschlagnahmen

confused adjective
= verwirrt

confusing *adjective*
= verwirrend

congratulate *verb*
= gratulieren
they congratulated me on passing the exam = sie gratulierten mir zur bestandenen Prüfung

congratulations *noun*
congratulations! = herzlichen Glückwunsch!

conjurer *noun*
= (der) Zauberer/(die) Zauberin

connection *noun*
• (*link*) = (der) Zusammenhang
in connection with = in Zusammenhang mit
• (*train, phone connection*) = (der) Anschluss

conquer *verb*
= erobern

conscientious *adjective*
= gewissenhaft

conscious *adjective*
• (*aware*) = bewusst
he's very conscious of his height = er ist sich (*dative*) seiner Größe sehr bewusst
• (*after an operation*)
to be conscious = bei Bewusstsein sein

consent *noun*
= (die) Zustimmung

consequence *noun*
= (die) Folge

considerate *adjective*
= rücksichtsvoll

consideration *noun*
to take the [price | accommodation | time ...] **into consideration** = [den Preis | die Unterkunft | die Zeit ...] berücksichtigen

construct *verb*
= bauen

consulate *noun*
= (das) Konsulat

consult *verb*
= um Rat fragen

consumer *noun*
= (der) Verbraucher/(die) Verbraucherin

contact
1 *noun* = (der) Kontakt
to be in contact with someone = mit jemandem in Kontakt sein
to lose contact = den Kontakt verlieren
2 *verb* = sich in Verbindung setzen mit (+ *dative*)

contact lens *noun*
= (die) Kontaktlinse

contain *verb*
= enthalten

container *noun*
= (der) Behälter

content *adjective*
= zufrieden

contents *noun*
= (der) Inhalt

contest *noun*
= (der) Wettbewerb

continent *noun*
= (der) Kontinent

continental quilt *noun* (*British*)
= (die) Daunendecke

continue *verb*
• = fortsetzen
to continue doing something = etwas weiterhin tun
if the bad weather continues, we'll have to cancel the picnic = wenn das schlechte Wetter anhält, müssen wir das Picknick absagen
• (*walk*) = weitergehen (✖ *sein*)
(*in a car*) = weiterfahren (✖ *sein*)
• (*go on doing something*) = weitermachen
• (*go on speaking*) = fortfahren (✖ *sein*)

continuous *adjective*
= ununterbrochen

contraception *noun*
= (die) Empfängnisverhütung

contract *noun*
= (der) Vertrag

contradict *verb*
= widersprechen (+ *dative*)
don't contradict! = widersprich mir nicht!

contradiction *noun*
= (der) Widerspruch

contribute *verb*
• (*give money*) = beisteuern
(*donate*) = spenden
• (*participate*) = beitragen
to contribute to a discussion = zu einer Diskussion beitragen

control
1 *noun* = (die) Kontrolle
to be in control of a business = ein Geschäft leiten
to take control of the situation = die Situation unter sich (*dative*) haben
to get out of control = außer Kontrolle geraten (✖ *sein*)
she lost control = sie verlor die Beherrschung
2 *verb*
to control a firm = eine Firma leiten
to control the traffic = den Verkehr regeln
to control a dog = einen Hund unter Kontrolle halten

convenient *adjective*
- (*useful, practical*) = praktisch
  it's more convenient to take the bus = es
  ist viel praktischer mit dem Bus zu
  fahren
- (*suitable*) = günstig
  to be convenient for someone =
  jemandem passen

conversation *noun*
= (das) Gespräch
  to be in conversation with someone = sich
  mit jemandem unterhalten

convertible *noun*
(*car*) = (das) Kabrio

convince *verb*
= überzeugen

cook
1 *verb* = kochen
2 *noun* = (der) Koch/(die) Köchin

cookbook *noun*
= (das) Kochbuch

cooker *noun* (*British*)
= (der) Kochherd

cookery book *noun* (*British*)
= (das) Kochbuch

cookie *noun* (*US*)
= (der) Keks

cooking *noun*
- (*food*) – (die) Küche
- (*preparing food*) = (das) Kochen

cool
1 *adjective*
- (*not hot*) = kühl
- (*calm*) = ruhig, = gelassen
  stay cool! = bleib ruhig!
- (*great*) = cool, = geil ✱
2 *noun*
  to lose one's cool = durchdrehen✱
  to keep one's cool = gelassen bleiben
  (**!** *sein*)
cool down
- (*get colder*) = sich abkühlen
- (*calm down*) = sich beruhigen

co-operate *verb*
= zusammenarbeiten

cope *verb*
= zurechtkommen (**!** *sein*)

copper *noun*
= (das) Kupfer

copy
1 *noun*
- (*imitation*) = (die) Kopie
- (*book, newspaper*) = (das) Exemplar
2 *verb*
- = kopieren
- (*in school*) = abschreiben
- (*imitate*) = nachahmen

cork *noun*
- (*material*) = (der) Kork
- (*for a bottle*) = (der) Korken

corkscrew *noun*
= (der) Korkenzieher

corn *noun*
- (*British: wheat*) = (das) Korn
- (*US: maize*) = (der) Mais
- (*on the foot*) = (das) Hühnerauge

corner *noun*
- (*of a street, building*) = (die) Ecke
  the post office is just round the corner =
  die Post ist gleich um die Ecke
- (*bend in the road*) = (die) Kurve
- (*in football, hockey*) = (der) Eckball

corpse *noun*
= (die) Leiche

correct
1 *adjective* = richtig
  that is correct = das stimmt
2 *verb* = verbessern
  (*in school, when typing*) = korrigieren

cost *verb*
= kosten

cost of living *noun*
= Lebenshaltungskosten (*plural*)

costume *noun*
= (das) Kostüm
  (*national costume*) = (die) Tracht

cosy *adjective* (*British*)
= gemütlich

cot *noun*
  (*British: for a baby*) = (das) Kinderbett
  (*US: camp bed*) = (das) Feldbett

cottage cheese *noun*
= (der) Hüttenkäse

cotton *noun*
- (*material*) = (die) Baumwolle
- (*thread*) = (das) Nähgarn

cotton wool *noun*
= (die) Watte

couch *noun*
= (die) Couch
  (*in a doctor's surgery*) = (die) Liege

cough
1 *verb* = husten
2 *noun* = (der) Husten
  to have a cough = Husten haben

could *verb*
- ▶ can

> **!** *The subjunctive of* **können** *is often used
> to translate* could, *expressing a
> speculation, wish, or suggestion.*

- (*as speculation*)
  it could well be true = es könnte ja wahr
  sein

C

Countries and cities

In German, most countries and cities are neuter, but the **das** is not normally used:

> *Austria* = Österreich
> *to come from Austria* = aus Österreich kommen (**!** *sein*)
> *Munich* = München
> *he lives in Munich* = er wohnt in München

A few countries are feminine, and the **die** is normally used:

> *Switzerland* = die Schweiz
> *we went to Switzerland* = wir sind in die Schweiz gefahren
> *Turkey* = die Türkei

A few countries are plural, and the **die** is normally used:

> *the United States* = die Vereinigten Staaten
> *the Netherlands* = die Niederlande
> *in the USA* = in den USA

Nationality

In German, when you refer to a person's nationality, you use a noun but leave out the article:

> *he is German* = er ist Deutscher
> *she is German* = sie ist Deutsche
> *he is English* = er ist Engländer
> *she is English* = sie ist Engländerin

Adjectives

When referring to countries, adjectives are written with a small letter:

> *English* = englisch
> *German* = deutsch
> *French* = französisch

To form adjectives, cities add an **-er**:

> *the Berlin shops* = die Berliner Geschäfte
> *Munich beer* = das Münchner Bier

- (*indicating uncertainty*)
  he could be right = er könnte Recht haben
- (*expressing a wish*)
  if only I could sing well = wenn ich nur gut singen könnte
- (*asking or suggesting*)
  could I speak to Anna? = könnte ich Anna sprechen?
  it would be nice if you could come = es wäre schön, wenn du kommen könntest

count *verb*
= zählen

count on
- (*rely on*) = sich verlassen auf (+ *accusative*)
- (*expect*) = rechnen mit (+ *dative*)

counter *noun*
- (*in a shop*) = (der) Ladentisch
  (*in a bank, post office*) = (der) Schalter
  (*in a bar*) = (die) Theke
- (*in board games*) = (die) Spielmarke

country
1 *noun*

- (*state*) = (das) Land
- (*scenery*) = (die) Landschaft
- (*not town*) = (das) Land
  to live in the country = auf dem Land wohnen
2 *adjective* = Land-
  country life = (das) Landleben

countryside *noun*
- (*scenery*) = (die) Landschaft
- (*not town*) = (das) Land

couple *noun*
- **a couple of days** (*two*) = zwei Tage, (*a few*) = ein paar Tage
- (*pair*) = (das) Paar

courage *noun*
= (der) Mut

courageous *adjective*
= mutig

course *noun*
- (*series of lessons*) = (der) Kurs
  a language course = ein Sprachkurs
- (*part of a meal*) = (der) Gang
- (*for golf*) = (der) Platz

✘ in informal situations

- (*other uses*)
  of course = natürlich
  in the course of = im Laufe (+ *genitive*)

court *noun*
- (*of law*) = (das) Gericht
  to go to court = vor Gericht gehen (**!** *sein*)
- (*for playing sports*) = (der) Platz
- (*of a monarch*) = (der) Hof

courtyard *noun*
  = (der) Hof

cousin *noun*
  (*male*) = (der) Vetter, (*female*) = (die) Kusine

cover
1 *verb*
- (*for protection*) = bedecken
  (*cover over*) = zudecken
  (*with a loose cover*) = beziehen
- (*spread over*) **to cover a cake with
  chocolate icing** = einen Kuchen mit
  Schokoladenguss überziehen
- (*be found on*)
  to be covered in dust = völlig verstaubt
  sein
- (*insure*) = versichern
  to be covered against theft = gegen
  Diebstahl versichert sein
- (*report*) = berichten über (+ *accusative*)
- (*pay for*) decken
  to cover expenses = die Kosten decken
2 *noun*
- (*lid*) = (der) Deckel
- (*for a cushion, duvet*) = (der) Bezug
- (*blanket*) = (die) Decke
- (*of a book*) = (der) Einband
- (*of a magazine*) = (der) Umschlag

coverage *noun*
  = der Empfangs-/Sendebereich

cow *noun*
  = (die) Kuh

coward *noun*
  = (der) Feigling

crab *noun*
  = (die) Krabbe

crack
1 *verb*
- (*break or damage*)
  (*if it's glass, china*) = anschlagen
  (*if it's wood*) = anknacksen
  (*if it's a nut, problem*) = knacken
  to crack something open = etwas
  aufbrechen
- (*get damaged*)
  (*of glass, china*) = einen Sprung
  bekommen
  (*of wood*) = einen Riss bekommen
2 *noun*
- (*narrow gap*) = (der) Spalt
- (*in a cup, mirror*) = (der) Sprung
- (*in wood, a wall*) = (der) Riss
- (*loud noise*) = (der) Knall

cradle *noun*
  = (die) Wiege

crafty *adjective*
  = gerissen

cramp *noun*
  = (der) Krampf

crane *noun*
- (*machine*) = (der) Kran
- (*bird*) = (der) Kranich

crash
1 *noun*
- (*collision*) = (der) Zusammenstoß
  to have a crash = einen Unfall haben
  a plane crash = ein Flugzeugunglück
- (*loud noise*) = (das) Krachen
2 *verb*
- (*collide*) = einen Unfall haben
  to crash into a lorry = mit einem Lastwagen
  zusammenstoßen (**!** *sein*)
  the plane crashed = das Flugzeug ist
  abgestürzt

crate *noun*
  = (die) Kiste

crawl *verb*
  = kriechen (**!** *sein*)

crayon *noun*
  (*wax*) = (der) Wachsstift
  (*pencil*) = (der) Buntstift

crazy *adjective*
  = verrückt
  to be crazy about someone = verrückt
  nach jemandem sein✱

cream
1 *noun*
- (*to eat*) = (die) Sahne
  strawberries and cream = Erdbeeren mit
  Sahne
- (*for face, burns*) = (die) Creme
2 *adjective* (*colour*) = cremefarben

create *verb*
  = schaffen
  to create difficulties = Schwierigkeiten
  machen
  to create a good impression = einen guten
  Eindruck machen

creative *adjective*
  = kreativ

crèche *noun*
  = (die) Kinderkrippe

credit
1 *noun*
  (*in banking*) = (der) Kredit
2 *verb* = gutschreiben

credit card *noun*
  = (die) Kreditkarte

crime *noun*
  = (das) Verbrechen

C

criminal
1 *noun* = (der/die) Kriminelle
2 *adjective* = kriminell

crisis *noun*
= (die) Krise

crisps *noun* (*British*)
= Chips (*plural*)

critical *adjective*
= kritisch

criticize *verb*
= kritisieren

crockery *noun*
= (das) Geschirr

crocodile *noun*
= (das) Krokodil

crooked *adjective*
• = schief
• (*bent*) = krumm

cross
1 *verb*
• (*go across*) = überqueren
  the train crossed the bridge = der Zug fuhr
    über die Brücke
• (*intersect*) = sich kreuzen
  our letters crossed = unsere Briefe haben
    sich gekreuzt
• (*other uses*)
  to cross one's legs = die Beine
    übereinander schlagen
  to cross a cheque = einen Scheck zur
    Verrechnung ausstellen
  it crossed my mind = es fiel mir ein
2 *noun* = (das) Kreuz
3 *adjective* = verärgert
  to get cross = ärgerlich werden (**!** *sein*)
cross off
= streichen
cross out
= ausstreichen

crossroads *noun*
= (die) Kreuzung

crossword *noun*
= (das) Kreuzworträtsel

crow *noun*
= (die) Krähe

crowd
1 *noun*
• (*large number of people*) =
    (die) Menschenmenge
  crowds of people = Menschenmassen
• (*spectators*) = Zuschauer (*plural*)
2 *verb* = sich drängen
  we crowded into a small room = wir
    drängten uns in ein kleines Zimmer

crowded *adjective*
= überfüllt

crown
1 *noun* = (die) Krone
2 *verb* = krönen

cruel *adjective*
= grausam

cruelty *noun*
= (die) Grausamkeit

cruise *noun*
= (die) Kreuzfahrt
to go on a cruise = eine Kreuzfahrt machen

crush *verb*
= quetschen

crust *noun*
= (die) Kruste

crutch *noun*
= (die) Krücke
to be on crutches = an Krücken gehen
  (**!** *sein*)

cry
1 *verb* = weinen
2 *noun*
  (*shout*) = (der) Schrei
cry out
= aufschreien

cuckoo *noun*
= (der) Kuckuck

cucumber *noun*
= (die) Gurke

cuddle *noun*
= (die) Liebkosung
to have a cuddle = schmusen

cuff *noun*
= (die) Manschette

cul-de-sac *noun*
= (die) Sackgasse

culprit *noun*
= (der) Täter/(die) Täterin

cultural *adjective*
= kulturell

culture *noun*
= (die) Kultur

cunning *adjective*
= listig

cup *noun*
• (*crockery*) = (die) Tasse
  a cup of coffee = eine Tasse Kaffee
• (*trophy*) = (der) Pokal
  the cup final = das Pokalendspiel
  the World Cup = die Weltmeisterschaft

cupboard *noun*
= (der) Schrank

curb *noun* (*US*) ▶ kerb

cure
1 *verb* = heilen
2 *noun*
  (*thing that cures*) = (das) Heilmittel

curious *adjective*
= neugierig

curl
1 *noun* = (die) Locke
2 *verb*
  (*go curly*) = sich locken

curly *adjective*
= lockig

currant *noun*
= (die) Korinthe

currency *noun*
= (die) Währung
foreign currency = Devisen (*plural*)

current *noun*
• (*water*) = (die) Strömung
• (*electricity*) = (der) Strom

curry *noun*
• (*powder*) = (das) *or* (der) Curry
• (*dish*) = (das) Currygericht

cursor *noun*
= (der) Cursor

curtain *noun*
= (der) Vorhang

cushion *noun*
= (das) Kissen

custard *noun* (*British*)
= (die) Vanillesoße

custom *noun*
• (*tradition*) = (der) Brauch
• (*habit*) = (die) Gewohnheit

customer *noun*
= (der) Kunde/(die) Kundin

customs *noun*
= (der) Zoll

customs officer *noun*
= (der) Zollbeamte/(die) Zollbeamtin

cut
1 *verb* = schneiden
  to cut an apple in half = einen Apfel
    halbieren
  to cut one's finger = sich in den Finger
    schneiden
  she cut herself = sie hat sich geschnitten
  to have one's hair cut = sich (*dative*) die
    Haare schneiden lassen
2 *noun*
• (*wound*) = (die) Schnittwunde
• (*hairstyle*) = (der) Schnitt
• (*reduction*) = (die) Kürzung
  (*in prices*) = (die) Senkung
cut out
• **to cut a photo out of a magazine** = ein Foto
  aus einer Zeitschrift ausschneiden
• **the engine cut out** = der Motor setzte aus
cut up
= zerschneiden

cute *adjective*
• (*sweet, attractive*) = niedlich
• (*US: cunning*) = schlau

cutlery *noun*
= (das) Besteck

CV *noun* (*British*)
= (der) Lebenslauf

cycle *verb*
= Rad fahren (**!** *sein*)
he cycles = er fährt Rad

cycle lane *noun*
= (die) Fahrradspur

cycling *noun*
= (das) Radfahren

cycling shorts *noun*
= (die) Radlerhose

cyclist *noun*
= (der) Radfahrer/(die) Radfahrerin

cynical *adjective*
= zynisch

Czech Republic *noun*
the Czech Republic = die Tschechische
  Republik

Dd

dad *noun*
= (der) Vati

daddy *noun*
= (der) Papa

daffodil *noun*
= (die) Osterglocke

daisy *noun*
= (das) Gänseblümchen

damage
1 *noun* = (der) Schaden
2 *verb*
• (*physically*) = beschädigen
  the building was damaged by fire = das
    Gebäude wurde durch ein Feuer
    beschädigt
• (*harm*) = schädigen
  it damaged his reputation = das hat seinen
    Ruf geschädigt

damp
1 *noun* = (die) Feuchtigkeit
2 *adjective* = feucht

dance
1 *noun* = (der) Tanz
2 *verb* = tanzen

dancer *noun*
= (der) Tänzer/(die) Tänzerin

dancing *noun*
= (das) Tanzen

dandruff *noun*
• Schuppen (*plural*)

Dane *noun*
= (der) Däne/(die) Dänin

danger *noun*
= (die) Gefahr

dangerous *adjective*
= gefährlich

Danish
1 *noun*
(*language*) = (das) Dänisch
2 *adjective* = dänisch ▶ **Countries p. 208**

dark
1 *noun* = (die) Dunkelheit
in the dark = im Dunkeln
2 *adjective*
= dunkel

> **!** *Adjectives ending in -el drop the e when followed by a vowel, so* dunkel *becomes* dunkler/dunkle/dunkles.

a dark night = eine dunkle Nacht
he's got dark hair = er ist dunkelhaarig

darkness *noun*
= (die) Dunkelheit

darling *noun*
= (der) Liebling

dart *noun*
= (der) Pfeil
(*game*) **darts** = (das) Darts

data *noun*
= Daten (*plural*)

database *noun*
• = (die) Datenbank

date
1 *noun*
• (*das*) Datum ▶ **Dates p. 213**
date of birth = (das) Geburtsdatum
• (*meeting*) = (die) Verabredung
2 *verb* = datieren
a letter dated 3rd August = ein vom dritten August datierter Brief

daughter *noun*
= (die) Tochter

daughter-in-law *noun*
= (die) Schwiegertochter

dawn *noun*
= (die) Morgendämmerung
at dawn = bei Tagesanbruch

day *noun*
= (der) Tag ▶ **Dates p. 213**
during the day = tagsüber
these days = heutzutage
the day after tomorrow = übermorgen
the day before yesterday = vorgestern
the next day = am nächsten Tag

daylight *noun*
= (das) Tageslicht

dazzle *verb*
= blenden

dead
1 *adjective* = tot
2 *noun*
the dead = die Toten

deaf
1 *adjective* = taub
2 *noun*
the deaf = die Tauben

deal
1 *noun*
• (*in business*) = (das) Geschäft
• **a great deal of** = viel
2 *verb*
• (*when playing cards*) = geben
to deal the cards = geben
deal with
• (*handle*) = sich befassen mit (+ *dative*)
• (*cope with*) = fertig werden mit (+ *dative*)
  (**!** *sein*)

dear
1 *adjective*
• (*expensive*) = teuer
• (*precious*) = lieb
• (*in letter-writing*) = Lieber/Liebe ▶ **Letter-writing p. 262**
2 *interjection*
oh dear! = oje!

death *noun*
= (der) Tod

debt *noun*
= (die) Schuld
(*money owed*) = Schulden (*plural*)
to be in debt = Schulden haben

decade *noun*
= (das) Jahrzehnt

December *noun*
= (der) Dezember ▶ **Dates p. 213**

decide *verb*
• (*make up one's mind*) = sich entschließen
she can never decide what to do = sie kann sich niemals entschließen, was sie tun soll
• (*come to a decision*) = sich entscheiden
to decide on doing something = sich entscheiden, etwas zu tun

decision *noun*
= (die) Entscheidung
to make a decision = eine Entscheidung treffen

declare *verb*
= erklären
(*at customs*) **anything to declare?** = etwas zu verzollen?

decorate *verb*
• (*with ornaments*) = schmücken
to decorate the Christmas tree = den Weihnachtsbaum schmücken

Dates

Days

The days of the week are all masculine:

Sunday	= Sonntag
Monday	= Montag
Tuesday	= Dienstag
Wednesday	= Mittwoch
Thursday	= Donnerstag
Friday	= Freitag
Saturday	= Samstag, = Sonnabend

To translate *on* with days, use **am**, the shortened form of **an dem**:

on Sunday = am Sonntag

Months

The months of the year are all masculine:

January	= Januar
February	= Februar
March	= März
April	= April
May	= Mai
June	= Juni
July	= Juli
August	= August
September	= September
October	= Oktober
November	= November
December	= Dezember

To translate *in* with months, use **im**, the shortened form of **in dem**:

in January	= im Januar
what day is it today?	= welchen Tag haben wir heute?, = welcher Tag ist heute?
what is the date today?	= den Wievielten haben wir heute?, = der Wievielte ist heute?
the ninth of May, 9th May	= der neunte Mai, = 9. Mai
it's the first of June	= heute ist der erste Juni
on the nineteenth of January	= am neunzehnten Januar

At the top of a letter, the date is in the accusative:

5th March   = den 5. März, = den fünften März

• **to decorate a room** (*with paint*) = ein Zimmer streichen, (*with wallpaper*) = ein Zimmer tapezieren

decoration *noun*
= (die) Verzierung

deed *noun*
= (die) Urkunde

deep *adjective*
= tief

deer *noun*
= (der) Hirsch

defeat
1 *noun* = (die) Niederlage
2 *verb* = schlagen

defense *noun* (*British*)
= (die) Verteidigung

defend *verb*
= verteidigen

defense (*US*) ▶ defence

definite *adjective*
• (*precise*) = klar
• (*obvious*) = eindeutig
• (*certain*) = sicher

definitely *adverb*
• (*certainly*) = bestimmt
I'm definitely coming = ich komme ganz bestimmt
• (*clearly*) = eindeutig

definition *noun*
= (die) Definition

degree *noun*
• (*from a university*) = (der) akademische Grad
• (*in measurements*) = (der) Grad
20 degrees = zwanzig Grad

deliberately *adverb*
= absichtlich

delicatessen *noun*
= (das) Feinkostgeschäft

delicious *adjective*
= köstlich

delighted *adjective*
= hocherfreut
she was delighted with her present = sie
  hat sich sehr über ihr Geschenk gefreut

deliver *verb*
  (*supply*) = liefern
  (*put through a letterbox*) = austragen

delivery *noun*
  (*of goods*) = (die) Lieferung
  (*of letters*) = (die) Zustellung

demand
1 *noun*
• (*request*) = (die) Nachfrage
  in demand = gefragt
• (*claim*) = (die) Forderung
2 *verb* = verlangen

democracy *noun*
= (die) Demokratie

democratic *adjective*
= demokratisch

demolish *verb*
= abreißen

demonstration *noun*
• (*by protesters*) = (die) Demonstration
• (*presentation*) = (die) Vorführung

Denmark *noun*
= (das) Dänemark ▶ **Countries p. 208**

dentist *noun*
= (der) Zahnarzt/(die) Zahnärztin
  ▶ **Professions p. 298**

deny *verb*
= bestreiten

department *noun*
• (*part of a firm or shop*) = (die) Abteilung
• (*division of government*) =
  (das) Ministerium

department store *noun*
= (das) Kaufhaus

departure *noun*
= (die) Abfahrt
  (*of a plane*) = (der) Abflug

depend *verb*
to depend on = abhängen von (+ *dative*)
it depends on him = das hängt von ihm ab
it depends = es kommt darauf an

deposit
1 *noun*
• (*initial payment*) = (die) Anzahlung
• (*when renting a house*) = (die) Kaution
• (*in a bank account*) = (das) Guthaben
2 *verb*
• **to deposit money in a bank** = Geld bei
  einer Bank einzahlen
• (*place down*) = ablegen

depressed *adjective*
= deprimiert

depressing *adjective*
= deprimierend

deprive *verb*
= entziehen

depth *noun*
= (die) Tiefe
I'm out of my depth (*when swimming*) = ich
  kann nicht mehr stehen

deputy
1 *noun* = (der) Stellvertreter/
  (die) Stellvertreterin
2 *adjective* = stellvertretend

describe *verb*
= beschreiben

description *noun*
= (die) Beschreibung

desert
1 *noun* = (die) Wüste
2 *verb* = verlassen

deserve *verb*
= verdienen
he deserves to be punished = er verdient
  Strafe

design
1 *noun*
• (*pattern*) = (das) Muster
• (*plan*) = (der) Entwurf
• (*construction*) = (die) Konstruktion
• (*subject of study*) = (das) Design
2 *verb*
• = entwerfen
• (*intend, plan*)
  to be designed for = vorgesehen sein für
  (+ *accusative*)

desire
1 *noun* = (der) Wunsch
2 *verb* = wünschen

desk *noun*
• (*piece of furniture*) = (der) Schreibtisch
• (*in the classroom*) = (das) Pult
• (*at an airport, station*) = (der) Schalter
• (*in a hotel*) = (der) Empfang

despair *noun*
= (die) Verzweiflung
in despair = verzweifelt

desperate *adjective*
= verzweifelt

dessert *noun*
= (der) Nachtisch

destroy *verb*
= zerstören

destruction *noun*
= (die) Zerstörung

detached *adjective*
• (*torn off*) = abgetrennt

- (*unemotional*) = distanziert
- (*separate*)
  a detached house = ein Einzelhaus

detail *noun*
= (die) Einzelheit
to go into details = auf Einzelheiten
  eingehen (! *sein*)
in detail = ausführlich

detective *noun*
= (der) Kriminalbeamte/
  (die) Kriminalbeamtin
private detective = (der) Detektiv/
  (die) Detektivin

determined *adjective*
= entschlossen
to be determined to do something = fest
  entschlossen sein, etwas zu tun

develop *verb*
- = entwickeln
- to develop into a row = sich zu einem Streit
  entwickeln

development *noun*
= (die) Entwicklung

devil *noun*
= (der) Teufel

dew *noun*
= (der) Tau

diagram *noun*
= (die) schematische Darstellung

dial
1 *noun*
- (*of a clock*) = (das) Zifferblatt
- (*of a telephone*) = (die) Wählscheibe
2 *verb*
  to dial a number = eine Nummer wählen

diamond *noun*
- (*precious stone*) = (der) Diamant
  (*in jewellery*) = (der) Brillant
- (*playing cards*) diamonds = (das) Karo

diaper *noun* (*US*)
= (die) Windel

diarrhoea *noun*
= (der) Durchfall

diary *noun*
- (*for writing personal thoughts*) =
  (das) Tagebuch
- (*for appointments*) = (der) Terminkalender

dice *noun*
= (der) Würfel
to throw the dice = würfeln

dictionary *noun*
= (das) Wörterbuch

die *verb*
- (*of a person*) = sterben (! *sein*)
  to die of pneumonia = an
  Lungenentzündung sterben
- (*of a plant*) = eingehen (! *sein*)
  (*of a flower*) = verwelken (! *sein*)

diet *noun*
= (die) Diät
(*for slimming*) = (die) Schlankheitskur
to go on a diet = eine Schlankheitskur
  machen

difference *noun*
= (der) Unterschied
it makes no difference = es ist egal

different *adjective*
= anderer/andere/anderes
a different book = ein anderes Buch
to be different = anders sein
he is different from his brother = er ist
  anders als sein Bruder

difficult *adjective*
= schwierig

difficulty *noun*
= (die) Schwierigkeit

dig *verb*
= graben
dig up
= ausgraben

dilute *verb*
= verdünnen

dining room *noun*
= (das) Esszimmer

dinner *noun*
= (das) Abendessen
dinner's ready = das Essen ist fertig

dinosaur *noun*
= (der) Dinosaurier

direct
1 *adjective* = direkt
2 *verb*
- (*give directions*)
  he directed me to the station = er hat mir
  den Weg zum Bahnhof gesagt
- (*in film or theatre*) = Regie führen
  to direct a film = bei einem Film Regie
  führen

direction *noun*
- (*the way*) = (die) Richtung
  to ask for directions = nach dem Weg
  fragen
- (*instructions*)
  directions (for use) =
  (die) Gebrauchsanweisung

director *noun*
- (*of a film, play*) = (der) Regisseur/
  (die) Regisseurin
- (*of a company*) = (der) Direktor/
  (die) Direktorin

dirt *noun*
= (der) Schmutz

dirty
1 *adjective* = schmutzig
2 *verb* = schmutzig machen

D

disadvantage *noun*
= (der) Nachteil

disagree *verb*
= nicht übereinstimmen

disappear *verb*
= verschwinden (**!** *sein*)

disappoint *verb*
= enttäuschen

disappointment *noun*
= (die) Enttäuschung

disapprove *verb*
to disapprove of something = gegen etwas
(*accusative*) sein

disaster *noun*
= (die) Katastrophe

discipline
1 *noun* = (die) Disziplin
2 *verb*
(*punish*) = bestrafen

disco *noun*
= (die) Disko

discover *verb*
= entdecken

discovery *noun*
= (die) Entdeckung

discuss *verb*
(*talk about*) = besprechen
to discuss politics = über Politik
diskutieren

disease *noun*
= (die) Krankheit

disguise
1 *noun* = (die) Verkleidung
2 *verb* = verkleiden
she disguised herself as a witch = sie hat
sich als Hexe verkleidet

disgust
1 *noun* = (der) Ekel
2 *verb* = anekeln

disgusting *adjective*
= eklig

dish *noun*
• (*bowl*) = (die) Schüssel
(*shallow*) = (die) Schale
to do the dishes = abwaschen
• (*food*) = (das) Gericht

dishonest *adjective*
= unehrlich

dishwasher *noun*
= (die) Geschirrspülmaschine

disk *noun*
= (die) Diskette

✻ in informal situations

dislike *verb*
= nicht mögen
I dislike him = ich mag ihn nicht

dismiss *verb*
• (*reject*) = ablehnen
• (*from a job*) = entlassen

disobey *verb*
= nicht gehorchen (+ *dative*)

display
1 *noun*
• (*of objects for sale*) = (die) Auslage
• (*exhibition*) = (die) Ausstellung
2 *verb*
• (*show*) = ausstellen
• (*show off*) = zur Schau stellen

dispute *noun*
= (der) Streit

disrupt *verb*
= unterbrechen

dissatisfied *adjective*
= unzufrieden

distance *noun*
= (die) Entfernung
from a distance = aus der Entfernung

distant *adjective*
= fern

distinguish *verb*
= unterscheiden
to distinguish between right and wrong =
das Richtige vom Falschen unterscheiden

distract *verb*
= ablenken

distribute *verb*
= verteilen

disturb *verb*
= stören
I hope I'm not disturbing you = hoffentlich
störe ich nicht

disturbing *adjective*
= beunruhigend

dive
1 *noun*
(*into water*) = (der) Kopfsprung
2 *verb*
• (*into water*) = einen Kopfsprung machen
• (*swim under water*) = tauchen

divide *verb*
= teilen
to divide something in two = etwas in zwei
Teile teilen
they divided the money between them =
sie teilten das Geld untereinander
six divided by two is three = sechs geteilt
durch zwei ist drei

diving board *noun*
= (das) Sprungbrett

division *noun*
- (*sharing*) = (die) Teilung
- (*separation*) = (die) Trennung
- (*in maths*) = (die) Division

divorce
1 *noun* = (die) Scheidung
2 *verb* = sich scheiden lassen
   his parents are divorced = seine Eltern
      sind geschieden

DIY *noun* (*British*)
= (das) Heimwerken

dizzy *adjective*
= schwindlig
I feel dizzy = mir ist schwindlig

do *verb*
- = tun, = machen
   he did his homework = er hat seine
      Hausaufgaben gemacht
   to do the [washing-up | cooking | cleaning ...] =
      [abwaschen | kochen | putzen ...]
   can you do me a favour? = kannst du mir
      einen Gefallen tun?
   to do one's hair = sich frisieren
- (*used as an auxiliary verb*)
   I don't like cats = ich mag Katzen nicht
   do you like strawberries?—yes, I do =
      magst du Erdbeeren?—ja, sehr gerne
   I love chocolate—so do I = ich esse
      Schokolade wahnsinnig gern—ich auch
   do you know her?—no, I don't = kennst du
      sie?—nein
   may I sit down?—yes, please do = darf ich
      mich setzen?—ja bitte
   he lives in London, doesn't he? = er wohnt
      in London, nicht wahr?
- (*be enough*) = reichen
   ten pounds will do = zehn Pfund reichen
- (*perform*)
   he did well = er hat gut abgeschnitten
   how is he doing? = wie geht es ihm?
- (*have a job*)
   what do you do? = was machen Sie
      beruflich?

do up
- (*fasten*) = zumachen
- (*renovate, adorn*)
   to do up a house = ein Haus renovieren
   to do oneself up = sich zurechtmachen

do without
   to do without something = ohne etwas
      (*accusative*) auskommen (**!** *sein*)

doctor *noun*
= (der) Arzt/(die) Ärztin ▶**Professions p. 298**
to go to the doctor's = zum Arzt gehen
   (**!** *sein*)

document *noun*
= (das) Dokument

dog *noun*
= (der) Hund

doghouse (*US*) ▶**kennel**

doll *noun*
= (die) Puppe

dollar *noun*
= (der) Dollar ▶**Money p. 274**

dolphin *noun*
= (der) Delphin

dominate *verb*
= beherrschen

domino *noun*
= (der) Dominostein
dominoes (*game*) = (das) Domino

donation *noun*
= (die) Spende

donkey *noun*
= (der) Esel

donut *noun* (*US*) ▶**doughnut**

door *noun*
= (die) Tür

dormitory *noun*
= (der) Schlafsaal

double
1 *adjective*
- (*twice as much*) = doppelt
   a room double the size = ein doppelt so
      großes Zimmer
   at double the cost = zum doppelten Preis
   to underline something with a double line
      = etwas doppelt unterstreichen
- (*with numbers or letters*)
   double eight = acht acht
- (*for two*) = Doppel-
   a double bed = ein Doppelbett
2 *adverb*
   (*twice*) = doppelt
3 *noun*
- (*twice the amount*) = (das) Doppelte
- (*in tennis, badminton*)
   to play a game of doubles = ein Doppel
      spielen
4 *verb* = verdoppeln
   his fortune has doubled = sein Vermögen
      hat sich verdoppelt

double-decker *noun*
(*bus*) = (der) Doppeldeckerbus

doubt
1 *noun* = (der) Zweifel
2 *verb* = bezweifeln
   I doubt (that) she will come = ich
      bezweifle, dass sie kommt

doughnut *noun* (*British*)
= (der) Berliner, = (der) Krapfen

down
1 *adverb*
- (*in a static position*) = unten
   it's down there = es ist da unten
- (*moving downwards*) = nach unten
   to jump down = hinunterspringen/
      herunterspringen (**!** *sein*), =
      runterspringen✻ (**!** *sein*)

D

! *Note that* hin *and* her *show direction. In written German,* hinunter *is used for movement away and* herunter *for movement towards the speaker. In everyday spoken German,* runter *can cover both.*

I'm coming down = ich komme runter✱
* (*when writing*)
  to write something down = etwas
  aufschreiben
2 *preposition*
  he ran down the hill = er lief den Hügel
  herunter
  to fall down the stairs = die Treppe
  runterfallen✱ (**!** *sein*)

! *Note that* hinunter, herunter*and* runter *are usually put after the noun, which is in the accusative: When used with a verb, they form new, compound verbs.*

downstairs
1 *adverb* = unten
  to go downstairs = nach unten gehen
  (**!** *sein*)
2 *noun* = (das) Erdgeschoss
3 *adjective*
  the downstairs bedroom = das
  Schlafzimmer im Erdgeschoss

dozen *noun*
  = (das) Dutzend

draft *noun* (*US*) ▶draught

drag *verb*
  = schleppen

drain
1 *noun* = (der) Abfluss
  the drains = die Kanalisation
2 *verb*
* (*when cooking*)
  to drain the vegetables = das Gemüse
  abgießen
* (*drain away*) = ablaufen (**!** *sein*)

drama *noun*
  = (das) Drama

dramatic *adjective*
  = dramatisch

drapes *noun* (*US*)
  = Vorhänge (*plural*)

draught *noun* (*British*)
  = (der) Luftzug
  there is a draught in here = hier zieht es

draughts *noun* (*British*)
  = (das) Damespiel
  to play draughts = Dame spielen

draw
1 *verb*
* (*with a pencil*) = zeichnen
  to draw a line = einen Strich ziehen

* (*pull*) = ziehen
  to draw the curtains (*open*) = die Vorhänge
  aufziehen, (*close*) = die Vorhänge
  zuziehen
* (*take out*) = herausziehen
  he drew a knife from his pocket = er zog
  ein Messer aus der Tasche
  to draw money from one's account = Geld
  von seinem Konto abheben
* (*attract*) = anziehen
  the circus drew a large crowd = der Zirkus
  hat viele Zuschauer angezogen
* (*in a lottery*) = ziehen
  to draw a ticket = ein Los ziehen
* (*in sports*) = unentschieden spielen
* (*of a date or an event*)
  to draw near = heranrücken (**!** *sein*)
  to draw to an end = zu Ende gehen (**!** *sein*)
2 *noun*
* (*in sport*) = (das) Unentschieden
* (*in a lottery*) = (die) Ziehung
draw back
  = zurückziehen
draw up
  to draw up a list = eine Liste aufstellen

drawer *noun*
  = (die) Schublade

drawing *noun*
* (*picture*) = (die) Zeichnung
* (*activity*) = (das) Zeichnen

dream
1 *noun* = (der) Traum
2 *verb* = träumen

dress
1 *noun*
* (*worn by women*) = (das) Kleid
* (*clothing*) = (die) Kleidung
2 *verb*
* (*clothe*) = anziehen
  to dress a child = ein Kind anziehen
* (*put one's clothes on*) = sich anziehen
dress up
* (*put smart clothes on*) = sich schön
  anziehen
* (*put on a disguise*) = sich verkleiden

dressing gown *noun*
  = (der) Morgenrock

drill
1 *noun*
  (*tool*) = (der) Bohrer
2 *verb* = bohren

drink *noun*
* = (das) Getränk
  (*alcoholic*) = (der) Drink
  to have a drink = etwas trinken
  a drink of water = ein Glas Wasser
* (*alcohol*) = (der) Alkohol
2 *verb* = trinken

drive
1 *noun*
* (*in a car*) = (die) Fahrt
  to go for a drive = eine Autofahrt machen
* (*driveway*) = (die) Einfahrt

✱ in informal situations

2 verb
- (in a vehicle) = fahren (**!** sein)
- (force) **to drive someone to do something**
  = jemanden dazu bringen, etwas zu tun

drive away
= wegfahren (**!** sein)

drive back
= zurückfahren (**!** sein)

drive out
= hinauswerfen

driver noun
= (der) Fahrer/(die) Fahrerin

driver's license (US), **driving licence** (British) noun
= (der) Führerschein

driving test noun
= (die) **Fahrprüfung**
Jill has passed her driving test = Jill hat den Führerschein gemacht

drop
1 noun
- (of liquid) = (der) Tropfen
- (decrease) = (der) Rückgang
  a drop in temperature = ein Temperaturrückgang
2 verb
- (fall) = fallen (**!** sein)
- (let fall) = fallen lassen
  she dropped her bag = sie ließ ihre Tasche fallen
- (lower) = senken
  he dropped his price = er hat den Preis gesenkt
- (fall lower) = sinken (**!** sein)
  prices are dropping = die Preise sinken
- (omit) = auslassen

drop in
(visit) = vorbeikommen (**!** sein)

drop out
he dropped out of school = er hat die Schule aufgegeben
he dropped out of the race = er ist aus dem Rennen ausgeschieden

drought noun
= (die) Dürre

drown verb
- (die) = ertrinken (**!** sein)
- (kill) = ertränken

drug
1 noun
- (addictive substance) = (die) Droge, = (das) Rauschgift
  to be on drugs = Drogen nehmen
- (medicine) = (das) Medikament
2 verb
  to drug someone = jemanden betäuben

drug addict noun
= (der/die) Drogensüchtige

drum noun
= (die) Trommel

drunk adjective
= betrunken
to get drunk = sich betrinken

dry
1 adjective = trocken
2 verb = trocknen
  to dry the dishes = das Geschirr abtrocknen
  he dried his hands = er trocknete sich (dative) die Hände ab

dryer noun
- (for washing) = (der) Wäschetrockner
- (for hair) = (der) Föhn

duchess noun
= (die) Herzogin

duck
1 noun = (die) Ente
2 verb
  (bend down) = sich ducken

due adjective
- (owing) = zustehend
  I am due some holidays = mir stehen Ferien zu
- (now payable) = fällig
- (expected)
  to be due to do something = etwas tun sollen
  the train is due at 2 o'clock = der Zug soll um zwei Uhr ankommen
- **due to** = aufgrund (+ genitive)

duke noun
= (der) Herzog

dull adjective
- (of a colour) = fahl
- (of a person or book) = langweilig
- (of the weather) = trüb

dumb adjective
(unable to speak) = stumm

dump
1 noun
  (for rubbish) = (die) Müllkippe
2 verb = werfen

during preposition
= während (+ genitive)
  during the summer = während des Sommers

dusk noun
= (die) Abenddämmerung

dust
1 noun = (der) Staub
2 verb = abstauben

dustbin noun
= (die) Mülltonne

dustman noun
= (der) Müllmann

dustpan noun
= (die) Kehrschaufel

D

Dutch
1 *noun*
- (*people*) the Dutch = die Holländer
- (*language*) = (das) Holländisch
2 *adjective* = holländisch ▶**Countries p. 208**

duty *noun*
- (*moral obligation*) = (die) Pflicht
  it is your duty to return the money = du
    hast die Pflicht, das Geld zurückzugeben
- (*task*) = (die) Aufgabe
- (*of a soldier or nurse*)
  to be on duty = Dienst haben
- (*tax*) = (der) Zoll

duvet *noun*
= (das) Federbett

dye
1 *noun* = (die) Farbe
2 *verb* = färben
  to dye one's hair = sich (*dative*) die Haare
    färben

Ee

each
1 *adjective* = jeder/jede/jedes

> **!** *Note that* jeder, jede *and* jedes *change
> their endings in the same way as*
> der/die/das.

each morning = jeden Morgen
2 *pronoun*
- (*each one*) = jeder/jede/jedes

> **!** *Note that* jeder (*masculine*), jede
> (*feminine*) *and* jedes (*neuter*) *agree in
> gender with the noun they stand for.*

each of you = jeder/jede von euch
each other = einander
- (*per*) = je
  oranges are 30p each = Orangen kosten je
    dreißig Pence
  £10 each (*per person*) = zehn Pfund pro
    Person, (*per item*) = zehn Pfund pro
    Stück

eager *adjective*
  to be eager to do something = etwas
    unbedingt tun wollen

eagle *noun*
= (der) Adler

ear *noun*
= (das) Ohr

earl *noun*
= (der) Graf

early
1 *adverb* = früh
  to be early = früh dran sein
  early in the morning = früh am Morgen
  early next week = Anfang nächster Woche
2 *adjective* = früh
  to have an early night = früh zu Bett gehen
    (**!** *sein*)

earn *verb*
= verdienen

earring *noun*
= (der) Ohrring

earth *noun*
= (die) Erde

earthquake *noun*
= (das) Erdbeben

easily *adverb*
= leicht

east
1 *noun* = (der) Osten
  to the east of London = östlich von London
2 *adjective* = östlich, = Ost-
  the east coast = die Ostküste
3 *adverb* = nach Osten

Easter *noun*
= (das) Ostern
  at Easter = zu Ostern

easy *adjective*
= leicht

eat *verb*
- (*of people*) = essen
- (*of animals*) = fressen

economic *adjective*
= wirtschaftlich

economical *adjective*
= sparsam

economy *noun*
- (*of a country*) = (die) Wirtschaft
- (*saving*) = (die) Sparsamkeit

economy class *noun*
= (die) Touristenklasse

edge *noun*
- (*of a road, paper*) = (der) Rand
  on the edge of town = am Stadtrand
- (*of a table, bed*) = (die) Kante
- (*of a knife*) = (die) Schneide

educate *verb*
= erziehen

education *noun*
- (*process*) = (die) Erziehung
- (*studies, training*) = (die) Ausbildung
- (*knowledge, result of good education*)
  = (die) Bildung

effect *noun*
= (die) Wirkung
  to take effect (*of law*) = in Kraft treten
    (**!** *sein*)

effective *adjective*
= wirksam

effort *noun*
= (die) Anstrengung
to make an effort = sich (*dative*) Mühe
geben

egg *noun*
= (das) Ei

eggcup *noun*
= (der) Eierbecher

Egypt *noun*
= (das) Ägypten ▶Countries p. 208

eight *adjective*
= acht ▶Numbers p. 282

eighteen *adjective*
= achtzehn ▶Numbers p. 282

eighth ▶Numbers p. 282, ▶Dates p. 213
1 *adjective* = achter/achte/achtes
2 *noun*
(*fraction*) = (das) Achtel

eighty *adjective*
= achtzig ▶Numbers p. 282

either
1 *pronoun*
• (*one or other*) = einer von beiden/eine von
beiden/eins von beiden
I don't like either of them = ich mag keinen
von beiden/keine von beiden/keins von
beiden
• (*both*) = beide (*plural*)
I can't see either (of them) = ich kann
beide nicht sehen
2 *adjective*
• (*one or other*) = einer von beiden/eine von
beiden/eins von beiden
• (*each*) = beide (*plural*)
on either side of the road = auf beiden
Seiten der Straße
either day is fine = beide Tage sind okay✗
3 *adverb*
I can't do it either = ich kann es auch nicht
machen
4 *conjunction*
• **either . . . or** = entweder . . . oder
**they are coming on either Monday or
Tuesday** = sie kommen entweder am
Montag oder am Dienstag
• (*after a negative*)
I didn't see either Helen or Paul = ich habe
weder Helen noch Paul gesehen

elbow *noun*
= (der) Ellbogen

elderly *adjective*
= älterer/ältere/älteres

eldest *adjective*
= ältester/älteste/ältestes

elect *verb*
= wählen

election *noun*
= (die) Wahl

electric *adjective*
= elektrisch

electrician *noun*
= (der) Elektriker/(die) Elektrikerin
▶Professions p. 298

electricity *noun*
• (*supply*) = (der) Strom
• (*in physics*) = (die) Elektrizität

elephant *noun*
= (der) Elefant

eleven *adjective*
= elf ▶Numbers p. 282

eliminate *verb*
= ausschalten

elm *noun*
= (die) Ulme

else *adverb*
= sonst
nothing else = sonst nichts
anything else? = sonst noch etwas?
what else did he say? = was hat er sonst
noch gesagt?
everything else = alles andere
anyone else = jeder andere
or else = sonst

elsewhere *adverb*
= woanders

email *noun*
= (die) E-Mail

email address *noun*
= (die) E-Mail-Adresse

embark *verb*
= an Bord gehen (! *sein*)

embarrass *verb*
to embarrass someone = jemanden in
Verlegenheit bringen
I feel embarrassed about it = das ist mir
peinlich

embarrassing *adjective*
= peinlich

embarrassment *noun*
= (die) Verlegenheit

embassy *noun*
= (die) Botschaft

emerald *noun*
= (der) Smaragd

emerge *verb*
• = herauskommen (! *sein*)
he emerged from the building = er kam aus
dem Gebäude heraus
• (*become apparent*) = sich herausstellen
the truth finally emerged = die Wahrheit
hat sich endlich herausgestellt

emergency *noun*
= (der) Notfall
in an emergency = im Notfall

emergency exit *noun*
= (der) Notausgang

emotion *noun*
= (das) Gefühl

emotional *adjective*
• (*of a person*) = gefühlsbetont
• (*of a situation*) = emotionsgeladen

emperor *noun*
= (der) Kaiser

emphasize *verb*
= betonen

employ *verb*
• (*keep in service*) = beschäftigen
• (*appoint*) = einstellen

employee *noun*
= (der/die) Angestellte

employer *noun*
= (der) Arbeitgeber/(die) Arbeitgeberin

employment *noun*
= (die) Arbeit

empress *noun*
= (die) Kaiserin

empty
1 *adjective* = leer
2 *verb* = leeren

encourage *verb*
= ermutigen

encyclopaedia *noun*
= (das) Lexikon

end
1 *noun* = (das) Ende
at the end of the year = am Ende des Jahres
at the end of May = Ende Mai
she read to the end of the page = sie hat
    die Seite zu Ende gelesen
in the end = schließlich
2 *verb*
• (*bring to an end*) = beenden
• (*come to an end*) = enden

endure *verb*
= ertragen

enemy *noun*
= (der) Feind

energy *noun*
= (die) Energie

engaged *adjective*
• (*of a couple*) = verlobt
to get engaged = sich verloben
• (*of a phone, lavatory*) = besetzt

engagement *noun*
• (*before marriage*) = (die) Verlobung
• (*appointment*) = (die) Verabredung

engine *noun*
• (*of a car, plane*) = (der) Motor
• (*of a ship*) = (die) Maschine
• (*of a train*) = (die) Lokomotive

engineer *noun*
= (der) Ingenieur/(die) Ingenieurin
▶**Professions p. 298**

England *noun*
= (das) England ▶**Countries p. 208**

English
1 *noun*
• (*people*) the English = die Engländer
• (*language*) = (das) Englisch
2 *adjective* = englisch ▶**Countries p. 208**

Englishman *noun*
= (der) Engländer

Englishwoman *noun*
= (die) Engländerin

enjoy *verb*
• (*like*)
to enjoy [reading | swimming | going to the
    cinema ...] = gerne [lesen | schwimmen | ins
    Kino gehen ...]
I enjoyed the [book | film | trip ...] = [das Buch |
    der Film | der Ausflug ...] hat mir gut
    gefallen
he enjoyed the meal = das Essen hat ihm
    geschmeckt
• to enjoy oneself = sich amüsieren

enormous *adjective*
= riesig

enough
1 *pronoun* = genug
we have enough to eat = wir haben genug
    zu essen
that's enough = das reicht
2 *adverb* = genug
3 *adjective* = genug
we haven't got enough room = wir haben
    nicht genug Platz

enquire, enquiry ▶inquire, inquiry

enter *verb*
• (*go in*) = gehen in (+ *accusative*) (**!** *sein*)
he entered the room = er ging in das
    Zimmer
• (*come in*) = hereinkommen (**!** *sein*)
• (*participate*) = teilnehmen an (+ *dative*)
to enter a competition = an einem
    Preisausschreiben teilnehmen

entertain *verb*
= unterhalten

entertainment *noun*
• (*amusement*) = (die) Unterhaltung
• (*show*) = (die) Veranstaltung

enthusiasm *noun*
= (die) Begeisterung

entrance *noun*
= (der) Eintritt

entry *noun*
= (der) Eintritt
to force an entry into a building = sich (*dative*) Zutritt zu einem Gebäude verschaffen
no entry (*to pedestrians*) = Zutritt verboten, (*to cars*) = Einfahrt verboten

envelope *noun*
= (der) Briefumschlag

environment *noun*
= (die) Umwelt

envy
1 *noun* = (der) Neid
2 *verb* = beneiden

episode *noun*
• (*event*) = (die) Episode
• (*on TV or radio*) = (die) Folge

equal
1 *adjective* = gleich
in equal amounts = gleich viel
of equal [size | strength | height …] = gleich [groß | stark | hoch …]
2 *verb* = gleichen (+ *dative*)

equality *noun*
= (die) Gleichberechtigung

equator *noun*
the equator = der Äquator

equipment *noun*
• = (die) Ausstattung
• (*things needed for an activity*) = (die) Ausrüstung
skiing equipment = (die) Skiausrüstung

error *noun*
= (der) Fehler

escalator *noun*
= (die) Rolltreppe

escape
1 *noun* = (die) Flucht
2 *verb*
• = entkommen (! *sein*)
to escape from something = aus etwas (*dative*) entkommen
to escape from someone = jemandem entkommen
• (*from prison*) = ausbrechen (! *sein*)

especially *adverb*
= besonders

essay *noun*
= (der) Aufsatz

essential *adjective*
= wesentlich

establish *verb*
• (*set up*) = gründen
• (*prove*) = beweisen

estate agent *noun*
= (der) Immobilienmakler/(die) Immobilienmaklerin

estimate
1 *noun*
(*quote*) = (der) Kostenvoranschlag
2 *verb* = schätzen

etc. *abbreviation*
= usw.

EU *noun*
= (die) EU

euro *noun*
= (der) Euro
to cost 20 euros = 20 Euro kosten

Europe *noun*
= (das) Europa ▶Countries p. 208

European
1 *noun* = (der) Europäer/(die) Europäerin
2 *adjective* = europäisch ▶Countries p. 208

Eurozone *noun*
= (die) Eurozone

even
1 *adjective*
• (*flat, smooth*) = eben
• (*regular*) = gleichmäßig
• **an even number** = eine gerade Zahl
• (*equal*) = gleich
2 *adverb*
• = sogar
she works even on holiday = sie arbeitet sogar in den Ferien
• (*with a negative*)
not even = nicht einmal
he didn't even try = er hat es nicht einmal versucht
• (*with a comparison*) = sogar noch
it is even colder today = es ist sogar noch kälter heute

evening *noun*
= (der) Abend
in the evening = am Abend

event *noun*
= (das) Ereignis

eventually *adverb*
= schließlich

ever *adverb*
• (*at any time*) = je
have you ever been to Rome? = warst du je in Rom?
not ever = nie
nothing ever happens = es passiert nie etwas
• (*always*) = immer
for ever = für immer

every
adjective = jeder/jede/jedes

> **!** Note that **jeder**, **jede** and **jedes** *change their endings in the same way as* **der/die/das**.

every other day = jeden zweiten Tag
every one = jeder Einzelne/jede Einzelne/jedes Einzelne
every few days = alle paar Tage

E

everybody *pronoun*
= alle (*plural*)
everybody knows that = das wissen alle
(*each one*) = jeder
everybody has their own method = jeder
macht es auf seine eigene Weise

everyday *adjective*
= alltäglich

everyone ▶ everybody

everything *pronoun*
= alles

everywhere *adverb*
= überall

evidence *noun*
• (*proof*) = (der) Beweis
• (*given in court*) = (die) Aussage
to give evidence = aussagen

evil
1 *noun* = (das) Böse
2 *adjective* = böse

exact *adjective*
= genau

exactly *adverb*
= genau

exaggerate *verb*
= übertreiben

exaggeration
= (die) Übertreibung

exam *noun*
= (die) Prüfung

examination *noun*
• (*at school*) = (die) Prüfung
• (*medical check-up*) = (die) Untersuchung

examine *verb*
• (*at school*) = prüfen
• (*medically*) = untersuchen

excellent *adjective*
= ausgezeichnet

except *preposition*
= außer (+ *dative*)
you couldn't hear anything except (for) the
clock ticking = man hörte nichts außer
dem Ticken der Uhr

exception *noun*
= (die) Ausnahme

exchange
1 *noun*
• (*of ideas, students*) = (der) Austausch
• (*of money, bought items*) = (der) Umtausch
2 *verb* = umtauschen
she exchanged the bag for a scarf = sie
tauschte die Tasche gegen einen Schal
um

exchange rate *noun*
= (der) Wechselkurs

excited *adjective*
= aufgeregt

exciting *adjective*
= aufregend

excuse
1 *noun*
• (*justifying something*) =
(die) Entschuldigung
• (*pretext*) = (die) Ausrede
2 *verb* = entschuldigen
excuse me! = Entschuldigung!

exercise
1 *noun*
• (*piece of work*) = (die) Übung
• (*to keep fit*) = (die) Bewegung
to do exercises = Gymnastik machen
to take exercise = sich bewegen
2 *verb*
(*keep fit*) = trainieren

exhaust *noun*
(*of a car*) = (der) Auspuff

exhausted *adjective*
= erschöpft

exhibition *noun*
= (die) Ausstellung

existence *noun*
= (die) Existenz

exit *noun*
• (*door*) = (der) Ausgang
• (*from a motorway*) = (die) Ausfahrt

expect *verb*
• = erwarten
she is expecting a baby = sie erwartet ein
Kind
the results were worse than expected =
die Ergebnisse waren schlechter als
erwartet
I expect so = wahrscheinlich
to expect someone to do something = von
jemandem erwarten, dass er/sie etwas tut
they are expected to be there on time =
man erwartet von ihnen, dass sie
pünktlich da sind
• (*suppose*) = glauben
I expect so = ich glaube schon

expense *noun*
= Kosten (*plural*)
at my expense = auf meine Kosten

expenses *noun*
• (*outgoings*) = Ausgaben (*plural*)
• (*of a businessman*) = Spesen (*plural*)

expensive *adjective*
= teuer

explain *verb*
= erklären

explanation *noun*
= (die) Erklärung

explode *verb*
- (*go off*) = explodieren (**!** *sein*)
- (*set off*) = zur Explosion bringen

exploit *verb*
= ausbeuten

explore *verb*
= erforschen

explosion *noun*
= (die) Explosion

export
1 *noun* = (der) Export
2 *verb* = exportieren

expose *verb*
- (*reveal*) = aufdecken
- (*expose to danger*) = aussetzen
- to expose a film = einen Film belichten

express
1 *adjective* = Eil-
  an express letter = ein Eilbrief
  an express train = ein Schnellzug
2 *adverb*
  to send a letter express = einen Brief per
    Eilboten schicken
3 *verb* = ausdrücken
  to express oneself = sich ausdrücken

expression *noun*
= (der) Ausdruck

extent *noun*
- (*of knowledge, power*) = (der) Umfang
- (*of damage*) = (das) Ausmaß
- (*degree*)
  to a certain extent = in gewissem Maße

external *adjective*
= äußerer/äußere/äußeres

extra
1 *noun*
- (*additional thing*) = (das) Extra
- (*actor*) = (der) Statist/(die) Statistin
2 *adjective* = zusätzlich
3 *adverb*
- (*additionally*) = extra
- (*especially*) = besonders
  you need to be extra careful = du musst
    besonders vorsichtig sein

extraordinary *adjective*
- (*wonderful*) = außerordentlich
- (*strange*) = seltsam

extreme
1 *noun* = (das) Extrem
2 *adjective*
- (*outermost*) = äußerster/äußerste/
  äußerstes
- (*radical*) = extrem

extremely *adverb*
= äußerst

extrovert *adjective*
= extravertiert

eye *noun*
= (das) Auge

eyebrow *noun*
= (die) Augenbraue

eyelash *noun*
= (die) Wimper

eyelid *noun*
= (das) Augenlid

eyeliner *noun*
= (der) Eyeliner

eye shadow *noun*
= (der) Lidschatten

eyesight *noun*
  to have good/bad eyesight =
    gute/schlechte Augen haben

F

Ff

fabric *noun*
= (der) Stoff

face
1 *noun*
- (*of a person*) = (das) Gesicht
  he has a scar on his face = er hat eine
    Narbe im Gesicht
  to make a face = ein Gesicht schneiden
- (*of a clock, watch*) = (das) Zifferblatt
2 *verb*
- (*be opposite*) = gegenüberstehen
  (+ *dative*)
  she was facing me = sie stand mir
    gegenüber
  the house facing the church = das Haus
    gegenüber der Kirche
- (*look towards*)
  my room faces the garden = mein Zimmer
    geht auf den Garten
- (*of a building*)
  to face south = nach Süden liegen
- (*confront*) = gegenüberstehen (+ *dative*)
  to be faced with difficulties =
    Schwierigkeiten gegenüberstehen
- (*bear*) = verkraften
  not to be able to face something = etwas
    nicht verkraften können

face up to
= ins Auge sehen (+ *dative*)
  to face up to the facts = den Tatsachen ins
    Auge sehen

fact *noun*
= (die) Tatsache
  in fact (*in reality*) = tatsächlich, (*actually*) =
    eigentlich

factory *noun*
= (die) Fabrik

fade *verb*
- (*of a fabric*) = verbleichen (**!** *sein*)
- (*of a colour, memory*) = verblassen (**!** *sein*)
- (*of a sound*) = abklingen (**!** *sein*)
- (*of a flower*) = verwelken (**!** *sein*)

fail *verb*
- (*not succeed*) = scheitern (**!** *sein*)
  to fail in something = mit etwas scheitern
  to fail to do something = etwas nicht tun
  (*in an exam*) = durchfallen (**!** *sein*)
- (*not succeed at*) = nicht bestehen
  I failed my driving test = ich habe meine
  Fahrprüfung nicht bestanden
- (*not allow to pass*)
  to fail a candidate = einen Prüfling
  durchfallen lassen
- (*not work*) = versagen
  the brakes failed = die Bremsen versagten

failure *noun*
- (*lack of success*) = (der) Misserfolg
- (*unsuccessful person*) = (der) Versager
- (*of electricity, an engine*) = (der) Ausfall
  a power failure = ein Stromausfall

faint
1 *verb* = ohnmächtig werden (**!** *sein*)
2 *adjective* = schwach

fair
1 *noun* = (der) Jahrmarkt
  (*trade fair*) = (die) Messe
2 *adjective*
- (*in colour*)
  to have fair hair = blonde Haare haben
  to have fair skin = helle Haut haben
- (*just, reasonable*) = fair, = gerecht
- (*of weather*) = gut

fair-haired *adjective*
= blond

fairy *noun*
= (die) Fee

fairy story, fairy tale *noun*
= (das) Märchen

faith *noun*
- (*religious belief*) = (der) Glaube
- (*confidence*) = (das) Vertrauen
  to have faith in someone = Vertrauen zu
  jemandem haben

faithful *adjective*
= treu
  to be faithful to someone = jemandem treu
  sein

fall
1 *noun*
- (*of an object*) = (der) Fall
- (*of a person, regime*) = (der) Sturz
- (*in prices, temperature*) = (das) Sinken
- (*US: autumn*)
  the fall = der Herbst

2 *verb*
- (*drop, decrease*) = fallen (**!** *sein*)
  to fall to the ground = auf den Boden fallen

> **!** *To indicate direction, a prefix is often
> added to the verb* fallen, *forming a
> separable verb such as* herunterfallen.

  to fall downstairs = die Treppe
  herunterfallen (**!** *sein*)
- (*become*)
  to fall asleep = einschlafen (**!** *sein*)
  to fall in love with someone = sich in
  jemanden verlieben

fall down
- (*of a person*) = hinfallen (**!** *sein*)
- (*of a building*) = einstürzen (**!** *sein*)
- (*of a tent, toy*) = umfallen (**!** *sein*)

fall off
= herunterfallen (**!** *sein*)

fall out
= herausfallen (**!** *sein*)

fall over
- (*of a person*) = hinfallen (**!** *sein*)
- (*stumble*)
  he fell over the stool = er fiel über den
  Hocker

fall through
  (*of an agreement*) = ins Wasser fallen
  (**!** *sein*)

false *adjective*
= falsch

false teeth *noun*
= (das) Gebiss

familiar *adjective*
= bekannt
  the name sounds familiar = der Name ist
  mir bekannt

family *noun*
= (die) Familie

famine *noun*
= (die) Hungersnot

famous *adjective*
= berühmt

fan *noun*
- (*held in the hand*) = (der) Fächer
- (*electric, for cooling*) = (der) Ventilator
- (*supporter*) = (der) Fan

fancy *adjective*
= extravagant

fancy dress *noun*
= (die) Verkleidung
  in fancy dress = verkleidet

fantastic *adjective*
  (*wonderful*) = phantastisch

fantasy *noun*
= (die) Phantasie

far
1 *adverb*
- (*in distance, time*) = weit
  how far is it to London? = wie weit ist es
    bis London?
  it's very far away = es ist sehr weit weg
  far into the future = bis weit in die Zukunft
  as far back as 1950 = schon 1950
- (*very much*) = viel
  far better = viel besser
2 *adjective*
- (*remote*) = weit entfernt
- (*remote in time*) = fern
- (*other*)
  at the far end = am anderen Ende
- (*other uses*)
  by far = bei weitem
  so far = bisher
  as far as I know = soweit ich weiß

fare *noun*
- (*on a bus, train*) = (der) Fahrpreis
- (*on a plane*) = (der) Flugpreis

farm *noun*
= (der) Bauernhof

farmer *noun*
= (der) Bauer/(die) Bäuerin ▶**Professions**
p. 298

fart *verb*
= furzen♦*

farther ▶further

fascination *noun*
= (die) Faszination

fashion *noun*
= (die) Mode
to be in fashion = in Mode sein
to go out of fashion = aus der Mode
  kommen (**!** sein)

fashionable *adjective*
= modisch

fast
1 *adjective* = schnell
to be fast (*of a clock*) = vorgehen (**!** sein)
my watch is fast = meine Uhr geht vor
2 *adverb* = schnell
to be fast asleep = fest schlafen

fasten *verb*
to fasten a zip = einen Reißverschluss
  zumachen
to fasten one's seatbelt = sich anschnallen

fat
1 *adjective*
- (*of a person, animal*) = dick, = fett✖
- (*of meat*) = fett
2 *noun* = (das) Fett

fatal *adjective*
a fatal accident = ein tödlicher Unfall
a fatal mistake = ein verhängnisvoller
  Fehler

fate *noun*
= (das) Schicksal

father *noun*
= (der) Vater

Father Christmas *noun*
= (der) Weihnachtsmann

father-in-law *noun*
= (der) Schwiegervater

fattening *adjective*
to be fattening = dick machen

faucet *noun* (*US*)
= (der) Wasserhahn

fault *noun*
- (*responsibility*) = (die) Schuld
  it's your fault = du hast Schuld
- (*flaw*) = (der) Fehler

favor (*US*) ▶favour

favorite (*US*) ▶favourite

favour (*British*)
1 *noun*
- (*kind act*) = (der) Gefallen
  to do someone a favour = jemandem einen
    Gefallen tun
- (*advantage*)
  that's in his favour = das ist zu seinen
    Gunsten
- (*support*)
  in favour of = zugunsten (+ *genitive*)
  to be in favour of something = für etwas
    (*accusative*) sein
  I am in favour = ich bin dafür
2 *verb*
- (*benefit*) = begünstigen
- (*prefer*) = bevorzugen

favourite (*British*)
1 *adjective* = Lieblings-
  my favourite film = mein Lieblingsfilm
2 *noun*
- (*in a race or contest*) = (der) Favorit/
    (die) Favoritin
- (*favoured person*) = (der) Liebling

fax
1 *noun* = (das) Fax
2 *verb* = faxen

fear
1 *noun* = (die) Angst
  fear of = Angst vor (+ *dative*)
2 *verb* = fürchten

feast *noun*
= (das) Festessen

feather *noun*
= (die) Feder

February *noun*
= (der) Februar ▶**Dates p. 213**

fed up *adjective*
I am fed up with him = ich habe die Nase
  voll von ihm✖

fee *noun* = (die) Gebühr
  (of a doctor, lawyer) = (das) Honorar
  school fees = (das) Schulgeld

feed *verb*
  = füttern

feel *verb*
* *(emotionally, physically)*
  to feel [sad | happy | tired …] = [traurig |
    glücklich | müde …] sein
  to feel [young | old | ill …] = sich [jung | alt |
    krank …] fühlen
  she felt a pain = sie spürte einen Schmerz
  I feel hot = mir ist heiß
* *(to the touch)* = fühlen
  to feel [soft | hard | damp …] = sich [weich |
    hart | feucht …] anfühlen
* *(want)*
  to feel like something = Lust auf etwas
    (accusative) haben
  I don't feel like it = ich habe keine Lust
    dazu

feel up to
  to feel up to work = sich der Arbeit
    gewachsen fühlen

feeling *noun*
  = (das) Gefühl
  I have a feeling he's right = ich habe das
    Gefühl, dass er Recht hat

female
1 *adjective* = weiblich
2 *noun*
* *(woman)* = (die) Frau
* *(animal)* = (das) Weibchen

feminine
1 *adjective* = weiblich, = feminin
2 *noun*
  (in grammar) = (das) Femininum

feminist
1 *noun* = (die) Feministin/(der) Feminist
2 *adjective* = feministisch

fence *noun*
  = (der) Zaun

fencing *noun*
  (sport) = (das) Fechten

ferry *noun*
  = (die) Fähre

fertile *adjective*
  = fruchtbar

festival *noun*
* *(holiday)* = (der) Feiertag
* *(artistic event)* = Festspiele *(plural)*

fetch *verb*
* *(go and get)* = holen
  (collect) = abholen
* *(be sold for)* = einbringen
  to fetch a good price = einen guten Preis
    einbringen

✻ in informal situations

few
1 *adjective*
* *(not many)* = wenige
  few people = wenige Leute
* *(several)* **a few** = ein paar
  every few days = alle paar Tage
  the first few weeks = die ersten paar
    Wochen
2 *pronoun* = wenige
  there are so few of them = es gibt nur so
    wenige
  a few of us = ein paar von uns
  quite a few = eine ganze Menge

fiddle *verb*
  to fiddle with something = an etwas
    (dative) fummeln

field *noun*
  = (das) Feld

fierce *adjective*
  = wild

fifteen *adjective*
  = fünfzehn ▶ Numbers p. 282

fifth ▶ Numbers p. 282, ▶ Dates p. 213
1 *adjective* = fünfter/fünfte/fünftes
2 *noun*
  (fraction) = (das) Fünftel

fifty *adjective*
  = fünfzig ▶ Numbers p. 282

fight
1 *noun*
* *(battle)* = (der) Kampf
* *(brawl)* = (die) Schlägerei
  (between children) = (die) Rauferei
* *(quarrel)* = (der) Streit
2 *verb*
* *(do battle)* = kämpfen
  to fight someone = mit jemandem
    kämpfen
* *(brawl)* = sich schlagen
  (of children) = sich raufen
* *(quarrel)* = sich streiten
* *(combat)* **to fight** [disease | poverty | a fire …] =
  [Krankheit | Armut | ein Feuer …] bekämpfen

figure *noun*
* *(number)* = (die) Zahl
* *(person)* = (die) Gestalt
* *(body shape)* = (die) Figur

file
1 *noun*
* *(for documents)* = (die) Akte
* *(in computing)* = (die) Datei
* *(for nails)* = (die) Feile
* *(line)* = (die) Reihe
  in single file = im Gänsemarsch
2 *verb*
* **to file documents** = Akten ablegen
* *(smooth)* = feilen
  to file one's nails = sich *(dative)* die Nägel
    feilen

filing cabinet *noun*
  = (der) Aktenschrank

fill verb
• (make full) = füllen
• **fill her up!** = voll tanken!
• (become full) = sich füllen
fill in
= ausfüllen

film
1 noun = (der) Film
2 verb = filmen

filthy adjective
= dreckig

final
1 adjective
• (last) = letzter/letzte/letztes
the final day = der letzte Tag
• (definitive) = endgültig
her final decision = ihre endgültige
Entscheidung
the final result = das Endresultat
2 noun
(in sport) = (das) Finale

finally adverb
= schließlich

finance
1 noun
• (funds) = Geldmittel (plural)
• (resources) = Finanzen (plural)
2 verb = finanzieren

financial adjective
= finanziell

find verb
= finden
find out
= herausfinden

fine
1 adjective
• (very good) = gut
I'm fine = mir geht es gut
to feel fine = sich wohl fühlen
a fine day = ein schöner Tag
• (delicate) = fein
2 adverb = gut
they get along fine = sie verstehen sich gut
3 noun = (die) Geldstrafe
4 verb
to fine someone = jemanden zu einer
Geldstrafe verurteilen
he was fined £10 = er musste zehn Pfund
Strafe bezahlen

finger noun
= (der) Finger

fingernail noun
= (der) Fingernagel

finish
1 verb
• (end) = beenden
• (eat up food, meal) = aufessen
(drink up) = austrinken
(use up) = aufbrauchen

• (complete)
to finish doing something = etwas zu Ende
tun
she finished (reading) the book = sie las
das Buch zu Ende
• **to be finished with something** = mit etwas
fertig sein
have you finished your work? = bist du mit
der Arbeit fertig?
• (come to an end) = aufhören
(of a performance, meeting) = zu Ende sein
2 noun
• = (der) Schluss
• (finishing line) = (das) Ziel

Finland noun
= (das) Finnland ▶ Countries p. 208

fir noun
= (die) Tanne

fire
1 noun = (das) Feuer
to be on fire = brennen
to catch fire = Feuer fangen
to light a fire = das Feuer anmachen
to set fire to a house = ein Haus in Brand
stecken
2 verb
• (shoot)
to fire at someone = auf jemanden
schießen
to fire a gun = ein Gewehr abfeuern
• (dismiss) = feuern✶

fire brigade noun
= (die) Feuerwehr

fire engine noun
= (das) Feuerwehrauto

fire extinguisher noun
= (der) Feuerlöscher

fireman noun
= (der) Feuerwehrmann

fireplace noun
= (der) Kamin

fire station noun
= (die) Feuerwache

firework noun
= (der) Feuerwerkskörper

fireworks display noun
= (das) Feuerwerk

firm
1 noun = (die) Firma
2 adjective
• (hard) = fest
• (strict) = streng

first ▶ Numbers p. 282, ▶ Dates p. 213
1 adjective = erster/erste/erstes
for the first time = zum ersten Mal
at first sight = auf den ersten Blick
2 adverb
• (before others, to begin with) = zuerst
who saw him first? = wer hat ihn zuerst
gesehen?

F

- (*for the first time*) = zum ersten Mal
  I first met him in Berlin = ich traf ihn zum
  ersten Mal in Berlin
  at first = zuerst
3 *noun*
- the first = der/die/das Erste
  she was the first to arrive = sie kam als
  Erste an
  Elizabeth the First = Elisabeth die Erste
- (*in dates*)
  it's the first today = heute ist der Erste

first aid *noun*
= (die) erste Hilfe

first class
1 *adjective* = erstklassig
  a first-class ticket = eine Fahrkarte erster
  Klasse
  a first-class stamp = eine Briefmarke für
  bevorzugt beförderte Post
2 *adverb*
  he travels first class = er reist erster Klasse

first floor *noun*
- (*British*) = (der) erste Stock
- (*US*) = (das) Erdgeschoss

firstly *adverb*
= zuerst

first name *noun*
= (der) Vorname

fish
1 *noun* = (der) Fisch
2 *verb*
  (*with a net*) = fischen
  (*with a rod*) = angeln

fisherman *noun*
= (der) Fischer

fishing *noun*
= (die) Fischerei

fishing rod *noun*
= (die) Angel

fist *noun*
= (die) Faust

fit
1 *adjective*
- (*suitable*) = geeignet
  fit to eat = essbar
  the house is not fit to live in = das Haus ist
  nicht bewohnbar
- (*healthy*) = gesund, = fit✱
  to keep fit = fit bleiben
2 *noun* = (der) Anfall
  a coughing fit = ein Hustenanfall
3 *verb*
- (*be the right size*) = passen
  these shoes don't fit me = diese Schuhe
  passen mir nicht
- (*install*) = einbauen
  to fit a carpet = einen Teppich legen

✱ in informal situations

- (*match*) = zutreffen auf (+ *accusative*)
fit in
- (*in a room or car*) = hineinpassen, =
  reinpassen✱
- (*adapt*) = sich einfügen
  to fit in with a group = sich in eine Gruppe
  einfügen

fitted kitchen *noun*
= (die) Einbauküche

five *adjective*
= fünf ▶ Numbers p. 282

fix *verb*
- (*repair*) = reparieren
- (*establish*) = festlegen
  to fix a [date | price …] = [einen Termin | einen
  Preis …] festlegen
- (*prepare*) = machen
  to fix someone a meal = jemandem etwas
  zu essen machen

fizzy *adjective*
= kohlensäurehaltig

flag *noun*
= (die) Fahne

flame *noun*
= (die) Flamme

flannel *noun* (*British*)
= (der) Waschlappen

flash
1 *noun* = (der) Blitz
  a flash of lightning = ein Blitz
2 *verb*
  his eyes flashed = seine Augen blitzten
  the light flashed all the time = das Licht
  blinkte die ganze Zeit
  to flash a warning = zur Warnung blinken

flask *noun*
  (*vacuum flask*) = (die) Thermosflasche®

flat
1 *adjective*
- (*not curved*) = flach
  (*of a surface*) = eben
- (*of a tyre*) = platt
  to have a flat tyre = eine Reifenpanne
  haben
2 *noun* (*British*) = (die) Wohnung

flatter *verb*
= schmeicheln (+ *dative*)

flavor (*US*), **flavour** (*British*)
1 *noun* = (der) Geschmack
2 *verb* = abschmecken

flaw *noun*
= (der) Fehler

flea *noun*
= (der) Floh

fleet *noun*
= (die) Flotte

flesh *noun*
= (das) Fleisch

flexible *adjective*
• (*bendable*) = biegsam
• (*adaptable*) = flexibel

flicker *verb*
= flackern

flight *noun*
= (der) Flug

float *verb*
• (*on water*) = treiben (**!** *sein*)
  (*of a person*) = sich treiben lassen
• (*in the air*) = schweben (**!** *sein*)

flock *noun*
• (*of sheep*) = (die) Herde
• (*of birds*) = (der) Schwarm

flood
1 *noun*
= (die) Überschwemmung
2 *verb*
• (*overflow*) = über die Ufer treten (**!** *sein*)
  the river floods every spring = der Fluss
  tritt jeden Frühling über die Ufer
• (*fill with water*) = überschwemmen
  the houses were flooded = die Häuser
  wurden überschwemmt

floor *noun*
• (*ground*) = (der) Boden
• (*storey*) = (der) Stock

floorboard *noun*
= (die) Diele

floppy disk *noun*
= (die) Diskette

florist *noun*
= (der) Blumenhändler/(die)
  Blumenhändlerin ▶**Professions p. 298**

flour *noun*
= (das) Mehl

flow *verb*
= fließen (**!** *sein*)

flower
1 *noun* = (die) Blume
2 *verb* = blühen

flu *noun*
= (die) Grippe
  to have flu = die Grippe haben

fluent *adjective*
= fließend
  she speaks fluent German = sie spricht
  fließend Deutsch

fluff *noun*
= Fusseln (*plural*)

fluid
1 *noun* = (die) Flüssigkeit
2 *adjective* = flüssig

flush
1 *noun*
  (*on the face*) = (das) Erröten
2 *verb*
  (*wash away*) = spülen

flute *noun*
= (die) Flöte

fly
1 *verb*
• (*of a pilot*) = fliegen
  to fly a plane = ein Flugzeug fliegen
  to fly a kite = einen Drachen steigen lassen
• (*of a bird, plane*) = fliegen (**!** *sein*)
  I flew Lufthansa = ich bin mit Lufthansa
  geflogen
• (*of a flag*) = wehen
  to fly the German flag = die deutsche Fahne
  führen
2 *noun* = (die) Fliege

foam *noun*
• (*on sea, drink*) = (der) Schaum
• (*rubber or plastic material*) =
  (der) Schaumstoff

focus
1 *noun*
• (*in photography*)
  in focus = scharf
• (*centre*) = (der) Brennpunkt
  to be the focus of attention = im
  Brennpunkt des Interesses stehen
2 *verb*
• to focus a camera on something = eine
  Kamera scharf auf etwas (*accusative*)
  einstellen
• (*concentrate*) = sich konzentrieren

fog *noun*
= (der) Nebel

foggy *adjective*
= neblig

fold
1 *verb* = falten
  he folded his arms = er verschränkte die
  Arme
2 *noun*
• (*in fabric, skin*) = (die) Falte
• (*in paper*) = (der) Kniff
fold up
= zusammenfalten
  to fold up a chair = einen Stuhl
  zusammenklappen

follow *verb*
= folgen (+ *dative*) (**!** *sein*)
  she followed him into the room = sie folgte
  ihm ins Zimmer
  as follows = wie folgt

follower *noun*
= (der) Anhänger/(die) Anhängerin

following
1 *adjective* = folgend
2 *preposition* = nach (+ *dative*)
  following the accident = nach dem Unfall

F

fond *adjective*
  to be fond of someone = jemanden gern
    haben

food *noun*
  • = (das) Essen
  to buy food = Lebensmittel einkaufen
  • (*for animals*) = (das) Futter

fool
  1 *noun* = (der) Dummkopf
  2 *verb*
  to fool someone = jemanden täuschen
fool around
  = herumalbern

foot *noun*
  = (der) Fuß
  on foot = zu Fuß

football *noun*
  • (*soccer, ball*) = (der) Fußball
  • (*American football*) = (der) Football

footballer *noun*
  = (der) Fußballspieler/(die) Fußballspielerin

footpath *noun*
  = (der) Fußweg

footprint *noun*
  = (der) Fußabdruck

footstep *noun*
  = (der) Schritt

for *preposition*
  • = für (+ *accusative*)
  to work for a firm = bei einer Firma
    arbeiten
  to go for a swim = schwimmen gehen
    (**!** *sein*)
  to go for a walk = spazieren gehen (**!** *sein*)
  something for [a cough | a cold | a headache] =
    etwas gegen [Husten | Schnupfen |
    Kopfschmerzen]
  he is for nuclear power = er ist für
    Kernenergie
  to ask for help = um Hilfe bitten
  for this reason = aus diesem Grund
  • (*in time expressions*) = seit (+ *dative*)
  she has lived here for 8 years = sie wohnt
    seit acht Jahren hier
  I've been waiting for 3 hours = ich habe
    drei Stunden lang gewartet
  for hours = stundenlang
  he will be in Paris for a year = er bleibt ein
    Jahr in Paris
  • (*indicating distance*)
  we drove for 80 kilometres = wir fuhren
    achtzig Kilometer
  for kilometres = kilometerweit
  • (*indicating cost or an amount*)
  he bought it for £10 = er hat es für zehn
    Pfund gekauft
  a cheque for £20 = ein Scheck über
    zwanzig Pfund
  for nothing = umsonst

  • (*representing*)
  T for Tom = T wie Tom
  what is the French for cat? = wie heißt
    Katze auf Französisch?
  • (*on the occasion of*) = zu (+ *dative*)
  I got a book for my birthday = ich habe ein
    Buch zu meinem Geburtstag bekommen
  what's for lunch? = was gibts zum
    Mittagessen?
  what for? = wozu?

forbid *verb*
  = verbieten
  to forbid someone to do something =
    jemandem verbieten, etwas zu tun

force
  1 *noun*
  • (*power*) = (die) Kraft
  • (*violence*) = (die) Gewalt
  • the police force = die Polizei
  the (armed) forces = die Streitkräfte
  • (*of a law*)
  to be in force = gültig sein
  to come into force = in Kraft treten (**!** *sein*)
  2 *verb* = zwingen
force open
  = aufbrechen

forecast
  1 *noun* = (die) Voraussage
  (*weather report*) = (die) Vorhersage
  2 *verb* = voraussagen
  to forecast rain = Regen vorhersagen

forehead *noun*
  = (die) Stirn

foreign *adjective*
  = ausländisch
  foreign countries = fremde Länder
  a foreign language = eine Fremdsprache

foreigner *noun*
  = (der) Ausländer/(die) Ausländerin

Foreign Secretary *noun* (*British*)
  = (der) Außenminister/(die) Außenministerin

forest *noun*
  = (der) Wald

forever *adverb*
  • (*for all time*) = ewig
  • (*continually*) = ständig
  he is forever complaining = er beklagt sich
    ständig

forge *verb*
  = fälschen

forgery *noun*
  = (die) Fälschung

forget *verb*
  = vergessen
  to forget about something = etwas
    vergessen
  he forgot to do the shopping = er hat
    vergessen einzukaufen

forgive verb
= verzeihen (+ dative)
he forgave her for lying to him = er hat ihr verziehen, dass sie ihn angelogen hatte

fork noun
= (die) Gabel

form
1 noun
• (type, shape, mood) = (die) Form
  a form of life = eine Lebensform
  to be in good form = gut in Form sein
  off form = nicht in Form
• (document) = (das) Formular
  to fill in a form = ein Formular ausfüllen
• (British: class in school) = (die) Klasse
2 verb
• (develop) = bilden
  to form a circle = einen Kreis bilden
  to form an opinion = sich (dative) ein Urteil bilden
  to form an impression = einen Eindruck gewinnen
• (be formed) = sich bilden
  bubbles form on the surface = Blasen bilden sich auf der Oberfläche

formal adjective
• (official) = formell
• (of manner, clothes, language) = förmlich
• (festive) = feierlich

former adjective
• (previous) = ehemalig
  the former minister = der ehemalige Minister
  in former times = früher
• (first of two)
  the former = der/die/das Erstere

fortnight noun
= vierzehn Tage (plural)

fortnightly adverb
= alle vierzehn Tage

fortunate adjective
= glücklich
to be fortunate = Glück haben

fortunately adverb
= glücklicherweise

fortune noun
• (wealth) = (das) Vermögen
• (luck) = (das) Glück

fortune-teller noun
= (die) Wahrsagerin

forty adjective
= vierzig ▶Numbers p. 282

forward
1 adverb
• (in the direction faced) = vorwärts
• (to the front) = nach vorn
2 adjective
• (at the front) = vorderer/vordere/vorderes
• (cheeky) = frech

3 verb = nachsenden
  to forward a letter = einen Brief nachsenden
4 noun
  (in sport) = (der) Stürmer

fossil noun
= (das) Fossil

foundation noun
• (basis) = (die) Grundlage
• (cosmetics) = (das) Make-up
• **foundations** (of a building) = (das) Fundament

fountain noun
= (der) Brunnen

four adjective
= vier ▶Numbers p. 282

fourteen adjective
= vierzehn ▶Numbers p. 282

fourth ▶Numbers p. 282, ▶Dates p. 213
1 adjective = vierter/vierte/viertes
2 noun (fraction) = (das) Viertel

fox noun
= (der) Fuchs

fraction noun
• (in maths) = (der) Bruch
• (small amount) = (der) Bruchteil

fracture
1 noun = (der) Bruch
2 verb = brechen

fragile adjective
= zerbrechlich

frame
1 noun
• (of a picture, window) = (der) Rahmen
• (of spectacles) = (das) Gestell
2 verb = einrahmen

France noun
= (das) Frankreich ▶Countries p. 208

frank adjective
= offen

fraud noun
= (der) Betrug

freckle noun
= (die) Sommersprosse

free
1 adjective
• (at liberty, available) = frei
  to set a prisoner free = einen Gefangenen freilassen
  he is free to do what he wants = er kann tun, was er will
  is this seat free? = ist dieser Platz frei?
  are you free on Monday? = bist du am Montag frei?
• (without charge) = kostenlos
2 adverb
• (without charge) = umsonst

F

students get their meals free = Studenten
bekommen das Essen umsonst
- (*without restriction*) = frei

freedom noun
= (die) Freiheit

freeze verb
- (*become covered with ice*) = zufrieren
(**!** sein)
the lake was frozen = der See war
zugefroren
- (*of food, liquid*) = gefrieren (**!** sein)
- (*preserve food*) = einfrieren
- (*feel cold*) = sehr frieren
I'm freezing = ich friere sehr
- (*fix at a certain level*) = einfrieren
to freeze prices = Preise einfrieren

freezer noun
- (*deep freeze*) = (der) Gefrierschrank
- (*part of a fridge*) = (das) Gefrierfach

freezing adjective
= eiskalt

French
1 noun
- (*people*) the French = die Franzosen
- (*language*) = (das) Französisch
2 adjective = französisch ▶**Countries p. 208**

French fries noun
= Pommes frites (*plural*)

Frenchman noun
= (der) Franzose

Frenchwoman noun
= (die) Französin

frequently adverb
= häufig

fresh adjective
= frisch

Friday noun
= (der) Freitag ▶**Dates p. 213**

fridge noun
= (der) Kühlschrank

friend noun
= (der) Freund/(die) Freundin
to be friends with someone = mit
jemandem befreundet sein
he made friends with her = er hat sich mit
ihr befreundet

friendly adjective
= freundlich
to be friendly with someone = mit
jemandem befreundet sein

friendship noun
= (die) Freundschaft

fright noun
= (der) Schreck
to give someone a fright = jemanden
erschrecken

frighten verb
- (*scare*) = Angst machen (+ *dative*)
- (*startle*) = erschrecken

frightened adjective
to be frightened = Angst haben
she is frightened of dogs = sie hat Angst
vor Hunden

frightening adjective
= beängstigend

fringe noun
(*hairstyle*) = (der) Pony

frog noun
= (der) Frosch

from preposition
- (*indicating a starting place*) = von
(+ *dative*)
the journey from London to Munich = die
Reise von London nach München
we live ten minutes from the city centre =
wir wohnen zehn Minuten vom
Stadtzentrum
! Note the contraction vom = von dem.

- (*indicating place of origin*) = aus (+ *dative*)
he comes from Germany = er kommt aus
Deutschland
the train from Berlin = der Zug aus Berlin
where is he from? = woher kommt er?
- (*referring to time*) = von (+ *dative*)
the shop is open from 8 to 12 = das
Geschäft hat von acht bis zwölf offen
from Sunday on = ab Sonntag
from then on = von da an
from that day = seit dem Tag
- (*according to*) = nach (+ *dative*)
from his description = nach seiner
Beschreibung
from what she said = nach dem, was sie
sagte
- (*ranging*)
there were from 20 to 30 people there = es
waren zwischen zwanzig und dreißig
Leute da
- different from = anders als

front
1 noun
- (*exterior*) = (die) Vorderseite
- (*of a house*) = (die) Vorderfront
- (*of a jacket, building*) = (das) Vorderteil
- (*of a train, queue*) = (das) vordere Ende
- at the front = vorne
in *or* at the front of = vorne in (+ *dative*)
to sit at the front = vorne sitzen
2 adjective = vorderer/vordere/vorderes
the front wheel = das Vorderrad
in front of = vor (+ *dative or accusative*)
! Note that vor is followed by a noun in the
dative when position is described. The
accusative follows when there is
movement towards something.

front door noun
= (die) Haustür

frontier noun
= (die) Grenze

front page noun
= (die) Titelseite

front seat *noun*
= (der) Vordersitz

frost *noun*
= (der) Frost

frosty *adjective*
= frostig

frown *verb*
= die Stirn runzeln

frozen *adjective*
• (*very cold*) = gefroren
I'm frozen = mir ist eiskalt
• (*of food*) = tiefgekühlt
frozen food = (die) Tiefkühlkost

fruit *noun*
• (*a single fruit or type*) = (die) Frucht
• (*collectively*) = (das) Obst

frustrating *adjective*
= frustrierend

fry *verb*
= braten

frying pan (*British*), **frypan** (*US*) *noun*
= (die) Bratpfanne

fuel *noun*
• (*for a car*) = (der) Kraftstoff
• (*for heating*) = (der) Brennstoff

fulfil (*British*), **fulfill** (*US*) *verb*
= erfullen
to fulfil an ambition = eine Ambition
verwirklichen

full *adjective*
= voll
at full speed = in voller Fahrt
full of = voller (+ *genitive*)
the streets were full of people = die
Straßen waren voller Menschen

full board *noun*
= (die) Vollpension

full moon *noun*
= (der) Vollmond

full stop *noun*
= (der) Punkt

fumes *noun*
= Dämpfe (*plural*)
(*from cars*) = Abgase (*plural*)

fun *noun*
= (der) Spaß
dancing is fun = Tanzen macht Spaß
for fun = aus Spaß
to have fun = sich amüsieren

function
1 *noun*
• (*purpose*) = (die) Funktion
• (*reception*) = (die) Veranstaltung
2 *verb* = funktionieren

funeral *noun*
= (die) Beerdigung

funny *adjective*
• (*amusing*) = lustig
• (*odd*) = komisch
it's funny that he hasn't phoned = es ist
komisch, dass er nicht angerufen hat

fur
1 *noun*
• (*on an animal*) = (das) Fell
• (*on a coat*) = (der) Pelz
2 *adjective* = Pelz-
a fur coat = ein Pelzmantel

furious *adjective*
= wütend

furnish *verb*
(*with furniture*) = einrichten
a furnished flat = eine möblierte Wohnung

furniture *noun*
= Möbel (*plural*)
a piece of furniture = ein Möbelstück

further
1 *adverb* = weiter
it was further than I thought = es war
weiter als ich dachte
further off = weiter entfernt
2 *adjective*
• (*more distant*) = weiter entfernt
at the further end of the street = am
anderen Ende der Straße
• (*additional*) = weiterer/weitere/weiteres
a further 50 people = weitere fünfzig Leute
3 *verb* = fördern
to further one's career = seine Karriere
fördern

fuss
1 *noun* = (das) Theater
to make a fuss about something = viel
Theater um etwas machen
2 *verb*
(*worry*) = sich aufregen
to fuss over someone = jemanden
bemuttern

future
1 *noun* = (die) Zukunft
in future = in Zukunft
2 *adjective* = zukünftig
his future wife = seine zukünftige Frau
at a future date = zu einem späteren
Zeitpunkt

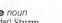

gale *noun*
= (der) Sturm

gallery *noun*
= (die) Galerie

G

game *noun*
= (das) Spiel
to have a game of football = Fußball
spielen
to play a game of chess with someone =
eine Partie Schach mit jemandem spielen
games (*at school*) = (der) Sport

gang *noun*
* (*group of friends*) = (die) Clique
* (*group of criminals*) = (die) Bande

gap *noun*
* (*space*) = (die) Lücke
* (*period of time*) = (die) Pause
* (*difference*) = (der) Unterschied
a big age gap = ein großer
Altersunterschied

garage *noun*
* (*for keeping cars*) = (die) Garage
* (*for repairing cars*) = (die) Autowerkstatt
* (*petrol station*) = (die) Tankstelle

garbage *noun* (*US*)
= (der) Müll

garden *noun*
= (der) Garten

gardener *noun*
= (der) Gärtner/(die) Gärtnerin

gardening *noun*
= (die) Gartenarbeit

garlic *noun*
= (der) Knoblauch

garment *noun*
= (das) Kleidungsstück

gas *noun*
* (*fuel*) = (das) Gas
to use gas for cooking = mit Gas kochen
* (*US: petrol*) = (das) Benzin

gasoline *noun* (*US*)
= (das) Benzin

gas station *noun* (*US*)
= (die) Tankstelle

gate *noun*
* (*entrance*) = (das) Tor
* (*in an airport*) = (der) Flugsteig

gather *verb*
* (*collect*) = sammeln
* (*come together*) = sich versammeln
people gathered in the park = die Leute
versammelten sich im Park

gay *adjective*
* (*happy*) = fröhlich
* (*homosexual*) = schwul✘

GCSE *noun* (*British*)
≈ (die) Abschlussprüfung

✘ in informal situations

gear *noun*
* (*in a car, on a bike*) = (der) Gang
to change gear = schalten
is the car in gear? = ist der Gang eingelegt?
* (*equipment*) = (die) Ausrüstung
* (*clothing*) = Sachen (*plural*), = (das) Zeug✘

Gemini *noun*
= Zwillinge (*plural*)

general
1 *noun* = (der) General
2 *adjective* = allgemein
in general = im Allgemeinen

generation *noun*
= (die) Generation

generous *adjective*
= großzügig

genetics *noun*
= (die) Genetik

Geneva *noun*
= (das) Genf ▶**Countries p. 208**
Lake Geneva = der Genfer See

genius *noun*
= (das) Genie

gentle *adjective*
= sanft

gentleman *noun*
= (der) Herr

genuine *adjective*
= echt
is that a genuine Picasso? = ist das ein
echter Picasso?

geography *noun*
= (die) Geographie, = (die) Erdkunde

German
1 *noun*
* (*person*) = (der) Deutsche/(die) Deutsche
the Germans = die Deutschen
* (*language*) = (das) Deutsch
I am learning German = ich lerne Deutsch
in German = auf Deutsch
2 *adjective* = deutsch ▶**Countries p. 208**

Germany *noun*
= (das) Deutschland ▶**Countries p. 208**

get *verb*

> **!** Note that *get* is a very common word in
> English and does not have a multi-
> purpose German equivalent. This entry
> covers most frequent uses, but to find
> translations for other expressions, such
> as *get well, get in shape, etc,* look up *well,*
> *shape, etc.*

* (*become*) = werden (**!** *sein*)
to get [old | wet | rich …] = [alt | nass | reich …]
werden
* (*ask or persuade*)
to get someone to do something =
jemanden dazu bringen, etwas zu tun

- (*cause to be done or happen*)
to get something done = etwas machen
lassen
to get one's hair cut = sich (*dative*) die
Haare schneiden lassen
to get dressed = sich anziehen
to get to know someone = jemanden
kennen lernen
- (*arrive*) = ankommen (**!** *sein*)
I'll let you know when we get there = ich
sage dir Bescheid, wenn wir ankommen
- (*obtain, receive*) = bekommen, = kriegen✶
to get a present from someone = ein
Geschenk von jemandem bekommen
to get a shock = einen Schreck kriegen✶
to get a good mark = eine gute Note
kriegen✶
- (*procure*) = besorgen
they can get you a car = sie können euch
ein Auto besorgen
- (*buy*) = kaufen
- (*fetch*) = holen
he's gone to get help = er holt Hilfe
to get someone from the station =
jemanden vom Bahnhof abholen
- (*prepare*) = machen
to get breakfast = Frühstück machen
- (*have illness*) = haben
I've got toothache = ich habe
Zahnschmerzen
- (*use for transport*) = nehmen
to get a taxi to the station = ein Taxi zum
Bahnhof nehmen
- (*answer the door or phone*)
I'll get it (*open the door*) = ich mache auf,
(*answer the phone*) = ich gehe ans
Telefon
to get someone (*on the phone*) =
jemanden erreichen
- (*start*)
to get working = sich an die Arbeit machen
to get talking = ins Gespräch kommen
(**!** *sein*)
- (*understand*) = verstehen, = kapieren✶
I don't get it = ich kapier es nicht✶

! *For translations of* got to, *see the entry* got.

get away
- (*leave*) = wegkommen (**!** *sein*)
- (*escape*) = entkommen (+ *dative*) (**!** *sein*)
- (*go unpunished*) = ungestraft
davonkommen (**!** *sein*)
get back
- (*return*) = zurückkommen (**!** *sein*)
- (*regain*) = zurückbekommen
get down to
to get down to something = sich an etwas
(*accusative*) machen
get off
- (*leave a bus, train*) = aussteigen (**!** *sein*)
- (*remove*) = entfernen
get on
- (*enter a bus, train*) = einsteigen (**!** *sein*)
- (*have a good relationship*) = sich verstehen
he gets on well with her = er versteht sich
gut mit ihr

- (*progress*) = vorankommen (**!** *sein*)
get out
- (*leave*) = herauskommen (**!** *sein*)
- (*bring out*) = herausbringen
- (*leave a car, train*) = aussteigen (**!** *sein*)
get through
- (*contact by phone*) = durchkommen
(**!** *sein*)
I couldn't get through to her = ich konnte
nicht zu ihr durchkommen
get up
= aufstehen (**!** *sein*)

ghost noun
= (der) Geist

giant noun
= (der) Riese

gift noun
- (*present*) = (das) Geschenk
- (*talent*) = (die) Begabung
he has a gift for languages = er ist
sprachbegabt

girl noun
= (das) Mädchen

girlfriend noun
= (die) Freundin

give verb
- = geben
to give someone something to eat =
jemandem etwas zu essen geben
to give a speech = einen Vortrag halten
to give one's name = seinen Namen
angeben
- (*donate*) = spenden
- (*give as a gift*) = schenken
to give someone a present = jemandem
etwas schenken
- (*pass on*)
give him my regards = richten Sie ihm
schöne Grüße von mir aus
to give someone a message = jemandem
eine Nachricht hinterlassen
to give the latest news = das Neueste
mitteilen

! *For translations of phrases such as* to
give someone a fright, a hand *or* a lift, *look
up the entries* fright, hand *or* lift.

give away
- (*get rid of*) = weggeben
(*give as a present*) = verschenken
- (*reveal*) = verraten
to give away a secret = ein Geheimnis
verraten
give back
= zurückgeben
give in
= nachgeben
to give in to someone = jemandem
nachgeben
give out
(*hand out*) = austeilen
give up
- (*stop*) = aufgeben

G

- (*surrender*) = sich stellen
  to give oneself up to the police = sich der
  Polizei stellen
give way
  (*British: when driving*) = die Vorfahrt
  beachten

glad *adjective*
  = froh
  we were glad to see him = wir haben uns
  gefreut, ihn zu sehen

glass *noun*
  = (das) Glas
  a glass of water = ein Glas Wasser

glasses *noun*
  = (die) Brille
  she wears glasses = sie trägt eine Brille

glitter *verb*
  = glitzern

global warming *noun*
  = (der) globale Temperaturanstieg

globe *noun*
  = (der) Globus

gloomy *adjective*
- (*dark*) = düster
- (*sad*) = pessimistisch

glove *noun*
  = (der) Handschuh

glow
1 *noun*
  = (der) Schein
2 *verb*
  (*of a candle*) = scheinen
  (*of a fire, cheeks*) = glühen

glue
1 *noun* = (der) Klebstoff
2 *verb* = kleben

> ! *Note that* **kleben** *forms a separable verb
> with prepositions such as* an, auf *and*
> zusammen.

  he glued them together = er klebte sie
  zusammen

go
1 *verb*
- (*on foot*) = gehen (**!** *sein*)
  (*by vehicle, bicycle*) = fahren (**!** *sein*)
  (*by plane*) = fliegen (**!** *sein*)
  to go to [town | the market | the beach | work …]
  = [in die Stadt | auf den Markt | zum Strand |
  zur Arbeit …] gehen
  to go for a [walk | jog | sleep …] = [spazieren |
  joggen | schlafen …] gehen
  we are going to Austria this year = dieses
  Jahr fahren wir nach Österreich
  to go on holiday = in die Ferien fahren
  to go [shopping | swimming | skiing …] =
  [einkaufen | schwimmen | Ski fahren …]
  gehen
  where are you going? = wo gehst du hin?

- (*leave*) = weggehen (**!** *sein*)
  (*in a vehicle*) = wegfahren (**!** *sein*)
  (*on a journey*) = abfahren (**!** *sein*)
- (*when talking about time*) = vergehen
  (**!** *sein*)
  time goes very slowly = die Zeit vergeht
  sehr langsam
- (*disappear*) = verschwinden (**!** *sein*), = weg
  sein✘
  my bike's gone = mein Rad ist weg✘
- (*belong*) = gehören
  the chair goes in the corner = der Stuhl
  gehört in die Ecke
- (*function*) = laufen (**!** *sein*)
  (*of a watch, clock*) = gehen (**!** *sein*)
  to get something going = etwas in Gang
  bringen
- (*in polite inquiries*) = gehen (**!** *sein*)
  how's it going? = wie gehts?
- (*become*) = werden (**!** *sein*)
  to go red = rot werden
- (*expressing the future*)
  to be going to do something = etwas tun
  werden
  I am going to [leave London | learn to drive |
  phone you …] = ich werde [London
  verlassen | fahren lernen | dich anrufen …]
- (*make a sound or signal*) = losgehen
  (**!** *sein*)
- (*US: take away*) **to go** = zum Mitnehmen
  one pizza to go = eine Pizza zum
  Mitnehmen
2 *noun*
- (*turn*)
  whose go is it? = wer ist dran?✘
- (*try*) = (der) Versuch
  have another go! = versuch es nochmal!
  to have a go at doing something =
  versuchen, etwas zu tun
go ahead
  (*take place*) = stattfinden
go away
  = weggehen (**!** *sein*)
  (*on a journey*) = wegfahren (**!** *sein*)
go back
  = zurückgehen (**!** *sein*)
  go back to sleep = wieder einschlafen
  (**!** *sein*)
  (*drive back*) = zurückfahren (**!** *sein*)
go down
- (*drop*) = fallen (**!** *sein*)
  the prices have gone down = die Preise
  sind gefallen
- (*come down*) = hinuntergehen (**!** *sein*)
  (*drive down*) = hinunterfahren (**!** *sein*)
- (*sink*) = untergehen (**!** *sein*)
go in
  (*enter*) = hineingehen (**!** *sein*)
  (*drive in*) = hineinfahren (**!** *sein*)
go off
- (*British: lose interest in*) = nicht mehr
  mögen
- (*of a gun or alarm*) = losgehen (**!** *sein*)
- (*leave*) = weggehen (**!** *sein*)
  (*drive off*) = wegfahren (**!** *sein*)

- (*go bad*) = schlecht werden (**!** *sein*)
- (*switch off*) = ausgehen (**!** *sein*)

go on
- (*continue*) = weitermachen
  to go on [talking | working | reading ...] = weiter [reden | arbeiten | lesen ...]
- (*happen*) = los sein
  what's going on? = was ist los?
- (*switch on*) = angehen (**!** *sein*)

go out
- (*leave*) = hinausgehen (**!** *sein*)
- (*have an evening out*) = ausgehen (**!** *sein*)
  to go out for a meal = essen gehen (**!** *sein*)
- (*switch off, stop burning*) = ausgehen (**!** *sein*)

go over
(*check*) = überprüfen

go through
- (*search*) = durchsuchen
- (*suffer*) = durchmachen
- (*check*) = durchgehen (**!** *sein*)
- **to go through a lot of money** = viel Geld ausgeben

go up
- (*by stairs*) = hinaufgehen (**!** *sein*)
  (*by lift*) = hochfahren (**!** *sein*)
- (*increase*) = steigen (**!** *sein*)

go with
(*match*) = passen zu (+ *dative*)
the jacket doesn't go with the skirt = die Jacke passt nicht zu dem Rock

go without
= verzichten auf (+ *accusative*)

goal *noun*
- (*in football, hockey*) = (das) Tor
  to score a goal = ein Tor schießen
- (*aim*) = (das) Ziel

goalkeeper *noun*
= (der) Torwart

goat *noun*
= (die) Ziege

god *noun*
= (der) Gott

goddaughter *noun*
= (die) Patentochter

goddess *noun*
= (die) Göttin

godfather *noun*
= (der) Pate

godmother *noun*
= (die) Patin

godson *noun*
= (der) Patensohn

gold
1 *noun* = (das) Gold
2 *adjective* = golden

golf *noun*
= (das) Golf

good
1 *adjective*

- = gut
  a good book = ein gutes Buch
  to have a good time = sich amüsieren
  to be good at chemistry = gut in Chemie sein
  to be good at doing something = etwas gut können
  that tastes good = das schmeckt gut
  good morning/night = guten Morgen/gute Nacht
  good afternoon = guten Tag
- (*healthy*) = gesund
  [fruit | fresh air | exercise ...] **is good for you** = [Obst | frische Luft | Bewegung ...] ist gesund
- (*well-behaved*) = artig, = brav
- (*kind*) = nett
  it was very good of you = es war sehr nett von Ihnen

2 *noun*
- (*use*) = (der) Nutzen
  it's no good [crying | complaining | shouting ...] = es nützt nichts [zu weinen | sich zu beschweren | zu schreien ...]
- **for good** = für immer

goodbye *interjection*
= auf Wiedersehen
(*on the phone*) = auf Wiederhören

Good Friday *noun*
= (der) Karfreitag

goods *noun*
= Waren (*plural*)

goose *noun*
= (die) Gans

gooseberry *noun*
= (die) Stachelbeere

gorilla *noun*
= (der) Gorilla

gossip
1 *noun* = (der) Klatsch
2 *verb* = klatschen

got *verb*
▶get
- **to have got** = haben
  I've got a lot of work = ich habe viel Arbeit
- **to have got to** = müssen
  I have got to [go | work | get dressed ...] = ich muss [gehen | arbeiten | mich anziehen ...]

government *noun*
= (die) Regierung

graceful *adjective*
= graziös

grade *noun*
- (*quality*) = (die) Klasse
- (*mark*) = (die) Note
  to get good grades = gute Noten bekommen
- (*US: class*) = (die) Klasse

grade school *noun* (*US*)
= (die) Grundschule

G

gradually *adverb*
= allmählich

gram *noun*
= (das) Gramm ▶ **Measures p. 270**
100 grams of butter = hundert Gramm
Butter

grammar *noun*
= (die) Grammatik

grandchild *noun*
= (das) Enkelkind

granddaughter *noun*
= (die) Enkelin

grandfather *noun*
= (der) Großvater

grandmother *noun*
= (die) Großmutter

grandparents *noun*
= Großeltern (*plural*)

grandson *noun*
= (der) Enkel

grape *noun*
= (die) Traube

grapefruit *noun*
= (die) Grapefruit, = (die) Pampelmuse

grass *noun*
• = (das) Gras
• (*lawn*) = (der) Rasen
to cut the grass = den Rasen mähen

grasshopper *noun*
= (die) Heuschrecke

grateful *adjective*
= dankbar
to be grateful to someone = jemandem
dankbar sein
I'd be very grateful to you = ich wäre Ihnen
sehr dankbar

grave *noun* = (das) Grab

graveyard *noun*
= (der) Friedhof

gray (*US*) ▶ grey

grease *noun*
• (*for a machine*) = (das) Schmierfett
• (*animal fat*) = (das) Fett

greasy *adjective*
= fettig

great *adjective*
• (*of size, importance*) = groß
to have a great advantage = einen großen
Vorteil haben
to have a great deal of free time = viel
Freizeit haben
• (*when showing enthusiasm*) = großartig, =
prima✱

Great Britain *noun*
= (das) Großbritannien ▶ **Countries p. 208**

great-grandfather *noun*
= (der) Urgroßvater

great-grandmother *noun*
= (die) Urgroßmutter

Greece *noun*
= (das) Griechenland ▶ **Countries p. 208**

greedy *adjective*
= gierig

Greek
1 *noun*
• (*person*) = (der) Grieche/(die) Griechin
• (*language*) = (das) Griechisch
2 *adjective* = griechisch ▶ **Countries p. 208**

green *adjective*
= grün ▶ **Colours p. 204**

greenhouse *noun*
= (das) Gewächshaus

greenhouse effect *noun*
= (der) Treibhauseffekt

grey *adjective* (*British*)
= grau ▶ **Colours p. 204**
to go grey = grau werden (! *sein*)

greyhound *noun*
= (der) Windhund

grill
1 *noun* = (der) Grill
2 *verb* = grillen

grin *verb*
= grinsen
to grin at someone = jemanden angrinsen

groan *verb*
• (*in pain*) = stöhnen
• (*when annoyed*) = sich beklagen

grocer *noun*
= (der) Lebensmittelhändler ▶ **Professions**
p. 298

groceries *noun*
= Lebensmittel (*plural*)

ground *noun*
• (*soil, surface, terrain*) = (der) Boden
• (*special area*) = (das) Gelände
sports ground = (der) Sportplatz
• (*position in a contest, debate*) = (der) Boden
to gain ground = Boden gewinnen
• (*US: electricity*) = (die) Erde

ground floor *noun* (*British*)
= (das) Erdgeschoss

grounds *noun*
• (*part of property*) = Anlagen (*plural*)
• (*reason*) = (der) Grund
to have grounds for something = einen
Grund für etwas (*accusative*) haben
to have no grounds for complaint = keinen
Grund zur Klage haben
to have grounds for divorce = einen
Scheidungsgrund haben

✱ in informal situations

group *noun*
= (die) Gruppe

grow *verb*
• (*get bigger*) = wachsen (**!** *sein*)
   the population is still growing = die
   Bevölkerung wächst noch
   to grow a beard = sich (*dative*) einen Bart
   wachsen lassen
• (*cultivate*) = anbauen
   to grow vegetables = Gemüse anbauen
• (*become*) = werden (**!** *sein*)
   to grow old = alt werden
grow up
= erwachsen werden (**!** *sein*)
   he grew up in London = er ist in London
   aufgewachsen

grumble *verb*
= murren

grumpy *adjective*
= grantig

guarantee
1 *verb* = garantieren
   to guarantee a watch for a year = ein Jahr
   Garantie auf eine Uhr geben
2 *noun* = (die) Garantie

guard
1 *verb*
• (*watch over*) = bewachen
   the dog guards the house = der Hund
   bewacht das Haus
• (**protect**) = beschützen
2 *noun*
• (*in a prison*) = (der) Wärter/(die) Wärterin
• (*in a bank, building*) = (der) Wächter
• (*in the army*) = (die) Wache
   to be on guard = Wache stehen

guard dog *noun*
= (der) Wachhund

guess *verb*
• = raten
• (*guess correctly*) = erraten
   I guessed right = ich habe es richtig
   erraten
• (*suppose*) = glauben
   I guess so = ich glaube schon

guest *noun*
= (der) Gast

guesthouse *noun*
= (die) Pension

guide
1 *noun*
• (*person*) = (der) Führer/(die) Führerin
   (*for tourists*) = (der) Fremdenführer/
   (die) Fremdenführerin
• (*book*) = (der) Reiseführer
• (*indicator*) = (der) Anhaltspunkt
2 *verb* = führen

guidebook *noun*
= (der) Reiseführer

guide dog *noun*
= (der) Blindenhund

guidelines *noun*
= Richtlinien (*plural*)

guilt *noun*
= (die) Schuld

guilty *adjective*
• = schuldig
   to be guilty of murder = des Mordes
   schuldig sein
   to feel guilty about something = ein
   schlechtes Gewissen wegen etwas
   (*genitive*) haben
• (*prompted by guilt*) = schuldbewusst

guitar *noun*
= (die) Gitarre

gulf *noun*
= (der) Golf

gum *noun*
(*in the mouth*) = (das) Zahnfleisch

gun *noun*
• (*rifle*) = (das) Gewehr
• (*pistol*) = (die) Pistole

gutter *noun*
• (*beside a road*) = (der) Rinnstein
• (*on a roof*) = (die) Regenrinne

gym *noun*
• (*gymnasium*) = (die) Turnhalle
• (*school lesson*) = (das) Turnen

gymnasium *noun*
= (die) Turnhalle

gymnastics *noun*
= (die) Gymnastik, = (das) Turnen

gypsy *noun*
= (der) Zigeuner/(die) Zigeunerin

Hh

habit *noun*
= (die) Gewohnheit
   (*bad habit*) = (die) Angewohnheit
   to do something out of habit = etwas aus
   Gewohnheit tun
   to be in the habit of doing something = die
   Gewohnheit *or* die Angewohnheit haben,
   etwas zu tun
   to get out of the habit of [watching TV |
   cooking | reading ...] = sich (*dative*)
   abgewöhnen [fernzusehen | zu kochen | zu
   lesen ...]

H

hail
1 *noun* = (der) Hagel
2 *verb* = hageln

hair *noun*
(*collectively*) = Haare (*plural*)
(*a single hair*) = (das) Haar

> **!** *A person's* hair *is normally translated by the plural* Haare.

to wash one's hair = sich (*dative*) die Haare waschen

hairbrush *noun*
= (die) Haarbürste

haircut *noun*
= (der) Haarschnitt
to have a haircut = sich (*dative*) die Haare schneiden lassen

hairdresser *noun*
• (*stylist*) = (der) Friseur/(die) Friseuse
  ▶**Professions p. 298**
• (*salon*) = Friseursalon
  to go to the hairdresser's = zum Friseur gehen (**!** *sein*)

hair-dryer *noun*
= (der) Föhn

hairstyle *noun*
= (die) Frisur

half ▶**Numbers p. 282**
1 *noun*
• (*fraction*) = (die) Hälfte
  half the money = die Hälfte des Geldes
• (*period in a game*) = (die) Spielhälfte
2 *adjective* = halb
  half a litre of milk = ein halber Liter Milch
  two and a half cups = zweieinhalb Tassen
  (at) half price = zum halben Preis
3 *pronoun*
• (*when talking about quantities, numbers*)
  half of his pocket money = die Hälfte von seinem Taschengeld
  you don't listen half the time = du hörst die halbe Zeit nicht zu
• (*when talking about time, age*)
  one and a half hours = anderthalb Stunden
  she is five and a half = sie ist fünfeinhalb

> **!** *When telling the time,* half past *is translated by* halb, *but in German the half-hour is 'half way to' the next hour.*

half past three = halb vier
4 *adverb* = halb
half as much = halb so viel

hall *noun*
• (*in a house, flat*) = (der) Flur
• (*in an airport, hotel*) = (die) Halle
• (*for public events*) = (der) Saal

ham *noun*
= (der) Schinken

---

hamburger *noun*
• = (der) Hamburger
• (*US: ground beef*) = (das) Hackfleisch

hammer
1 *noun* = (der) Hammer
2 *verb* = hämmern

hamster *noun*
= (der) Hamster

hand
1 *noun*
• (*part of the body*) = (die) Hand
  to hold someone's hand = jemandem die Hand halten
• (*on a clock*) = (der) Zeiger
• (*other uses*)
  to give someone a hand = jemandem helfen
  on the one hand . . ., on the other hand . . .
  = einerseits . . ., andererseits . . .
  to get out of hand = außer Kontrolle geraten (**!** *sein*)
2 *verb* = reichen
  to hand someone a book = jemandem ein Buch reichen

hand in
to hand in homework = die Hausaufgaben abgeben
to hand in an application = einen Antrag einreichen

hand out
= austeilen

hand over
= übergeben

handbag *noun*
= (die) Handtasche

handbrake *noun*
= (die) Handbremse

handicapped *adjective*
= behindert

handkerchief *noun*
= (das) Taschentuch

handle
1 *noun*
• (*on a drawer, bag, cutlery*) = (der) Griff
• (*on a door*) = (die) Klinke
• (*of a cup*) = (der) Henkel
• (*of a broom, saucepan*) = (der) Stiel
2 *verb*
• (*deal with*) = fertig werden mit (+ *dative*)
  (**!** *sein*)
  to handle a situation = mit einer Situation fertig werden
• (*control*) = handhaben

handlebars *noun*
= (die) Lenkstange

hand luggage *noun*
= (das) Handgepäck

handsome *adjective*
= gut aussehend

handwriting noun
= (die) Handschrift

handy adjective
• (of an object) = praktisch
• (of a person) = geschickt
  to have something handy = etwas
  griffbereit haben
  to come in handy = nützlich sein

hang verb
• (attach to a hook, line) = aufhängen
  to hang a picture on the wall = ein Bild an
  der Wand aufhängen
• (be attached) = hängen
• (kill) = hängen

hang around
• (wait) = warten
  to keep someone hanging around =
  jemanden warten lassen
• (waste time) = rumhängen*

hang on
• (grasp) = sich festhalten
  to hang on to something = sich an etwas
  (dative) festhalten
• (wait) = warten

hang up
• (put the phone down) = auflegen
• (attach to a hook, line) = aufhängen

hang-gliding noun
= (das) Drachenfliegen

hangover noun
= (der) Kater*

happen verb
• (occur) = passieren (! sein), = geschehen
  (! sein)
  when did it happen? = wann ist es passiert?
  what's happening? = was ist los?
• (by chance)
  I happened to meet him = ich habe ihn
  zufällig getroffen
  as it happens = zufälligerweise

happy adjective
= glücklich
  to be happy with [the new job | her work | one's
  life ...] = mit [der neuen Stelle | ihrer Arbeit |
  seinem Leben ...] zufrieden sein
  to be happy to do something = gerne etwas
  tun

harbor (US), **harbour** (British) noun
= (der) Hafen

hard
1 adjective
• = hart
  to be hard on someone = hart zu
  jemandem sein
• (difficult) = schwer
2 adverb
  to listen hard = gut zuhören
  to pull hard = kräftig ziehen
  to try hard = sich sehr bemühen
  to rain hard = stark regnen
  it hit him hard = es hat ihn schwer getroffen
  to be hard up = knapp bei Kasse sein

hard-boiled egg noun
= (das) hart gekochte Ei

hard disk noun
= (die) Festplatte

hardly adverb
= kaum

hardware noun
• (for computers) = (die) Hardware
• (for use in the home, garden) =
  Haushaltsgeräte (plural)

hardware shop (British), **hardware
store** (US) noun
= (das) Haushaltswarengeschäft

hard-working adjective
= fleißig

hare noun
= (der) Hase

harm
1 verb
• (injure a person) = verletzen
  to harm someone = jemanden verletzen
• (hurt reputation, environment, health) =
  schaden (+ dative)
2 noun = (der) Schaden
  there's no harm in asking = es kann nichts
  schaden zu fragen
  no harm done = nichts ist passiert

harmful adjective
= schädlich

harmless adjective
= unschädlich

harp noun
= (die) Harfe

harvest
1 noun = (die) Ernte
2 verb = ernten

hat noun
= (der) Hut

hatch verb
• to hatch eggs = Eier ausbrüten
• when will the eggs hatch? = wann
  schlüpfen die Jungen aus?

hate
1 verb = hassen
  I hate having to get up early = ich hasse es,
  früh aufstehen zu müssen
  the two brothers hate each other = die
  beiden Brüder hassen sich
2 noun = (der) Hass

hatred noun
= (der) Hass

haunted adjective
  a haunted castle = ein Spukschloss
  this house is haunted = in diesem Haus
  spukt es

have
1 verb
• (possess) = haben
  have got = haben
  she has (got) a dog = sie hat einen Hund

H

- (*eat, do*)

> **!** *The general verb* **have** *is usually translated by a more specific German verb.*

to have a meal = etwas essen
to have a game of football = Fußball spielen
- (*get*) = bekommen, = kriegen✻
I had a letter from Bob yesterday = gestern bekam ich einen Brief von Bob
- (*experience, suffer*) = haben
to have flu = die Grippe haben
to have a good time = sich amüsieren
- (*get done*)
to have something done = etwas machen lassen
- to have to = müssen
2 *auxiliary verb*
= haben, (*with some verbs*) = sein

> **!** *The auxiliary verb is used to form the perfect tense. Most German verbs form the perfect with* **haben**. *Some take* **sein**, *and these are mainly verbs expressing motion and involving a change of place.*

I have lost my bag = ich habe meine Tasche verloren
they have arrived = sie sind angekommen
you've been there, haven't you? = du warst schon mal dort, nicht?

> **!** *Note that* **nicht** *is only used in this way in spoken German; it is short for* **nicht wahr.**

to have a [coat | sweater | skirt ...] on = einen [Mantel | Pullover | Rock ...] anhaben
he had nothing on = er hatte nichts an

hay *noun*
= (das) Heu

hazelnut *noun*
= (die) Haselnuss

he *pronoun*
= er

head
1 *noun*
- (*part of the body*) = (der) Kopf
from head to foot = von Kopf bis Fuß
to have a good head for figures = gut rechnen können
- (*person in charge*) = (der) Leiter/ (die) Leiterin
(*of a firm*) = (der) Chef/(die) Chefin
the head of state = das Staatsoberhaupt
the head of a family = das Familienoberhaupt
- (*British: principal*) = (der) Direktor/ (die) Direktorin
- (*top part of a table, bed*) = (das) Kopfende
- (*when counting*) (*person*) = (der) Kopf
£10 per head = zehn Pfund pro Kopf
(*animal*) = (das) Stück

2 *verb*
- (*be in charge of*) = leiten
- (*be bound*)
to head for = zusteuern auf (+ *accusative*) (**!** *sein*)
to head (off) home = nach Hause fahren (**!** *sein*)
- (*in football*) = köpfen

headache *noun*
= Kopfschmerzen (*plural*)
I've got a headache = ich habe Kopfschmerzen

headlamp, headlight *noun*
= (der) Scheinwerfer

headline *noun*
= (die) Schlagzeile

headphones *noun*
= (der) Kopfhörer

heal *verb*
= heilen

health *noun*
= (die) Gesundheit
to be in good health = guter Gesundheit sein
to be in poor health = kränklich sein

health club *noun*
= (das) Fitnesscenter

healthy *adjective*
= gesund

hear *verb*
= hören
I've heard a lot about it = ich habe viel davon gehört
to have heard of something = schon mal von etwas (*dative*) gehört haben

heart *noun*
- (*organ, or heart shape*) = (das) Herz
to learn something by heart = etwas auswendig lernen
she took his warning to heart = sie hat sich (*dative*) seine Warnung zu Herzen genommen
- (*courage*) = (der) Mut
to lose heart = den Mut verlieren
- (*playing cards*) hearts = (das) Herz

heart attack *noun*
= (der) Herzanfall

heat
1 *noun*
- (*temperature*) = (die) Hitze
I can't stand the heat = ich kann die Hitze nicht aushalten
to cook at a low heat = bei niedriger Temperatur kochen
- (*qualifying round*) = (der) Vorlauf
2 *verb*
to heat food = Essen heiß machen
to heat a room = einen Raum heizen

✻ in informal situations

heat up
= aufwärmen

heater noun
= (das) Heizgerät

heating noun
= (die) Heizung

heaven noun
= (der) Himmel

heavily adverb
to sleep heavily = tief schlafen
to rain heavily = stark regnen

heavy adjective
• = schwer
heavy losses have been reported =
schwere Verluste wurden gemeldet
a heavy coat = ein dicker Mantel
to wear heavy shoes = feste Schuhe tragen
• (in quantity, intensity) = stark
heavy traffic = starker Verkehr

hedge noun
= (die) Hecke

hedgehog noun
= (der) Igel

heel noun
• (part of the foot, sock) = (die) Ferse
• (part of a shoe) = (der) Absatz

height noun
• (of a person) = (die) Größe
what height are you? = wie groß bist du?
• (of a building, tree) = (die) Höhe
what height is it? = wie hoch ist es?

helicopter noun
= (der) Hubschrauber

hell noun
= (die) Hölle
to make someone's life hell = jemandem
das Leben zur Hölle machen

helmet noun
= (der) Helm

help
1 verb
• (be of assistance) = helfen (+ dative)
to help someone (to) do something =
jemandem helfen, etwas zu tun
to help someone [with the shopping | with their
homework ...] = jemandem [beim
Einkaufen | bei den Hausaufgaben ...] helfen
can I help you? = kann ich dir helfen?, (in a
shop) = kann ich Ihnen behilflich sein?
• (serve)
to help oneself = sich (dative) etwas
nehmen
I helped myself to more potatoes = ich
habe mir mehr Kartoffeln genommen
help yourself! = greif zu!

• (avoid)
I couldn't help [laughing | thinking about it |
crying ...] = ich musste einfach [lachen |
darüber nachdenken | weinen ...]
I can't help it = ich kann nichts dafür
it can't be helped = es lässt sich nicht
ändern
2 interjection = Hilfe!
3 noun
(assistance) = (die) Hilfe
to ask someone for help = jemanden um
Hilfe bitten

helpful adjective
• (willing to help) = hilfbereit
• (useful) = nützlich

helpless adjective
= hilflos

hem noun
= (der) Saum

hen noun
= (die) Henne

her
1 adjective = ihr

> ! Note that ihr changes its endings in the
> same way as ein.

I hate her dog = ich hasse ihren Hund
2 pronoun

> ! In German this pronoun changes
> according to its function in the sentence.
> As a direct object it is in the accusative,
> sie, and as an indirect object it is in the
> dative, ihr.

• (in the accusative) = sie
I know her = ich kenne sie
I've read a lot about her = ich habe viel
über sie gelesen
• (in the dative) = ihr
you must help her = du musst ihr helfen
he gave her the money = er hat ihr das
Geld gegeben
• (in the nominative, as a complement) = sie
it was her = sie war es
if I were her = wenn ich sie wäre

herb noun
= (das) Kraut

herd noun
= (die) Herde

here adverb
• = hier
is it far from here? = ist es weit von hier?
here's my telephone number = hier ist
meine Telefonnummer
in here = hier drinnen
• (to this place) = hierher
when she came here = als sie hierher kam
to bring something here = etwas hierher
bringen
come here! = komm her!

heritage tourism noun
= (die) Kulturturismus

H

hers *pronoun*
= ihrer/ihre/ihrs

> **!** *Note that the pronoun agrees in number and gender with the noun it stands for:* hers *(meaning the pencil)* is red = ihrer *(der Bleistift)* ist rot; hers *(meaning the shoes)* are new = ihre *(die Schuhe)* sind neu.

my shirt is white but hers is blue = mein Hemd ist weiß, aber ihrs ist blau
the gloves are hers = die Handschuhe gehören ihr
a friend of hers = ein Freund von ihr

herself *pronoun*
• *(when translated by a reflexive verb in German)* = sich
she wants to enjoy herself = sie möchte sich amüsieren
• *(used for emphasis)* = selbst
she said it herself = sie hat es selbst gesagt
• by herself = allein
she did it all by herself = sie hat es ganz allein gemacht

hesitate *verb*
= zögern

heterosexual *noun*
= (der/die) Heterosexuelle

hi *interjection*
= hallo!

hiccup *noun*
= (der) Schluckauf
to have hiccups = einen Schluckauf haben

hide *verb*
• = verstecken
to hide (oneself) = sich verstecken
• *(keep secret)* = verheimlichen
to hide the facts = die Tatsachen verheimlichen

hi-fi *noun*
= (die) Hi-Fi-Anlage

high
1 *adjective* = hoch
the wall is high = die Mauer ist hoch

> **!** *The adjective* hoch *loses its c when it has an ending, becoming* hoher/hohe/hohes.

a high wall = eine hohe Mauer
a tower 200 metres high = ein zweihundert Meter hoher Turm
high tide = (die) Flut
to get high marks = sehr gute Noten bekommen
he was high *(on drugs)* = er war high
2 *adverb* = hoch

high heels *noun*
= hochhackige Schuhe (*plural*)

highlights *noun*
• *(on TV, radio)* = Highlights (*plural*)
• *(in hair)* = Strähnchen (*plural*)

high school *noun*
≈ (die) Oberschule

highway *noun*
• *(British: public road)* = (die) öffentliche Straße
• *(US: main road)* = (der) Highway

hijack *verb*
= entführen

hike
1 *noun* = (die) Wanderung
2 *verb* = wandern (**!** *sein*)

hill *noun*
= (der) Hügel
(higher) = (der) Berg

him *pronoun*

> **!** *In German this pronoun changes according to its function in the sentence. As a direct object it is in the accusative,* ihn, *and as an indirect object it is in the dative,* ihm.

• *(in the accusative)* = ihn
she loves him = sie liebt ihn
I've got nothing against him = ich habe nichts gegen ihn
• *(in the dative)* = ihm
you must help him = du musst ihm helfen
give him the money = gib ihm das Geld
• *(in the nominative, as a complement)* = er
it was him = er war es
if I were him = wenn ich er wäre

himself *pronoun*
• *(when translated by a reflexive verb in German)* = sich
he enjoyed himself = er hat sich amüsiert
• *(used for emphasis)* = selbst
he said it himself = er hat es selbst gesagt
• by himself = allein
he was all by himself = er war ganz allein

hip *noun*
= (die) Hüfte

hire
1 *verb*
• *(rent)* = mieten
to hire a car = ein Auto mieten
• *(hire out)* = vermieten
they hire boats (out) here = Boote werden hier vermietet
• *(employ)* = einstellen
to hire staff = Personal einstellen
2 *noun*
car hire = (die) Autovermietung
for hire = zu vermieten

hire car *noun*
= (der) Mietwagen, = (der) Leihwagen

his
1 *adjective* = sein

> **!** *Note that* sein *changes its endings in the same way as* ein.

I hate his dog = ich hasse seinen Hund

2 *pronoun* = seiner/seine/seins

> ! Note that the pronoun agrees in number and gender with the noun it stands for: his (*meaning the pencil*) is red = seiner (*der Bleistift*) ist rot; his (*meaning the shoes*) are new = seine (*die Schuhe*) sind neu.

my shirt is white but his is blue = mein Hemd ist weiß, aber seins ist blau
these books are his = diese Bücher gehören ihm
a friend of his = ein Freund von ihm

history *noun*
= (die) Geschichte

hit
1 *verb*
* (*strike*) = schlagen
  to hit someone = jemanden schlagen
* (*come into contact with*) = anstoßen
  to hit one's head on the door = sich (*dative*) den Kopf an der Tür stoßen
* (*collide with*) = prallen gegen (+ *accusative*) (! *sein*)
  to hit a wall = gegen eine Wand prallen
* (*strike with a missile, affect*) = treffen
  to hit the target = das Ziel treffen
  it hit him hard = es hat ihn schwer getroffen
2 *noun*
  (*song*) = (der) Hit
  (*film, book*) = (der) Erfolg

hitchhike *verb*
= per Anhalter fahren (! *sein*)

hitchhiker *noun*
= (der) Anhalter/(die) Anhalterin

hoarse *adjective*
= heiser

hobby *noun*
= (das) Hobby

hockey *noun*
= (das) Hockey

hold
1 *verb*
* = halten
  to hold hands = sich an der Hand halten
* (*arrange*) = abhalten
  to hold a meeting = eine Versammlung abhalten
* (*keep*) = festhalten
  to hold someone for several days = jemanden mehrere Tage lang festhalten
  to hold someone prisoner = jemanden gefangen halten
* (*have*) = haben
  to hold a German passport = einen deutschen Pass haben
* (*contain*) = enthalten
* (*other uses*)
  to hold someone responsible for something = jemanden für etwas (*accusative*) verantwortlich machen

(*on the phone*) to hold (the line) = warten
hold the line please = warten Sie bitte
2 *noun*
* (*grip*) = (der) Griff
  to keep hold of something = etwas festhalten
* (*contact*)
  to get hold of someone = jemanden erreichen
  to get hold of something = etwas bekommen
hold back
= zurückhalten
hold on
* (*wait*) = warten
* (*so as not to fall*) = festhalten
  to hold on to something = sich an etwas (*dative*) festhalten
hold up
* (*raise*) = hochhalten
* (*delay*) = aufhalten
  to hold up the traffic = den Verkehr aufhalten
* (*rob*) = überfallen

hole *noun*
= (das) Loch
  to be full of holes = voller Löcher sein

holiday *noun*
* (*British: vacation*) = (der) Urlaub, = Ferien (*plural*)

> ! People with paid jobs usually have Urlaub, schoolchildren and students have Ferien.

  to go on holiday = in Urlaub *or* in die Ferien fahren
  the school holidays = die Schulferien
* (*national festival*) = (der) Feiertag
* (*British: day off*) = (der) freie Tag

Holland *noun*
= (das) Holland ▶Countries p. 208

home
1 *noun*
* = (das) Zuhause
  he has no home = er hat kein Zuhause
  to go home = nach Hause gehen (! *sein*)
  to live at home = im Elternhaus wohnen
* (*flat*) = (die) Wohnung, (*house*) = (das) Haus
* (*own country*) = (die) Heimat
  to be far from home = fern der Heimat sein
* (*for elderly or ill people*) = (das) Heim
  a retirement home = ein Altersheim
* (*in sports*)
  a home win = ein Heimsieg
2 *adverb*
* (*to home*) = nach Hause
  to go home = nach Hause gehen (! *sein*)
  I met her on my way home = ich habe sie auf dem Weg nach Hause getroffen
* (*at home*) = zu Hause
  I've got to stay (at) home = ich muss zu Hause bleiben

H

• **to feel at home** (*comfortable*) = sich wohl
  fühlen
  to make oneself at home = es sich (*dative*)
  bequem machen

homeless *noun*
  the homeless = die Obdachlosen (*plural*)

homesick *adjective*
  to be homesick = Heimweh haben

homework *noun*
  = Hausaufgaben (*plural*)

homosexual *noun*
  = (der/die) Homosexuelle

honest *adjective*
  = ehrlich
  to be honest with someone = ehrlich zu
  jemandem sein

honestly *adverb*
  = ehrlich

honey *noun*
  = (der) Honig

honeymoon *noun*
  = Flitterwochen (*plural*)

honor (*US*), **honour** (*British*)
  1 *noun* = (die) Ehre
  2 *verb*
  • (*show respect for*) = ehren
  • (*fulfil*) = sich halten an (+ *accusative*)
  to honour a cheque = einen Scheck
  honorieren

hood *noun*
  • (*headwear*) = (die) Kapuze
  • (*on a convertible car*) = (das) Verdeck
  • (*US: car bonnet*) = (die) Motorhaube

hoof *noun*
  = (der) Huf

hook *noun*
  = (der) Haken
  the phone was off the hook = das Telefon
  war ausgehängt

hooligan *noun*
  = (der) Hooligan

hoover *verb* (*British*)
  = saugen

hop *verb*
  = hüpfen (**!** *sein*)

hope
  1 *verb* = hoffen
  to hope for something = auf etwas
  (*accusative*) hoffen
  I hope to [meet her | speak fluent German | get
  the job …] = ich hoffe, [sie zu treffen |
  fließend Deutsch zu sprechen | die Stelle zu
  bekommen …]
  I hope so = hoffentlich

2 *noun*
  = (die) Hoffnung
  to give up hope = die Hoffnung aufgeben
  in the hope of something = in der
  Hoffnung auf etwas (*accusative*)

horizon *noun*
  = (der) Horizont

horn *noun*
  • (*on a car*) = (die) Hupe
  • (*of an animal, instrument*) = (das) Horn

horoscope *noun*
  = (das) Horoskop

horrible *adjective*
  = furchtbar

horror *noun*
  = (das) Entsetzen
  to have a horror of doing something =
  einen Horror davor haben, etwas zu tun

horse *noun*
  = (das) Pferd

horseriding *noun*
  = (das) Reiten

horseshoe *noun*
  = (das) Hufeisen

hose *noun*
  = (der) Schlauch

hospital *noun*
  = (das) Krankenhaus

hospitality *noun*
  = (die) Gastfreundschaft

host *noun*
  • (*to guests*) = (der) Gastgeber
  • (*on a TV programme*) = (der) Moderator

hostage *noun*
  = (die) Geisel
  to take someone hostage = jemanden als
  Geisel nehmen

hostel *noun*
  (*for refugees, workers*) = (das) Wohnheim

hostess *noun*
  • (*to guests*) = (die) Gastgeberin
  • (*on a TV programme*) = (die) Moderatorin
  • (*air hostess*) = (die) Stewardess

hostile *adjective*
  • (*opposing*) = feindlich
  • (*unfriendly*) = feindselig
  to give someone a hostile look =
  jemanden feindselig ansehen

hot *adjective*
  • (*very warm*) = heiß
  I'm very hot = mir ist sehr heiß
  a hot meal = ein warmes Essen
  • (*spicy*) = scharf

hot dog *noun*
  = (der) *or* (das) Hotdog

hotel *noun*
= (das) Hotel

hour *noun*
= (die) Stunde ▶**Time p. 331**
I earn £5 an hour = ich verdiene fünf Pfund
    pro Stunde

house
1 *noun* = (das) Haus
    I went to my friend's house = ich bin zu
        meinem Freund nach Hause gegangen
    at my house = bei mir (zu Hause)
2 *verb* = unterbringen

housework *noun*
= (die) Hausarbeit

housing estate *noun*
= (die) Wohnsiedlung

hovercraft *noun*
= (das) Luftkissenboot

how *adverb*
• = wie
    how do you spell his name? = wie wird
        sein Name geschrieben?
    how are you? = wie gehts dir?, (*formal*) wie
        geht es Ihnen?

    ! Note that gehts, written as one word, is
    short for geht es.

    how do you do? = guten Tag
    how about something to eat? = wie wäre es
        mit etwas zu essen?
• (*asking about amount*) = wie
    how far? = wie weit?
    how many? = wie viele?
    how much? = wie viel?
    how much is it? = wie viel kostet es?

however *adverb*
• = jedoch, = aber
• however rich he is = wie reich er auch sein
        mag
    however long it takes = egal, wie lange es
        dauert

huge *adjective*
= riesig

humid *adjective*
= feucht

humor (*US*) ▶humour

humorous *adjective*
= lustig

humour *noun* (*British*)
= (der) Humor
to have a sense of humour = Humor haben

hundred *adjective*
= hundert ▶**Numbers p. 282**

Hungary *noun*
= (das) Ungarn ▶**Countries p. 208**

hunger *noun*
= (der) Hunger

hungry *adjective*
= hungrig
I am hungry = ich habe Hunger

hunting *noun*
= (die) Jagd

hurdles *noun*
(*race*) = (der) Hürdenlauf

hurrah, hurray *interjection*
= hurra!

hurry
1 *verb*
• (*hurry up*) = sich beeilen
    you'll have to hurry to catch the train = du
        musst dich beeilen, um den Zug zu
        erwischen
    you must hurry home = du musst schnell
        nach Hause
• (*hurry along*)
    to hurry someone = jemanden zur Eile
        antreiben
2 *noun* = (die) Eile
    to be in a hurry = es eilig haben
    there's no hurry = es eilt nicht

hurt *verb*
• (*injure*) = verletzen
    to hurt oneself = sich verletzen
    I hurt my arm playing tennis = ich habe mir
        den Arm beim Tennisspielen verletzt
• (*be painful*) = wehtun (+ *dative*)
    my arm is hurting = der Arm tut mir weh
• (*cause emotional pain*) = kränken
    to feel hurt = sich gekränkt fühlen

husband *noun*
= (der) Ehemann

hut *noun*
= (die) Hütte

hygienic *adjective*
= hygienisch

hypnotize *verb*
= hypnotisieren

hysterical *adjective*
= hysterisch

I **i**

I *pronoun*
= ich
I've got to go now = ich muss jetzt gehen

ice *noun*
= (das) Eis

ice cream *noun*
= (das) Eis
two ice creams, please = zwei Eis bitte

ice hockey *noun*
= (das) Eishockey

ice-skating *noun*
= (das) Schlittschuhlaufen

icing *noun*
= (der) Zuckerguss

idea *noun*
= (die) Idee
what a good idea = was für eine gute Idee
I haven't the slightest idea = ich habe
  keine Ahnung

identity card *noun*
= (der) Personalausweis

idiot *noun*
= (der) Idiot

if *conjunction*
* = wenn
if you meet him, don't tell him = wenn du
  ihn triffst, sage nichts
if you like = wenn du willst

> **!** *The subjunctive is often used in clauses
> following* if. *For information on the
> subjunctive,* ▶ **p. 349**

if I were you = wenn ich du wäre
* (*whether, usually following to know or to
  wonder*) = ob
I don't know if he is coming = ich weiß
  nicht, ob er kommt
as if = als ob

ignore *verb*
= ignorieren

ill *adjective*
= krank
to be ill with flu = die Grippe haben

illegal *adjective*
= illegal

illness *noun*
= (die) Krankheit

illustration *noun*
= (die) Illustration

imagination *noun*
* (*ability to imagine*) = (die) Phantasie
* (*fancy*) = (die) Einbildung
it's all in your imagination = das bildest du
  dir nur ein

imagine *verb*
= sich (*dative*) vorstellen
I imagine it's easy = ich stelle mir das
  leicht vor
can you imagine? = stell dir vor!

imitate *verb*
= nachahmen

immediately *adverb*
= sofort

✗ in informal situations

immigrant
1 *noun* = (der) Einwanderer/(die) Einwanderin
2 *adjective* = Einwanderer-

> **!** *Note that* Einwanderer- *forms the first
> part of a compound noun.*

an immigrant child = ein Einwandererkind

impatient *adjective*
= ungeduldig

important *adjective*
= wichtig

impossible *adjective*
= unmöglich

impress *verb*
= beeindrucken
to be impressed by something = von etwas
  (*dative*) beeindruckt sein

impression *noun*
= (der) Eindruck

improve *verb*
* (*make better*) = verbessern
to improve one's financial situation = seine
  finanzielle Lage verbessern
* (*get better*) = besser werden (**!** *sein*)
your German is improving = dein Deutsch
  wird besser
* (*of an ill or injured person*)
he has greatly improved = es geht ihm viel
  besser

improvement *noun*
= (die) Verbesserung

in
1 *preposition*
* (*in a place or position*) = in (+ *dative or
  accusative*)

> **!** *Note that* in *is followed by a noun in the
> dative when position is described. The
> accusative follows when there is
> movement towards something.*

to sit in the garden = im Garten sitzen

> **!** *Note that* im *is the shortened form of* in
> dem; *in* das *can also be shortened, to* ins.

to go in the garden = in den Garten gehen
  (**!** *sein*)
in the street = auf der Straße
in the world = auf der Welt
in Japan = in Japan
* (*among*) = bei (+ *dative*)
it's normal in children of that age = das ist
  normal bei Kindern in dem Alter
* (*wearing, with colours*) = in (+ *dative*)
she was dressed in black = sie war in
  Schwarz
* (*the way something is done*)
they were sitting in a circle = sie saßen im
  Kreis
in German = auf Deutsch
he spoke in a soft voice = er sprach mit
  leiser Stimme
we'll pay in cash = wir zahlen bar

- (*during*) = in (+ *dative*)
  in 1995 = (im Jahre) 1995
  in October = im Oktober
  at 2 o'clock in the morning = um zwei Uhr
    morgens
- (*with an occupation*)
  he is in banking = er ist im Bankwesen
  he is in the army = er ist beim Militär
- (*other uses*)
  one in ten (**people**) = jeder Zehnte
  a rise in prices = ein Preisanstieg
2 *adverb*
- (*indoors*) = herein-/hinein-, = rein-✶

! Note that herein-, hinein- and rein- *form
the prefixes to separable verbs; herein-
has the sense of* towards *the speaker,
and* hinein- *has the sense of* away from.
So herein- *often goes with verbs like*
kommen (*to come in* = hereinkommen),
and hinein- *goes with verbs like* gehen (*to
go in* = hineingehen). *The less formal* rein-
*can be used for both movements, towards
and away.*

you can come in = du kannst
  hereinkommen
can I go in? = kann ich reingehen?✶

- (*at home*) = zu Hause
  she's not in = sie ist nicht zu Hause
- (*indoors*) = drinnen
  in here = hier drinnen
  in there = da drinnen
- (*arrived*) = da
  he's not in yet = er ist noch nicht da
- (*other uses*)
  to keep in with someone = sich mit
    jemandem gut stellen
  to let oneself in for something = sich auf
    etwas (*accusative*) einlassen
3 *adjective*
  (*in fashion*) = in Mode, = in✶

inch *noun*
= (der) Inch ▶**Measures p. 270**

incident *noun*
= (der) Vorfall

include *verb*
= einschließen
service is included in the price = die
  Bedienung ist im Preis eingeschlossen

including *preposition*
= einschließlich (+ *genitive*)
they were all invited, including the
children = sie waren alle eingeladen,
  einschließlich der Kinder

income *noun*
= (das) Einkommen

income tax *noun*
= (die) Einkommenssteuer

incompetent *adjective*
= unfähig

inconsiderate *adjective*
= rücksichtslos

inconvenient *adjective*
= ungünstig
at an inconvenient time = zu einem
  ungünstigen Zeitpunkt

incorrect *adjective*
= unrichtig
that is incorrect = das stimmt nicht

increase
1 *verb*
- (*raise*) = erhöhen
  they increased his salary = sie erhöhten
    sein Gehalt
- (*rise*) = steigen (**!** *sein*)
  to increase in value = im Wert steigen
- (*get bigger*) = größer werden (**!** *sein*)
2 *noun*
- (*becoming greater*) = (die) Zunahme
- (*amount*) = (die) Erhöhung
  a price increase = eine Preiserhöhung

incredible *adjective*
= unglaublich

India *noun*
= (das) Indien ▶**Countries p. 208**

Indian
1 *noun*
- (*a person from India*) = (der) Inder/
  (die) Inderin
- (*a Native American*) = (der) Indianer/
  (die) Indianerin
2 *adjective*
- (*of India*) = indisch
  (*Native American*) = indianisch ▶**Countries
p. 208**

indicate *verb*
- (*point to*) = zeigen auf (+ *accusative*)
- (*of a car, driver*) = blinken

indigestion *noun*
= (die) Magenverstimmung
to have indigestion = eine
  Magenverstimmung haben

individual
1 *noun* = (der/die) Einzelne
2 *adjective*
- (*single*) = einzeln
- (*distinctive*) = individuell

indoor *adjective*
- (*of a pool, court*) = Hallen-
  an indoor swimming pool = ein Hallenbad
- (*taking place inside*) = im Haus

indoors *adverb*
= drinnen, = im Haus
to stay indoors = drinnen bleiben (**!** *sein*)
to go indoors = ins Haus gehen (**!** *sein*)

industry *noun*
= (die) Industrie

inevitable *adjective*
= unvermeidlich

infant *noun*
- (*baby*) = (der) Säugling
- (*small child*) = (das) kleine Kind

infant school *noun*
= (die) Vorschule

infection *noun*
= (die) Infektion

influence
1 *noun* = (der) Einfluss
2 *verb* = beeinflussen

inform *verb*
- (*tell*) = informieren
  to inform someone of something =
    jemanden über etwas (*accusative*)
    informieren
  we are pleased to inform you that ... = wir
    freuen uns, Ihnen mitteilen zu können,
    dass ...
  to keep someone informed = jemanden
    auf dem Laufenden halten
- (*denounce*)
  to inform on someone = jemanden
    anzeigen

informal *adjective*
- (*of manner, discussion*) = zwanglos
- (*of language, tone*) = ungezwungen

information *noun*
= (die) Auskunft
  a piece of information = eine Auskunft
  to give someone information about
    something = jemandem Auskunft über
    etwas (*accusative*) geben

information desk *noun*
= (das) Auskunftsbüro, = (die) Information

information technology *noun*
= (die) Informatik

ingredient *noun*
= (die) Zutat

inhabitant *noun*
= (der) Einwohner/(die) Einwohnerin

inheritance tax *noun*
= (die) Erbschaftssteuer

injection *noun*
= (die) Spritze

injured *adjective*
= verletzt

injury *noun*
= (die) Verletzung

injury time *noun*
= (die) Nachspielzeit

ink *noun*
= (die) Tinte

inn *noun*
= (das) Gasthaus

✻ in informal situations

innocent *adjective*
= unschuldig

inquire *verb*
  to inquire about something = sich nach
    etwas (*dative*) erkundigen

inquiry *noun*
- (*question*) = (die) Erkundigung
  to make inquiries about something = sich
    nach etwas (*dative*) erkundigen
- (*asking*) = (die) Anfrage
- (*investigation*) = (die) Untersuchung

insect *noun*
= (das) Insekt

inside
1 *preposition*
= in (+ *dative or accusative*)

> **!** *Note that* in *is followed by a noun in the
> dative when position is described. The
> accusative follows when there is
> movement towards something.*

  to be inside the house = im Haus sein

> **!** *Note that* im *is the shortened form of* in
> dem; in das *can also be shortened, to* ins.

  to go inside the house = ins Haus gehen
    (**!** *sein*)
2 *adjective* = Innen-

> **!** *Note that* Innen- *forms the first part of a
> compound noun.*

  inside pocket = (die) Innentasche
3 *adverb*
- (*on or in the inside*) = innen
  inside out = links (herum)
- (*indoors*) = drinnen
  he's inside = er ist drinnen
- (*to the inside*) = nach innen hinein/herein,
  = nach innen rein✻

> **!** *Note that* herein *has the sense of
> towards the speaker, and* hinein *has the
> sense of away from. The less formal* rein
> *can be used for both movements,
> towards and away.*

  we brought the chairs inside = wir haben
    die Stühle reingebracht✻

inspect *verb*
- (*look at closely*) = inspizieren
- (*test*) = prüfen
- (*check tickets, passport*) = kontrollieren

inspector *noun*
- (*of passengers' tickets*) =
    (der) Kontrolleur/(die) Kontrolleurin
- (*in the police*) = (der) Kommissar/
    (die) Kommissarin

instead *adverb*
- = stattdessen
  I don't feel like going to the cinema, we
    could play tennis instead = ich habe
    keine Lust, ins Kino zu gehen, stattdessen
    könnten wir Tennis spielen

- **instead of** = (an)statt (+ *genitive*)
  he hired a bicycle instead of a car = er hat
  ein Fahrrad statt eines Autos gemietet
  instead of working he watched television =
  anstatt zu arbeiten, hat er ferngesehen
  his wife came instead of him = seine Frau
  kam an seiner Stelle

instruction *noun*
= (die) Anweisung
instructions for use =
(die) Gebrauchsanweisung

instrument *noun*
= (das) Instrument

insult
1 *noun* = (die) Beleidigung
2 *verb* = beleidigen

insurance *noun*
= (die) Versicherung
travel insurance = (die) Reiseversicherung

insure *verb*
= versichern
to insure against theft = sich gegen
Diebstahl versichern

intelligent *adjective*
= intelligent

intend *verb*
- = beabsichtigen
  to intend to do something = beabsichtigen,
  etwas zu tun
- **to be intended for something** = für etwas
  (*accusative*) gedacht sein
  this course is intended for adults = dieser
  Kurs ist für Erwachsene

intensive care *noun*
= (die) Intensivpflege
to be in intensive care = auf der
Intensivstation sein

interest
1 *noun*
- = (das) Interesse
  to show interest in something = Interesse
  an etwas (*dative*) zeigen
  he has lost interest in politics = er hat das
  Interesse an Politik verloren
- (*financial*) = Zinsen (*plural*)
  the rate of interest = der Zinssatz
  2 *verb* = interessieren

interested *adjective*
= interessiert
to be interested in politics = sich für Politik
interessieren

interesting *adjective*
= interessant

interfere *verb*
- (*meddle*) = sich einmischen
- (*damage*)
  to interfere with something = etwas
  beeinträchtigen

interior decoration *noun*
= (die) Innenausstattung

international *adjective*
= international

Internet *noun*
= (das) Internet
on the Internet = im Internet

interpreter *noun*
= (der) Dolmetscher/(die) Dolmetscherin

interrupt *verb*
= unterbrechen
he interrupted me = er hat mich
unterbrochen

interval *noun*
- (*in time or space*) = (der) Abstand
  at regular intervals = in regelmäßigen
  Abständen
  at 30-minute intervals = in Abständen von
  dreißig Minuten
  at two-hourly intervals = alle zwei Stunden
- (*break during a performance*) = (die) Pause

interview
1 *noun*
- (*for a job*) = (das) Vorstellungsgespräch
  to go for an interview = sich vorstellen
- (*with a journalist*) = (das) Interview
  2 *verb*
- (*for a job*)
  to interview someone = ein
  Vorstellungsgespräch mit jemandem
  führen
- (*of a journalist*) = interviewen
- (*of the police*) = vernehmen

into *preposition*
- (*when referring to a place or location*) = in
  (+ *accusative*)

  > **!** Note that in the meaning of *into*, *in* is
  > always followed by a noun in the
  > accusative, because there is movement
  > towards something.

  to go into the garden = in den Garten
  gehen (**!** *sein*)
  to get into the car = ins Auto steigen
  (**!** *sein*)

  > **!** Note that *ins* is a shortened form of *in
  > das*.

- (*against*) = gegen (+ *accusative*)
  he drove into the tree = er ist gegen den
  Baum gefahren
- (*indicating change*) = in (+ *accusative*)
  to translate a letter into German = einen
  Brief ins Deutsche übersetzen
- (*in division*) = durch (+ *accusative*)
  five into twenty goes four = zwanzig durch
  fünf ist vier

introduce *verb*
- (*when people meet*) = vorstellen
  he introduced me to Peter = er hat mich
  Peter vorgestellt
  to introduce oneself = sich vorstellen

- (*on radio or TV*)
  to introduce a programme = ein Programm
  ankündigen
- (*bring into operation*)
  to introduce a [law | reform | change …] = [ein
  Gesetz | eine Reform | eine Änderung …]
  einführen

introduction *noun*
- (*of one person to another*) =
  (die) Vorstellung
- (*in a book, speech*) = (die) Einleitung
- (*of a law, reform*) = (die) Einführung

invent *verb*
= erfinden

invention *noun*
= (die) Erfindung

investigate *verb*
= untersuchen

investigation *noun*
= (die) Untersuchung

investment *noun*
= (die) Investion, (die) Anlage

invisible *adjective*
= unsichtbar

invitation *noun*
= (die) Einladung

invite *verb*
= einladen
  to invite someone round = jemanden zu
  sich (*dative*) einladen

involved *adjective*
= verwickelt
  he was involved in an accident = er war in
  einen Unfall verwickelt

Ireland *noun*
= (das) Irland ▶Countries p. 208

Irish
1 *noun*
- (*people*) **the Irish** = die Iren
- (*language*) = (das) Irisch
2 *adjective* = irisch ▶Countries p. 208

iron *noun*
- (*metal*) = (das) Eisen
- (*for clothes*) = (das) Bügeleisen

island *noun*
= (die) Insel

it *pronoun*

! Note that the German translation for it
can be masculine, feminine or neuter,
depending on the gender of the noun it
represents.

- (*as the subject of a sentence, in the
  nominative*) = er/sie/es
  it's gone = er/sie/es ist weg
  where is the newspaper?—it's on the table
  = wo ist die Zeitung?—sie ist auf dem
  Tisch
- (*as the object of a sentence, in the
  accusative*) = ihn/sie/es
  have you found it? = hast du ihn/sie/es
  gefunden?
  that's my newspaper, give it to me = das ist
  meine Zeitung, gib sie mir
- (*used to represent something general*)
  it's [difficult | easy | awful …] = es ist [schwierig |
  einfach | furchtbar …]
  it's a nice house = das ist ein hübsches
  Haus
  it's me = ich bins
  we talked about it = wir haben darüber
  gesprochen
  of it/from it/about it = davon
  out of it = daraus
  who is it? = wer ist da?
  what is it? = was ist los?

IT *noun*
= (die) Informatik

Italian
1 *noun*
- (*person*) = (der) Italiener/(die) Italienerin
- (*language*) = (das) Italienisch
2 *adjective* = italienisch ▶Countries p. 208

Italy *noun*
= (das) Italien ▶Countries p. 208

itchy *adjective*
  my back is itchy = mein Rücken juckt

its *adjective*
  (*masculine*) = sein
  (*feminine*) = ihr
  (*neuter*) = sein

! Note that sein and ihr change their
endings in the same way as ein. Gender
depends on the noun to which the
adjective refers.

  the dog was black and its tail was white =
  der Hund war schwarz und sein Schwanz
  war weiß
  the cat is black and its eyes are green =
  die Katze ist schwarz und ihre Augen
  sind grün

itself *pronoun*
- (*when translated by a reflexive verb in
  German*) = sich
  the cat hurt itself = die Katze hat sich
  wehgetan
- (*used for emphasis*) = selbst
  the garden itself is quite large = der Garten
  selbst ist ziemlich groß
- **by itself** (*automatically*) = von selbst,
  (*alone*) = allein
  the heating comes on by itself = die
  Heizung geht von selbst an

Jj

jacket *noun*
* (*clothing*) = (die) Jacke
* (*on a book*) = (der) Umschlag

jail *noun*
= (das) Gefängnis
to be sent to jail = ins Gefängnis kommen
(**!** *sein*)

jam *noun*
* (*food*) = (die) Marmelade
* (*traffic*) = (der) Stau

January *noun*
= (der) Januar ▶ **Dates p. 213**

Japan *noun*
= (das) Japan ▶ **Countries p. 208**

Japanese
1 *noun*
* (*person*) = (der) Japaner/(die) Japanerin
* (*language*) = (das) Japanisch
2 *adjective* = japanisch ▶ **Countries p. 208**

jar *noun*
* (*for jam, sweets*) = (das) Glas
* (*larger, earthenware*) = (der) Topf

jaw *noun*
= (der) Kiefer

jazz *noun*
= (der) Jazz

jealous *adjective*
= eifersüchtig
he is jealous of her = er ist eifersüchtig auf
sie

jeans *noun*
= Jeans (*plural*)

jet *noun*
(*plane*) = (das) Düsenflugzeug, = (der) Jet**✗**

Jew *noun*
= (der) Jude/(die) Jüdin

jewel *noun*
= (der) Edelstein

jewellery (*British*), **jewelry** (*US*) *noun*
= (der) Schmuck
a piece of jewellery = ein Schmuckstück

Jewish *adjective*
= jüdisch

jigsaw *noun*
= (das) Puzzle

job *noun*
* (*post*) = (die) Stelle, = (der) Job**✗**
to look for a job = einen Job suchen**✗**

* (*task*) = (die) Arbeit
he made a good job of it = er hat es gut
gemacht
* (*duty*) = (die) Aufgabe

jogging *noun*
= (das) Jogging
to go jogging = joggen gehen (**!** *sein*)

join *verb*
* (*meet*) = treffen
I'll join you in half an hour = ich treffe dich
in einer halben Stunde
* (*accompany*) = mitkommen mit (+ *dative*)
(**!** *sein*)
* (*take part*) = sich anschließen (+ *dative*)
to join a demonstration = sich einer
Demonstration anschließen
* (*become a member of a club, party*) =
beitreten (+ *dative*) (**!** *sein*)
* (*become a member of a firm, the army*) =
eintreten in (+ *accusative*) (**!** *sein*)
* (*fasten together*) = verbinden
join in
= mitmachen
to join in a game = bei einem Spiel
mitmachen

joke
1 *noun* = (der) Witz
to play a joke on someone = jemandem
einen Streich spielen
2 *verb* = Witze machen

journalist *noun*
= (der) Journalist/(die) Journalistin

journey *noun*
= (die) Reise
to go on a journey = verreisen (**!** *sein*)

joy *noun*
= (die) Freude

judge
1 *noun*
* (*in court*) = (der) Richter
* (*at a sporting event*) = (der) Schiedsrichter
* (*in a competition*) = (der) Preisrichter
2 *verb*
* (*form an opinion about*) = beurteilen
* (*make a judgement*) = urteilen
to judge by = urteilen nach (+ *dative*)

jug *noun*
= (der) Krug

juice *noun*
= (der) Saft

July *noun*
= (der) Juli ▶ **Dates p. 213**

jump
1 *verb* = springen (**!** *sein*)
he jumped across the stream = er sprang
über den Bach
to jump the queue = sich vordrängen
2 *noun* = (der) Sprung

J

jump out
= herausspringen/hinausspringen (**!** *sein*),
= rausspringen✗ (**!** *sein*)

> **!** *Note that* **heraus-** *has the sense of* **towards** *the speaker, and* **hinaus-** *has the sense of* **away** *from. The less formal* **raus-** *can be used for both movements, towards and away.*

jumper *noun*
= (der) Pullover

June *noun*
= (der) Juni ▶Dates p. 213

junior *adjective*
• (*younger*) = jünger
• (*of lower rank*) = untergeordnet
• (*US: after name*) = junior

jury *noun*
• (*in court*)
  the jury = die Geschworenen (*plural*)
• (*in a competition*) = (die) Jury

just¹
1 *adverb*
• (*very recently*) = gerade
  I saw him just now = ich habe ihn gerade
  eben gesehen
• (*exactly*) = genau
  it's just as good = das ist genauso gut
• (*immediately*)
  it was just after 6 o'clock = es war kurz
  nach sechs Uhr
• (*only*) = nur
  I've come just to say goodbye = ich bin
  nur gekommen, um auf Wiedersehen zu
  sagen
• (*barely*) = gerade noch
  I got there just in time = ich kam gerade
  noch rechtzeitig an
• (*simply*) = einfach
  just tell the truth = sag einfach die
  Wahrheit
• (*equally*)
  he is just as tall as you = er ist genauso
  groß wie du
• (*at that very moment*)
  to be just about to do something = dabei
  sein, etwas zu tun
  I was just about to phone you = ich war
  gerade dabei, dich anzurufen
  just a minute! = einen Moment!

just² *adjective*
= gerecht

justice *noun*
= (die) Gerechtigkeit

justify *verb*
= rechtfertigen

Kk

kangaroo *noun*
= (das) Känguru

karate *noun*
= (das) Karate

keen *adjective*
• (*eager*) = begeistert
  to be keen on [tennis | swimming | sweets ...] =
    [Tennis | Schwimmen | Bonbons ...] mögen
  to be keen to do something = etwas
    unbedingt tun wollen
  he is very keen for you to come along = er
    will unbedingt, dass du mitkommst
• (*sharp*) = scharf

keep *verb*
• (*retain*) = behalten
  you can keep the change = du kannst das
    Wechselgeld behalten
• (*maintain*) = halten
  to keep something hot = etwas warm
    halten
• (*store*) = aufbewahren
  to keep the wine in the cellar = den Wein
    im Keller aufbewaren
  (*not throw away*) = aufheben
• (*detain*) = aufhalten
  I won't keep you long = ich will dich nicht
    lange aufhalten
  to keep someone waiting = jemanden
    warten lassen
  to keep a seat = einen Platz freihalten
• (*not break*) = einhalten
  to keep an appointment = eine
    Verabredung einhalten
• (*carry on, manage*) = führen
  to keep the accounts = Buch führen
• (*continue*)
  to keep walking = weitergehen (**!** *sein*)

> **!** *Note that the prefix* **weiter-** *forms a separable verb.*

  keep going! = mach weiter!
• (*do repeatedly*)
  to keep (on) interrupting = dauernd
    unterbrechen
• (*remain*) = bleiben (**!** *sein*)
  to keep calm = ruhig bleiben (**!** *sein*)
• (*of food, stay in good condition*) = sich
    halten
• (*prevent*)
  to keep someone from doing something =
    jemanden davon abhalten, etwas zu tun
  to keep something from falling down =
    verhindern, dass etwas herunterfällt

keep away
= sich fernhalten, = wegbleiben✗ (**!** *sein*)

keep back
= zurückhalten
the police kept the crowd back = die
Polizei hielt die Menschenmenge zurück
keep down
to keep [prices | unemployment | wages ...]
down = [Preise | Arbeitslosigkeit | Löhne ...]
niedrig halten
keep your voice down = rede nicht so laut
keep off
to keep off the grass = den Rasen nicht
betreten
keep on
= weitermachen

> ! Note that the prefix **weiter-** forms a
> separable verb when the action carries
> on continuously. But **weiter** and the verb
> are written as two separate words if the
> action carries on over a long period of
> time, with interruptions.

to keep on [talking | playing | reading ...] =
[weiterreden | weiterspielen | weiterlesen ...]
you must keep on practising = du musst
weiter üben
keep out
to keep out of a building = ein Gebäude
nicht betreten
to keep out of the sun = nicht in die Sonne
gehen (! sein)
the curtain is supposed to keep the flies
out = der Vorhang soll die Fliegen
abhalten

kennel noun
(British: doghouse) = (die) Hundehütte

kerb noun (British)
= (der) Randstein

kettle noun
= (der) Kessel

key
1 noun
• = (der) Schlüssel
• (on a computer, piano) = (die) Taste
2 verb = eintasten, = eingeben
to key (in) data = Daten eintasten

keyboard noun
= (die) Tastatur

keyhole noun
= (das) Schlüsselloch

kick
1 verb
to kick someone = jemandem einen Tritt
geben
to kick the ball = den Ball schließen
2 noun = (der) Tritt
kick off
= anstoßen
kick out
to kick someone out = jemanden
rausschmeißen✱

kid noun
• (young goat) = (das) Kitz
• (child) = (das) Kind

kidnap verb
= entführen, = kidnappen

kill verb
= töten
to kill an animal = ein Tier töten
to kill a man = einen Mann umbringen
he killed himself = er hat sich umgebracht

killer noun
= (der) Mörder/(die) Mörderin

kilometer (US), **kilometre** (British)
noun
= (der) Kilometer ▶Measures p. 270

kind
1 adjective
• (friendly) = nett
it is very kind of you to help me = es ist
sehr nett von Ihnen, mir zu helfen
• (affectionate) = lieb
a kind act = eine gute Tat
2 noun
• (type) = (die) Art
a kind of [novel | game | fish ...] = so eine Art
[Roman | Spiel | Fisch ...]
all kinds of [people | excuses | games ...] = alle
möglichen [Leute | Ausreden | Spiele ...]
• (brand) = (die) Sorte
a new kind of cheese = eine neue Käsesorte
what kind of car does he drive? = was für
ein Auto hat er?

kindness noun
= (die) Freundlichkeit

king noun
= (der) König

kingdom noun
= (das) Königreich

kiss
1 verb = küssen
they kissed (each other) = sie küssten sich
2 noun = (der) Kuss

kitchen noun
= (die) Küche

kite noun
= (der) Drachen

knee noun
= (das) Knie

kneel verb
= knien
(go down on one's knees) = niederknien
to kneel (down) to do something = sich
hinknien, um etwas zu tun

knife noun
= (das) Messer

knit verb
= stricken

knock
1 verb
• (strike lightly) = klopfen an (+ accusative)
he knocked on the door = er klopfte an die
Tür

K

* (*hit*) = stoßen
  he knocked his head = er hat sich (*dative*)
  den Kopf gestoßen
2 *noun*
* (*blow*) = (der) Schlag
* (*at the door*) = (das) Klopfen
  there is a knock at the door = es klopft an
  der Tür
knock down
* = herunterwerfen
  (*punch*) = niederschlagen
  (*in a car*) **he was knocked down by a car** =
  er ist von einem Auto angefahren worden
* (*demolish a building*) = abreißen
knock out
  = bewusstlos schlagen
  (*in boxing*) = k.o. schlagen
knock over
  = umstoßen

knot
1 *noun* = (der) Knoten
2 *verb* = knoten

know *verb*
* (*be acquainted with*) = kennen
  I don't know her = ich kenne sie nicht
  to get to know someone = jemanden
  kennen lernen
* (*have knowledge of*) = wissen
  how do you know that? = woher weißt du
  das?
  to let someone know something =
  jemandem über etwas (*accusative*)
  Bescheid sagen
* (*have an understanding of*) = können
  to know how to do something = etwas tun
  können
  do you know any German? = können Sie
  etwas Deutsch?

knowledge *noun*
* (*learning*) = Kenntnisse (*plural*)
  his scientific knowledge = seine
  wissenschaftlichen Kenntnisse
* (*awareness*) = (das) Wissen
  to my knowledge = meines Wissens
  not to my knowledge = meines Wissens
  nicht

L l

laboratory *noun*
  = (das) Labor

lace *noun*
* (*material*) = (die) Spitze
* (*shoelace*) = (der) Schnürsenkel
  to tie one's laces = sich (*dative*) die
  Schnürsenkel binden

lack
1 *noun* = (der) Mangel
  lack of |money | interest | tact ...] = Mangel an
  [Geld | Interesse | Takt ...]
2 *verb* = fehlen an (+ *dative*)
  he lacks confidence = ihm fehlt es an
  Selbstvertrauen

ladder *noun*
  = (die) Leiter

lady *noun*
  = (die) Dame

lake *noun*
  = (der) See

lamb *noun*
  = (das) Lamm

lamp *noun*
  = (die) Lampe

lampshade *noun*
  = (der) Lampenschirm

land
1 *noun*
* = (das) Land
* (*property*) = (der) Grundbesitz
2 *verb*
  = landen (**!** *sein*)

landlady *noun*
* (*of a house, room*) = (die) Vermieterin
* (*of a pub*) = (die) Gastwirtin

landlord *noun*
* (*of a house, room*) = (der) Vermieter
* (*of a pub*) = (der) Gastwirt

landscape *noun*
  = (die) Landschaft

language *noun*
  = (die) Sprache

language laboratory *noun*
  = (das) Sprachlabor

lap *noun*
* (*part of the body*) = (der) Schoß
* (*in a race*) = (die) Runde

laptop *noun*
  = (der) Laptop

large *adjective*
  = groß

last
1 *adjective* = letzter/letzte/letztes
  for the last time = zum letzten Mal
2 *pronoun*
  the last = der Letzte/die Letzte/das Letzte
  the night before last = vorgestern Nacht
3 *adverb*
* (*at the end*) = zuletzt
  I'll do the packing last = ich packe die
  Koffer zuletzt
* (*in final position*) = als Letzter/als Letzte
  they were last to arrive = sie kamen als
  Letzte an
  he spoke last = er hat als Letzter
  gesprochen

- (*most recently*) = das letzte Mal
  I last saw him in June = ich habe ihn das
  letzte Mal im Juni gesehen
  4 *verb* = dauern
  the film lasted 3 hours = der Film dauerte
  drei Stunden

late
1 *adjective*
- (*not on time*) = verspätet
  to be late = sich verspäten
  the train was 10 minutes late = der Zug
  hatte zehn Minuten Verspätung
  to make someone late = jemanden
  aufhalten
- (*far into the day or night*) = spät
  at this late hour = zu dieser späten Stunde
- (*towards the end of*)
  in late September = Ende September
- (*most recent*)
  the latest fashion = die neueste Mode
2 *adverb*
- (*not on time*) = zu spät
  they arrived an hour late = sie kamen eine
  Stunde zu spät an
- (*far into the day or night*) = spät
  to stay up late = bis spät aufbleiben (**!** *sein*)

later *adverb*
= später
later on = später
see you later = bis später

Latin *noun*
= (das) Latein

Latin America *noun*
= (das) Lateinamerika ▶Countries p. 208

Latvia *noun*
= (das) Lettland ▶Countries p. 208

laugh
1 *verb* = lachen
  to laugh at something = über etwas
  (*accusative*) lachen
  (*mock*) to laugh at someone = jemanden
  auslachen
2 *noun* = (das) Lachen
  with a laugh = lachend

laughter *noun*
= (das) Gelächter

launderette *noun*
= (der) Waschsalon

laundry *noun*
- (*place*) = (die) Wäscherei
- (*washing*) = (die) Wäsche
  to do the laundry = Wäsche waschen

law *noun*
- (*regulation*) = (das) Gesetz
  to break the law = gegen das Gesetz
  verstoßen
- (*set of rules in a country*) = (das) Recht
  according to German law = nach
  deutschem Recht
  it's against the law = das ist verboten

- (*as a university subject*) = Jura (*plural*)
  to study law = Jura studieren

lawn *noun*
= (der) Rasen

lawnmower *noun*
= (der) Rasenmäher

lawyer *noun*
= (der) Rechtsanwalt/(die) Rechtsanwältin
  ▶Professions p. 298

lay *verb*
- (*put, fit*) = legen
  she laid her hand on his shoulder = sie
  legte ihre Hand auf seine Schulter
  to lay a carpet = einen Teppich legen
  (*of a bird*) to lay an egg = ein Ei legen
- (*set*) = decken
  to lay the table = den Tisch decken
lay down
- (*put down*) = hinlegen
  to lay something down on the table =
  etwas auf den Tisch legen
- (*impose*) = festlegen
  to lay down rules = Regeln festlegen
lay off
  to lay off workers = Arbeiter
  vorübergehend entlassen

lazy *adjective*
= faul

lead¹
1 *verb*
- (*guide, have or conduct*) = führen
  he led me into the garden = er führte mich
  in den Garten
  to lead someone into difficulties =
  jemanden in Schwierigkeiten bringen
  to lead the way = vorangehen (**!** *sein*)
- (*be at the head of*) = anführen
  to lead a [team | demonstration | parade ...] =
  [eine Mannschaft | eine Demonstration | einen
  Umzug ...] anführen
- (*be ahead*) = führen
  to lead by 5 points = mit fünf Punkten
  führen
- (*cause*)
  to lead someone to do something =
  jemanden dazu bringen, etwas zu tun
  to be easily led = sich leicht beeinflussen
  lassen
- (*result in*)
  to lead to = führen zu (+ *dative*)
  to lead to an accident = zu einem Unfall
  führen
- (*in cards*) = ausspielen
2 *noun*
- (*in a match, contest*) = (die) Führung
  to take the lead = in Führung gehen
  (**!** *sein*)
- (*leading role*) = (die) Hauptrolle
- (*wire*) = (die) Schnur
- (*British: for a dog*) = (die) Leine

lead² *noun*
- (*metal*) = (das) Blei
- (*in a pencil*) = (die) Mine

L

leader *noun*
- (*of an army, movement*) = (der) Führer/(die) Führerin
- (*of a political party*) = (der/die) Vorsitzende
- (*of an expedition, group*) = (der) Leiter/(die) Leiterin
- (*of a gang*) = (der) Anführer/(die) Anführerin

leaf *noun*
= (das) Blatt

leak
1 *verb*
- (*of a roof, container*) = undicht sein
- (*of a boat*) = leck sein
2 *noun*
- (*in a roof, container*) = (die) undichte Stelle
- (*in a boat*) = (das) Leck
- (*of gas*) = (der) Gasausfluss

lean
1 *verb*
- = lehnen
 to lean against/on something = an etwas (+ *accusative*) lehnen
- (*of a person*) = sich lehnen
 he leant out of the window = er lehnte sich aus dem Fenster
2 *adjective*
= mager
lean on
= sich stützen auf (+ *accusative*)
he leaned on his stick = er stützte sich auf seinen Stock

leap
1 *verb* = springen (**!** *sein*)
2 *noun* = (der) Sprung

learn *verb*
= lernen

leash *noun*
= (die) Leine

least
1 *adjective* = wenigster/wenigste/wenigstes
 they have the least money = sie haben das wenigste Geld
 to have least time = am wenigsten Zeit haben
2 *pronoun* = das wenigste
 that is the least you can do = das ist das wenigste, was man tun kann
3 *adverb* = am wenigsten
 I like that colour (the) least = die Farbe gefällt mir am wenigsten

> **!** Note that **least** *is often translated into German by forming the superlative of the opposite adjective:* the least expensive (*the cheapest*) = der/die/das billigste.

 the least expensive shop = der billigste Laden
 the least difficult question = die einfachste Frage

at least
- (*at the minimum*) = mindestens
 he's at least 30 = er ist mindestens dreißig
- (*if nothing more, anyway*) = wenigstens
 they could at least have phoned = sie hätten wenigstens anrufen können
 he's gone out, at least I think he has = er ist rausgegangen, glaube ich wenigstens

leave *verb*
- = verlassen
 she left her husband = sie hat ihren Mann verlassen
 the train leaves London at 11 o'clock = der Zug fährt um elf Uhr von London ab
- (*depart*) = (weg)gehen (**!** *sein*), (*by car*) = (weg)fahren (**!** *sein*), (*by plane*) = abfliegen (**!** *sein*)
 we are leaving now = wir gehen jetzt
 she leaves home at 8 o'clock = sie geht um acht Uhr von zu Hause weg
- (*let remain, deposit, in will*) = hinterlassen
 he didn't leave a message = er hat keine Nachricht hinterlassen
- (*forget*) = vergessen
 I left my gloves = ich habe meine Handschuhe vergessen
- (*postpone*) = lassen
 leave it until tomorrow = lass es bis morgen
- (*allow to remain*) = lassen
 to leave the light on = das Licht anlassen
 to leave the door open = die Tür offen lassen
- (*remain*) = übrig bleiben (**!** *sein*)
 was there any food left? = ist von dem Essen etwas übrig geblieben?
- (*entrust*) = überlassen
 leave it to me = überlassen Sie es mir
leave behind
- (*not take with one*) = zurücklassen
- (*by mistake*) = vergessen
leave out
- (*not show or mention*) = auslassen
- (*exclude a person*) = ausschließen
- (*allow to remain outdoors*) = draußen lassen
 they leave the cat out all night = sie lassen die Katze die ganze Nacht draußen

Lebanon *noun*
 (the) Lebanon = der Libanon ▶ Countries p. 208

lecture *noun*
- (*British: at university*) = (die) Vorlesung
 to give a lecture = eine Vorlesung halten
- (*public talk*) = (der) Vortrag

left
1 *noun* = (die) linke Seite
 the first street on your left = die erste Straße links
2 *adjective* = linker/linke/linkes
 his left hand = seine linke Hand
3 *adverb* = links
 to turn left = nach links abbiegen (**!** *sein*)

left-click *verb*
= linksklicken

leg *noun*
= (das) Bein
a leg of lamb = eine Hammelkeule

legal *adjective*
• (*concerning the law*) = rechtlich
• (*lawful*) = gesetzlich

leisure *noun*
= (die) Freizeit

lemon *noun*
= (die) Zitrone

lemonade *noun*
= (die) Limonade

lend *verb*
= leihen
to lend someone money = jemandem Geld leihen

length *noun*
• = (die) Länge
to be 30 metres in length = dreißig Meter lang sein ▶ **Measures p. 270**
• (*of an event*) = (die) Dauer

lens *noun*
• (*of a camera*) = (das) Objektiv
• (*of spectacles*) = (das) Brillenglas
• (*contact lens*) = (die) Linse

Leo *noun*
= (der) Löwe

leopard *noun*
= (der) Leopard

less
1 *adjective* = weniger

! Note that **weniger** *never changes.*

less [money | time | love ...] = weniger [Geld | Zeit | Liebe ...]
2 *pronoun* = weniger
he reads less than she does = er liest weniger als sie
3 *adverb* = weniger
we travel less in winter = wir reisen weniger im Winter
less and less = immer weniger

lesson *noun*
= (die) Stunde
a driving lesson = eine Fahrstunde

let¹ *verb*
• (*used in a suggestion*)
let's eat = essen wir
let's go home = gehen wir nach Hause
• (*allow*) = lassen
she lets her do what she likes = sie lässt sie tun, was sie will
to let someone in = jemanden hereinlassen

! Note the use of the separable verb formed with the prefix **herein-**.

• **let alone** = geschweige denn
he can't read, let alone write = er kann nicht lesen, geschweige denn schreiben
let down
• (*disappoint*) = enttäuschen
• (*lengthen*) = länger machen
let go
• (*stop holding*) = loslassen
let go of my arm! = lass meinen Arm los!
• (*release from captivity*) = freilassen
let in
• (*into a room or house*) = hereinlassen
let me in! = lass mich herein!
• (*unintentionally*) = durchlassen
to let in water = Wasser durchlassen
let off
• (*not punish*) = frei ausgehen lassen
• (*allow to explode*)
to let off a bomb = eine Bombe hochgehen lassen
let out
• (*allow out*) = hinauslassen, = rauslassen✱
• (*utter*) = ausstoßen
• (*make wider*) = auslassen
• (*release*)
to let a prisoner out = einen Gefangenen entlassen

let² *verb*
= vermieten
to let a room to someone = jemandem ein Zimmer vermieten
'to let' = 'zu vermieten'

letter *noun*
• (*written message*) = (der) Brief
• (*of the alphabet*) = (der) Buchstabe

letterbox *noun*
= (der) Briefkasten

lettuce *noun*
= (der) Salat
a lettuce = ein Kopf Salat

level
1 *noun* = (die) Höhe
at sea level = auf Meereshöhe
2 *adjective*
• (*flat*) = eben
a level surface = eine ebene Oberfläche
a level teaspoon of sugar = ein gestrichener Teelöffel Zucker
• (*at the same height*) = auf gleicher Höhe

liar *noun*
= (der) Lügner/(die) Lügnerin

Libra *noun*
= (die) Waage

library *noun*
= (die) Bibliothek

licence (*British*), **license** (*US*) *noun*
= (die) Genehmigung

lick *verb*
= lecken

L

Letter-writing

Addressing the envelope

The addressed person's title appears on a separate line, in the accusative:

Mr = Herrn
Mrs = Frau
Miss = Fräulein
Ms = Frau

On the next line comes the person's name, and on the next the name of the street, followed by the house number. Then comes the postcode (= **die Postleitzahl**), followed by the town. The German postcode refers to a town or to part of a larger town or city.

Frau
Elisabeth Becker
Oderstraße 28
82577 München
Germany

Beginnings

To someone you know well:

Dear Hans, = Lieber Hans!
Dear Gabi, = Liebe Gabi!

The letter itself starts on the next line with a capital. Or you can use a comma instead of the exclamation mark, as in English, and this is followed by a small letter:

Dear Natalie and Peter, = Liebe Natalie, lieber Peter,

To someone you do not know:

Dear Mr Braun = Lieber Herr Braun
Dear Ms Fischer = Liebe Frau Fischer

In a formal business letter:

Dear Mr Schneider = Sehr geehrter Herr Schneider
Dear Sir or Madam = Sehr geehrte Damen und Herren

Endings

To someone you know well:

Yours = Herzliche Grüße

To someone you do not know:

Yours sincerely = Mit freundlichen Grüßen

In a formal business letter:

Yours faithfully = Mit freundlichen Empfehlungen, = Hochachtungsvoll

---

lid *noun*
= (der) Deckel

lie
1 *verb*
- = liegen
  he is lying on the carpet = er liegt auf dem Teppich
  to lie down on the sofa = sich auf das Sofa legen
- (*be situated*) = liegen (**!** *sein*)
  the village lies in the valley = das Dorf liegt im Tal
- (*not tell the truth*) = lügen
  to lie to someone = jemanden belügen
2 *noun* = (die) Lüge
  to tell a lie = lügen
lie down
= sich hinlegen

life *noun*
= (das) Leben
  throughout his life = sein ganzes Leben lang

lift
1 *verb* = heben
2 *noun*
- (*British: elevator*) = (der) Aufzug
- **to give someone a lift** (*in a car*) = jemanden mitnehmen
lift up
= hochheben

light
1 *noun*
- = (das) Licht
  turn the light on = mach das Licht an
- (*lamp*) = (die) Lampe

* (*in the street*) = (die) Straßenlampe
* (**traffic**) **lights** = (die) Ampel
  the lights are green = die Ampel ist grün
* **have you got a light?** (*for a cigarette*) =
  haben Sie Feuer?
2 *adjective*
* (*not dark*) = hell
  light blue = hellblau ▶**Colours p. 204**
  it's still light outside = es ist immer noch
  hell draußen
* (*not heavy*) = leicht
3 *verb*
* (*with a match*) = anzünden
* (*illuminate*) = beleuchten

lighter *noun*
= (das) Feuerzeug

light bulb *noun*
= (die) Glühbirne

lightning *noun*
= (der) Blitz

like¹ *preposition*
* = wie (+ *nominative*)
  what's it like? = wie ist es?
  he cried like a child = er hat wie ein Kind
  geweint
  like this/that = so
* (*similar to*) = ähnlich (+ *dative*)
  she looks like her mother = sie sieht ihrer
  Mutter ähnlich

like² *verb*
* = mögen
  I like Paul but I don't like Peter = ich mag
  Paul, aber Peter mag ich nicht
  I like [reading | dancing | working ...] = ich
  [lese | tanze | arbeite ...] gerne
  do you like the dress? = gefällt dir das
  Kleid?
  I like chocolate/tea = ich esse gerne
  Schokolade/ich trinke gerne Tee
* (*want*)
  would you like some cake? = möchten Sie
  ein Stück Kuchen?
  I'd like a drink = ich würde gerne etwas
  trinken
  if you like = wenn du willst

likely *adjective*
= wahrscheinlich
it is likely that he will come =
wahrscheinlich kommt er
! *Note that the future is often translated
by the German present tense.*

limit
1 *noun* = (die) Grenze
2 *verb* = begrenzen

limited *adjective*
= begrenzt
a limited company = eine Gesellschaft mit
beschränkter Haftung

line
1 *noun*

* = Linie
  a straight line = eine gerade Linie
* (*in writing*) = (die) Zeile
* (*US: queue*) = (die) Schlange
  to stand in line = Schlange stehen
* (*row*) = (die) Reihe
* (*wrinkle*) = (die) Falte
* (*for fishing*) = (die) Leine
* (*phone line*) = (die) Leitung
  it's a bad line = die Verbindung ist schlecht
* (*railway track*) = (das) Gleis
* (*line of business*) = (die) Branche
2 *verb*
= füttern
to line a coat = einen Mantel füttern

line up
* = aufstellen
* **the children lined up** = die Kinder stellten
  sich auf

linen *noun*
* (*fabric*) = (das) Leinen
* (*for household use*) = (die) Wäsche

link
1 *noun*
* (*connection*) = (die) Verbindung
* (*in a chain*) = (das) Glied
2 *verb* = verbinden

lion *noun*
= (der) Löwe

lioness *noun*
= (die) Löwin

lip *noun*
= (die) Lippe

lipstick *noun*
= (der) Lippenstift

Lisbon *noun*
= (das) Lissabon ▶**Countries p. 208**

list
1 *noun* = (die) Liste
2 *verb* = auflisten

listen *verb*
= zuhören (+ *dative*)
to listen to the teacher = dem Lehrer
zuhören
to listen to the radio = Radio hören

liter (*US*) ▶**litre**

literature *noun*
= (die) Literatur

Lithuania *noun*
= (das) Litauen ▶**Countries p. 208**

litre *noun* (*British*)
= (der) Liter ▶**Measures p. 270**

litter *noun*
* (*rubbish*) = (der) Abfall
* (*baby animals*) = (der) Wurf

little
1 *adjective*
* (*small*) = klein
* (*not much*) = wenig

L

2 *pronoun*
a little = ein wenig

> **!** Note that ein wenig *never changes.*

I have a little left = ich habe ein wenig
übrig
3 *adverb* = wenig
he writes little now = er schreibt nur noch
wenig
a little (bit) slow = ein bisschen langsam

live¹ *verb*
• (*exist*) = leben
you can't live on that = davon kann man
nicht leben
• (*reside*) = wohnen
he lives in a small village = er wohnt in
einem kleinen Dorf
he lives in Rome = er lebt in Rom

live²
1 *adjective*
• (*alive*) = lebendig
• (*of a performance*) = Live-
a live broadcast = eine Livesendung
• (*of a wire*) = Strom führend
2 *adverb*
to broadcast a concert live = ein Konzert
live senden

lively *adjective*
= lebhaft

living room *noun*
= (das) Wohnzimmer

load
1 *noun*
• (*cargo*) = (die) Ladung
• loads of [money | work | toys ...] = jede Menge
or ein Haufen✱ [Geld | Arbeit | Spielzeug ...]
2 *verb*
to load a truck with wood = einen
Lastwagen mit Holz beladen
to load a camera = einen Film einlegen

loaf *noun*
= (das) Brot
a loaf of bread = ein Brot

loan
1 *noun*
• = (die) Leihgabe
• (*money*) = (das) Darlehen
2 *verb* = leihen

lobster *noun*
= (der) Hummer

local *adjective*
= lokal
the local newspaper = die Lokalzeitung
the local people = die Einheimischen
our local shops = die Geschäfte bei uns in
der Nähe
a local call = ein Ortsgespräch

location *noun*
= (die) Lage

lock
1 *verb* = abschliessen
2 *noun* = (das) Schloss
lock in
= einschließen
lock up
• = abschließen
• (*imprison*) = einsperren

locker *noun*
= (das) Schließfach

log *noun*
= (der) Baumstamm
(*for a fire*) = (das) Holzscheit

logical *adjective*
= logisch

lonely *adjective*
= einsam

long
1 *adjective* = lang
10 metres long = zehn Meter lang
a long journey = eine weite Reise
it's quite a long way = es ist ziemlich weit
a long time = lange
the film is two hours long = der Film dauert
zwei Stunden
2 *adverb* = lange
it won't take long = es dauert nicht lange
I won't be long = ich bin gleich fertig
all day long = den ganzen Tag
as long as = solange

long-sighted *adjective*
= weitsichtig

look
1 *verb*
• = sehen, = schauen
he looked out of the window = er sah aus
dem Fenster
to look at someone = jemanden ansehen
• (*appear*) = aussehen
what does he look like? = wie sieht er aus?
2 *noun*
• (*appearance*) = (das) Aussehen
to have a look at something = sich (*dative*)
etwas ansehen
• (*expression*) = (der) Blick
a look of sadness = ein trauriger Blick
look after
• (*attend to*) = sich kümmern um
(+ *accusative*)
• (*keep in good condition*) = pflegen
look around
= sich umsehen
look back
• (*glance back*) = sich umsehen
• (*recall*)
to look back on something = auf etwas
(*accusative*) zurückblicken
look for
= suchen
he is looking for a job = er sucht eine Stelle

look forward to
= sich freuen auf (+ *accusative*)
to look forward to doing something = sich
darauf freuen, etwas zu tun
look on to
= gehen auf (+ *accusative*) (**!** *sein*)
my bedroom looks on to the garden =
mein Schlafzimmer geht auf den Garten
look out for
= aufpassen auf (+ *accusative*)
look out! = Vorsicht!
look up
• (*in a book*) = nachschlagen
to look up a word = ein Wort nachschlagen
• (*raise one's eyes*) = aufsehen
• **to look up to someone** = zu jemandem
aufsehen

loose *adjective*
• (*of a knot, screw, tooth*) = locker
• (*of a page*) = lose
• (*of clothes*) = weit

lord *noun*
= (der) Lord

lorry *noun* (*British*)
= (der) Lastwagen

lose *verb*
= verlieren
to lose weight = abnehmen
the clock loses (**time**) = die Uhr geht nach

loss *noun*
= (der) Verlust

lost *adjective*
= verloren
(*of a person*) = vermisst
to get lost = sich verlaufen

lot *pronoun*
a lot = viel
he drinks a lot = er trinkt viel
a lot of = viel, (*many*) = viele
to have a lot of [energy | time | money …] =
viel [Energie | Zeit | Geld …] haben
a lot of [children | dresses | books …] = viele
[Kinder | Kleider | Bücher …]

lottery *noun*
= (die) Lotterie, = (das) Lotto

loud *adjective*
• (*of sounds*) = laut
• (*of colours*) = grell

loudspeaker *noun*
= (der) Lautsprecher

lounge *noun*
• (*in a house*) = (das) Wohnzimmer
• (*in a hotel, airport*) = (die) Halle
the departure lounge = die Abflughalle
• (*US: bar*) = (die) Bar

love
1 *verb*
• = lieben
they love each other = sie lieben sich

• (*enjoy*)
to love doing something = etwas sehr
gerne tun
I love chocolate = ich mag Schokolade sehr
gerne
I'd love to come = ich würde sehr gerne
kommen
2 *noun* = (die) Liebe
to be in love with someone = in jemanden
verliebt sein

lovely *adjective*
• (*beautiful*) = schön
• (*pleasant*) = nett

low
1 *adjective*
• = niedrig
a low ceiling = eine niedrige Decke
low tide = (die) Ebbe
• (*of a sound, cloud, note*) = tief
2 *adverb*
• (*in a low position*) = niedrig
lower down the page = weiter unten auf
der Seite
• (*not loud*) = leise
(*at a low pitch*) = tief

loyal *adjective*
= treu

loyalty card *noun*
= (die) Treukarte

luck *noun*
= (das) Glück
to bring someone (**good**) **luck** = jemandem
Glück bringen
good luck! = viel Glück!
bad luck = (das) Pech

lucky *adjective*
= glücklich
to be lucky = Glück haben

luggage *noun*
= (das) Gepäck

lump *noun*
• (*on the body*) = (die) Beule
• (*of sugar, coal*) = (das) Stück

lunch *noun*
= (das) Mittagessen
to have lunch = zu Mittag essen

lung *noun*
= (der) Lungenflügel
lungs = (die) Lunge

Luxembourg *noun*
= (das) Luxemburg ▶**Countries p. 208**

luxury
1 *noun* = (der) Luxus
2 *adjective* = Luxus-
a luxury hotel = ein Luxushotel

L

Mm

machine noun
- = (die) Maschine
- (slot-machine) = (der) Automat

mad adjective
- (crazy) = verrückt
  are you mad? = bist du verrückt
  geworden?
- (angry) = wütend
  to be mad at someone = auf jemanden
  wütend sein
- (keen)
  to be mad about something = ganz wild
  auf etwas (accusative) sein✗

magazine noun
= (die) Zeitschrift
(containing mostly photos) = (das) Magazin

magic
1 adjective
- (supernatural) = magisch
- (in tricks) = Zauber-
  magic wand = (der) Zauberstab
2 noun
- (witchcraft) = (die) Magie
- (tricks) = (die) Zauberei

magnet noun
= (der) Magnet

magnificent adjective
= herrlich

magnifying glass noun
= (die) Lupe

maiden name noun
= (der) Mädchenname

mail
1 noun
(post) = (die) Post
2 verb
- = mit der Post schicken
- (send off) = abschicken
  (put in a postbox) = einwerfen

mailbox noun (US)
= (der) Briefkasten

mailman noun (US)
= (der) Briefträger

main adjective
= Haupt-
the main problem = das Hauptproblem

main course noun
= (das) Hauptgericht

main road noun
= (die) Hauptstraße

✗ in informal situations

maintain verb
- (preserve) = aufrechterhalten
- (take care of) = instand halten

maize noun
= (der) Mais

major
1 adjective
- (important) = groß
  of major importance = von großer
  Bedeutung
- (serious) = schwer
2 noun = (der) Major
3 verb (US)
  to major in English = Englisch als
  Hauptfach studieren

majority noun
= (die) Mehrheit

make
1 verb
- (do, cause to be) = machen
  to make [the bed | a noise | breakfast ...] = [das
  Bett | Lärm | Frühstück ...] machen
  it makes you [thirsty | tired | sad ...] = das
  macht einen [durstig | müde | traurig ...]
  to make someone laugh = jemanden zum
  Lachen bringen

> ! Note that the general verb make is often
> translated by a German verb relating
> more specifically to the action.

  to make a cake = einen Kuchen backen
  to make a speech = eine Rede halten
  to make a dress = ein Kleid nähen
  to make a film = einen Film drehen
  to make a phone call = telefonieren
  to make friends with someone = sich mit
  jemandem anfreunden
  to make room = Platz schaffen
- (manufacture) = herstellen
  to make wine from grapes = aus Trauben
  Wein machen
  made in Germany = in Deutschland
  hergestellt
  made of [gold | cotton | plastic ...] = aus [Gold |
  Baumwolle | Plastik ...]
- (cause to do)
  to make someone do something =
  jemanden dazu bringen, etwas zu tun
  to make someone wait = jemanden warten
  lassen
- (force) = zwingen
  they made me give them the money = sie
  haben mich gezwungen, ihnen das Geld
  zu geben
- (earn) = verdienen
  to make a lot of money = viel Geld
  verdienen
2 noun = (die) Marke
make do
= zurechtkommen (! sein)
make out
- (understand) = verstehen
  I can't make him out = ich kann ihn nicht
  verstehen

- (*write out*) = ausstellen
  to make a cheque out to someone = jemandem einen Scheck ausstellen

make up
- (*be friends again*) = sich versöhnen
- (*invent*) = erfinden
- (*compile*) = zusammenstellen
- **to make up one's mind** = sich entschließen

make-up *noun*
= (das) Make-up
to put on make-up = sich schminken

male
1 *adjective* = männlich
2 *noun*
- (*man*) = (der) Mann
- (*animal*) = (das) Männchen

man *noun*
- = (der) Mann
- (*human race*) = (der) Mensch

manage *verb*
- (*run*) = leiten
  he manages the hotel = er leitet das Hotel
- (*be able to*)
  to manage to [finish one's homework | find a job | be on time …] = es schaffen, [seine Hausaufgaben fertig zu machen | eine Stelle zu finden | pünktlich zu sein …]
- (*cope*) = zurechtkommen (**!** *sein*)
  can you manage? = kommst du zurecht?

manager *noun*
- (*of a company, bank*) = (der) Direktor
- (*of a shop*) = (der) Geschäftsführer
- (*of a soccer team*) = (der) Trainer

manageress *noun*
- (*of a company, bank*) = (die) Direktorin
- (*of a shop*) = (die) Geschäftsführerin
- (*of a soccer team*) = (die) Trainerin

manner *noun*
= (die) Art

manners *noun*
= Manieren (*plural*)
to have good manners = gute Manieren haben
it's bad manners to grin = es gehört sich nicht zu grinsen

manual *noun*
= (das) Handbuch

manufacture *verb*
= herstellen

many
1 *adjective* = viele
how many people were there? = wie viele Leute waren da?
so many = so viele
2 *pronoun* = viele
many find work abroad = viele finden Arbeit im Ausland
how many? = wie viele?

map *noun*
= (die) Karte
(*of a town*) = (der) Stadtplan

marble *noun*
= (der) Marmor

march *noun*
1 *verb* = marschieren (**!** *sein*)
2 *noun* = (der) Marsch

March *noun*
= (der) März ▶ Dates p. 213

margarine *noun*
= (die) Margarine

mark
1 *noun*
- (*stain*) = (der) Fleck
  (*scratch*) = (der) Kratzer
- (*on the body*) = (das) Mal
- (*grade*) = (die) Note
  to get good marks = gute Noten bekommen
- (*German money*) = (die) Mark
- (*in races*)
  on your marks! = auf die Plätze!
2 *verb*
- (*stain*) = Flecken machen auf (+ *dative*)
  (*damage*) = beschädigen
- (*correct*) = korrigieren
- (*indicate*) = markieren
- (*in sports*) = decken

market
1 *noun* = (der) Markt
  the job market = der Arbeitsmarkt
2 *verb*
  (*sell*) = vertreiben

marketing *noun*
= (das) Marketing

marmalade *noun*
= (die) Orangenmarmelade

marriage *noun*
- = (die) Ehe
- (*wedding*) = (die) Hochzeit

married *adjective*
= verheiratet
to be married to someone = mit jemandem verheiratet sein

marry *verb*
= heiraten
to get married to someone = jemanden heiraten

marvellous (*British*), **marvelous** (*US*) *adjective*
= wunderbar

marzipan *noun*
= (das) Marzipan

mascara *noun*
= (die) Wimperntusche

masculine
1 *adjective* = männlich
2 *noun*
(*in grammar*) = (das) Maskulinum

M

mash *verb*
= stampfen

mashed potatoes *noun*
= (der) Kartoffelbrei

mask *noun*
= (die) Maske

mass *noun*
• (*large number*) = (die) Masse
  a mass of people = eine große
  Menschenmenge
• (*in church*) = (die) Messe

massive *adjective*
= riesig

mast *noun*
= (der) Mast

master
1 *noun*
• = (der) Herr
  (*dog owner*) = (das) Herrchen
• (*artist*) = (der) Meister
• (*British: teacher*) = (der) Lehrer
2 *verb* = beherrschen

mat *noun*
= (die) Matte

match
1 *noun*
• (*game*) = (das) Spiel
• (*matchstick*) = (das) Streichholz
2 *verb* = passen zu (+ *dative*)
  the shoes match the skirt = die Schuhe
  passen zu dem Rock

matchbox *noun*
= (die) Streichholzschachtel

mate
1 *noun*
• (der) Gehilfe
• (*British: friend*) = (der) Freund,
  = (der) Kumpel✘
2 *verb* = sich paaren

material *noun*
• (*substance*) = (das) Material
• (*cloth, information for a novel*) = (der) Stoff

math *noun* (*US*)
= (die) Mathe✘

mathematics *noun*
= (die) Mathematik

maths *noun* (*British*)
= (die) Mathe✘

matter
1 *noun*
• (*affair*) = (die) Angelegenheit, = (die) Sache
  money matters = Geldangelegenheiten
  it's a private matter = das ist eine
  Privatsache

• (*question*) = (die) Frage
  a matter of = eine Frage (+ *genitive*)
  it's only a matter of time = es ist nur noch
  eine Frage der Zeit
• (*problem*)
  what's the matter with her? = was ist mit
  ihr los?
2 *verb* = etwas ausmachen
  it doesn't matter = das macht nichts
  does it really matter? = ist das wirklich so
  wichtig?

mattress *noun*
= (die) Matratze

mature *adjective*
= reif

maximum *adjective*
= maximal
  a maximum temperature of 40° = eine
  Höchsttemperatur von vierzig Grad

may *verb*
• (*stating possibility*) = können
  they may be able to come after all = sie
  können vielleicht doch kommen
• (*when asking for or giving permission*) =
  dürfen
  may I come in? = darf ich reinkommen✘?

May *noun*
= (der) Mai ▶ **Dates p. 213**

maybe *adverb*
= vielleicht

mayor *noun*
= (der) Bürgermeister/(die) Bürgermeisterin

maze *noun*
= (der) Irrgarten

me *pronoun*

> ❗ *In German this pronoun changes
> according to its function in the sentence.
> As a direct object it is in the accusative,
> mich, and as an indirect object it is in the
> dative, mir.*

• (*in the accusative*) = mich
  she loves me = sie liebt mich
  did you do it for me? = hast du das für
  mich getan?
• (*in the dative*) = mir
  give me the money = gib mir das Geld
  he never talks to me = er redet nie mit mir
• (*in the nominative, as a complement*) = ich
  it's me = ich bins

> ❗ *Note that bins, written as one word, is
> short for bin es.*

meadow *noun*
= (die) Wiese

meal *noun*
• = (die) Mahlzeit
• (*food*) = (das) Essen
  to cook a meal = Essen kochen
  to go out for a meal = essen gehen

✘ in informal situations

mean
1 *verb*
- = bedeuten
  what does that mean? = was bedeutet das?
- (*intend*) = beabsichtigen
  I meant to [invite them for dinner | order a pizza |
  go to the cinema ...] = ich wollte [sie zum
  Essen einladen | eine Pizza bestellen | ins Kino
  gehen ...]
  she meant well = sie meinte es gut
- (*be supposed to*)
  to be meant for something = für etwas
  (*accusative*) bestimmt sein
  she is meant to be doing her homework =
  sie soll ihre Hausaufgaben machen
- (*intend to say*) = meinen
  do you see what I mean? = verstehst du,
  was ich meine?
2 *adjective*
- (*not generous*) = geizig
- (*nasty*) = gemein

meaning *noun*
= (die) Bedeutung

means *noun*
- (*way*) = (das) Mittel, = (die) Möglichkeit
  means of transport = (das) Verkehrsmittel
  a means of earning money = eine
  Möglichkeit, Geld zu verdienen
  by means of = mit Hilfe (+ *genitive*)
- (*money*) = Mittel (*plural*)

meanwhile *adverb*
= inzwischen

measles *noun*
= Masern (*plural*)

measure
1 *verb* = messen
  to measure a room = ein Zimmer
  ausmessen
2 *noun*
  (*step*) = (die) Maßnahme
  to take measures = Maßnahmen ergreifen

measurement *noun*
= (das) Maß
  to take someone's measurements = bei
  jemandem Maß nehmen

meat *noun*
= (das) Fleisch

mechanical *adjective*
= mechanisch

medal *noun*
= (der) Orden
  (*in sport*) = (die) Medaille

media *noun*
  the media = die Medien (*plural*)

medical *adjective*
= medizinisch
  (*of treatment*) = ärztlich
  to have medical treatment = in ärztlicher
  Behandlung sein

medicine *noun*
- (*subject, profession*) = (die) Medizin
- (*drug*) = (das) Medikament

Mediterranean
1 *noun*
  the Mediterranean (Sea) = das Mittelmeer
2 *adjective* = Mittelmeer-
  a Mediterranean climate = ein
  Mittelmeerklima

medium *adjective*
= mittlerer/mittlere/mittleres
  a medium size = eine mittlere Größe

meet *verb*
- (*by chance*) = treffen
  she met him in the shopping centre = sie
  hat ihn im Einkaufszentrum getroffen
  they met in the street = sie trafen sich auf
  der Straße
- (*by arrangement*) = sich treffen mit
  (+ *dative*)
  I meet her every Tuesday = ich treffe mich
  jeden Dienstag mit ihr
  to meet again = sich wieder treffen
- (*get to know*) = kennen lernen
  she met him on holiday = sie hat ihn auf
  Urlaub kennen gelernt
  I've never met her = ich kenne sie nicht
- (*collect*) = abholen
  she's meeting me at the airport = sie holt
  mich vom Flughafen ab
- (*fulfil*) = erfüllen
  to meet a condition = eine Bedingung
  erfüllen
meet up
= sich treffen

meeting *noun*
- = (das) Treffen
- (*discussion*) = (die) Besprechung

melon *noun*
= (die) Melone

melt *verb*
= schmelzen (**!** *sein*)

member *noun*
= (das) Mitglied
  family member = (der/die) Angehörige

memory *noun*
- (*ability to remember*) = (das) Gedächtnis
- (*thing remembered*) = (die) Erinnerung
- (*of a computer*) = (der) Speicher
- memory stick = (der) Speicherstab

mend *verb*
  (*fix*) = reparieren
  (*by sewing*) = ausbessern

mental *adjective*
= geistig
  mental illness = (die) Geisteskrankheit

mention *verb*
= erwähnen
  thank you very much—don't mention it =
  herzlichen Dank—bitte

M

Measures

The metric system of measures is used in German.

Length

millimetre = (der) Millimeter (mm)	metre = (der) Meter (m)
centimetre = (der) Zentimeter (cm)	kilometre = (der) Kilometer (km)

Note that German uses a comma instead of a decimal point:

1 inch = 2,54 cm	1 yard = 91,44 cm
1 foot = 30,48 cm	1 mile = 1,61 km

how long is the rope? = wie lang ist das Seil?
it's 3 metres too long = es ist um drei Meter zu lang

Height

When talking about people:

how tall is he? = wie groß ist er?
he's six feet (1.83 metres) tall = er ist 1,83 groß, = er ist ein Meter dreiundachtzig groß
he's taller than me = er ist größer als ich
at a height of 2 metres = in zwei Meter Höhe

Distance

how far is it from Frankfurt to Munich? = wie weit is es von Frankfurt bis München?
it's about 300 kilometres = es sind ungefähr dreihundert Kilometer
the distance between the houses is 12 metres = die Entfernung zwischen den Häusern beträgt zwölf Meter
at a distance of 5 kilometres = in einer Entfernung von fünf Kilometern

Speed

kilometres per hour = Stundenkilometer (km/h)
he was doing 120 k.p.h. = er fuhr hundertzwanzig Stundenkilometer

Width/depth

how wide is it? = wie breit is es?
how deep is it? = wie tief ist es?
at a depth of 10 metres = in zehn Meter Tiefe

Weight

gram = (das) Gramm (g)	1 oz = 28,35 g
kilogram = (das) Kilogramm (kg)	1 lb = 453,6 g
kilo = (das) Kilo	
tonne = (die) Tonne (t)	

Note that a pound is translated by **ein Pfund**, but in German this is the equivalent of 500 grams (half a kilo).

When you are expressing a quantity of something in German, masculine and neuter nouns stay in the singular:

250 grams of cheese = zweihundertfünfzig Gramm Käse
3 pieces of cake = drei Stück Torte

But feminine nouns are in the plural:

2 bottles of coke = zwei Flaschen Cola

how much does it weigh? = wie viel wiegt es?
it weighs 3 pounds = es wiegt drei Pfund
to get 4 apples to the pound = vier Äpfel je Pfund bekommen

Capacity

litre = (der) Liter (l)
1 pint (British) = 0,568 Liter, (US) = 0,473 Liter
half a litre of mineral water = ein halber Liter Mineralwasser

Note that both **Liter** and **Meter** can be neuter as well as masculine.

Temperature

20 degrees Celsius or centigrade = zwanzig Grad Celsius

menu *noun*
- (*in a restaurant*) = (die) Speisekarte
- (*in computing*) = (das) Menü

mercy *noun*
= (die) Gnade
to be at someone's mercy = jemandem
ausgeliefert sein

mess *noun*
- (*untidiness*) = (das) Durcheinander
your room is in a mess = dein Zimmer ist
unordentlich
to make a mess on something = etwas
schmutzig machen
- (*difficult situation*) = Schwierigkeiten
(*plural*)
mess around
(*be silly*) = herumalbern
mess up
- (*botch*) = verpfuschen
- (*make dirty*) = schmutzig machen
(*untidy*) = in Unordnung bringen

message *noun*
= (die) Nachricht

messenger *noun*
= (der) Bote/(die) Botin

metal *noun*
= (das) Metall

meter *noun*
- (*for gas, electricity*) = (der) Zähler
- (*for parking*) = (die) Parkuhr
- (*US*) ▶metre

method *noun*
= (die) Methode

metre *noun* (*British*)
= (der) Meter ▶**Measures p. 270**

Mexico *noun*
= (das) Mexiko ▶**Countries p. 208**

microphone *noun*
= (das) Mikrofon

microscope *noun*
= (das) Mikroskop

microwave *noun*
(*oven*) = (der) Mikrowellenherd

midday *noun*
= (der) Mittag
at midday = mittags

middle *noun*
= (die) Mitte
in the middle of the night = mitten in der
Nacht
in the middle of August = Mitte August
to be in the middle of [writing a letter |
cooking ...] = gerade dabei sein [, einen Brief
zu schreiben | zu kochen ...]

Middle Ages *noun*
the Middle Ages = das Mittelalter

middle class
1 *noun*
= (der) Mittelstand
2 *adjective* = bürgerlich

midnight *noun*
= (die) Mitternacht

midwife *noun*
= (die) Hebamme

might *verb*

> **!** *The subjunctive of* **können** *is usually
> used to translate* **might**, *expressing a
> possibility or suggestion.*

- (*talking about a possibility*)
she might be right = sie könnte Recht
haben
will you come?—I might = kommst du?
—vielleicht
- (*referring to something that did not happen*)
she might have warned us = sie hätte uns
warnen können
- (*making a polite suggestion*)
you might try leaving a message = Sie
könnten versuchen, eine Nachricht zu
hinterlassen

mild *adjective*
- (*gentle*) = mild
- (*not serious*) = leicht
a mild infection = eine leichte Infektion

mile *noun*
= (die) Meile ▶**Measures p. 270**
it's miles too big = es ist viel zu groß

military *adjective*
= militärisch

milk
1 *noun* = (die) Milch
2 *verb* = melken

mill *noun*
= (die) Mühle

millennium *noun*
= (das) Jahrtausend

million *noun*
= (die) Million ▶**Numbers p. 282**
a million marks = eine Million Mark

millionaire *noun*
= (der) Millionär/(die) Millionärin

mince
1 *noun* (*British*) = (das) Hackfleisch
2 *verb* = durchdrehen

mind
1 *noun*
- (*a person's thoughts*) = (der) Verstand
to have a logical mind = logisch denken
to take someone's mind off things =
jemanden auf andere Gedanken bringen
to bear something in mind = etwas nicht
vergessen

- (*a person's opinions or attitudes*)
to make up one's mind to [live in Germany | change jobs | move …] = sich entschließen [, in Deutschland zu leben | , die Stelle zu wechseln | umzuziehen …]
I've made up my mind = ich habe mich entschieden
I've changed my mind = ich habe es mir anders überlegt
she knows her own mind = sie weiß, was sie will
2 *verb*
- (*when expressing an opinion*)
where would you like to sit?—I don't mind = wo willst du sitzen?–das ist mir egal
I don't mind where I sit = mir ist egal, wo ich sitze
she doesn't mind the heat = die Hitze macht ihr nichts aus
- (*in polite questions or requests*)
would you mind [closing the window | turning the radio down | waiting …]? = würden Sie bitte [das Fenster zumachen | warten | das Radio leiser stellen …]?
- (*be careful*) = aufpassen
mind the step! = Achtung Stufe!
mind you don't fall = pass auf, dass du nicht stolperst
- (*take care of*) = sich kümmern um (+ *accusative*)
- (*worry*)
never mind! = macht nichts!

mine¹ *pronoun*
= meiner/meine/meins

> **!** *Note that the pronoun agrees in number and gender with the noun it represents:* mine (*meaning the pencil*) is red = meiner (*der Bleistift*) ist rot; mine (*meaning the shoes*) are new = meine (*die Schuhe*) sind neu.

his shirt is white but mine is blue = sein Hemd ist weiß, aber meins ist blau
his sister is the same age as mine = seine Schwester ist genauso alt wie meine
a friend of mine = ein Freund von mir

mine²
1 *noun*
- (*for coal, metals*) = (das) Bergwerk
to work down the mines = unter Tage arbeiten
- (*explosive*) = (die) Mine
2 *verb* = abbauen
to mine for coal = Kohle abbauen

miner *noun*
= (der) Bergarbeiter

mineral water *noun*
= (das) Mineralwasser

minimum *adjective*
= Mindest-
to pay the minimum price = den Mindestpreis zahlen

minister *noun*
- (*in government*) = (der) Minister/ (die) Ministerin
- (*of religion*) = (der/die) Geistliche

minor
1 *adjective* = kleinerer/kleinere/kleineres
a minor injury = eine kleinere Verletzung
a minor role = eine Nebenrolle
2 *noun* = (der/die) Minderjährige

minority *noun*
= (die) Minderheit

mint *noun*
- (*herb*) = (die) Minze
- (*sweet*) = (der) *or* (das) Pfefferminzbonbon

minus *preposition*
= minus (+ *genitive*)
six minus two is four = sechs minus zwei ist vier
it's minus four degrees = es ist minus vier Grad

minute *noun*
- = (die) Minute ▶ **Time p. 331**
- (*moment*) = (der) Moment
in a minute = gleich
wait a minute! = einen Moment bitte!

minutes *noun*
= (das) Protokoll
to take the minutes = das Protokoll führen

miracle *noun*
= (das) Wunder

mirror *noun*
= (der) Spiegel

miserable *adjective*
- (*unhappy*) = unglücklich
to look miserable = unglücklich aussehen
to feel miserable = sich elend fühlen
- (*awful*)
the weather is miserable = das Wetter ist fürchterlich

miss *verb*
- (*fail to hit*) = nicht treffen
the stone missed his head = der Stein hat seinen Kopf nicht getroffen
to miss the target = das Ziel verfehlen
- (*fail to see*) = übersehen
- (*fail to take, catch*) = verpassen
to miss the train = den Zug verpassen
- (*fail to understand*) = nicht mitbekommen
- (*feel sad not to see*) = vermissen
I miss you = ich vermisse dich
- (*fail to go to*) = versäumen
to miss school = in der Schule fehlen

Miss *noun*
- = Fräulein, = Frau

> **!** *It is now usual to address adult women as* Frau, *whether or not they are married.*

good morning, Miss Jones (*to a girl*) = guten Morgen, Fräulein Jones, (*to a woman*) = guten Morgen, Frau Jones

- (*in a letter*)
  Dear Miss Jones (*to a girl*) = Sehr geehrtes Fräulein Jones, (*to a woman*) = Sehr geehrte Frau Jones ▶ **Letter-writing p. 262**

missing *adjective*
- = fehlend
  to be missing = fehlen
- (*lost*) = verschwunden
  he went missing yesterday = er wird seit gestern vermisst

mist *noun*
= (der) Nebel

mistake *noun*
= (der) Fehler
spelling mistake = (der) Rechtschreibfehler
by mistake = aus Versehen

misunderstand *verb*
= missverstehen

misunderstanding *noun*
= (das) Missverständnis

mix
1 *verb*
- (*put together*) = mischen
  to mix wine and water = Wein und Wasser mischen
  to mix cream into the sauce = Sahne in die Soße rühren
- (*go together*) = sich mischen
  oil doesn't mix with water = Öl mischt sich nicht mit Wasser
- (*be sociable*) = Kontakt mit anderen Menschen haben
2 *noun* = (die) Mischung
mix up
- (*get confused*) = durcheinander bringen
- (*mistake for*) = verwechseln
  I'm always mixing him up with his brother = ich verwechsele ihn immer mit seinem Bruder

mixture *noun*
= (die) Mischung

moan *verb*
- (*groan*) = stöhnen
- (*complain*) = jammern

mobile phone *noun*
= (das) Mobiltelefon, = (das) Handy

model *noun*
- (*of a train, building*) = (das) Modell
- (*fashion model*) = (das) Mannequin

modem *noun*
= (der) Modem

modern *adjective*
= modern

module *noun*
= (die) Unterrichtseinheit (*Educ*)

mole *noun*
- (*animal*) = (der) Maulwurf
- (*spot on the skin*) = (der) Leberfleck

moment *noun*
= (der) Moment
it will be ready in a moment = es ist gleich fertig
there's no one there at the moment = im Moment ist niemand da

Monday *noun*
= (der) Montag ▶ **Dates p. 213**

money *noun*
= (das) Geld

monkey *noun*
= (der) Affe

monster *noun*
= (das) Ungeheuer

month *noun*
= (der) Monat

monument *noun*
= (das) Denkmal

mood *noun*
= (die) Laune
to be in a good mood = gute Laune haben
to not be in the mood for working = keine Lust zum Arbeiten haben

moody *adjective*
= launisch

moon *noun*
= (der) Mond

moor
1 *noun* = (das) Moor
2 *verb* = festmachen

moped *noun*
= (das) Moped

moral *adjective*
= moralisch

morals *noun*
= (die) Moral

more
1 *adjective*
- = mehr

  | **!** Note that **mehr** *never changes.* |

  more [friends | time | work ...] = mehr [Freunde | Zeit | Arbeit ...]
  there's no more bread = es ist kein Brot mehr da
- (*in addition*) = noch
  he's buying two more tickets = er kauft noch zwei Karten
  more coffee? = noch etwas Kaffee?
2 *pronoun* = mehr
  to cost more = mehr kosten
3 *adverb*
- (*when comparing*)

  | **!** *The comparative of adjectives, such as* **more difficult**, *is formed in German by adding the ending* **-er** (**schwieriger**). |

  it is more interesting than I thought = es ist interessanter als ich dachte

M

Money

The German unit of currency is the euro (der Euro). There are 100 cents in a euro.

Note that when you are expressing an amount of money, the noun stays in the singular:

2 euros = zwei Euro (2 €)
a hundred euros = hundert Euro (100 €)
one euro ninety cents = ein Euro und neunzig Cent (1,90 €)
one euro ninety = ein Euro neunzig (1,90 €)

a 50 cent coin = ein Fünfcentstück
a 20 euro note = ein Zwanzigeuroschein

pound = (das) Pfund
£5 = fünf Pfund, = fünf englische Pfund
dollar = (der) Dollar
dollar bill = (der) Dollarschein

Until recently, the German unit of currency was the mark. There were 100 pfennigs in a mark.

one Deutschmark = eine Deutsche Mark (1,— DM)
50 pfennigs = fünfzig Pfennig (0,50 DM)

In Austria the unit of currency is the **Euro**, and in Switzerland it is the **Franken** (der).

Talking about money

how much is it? = wie viel kostet das?
the dress is 40 euros = das Kleid kostet 40 Euro
to pay cash = bar zahlen
1·6 euros to the pound = 1,6 Euro für ein Pfund
do you cash traveller's cheques? = lösen Sie Reiseschecks ein?
a £50 cheque = ein Scheck über fünfzig Pfund
two 1 euro stamps = zwei Briefmarken zu 1 Euro

---

* (*when talking about time*) = mehr
  he doesn't live here any more = er wohnt hier nicht mehr
* (*more often*) = öfter
  I'd like to go to the theatre more = ich würde gerne öfter ins Theater gehen
* (*other uses*)
  more and more = immer mehr
  more or less = mehr oder weniger

morning *noun*
= (der) Morgen
in the morning = am Morgen
3 o'clock in the morning = drei Uhr morgens
good morning! = guten Morgen!
this morning = heute Morgen
on Friday morning = am Freitagmorgen
tomorrow morning = morgen früh

mosquito *noun*
= (die) Mücke
(*tropical*) = (der) Moskito

most
1 *adjective*
* (*majority of*) = die meisten
  most shops are closed = die meisten Geschäfte haben zu

* (*largest amount of*) = der meiste/ die meiste/das meiste
  who has the most money? = wer hat das meiste Geld?
2 *pronoun*
* (*majority*) = die meisten
  most of the time = die meiste Zeit
* (*largest amount*) = das meiste
  he earns the most money = er verdient das meiste Geld
3 *adverb*
* (*when comparing*)

  ! *The superlative of adjectives, such as* **most difficult,** *is formed in German by adding the ending* -(e)st (der/die/das schwierigste).

  the most [expensive shop | difficult problem | interesting programme …] = das teuerste Geschäft | das schwierigste Problem | die interessanteste Sendung …]
* (*to the greatest degree*) = am meisten
  I drank most = ich habe am meisten getrunken
* (*very*) = äußerst
  a most enjoyable evening = ein äußerst angenehmer Abend
* (*other uses*)
  at most = höchstens
  most of all = am allermeisten

---

mostly adverb
= hauptsächlich

moth noun
= (der) Nachtfalter
(in clothes) = (die) Motte

mother noun
= (die) Mutter

mother-in-law noun
= (die) Schwiegermutter

motor noun
= (der) Motor

motorbike, motorcycle noun
= (das) Motorrad

motorcyclist noun
= (der) Motorradfahrer/
(die) Motorradfahrerin

motorist noun
= (der) Autofahrer/(die) Autofahrerin

motor racing noun
= (das) Autorennen

motorway noun (British)
= (die) Autobahn

mountain noun
= (der) Berg

mountain bike noun
= (das) Mountainbike

mountaineering noun
= (das) Bergsteigen

mourning noun
= (die) Trauer
to be in mourning = in Trauer sein

mouse noun
= (die) Maus

moustache (British) noun
= (der) Schnurrbart

mouth noun
• (of a person) = (der) Mund
to have a big mouth = einen großen Mund
haben*
• (of an animal) = (das) Maul
• (of a river) = (die) Mündung

mouth organ noun
= (die) Mundharmonika

move
1 verb
• (of a person) = sich bewegen
he can't move = er kann sich nicht
bewegen
don't move! = still halten!
• (of a vehicle) = fahren (**!** sein)
• (put elsewhere)
to move the furniture = die Möbel rücken
to move something somewhere else =
etwas woandershin tun

• (make a move) = bewegen
I can't move my leg = ich kann mein Bein
nicht bewegen
can you move your head to the side? =
kannst du deinen Kopf zur Seite tun?
• (touch emotionally) = rühren
he was deeply moved = er war sehr
gerührt
• (act) = handeln
to move fast = schnell handeln
• (change location) = umziehen (**!** sein)
to move to London = nach London
umziehen
to move house = umziehen (**!** sein)
2 noun
• (movement) = (die) Bewegung
to make a move = aufbrechen (**!** sein)
• (step, decision) = (der) Schritt
to make the first move = den ersten Schritt
tun
• (change of location) = (der) Umzug
• (in a game) = (der) Zug
it's your move = du bist am Zug
move around
• (travel around) = unterwegs sein
• (put elsewhere) = herumräumen
to move the furniture around = umräumen
move away
• (live elsewhere) = wegziehen (**!** sein)
• (make a movement away) = wegrücken
(**!** sein)
to move away from the window = vom
Fenster wegrücken
move back
= zurückrücken (**!** sein)
(of a vehicle) = zurückfahren (**!** sein)
move forward
= vorrücken (**!** sein)
(of a vehicle) = vorwärts fahren (**!** sein)
move in
= einziehen (**!** sein)
to move in with friends = bei Freunden
einziehen
move off
= sich in Bewegung setzen
(of a vehicle) = losfahren (**!** sein)
move out
= ausziehen (**!** sein)
move over
= zur Seite rücken (**!** sein)

movement noun
= (die) Bewegung
a movement of the hand = eine
Handbewegung
the women's movement = die
Frauenbewegung

movie noun (US)
= (der) Film
at the movies = im Kino

mow verb
= mähen

MP noun (British)
= (der/die) Abgeordnete

M

Mr *noun*
* = (der) Herr
   good morning, Mr Jones = guten Morgen,
      Herr Jones
   we are waiting for Mr Brown's call = wir
      warten auf Herrn Browns Anruf
* (*in a letter*)
   Dear Mr Jones = Sehr geehrter Herr Jones
   ▶Letter-writing p. 262

Mrs *noun*
* = (die) Frau
   good morning, Mrs White = guten Morgen,
      Frau White, (*very formal*) = guten
      Morgen, gnädige Frau
* (*in a letter*)
   Dear Mrs Black = Sehr geehrte Frau Black
   ▶Letter-writing p. 262

Ms *noun*
   = (die) Frau
   Dear Ms Jones = Sehr geehrte Frau Jones
   ▶Letter-writing p. 262

much
1 *adverb*
* (*a lot*) = viel
   he doesn't read much = er liest nicht viel
   I'd much rather stay here = ich bleibe viel
      lieber hier
   she earns twice as much as me = sie
      verdient doppelt so viel wie ich
* (*often*) = oft
   they don't go to the cinema much = sie
      gehen nicht oft ins Kino
* (*when used with* **very, too, so**) = sehr
   he misses her very much = er vermisst sie
      sehr
   I don't like driving very much = ich fahre
      nicht sehr gerne Auto
2 *pronoun* = viel

> **!** Note that viel *never changes.*

   I don't need much = ich brauche nicht viel
   as much as you like = so viel du willst
   how much is it? = wie viel kostet es?
   not too much = nicht zu viel
3 *adjective* = viel
   I haven't got much time = ich habe nicht
      viel Zeit
   we have too much work = wir haben zu
      viel Arbeit

mud *noun*
   = (der) Schlamm

mudguard *noun*
   (*on a bike*) = (das) Schutzblech

mug
1 *noun* = (der) Becher
2 *verb* = überfallen
   to be mugged = überfallen und beraubt
      werden (**!** *sein*)

mule *noun*
   = (das) Maultier

multiply *verb*
   (*in maths*) = multiplizieren
   2 multiplied by 3 is 6 = drei mal zwei ist
      sechs

mum *noun*
   = (die) Mutti

mumble *verb*
   = murmeln

mummy *noun*
* (*mother*) = (die) Mama
* (*body*) = (die) Mumie

murder
1 *noun* = (der) Mord
   to be accused of murder = des Mordes
      beschuldigt werden
2 *verb* = ermorden
3 *adjective* = Mord-
   murder suspect = (der/die) Mordverdächtige

murderer *noun*
   = (der) Mörder/(die) Mörderin

muscle *noun*
   = (der) Muskel

museum *noun*
   = (das) Museum

mushroom *noun*
   = (der) Pilz

music *noun*
* = (die) Musik
* (*score*) = Noten (*plural*)

musical
1 *adjective* = musikalisch
2 *noun* = (das) Musical

musical instrument *noun*
   = (das) Musikinstrument

musician *noun*
   = (der) Musiker/(die) Musikerin

Muslim
1 *noun* = (der) Moslem/(die) Moslime
2 *adjective* = moslemisch

mussel *noun*
   = (die) Muschel

must *verb*
* = müssen, (*with a negative*) = dürfen
   we must go = wir müssen gehen
   we mustn't be late = wir dürfen nicht zu
      spät kommen
* (*when assuming something is true*) =
      müssen
   you must be Peter's sister = du musst
      Peters Schwester sein

mustache (*US*) ▶moustache

mustard *noun*
   = (der) Senf

mutton *noun*
   = (das) Hammelfleisch

my *adjective*
= mein

> ! *Note that* mein *changes its endings in the same way as* ein.

they don't like my dog = sie mögen meinen Hund nicht

myself *pronoun*
* *(when translated by a reflexive verb in German)* = mich
  I've cut myself = ich habe mich geschnitten
* *(reflexive dative pronoun)* = mir
  I hurt myself = ich habe mir wehgetan
  I thought to myself = ich habe mir gedacht
* *(used for emphasis)* = selbst
  I told them myself = ich habe es ihnen selbst gesagt
  all by myself = ganz allein

mysterious *adjective*
= rätselhaft

mystery *noun*
* *(puzzle)* = (das) Rätsel
* *(secret)* = (das) Geheimnis

Nn

nail
1 *noun*
  = (der) Nagel
2 *verb* = nageln
  to nail a picture to the wall = ein Bild an die Wand nageln

nail varnish *noun*
= (der) Nagellack

naked *adjective*
= nackt

name
1 *noun*
* *(of a person)* = (der) Name
  what's your name? = wie heißt du?,
    (polite) = wie heißen Sie?
  my name is Sam = ich heiße Sam
* *(of a book, film)* = (der) Titel
2 *verb* = nennen

napkin *noun*
= (die) Serviette

nappy *noun* *(British)*
= (die) Windel

narrow
1 *adjective*
* = schmal
  a narrow road = eine schmale Straße
* *(restricted)* = eng
  the shoe is too narrow = der Schuh ist zu eng
2 *verb*
* *(become less wide)* = sich verengen
* *(reduce)* = verkleinern
  to narrow the gap = den Abstand verkleinern

narrow-minded *adjective*
= engstirnig

nasty *adjective*
* *(spiteful)* = gemein
  to be nasty to someone = gemein zu jemandem sein
* *(unpleasant)* = scheußlich
  a nasty smell = ein scheußlicher Geruch
* *(serious)* = schlimm
  a nasty accident = ein schlimmer Unfall

nation *noun*
* *(state)* = (die) Nation
* *(people)* = (das) Volk

national
1 *adjective* = national
  a national newspaper = eine überregionale Zeitung
  a national strike = ein landesweiter Streik
2 *noun*
  (citizen) = (der) Staatsbürger/
    (die) Staatsbürgerin

national anthem *noun*
= (die) Nationalhymne

nationality *noun*
= (die) Nationalität

native
1 *adjective*
  my native land = mein Heimatland
  his native language = seine Muttersprache
  she is a native German speaker = Deutsch ist ihre Muttersprache
2 *noun*
  (person born in a place) =
    (der/die) Eingeborene
  (local inhabitant) = (der/die) Einheimische

natural *adjective*
= natürlich

naturally *adverb*
= natürlich
  naturally, we're delighted = natürlich freuen wir uns

nature *noun*
* = (die) Natur
  to protect nature = die Natur schützen
  to be suspicious by nature = von Natur aus misstrauisch sein
* *(sort, character)* = (die) Art

naughty *adjective*
= unartig

navel *noun*
= (der) Nabel

N

navy *noun*
= (die) Marine

navy blue *adjective*
= marineblau ▶Colours p. 204

near
1 *preposition* = nahe an (+ *dative*)
the cinema is near the station = das Kino
ist nahe am Bahnhof
! *Note that* am *is the shortened form of* an
dem.

2 *adverb* = nahe, = nah✱

! *Note that in spoken German* nahe *is
often shortened to* nah.

they live quite near = sie wohnen ganz
nah✱
near by = nicht weit weg
3 *adjective* = nahe, = nah✱

! *The superlative of* nah(e) *is* der/die/das
nächste.

the nearest supermarket is just round the
corner = der nächste Supermarkt ist
gleich um die Ecke
in the near future = demnächst

nearby *adverb*
= in der Nähe
is there a chemist nearby? = gibt es eine
Drogerie hier in der Nähe?

nearly *adverb*
= fast
we're nearly there = wir sind fast da
I nearly screamed = ich hätte fast
geschrien

neat *adjective*
• (*tidy*) = ordentlich
her room is always very neat = ihr Zimmer
ist immer sehr ordentlich
neat handwriting = eine saubere
Handschrift
• (*describing a person's looks*) = adrett
• (*clever*) = geschickt
to find a neat solution = eine geschickte
Lösung finden

necessary *adjective*
= nötig, = notwendig
to do no more than is necessary = nicht
mehr tun, als nötig ist

neck *noun*
• (*of a person*) = (der) Hals
back of the neck = (der) Nacken
• (*of a garment*) = (der) Kragen

necklace *noun*
= (die) Halskette

need
1 *verb*

• (*have to*) = müssen, (*with a negative*) =
brauchen
to need to do something = etwas tun
müssen
I need to know = ich muss es wissen
you don't need to ask for permission = du
brauchst nicht um Erlaubnis zu fragen
• (*want*) = brauchen
to need [money | friends | time ...] = [Geld |
Freunde | Zeit ...] brauchen
2 *noun*
there's no need = das ist nicht nötig
there's no need to worry = du brauchst dir
keine Sorgen zu machen

needle *noun*
= (die) Nadel

negative
1 *adjective* = negativ
to have a negative influence on someone
= jemanden negativ beeinflussen
2 *noun*
(*of a photo*) = (das) Negativ

neglect *verb*
= vernachlässigen

negotiations *noun*
= Verhandlungen (*plural*)

neighbor (*US*), **neighbour** (*British*)
noun
= (der) Nachbar/(die) Nachbarin

neither
1 *conjunction*
• neither ... nor = weder ... noch
she speaks neither German nor English =
sie spricht weder Deutsch noch Englisch
• (*nor*) = auch nicht
I can't sleep—neither can I = ich kann
nicht schlafen—ich auch nicht
you don't like her and neither do I = du
magst sie nicht, und ich mag sie auch
nicht
2 *adjective* = keiner der beiden/keine der
beiden/keins der beiden
neither book is interesting = keins der
beiden Bücher ist interessant
3 *pronoun* = keiner von beiden/keine von
beiden/keins von beiden
neither of them is coming = keiner von
beiden kommt
neither of us = keiner von uns beiden

nephew *noun*
= (der) Neffe

nerve *noun*
• = (der) Nerv
• (*courage*) = (der) Mut

nervous *adjective*
• (*anxious*) = ängstlich
to be nervous of *or* about something =
Angst vor etwas (*dative*) haben
to be nervous about making a mistake =
Angst davor haben, einen Fehler zu
machen
• (*as a personality*) = nervös

nest *noun*
= (das) Nest

net
1 *noun*
= (das) Netz
2 *adjective* = netto, = Netto-
net income = (das) Nettoeinkommen

Netherlands *noun*
the Netherlands = die Niederlande (*plural*)
▶Countries p. 208

nettle *noun*
= (die) Nessel

network *noun*
= (das) Netz

neutral
1 *adjective* = neutral
2 *noun*
(*when driving*) to be in neutral = im
Leerlauf sein

never *adverb*
• (*not ever*) = nie, niemals
never again = nie wieder
• (*used for emphasis*) = noch nie
I never knew that = das habe ich noch nie
gewusst
• never mind = macht nichts

nevertheless *adverb*
= trotzdem

new *adjective*
= neu

news *noun*
• (*new information*) = (die) Nachricht
piece of news = (die) Neuigkeit
what's the latest news? = was gibt es
Neues?
we haven't had any news from her for
weeks = wir haben schon wochenlang
nichts mehr von ihr gehört
• (*on TV, radio*) = Nachrichten (*plural*)
I saw it on the news = ich habe es in den
Nachrichten gesehen

newsagent *noun*
= (der) Zeitungshändler

newsflash *noun*
= (die) Kurzmeldung

newspaper *noun*
= (die) Zeitung
the Sunday newspaper = die
Sonntagszeitung

newsreader *noun*
= (der) Nachrichtensprecher/
(die) Nachrichtensprecherin

New Year *noun*
= (das) Neujahr
Happy New Year! = ein gutes neues Jahr!

New Year's (*US*), **New Year's Day**
(*British*) *noun*
= (das) Neujahr

New Year's Eve *noun*
= (das) Silvester

New Zealand *noun*
= (das) Neuseeland ▶Countries p. 208

next
1 *adjective*
• = nächster/nächste/nächstes
she's leaving next Friday = sie fährt
nächsten Freitag ab
• (*in a sequence*)
who's next? = wer ist der Nächste?
I'm next = ich bin an der Reihe, = ich bin
dran✱
next! = der Nächste!/die Nächste!
2 *adverb*
• (*in the past*) = danach
what happened next? = was geschah
danach?
• (*now*) = als nächstes
what shall we do next? = was machen wir
als Nächstes?
• (*in the future*) = das nächste Mal
when you next go to Paris, give Gary a call
= wenn du nächstes Mal nach Paris
fährst, ruf Gary an
• next to = neben (+ *dative or accusative*)

> ! Note that neben is followed by a noun in
> the dative when position is described.
> The accusative follows when there is
> movement towards something.

we live next to the school = wir wohnen
neben der Schule
she sat down next to him = sie hat sich
neben ihn gesetzt
3 *pronoun*
she was (the) next to be examined = sie
wurde als Nächste geprüft
the week after next = übernächste Woche

next door *adverb*
= nebenan

nice *adjective*
• (*enjoyable*) = schön
it's nice to be able to relax = es ist schön,
wenn man sich entspannen kann
have a nice day! = viel Spaß!
• (*kind*) = nett
to be nice to someone = zu jemandem nett
sein
• (*attractive*) = hübsch
to look very nice (*of a woman*) = sehr
hübsch sein, (*of a man*) = gut aussehen
• (*tasty*) = gut

nickname *noun*
= (der) Spitzname

niece *noun*
= (die) Nichte

night *noun*
• (*as opposed to day*) = (die) Nacht
he's staying the night with friends = er
bleibt über Nacht bei Freunden
I couldn't sleep last night = ich konnte
heute Nacht nicht schlafen
to work at night = nachts arbeiten

N

• (*evening*) = (der) Abend
  he arrived last night = er kam gestern
  Abend an

nightdress *noun*
  = (das) Nachthemd

nightmare *noun*
  = (der) Alptraum

nil *noun*
  (*in sport*) = null
  to win one nil = eins zu null gewinnen

nine *adjective*
  = neun ▶**Numbers p. 282**

nineteen *adjective*
  = neunzehn ▶**Numbers p. 282**

ninety *adjective*
  = neunzig ▶**Numbers p. 282**

ninth *adjective*
  = neunter/neunte/neuntes
    ▶**Numbers p. 282,** ▶**Dates p. 213**

no
1 *adjective*
• (*not any*) = kein

  > ! *Note that* **kein** *changes its endings in
  > the same way as* **ein**.

  we have no money = wir haben kein Geld
  it's no use = das hat keinen Zweck
  I've no idea = ich habe keine Ahnung
• (*forbidden*)
  no [parking | smoking | dogs] = [Parken |
  Rauchen | Hunde] verboten
2 *adverb*
• = nein
  to say no = nein sagen
• (*not*) = nicht
  he no longer works here = er arbeitet nicht
  mehr hier

nobody ▶ no one

nod *verb*
  = nicken
  to nod one's head = mit dem Kopf nicken

noise *noun*
• (*loud*) = (der) Lärm
  don't make too much noise = sei nicht zu
  laut
• (*any sound*) = (das) Geräusch

noisy *adjective*
  = laut

non-alcoholic *adjective*
  = alkoholfrei

none *pronoun*
  = keiner/keine/keins
  **none of [us | you | them …] can speak
  Russian** = keiner von [uns | euch |
  ihnen …] spricht Russisch
  have you got any money?—none at all =
  hast du Geld?—überhaupt keins
  none of it is true = nichts davon ist wahr
  there's none left = es ist nichts mehr übrig

nonsense *noun*
  = (der) Unsinn

non-smoker *noun*
  = (der) Nichtraucher/(die) Nichtraucherin

noon *noun*
  = (der) Mittag
  at noon = um zwölf (Uhr mittags)

no one *pronoun*
  = niemand
  no one saw him = niemand hat ihn
  gesehen

nor *conjunction*
• **neither … nor** = weder … noch
  she speaks neither German nor English =
  sie spricht weder Deutsch noch Englisch
• = auch nicht
  nor do we = wir auch nicht

normal
1 *adjective* = normal
  at the normal time = zur normalen Zeit
2 *noun*
  to get back to normal = sich normalisieren

normally *adverb*
• (*usually*) = normalerweise
• (*properly*) = normal

north
1 *noun* = (der) Norden
  to the north of London = nördlich von
  London
2 *adjective* = nördlich, = Nord-
  a north wind = ein Nordwind
3 *adverb* = nach Norden

North America *noun*
  = (das) Nordamerika ▶**Countries p. 208**

Northern Ireland *noun*
  = (das) Nordirland ▶**Countries p. 208**

Norway *noun*
  = (das) Norwegen ▶**Countries p. 208**

Norwegian
1 *noun*
• (*person*) = (der) Norweger/(die) Norwegerin
• (*language*) = (das) Norwegisch
2 *adjective* = norwegisch ▶**Countries p. 208**

nose *noun*
  = (die) Nase
  to nose around = herumschnüffeln

nostril *noun*
• (*of a person*) = (das) Nasenloch
• (*of a horse*) = (die) Nüster

not *adverb*
  = nicht
  hasn't he phoned you? = hat er dich nicht
  angerufen?
  we won't need a car = wir brauchen kein
  Auto
  not a chance = keine Möglichkeit
  not at all = überhaupt nicht, = gar nicht
  thanks a lot—not at all = vielen Dank—gern
  geschehen

note
1 *noun*
- (*written comment*) = (die) Notiz
  to take notes = sich (*dative*) Notizen machen
  to make a note of an address = sich (*dative*) eine Adresse notieren
- (*short letter*) = (der) kurze Brief, = (der) Zettel✱
  I left you a note = ich hab dir einen Zettel dagelassen✱
  to write a quick note = ein paar Zeilen schreiben
- (*British: banknote*) = (der) Schein
  a £10 note = ein Zehnpfundschein
- (*in music*) = (die) Note
2 *verb*
- (*notice*) = bemerken
- (*pay attention to*) = beachten
- (*write down*) = notieren
note down
= sich (*dative*) notieren

notebook *noun*
= (das) Notizbuch

nothing
1 *pronoun* = nichts
  to have nothing to do with something = nichts mit etwas (*dative*) zu tun haben
  there's nothing left = es ist nichts mehr übrig
2 *adverb*
  it's nothing like as difficult as Russian = es ist längst nicht so schwer wie Russisch
3 (*other uses*)
  it's caused me nothing but trouble = es hat mir nur Ärger gemacht
  for nothing = umsonst

notice
1 *verb* = bemerken
  I noticed he wasn't wearing glasses = ich bemerkte, dass er keine Brille trug
2 *noun*
- (*written sign*) = (der) Anschlag
- (*public announcement*) = (die) Bekanntmachung
- (*advance warning*) = (die) Ankündigung
  without any notice = ohne irgendwelche Ankündigung
  to be cancelled at short notice = kurzfristig abgesagt werden
  to hand in one's notice = kündigen
  to give someone notice = jemandem kündigen
- (*announcement of birth, marriage, death*) = (die) Anzeige
- (*attention*) = (die) Beachtung
  to take notice of something = etwas beachten
  to take no notice of someone = keine Notiz von jemandem nehmen

noticeable *adjective*
= bemerkenswert

novel
1 *noun* = (der) Roman
2 *adjective* = neu

November *noun*
= (der) November ▶Dates p. 213

now *adverb*
= jetzt
  do it right now = mach es sofort
  it hasn't been a problem until now = bis jetzt war es kein Problem
  I should have told you before now = ich hätte es dir vorher sagen sollen
  he left just now = er ist gerade gegangen
  between now and next Monday = bis nächsten Montag
  now and again = hin und wieder
  it's now or never = jetzt oder nie

nowhere *adverb*
= nirgends
  there is nowhere to [shop | change | eat ...] = man kann [nirgends einkaufen | sich nirgends umziehen | nirgends essen ...]

nuclear *adjective*
= Kern-
  nuclear energy = (die) Kernenergie
  nuclear deterrent = (das) nukleare Abschreckungsmittel

nude
1 *adjective* = nackt
2 *noun* = (der/die) Nackte
  in the nude = nackt

nuisance *noun*
- (*annoying person*) = (der) Quälgeist✱
  stop making a nuisance of yourself = hör auf, alle verrückt zu machen
- (*annoying thing*) = (die) Plage
  the flies are a real nuisance = die Fliegen sind eine richtige Plage
  what a nuisance = wie ärgerlich

number
1 *noun*
- (*figure*) = (die) Zahl
  (*of a house, bus, telephone*) = (die) Nummer
  to dial the wrong number = sich verwählen
- (*quantity*) = (die) Anzahl
  we have received a number of applications = wir haben eine Anzahl Bewerbungen erhalten
  a number of [people | things | books ...] = einige [Leute | Dinge | Bücher ...]
  for a number of reasons = aus mehreren Gründen
  any number of = beliebig viele
- (*performance*) = (die) Nummer
2 *verb* = nummerieren
  the seats are numbered = die Plätze sind nummeriert

numberplate *noun* (*British*)
= (das) Nummernschild

N

Numbers

1	eins	1st	erster / erste / erstes
2	zwei	2nd	zweiter / zweite / zweites
3	drei	3rd	dritter / dritte / drittes
4	vier	4th	vierter / vierte / viertes
5	fünf	5th	fünfter / fünfte / fünftes
6	sechs	6th	sechster / sechste / sechstes
7	sieben	7th	siebter / siebte / siebtes
8	acht	8th	achter / achte / achtes
9	neun	9th	neunter / neunte / neuntes
10	zehn	10th	zehnter / zehnte / zehntes
11	elf	11th	elfter / elfte / elftes
12	zwölf	12th	zwölfter / zwölfte / zwölftes
13	dreizehn	13th	dreizehnter / dreizehnte / dreizehntes
14	vierzehn	14th	vierzehnter / vierzehnte / vierzehntes
15	fünfzehn	15th	fünfzehnter / fünfzehnte / fünfzehntes
16	sechzehn	16th	sechzehnter / sechzehnte / sechzehntes
17	siebzehn	17th	siebzehnter / siebzehnte / siebzehntes
18	achtzehn	18th	achtzehnter / achtzehnte / achtzehntes
19	neunzehn	19th	neunzehnter / neunzehnte / neunzehntes
20	zwanzig	20th	zwanzigster / zwanzigste / zwanzigstes
21	einundzwanzig	21st	einundzwanzigster / einundzwanzigste / einundzwanzigstes
30	dreißig	30th	dreißigster / dreißigste / dreißigstes
40	vierzig	40th	vierzigster / vierzigste / vierzigstes
50	fünfzig	50th	fünfzigster / fünfzigste / fünfzigstes
60	sechzig	60th	sechzigster / sechzigste / sechzigstes
70	siebzig	70th	siebzigster / siebzigste / siebzigstes
80	achtzig	80th	achtzigster / achtzigste / achtzigstes
90	neunzig	90th	neunzigster / neunzigste / neunzigstes
100	hundert	100th	hundertster / hundertste / hundertstes

In German, the endings of the ordinal numbers (*erster / erste / erstes*, etc.) change according to the gender and case of the noun which they describe:

the fourth goal = das vierte Tor   *in the third week* = in der dritten Woche

With large numbers, full stops or spaces are used instead of the English commas:

1,000,000 = 1.000.000 *or* 1 000 000

Ordinal numbers are usually written as figures followed by a full stop:

3rd = 3.

Fractions

When used as nouns, fractions have a capital letter:

half = (die) Hälfte   *fifth* = (das) Fünftel
third = (das) Drittel   *eighth* = (das) Achtel
quarter = (das) Viertel   *two thirds* = zwei Drittel

I've paid a third of the amount = ich habe ein Drittel des Betrages gezahlt

They are written with a small letter when used as an adjective:

$\frac{1}{2}$ = ein halb $\frac{5}{8}$ = fünf achtel
$1\frac{1}{2}$ = eineinhalb $\frac{2}{3}$ = zwei drittel

half a litre of milk = ein halber Liter Milch

Decimals

Note that German uses a comma instead of a decimal point:

0.1 (nought point one) = 0,1 (null Komma eins)
1.43 (one point four three) = 1,43 (eins Komma vier drei)

Calculations in German

4 + 5 = 9 (vier und fünf ist neun)   10 × 3 = 30 (zehn mal drei ist dreißig)
10 − 3 = 7 (zehn weniger drei ist sieben)   30 : 3 = 10 (dreißig geteilt durch drei ist zehn)

Note that the German division sign is a colon.

nurse
1 *noun* = (die) Krankenschwester
(*male*) = (der) Pfleger
2 *verb*
- (*look after*) = pflegen
- (*breast-feed*) = stillen

nursery *noun*
- (*children's room*) = (das) Kinderzimmer
- (*day nursery*) = (die) Kindertagesstätte
- (*for plants*) = (die) Gärtnerei

nursery school *noun*
= (der) Kindergarten

nursing home *noun*
= (das) Pflegeheim

nut *noun*
- (*for eating*) = (die) Nuss
- (*for use with a bolt*) = (die) Mutter

Oo

oak *noun*
= (die) Eiche

oar *noun*
= (das) Ruder

obedient *adjective*
= gehorsam

obey *verb*
= gehorchen (+ *dative*)
to obey someone = jemandem gehorchen
to obey the law = sich an das Gesetz halten

object
1 *noun*
- (*thing*) = (der) Gegenstand
- (*aim*) = (der) Zweck
2 *verb* = Einwände erheben
to object to something = Einwände gegen
etwas (*accusative*) erheben
no one objected = keiner war dagegen

objection *noun*
= (der) Einwand

oblige *verb*
- (*have to*)
to be obliged to give up work = gezwungen
sein, die Arbeit aufzugeben
- (*be helpful*)
to oblige someone = jemandem einen
Gefallen tun
- (*be grateful*)
to be obliged to someone for something =
jemandem für etwas (*accusative*) sehr
verbunden sein

obscene *adjective*
= obszön

obsessed *adjective*
= besessen

obsession *noun*
- = (die) Besessenheit
- (*persistent idea*) = (die) fixe Idee

obstacle *noun*
= (das) Hindernis

obstinate *adjective*
= starrsinnig

obstruct *verb*
- (*impede*) = behindern
to obstruct a player = einen Spieler
behindern
- (*block*) = versperren
to obstruct someone's view = jemandem
die Sicht versperren

obtain *verb*
= erhalten

obvious *adjective*
= eindeutig

obviously
1 *adverb* = offensichtlich
he obviously needs help = er braucht
offensichtlich Hilfe
2 *interjection* = natürlich!

occasion *noun*
= (die) Gelegenheit
on special occasions = zu besonderen
Gelegenheiten
on a number of occasions = mehrmals

occasionally *adverb*
= gelegentlich

occupy *verb*
- (*live in*) = bewohnen
- (*take*) = besetzen
the seats are occupied = die Plätze sind
besetzt
- (*keep busy*) = beschäftigen
to keep oneself occupied = sich
beschäftigen
- (*conquer*) = einnehmen

occur *verb*
- (*take place*) = sich ergeben
- (*cross someone's mind*)
to occur to someone = jemandem
einfallen (**!** sein)

ocean *noun*
= (der) Ozean

o'clock *adverb*
at five o'clock = um fünf Uhr ▶ Time p. 331

October *noun*
= (der) Oktober ▶ Dates p. 213

octopus *noun*
= (der) Tintenfisch

odd *adjective*
- (*strange*) = seltsam

O

- (*not matching*) = einzeln
  odd socks/gloves = nicht zusammengehörende Socken/Handschuhe
  the odd one out = die Ausnahme
- **an odd number** = eine ungerade Zahl

odor (*US*), **odour** (*British*) *noun*
= (der) Geruch

of *preposition*
- von (+ *dative*)

> **!** Note that instead of translating of with von, the genitive case can be used.

the father of the child = der Vater des Kindes *or* der Vater von dem Kind
the names of the pupils = die Namen der Schüler
- (*with quantities*)
  a kilo of potatoes = ein Kilo Kartoffeln
  a child of ten = ein zehnjähriges Kind

> **!** Note that davon can be used to translate it or of them when talking about things, but not when referring to people.

half of it = die Hälfte davon
I didn't have any of it = ich habe nichts davon bekommen
how many of them? (*of things*) = wie viele davon?, (*of people*) = wie viele von ihnen?
there are six of us = wir sind zu sechst
some of us = einige von uns
the whole of the town = die ganze Stadt
- (*made from*) = aus (+ *dative*)
  it's made of plastic = es ist aus Plastik

off
1 *adverb*
- (*leaving*)
  to be off = gehen (**!** *sein*), (*in a vehicle*) = fahren (**!** *sein*)
  I'm off now = ich gehe jetzt
  they are off to Italy tomorrow = sie fahren morgen nach Italien
- (*away*)
  the coast is a long way off = die Küste ist weit entfernt
  summer isn't far off now = bis zum Sommer ist es jetzt nicht mehr lange hin
- (*free*)
  to take a day off = sich (*dative*) einen Tag frei nehmen
  to have a day off = einen freien Tag haben
- (*on an appliance*)
  on/off = ein/aus
- (*turned off*)
  the lights are off = das Licht ist aus
  the water is off = das Wasser ist abgestellt
- (*cancelled*) = abgesagt
  the match is off = das Spiel ist abgesagt worden

2 *adjective*
  the milk is off = die Milch ist sauer
  the meat is off = das Fleisch ist schlecht
3 *preposition*
- (*near*)
  there's a florist just off the station = ganz in der Nähe vom Bahnhof ist ein Blumengeschäft
  the kitchen is just off the dining room = die Küche ist direkt neben dem Esszimmer
- (*not interested in*)
  to be off something = etwas (*accusative*) leid sein
  he's off his food = er hat keinen Appetit

> **!** Note that off is often used with verbs—fall off, get off, turn off, etc. You will find translations for these under the entries fall, get, turn, etc.

offence *noun* (*British*)
- (*crime*) = (die) Straftat
- (*insult*) = (die) Beleidigung
  to take offence = beleidigt sein

offend *verb*
= beleidigen

offense (*US*) ▶offence

offer
1 *verb* = anbieten
  to offer someone a job = jemandem eine Stelle anbieten
  to offer to [water the flowers | mind the children | feed the cat …] = anbieten, [die Blumen zu gießen | auf die Kinder aufzupassen | die Katze zu füttern …]
2 *noun* = (das) Angebot
  on special offer = im Sonderangebot

office *noun*
= (das) Büro

office hours *noun*
= Dienststunden (*plural*)

officer *noun*
- (*in the army*) = (der) Offizier
- (*in the police*) = (der) Beamte/(die) Beamtin

office worker *noun*
= (der/die) Büroangestellte

official
1 *adjective* = offiziell
2 *noun* = (der) Repräsentant/(die) Repräsentantin

often *adverb*
= oft

oil
1 *noun* = (das) Öl
2 *verb* = ölen

oil rig *noun*
= (die) Bohrinsel

okay, OK
1 *adjective*
- = in Ordnung, = okay✖

---

that's OK by me = mir ist es recht
is it OK if I come a little later? = ist es okay,
wenn ich etwas später komme?✱
• (when talking about health)
he's OK at the moment = es geht ihm im
Moment ganz gut
how are you?—OK = wie gehts?—ganz gut
2 interjection = gut!, = okay!✱

old adjective
• = alt
old people = alte Leute
how old are you? = wie alt bist du?
he's 40 years old = er ist vierzig Jahre alt
to get old = alt werden (! sein)
• (previous)
that's my old address = das ist meine alte
Adresse
in the old days = früher

old-fashioned adjective
= altmodisch

old people's home noun
= (das) Altersheim

olive noun
= (die) Olive

olive oil noun
= (das) Olivenöl

Olympic Games noun
the Olympic Games = die Olympischen Spiele

on
1 preposition
• (showing location) = auf (+ dative or
accusative)
(on a vertical surface) = an (+ dative or
accusative)

> ! Note that auf and an are followed by a
> noun in the dative when position is
> described. The accusative follows when
> there is movement towards something.

put the cups on the table = stelle die Tassen
auf den Tisch
I like the picture on the wall = mir gefällt
das Bild an der Wand
on the right/left = rechts/links
• (when talking about transport)
to travel on the coach = mit dem Bus
fahren (! sein)
the baggage is already on the plane = das
Gepäck ist schon im Flugzeug
• (about) = über (+ accusative)
a book on drugs = ein Buch über Drogen
• (when talking about time) = an (+ dative)
on the 6th of December = am sechsten
Dezember

> ! Note that am is a shortened form of an
> dem.

• on television = im Fernsehen
on tape = auf Band
• (using)
to be on antibiotics = Antibiotika nehmen

• (earning)
to be on a low income = wenig verdienen
I couldn't live on it = davon könnte ich
nicht leben
2 adverb
• (when talking about clothes)
to have a [coat | sweater | bra ...] on = einen
[Mantel | Pullover | BH ...] anhaben
to have a hat on = einen Hut aufhaben
• (on an appliance)
on/off = ein/aus
• (turned on)
why are the lights on? = warum ist das
Licht an?
• (showing)
is there anything good on? (TV) = gibt es
irgendwas Gutes im Fernsehen?
what's on at the cinema? = was läuft im
Kino?
• (when talking about time)
from Tuesday on = ab Dienstag
from then on = von da an
a little later on = etwas später
• (when talking about distance)
a little further on = etwas weiter weg
• (other uses)
I've nothing on tonight = ich habe heute
Abend nichts vor
it's on me = das spendiere ich

> ! Note that on is often used with
> verbs—count on, keep on, turn on, etc.
> You will find translations for these under
> the entries count, keep, turn, etc.

O

once
1 adverb
• (one time) = einmal
once a day = einmal täglich
once and for all = ein für alle Mal
at once (immediately) = sofort, (at the same
time) = gleichzeitig
• (in the old days) = früher
(in fairy tales) once upon a time there was
= es war einmal
2 conjunction = sobald
it will be easier once we have found a
house = es wird einfacher sein, sobald
wir ein Haus gefunden haben

one
1 noun
(number) = (die) Eins ▶Numbers p. 282
2 adjective
• (when counting) = eins, (with a noun) = ein
one child = ein Kind
one day = eines Tages
one of my colleagues = einer meiner
Kollegen
• (only) = einzig
it's the one thing that annoys me = das ist
das Einzige, das mich ärgert
• (same) = ein
to keep all the keys in one drawer = alle
Schlüssel in einer Schublade
aufbewahren

3 *pronoun*
- (*person or thing*) = einer/eine/eins
  not one = keiner/keine/keins
  the biscuits are delicious, I'll have another one = die Kekse sind köstlich, ich nehme mir noch einen
  not one of them came = keiner von ihnen kam

! *The pronoun is often translated by an adjective for the person or thing.*

I like the new house but she prefers the old one = mir gefällt das neue Haus, aber sie mag das alte lieber
I'm going to wear the black one (*dress = das Kleid*) = ich ziehe das schwarze an
which one? = welcher/welche/welches?
this one = dieser/diese/dieses
I like that one = ich mag den da/die da/das da

! *The gender depends on the noun referred to.*

- (*you*) = man
  one never knows = man kann nie wissen

one another *pronoun*
= einander

! *Note that* one another *is translated with the reflexive pronoun* sich.

to love one another = sich lieben

oneself *pronoun*
- (*when used as a reflexive pronoun*) = sich
  to enjoy oneself = sich amüsieren
- (*used for emphasis*) = selbst
- by oneself = allein

one-way street *noun*
= (die) Einbahnstraße

onion *noun*
= (die) Zwiebel

online banking *noun*
= (das) Onlinebanking

only
1 *adverb* = nur
  you only have to ask = du brauchst nur zu fragen
2 *adjective* = einziger/einzige/einziges
  they are our only neighbours = sie sind unsere einzigen Nachbarn
  an only child = ein Einzelkind
3 *conjunction* = nur
  they need a car, only they can't afford it = sie brauchen ein Auto, nur können sie es sich nicht leisten

only just
- (*very recently*) = gerade erst
- (*by a narrow margin*) = gerade noch
  we only just caught the train = wir haben gerade noch den Zug erwischt

open
1 *verb*
- = öffnen, = aufmachen

---

to open [the door | a letter | the garage ...] = [die Tür | einen Brief | die Garage ...] öffnen *or* aufmachen
the shop opens at 8 = das Geschäft öffnet um acht, = das Geschäft macht um acht auf
- (*open up*) = sich öffnen
- (*set up, start*) = eröffnen
  to open an account = ein Konto eröffnen
- (*be started*) = eröffnet werden (! *sein*)
2 *adjective*
- = offen
  the door is open = die Tür ist offen
  are the shops open today? = haben die Geschäfte heute auf?
- (*public*) = öffentlich
- (*frank*) = offen
- (*other uses*)
  to keep an open mind = alles offen lassen
  to leave the date open = das Datum offen lassen
3 *noun*
  in the open = im Freien
  to come into the open = herauskommen (! *sein*), = an den Tag kommen✘ (! *sein*)

open up
- (*for business*) = öffnen
- (*talk*) = gesprächig werden (! *sein*)

opener *noun*
= (der) Öffner

opening hours *noun*
= Öffnungszeiten (*plural*)

open-minded *adjective*
= aufgeschlossen

opera *noun*
= (die) Oper

operate *verb*
- (*run*) = verkehren (! *sein*)
  the bus service does not operate after 8 pm = Busse verkehren nicht nach zwanzig Uhr
- (*make a machine work*) = bedienen
- (*of a surgeon*) = operieren
  to operate on someone = jemanden operieren

operation *noun*
= (die) Operation
to have an operation = sich operieren lassen

operator *noun*
(*on the phone*) = (die) Vermittlung

opinion *noun*
= (die) Meinung
in my opinion = meiner Meinung nach

opponent *noun*
= (der) Gegner

opportunity *noun*
= (die) Gelegenheit

oppose *verb*
to oppose a plan = gegen einen Plan sein
to be opposed to nuclear weapons =
   gegen Kernwaffen sein

opposite
1 *preposition* = gegenüber (+ *dative*)
  she was sitting opposite me = sie saß mir
    gegenüber
2 *adjective*
• (*totally different*) = entgegengesetzt
  he was walking in the opposite direction =
    er ging in die entgegengesetzte Richtung
  the opposite sex = das andere Geschlecht
• (*other side*) = gegenüberliegend
  on the opposite side of the room = auf der
    gegenüberliegenden Zimmerseite
3 *adverb*
who lives opposite? = wer wohnt
    gegenüber?
4 *noun* = (das) Gegenteil

opposition *noun*
= (der) Widerstand
(*in sport*) = (der) Gegner

optician *noun*
= (der) Optiker/(die) Optikerin

optimistic *adjective*
= optimistisch

option *noun*
= (die) Wahl
I don't have any option = ich habe keine
    andere Wahl
to have the option of [going abroad | buying a
  house ...] = die Möglichkeit haben, [ins
  Ausland zu gehen | ein Haus zu kaufen ...]

or *conjunction*
• = oder
• (*in negative sentences*) = noch
  I can't come today or tomorrow = ich kann
    weder heute noch morgen kommen
• (*otherwise*) = sonst
  be careful or it will break = sei vorsichtig,
    sonst geht es kaputt✱

oral *adjective*
= mündlich

orange
1 *noun*
  (*fruit*) = (die) Orange
2 *adjective* = orange ▶ **Colours p. 204**

orange juice *noun*
= (der) Orangensaft

orchard *noun*
= (der) Obstgarten

orchestra *noun*
= (das) Orchester

order
1 *verb*
• (*tell*) = befehlen (+ *dative*)
  they ordered him to leave the country = sie
    befahlen ihm, das Land zu verlassen

• (*call for*) = anordnen
  to order the evacuation of a building = die
    Räumung eines Gebäudes anordnen
• (*ask for, book*) = bestellen
  I've ordered = ich habe schon bestellt
2 *noun*
• (*instruction*) = (der) Befehl
• (*in a shop, restaurant*) = (die) Bestellung
  to place an order = eine Bestellung
    aufgeben
  the books are on order = die Bücher sind
    bestellt
• (*arrangement*) = (die) Reihenfolge
  in alphabetical order = in alphabetischer
    Reihenfolge
• (*control*) = (die) Ordnung
  out of order = außer Betrieb
  in order to = um zu
  I phoned in order to book tickets = ich
    habe angerufen, um Karten zu buchen

ordinary *adjective*
• (*not unusual*) = normal
• (*not exceptional*) = gewöhnlich

organ *noun*
• (*musical instrument*) = (die) Orgel
• (*part of the body*) = (das) Organ

organization *noun*
= (die) Organisation

original *adjective*
• (*first*) = ursprünglich
• (*not an imitation*) = original
  an original (painting) = ein Original
• (*new*) = originell
  an original idea = eine originelle Idee

orphan *noun*
= (die) Waise

ostrich *noun*
= (der) Strauß

other
1 *adjective* = anderer/andere/anderes
  the other pupils = die anderen Schüler
  we met them the other day = wir haben sie
    neulich getroffen
  the other evening = neulich abends
  every other day = jeden zweiten Tag
  any other questions? = sonst noch Fragen?
2 *pronoun* = anderer/andere/anderes
  the others = die anderen
  not any other = kein anderer/keine
    andere/kein anderes
  they came in one after the other = sie
    kamen hintereinander herein
  someone or other told me = irgendjemand
    hat es mir gesagt
  other than = außer (+ *dative*)

otherwise *adverb*
= sonst

ought *verb*
• = sollen
  I ought to do my homework, but I'm too
    lazy = ich soll meine Hausaufgaben
    machen, aber ich bin zu faul

O

! *The subjunctive of* **sollen** *is usually used to translate* ought, *when making polite suggestions or when something is likely to happen.*

he ought to arrive tomorrow = er sollte morgen ankommen

• (*when implying that something was not right*)
he ought to have been more polite = er hätte höflicher sein sollen
you ought not to have done it = du hättest es nicht machen sollen

our *adjective*
= unser

! *Note that* **unser** *changes its endings in the same way as* **ein.**

he ran over our dog = er hat unseren Hund überfahren

ours *pronoun*
= unserer/unsere/unsers

! *Note that* **unserer** *and other forms sometimes drop an* e *in informal use, to become* **unsrer,** *etc. The pronoun agrees in number and gender with the noun it stands for.*

their garden is bigger than ours = ihr Garten ist größer als unserer
the grey car is ours = das graue Auto gehört uns
he's a friend of ours = er ist ein Freund von uns

ourselves *pronoun*
• (*when translated by a reflexive verb in German*) = uns
we want to enjoy ourselves = wir wollen uns amüsieren
• (*used for emphasis*) = selbst
we organized everything ourselves = wir haben alles selbst organisiert
• by ourselves = allein

out
1 *adverb*
• (*outside*) = draußen
it's quite cold out = es ist ziemlich kalt draußen
• (*absent*) = weg
he is out = er ist nicht da
he's been out all night = er war die ganze Nacht weg
• (*seen or heard*) = heraus, = raus✶
the book will be out in November = das Buch kommt im November heraus
the sun is out = die Sonne scheint
the ball was out (*out of play*) = der Ball war aus
out with it! = raus damit!✶
• (*not on*) = aus
the fire is out = das Feuer ist aus
• (*unconscious*) = bewusstlos

2 *preposition*
out of = aus (+ *dative*)
to walk out of the building = aus dem Gebäude gehen (**!** *sein*)
to stay out of the sun = aus der Sonne bleiben (**!** *sein*)

! *Note that* **out** *is often used with verbs—blow out, find out, go out, etc. You will find translations for these under the entries* **blow, find, go,** *etc.*

outdoor *adjective*
outdoor games = Spiele im Freien
outdoor swimming pool = (das) Freibad
to lead an outdoor life = viel im Freien sein

outdoors *adverb*
= draußen

outlook *noun*
• (*attitude*) = (die) Einstellung
• (*for the future*) = Aussichten (*plural*)

outside
1 *noun* = (die) Außenseite
2 *preposition*
• (*in front of*) = vor (+ *dative*)
to wait outside the school = vor der Schule warten
• (*beyond*) = außerhalb (+ *genitive*)
outside the city = außerhalb der Stadt
3 *adverb*
• (*on the outside*) = draußen
they are sitting outside = sie sitzen draußen
• (*to the outside*) = nach draußen
to go outside = nach draußen gehen (**!** *sein*)
4 *adjective* = Außen-
outside wall = (die) Außenwand

oven *noun*
= (der) Ofen

over
1 *preposition*
• (*across, above*) = über (+ *dative or accusative*)

! *Note that* **über** *is followed by a noun in the dative when position is described. The accusative follows when there is movement towards something.*

to wear a sweater over a shirt = einen Pullover über dem Hemd anhaben
to climb over a fence = über einen Zaun klettern (**!** *sein*)
over there = da drüben
• (*during*) = über (+ *accusative*)
over the weekend = übers Wochenende

! *Note that* **übers** *is a shortened form of* **über das.**

• all over (*everywhere*) = überall, (*finished*) = zu Ende
2 *adverb*
• (*finished*) = zu Ende
when the film is over = wenn der Film zu Ende ist

✶ in informal situations

- (*to one's home*)
  to invite someone over = jemanden zu sich
  (*dative*) einladen
  come over tomorrow evening = komm
  morgen Abend zu uns herüber
- (*remaining*) = übrig
  to be left over = übrig bleiben (**!** *sein*)
- (*repeated*)
  over again = noch einmal

  ! *Note that* over *is often used with
  verbs—*hand over, move over, *etc. You
  will find translations for these under the
  entries* hand, move, *etc.*

overdraft *noun*
= (die) Kontoüberziehung
to have an overdraft = sein Konto
überzogen haben

overtake *verb*
= überholen

overthrow *verb*
= stürzen

overweight *adjective*
to be overweight = Übergewicht haben

owe *verb*
= schulden
to owe someone money = jemandem Geld
schulden

owl *noun*
= (die) Eule

own
1 *adjective* = eigen
he would like his own car = er hätte gerne
ein eigenes Auto
2 *pronoun* = eigen
I don't need his pencil, I've got my own =
ich brauche seinen Bleistift nicht, ich
habe meinen eigenen
on one's own = allein
3 *verb* = besitzen, = haben
she owns two cars = sie hat zwei Autos
own up
to own up to something = etwas
(*accusative*) zugeben

owner *noun*
= (der) Eigentümer/(die) Eigentümerin

oxygen *noun*
= (der) Sauerstoff

ozone layer *noun*
= (die) Ozonschicht

P p

Pacific *noun*
the Pacific, the Pacific Ocean = der Pazifik

pack
1 *verb*
(*fill*) = packen
(*put into a container*) = einpacken
2 *noun* = (die) Packung
pack of cards = (das) Kartenspiel
pack up
= packen
to pack up one's belongings = seine
Sachen packen

package *noun*
= (das) Paket

packet *noun*
= (das) Päckchen

paddle *noun*
= (das) Paddel

page *noun*
= (die) Seite

pain *noun*
= (der) Schmerz
to be in pain = Schmerzen haben

painful *adjective*
= schmerzhaft

paint
1 *noun* = (die) Farbe
2 *verb*
- (*in art*) = malen
- (*decorate*) = streichen

paintbrush *noun*
= (der) Pinsel

painter *noun*
= (der) Maler/(die) Malerin

painting *noun*
- (*picture*) = (das) Gemälde
- (*activity*) = (die) Malerei
- (*by a decorator*) = Malerarbeiten (*plural*)

pair *noun*
= (das) Paar

pajamas (*US*) ▶ pyjamas

Pakistan *noun*
= (das) Pakistan ▶ **Countries p. 208**

palace *noun*
= (der) Palast

pale *adjective*
= blass
to go *or* **turn pale** = blass werden (**!** *sein*)

P

pan noun
  (*for frying*) = (die) Pfanne
  (*saucepan*) = (der) Topf

pancake noun
  = (der) Pfannkuchen

panic verb
  = in Panik geraten (**!** *sein*)

pants noun
• (*British: underwear*) = (die) Unterhose,
  (*woman's*) = (der) Schlüpfer
• (*US: trousers*) = (die) Hose

paper noun
• = (das) Papier
  a piece of paper = ein Blatt Papier
• (*newspaper*) = (die) Zeitung

paperback noun
  = (das) Taschenbuch

parachute noun
  = (der) Fallschirm

parade noun
  = (der) Umzug

paralysed (*British*), **paralyzed** (*US*)
  adjective
  = gelähmt

paramedic noun
  = (der) Sanitäter/(die) Sanitäterin

parcel noun
  = (das) Paket

parents noun
  = Eltern (*plural*)

park
1 *noun* = (der) Park
2 *verb* = parken

parking meter noun
  = (die) Parkuhr

parking ticket noun
  = (der) Strafzettel

parliament noun
  = (das) Parlament

parrot noun
  = (der) Papagei

part noun
• (der) Teil
  part of the [book | work | story ...] = ein Teil
  [des Buches | der Arbeit | der Geschichte ...]
• (*piece for a machine, car*) = (das) Teil
  the different parts of an engine = die
  einzelnen Teile eines Motors
• (*area*) = (die) Gegend
• (*role*) = (die) Rolle
• to take part in a demonstration = an einer
  Demonstration teilnehmen

participate verb
  = teilnehmen
  to participate in something = an etwas
  (*dative*) teilnehmen

particular adjective
  = besonderer/besondere/besonderes
  nothing in particular = nichts Besonderes
  in particular = besonders

partner noun
  = (der) Partner/(die) Partnerin

part-time
1 *adjective* = Teilzeit-
  part-time work = (die) Teilzeitarbeit
2 *adverb*
  to work part-time = Teilzeit arbeiten

party noun
• (*social event*) = (die) Party, = (das) Fest
• (*political organization*) = (die) Partei

pass verb
• (*go past*) = vorbeigehen an (+ *dative*)
  (**!** *sein*)
  (*drive past*) = vorbeifahren an (+ *dative*)
  (**!** *sein*)
  to let someone pass = jemanden
  vorbeilassen
• (*overtake*) = überholen

  > **!** Note that überholen is an inseparable
  > verb.

  the car passed the lorry = das Auto
  überholte den Lastwagen
• (*hand over*) = reichen
• (*spend*) = verbringen
  to pass the time [reading | listening to the
  radio | playing the piano ...] = sich (*dative*)
  die Zeit mit [Lesen | Radiohören |
  Klavierspielen ...] vertreiben
• (*succeed in an exam*) = bestehen
• (*of time*) = vergehen (**!** *sein*)
  time passes quickly on holiday = auf
  Ferien vergeht die Zeit schnell
pass on
  = weitergeben
  to pass a message on to someone = eine
  Nachricht an jemanden weitergeben
pass out
  = ohnmächtig werden (**!** *sein*)

passage noun
• (*corridor*) = (der) Gang
• (*voyage*) = (die) Überfahrt

passenger noun
  = (der) Passagier/(die) Passagierin

passport noun
  = (der) Reisepass

password noun
  (*in computing*) = (das) Passwort

past
1 *noun* = (die) Vergangenheit
2 *adjective*
  (*last*) = letzter/letzte/letztes
  in the past few days = in den letzten paar
  Tagen
3 *preposition*
• (*when talking about time*) = nach (+ *dative*)
  ▶ Time p. 331

- (*by*)
  past something = an etwas (*dative*) vorbei
  to go past someone = an jemandem
  vorbeigehen (**!** *sein*)
- (*after*) = nach (+ *dative*)
  it's just past the traffic lights = es ist kurz
  nach der Ampel
  4 *adverb* = vorbei
  to go past = vorbeigehen (**!** *sein*)

pasta *noun*
  = Nudeln (*plural*)

pastry *noun*
- (*for baking*) = (der) Teig
- (*cake*) = (das) Gebäck

patch *noun*
- (*on a garment*) = (der) Flicken
- (*spot*) = (der) Fleck
- (*area*) = (die) Stelle
  patches of ice = stellenweise Eis

path *noun*
  = (der) Weg
  (*narrower*) = (der) Pfad

patience *noun*
  = (die) Geduld

patient
  1 *noun* = (der) Patient/(die) Patientin
  2 *adjective* = geduldig

patrol car *noun*
  = (der) Streifenwagen

pattern *noun*
- (*design*) = (das) Muster
- (*for making garments*) = (der) Schnitt

pavement *noun* (*British*)
  = (der) Bürgersteig

paw *noun*
  = (die) Pfote

pay
  1 *verb*
- = bezahlen, = zahlen

  ! Note that **bezahlen** is used when you
  pay a person, a fine or a bill, and **zahlen**
  when the object of the verb is money or
  there is no object.

  he paid for the meal = er hat das Essen
  bezahlt
  the work doesn't pay very well = die Arbeit
  wird schlecht bezahlt
  to pay by credit card = mit Kreditkarte
  zahlen
  they pay £5 an hour = sie zahlen fünf
  Pfund pro Stunde
- (*give*)
  to pay someone a visit = jemanden
  besuchen
  to pay someone a compliment =
  jemandem ein Kompliment machen
  2 *noun* = (das) Gehalt
  pay back
  = zurückzahlen

PC *noun*
  = (der) PC

pea *noun*
  = (die) Erbse

peace *noun*
  = (der) Frieden
  for my own peace of mind = zu meiner
  eigenen Beruhigung

peach *noun*
  = (der) Pfirsich

peacock *noun*
  = (der) Pfau

peanut *noun*
  = (die) Erdnuss

pear *noun*
  = (die) Birne

pearl *noun*
  = (die) Perle

pebble *noun*
  = (der) Kieselstein

pedestrian *noun*
  = (der) Fußgänger/(die) Fußgängerin

pedestrian crossing *noun*
  = (der) Fußgängerüberweg

peel *verb*
  = schälen
  I'm peeling = ich schäle mich

pen *noun*
  (*ballpoint*) = (der) Kugelschreiber
  (*fountain*) = (der) Füller

penalty *noun*
- (*fine*) = (die) Geldstrafe
- (*in soccer*) = (der) Elfmeter

pencil *noun*
  = (der) Bleistift

pencil case *noun*
  = (das) Federmäppchen

pencil sharpener *noun*
  = (der) Bleistiftspitzer

pen friend *noun*
  = (der) Brieffreund/(die) Brieffreundin

penguin *noun*
  = (der) Pinguin

penknife *noun*
  = (das) Taschenmesser

pensioner *noun*
  = (der) Rentner/(die) Rentnerin

people *noun*
  = Leute (*plural*)
  most people = die meisten Leute
  for three people = für drei Personen

pepper *noun*
- (*spice*) = (der) Pfeffer
- (*vegetable*) = (der) Paprika

P

per *preposition*
= pro (+ *accusative*)
per person = pro Person

per cent *noun*
= (das) Prozent

perfect *adjective*
= perfekt

perform *verb*
• (*do*)
to perform a task = eine Arbeit ausführen
• (*act*) = spielen
• (*a play*) = aufführen

perfume *noun*
= (das) Parfüm

perhaps *adverb*
= vielleicht

period *noun*
• (*in time*) = (die) Zeit
trial period = (die) Probezeit
• (*school lesson*) = (die) Stunde
• (*in history, woman's cycle*) = (die) Periode
• (*punctuation*) = (der) Punkt

permanent *adjective*
= ständig
a permanent job = eine feste Stelle

permission *noun*
= (die) Erlaubnis

person *noun*
= (der) Mensch, = (die) Person
an old person = ein alter Mensch

> **!** Note that **Person** *is mainly used when
> counting people or as a grammatical
> term. Referring to a* **person**, *the word
> may seem rude and so is untranslated*

he's not a very patient person = er ist nicht
sehr geduldig
a sick person = ein Kranker/eine Kranke

personal *adjective*
= persönlich

personal organizer *noun*
= (der) Terminplaner

personality *noun*
= (die) Persönlichkeit

persuade *verb*
= überreden
(*convince*) = überzeugen
to persuade someone to [come | buy a car |
help ...] = jemanden überreden [zu
kommen | , ein Auto zu kaufen | zu helfen ...]

pessimistic *adjective*
= pessimistisch

pet *noun*
= (das) Haustier

petrol *noun* (*British*)
= (das) Benzin

petrol station *noun* (*British*)
= (die) Tankstelle

pet shop *noun*
= (die) Tierhandlung

pharmacy *noun*
= (die) Apotheke

pheasant *noun*
= (der) Fasan

phone
1 *noun* = (das) Telefon
he's on the phone = er telefoniert
to pick up the phone = den Hörer
abnehmen
2 *verb* = anrufen

phone book *noun*
= (das) Telefonbuch

phone booth *noun*
= (die) Telefonzelle

phone call *noun*
= (der) Telefonanruf

phone card *noun*
= (die) Telefonkarte

photo *noun*
= (das) Foto
to take a photo of someone = ein Foto von
jemandem machen

photocopier *noun*
= (das) Fotokopiergerät

photocopy *noun*
= (die) Fotokopie

photograph
1 *noun* = (die) Fotografie
2 *verb* = fotografieren

photographer *noun*
= (der) Fotograf/(die) Fotografin

physical *adjective*
= körperlich

physics *noun*
= (die) Physik

piano *noun*
= (das) Klavier

pick *verb*
• (*choose*) = aussuchen, (*for oneself*) = sich
(*dative*) aussuchen
• (*collect*) = pflücken
• (*take*)
to pick a book off the shelf = ein Buch aus
dem Regal nehmen
pick up
• (*lift*)
to pick the toys up off the floor = die
Spielsachen vom Boden aufheben
to pick a baby up = ein Baby hochnehmen
to pick up the phone = den Hörer
abnehmen

✗ in informal situations

- (*collect*) = abholen
  he's picking me up from the station = er
  holt mich vom Bahnhof ab
- (*buy*) = kaufen
- (*learn*) = lernen
  to pick up a little French = ein bisschen
  Französisch lernen

picnic *noun*
= (das) Picknick

picture *noun*
- = (das) Bild
- (*film*) = (der) Film

piece *noun*
- (*bit*) = (das) Stück
  a piece of cheese = ein Stück Käse
- (*part of a machine or set*) = (das) Teil
  to take something to pieces = etwas in
    Einzelteile zerlegen, = etwas auseinander
    nehmen
  to fall to pieces = zerbrechen (**!** *sein*), =
    kaputtgehen✱ (**!** *sein*)
- (*coin*) = (das) Stück
  a 50-pence piece = ein Fünfzig-Pence-Stück

pierce *verb*
= durchstechen

pig *noun*
= (das) Schwein

pigeon *noun*
= (die) Taube

pile *noun*
- = (der) Haufen
  (*neat stack*) = (der) Stapel
- (*lots*) = (die) Menge
  piles of [CDs | books | magazines ...] = eine
    Menge | CDs | Bücher | Zeitschriften ...]

pill *noun*
= (die) Pille

pillow *noun*
= (das) Kopfkissen

pilot *noun*
= (der) Pilot/(die) Pilotin

pin
1 *noun* = (die) Stecknadel
2 *verb* = stecken

pinball *noun*
= (das) Flippern

pinch *verb*
- = kneifen
- (*hurt by being too tight*) = drücken

pineapple *noun*
= (die) Ananas

pine tree *noun*
= (die) Kiefer

pink *adjective*
= rosa ▶ **Colours p. 204**

pint *noun*
= (das) Pint
let's go for a pint = gehen wir auf ein Bier

pipe *noun*
- = (das) Rohr
- (*for smoking*) = (die) Pfeife

pirate *noun*
= (der) Pirat

Pisces *noun*
= Fische (*plural*)

pitch *noun* (*British*)
= (das) Feld
football pitch = (der) Fußballplatz

pity
1 *noun*
- = (das) Mitleid
- (*when showing regret*)
  it's a pity you [can't come | have to go | didn't
    tell me ...] = schade, dass du [nicht kommen
    kannst | gehen musst | mir das nicht gesagt
    hast ...]
  what a pity! = wie schade!
2 *verb* = bemitleiden

pizza *noun*
= (die) Pizza

place *noun*
- (*location, town*) = (der) Ort
  Oxford is a nice place = Oxford ist ein
    netter Ort
  they come from all over the place = sie
    kommen von überall her
  this place is very dirty = es ist sehr
    schmutzig hier
- (*spot*) = (die) Stelle
- (*house*) = (das) Haus, (*flat*) = (die) Wohnung
  I've got my own place = ich habe meine
    eigene Wohnung
  at Alison's place = bei Alison
- (*in a queue*) = (der) Platz
  to find a place to park = einen Platz zum
    Parken finden
  out of place = fehl am Platz
- (*in a contest, team*) = (der) Platz
  to gain third place = den dritten Platz
    belegen
  a university place = ein Studienplatz

plain
1 *adjective*
- (*simple*) = einfach
- (*without pattern*) = einfarbig
- (*not good-looking*) = nicht hübsch
2 *noun* = (die) Ebene

plait *noun*
= (der) Zopf

plan
1 *noun* = (der) Plan
  I don't have any plans for tonight = ich
    habe heute Abend nichts vor

P

2 *verb*
* (*prepare*) = planen
  to plan a [trip | meeting | party ...] = [einen
  Ausflug | ein Treffen | eine Party ...] planen
* (*intend*) = vorhaben
  I'm planning to [visit Scotland | go to
  university ...] = ich habe vor, [nach
  Schottland zu fahren | auf die Universität zu
  gehen ...]

plane *noun*
  = (das) Flugzeug

planet *noun*
  = (der) Planet

plant
1 *noun* = (die) Pflanze
2 *verb* = pflanzen

plaster *noun*
* (*material*) = (der) Gips
  his leg is in plaster = er hat das Bein in
  Gips
* (*for walls*) = (der) Verputz
* (*sticking plaster*) = (das) Pflaster

plastic
1 *noun* = (das) Plastik
2 *adjective* = Plastik-
  plastic bag = (die) Plastiktüte

plate *noun*
  = (der) Teller

platform *noun*
  = (der) Bahnsteig
  on platform 4 = auf Gleis 4

play
1 *verb*
  = spielen
  to play [football | cards | a game ...] = [Fußball |
  Karten | ein Spiel ...] spielen
  Germany are playing Ireland =
  Deutschland spielt gegen Irland

> **!** *Note that in German the article is not
> translated when playing musical
> instruments.*

  to play the [piano | flute | guitar ...] = [Klavier |
  Flöte | Gitarre ...] spielen
  the film is playing at the Odeon = der Film
  läuft im Odeon
  to play a trick on someone = jemandem
  einen Streich spielen
2 *noun*
  = (das) Theaterstück
play around
  = Blödsinn machen
play back
  = abspielen

player *noun*
  = (der) Spieler/(die) Spielerin

playground *noun*
  = (der) Spielplatz
  school playground = (der) Schulhof

please *adverb*
  = bitte
  please come in = kommen Sie bitte herein

pleased *adjective*
* (*happy*) = erfreut
  to be pleased about something = sich über
  etwas (*accusative*) freuen
  I'm pleased to hear that you are well = ich
  freue mich zu hören, dass es euch gut
  geht
* (*satisfied*) = zufrieden

plenty *pronoun*
  to have plenty of [time | friends | money ...] =
  [viel Zeit | viele Freunde | viel Geld ...] haben

plot *noun*
* (*story*) = (die) Handlung
* (*plan*) = (das) Komplott
* **a plot of land** = ein Grundstück

plug *noun*
* (*electric*) = (der) Stecker
* (*in a sink, bath*) = (der) Stöpsel
plug in
  = einstecken

plum *noun*
  = (die) Pflaume

plumber *noun*
  = (der) Installateur

plus *preposition*
  = plus (+ *dative*)

pneumonia *noun*
  = (die) Lungenentzündung

pocket *noun*
  = (die) Tasche

pocketbook *noun* (*US*)
  = (die) Handtasche

poem *noun*
  = (das) Gedicht

point
1 *noun*
* = (der) Punkt
  a point of view = ein Standpunkt
* (*in a contest, game*) = (der) Punkt
* (*most important thing, meaning*) = (der) Sinn
  that's not the point = darum geht es nicht
  what's the point? = wozu?
  there's no point in [shouting | protesting ...] =
  es hat keinen Sinn zu [schreien |
  protestieren ...]
* (*talking about time*)
  to be on the point of [moving | selling the
  house | changing jobs ...] = im Begriff sein
  [umzuziehen | , das Haus zu verkaufen | , die
  Stelle zu wechseln ...]
* (*sharp end*) = (die) Spitze
* (*in numbers*)
  one point five = eins Komma fünf

2 verb
• (indicate)
to point one's finger at someone = mit dem Finger auf jemanden zeigen
to point at a [house | street …] = auf [ein Haus | eine Straße …] zeigen
to point the way to the station = den Weg zum Bahnhof zeigen
• (aim) = richten
to point a gun at someone = ein Gewehr auf jemanden richten
point out
= zeigen auf (+ accusative)
to point something out to someone = jemanden auf etwas (accusative) hinweisen

poison
1 noun = (das) Gift
2 verb = vergiften

Poland noun
= (das) Polen ▶ Countries p. 208

Pole noun
(der) Pole/(die) Polin

pole noun
= (die) Stange

police noun
= (die) Polizei

policeman noun
= (der) Polizist

police station noun
= (die) Polizeiwache

policewoman noun
= (die) Polizistin

polish verb
= polieren
to polish the floor = den Fußboden bohnern

polite adjective
= höflich

political adjective
= politisch

politician noun
= (der) Politiker/(die) Politikerin

politics noun
= (die) Politik

pollute verb
= verschmutzen

pollution noun
= (die) Verschmutzung

pond noun
= (der) Teich

pony noun
= (das) Pony

ponytail noun
= (der) Pferdeschwanz

pool noun
• (swimming pool) = (das) Schwimmbecken

• (on the ground, floor) = (die) Lache
• (game) = (das) Poolbillard

poor adjective
• = arm
• (not satisfactory) = schlecht

population noun
= (die) Bevölkerung

pork noun
= (das) Schweinefleisch

port noun
= (der) Hafen

porter noun
(in a station, airport) = (der) Gepäckträger
(in a hotel) = (der) Portier

Portugal noun
= (das) Portugal ▶ Countries p. 208

positive adjective
• (definite) = eindeutig
• (convinced) = sicher
• (of a result, attitude) = positiv

possibility noun
= (die) Möglichkeit

possible adjective
= möglich
as quickly as possible = so schnell wie möglich

post (British)
1 noun = (die) Post
by post = per Post, = mit der Post
2 verb
to post a letter = einen Brief abschicken

postbox noun (British)
= (der) Briefkasten

postcode noun (British)
= die Postleitzahl

poster noun
= (das) Plakat
(used as a picture) = (das) or (der) Poster

postman noun (British)
= (der) Briefträger

post office noun
= (die) Post

postpone verb
= verschieben
to postpone the party until next week = die Party auf nächste Woche verschieben

pot noun
= (der) Topf
(for tea, coffee) = (die) Kanne
a pot of tea = eine Kanne Tee

potato noun
= (die) Kartoffel

pottery noun
• (craft) = (die) Töpferei
• (objects) = Töpferwaren (plural)

P

pound *noun*
= (das) Pfund ▶Measures p. 270, ▶Money
p. 274

pour *verb*
- *(from a container)* = gießen
- *(serve a drink)* = eingießen
  to pour someone a cup of tea = jemandem
  eine Tasse Tee eingießen
- *(flow)* = fließen (**!** *sein*)
- *(enter or leave in large numbers)* = strömen
  (**!** *sein*)
  refugees were pouring out of the city = die
  Flüchtlinge strömten aus der Stadt
- *(rain)*
  it's pouring = es gießt

powder *noun*
= (das) Pulver
(cosmetics) = (der) Puder

power *noun*
- *(control)* = (die) Macht
  to be in power = an der Macht sein
- *(influence)*
  to have great power = großen Einfluss
  haben
- *(strength)* = (die) Kraft
- *(electricity)* = (der) Strom

power cut *noun*
= (die) Stromsperre

practical *adjective*
= praktisch

practice
1 *noun (British)*
- = (die) Übung
- *(of a doctor, lawyer)* = (die) Praxis
2 *verb (US)* ▶practise

practise
1 *verb (British)*
- = üben
- *(rehearse)* = proben
2 *noun (US)* ▶practice

praise *verb*
= loben

pram *noun (British)*
= (der) Kinderwagen

prawn *noun*
= (die) Garnele

prayer *noun*
= (das) Gebet

precaution *noun*
= (die) Vorsichtsmaßnahme

precious *adjective*
= kostbar

precise *adjective*
= genau

prefer *verb*
= vorziehen
I prefer him to his brother = ich ziehe ihn
seinem Bruder vor
I prefer to phone = ich rufe lieber an

pregnant *adjective*
= schwanger

prejudice *noun*
- = (das) Vorurteil
- *(bias)* = (die) Voreingenommenheit

prepare *verb*
- *(get ready)* = vorbereiten
  to prepare pupils for an exam = Schüler
  auf eine Prüfung vorbereiten
- *(get oneself ready)* = sich vorbereiten
  to prepare for an exam = sich auf eine
  Prüfung vorbereiten

prepared *adjective*
- *(willing)*
  to be prepared to wait = bereit sein zu
  warten
- *(ready)* = vorbereitet
  to be prepared for an exam = auf eine
  Prüfung vorbereitet sein

prescription *noun*
= (das) Rezept

present
1 *noun*
- *(gift)* = (das) Geschenk
  to give someone a present = jemandem
  ein Geschenk machen
- *(now)*
  the present = die Gegenwart
  at present = zur Zeit
2 *verb*
- *(give)* = überreichen
  to present a prize to someone = jemandem
  einen Preis überreichen
- *(on TV, radio)* = moderieren

president *noun*
= (der) Präsident/(die) Präsidentin

press
1 *verb*
- = drücken
- *(on something)* = drücken auf
  (+ *accusative*)
  to press the bell = auf die Klingel drücken
2 *noun*
  the press = die Presse

pressure *noun*
= (der) Druck
to put pressure on someone = jemanden
unter Druck setzen

pretend *verb*
= vorgeben
he's pretending to be annoyed = er gibt
vor, böse zu sein
to pretend that . . . = so tun, als ob . . .

pretty
1 *adjective* = hübsch
2 *adverb*
  (quite) = ziemlich

prevent *verb*
  to prevent an accident = einen Unfall
    verhindern
  to prevent someone from working =
    jemanden daran hindern zu arbeiten

previous *adjective*
• (*earlier*) = früher
  in previous years = in früheren Jahren
• (*preceding*) = vorig
  the previous owner = der vorige Besitzer

price *noun*
  = (der) Preis

pride *noun*
  = (der) Stolz

priest *noun*
  = (der) Priester

primary school *noun*
  = (die) Grundschule

prime minister *noun*
  = (der) Premierminister/
    (die) Premierministerin

prince *noun*
  = (der) Prinz

princess *noun*
  = (die) Prinzessin

principal *noun*
  (*of a senior school*) = (der) Direktor/
    (die) Direktorin
  (*of a junior school*) = (der) Rektor/
    (die) Rektorin

print
1 *verb*
  = drucken
  (*in computing*) = ausdrucken
2 *noun*
• (*photo*) = (der) Abzug
• (*in a book*) = (der) Druck
• (*of a finger, foot*) = (der) Abdruck

printer *noun*
  (*for a computer*) = (der) Drucker

printout *noun*
  = (der) Ausdruck

prison *noun*
  = (das) Gefängnis

prisoner *noun*
  = (der/die) Gefangene

private *adjective*
  = privat, = Privat-
  my private life = mein Privatleben
  in private = privat

prize *noun*
  = (der) Preis

probably *adverb*
  = wahrscheinlich

problem *noun*
  = (das) Problem
  no problem! = kein Problem!

process *noun*
  = (der) Prozess
  to be in the process of writing a letter =
    dabei sein, einen Brief zu schreiben

produce
1 *verb*
• (*make*) = herstellen
  the company produces soft drinks = die
    Firma stellt alkoholfreie Getränke her
• (*create*)
  to produce a film = einen Film produzieren
  to produce a play = ein Theaterstück
    inszenieren
2 *noun* = Erzeugnisse (*plural*)

product *noun*
  = (das) Produkt

production *noun*
  = (die) Produktion

profession *noun*
  = (der) Beruf

professional *adjective*
• (*relating to work*) = beruflich
• (*expert*) = fachmännisch
• (*not amateur*) = Berufs-
  (*in sport*) = professionell
  a professional musician = ein
    Berufsmusiker

profit *noun*
  = (der) Gewinn
  to sell something at a profit = etwas mit
    Gewinn verkaufen

program
1 *noun*
• (*for a computer*) = (das) Programm
• (*US*) ▶ programme
2 *verb* = programmieren

programme *noun* (*British*)
• (*on TV, radio*) = (die) Sendung
• (*booklet, schedule*) = (das) Programm

progress *noun*
  = (der) Fortschritt
  to make progress = Fortschritte machen

project *noun*
  (*at school*) = (die) Arbeit

promise
1 *verb* = versprechen
  to promise to [write a letter | say nothing | come
    back soon …] = versprechen, [einen Brief zu
    schreiben | nichts zu sagen | bald
    wiederzukommen …]
  to promise someone a letter = jemandem
    einen Brief versprechen
2 *noun* = (das) Versprechen

pronounce *verb*
  = aussprechen

proof *noun*
  = (der) Beweis
  I have proof that they lied = ich kann
    beweisen, dass sie gelogen haben

P

Professions

Shops

In English you can say *at the baker's* or *at the baker's shop*. In German, you can also use the name of the trader or the shop.

he is at the baker's = er ist beim Bäcker, = er ist in der Bäckerei
to go to the chemist's = zum Apotheker *or* Drogisten gehen, = in die Apotheke *or* Drogerie gehen (**!** *sein*)

Note that in German you go to the **Apotheke** for medicines and to the **Drogerie** for toiletries.

to work at the hairdresser's = beim Friseur arbeiten, = im Friseursalon arbeiten
to go to the hairdresser's = zum Friseur gehen (**!** *sein*)

People

In sentences describing a person's profession, the article (*a* / *an*) is not translated in German:

my father is a doctor = mein Vater ist Arzt
my mother is a teacher = meine Mutter ist Lehrerin

But if an adjective describes the profession, the article is used with the adjective:

she is a good dentist = sie ist eine gute Zahnärztin

Bei and **zu** are also used with professions:

at the lawyer's = beim Anwalt / bei der Anwältin
to go to the doctor's = zum Arzt / zur Ärztin gehen (**!** *sein*)

Useful shopping expressions

can I help you? = kann ich Ihnen helfen?
what would you like? = was wünschen Sie, bitte?
anything else? = sonst noch etwas?
I'd like ... = ich möchte ...
have you got ...? = haben Sie ...?

---

properly *adverb*
= richtig

property *noun*
• (*possessions*) = (das) Eigentum
• (*land*) = (der) Besitz
  (*house*) = (das) Haus

protect *verb*
= schützen
to protect someone from something =
jemanden vor etwas (*dative*) schützen

protest *verb*
= protestieren
to protest about something = gegen etwas
(*accusative*) protestieren

protester *noun*
(*at a demonstration*) = (der)
Demonstrant/(die) Demonstrantin

proud *adjective*
= stolz
she is proud of her work = sie ist auf ihre
Arbeit stolz

prove *verb*
= beweisen
to prove to be wrong = sich als falsch
erweisen

✱ in informal situations

provide *verb*
to provide [work | food | entertainment ...] = für
[Arbeit | Essen | Unterhaltung ...] sorgen
to provide a car = ein Auto zur Verfügung
stellen

provided *conjunction*
provided (that) = vorausgesetzt, (dass)

psychiatrist *noun*
= (der) Psychiater/(die) Psychiaterin

pub *noun* (*British*)
= (die) Kneipe✱

public
1 *noun*
the public = die Öffentlichkeit
in public = öffentlich
2 *adjective*
= öffentlich
public holiday = (der) gesetzliche Feiertag

public transport *noun*
= öffentliche Verkehrsmittel (*plural*)

pudding *noun* (*British*)
= (der) Nachtisch

puddle *noun*
= (die) Pfütze

pull *verb*
• = ziehen

(*pull on*) = ziehen an (+*dative*)
to pull a rope = an einem Seil ziehen
to pull someone's sleeve = jemanden am Ärmel ziehen
he pulled a handkerchief out of his pocket = er zog ein Taschentuch aus der Tasche
to pull a face = eine Grimasse schneiden
• (*injure*)
to pull a muscle = sich (*dative*) einen Muskel zerren

pull down
• (*demolish*) = abreißen
• (*lower*) = herunterziehen

pull out
• to pull out a tooth = einen Zahn ziehen
• the train is pulling out = der Zug fährt ab

pull up
• (*raise*) = hochziehen
• (*stop*) = anhalten
• (*remove*) = herausziehen, = rausziehen✱

pullover *noun*
= (der) Pullover

pump *noun*
= (die) Pumpe
pump up
= aufpumpen

pumpkin *noun*
= (der) Kürbis

punch *verb*
= boxen

punctual *adjective*
= pünktlich

puncture *noun*
• (*hole*) = (das) Loch
• (*flat tyre*) = (die) Reifenpanne

punish *verb*
= bestrafen

pupil *noun*
= (der) Schüler/(die) Schülerin

puppet *noun*
= (die) Puppe

puppy *noun*
= (der) junge Hund

pure *adjective*
= rein

purple *adjective*
= lila ▶Colours p. 204
the purple dress = das lila Kleid

purpose *noun*
= (der) Zweck
on purpose = absichtlich

purse *noun*
• (*for money*) = (das) Portemonnaie
• (*US: handbag*) = (die) Handtasche

push *verb*
• (*move by pushing*) = schieben
to push a car = ein Auto schieben, (*to get it started*) = ein Auto anschieben

• (*roughly*) = schubsen
she pushed him down the stairs = sie schubste ihn die Treppe herunter
• (*press*) = drücken
to push a button = auf einen Knopf drücken
• (*sell*) = pushen✱
to push drugs = Rauschgift pushen

pushchair *noun* (*British*)
= (der) Sportwagen

put *verb*
• (*place*) = tun
to put sugar in one's coffee = sich (*dative*) Zucker in den Kaffee tun
• (*lay flat*) = legen
she put the pencil on the table = sie legte den Bleistift auf den Tisch
• (*place upright*) = stellen
I put the vase on the shelf = ich habe die Vase auf das Regal gestellt
• (*push in*) = stecken
she put her hands in her pockets = sie steckte die Hände in die Taschen

put away
= wegräumen

put back
• (*return to its place*) = zurücktun
• (*turn back*) = zurückstellen
to put the clocks back = die Uhren zurückstellen

put down
• (*vertically*) = hinstellen, (*horizontally*) = hinlegen
to put the phone down = den Hörer auflegen
• (*kill an animal painlessly*) = einschläfern

put forward
= vorstellen
to put the clocks forward = die Uhren vorstellen

put off
• (*postpone*) = verschieben
we'll have to put the party off till next week = wir müssen die Party auf nächste Woche verschieben
• (*switch off*) = ausmachen

put on
• (*when dressing*) = anziehen
to put jeans on = Jeans anziehen
to put a hat on = einen Hut aufsetzen
• (*switch on*)
to put the light on = das Licht anmachen
to put the kettle on = Wasser aufsetzen
to put a CD on = eine CD auflegen
• to put on weight = zunehmen
• to put on a play = ein Theaterstück aufführen

put out
• (*extinguish*) = ausmachen
to put out the fire = das Feuer löschen
• (*take outside*) = hinaustun, = raustun✱

put up
• (*lift*) = heben
to put one's hand up = die Hand heben
• (*attach*) = anbringen

P

- (*pitch*)
  to put up a tent = ein Zelt aufschlagen
- (*raise*) = erhöhen
  to put the rent up = die Miete erhöhen
- (*give a place to stay*) = unterbringen
- to put up with someone = jemanden dulden

puzzle *noun*
= (das) Rätsel

pyjamas *noun* (*British*)
= (der) Schlafanzug

Qq

qualified *adjective*
= ausgebildet

quality *noun*
= (die) Qualität

quantity *noun*
= (die) Menge

quarrel
1 *noun* = (der) Streit
2 *verb* = sich streiten

quarter *noun*
= (das) Viertel ▶Time p. 331
a quarter of an hour = eine Viertelstunde
an hour and a quarter = eineinviertel Stunden

quay *noun*
= (der) Kai

queen *noun*
= (die) Königin
(*in chess, cards*) = (die) Dame

question
1 *noun*
= (die) Frage
to ask someone a question = jemandem eine Frage stellen
2 *verb*
- (*ask questions*) = befragen
- (*doubt*) = bezweifeln

questionnaire *noun*
(der) Fragebogen

queue (*British*)
1 *noun*
= (die) Schlange
to join the queue = sich anstellen
2 *verb* = Schlange stehen

quick *adjective*
= schnell
to have a quick meal = schnell etwas essen
be quick! = mach schnell!

quickly *adverb*
= schnell

quiet
1 *adjective*
- (*silent, not talkative*) = still
  to keep quiet = still sein
  be quiet! = sei still!
  to have a quiet voice = eine leise Stimme haben
- (*calm*) = ruhig
2 *noun* = (die) Ruhe

quietly *adverb*
to speak quietly = leise reden

quit *verb*
- (*resign*) = kündigen
- (*US: give up*)
  to quit smoking = aufhören zu rauchen

quite *adverb*
- (*rather*) = ziemlich
- (*completely*) = ganz
  I'm not quite ready yet = ich bin noch nicht ganz fertig
- (*exactly*)
  I don't quite know what he does = ich weiß nicht genau, was er macht
  quite! = genau!

quiz *noun*
= (das) Quiz

Rr

rabbit *noun*
= (das) Kaninchen

rabies *noun*
= (die) Tollwut

race
1 *noun*
- (*contest*) = (das) Rennen
  to have a race (*running*) = um die Wette laufen (**!** *sein*), (*swimming*) = um die Wette schwimmen (**!** *sein*)
  the races = das Pferderennen
- (*ethnic group*) = (die) Rasse
2 *verb*
- (*compete with*)
  to race someone = mit jemandem um die Wette laufen
- (*take part in a contest*)

  ! Note that the translation can change according to the type of race.

  (*running*) = laufen, (*swimming*) = schwimmen, (*sailing*) = segeln (**!** *all sein*)

racetrack *noun*
= (die) Rennbahn

racket, racquet *noun*
= (der) Schläger

radiator *noun*
• (*heater*) = (der) Heizkörper
• (*in a car*) = (der) Kühler

radio *noun*
= (das) Radio
I heard it on the radio = ich habe es im
Radio gehört

radish *noun*
= (das) Radieschen

rage *noun*
= (die) Wut
to fly into a rage = in Wut geraten (**!** *sein*)

raid
1 *verb*
to raid a bank = eine Bank überfallen
the police raided the house = die Polizei
hat in dem Haus eine Razzia gemacht
2 *noun*
(*by thieves*) = (der) Überfall
(*by the police*) = (die) Razzia

rail *noun*
• (*for holding on to*) = (das) Geländer
• (*for trains*) = (die) Schiene
to go by rail = mit der Bahn fahren (**!** *sein*)

railroad (*US*), **railway** (*British*) *noun*
• (*track*) = (die) Bahnstrecke
• (*system*) = (die) Eisenbahn, = (die) Bahn

railway station *noun*
= (der) Bahnhof

rain
1 *noun* = (der) Regen
2 *verb* = regnen
it's raining = es regnet

rainbow *noun*
= (der) Regenbogen

raincoat *noun*
= (der) Regenmantel

raise *verb*
• (*lift*) = heben
to raise one's hand = die Hand heben
• (*increase*) = erhöhen
to raise prices = die Preise erhöhen
• (*talk about*) = aufwerfen
to raise a question = eine Frage aufwerfen
• (*bring up*) = aufziehen
to raise children = Kinder aufziehen

range *noun*
• (*selection*) = (die) Auswahl
to have a range of something = eine
Auswahl an etwas (*dative*) haben
to have a range of options = verschiedene
Möglichkeiten haben
a range of subjects = verschiedene Fächer
in this price range = in dieser Preislage
• (*of mountains*) = (die) Kette

rarely *adverb*
= selten

rasher *noun*
(*of bacon*) = (die) Speckscheibe

raspberry *noun*
= (die) Himbeere

rat *noun*
= (die) Ratte

rather *adverb*
• (*when saying what one would prefer*)
= lieber
I'd rather [stay here | read the paper | wait …] =
ich würde lieber [hier bleiben | die Zeitung
lesen | warten …]
I'd rather you came with me = es wäre mir
lieber, wenn du mitkämst
• (*quite*) = ziemlich
she's rather young = sie ist ziemlich jung

raw *adjective*
= roh

razor *noun*
= (der) Rasierapparat

reach *verb*
• (*arrive at*) = ankommen in (+ *dative*)
(**!** *sein*)
they reached the town at 8 o'clock = sie
kamen um acht Uhr in der Stadt an
• (*be delivered to, contact by phone*)
= erreichen
the letter never reached her = der Brief hat
sie nie erreicht
• (*by stretching*) = reichen an (+ *accusative*)
to be able to reach the shelf = an das Regal
reichen können
can you reach? = kommst du daran?
• (*come to*) = kommen zu (+ *dative*) (**!** *sein*)
to reach a decision = zu einer
Entscheidung kommen
reach for
= greifen nach (+ *dative*)
reach out
= die Hand ausstrecken

react *verb*
= reagieren

read *verb*
= lesen
his writing is difficult to read = seine Schrift
ist schwer zu lesen
to read a story to someone = jemandem
eine Geschichte vorlesen
read out
= laut vorlesen
read through
= durchlesen

ready *adjective*
• (*prepared*) = fertig
to get ready = sich fertig machen
• (*willing*) = bereit
I'm ready to help them = ich bin bereit,
ihnen zu helfen

real *adjective*
• (*not imagined*) = wirklich

R

- (*not artificial*) = echt
  are they real diamonds? = sind das echte Brillanten?
- (*great*) = wirklich
  it's a real shame = das ist wirklich schade

reality *noun*
= (die) Wirklichkeit

realize *verb*
(*know*) = wissen

really *adverb*
= wirklich
it's really easy = es ist wirklich einfach
I don't really know him = ich kenne ihn eigentlich nicht

rear
1 *noun* = (der) hintere Teil
2 *adjective* = hinterer/hintere/hinteres
rear wheel = (das) Hinterrad
3 *verb* = aufziehen

reason *noun*
= (der) Grund

receipt *noun*
= (die) Quittung

receive *verb*
= erhalten

recent *adjective*
(*not long past*) = jüngst
in recent years = in den letzten Jahren
recent research = die neueste Forschung

recently *adverb*
= kürzlich

reception *noun*
- (*in a hotel, company*) = (der) Empfang, = (die) Rezeption
- (*in a hospital*) = (die) Aufnahme
- (*formal event*) = (der) Empfang

receptionist *noun*
= (die) Empfangsdame
(*at the doctor's*) = (die) Sprechstundenhilfe

recipe *noun*
= (das) Rezept

recharge *verb*
= aufladen

recognize *verb*
= erkennen

recommend *verb*
= empfehlen

record
1 *noun*
- (*of events*) = (die) Aufzeichnung
- (*information*)
  records = Unterlagen (*plural*)
- (*musical disc*) = (die) Platte
- (*in sport*) = (der) Rekord
2 *verb*
- (*keep account of*) = aufzeichnen
- (*on tape*) = aufnehmen

recorder *noun*
= (die) Blockflöte

record player *noun*
= (der) Plattenspieler

recover *verb*
= sich erholen
to recover from an illness = sich von einer Krankheit erholen

recycle *verb*
= recyceln

red *adjective*
= rot ▶ Colours p. 204
to go red, to turn red = rot werden (**!** *sein*)

red-haired *adjective*
= rothaarig

reduce *verb*
to reduce the size of something = etwas verkleinern
to reduce speed = die Geschwindigkeit verringern
to reduce prices = die Preise herabsetzen

reduction *noun*
- (*in size*) = (die) Verkleinerung
- (*in number*) = (die) Verringerung
- (*in price*) = (die) Ermäßigung

redundant *adjective* (*British*)
to be made redundant = entlassen werden (**!** *sein*)

referee *noun*
= (der) Schiedsrichter/(die) Schiedsrichterin

reflect *verb*
= spiegeln
the lights were reflected in the water = die Lichter spiegelten sich im Wasser

reflection *noun*
= (das) Spiegelbild

refreshing *adjective*
= erfrischend

refrigerator *noun*
= (der) Kühlschrank

refugee *noun*
= (der) Flüchtling

refuse[1] *verb*
(*not allow*) = verweigern
to refuse someone admission = jemandem den Zutritt verweigern
to refuse to [stop | pay | go …] = sich weigern [aufzuhören | zu zahlen | zu gehen …]

refuse[2] *noun* (*British*)
= (der) Abfall, = (der) Müll

regards *noun*
= Grüße (*plural*)
give her my regards = grüße sie von mir

region *noun*
= (das) Gebiet

register *noun*
(*at school*) = (das) Klassenbuch
to take the register = die Anwesenheit der
Schüler überprüfen

registration number *noun* (*British*)
= (die) Autonummer

regret
1 *verb* = bedauern
I regret not seeing him again = ich
bedauere es, dass ich ihn nicht mehr
gesehen habe
2 *noun* = (das) Bedauern
to have regrets = es bereuen

regular *adjective*
• = regelmäßig
• (*usual*) = üblich

regularly *adverb*
= regelmäßig

rehearsal *noun*
= (die) Probe

rehearse *verb*
= proben

reject *verb*
= ablehnen

relationship *noun*
= (die) Beziehung
**to have a good relationship with one's
parents** = eine gute Beziehung zu seinen
Eltern haben

relative *noun*
= (der/die) Verwandte

relax *verb*
= sich entspannen

relaxed *adjective*
= entspannt

relay race *noun*
= (die) Staffel

release *verb*
(*free*) = freilassen

reliable *adjective*
= zuverlässig

relieved *adjective*
I was relieved to get a letter from him = ich
war erleichtert, als ich seinen Brief
erhielt

religion *noun*
= (die) Religion

religious *adjective*
= religiös

religious education *noun*
= (der) Religionsunterricht

rely *verb*
to rely on (*be dependent on*) = angewiesen
sein auf (+ *accusative*), (*count on*) = sich
verlassen auf (+ *accusative*)
can we rely on you? = können wir uns auf
euch verlassen?

remain *verb*
= bleiben (**!** *sein*)
(*be left over*) = übrig bleiben (**!** *sein*)

remark *noun*
= (die) Bemerkung

remarkable *adjective*
= bemerkenswert

remember *verb*
= sich erinnern an (+ *accusative*)
do you remember her? = kannst du dich
an sie erinnern?
to remember to [post the letters | switch off the
lights | lock the door …] = daran denken, [die
Briefe abzuschicken | das Licht auszumachen |
abzuschließen …]

remind *verb*
= erinnern
she reminds me of my sister = sie erinnert
mich an meine Schwester
to remind someone to buy milk =
jemanden daran erinnern, Milch zu
kaufen

remote control *noun*
• (*of a car or plane*) = (die) Fernlenkung
• (*of a TV or video*) = (die) Fernbedienung

remove *verb*
= entfernen

rent
1 *verb* = mieten
2 *noun* = (die) Miete
rent out
= vermieten

repair *verb*
= reparieren
to have a bicycle repaired = ein Fahrrad
reparieren lassen

repeat *verb*
= wiederholen

replace *verb*
• (*substitute*) = ersetzen
• (*put back*) = zurücktun

reply
1 *verb* = antworten
to reply to someone = jemandem
antworten
to reply to a letter = auf einen Brief
antworten
2 *noun* = (die) Antwort

report
1 *verb*
• (*notify*) = melden
to report someone to the police =
jemanden anzeigen
• (*in the news*) = berichten
to report on an event = über ein Ereignis
berichten
2 *noun*
• = (der) Bericht
• (*British: at school*) = (das) Zeugnis

R

report card *noun* (*US*)
= (das) Zeugnis

reporter *noun*
= (der) Reporter/(die) Reporterin

represent *verb*
* (*act for*) = vertreten
* (*symbolize*) = darstellen

republic *noun*
= (die) Republik

request *noun*
= (die) Bitte

rescue *verb*
= retten

resemble *verb*
= ähneln (+ *dative*)
to resemble each other = sich (*dative*)
ähneln

resent *verb*
= übel nehmen
she resented his remark = sie hat ihm
seine Äußerung übel genommen
he resents her for winning = er nimmt es
ihr übel, dass sie gewonnen hat

reserve *verb*
* (*keep*) = reservieren
* (*book*) = reservieren lassen

resign *verb*
(*from one's job*) = kündigen
(*from public office*) = zurücktreten (**!** *sein*)

resist *verb*
= widerstehen (+ *dative*)

respect
1 *verb* = respektieren
2 *noun* = (der) Respekt
to have respect for someone = Respekt vor
jemandem haben

responsibility *noun*
= (die) Verantwortung

responsible *adjective*
* (*the cause of*) = verantwortlich
* (*in charge*) = verantwortlich
* (*sensible*) = verantwortungsbewusst

rest
1 *noun*
* (*what is left*) = (der) Rest
* (*break*) = (die) Pause
to have a rest = eine Pause machen
2 *verb* = sich ausruhen

restaurant *noun*
= (das) Restaurant

result *noun*
* (*outcome*) = (das) Ergebnis
the exam results = die Prüfungsergebnisse
* (*consequence*) = (die) Folge
as the result of an accident = als Folge
eines Unfalls
as a result of this = infolgedessen

retire *verb*
= in den Ruhestand treten (**!** *sein*)

return *verb*
* (*go back*) = zurückgehen (**!** *sein*),
(*drive*) = zurückfahren (**!** *sein*)
* (*come back*) = zurückkommen (**!** *sein*)
* (*give back*) = zurückgeben
* (*send back*) = zurückschicken
* (*put back*) = zurückstellen, = zurücklegen
! *Note that* zurückstellen *is used if
something is put down in a vertical
position and* zurücklegen *if it is put down
in a horizontal position.*

* (*start again*)
to return to school = wieder in die Schule
gehen (**!** *sein*)

return ticket *noun*
= (die) Rückfahrkarte
(*by air*) = (der) Rückflugschein

reunification *noun*
= (die) Wiedervereinigung

reveal *verb*
to reveal a secret = ein Geheimnis
enthüllen

revenge *noun*
= (die) Rache
to get one's revenge = sich rächen

revolution *noun*
= (die) Revolution

reward
1 *noun* = (die) Belohnung
2 *verb* = belohnen

rhinoceros *noun*
= (das) Nashorn

rhythm *noun*
= (der) Rhythmus

rib *noun*
= (die) Rippe

ribbon *noun*
= (das) Band

rice *noun*
= (der) Reis

rich *adjective*
= reich

rid *verb*
to get rid of = loswerden (**!** *sein*)

ride
1 *verb*
to ride a horse = reiten (**!** *sein*)
to ride a bike = Rad fahren (**!** *sein*)
he's riding his bike = er fährt Rad
2 *noun*
to go for a ride (*in a car*) = eine Fahrt
machen, (*on a horse*) = ausreiten
(**!** *sein*), (*on a bike*) = Rad fahren (**!** *sein*)

ridiculous *adjective*
= lächerlich

riding *noun*
= (das) Reiten

rifle *noun*
= (das) Gewehr

right
1 *adjective*
* (*not left*) = rechter/rechte/rechtes
  his right hand = seine rechte Hand
* (*correct*) = richtig
  the right answer = die richtige Antwort
  you're right = du hast Recht
  that's right = das stimmt
2 *noun*
* (*not left*) = (die) rechte Seite
  the first street on the right = die erste
    Straße rechts
* (*entitlement*) = (das) Recht
  to have a right to something = ein Recht
    auf etwas (*accusative*) haben
3 *adverb*
= rechts
  to turn right = rechts abbiegen (**!** *sein*)

ring
1 *verb*
* (*British: phone*) = anrufen
* (*make a sound*) = klingeln
  I rang the bell = ich habe geklingelt
  the bell rang = es hat geklingelt
2 *noun*
* (*piece of jewellery*) = (der) Ring
  wedding ring = (der) Ehering
* (*circle*) = (der) Kreis
  to stand in a ring = im Kreis stehen
* (*in a circus*) = (die) Manege
ring back (*British*)
= zurückrufen
ring up (*British*)
= anrufen

rinse *verb*
= spülen

ripe *adjective*
= reif

rise *verb*
* = steigen (**!** *sein*)
* (*of the sun or moon*) = aufgehen (**!** *sein*)

risk
1 *noun* = (das) Risiko
  I took a risk = ich bin ein Risiko
    eingegangen
2 *verb* = riskieren
  to risk losing one's job = es riskieren, seine
    Stelle zu verlieren

rival *noun*
* (*person*) = (der) Rivale/(die) Rivalin
* (*company*) = (die) Konkurrenz

river *noun*
= (der) Fluss

road *noun*
= (die) Straße

road sign *noun*
= (das) Straßenschild

roadworks *noun*
= Straßenarbeiten (*plural*)

roar *verb*
  (*of a lion or person*) = brüllen
  (*of traffic*) = donnern
  (*of an engine*) = dröhnen

roast
1 *verb* = braten
2 *adjective* = gebraten
  roast beef = (der) Rinderbraten
  roast potatoes = Bratkartoffeln (*plural*)
3 *noun* = (der) Braten

rob *verb*
  to rob a bank = eine Bank ausrauben
  to rob someone = jemanden berauben

robbery *noun*
= (der) Raub

robin *noun*
= (das) Rotkehlchen

robot *noun*
= (der) Roboter

rock *noun*
* (*substance*) = (der) Fels
* (*large stone*) = (der) Felsen
* (*music*) = (der) Rock

rocket *noun*
= (die) Rakete

rocking chair *noun*
= (der) Schaukelstuhl

role *noun*
= (die) Rolle

roll
1 *verb* = rollen (**!** *sein*)
2 *noun*
* (*of paper, cloth, plastic*) = (die) Rolle
  a roll of film = eine Rolle Film
* (*bread*) = (das) Brötchen, = (die) Semmel
roll about, roll around
  (*of an object*) = herumrollen (**!** *sein*)
  (*of a person*) = sich wälzen
roll over
= sich umdrehen
roll up
* to roll up a carpet = einen Teppich
    aufrollen
  to roll up a newspaper = eine Zeitung
    zusammenrollen
* to roll up one's sleeves = sich (*dative*) die
    Ärmel hochkrempeln

roller coaster *noun*
= (die) Achterbahn

roller-skate *noun*
= (der) Rollschuh

roller-skating *noun*
= (das) Rollschuhlaufen

R

Romania *noun*
= (das) Rumänien ▶Countries p. 208

romantic *adjective*
= romantisch

roof *noun*
= (das) Dach

room *noun*
• = (das) Zimmer
• (*space*) = (der) Platz
to make room = Platz machen

root *noun*
= (die) Wurzel

rope *noun*
= (das) Seil

rose *noun*
= (die) Rose

rosy *adjective*
= rosig

rot *verb*
= verfaulen (! *sein*)

rotten *adjective*
= verfault

rough *adjective*
• (*not smooth*) = rau
(*of a road, ground*) = uneben
• (*not gentle, not exact*) = grob
a rough estimate = eine grobe Schätzung
• (*difficult*) = schwer
to have a rough time = es schwer haben
• (*stormy*)
a rough sea = eine stürmische See

round
1 *preposition* = um (+ *accusative*)
to go round the corner = um die Ecke
gehen (! *sein*)
to go round a museum = ein Museum
besuchen
2 *adverb*
to go round and round = sich im Kreis
drehen
to invite someone round = jemanden zu
sich (*dative*) einladen
to go round to John's = zu John gehen
(! *sein*)
to look round = sich umsehen

> ! Note that round *is often used with*
> *verbs*—come round, show round, *etc. You
> will find translations for these under the*
> *entries* come, show, *etc.*

3 *adjective* = rund
4 *noun* = (die) Runde

roundabout *noun* (*British*)
• (*at a fair*) = (das) Karussell
• (*for traffic*) = (der) Kreisverkehr

routine *noun*
= (die) Routine

row[1]
1 *noun*
• = (die) Reihe
• (*sequence*)
in a row = hintereinander
to be absent for five days in a row = fünf
Tage hintereinander fehlen
2 *verb* = rudern (! *sein*)

row[2] *noun*
= (der) Streit, = (der) Krach✱
to have a row with someone = sich mit
jemandem streiten

rowboat (*US*) ▶rowing boat

rowing *noun*
= (das) Rudern

rowing boat *noun* (*British*)
= (das) Ruderboot

royal *adjective*
= königlich

rub *verb*
= reiben
to rub one's eyes = sich (*dative*) die Augen
reiben
rub off
= abreiben
rub out
= ausradieren

rubber *noun*
• (*material*) = (der) *or* (das) Gummi
• (*British: eraser*) = (der) Radiergummi

rubber band *noun*
= (das) Gummiband

rubbish *noun* (*British*)
• (*refuse*) = (der) Abfall, = (der) Müll
• (*poor goods*) = (der) Schund✱
• (*nonsense*) = (der) Quatsch✱

rucksack *noun*
= (der) Rucksack

rude *adjective*
• (*impolite*) = unhöflich
• (*vulgar*) = unanständig

rug *noun*
• (*carpet*) = (der) Teppich
• (*blanket*) = (die) Decke

rugby *noun*
= (das) Rugby

ruin
1 *verb* = ruinieren
2 *noun* = (die) Ruine

rule[1]
1 *noun* = (die) Regel
the rules of the game = die Spielregeln
as a rule = in der Regel
2 *verb* = regieren

ruler *noun*
• (*for measuring*) = (das) Lineal
• (*person*) (der) Herrscher/(die) Herrscherin

rumor (*US*), **rumour** (*British*) *noun*
= (das) Gerücht

run
1 *verb*
- = laufen (**!** *sein*), (*run fast*) = rennen (**!** *sein*)
to run a race = ein Rennen laufen
- (*flee from danger*) = weglaufen (**!** *sein*),
= wegrennen (**!** *sein*)
- (*manage*) = führen
to run a shop = ein Geschäft führen
- (*work, operate*) = laufen (**!** *sein*)
to leave the engine running = den Motor
laufen lassen
the car runs on unleaded petrol = das Auto
fährt mit bleifreiem Benzin
- (*organize*) = leiten
- (*when talking about transport*) = fahren
(**!** *sein*)
the train runs every hour = der Zug fährt
jede Stunde
the train is running 20 minutes late = der
Zug hat zwanzig Minuten Verspätung
- (*flow*) = laufen (**!** *sein*)
(*of a river*) = fließen (**!** *sein*)
his nose is running = ihm läuft die Nase
- to run a bath = sich (*dative*) ein Bad
einlaufen lassen
- (*of colours*)
(*in the wash*) = auslaufen (**!** *sein*)
(*on a painting*) = ineinander laufen (**!** *sein*)
- (*remain valid, showing*) = laufen (**!** *sein*)
the contract runs until June = der Vertrag
läuft bis Juni
- (*drive*) = fahren
I ran her home = ich habe sie nach Hause
gefahren
- (*in an election*) = kandidieren
to run for president = für das Amt des
Präsidenten kandidieren
2 *noun* (*on foot*) = (der) Lauf
(*in a car*) = (die) Fahrt
(*of a play, show*) = (die) Laufzeit

run away
= weglaufen (**!** *sein*), = wegrennen (**!** *sein*)
run off
= weglaufen (**!** *sein*)
run out
= ausgehen (**!** *sein*)
we've run out of petrol = wir haben kein
Benzin mehr
run over
(*injure*) = überfahren

runner *noun*
(*person*) = (der) Läufer/(die) Läuferin

rush
1 *verb*
- (*run*) = rasen (**!** *sein*)
she rushed out of the house = sie raste aus
dem Haus
- (*hurry*) = sich beeilen
he rushed to finish his homework = er
beeilte sich, seine Hausaufgaben fertig zu
machen
to rush something = etwas zu schnell
machen

to be rushed into hospital = schnellstens
ins Krankenhaus gebracht werden
(**!** *sein*)
- (*pressurize*) = hetzen
2 *noun* = (die) Eile
to be in a rush = in Eile sein

rush hour *noun*
= (die) Stoßzeit

Russia *noun*
= (das) Russland ▶**Countries p. 208**

Russian
1 *noun*
- (*person*) = (der) Russe/(die) Russin
- (*language*) = (das) Russisch
2 *adjective* = russisch ▶**Countries p. 208**

rusty *adjective*
= rostig
to go rusty = rosten

Ss

sad *adjective*
= traurig

saddle *noun*
= (der) Sattel

safe
1 *adjective*
- (*not dangerous*) = sicher
to feel safe from something = sich vor
etwas (*dative*) sicher fühlen
is the water safe to drink? = kann man das
Wasser ohne Risiko trinken?
have a safe journey! = gute Reise!
- (*out of harm*) = in Sicherheit
he's safe = er ist in Sicherheit
2 *noun* = (der) Safe

safety *noun*
= (die) Sicherheit

safety pin *noun*
= (die) Sicherheitsnadel

Sagittarius *noun*
= (der) Schütze

sail
1 *noun* = (das) Segel
to set sail = Segel setzen
2 *verb*
(*travel on water*) = fahren (**!** *sein*)
(*in a sailing boat*) = segeln (**!** *sein*)

sailboat (*US*) ▶**sailing boat**

sailing *noun*
= (das) Segeln

sailing boat *noun* (*British*)
= (das) Segelboot

sailor *noun*
= (der) Seemann
(*in the navy*) = (der) Matrose

saint *noun*
= (der/die) Heilige

salad *noun*
= (der) Salat

salary *noun*
= (das) Gehalt

sale *noun*
• = (der) Verkauf
  for sale = zu verkaufen
  to put a house up for sale = ein Haus zum
    Verkauf anbieten
  on sale at your bookshop = in Ihrer
    Buchhandlung erhältlich
• (*at reduced prices*) = (der) Ausverkauf

sales assistant *noun* (*British*)
= (der) Verkäufer/(die) Verkäuferin

salmon *noun*
= (der) Lachs

salt *noun*
= (das) Salz

same
1 *adjective*
• **the same** = der gleiche/die gleiche/das
    gleiche
  I've got the same picture = ich habe das
    gleiche Bild
• (*one and the same*) =
    derselbe/dieselbe/dasselbe
  they go to the same school = sie gehen in
    dieselbe Schule
2 *adverb*
  the same = gleich
  the houses all look the same = die Häuser
    sehen alle gleich aus
3 *pronoun*
• **the same** = der Gleiche/
    die Gleiche/das Gleiche
  I'll have the same = ich nehme das Gleiche
  Happy New Year—the same to you = ein
    gutes neues Jahr—danke gleichfalls
• (*one and the same*) =
    derselbe/dieselbe/dasselbe
  to do the same as the others = dasselbe
    wie die anderen machen

sand *noun*
= (der) Sand

sandal *noun*
= (die) Sandale

Santa Claus *noun*
= (der) Weihnachtsmann

sardine *noun*
= (die) Sardine

satellite dish *noun*
= (die) Parabolantenne, =
  (die) Satellitenschüssel

satellite TV *noun*
= (das) Satellitenfernsehen

satisfactory *adjective*
= befriedigend

satisfied *adjective*
= zufrieden

Saturday *noun*
= (der) Samstag, = (der) Sonnabend ▶ Dates
  p. 213

sauce *noun*
= (die) Soße

saucepan *noun*
= (der) Kochtopf

saucer *noun*
= (die) Untertasse

sausage *noun*
= (die) Wurst

save *verb*
• (*rescue*) = retten
  to save someone from something =
    jemanden vor etwas (*dative*) retten
  they saved his life = sie haben ihm das
    Leben gerettet
• (*avoid spending, wasting*) = sparen
  to save [time | money | energy …] = [Zeit |
    Geld | Energie …] sparen
  to save up for something = auf etwas
    (*accusative*) sparen
• (*keep*) = aufheben
  to save a piece of cake for someone =
    jemandem ein Stück Kuchen aufheben
• (*spare*) = ersparen
  to save someone a lot of work =
    jemandem viel Arbeit ersparen
• (*stop*) = abwehren
  to save a penalty = einen Elfmeter
    abwehren
• (*in computing*) = speichern

savings *noun*
= Ersparnisse (*plural*)

saw *noun*
= (die) Säge

say *verb*
= sagen
  he didn't say that = er hat das nicht gesagt
  what does the paper say? = was steht in
    der Zeitung?
  that is to say = das heißt
  that goes without saying = das versteht
    sich von selbst

scandal *noun*
= (der) Skandal

scare *verb*
  (*startle*) = erschrecken
  (*frighten*) = Angst machen (+ *dative*)

scare away
= verscheuchen

scared *adjective*
to be scared of someone = vor jemandem
Angst haben

scarf *noun*
(*long*) = (der) Schal
(*square*) = (das) Tuch

scenery *noun*
= (die) Landschaft

school
1 *noun* = (die) Schule
to be at school = in der Schule sein
to go to school = zur Schule gehen (**!** *sein*)
2 *adjective* = Schul-
school uniform = (die) Schuluniform

schoolboy *noun*
= (der) Schüler

schoolgirl *noun*
= (die) Schülerin

schoolwork *noun*
= Schularbeiten (*plural*)

science *noun*
= (die) Wissenschaft
to study science = Naturwissenschaften
studieren

scientist *noun*
= (der) Wissenschaftler/
(die) Wissenschaftlerin

scissors *noun*
= (die) Schere
a pair of scissors = eine Schere

score *verb*
to score a goal = ein Tor schießen

Scorpio *noun*
= (der) Skorpion

Scotland *noun*
= (das) Schottland ▶**Countries p. 208**

Scottish *adjective*
= schottisch ▶**Countries p. 208**

scratch *verb*
• (*when itchy*) = sich kratzen
• (*hurt*) = kratzen
• (*mark, damage*) = zerkratzen

scream *verb*
= schreien

screen *noun*
• (*of a TV, computer*) = (der) Bildschirm
(*in the cinema*) = (die) Leinwand
• (*partition*) = (die) Trennwand

screw *noun*
= (die) Schraube

scroll *verb*
= scrollen

sea *noun*
= (das) Meer, = (die) See

seafood *noun*
= Meeresfrüchte (*plural*)

seagull *noun*
= (die) Möwe

seal *noun*
• (*animal*) = (der) Seehund
• (*official mark, stamp*) = (das) Siegel

search *verb*
• = suchen
to search for someone = jemanden suchen
• (*examine*) = durchsuchen
to search a building for something = ein
Gebäude nach etwas (*dative*)
durchsuchen

seashell *noun*
= (die) Muschel

seasick *adjective*
= seekrank

season *noun*
= (die) Jahreszeit
(*holiday period, sporting*) = (die) Saison
strawberries are in season = es ist die Zeit
für Erdbeeren

season ticket *noun*
(die) Dauerkarte

seat *noun*
• (*chair, bench*) = (der) Sitzplatz
have a seat = setz dich, (*formal*) = setzen
Sie sich
• (*on a bus, in the theatre*) – (der) Platz

seatbelt *noun*
= (der) Sicherheitsgurt

second
1 *adjective* = zweiter/zweite/zweites
it's the second time I've called her = ich
habe sie schon zum zweiten Mal gerufen
every second Monday = jeden zweiten
Montag
to be second = Zweiter/Zweite sein
2 *noun*
• (*in a sequence*)
the second = der/die/das Zweite
the second of May = der zweite Mai
▶**Dates p. 213**
• (*part of a minute*) = (die) Sekunde

secondary school *noun*
= (die) höhere Schule

second-hand *adjective*
= gebraucht
a second-hand car = ein Gebrauchtwagen

secret
1 *adjective* = geheim
2 *noun* = (das) Geheimnis
to tell someone a secret = jemandem ein
Geheimnis verraten
in secret = heimlich

secretary *noun*
= (der) Sekretär/(die) Sekretärin

S

see *verb*
- = sehen
  do they see each other often? = sehen sie
  sich oft?
  he saw it happen = er hat gesehen, wie es
  passiert ist
  see you soon = bis bald
  see you! = tschüss!
- (*check*) = nachsehen
  I'll go and see = ich sehe nach
- (*visit*) = besuchen
  (*see a doctor, solicitor*) = gehen zu
  (+ *dative*) (**!** *sein*)
- (*speak to*) = sprechen
  I want to see him about the flat = ich
  möchte ihn wegen der Wohnung
  sprechen
- (*make sure*)
  to see that the work is finished = zusehen,
  dass die Arbeit fertig wird
- (*accompany*) = begleiten
  I'll see you home = ich begleite dich nach
  Hause
- (*understand*) = verstehen

see off
(*say goodbye to*) = verabschieden

see through
to see through someone = jemanden
durchschauen

see to
= sich kümmern um (+ *accusative*)

seem *verb*
= scheinen
  she seems [happy | tired | depressed ...] = sie
  scheint [glücklich | müde | deprimiert ...] zu
  sein
  it seems there are a lot of problems =
  anscheinend gibt es viele Probleme

seldom *adverb*
= selten

self-confident *adjective*
= selbstbewusst

selfish *adjective*
= egoistisch

sell *verb*
= verkaufen
It sells well = es verkauft sich gut

send *verb*
= schicken
  to send a parcel to someone = jemandem
  ein Paket schicken
  to send someone to do the shopping =
  jemanden einkaufen schicken
send away
= wegschicken
send back
= zurückschicken
send for
  to send for the doctor = den Arzt rufen
  to send for a catalogue = einen Katalog
  anfordern

send off
- **to send a player off** = einen Spieler vom
  Platz stellen
- **to send off for something** = sich (*dative*)
  etwas schicken lassen
send on
= nachsenden

senior *adjective*
- (*in age*) = älter
- (*in rank*) = höher

senior high school *noun* (*US*)
= (die) höhere Schule

sense *noun*
- (*common sense*) = (der) Verstand
- (*one of the five senses, meaning*)
  = (der) Sinn
  sense of taste = (der) Geschmackssinn
  it doesn't make sense = es ergibt keinen
  Sinn

sensible *adjective*
- (*reasonable*) = vernünftig
- (*practical*) = praktisch

sensitive *adjective*
= empfindlich

sentence
1 *noun*
- (*in grammar*) = (der) Satz
- (*punishment*) = (die) Strafe
  a prison sentence = eine Gefängnisstrafe
2 *verb* = verurteilen
  to sentence someone to a year in prison =
  jemanden zu einem Jahr Gefängnis
  verurteilen

separate
1 *adjective*
- (*apart*)
  separate bedrooms
  = getrennte Schlafzimmer
  a separate toilet = eine separate Toilette
  all the children have separate rooms = die
  Kinder haben alle ihr eigenes Zimmer
- (*different*) = verschieden
  there are two separate problems = es gibt
  zwei verschiedene Probleme
2 *verb*
- = trennen
- (*of a couple*) = sich trennen

separated *adverb*
= getrennt
  the couple are separated = das Paar lebt
  getrennt

separately *adverb*
- (*individually*) = einzeln
- (*alone*) = getrennt

September *noun*
= (der) September ▶ Dates p. 213

serial *noun*
= (die) Fortsetzungsgeschichte
(*on TV, radio*) = (die) Serie

series *noun*
= (die) Serie

serious *adjective*
* = ernst
  to be serious about sport = Sport ernst
  nehmen
  [auf die Universität gehen | heiraten | einen Job
  finden ...] wollen
* (*of an illness, accident*) = schwer

serve *verb*
* (*in a shop*) = bedienen
  are you being served? = werden Sie schon
  bedient?
* (*at table*) = servieren
* (*in tennis*) = aufschlagen

server *noun*
= (der) Server

service *noun*
* (*work, helping others*) = (der) Dienst
* (*in a shop, restaurant*) = (die) Bedienung
* (*religious ceremony*) = (der) Gottesdienst
* (*car maintenance*) = (die) Wartung
* (*system of transport*) = (die) Verbindung

service station *noun*
= (die) Tankstelle

set
1 *noun*
* (*collection, in tennis*) = (der) Satz
  a chess set = ein Schachspiel
* (*TV*) = (das) Gerät
2 *verb*
* (*decide on*) = festlegen
  to set a [date | price ...] = [einen Termin | einen
  Preis ...] festlegen
* (*adjust controls*) = einstellen
  to set an alarm clock = einen Wecker
  stellen
* (*at school*)
  to set homework = Hausaufgaben aufgeben
* (*be responsible for*)
  to set a record = einen Rekord aufstellen
  to set an example to someone =
  jemandem ein Beispiel geben
* (*locate*)
  the film is set in Paris = der Film spielt in
  Paris
* (*of the sun*) = untergehen (**!** *sein*)
* **to set the table** = den Tisch decken
set off
* (*leave*) = aufbrechen (**!** *sein*)
* (*cause to go off*)
  to set off an alarm = eine Alarmanlage
  auslösen
  to set off a bomb = eine Bombe explodieren
  lassen
set up
= aufbauen

settle *verb*
* (*end*)
  to settle an argument = einen Streit
  beilegen
* (*pay*) = bezahlen
  to settle a bill = eine Rechnung bezahlen

* (*decide on*) = entscheiden
* (*make one's home*) = sich niederlassen
settle down
* (*sit comfortably*) = sich gemütlich
  hinsetzen
* (*become established in a place*)
  = sich einleben
* (*calm down*) = sich beruhigen
  to settle down to work = mit der Arbeit
  anfangen
* (*marry*) = häuslich werden (**!** *sein*)

seven *adjective*
= sieben ▶**Numbers p. 282**

seventeen *adjective*
= siebzehn ▶**Numbers p. 282**

seventh *adjective*
= siebter/siebte/siebtes ▶**Numbers p. 282**,
▶**Dates p. 213**

seventy *adjective*
= siebzig ▶**Numbers p. 282**

several *adjective, pronoun*
= mehrere

severe *adjective*
* (*of an illness, conditions*) = schwer
* (*of a person, criticism*) = hart

sew *verb*
= nähen

sewing machine *noun*
= (die) Nähmaschine

sex *noun*
* (*gender*) = (das) Geschlecht
* (*sexuality*) = (der) Sex

shade *noun*
* (*out of the sun*) = (der) Schatten
  to sit in the shade = im Schatten sitzen
* (*of colour*) = (der) Ton
* (*for a lamp*) = (der) Schirm

shadow *noun*
= (der) Schatten

shake *verb*
* schütteln
  to shake one's head = den Kopf schütteln
  to shake hands with someone =
  jemandem die Hand geben
* (*cause to tremble, shock*) = erschüttern
* (*with cold, shock*) = zittern
  he was shaking with fear = er zitterte vor
  Angst
* (*from an explosion, earthquake*) = beben

shall *verb*

> **!** *Note that* shall *is normally translated by*
> werden, *since in German the future tense
> is formed by* werden *and the infinitive of
> the main verb. However, the present
> tense and verbs implying the future, such
> as* können (= can), sollen (= should) *and*
> müssen (= must), *are often used to
> express the future tense.*

S

• I shall certainly come = ich werde ganz
  bestimmt kommen *or* ich komme ganz
  bestimmt

> **!** *Note that* werden *is always used when
> some doubt is expressed about the
> future.*

I shall probably spend Christmas at home
  = ich werde wahrscheinlich Weihnachten
  zu Hause verbringen
• (*in questions*) = sollen
  shall I set the table? = soll ich den Tisch
  decken?

shame *noun*
• (*disgrace*) = (die) Schande
• **what a shame** = wie schade
  it's a shame he can't come = schade, dass
  er nicht kommen kann

shampoo *noun*
  = (das) Shampoo

shape *noun*
  = (die) Form
  to be in good shape = gut in Form sein
  to get in shape = in Form kommen (**!** *sein*)

share
1 *verb* = teilen
2 *noun* = (der) Teil
  to pay one's share = seinen Teil zahlen
share out
  = aufteilen

shark *noun*
  = (der) Hai

sharp *adjective*
• (*used for cutting*) = scharf
• (*with a point*) = spitz
• (*sudden*) = steil
  a sharp rise = ein steiler Anstieg
  a sharp bend = eine scharfe Kurve
• (*clever*) = clever
• (*severe, painful*) = heftig
• (*unscrupulous*) = gerissen
• (*in taste*) = sauer

shave *verb*
  = sich rasieren

she *pronoun*
  = sie

sheep *noun*
  = (das) Schaf

sheet *noun*
• (*for a bed*) = (das) Laken
• (*of paper*) = (das) Blatt
• (*of glass*) = (die) Platte

shelf *noun*
• (*single board*) = (das) Brett
  (*set of shelves*) = (das) Regal
  the book is on the shelf = das Buch steht
  im Regal
• (*in an oven*) = (die) Schiene

shell *noun*
• (*of an egg, nut*) = (die) Schale
  (*of a snail*) = (das) Haus
  (*of a tortoise*) = (der) Panzer
  (*on a beach*) = (die) Muschel
• (*bomb*) = (die) Granate

shelter
1 *noun*
• (*from rain, danger*) = (der) Schutz
• (*for homeless people*) = (die) Unterkunft
2 *verb*
  (*take shelter*) = Schutz suchen
  (*from the rain*) = sich unterstellen
  to shelter someone from something =
  jemanden vor etwas (*dative*) schützen

shin *noun*
  = (das) Schienbein

shine *verb*
• (*to give out light*) = leuchten
  (*of the sun, moon, a lamp*) = scheinen
  the sun shone in his eyes = die Sonne
  schien ihm in die Augen
• (*point*) = leuchten
  to shine a torch at something = etwas
  anleuchten

> **!** *Note that it is not necessary to translate*
> torch.

• (*reflect light*) = glänzen

ship *noun*
  = (das) Schiff

shirt *noun*
  = (das) Hemd

shit *noun* = (die) Scheiße✶

shiver *verb*
  = zittern

shock
1 *noun*
• = (der) Schock
  to get a shock = einen Schock bekommen
  to give someone a shock = jemandem
  einen Schock versetzen
  to be in shock = unter Schock stehen
• (*from electricity*) = (der) Schlag
  to get a shock = einen Schlag bekommen
2 *verb*
• (*upset*) = erschüttern
• (*cause scandal*) = schockieren

shoe *noun*
  = (der) Schuh

shoelace *noun*
  = (der) Schnürsenkel

shoot *verb*
• (*using a weapon*) = schießen
  (*kill*) = erschießen
• (*move very fast*) = schießen�ると (**!** *sein*)
  to shoot past = vorbeischießen✶ (**!** *sein*)
• **to shoot a film** = einen Film drehen
shoot up
  (*grow*) = in die Höhe schießen (**!** *sein*)

---

shop
1 *noun* = (das) Geschäft, = (der) Laden
2 *verb* = einkaufen
  to go shopping = einkaufen gehen
  (**!** *sein*)

shop assistant *noun* (*British*)
= (der) Verkäufer/(die) Verkäuferin

shopkeeper *noun*
= (der) Geschäftsinhaber/
  (die) Geschäftsinhaberin, = (der)
  Ladenbesitzer/(die) Ladenbesitzerin

shopping *noun*
• (*activity*) = (das) Einkaufen
  to do the shopping = einkaufen
• (*things bought*) = Einkäufe (*plural*)

shopping cart *noun* (*US*)
  (der) Einkaufswagen

shopping centre (*British*), **shopping
  mall** (*US*) *noun*
= (das) Einkaufszentrum

shopping trolley *noun* (*British*)
= (der) Einkaufswagen

shop window *noun*
= (das) Schaufenster

shore *noun*
• (*coast*) = (die) Küste
  (*beach*) = (der) Strand
  to be on shore = an Land sein
• (*of a lake, river*) = (das) Ufer

short *adjective*
• (*not long*) = kurz
  to have short hair = kurze Haare haben
• (*not tall*) = klein
• (*lacking*)
  to be short of [money | time | paper ...] = zu
  wenig [Geld | Zeit | Papier ...] haben
  to be short of breath = außer Atem sein
  in short = kurz

short cut *noun*
= (die) Abkürzung

shortly *adverb*
• (*soon*) = in Kürze
• (*not long*) = gleich
  shortly before = kurz bevor
  shortly after = kurz danach

shorts *noun*
= Shorts (*plural*)

short-sighted *adjective*
= kurzsichtig

shot *noun*
• (*from a gun, in football*) = (der) Schuss
  to fire a shot at someone = einen Schuss
  auf jemanden abfeuern
• (*photo*) = (die) Aufnahme

should *verb*

! *Note that* should *is usually translated by
the imperfect subjunctive of* sollen. *For
more about the subjunctive* ▶**p. 349**.

• (*ought*)
  one should always tell the truth = man
  sollte immer die Wahrheit sagen
  shouldn't he be at school? = sollte er nicht
  in der Schule sein?
• (*when something is likely to happen*)
  they should be home soon = sie müssten
  bald zu Hause sein
  that should be enough = das müsste
  reichen
• (*implying that something didn't happen*)
  the letter should have arrived yesterday =
  der Brief hätte gestern ankommen
  müssen
• (*when asking for advice*)
  should I call the doctor? = soll ich den Arzt
  rufen?
• (*expressing a wish*)
  I should like to know = ich möchte gerne
  wissen

shoulder *noun*
= (die) Schulter

shout
1 *verb* = schreien

! *Note that* schreien *forms a separable
verb with prepositions such as* an.

  to shout at someone = jemanden
  anschreien
2 *noun* = (der) Schrei

shovel *noun*
= (die) Schaufel

show
1 *verb*
• (*let someone see, indicate*) = zeigen
  to show someone a photo = jemandem ein
  Foto zeigen
  to show one's passport = den Pass
  vorzeigen
• (*go with*) = begleiten
  I'll show you to your room = ich begleite
  Sie auf Ihr Zimmer
  she showed him to his seat = sie führte
  ihn an seinen Platz
• (*be on*) = laufen (**!** *sein*)
  the film is showing at the Odeon = der
  Film läuft im Odeon
  to be shown on TV = im Fernsehen
  kommen (**!** *sein*)
2 *noun*
• (*on stage, TV*) = (die) Schau, = (die) Show
• (*exhibition*) = (die) Ausstellung
  to be on show = ausgestellt sein
show off
= angeben
show round
  to show someone round the town =
  jemandem die Stadt zeigen

shower *noun*
• (*for washing*) = (die) Dusche
  to have a shower = sich duschen
• (*rain*) = (der) Schauer

S

shrimp noun
= (die) Krabbe

shrink verb
(get smaller) = schrumpfen (**!** sein)
(of clothes) = einlaufen (**!** sein)

shut
1 adjective = zu
to stay shut = zubleiben (**!** sein)
2 verb
(close) = zumachen
(of a door, mouth, eyes) = schließen
the door won't shut = die Tür schließt nicht
the door shut after her = die Tür schloss
sich hinter ihr
shut up
• (be quiet) = den Mund halten✘
shut up! = halt den Mund!✘
• (lock in) = einsperren

shy adjective
= schüchtern

sick adjective
• (ill) = krank
to be sick (vomit) = sich übergeben
I feel sick = mir ist schlecht
• (fed up)
to be sick of [work | the neighbours | the
noise ...] = [die Arbeit | die Nachbarn | den
Lärm ...] satt haben
to be sick of doing something = es satt
haben, etwas zu tun

sickness noun
= (die) Krankheit
(vomiting) = (das) Erbrechen

side noun
• = (die) Seite
on the wrong side of the road = auf der
falschen Straßenseite
at or by the side of = neben (+ dative)
to take sides against someone = gegen
jemanden Partei ergreifen
to stand side by side = nebeneinander
stehen
• (team) = (die) Mannschaft
side with
= Partei ergreifen für (+accusative)

sidewalk noun (US)
= (der) Bürgersteig

sigh verb
= seufzen

sight noun
to have good sight = gute Augen haben
to catch sight of someone = jemanden
sehen
to lose sight of someone = jemanden aus
dem Auge verlieren
to be out of sight = außer Sicht sein
at first sight = auf den ersten Blick

sights noun
= Sehenswürdigkeiten (plural)

sightseeing noun
to go sightseeing = die
Sehenswürdigkeiten besichtigen

sign
1 noun
• = (das) Zeichen
the dollar sign = das Dollarzeichen
• (notice) = (das) Schild
2 verb = unterschreiben
sign on
(when unemployed) = sich arbeitslos
melden

signal
1 noun = (das) Signal
2 verb
• (make signs) = signalisieren
to signal to someone = jemandem ein
Signal geben
• (when driving) = die Fahrtrichtung
anzeigen

signature noun
= (die) Unterschrift

silence noun
(quiet) = (die) Stille
(saying nothing) = (das) Schweigen

silent adjective
(quiet) = still
(saying nothing) = schweigend

silk noun
= (die) Seide

silly adjective
= dumm

silver
1 noun
= (das) Silber
2 adjective = silbern
silver paper = (das) Silberpapier

SIM-card noun
= (die) SIM-Karte

similar adjective
= ähnlich

simple adjective
= einfach

since
1 preposition = seit (+ dative)

> **!** For an action starting in the past and
> going on to the present, the present tense
> is used after **seit**. But with a negative, the
> perfect tense is used.

she has been living in Germany since
1990 = sie lebt schon seit 1990 in
Deutschland
I haven't seen him since yesterday = ich
habe ihn seit gestern nicht gesehen
2 conjunction
• = seit
since she's known him = seit sie ihn kennt
• (because) = da
since she was ill, she couldn't come = da
sie krank war, konnte sie nicht kommen

3 *adverb* = seitdem
I haven't seen him since = ich habe ihn
seitdem nicht mehr gesehen
ever since = seither

sincere *adjective*
= aufrichtig

sincerely *adverb*
= aufrichtig
Yours sincerely (*British*), Sincerely yours
(*US*) = Mit freundlichen Grüßen ▶Letter-
writing p. 262

sing *verb*
= singen

singer *noun*
= (der) Sänger/(die) Sängerin

single *adjective*
• (*just one*) = einzig
we visited three museums in a single day
= wir haben drei Museen an einem
einzigen Tag besucht
not a single word = kein einziges Wort
• (*individual*) = einzeln
every single one = jeder/jede/jedes
Einzelne
• (*unmarried*) = ledig, = allein stehend

single bed *noun*
= (das) Einzelbett

single parent *noun*
= (der/die) Alleinerziehende

single room *noun*
= (das) Einzelzimmer

single ticket *noun* (*British*)
= (die) einfache Fahrkarte

sink
1 *noun* = (das) Spülbecken
2 *verb* = sinken

sister *noun*
= (die) Schwester

sister-in-law *noun*
= (die) Schwägerin

sit *verb*
• (*take a seat*) = sich setzen
sit over there = setzt euch da drüben hin
• (*be seated*) = sitzen
to sit on the floor = auf dem Boden sitzen
• to sit an exam = eine Prüfung machen
sit down
= sich hinsetzen
to be sitting down = sitzen
sit up
• (*after lying down*) = sich aufsetzen
to sit up straight = gerade sitzen
• (*stay up late*) = aufbleiben (**!** *sein*)

sitting room *noun*
= (das) Wohnzimmer

situated *adjective*
to be situated in the town centre = in der
Stadtmitte liegen

situation *noun*
• = (die) Lage
• (*job*) = (die) Stelle

six *adjective*
= sechs ▶Numbers p. 282

sixteen *adjective*
= sechzehn ▶Numbers p. 282

sixth *adjective*
= sechster/sechste/sechstes ▶Numbers
p. 282, ▶Dates p. 213

sixty *adjective*
= sechzig ▶Numbers p. 282

size *noun*
= (die) Größe
what size do you take? = welche Größe
haben Sie?
she's about your size = sie ist ungefähr so
groß wie du

skateboard *noun*
= (das) Skateboard

skating *noun*
(*ice-skating*) = (das) Schlittschuhlaufen, =
(das) Eislaufen
(*roller-skating*) = (das) Rollschuhlaufen
to go skating = Schlittschuh laufen/
Rollschuh laufen (**!** *sein*)

skating rink *noun*
(*for ice-skating*) = (die) Eisbahn
(*for roller-skating*) = (die) Rollschuhbahn

skeleton *noun*
= (das) Skelett

sketch *noun*
• (*drawing*) = (die) Skizze
• (*funny scene*) = (der) Sketch

ski
1 *noun* = (der) Ski
2 *verb* = Ski fahren, = Ski laufen (**!** *sein*)

skiing *noun*
= (das) Skifahren, = (das) Skilaufen

skilful *adjective* (*British*)
= geschickt

skill *noun*
= (das) Geschick
(*ability*) = (die) Fähigkeit

skilled *adjective*
(*trained*) = ausgebildet

skillful (*US*) ▶skilful

skin *noun*
• = (die) Haut
• (*on fruit*) = (die) Schale

skinny *adjective*
= dünn

skip *verb*
• (*hop*) = hüpfen (**!** *sein*)
• (*with a rope*) = seilspringen (**!** *sein*)
• to skip lunch = das Mittagessen auslassen

S

skirt *noun*
= (der) Rock

sky *noun*
= (der) Himmel

skydiving *noun*
= (das) Fallschirmspringen

skyscraper *noun*
= (der) Wolkenkratzer

slap *verb*
to slap someone = jemanden schlagen,
(across the face) = jemanden ohrfeigen

sled (US), **sledge** (British)
1 *noun* = (der) Schlitten
2 *verb* = Schlitten fahren (**!** *sein*)

sleep
1 *noun* = (der) Schlaf
to go to sleep = einschlafen (**!** *sein*)
to go back to sleep = wieder einschlafen
2 *verb* = schlafen

sleeping bag *noun*
= (der) Schlafsack

sleet *noun*
= (der) Schneeregen

sleeve *noun*
= (der) Ärmel

slice
1 *noun*
(of bread, meat) = (die) Scheibe
(of cake, cheese) = (das) Stück
2 *verb*
(cut bread, meat) = in Scheiben schneiden
(cut cake, vegetable) = in Stücke
schneiden

slide
1 *verb* = rutschen (**!** *sein*)
2 *noun*
• (transparency) = (das) Dia
• (in a playground) = (die) Rutschbahn

slim
1 *adjective* = schlank
2 *verb* (British)
= abnehmen

slip *verb*
• (slide) = rutschen (**!** *sein*)
the glass slipped out of my hand = das
Glas ist mir aus der Hand gerutscht
• (fall) = ausrutschen (**!** *sein*)
she slipped and broke her leg = sie
rutschte aus und brach sich (dative) das
Bein
• to slip out of the room = aus dem Zimmer
schlüpfen (**!** *sein*)
to slip a letter to someone = jemandem
einen Brief zustecken
it slipped my mind = es ist mir entfallen

slipper *noun*
= (der) Hausschuh

slippery *adjective*
(of a road, surface) = glatt
(of an object) = schlüpfrig

Slovakia *noun*
= (die) Slowakei ▶Countries p. 208

slow *adjective*
• = langsam
to make slow progress = langsam vorwärts
kommen (**!** *sein*)
• to be slow (of a clock) = nachgehen (**!** *sein*)
my watch is slow = meine Uhr geht nach
slow down
= langsamer werden (**!** *sein*)

slowly *adverb*
= langsam

sly *adjective*
= schlau

small *adjective*
= klein

small ads *noun* (British)
= Kleinanzeigen (plural)

smart *adjective*
• (British: elegant) = elegant
• (clever) = clever

smash *verb*
• (break) = zerschlagen
• (get broken) = zerbrechen (**!** *sein*)
smash up
= zertrümmern

smell
1 *noun*
• (odour) = (der) Geruch
• (sense) = (der) Geruchssinn
2 *verb* = riechen
(sniff at) = riechen an (+dative)
to smell of soap = nach Seife riechen

smelly *adjective*
= stinkend
to be smelly = stinken

smile
1 *verb* = lächeln
to smile at someone = jemanden
anlächeln
2 *noun* = (das) Lächeln

smoke
1 *noun* = (der) Rauch
2 *verb* = rauchen

smooth *adjective*
= glatt
a smooth crossing = eine ruhige Überfahrt

snack *noun*
= (der) Imbiss

snail *noun*
= (die) Schnecke

snake *noun*
= (die) Schlange

snapshot *noun*
= (der) Schnappschuss

sneeze *verb*
= niesen

snore *verb*
= schnarchen

snorkel
1 *noun* = (der) Schnorchel
2 *verb* = schnorcheln (**!** *sein*)

snow
1 *noun* = (der) Schnee
2 *verb* = schneien
it's snowing = es schneit

snowboarding *noun*
= (das) Snowboarding

snowflake *noun*
= (die) Schneeflocke

snowman *noun*
= (der) Schneemann

so
1 *adverb*
• so
  I have so much to do = ich habe so viel zu
  tun
• (*also*) = auch
  I'm 15 and so is he = ich bin fünfzehn und
  er auch
• (*other uses*)
  I think so = ich glaube schon
  I'm afraid so = leider ja
  so what? = na und?
  who says so? = wer hat das gesagt?
  so long! = tschüss!
2 *conjunction*
• (*therefore*) = also
  he's on holiday so he won't be able to
  come = er ist auf Urlaub, also kann er
  nicht kommen
• (*for a purpose*)
  be quiet so that I can work = sei still, damit
  ich arbeiten kann
  we left early so as not to miss the train =
  wir sind früh weggegangen, um den Zug
  nicht zu verpassen

soap *noun*
= (die) Seife

soap opera *noun*
= (die) Seifenoper

soccer *noun*
= (der) Fußball

social *adjective*
• = sozial
• (*sociable*) = gesellig

social studies *noun*
= (die) Gemeinschaftskunde

social worker *noun*
= (der) Sozialarbeiter/(die) Sozialarbeiterin

sock *noun*
= (die) Socke
(*knee-length*) = (der) Kniestrumpf

sofa *noun*
= (das) Sofa

soft *adjective*
• (*not hard or tough*) = weich
• (*not harsh or severe*) = sanft
• (*not strict*) = nachsichtig

soft drink *noun*
= (das) alkoholfreie Getränk

software *noun*
= (die) Software

soil *noun*
= (die) Erde

solar energy *noun*
= (die) Sonnenenergie

soldier *noun*
= (der) Soldat

sole *noun*
(*of the foot*) = (die) Fußsohle
(*of a shoe*) = (die) Sohle

solicitor *noun* (*British*)
= (der) Rechtsanwalt/(die) Rechtsanwältin

solution *noun*
= (die) Lösung

solve *verb*
= lösen

some
1 *adjective*
• (*an amount*) = etwas
  can you lend me some money? = kannst
  du mir etwas Geld leihen?

  ! Note that some *is often not translated,
  unless it is emphasized.*

  we bought some beer = wir haben Bier
  gekauft
• (*a certain number of*) = einige
  some of his books are very old = einige
  von seinen Büchern sind sehr alt
• (*a few*) = ein paar
• (*certain*) = manche
  some people don't like flying = manche
  Leute fliegen nicht gerne
2 *pronoun*
• (*an amount*) = etwas
  have some more = nimm dir noch etwas
  some of it is quite good = manches ist
  nicht schlecht
• (*a number of them*) = einige
  some left very late = einige gingen sehr
  spät
  I know where you can find some = ich
  weiß, wo du welche finden kannst
• (*certain people or things*) = manche
  some think differently = manche sind
  anderer Meinung

S

somebody, someone *pronoun*
= jemand
someone or other = irgendjemand

something *pronoun*
= etwas
there's something wrong = irgendetwas
stimmt nicht

sometimes *adverb*
= manchmal

somewhere *adverb*
= irgendwo
(*go, travel*) = irgendwohin

son *noun*
= (der) Sohn

song *noun*
= (das) Lied

son-in-law *noun*
= (der) Schwiegersohn

soon *adverb*
• (*in a short time*) = bald
see you soon! = bis bald!
• (*quickly*) = schnell
you must come as soon as possible = du
musst so schnell wie möglich kommen
• (*early*) = früh
sooner or later = früher oder später

sore *adjective*
(*painful*) = schmerzhaft
(*inflamed*) = wund
to have a sore throat = Halsschmerzen
haben

sorry
1 *interjection*
• (*when apologizing*) = Entschuldigung!
• (*when asking someone to repeat*) = wie
bitte?
2 *adjective*
• (*sad, upset*) = traurig
• (*when apologizing*)
to say sorry = sich entschuldigen
sorry I'm late = es tut mir Leid, dass ich zu
spät komme
• (*feeling pity*)
she feels sorry for him = er tut ihr Leid

sort
1 *noun* = (die) Art
it's a sort of [game | bird | toy ...] = es ist so
eine Art [|Spiel | Vogel | Spielzeug ...]
all sorts of things = alles Mögliche
he's a funny sort of person = er ist ein
komischer Typ
2 *verb* = sortieren
sort out
• (*solve, deal with*) = klären
• (*organize*) = sortieren
• (*pick out*) = aussortieren

sound
1 *noun*

• (*noise*) = (das) Geräusch
they left without a sound = sie sind lautlos
gegangen
• (*of a bell, voice*) = (der) Klang
• (*of TV, radio*) = (der) Ton
2 *verb*
it sounds [funny | interesting | exciting ...] = es
hört sich [komisch | interessant |
aufregend ...] an

soup *noun*
= (die) Suppe

sour *adjective*
= sauer

south
1 *noun* = (der) Süden
to the south of London = südlich von
London
2 *adjective* = südlich, = Süd-
the south coast = die Südküste
3 *adverb* = nach Süden

South Africa *noun*
= (das) Südafrika ▶ **Countries p. 208**

souvenir *noun*
= (das) Andenken, = (das) Souvenir

space *noun*
• (*room*) = (der) Platz
• (*outer space*) = (der) Weltraum
• (*gap*) = (der) Zwischenraum
(*for parking*) = (die) Lücke

spacecraft *noun*
= (das) Raumschiff

spade *noun*
• = (der) Spaten
• (*playing cards*) **spades** = (das) Pik

Spain *noun*
= (das) Spanien ▶ **Countries p. 208**

Spanish
1 *noun*
• (*people*) **the Spanish** = die Spanier
• (*language*) = (das) Spanisch
2 *adjective* = spanisch ▶ **Countries p. 208**

spare
1 *adjective*
• (*extra*) = Extra-
to have a spare key = einen Extraschlüssel
haben
• (*not in use*) = übrig
there is one spare ticket = eine Karte ist
noch übrig
2 *verb*
• **to have money to spare** = Geld übrig
haben
to have time to spare = Zeit haben

spare part *noun*
= (das) Ersatzteil

spare room *noun*
= (das) Gästezimmer

spare time *noun*
= (die) Freizeit

speak *verb*
= sprechen
to speak to someone about something =
mit jemandem über etwas (*accusative*)
sprechen
who's speaking? (*on the phone*) = wer ist
am Apparat?
speak up
= lauter sprechen

special *adjective*
= besonderer/besondere/besonderes
= speziell

> **!** speziell *is mainly used to talk about an
> interest, question or subject.*

my special interests = meine speziellen
Interessen
special offer = (das) Sonderangebot

speciality *noun* (*British*)
= (die) Spezialität

specially *adverb*
(*especially*) = besonders

specialty (*US*) ▶speciality

spectator *noun*
= (der) Zuschauer/(die) Zuschauerin

speech *noun*
• (*manner of speaking*) = (die) Sprache
• (*talk*) = (die) Rede

speed
1 *noun* = (die) Geschwindigkeit
2 *verb*
• (*travel fast*) = schnell fahren (**!** sein)
• (*drive too fast*) = zu schnell fahren (**!** sein)
speed up
= beschleunigen

speed camera *noun*
= (die) Geschwindigkeitsüberwachungs-
kamera

speed limit *noun*
= (die) Geschwindigkeitsbeschränkung

spell *verb*
(*when speaking*) = buchstabieren
(*when writing*) = schreiben
how do you spell that? = wie schreibt man
das?

spelling *noun*
= (die) Rechtschreibung

spend *verb*
• (*pay money*) = ausgeben
• (*pass time*) = verbringen

spider *noun*
= (die) Spinne

spill *verb*
• = verschütten
• (*of a liquid*) = überlaufen (**!** sein)

spinach *noun*
= (der) Spinat

spine *noun*
= (die) Wirbelsäule

spit *verb*
= spucken

spite *noun*
in spite of = trotz (+ *genitive*)

spiteful *adjective*
= boshaft

spoil *verb*
• (*ruin*) = verderben
he spoiled our evening = er hat uns
(*dative*) den Abend verdorben
• (*pamper*) = verwöhnen

sponge *noun*
= (der) Schwamm

spoon *noun*
= (der) Löffel

sport *noun*
= (der) Sport

sportsman *noun*
= (der) Sportler

sportswoman *noun*
= (die) Sportlerin

spot
1 *noun*
• (*stain*) = (der) Fleck
• (*pimple*) = (der) Pickel
• (*drop*) = (der) Tropfen
• (*place*) = (die) Stelle
on the spot = auf der Stelle
2 *verb* = entdecken

sprain *verb*
= verstauchen
to sprain one's wrist = sich (*dative*) das
Handgelenk verstauchen

spring *noun*
= (der) Frühling
in spring = im Frühling

spy
1 *noun* = (der) Spion/(die) Spionin
2 *verb*
to spy on someone = jemandem
nachspionieren

square
1 *noun*
• (*shape*) = (das) Quadrat
• (*in a town*) = (der) Platz
2 *adjective* = quadratisch
square metre = (der) Quadratmeter

squash
1 *noun*
• (*game*) = (das) Squash
• (*drink*) = (das) Fruchtsaftgetränk
2 *verb* = zerquetschen

squeak *verb*
= quietschen

S

squeeze *verb*
to squeeze a lemon = eine Zitrone
auspressen
to squeeze someone's hand = jemandem
die Hand drücken

squirrel *noun*
= (das) Eichhörnchen

stable *noun*
= (der) Stall

stadium *noun*
= (das) Stadion

staff *noun*
(*of a company*) = (das) Personal
(*of a school, college*) = Lehrkräfte
(*plural*)

staff room *noun*
= (das) Lehrerzimmer

stage *noun*
= (die) Bühne

stain
1 *noun* = (der) Fleck
2 *verb* = beflecken

stairs *noun*
= (die) Treppe

stamp *noun*
• (*for postage*) = (die) Briefmarke
• (*on a document*) = (der) Stempel

stand *verb*
• = stehen
to remain standing = stehen bleiben
(**!** *sein*)
• (*put*) = stellen
to stand a vase on the table = eine Vase auf
den Tisch stellen
• (*bear*) = ausstehen
I can't stand German = ich kann Deutsch
nicht ausstehen
I can't stand the noise any more = ich
kann den Krach nicht mehr aushalten
• (*other uses*)
to stand someone a coke = jemandem
eine Cola spendieren
to stand one's ground = nicht nachgeben
stand back
= zurücktreten (**!** *sein*)
stand for
• (*represent*) = vertreten
• (*mean*) = bedeuten
stand out
• (*be conspicuous*) = auffallen (**!** *sein*)
• (*be outstanding*) = hervorstechen
stand up = aufstehen (**!** *sein*)
to stand someone up = jemanden
versetzen

star *noun*
• (*in space*) = (der) Stern
• (*famous person*) = (der) Star

× in informal situations

stare *verb*
to stare at someone = jemanden anstarren

start
1 *verb*
• = anfangen
to start crying = anfangen zu weinen
to start with = zuerst
• (*set up*) = gründen
to start a shop = einen Laden aufmachen
• (*cause*) = auslösen
• to start a car = ein Auto starten
the car won't start = das Auto springt nicht
an
2 *noun*
• = (der) Anfang
from the start = von Anfang an
• (*in sport*) = (der) Start
start off
• (*begin*) = anfangen
• (*set off*) = aufbrechen (**!** *sein*)
start over (*US*)
= noch einmal von vorn anfangen

state *noun*
• (*territory*) = (der) Staat
• (*condition*) = (der) Zustand
don't get in a state! = reg dich nicht auf!**×**

statement *noun*
= (die) Erklärung

station *noun*
• (*railway*) = (der) Bahnhof
• (*TV*) = (der) Sender

stationer *noun*
stationer('s) = (das) Schreibwarengeschäft

stationery *noun*
= Schreibwaren (*plural*)

statue *noun*
= (die) Statue

stay
1 *verb*
• (*remain*) = bleiben (**!** *sein*)
we stayed for a week = wir sind eine
Woche geblieben
• (*have accommodation*) = wohnen
(*for a night*) = übernachten
to stay the night with friends = bei
Freunden übernachten
2 *noun* = (der) Aufenthalt
stay away
= wegbleiben (**!** *sein*)
to stay away from school = nicht zur
Schule gehen (**!** *sein*)
stay in
= zu Hause bleiben (**!** *sein*)
stay up
= aufbleiben (**!** *sein*)

steady *adjective*
• (*constant*) = stetig
• (*stable*) = stabil

steak *noun*
= (das) Steak

steal verb
= stehlen
to steal money from someone = jemandem
Geld stehlen

steam noun
= (der) Dampf
steam up
= beschlagen (**!** sein)

steel noun
= (der) Stahl

steep adjective
= steil

steering wheel noun
= (das) Lenkrad

step
1 noun
• = (der) Schritt
to take a step = einen Schritt machen
to take steps to do something = Schritte
unternehmen, um etwas zu tun
• (stair) = (die) Stufe
2 verb = treten (**!** sein)
step aside
= zur Seite treten (**!** sein)

stepbrother noun
= (der) Stiefbruder

stepfather noun
= (der) Stiefvater

stepmother noun
= (die) Stiefmutter

stepsister noun
= (die) Stiefschwester

stereo noun
• (sound) = (das) Stereo
• (equipment) = (die) Stereoanlage

stewardess noun
= (die) Stewardess

stick
1 verb
• (glue, tape) = kleben
• (become attached) = kleben
to stick to something = an etwas (dative)
kleben
• (jam) = klemmen
the door is stuck = die Tür klemmt
I'm stuck = ich kann nicht weiter
• (pin, insert) = stecken
2 noun = (der) Stock
stick out
• **his ears stick out** = seine Ohren stehen ab
• **to stick one's tongue out** = die Zunge
herausstrecken

sticker noun
= (der) Aufkleber

sticky tape noun (British)
= (der) Tesafilm®, = (der) Klebestreifen

stiff adjective
= steif
to be stiff (after sport) = Muskelkater haben
to be bored stiff = sich zu Tode langweilen

still¹ adverb
• = noch
does she still play the piano? = spielt sie
noch Klavier?
• (even now) = immer noch

still²
1 adverb
to sit still = stillsitzen
to keep still = stillhalten
2 adjective = ruhig

stir verb
= rühren
he didn't stir = er hat sich nicht gerührt

stomach noun
= (der) Magen

stomach ache noun
= Magenschmerzen (plural)

stone noun
= (der) Stein

stop
1 verb
• (put an end to) = aufhören
to stop [laughing | crying | working ...] =
aufhören zu [lachen | weinen | arbeiten ...]
stop it! = hör auf damit!
• (prevent) = verhindern
to stop something happening =
verhindern, dass etwas geschieht
to stop someone from phoning =
jemanden daran hindern anzurufen
• (not move) = halten
(of a person, watch) = stehen bleiben
(**!** sein)
the bus didn't stop = der Bus hat nicht
gehalten
• (make stop) = anhalten
the policeman stopped the car = der
Polizist hielt den Wagen an
• (of a machine, noise) = aufhören
2 noun
(for a bus) = (die) Haltestelle

store noun
(shop) = (der) Laden
(department store) = (das) Kaufhaus

storm noun
= (der) Sturm

story noun
• = (die) Geschichte
• (in a newspaper) = (der) Bericht

straight
1 adjective
• = gerade
a straight line = eine gerade Linie
the picture isn't straight = das Bild hängt
nicht gerade
• (not curly) = glatt

S

- (*honest*) = ehrlich
  to be straight with someone = zu jemandem offen sein
- (*clear, logical*) = klar

2 *adverb*
- = gerade
  to go straight ahead = immer geradeaus gehen (**!** *sein*)
- (*directly*) = direkt
- (*without delay*) = sofort
  to go straight home = sofort nach Hause gehen (**!** *sein*)

straight away *adverb*
= sofort

strange *adjective*
- (*odd*) = seltsam
- (*unfamiliar*) = fremd

stranger *noun*
= (der/die) Fremde

straw *noun*
- (*for drinking*) = (der) Strohhalm
- (*grain*) = (das) Stroh

strawberry *noun*
= (die) Erdbeere

stream *noun*
= (der) Bach

street *noun*
= (die) Straße

streetlamp *noun*
= (die) Straßenlampe

strength *noun*
- (*power of a person or an animal*) = (die) Kraft
- (*force, intensity*) = (die) Stärke

stress *noun*
= (der) Stress

stressful *adjective*
= stressig**✗**

stretch *verb*
to stretch one's arms = die Arme strecken
the jeans have stretched = die Jeans haben sich gedehnt

strict *adjective*
= streng

strike
1 *noun* = (der) Streik
2 *verb*
- (*hit*) = schlagen
- (*go on strike*) = streiken

string *noun*
= (die) Schnur
a piece of string = eine Schnur

striped *adjective*
= gestreift

✗ in informal situations

stroke *verb*
= streicheln

stroller *noun* (*US*)
= (der) Sportwagen

strong *adjective*
- = stark
  a strong French accent = ein starker französischer Akzent
  a strong child = ein kräftiges Kind
- (*not easily damaged*) = stabil
- **a strong argument** = ein gutes Argument

stubborn *adjective*
= starrsinnig, = stur**✗**

student *noun*
(*at school*) = (der) Schüler/(die) Schülerin
(*at university*) = (der) Student/(die) Studentin

study
1 *verb* = lernen
(*at university*) = studieren
2 *noun*
- = (das) Studium
- (*room*) = (das) Arbeitszimmer

stuff
1 *noun* = (das) Zeug
2 *verb*
- = stopfen
  she stuffed the socks in a drawer = sie hat die Socken in eine Schublade gestopft
- (*fill*) = vollstopfen**✗**
  to stuff oneself = sich vollstopfen**✗**

stuffing *noun*
= (die) Füllung

stupid *adjective*
= dumm

style *noun*
- = (der) Stil
- (*fashion*) = (die) Mode

stylish *adjective*
= elegant

subject *noun*
- = (das) Thema
  to change the subject = das Thema wechseln
- (*at school*) = (das) Fach

subscription *noun*
= (das) Abonnement

subtitles *noun*
= Untertitel (*plural*)

suburb *noun*
= (der) Vorort
to live in the suburbs = am Stadtrand wohnen

subway *noun*
- (*British: passage*) = (die) Unterführung
- (*US: underground railway*) = (die) U-Bahn

succeed *verb*
= gelingen (**!** *sein*)
I succeeded in persuading him = es ist mir gelungen, ihn zu überzeugen

success *noun*
= (der) Erfolg

successful *adjective*
= erfolgreich

such
1 *adjective* = solcher/solche/solches

> **!** *Note that* solcher, solche *and* solches *change their endings in the same way as* der/die/das.

such a thing should not have happened = so etwas hätte nicht passieren dürfen
2 *adverb*
they have such a lot of money = sie haben so viel Geld

suddenly *adverb*
= plötzlich

suede *noun*
= (das) Wildleder

suffer *verb*
= leiden

sugar *noun*
= (der) Zucker

suggestion *noun*
= (der) Vorschlag

suit
1 *noun*
(*man's*) = (der) Anzug
(*woman's*) = (das) Kostüm
2 *verb*
• (*be convenient*) = passen (+ *dative*)
does Friday suit you? = passt Ihnen Freitag?
• (*look good on*)
the hat suits you = der Hut steht Ihnen gut

suitable *adjective*
= geeignet
to be suitable for children = für Kinder geeignet sein

suitcase *noun*
= (der) Koffer

sum *noun*
• (*amount*) = (die) Summe
• (*in maths*) = (die) Rechenaufgabe
to be good at sums = gut im Rechnen sein
sum up
= zusammenfassen

summer *noun*
= (der) Sommer
in summer = im Sommer

sun *noun*
= (die) Sonne

sunbathe *verb*
= sich sonnen

sunburn *noun*
= (der) Sonnenbrand

sunburnt *adjective*
to get sunburnt = einen Sonnenbrand bekommen

Sunday *noun*
= (der) Sonntag ▶ Dates p. 213

sunglasses *noun*
= (die) Sonnenbrille

sunny *adjective*
= sonnig

sunrise *noun*
= (der) Sonnenaufgang

sunset *noun*
= (der) Sonnenuntergang

sunshade *noun*
= (der) Sonnenschirm

sunshine *noun*
= (der) Sonnenschein

suntan *noun*
= (die) Bräune
to get a suntan = braun werden (**!** *sein*)

superintendent *noun*
(*in the police*) = (der) Kommissar/ (die) Kommissarin

supermarket *noun*
= (der) Supermarkt

superstitious *adjective*
= abergläubisch

supper *noun*
= (das) Abendessen

support *verb*
• (*help, give money to*) = unterstützen
• (*hold, help physically*) = stützen

supporter *noun*
(*of a team*) = (der) Fan
(*of a party*) = (der) Anhänger/ (die) Anhängerin

suppose *verb*
• (*imagine*) = annehmen
I suppose so = ich nehme es an, (*doubtfully*) = ja, vermutlich
• (*be meant to*)
to be supposed to do something = etwas tun sollen

sure *adjective*
• (*certain*) = sicher
are you sure? = bist du dir sicher?
to make sure the door is shut = nachprüfen, dass die Tür zu ist
• (*bound*)
he's sure to [win | forget it | meet him ...] = er [gewinnt | vergisst es | trifft ihn ...] bestimmt
• sure of oneself = selbstsicher

surf *verb*
= surfen (**!** *sein*)

S

surface
1 *noun* = (die) Oberfläche
2 *verb* = auftauchen (**!** *sein*)

surfboard *noun*
= (das) Surfbrett

surgeon *noun*
= (der) Chirurg/(die) Chirurgin

surgery *noun*
• (*British: place*) = (die) Praxis
• to have surgery = operiert werden

surname *noun*
= (der) Nachname

surprise
1 *noun* = (die) Überraschung
it came as a surprise to us = es hat uns
überrascht
2 *verb* = überraschen

surprised *adjective*
= überrascht
I'm not surprised = das wundert mich gar
nicht

surround *verb*
= umgeben

surroundings *noun*
= (die) Umgebung

survey *noun*
(*poll*) = (die) Umfrage
(*investigation*) = (die) Untersuchung

survive *verb*
= überleben

suspect
1 *verb*
• = verdächtigen
she is suspected of stealing the money =
man verdächtigt sie, das Geld gestohlen
zu haben
• (*assume*) = vermuten
2 *noun* = (der/die) Verdächtige

suspicious *adjective*
• (*feeling suspicion*) = misstrauisch
to be suspicious of someone = jemandem
misstrauen
• (*causing suspicion*) = verdächtig

swan *noun*
= (der) Schwan

swap *verb*
= tauschen
to swap something for something = etwas
gegen etwas (*accusative*) eintauschen

sweat
1 *noun* = (der) Schweiß
2 *verb* = schwitzen

sweater *noun*
= (der) Pullover

Sweden *noun*
= (das) Schweden ▶ Countries p. 208

Swedish
1 *noun*
(*language*) = (das) Schwedisch
2 *adjective* = schwedisch ▶ Countries p. 208

sweep *verb*
= kehren, = fegen

sweet
1 *adjective*
• = süß
to have a sweet tooth = gern Süßes mögen
• (*kind, gentle*) = lieb
2 *noun* = (der) *or* (das) Bonbon

swim *verb*
= schwimmen (**!** *sein*)

swimming *noun*
= (das) Schwimmen

swimming pool *noun*
= (das) Schwimmbecken

swimsuit *noun*
= (der) Badeanzug

swing
1 *verb*
• (*move back and forth*) = schwingen
• (*on a swing*) = schaukeln
• (*dangle*) = baumeln
to swing from a branch = an einem Ast
baumeln
2 *noun* = (die) Schaukel

swipe card *noun*
= (die) Magnetkarte

Swiss
1 *noun*
(*person*) = (der) Schweizer/(die) Schweizerin
2 *adjective* = schweizerisch ▶ Countries p. 208

switch
1 *noun* = (der) Schalter
2 *verb* = wechseln
to switch to another programme = auf ein
anderes Programm umschalten

switch off
= ausschalten

switch on
= einschalten

Switzerland *noun*
= die Schweiz ▶ Countries p. 208

syllabus *noun*
= (der) Lehrplan

sympathetic *adjective*
(*showing understanding*) = verständnisvoll
(*showing pity*) = mitfühlend

syringe *noun*
= (die) Spritze

system *noun*
= (das) System

Tt

table *noun*
= (der) Tisch

tablet *noun*
= (die) Tablette

table tennis *noun*
= (das) Tischtennis

tackle *verb*
(*in soccer, hockey*) = angreifen
(*in American football, rugby*) = fassen
to tackle a problem = ein Problem in
Angriff nehmen

tactful *adjective*
= taktvoll

tail *noun*
= (der) Schwanz

take *verb*
• (*take hold of*) = nehmen
  to take someone by the hand = jemanden
  bei der Hand nehmen
• (*carry with one*) = mitnehmen
  I took my umbrella = ich habe meinen
  Regenschirm mitgenommen
• (*take to a place*) = bringen
  to take someone home = jemanden nach
  Hause bringen
  to take the children for a walk = mit den
  Kindern spazieren gehen (**!** *sein*)
• (*steal*) = stehlen
• (*cope with*) = aushalten
  I can't take the pain = ich kann die
  Schmerzen nicht aushalten
• (*need*) = brauchen
  it won't take long = es wird nicht lange
  dauern
• (*accept*) = annehmen
  we don't take cheques = wir nehmen
  keine Schecks an
• (*react to*) = aufnehmen
  to take something calmly = etwas gelassen
  aufnehmen
• (*use when travelling*) = nehmen
  to take a taxi = ein Taxi nehmen
• (*do, have*)
  to take driving lessons = Fahrstunden
  nehmen
  to take an exam = eine Prüfung machen
  to take a holiday = Ferien machen
  to take a photo = eine Aufnahme machen
• (*wear*) = haben
  to take size 10 = Größe zehn haben
take apart
= auseinander nehmen
take away
(*remove*) = wegnehmen
(*of food*) **'to take away'** = 'zum
  Mitnehmen'

take back
= zurückbringen
take down
• (*from a shelf*) = herunternehmen
• (*write down*) = aufschreiben
take off
• (*from an airport*) = abfliegen (**!** *sein*)
• (*remove*) = ausziehen
  to take one's clothes off = sich ausziehen
• **to take time off** = sich (*dative*) freinehmen
take out
• (*from a container, pocket*) = herausnehmen
• (*from a bank account*) = abheben
• **to take someone out** = mit jemandem
  ausgehen (**!** *sein*)
• **to take it out on someone** = seinen Ärger
  an jemandem auslassen
take part = teilnehmen
  to take part in a game = an einem Spiel
  teilnehmen
take place
= stattfinden
take up
• **to take up German** = anfangen, Deutsch zu
  lernen
• **to take up time** = Zeit in Anspruch nehmen

talented *adjective*
= talentiert

talk
1 *verb*
• = reden, = sprechen
  to talk to someone = mit jemandem
  sprechen *or* reden
  to talk in German = Deutsch sprechen
• (*gossip*) = reden
  they were talking about him = sie haben
  über ihn geredet
2 *noun*
• (*conversation*) = (das) Gespräch
• (*speech*) = (der) Vortrag

talkative *adjective*
= gesprächig

tall *adjective*
(*of a person*) = groß
(*of a building, tree*) = hoch

tame *adjective*
= zahm

tampon *noun*
(der) Tampon

tan *noun*
= (die) Bräune
to get a tan = braun werden (**!** *sein*)

tank *noun*
• (*in a car*) = (der) Tank
  (*for water*) = (der) Wasserspeicher
• (*in war*) = (der) Panzer

tap
1 *noun* (*British*) = (der) Wasserhahn
2 *verb* = klopfen
  to tap on the door = an die Tür klopfen

T

tape

1 *noun*
- *(cassette)* = (die) Kassette
  to record something on tape = etwas auf
  Band aufnehmen
- *(for sticking)* = (der) Klebestreifen
  (strip of material) = (das) Band

2 *verb*
- *(record)* = aufnehmen
- *(stick)* = kleben

tape measure *noun*
= (das) Metermaß

tape recorder *noun*
= (das) Tonbandgerät

target

1 *noun* = (das) Ziel
  (board) = (die) Zielscheibe

2 *verb* = zielen auf (+ *accusative*)

tart *noun* (*British*)
= (das) Törtchen
an apple tart = ein Apfelkuchen

task *noun*
= (die) Aufgabe

taste

1 *noun* = (der) Geschmack

2 *verb*
- *(describing flavour)* = schmecken
  it tastes good = es schmeckt gut
- *(sample when eating or drinking)* =
  probieren

Taurus *noun*
= (der) Stier

tax *noun*
= (die) Steuer

taxi *noun*
= (das) Taxi

taxi rank (*British*), **taxi stand** (*US*)
noun
= (der) Taxistand

tea *noun*
- = (der) Tee
- *(meal)* = (das) Abendessen

teach *verb*
- **to teach someone to** [read | drive | swim …] =
  jemandem [Lesen | Autofahren |
  Schwimmen …] beibringen
- *(work as a teacher)* = unterrichten
  to teach German = Deutsch unterrichten

teacher *noun*
= (der) Lehrer/(die) Lehrerin

team *noun*
  (group) = (das) Team
  (in sport) = (die) Mannschaft

teapot *noun*
= (die) Teekanne

tear¹ *verb*
- *(rip)* = zerreißen
  to tear a page out of a book = eine Seite
  aus einem Buch reißen
- *(get damaged)* = zerreißen (**!** *sein*)
  the string has torn = die Schnur ist
  zerrissen

> **!** *A verb like* zerreißen *that normally takes*
> sein *in the perfect tense takes* haben
> *when it has a direct object.*

  I have torn the string = ich habe die Schnur
  zerrissen
  I tore my dress = ich habe mir mein Kleid
  zerrissen

tear off
= abreißen

tear up
= zerreißen

tear² *noun*
  (when crying) = (die) Träne

tease *verb*
= necken

teaspoon *noun*
= (der) Teelöffel

technical *adjective*
= technisch

teenager *noun*
= (der) Teenager

telegram *noun*
= (das) Telegramm

telephone *noun*
= (das) Telefon

telephone directory *noun*
= (das) Telefonbuch

television *noun*
= (das) Fernsehen
  (set) = (der) Fernseher
  I saw it on television = ich habe es im
  Fernsehen gesehen
  to watch television = fernsehen

tell *verb*
- *(say to, inform)* = sagen
  to tell someone something = jemandem
  etwas sagen
  **could you tell me how to get to the
  station?** = könnten Sie mir sagen, wie ich
  zum Bahnhof komme?
  to tell someone how to do something =
  jemandem sagen, wie man etwas tut
- *(relate)* = erzählen
  to tell someone a story = jemandem eine
  Geschichte erzählen
- *(work out, know)* = wissen
  I can tell she doesn't like me = ich weiß,
  dass sie mich nicht mag
- *(make a distinction)* = erkennen
  to tell the difference = den Unterschied
  erkennen
  its difficult to tell the twins apart = die
  Zwillinge sind schwer zu unterscheiden

tell off
= ausschimpfen

temper *noun*
to lose one's temper = wütend werden
(**!** *sein*)

temperature *noun*
= (die) Temperatur
to have a temperature = Fieber haben

temporary *adjective*
= vorübergehend
temporary worker = (die) Aushilfe

ten *adjective*
= zehn ▶Numbers p. 282

tennis *noun*
= (das) Tennis

tennis court *noun*
= (der) Tennisplatz

tense *adjective*
= gespannt

tent *noun*
= (das) Zelt

tenth
1 *adjective* = zehnter/zehnte/zehntes
▶Numbers p. 282, ▶Dates p. 213
2 *noun*
(*fraction*) = (das) Zehntel

term *noun*
(*at school*) = (das) Halbjahr
(*at university*) = (das) Semester

terrible *adjective*
= schrecklich

terrified *adjective*
= verängstigt

terror *noun*
• (*fear*) = (die) panische Angst
• (*thing or person causing fear*) =
(der) Schrecken

terrorist *noun*
= (der) Terrorist/(die) Terroristin

test
1 *verb*
• (*try out*) = testen
• (*at school*) = prüfen
2 *noun*
• (*of a person's ability*) = (der) Test
(*at school*) = (die) Klassenarbeit
driving test = (die) Fahrprüfung
• (*medical*)
eye test = (der) Sehtest
to have a blood test = eine Blutprobe
machen

textbook *noun*
= (das) Lehrbuch

text message *noun*
= (die) Textnachricht

than *conjunction*
= als
he is older than me = er ist älter als ich

thank *verb*
= danken (+ *dative*)
thank you = danke schön
thank you for coming = danke, dass du
gekommen bist

thanks
1 *interjection* = danke!
2 *noun* = (der) Dank
many thanks = vielen Dank

that
1 *adjective*
= der/die/das, (*stressed*) =
dieser/diese/dieses

> **!** *Note that* dieser, diese *and* dieses
> *change their endings in the same way as*
> der/die/das.

I prefer that shirt = mir gefällt das Hemd
besser
that one = der da/die da/das da
I'll take that one = ich nehme das da
that poor child = dieses arme Kind
2 *pronoun*
• = das
what's that? = was ist das?
who's that? = wer ist das?, (*on the phone*) =
wer ist am Apparat?
is that John? = ist das John?
that's not true = das stimmt nicht
• (*of the kind or in the way mentioned*) = so
just like that = einfach so
that's right! = gut so!
a man like that = so ein Mann
• (*introducing a relative clause*) = der/die/das

> **!** *Note that* der, die *and* das *agree in*
> *gender with the noun they stand for.*

a shop that sells jewellery = ein Geschäft,
das Schmuck verkauft
3 *adverb* = so
it wasn't that hot = es war nicht so heiß
4 *conjunction* = dass
I know that it's not easy = ich weiß, dass es
nicht leicht ist
he drove so slowly that he caused a traffic
jam = er fuhr so langsam, dass er einen
Stau verursachte

> **!** *Note that there is always a comma*
> *before the conjunction* dass.

the
1 *article* = der/die/das, (*plural*) = die

> **!** *Note that the article changes according*
> *to the gender of the noun it goes with:* the
> table = der Tisch (*masculine*); the flower =
> die Blume (*feminine*); the house = das
> Haus (*neuter*); the children = die Kinder
> (*plural*).

the fifth of March = der fünfte März
2 *adverb*
the more the better = je mehr, desto besser
all the better = umso besser

theater (US), **theatre** (British) noun
= (das) Theater

their adjective
= ihr

> ! Note that ihr changes its endings in the same way as ein.

they are selling their car = sie verkaufen ihr Auto

theirs pronoun
= ihrer/ihre/ihrs

> ! Pronouns agree in number and gender with the noun they stand for: theirs (meaning the garden) is small = ihrer (der Garten) ist klein; theirs (meaning the shoes) are new = ihre (die Schuhe) sind neu.

the new house is theirs = das neue Haus gehört ihnen
a friend of theirs = ein Freund von ihnen

them pronoun

> ! In German this pronoun changes according to its function in the sentence. As a direct object it is in the accusative, sie, and as an indirect object it is in the dative, ihnen.

* (in the accusative) = sie
  I know them = ich kenne sie
* (in the dative) = ihnen
  he gave them the money = er hat ihnen das Geld gegeben
* (in the nominative, for emphasis)
  it's them who stole it = sie haben es gestohlen

themepark noun
= (der) Themenpark

themselves pronoun
* (when translated by a reflexive verb in German) = sich
  they want to enjoy themselves = sie möchten sich amüsieren
* (used for emphasis) = selbst
  they did it themselves = sie haben es selbst gemacht
* by themselves = allein

then adverb
* (at that time) = damals
  we met a lot then = wir trafen uns damals oft
  from then on = von da an
  since then = seitdem
* (after, next) = dann

there
1 pronoun
  there is = da ist, = es gibt
  there is no room = da ist kein Platz
  there will be a lot of people = es werden viele Leute da sein
2 adverb
* (when talking about location) = da

(with movement to a place) = dahin
who's there? = wer ist da?
put the books there = leg die Bücher dahin
they don't go there often = sie fahren nicht oft dahin
* (when drawing attention)
  there they are! = da sind sie ja!
  there you are (when giving something) = bitte schön
  there, there = nun, nun

therefore adverb
= deshalb

thermometer noun
= (das) Thermometer

these
1 adjective = diese

> ! Note that diese changes its endings in the same way as the plural article die.

these books aren't mine = diese Bücher gehören mir nicht
these ones = diese (da)
2 pronoun
* = die
  I prefer these = die gefallen mir besser
  these are your things = das sind deine Sachen
* (referring to near things or people) = diese

they pronoun
* = sie
  they want to come too = sie wollen auch kommen
* (indefinite use) = man
  they say = man sagt

thick adjective
* (not thin) = dick
* (stupid) = dumm

thief noun
= (der) Dieb/(die) Diebin

thigh noun
= (der) Oberschenkel

thin adjective
= dünn

thing noun
* (object) = (das) Ding
* (action, subject) = (die) Sache
  the thing is, he wants money for it = die Sache ist, dass er Geld dafür haben will
  the best thing would be to call him = am besten wäre es, ihn anzurufen
  how are things? = wie gehts?

> ! Note that gehts, written as one word, is short for geht es.

* things (belongings) = Sachen (plural)

think verb
* = denken
  to think of something = an etwas (accusative) denken
  we didn't think of closing the window = wir haben nicht daran gedacht, das Fenster zuzumachen

- (*believe*) = meinen
  what do you think? = was meinen Sie?
  I think so = ich glaube schon
  I don't think so = ich glaube nicht
- (*consider*) = nachdenken
  to think about something = über etwas
    (*accusative*) nachdenken
  what do you think of his proposal? = was
    halten Sie von seinem Vorschlag?
- (*regard as*) = halten für (+ *accusative*)
- (*remember*)
  I can't think of his name = ich kann mich
    nicht an seinen Namen erinnern

think over
= sich (*dative*) überlegen
I have to think it over first = ich muss es
  mir erst überlegen

think up
= sich (*dative*) ausdenken

third
1 *adjective* = dritter/dritte/drittes ▶**Numbers**
  p. 282, ▶**Dates p. 213**
2 *noun*
  (*fraction*) = (das) Drittel

thirsty *adjective*
= durstig
I am thirsty = ich habe Durst

thirteen *adjective*
= dreizehn ▶**Numbers p. 282**

thirty *adjective*
= dreißig ▶**Numbers p. 282**

this
1 *adjective* = dieser/diese/dieses

> **!** *Note that* dieser, diese *and* dieses
> *change their endings in the same way as*
> der/die/das.

he wants to come this week = er will diese
  Woche kommen
I'll take this one = ich nehme
  diesen/diese/dieses
this morning = heute Morgen
2 *pronoun*
- = das
  what's this? = was ist das?
  who's this? = wer ist das?
  how much is this? = wie viel kostet das?
  like this = so
- (*referring to a near thing or person*) =
    dieser/diese/dieses
  this is the best = dieser ist der beste

thorn *noun*
= (der) Dorn

those
1 *adjective* = diese, = die

> **!** *Note that* diese *changes its endings in*
> *the same way as the plural article* die.

those books are yours = diese Bücher
  gehören dir

2 *pronoun* = die (da)
  can I have those? = kann ich die da haben?
  those are my letters = das sind meine
    Briefe
  one of those = einer von denen

though *conjunction*
= obwohl

thought *noun*
= (der) Gedanke

thousand *adjective*
= tausend
one thousand, a thousand = eintausend
  ▶**Numbers p. 282**

thread *noun*
= (der) Faden

threat *noun*
- = (die) Drohung
- (*danger*) = (die) Gefahr

threaten *verb*
= drohen (+ *dative*)
(*with a weapon*) = bedrohen

three *adjective*
= drei ▶**Numbers p. 282**

throat *noun*
= (der) Hals

through *preposition*
- durch (+ *accusative*)
  to drive through the desert = durch die
    Wüste fahren (**!** *sein*)
- (*when talking about time*)
  right through the day = den ganzen Tag
    hindurch
  open April through September (*US*) = von
    April bis September geöffnet

> **!** *Note that* through *is often used with*
> *verbs*—get through, go through, see
> through, *etc. You will find translations for*
> *these under the entries* get, go, see, *etc.*

throw *verb*
- = werfen
  to throw a book on the floor = ein Buch auf
    den Boden werfen
  to throw stones at someone = mit Steinen
    nach jemandem werfen
  throw me the ball = wirf mir den Ball zu
  to throw oneself to the ground = sich auf
    den Boden werfen
- (*other uses*)
  to throw a party = eine Party schmeißen**✱**
throw away, throw out
= wegwerfen

thumb *noun*
= (der) Daumen

thunder *noun*
= (der) Donner

thunderstorm *noun*
= (das) Gewitter

T

Thursday *noun*
= (der) Donnerstag ▶Dates p. 213

ticket *noun*
(*for the theatre, an exhibition*) = (die) Karte
(*for a bus, train*) = (die) Fahrkarte
(*for a plane*) = (der) Flugschein
(*for a locker, parking*) = (der) Schein

tickle *verb*
= kitzeln

tide *noun*
= Gezeiten (*plural*)
the tide is in/out = es is Flut/es ist Ebbe

tidy *adjective*
= ordentlich
tidy up
= aufräumen

tie
1 *verb* = binden
to tie the horse to the fence = das Pferd an
den Zaun binden
to tie a knot = einen Knoten machen
2 *noun*
• (*necktie*) = (die) Krawatte, = (der) Schlips
• (*draw*) = (das) Unentschieden
tie up
to tie someone up = jemanden fesseln
to tie a boat up = ein Boot festbinden

tiger *noun*
= (der) Tiger

tight *adjective*
• (*firm*) = fest
• (*close-fitting*) = eng

tights *noun*
= (die) Strumpfhose
a pair of tights = eine Strumpfhose

tile *noun*
(*on the wall*) = (die) Kachel
(*on the floor*) = (die) Fliese
(*on the roof*) = (der) Ziegel

till¹ ▶until

till² *noun*
= (die) Kasse

timber *noun*
= (das) Holz

time *noun*
• = (die) Zeit
I don't have time to visit them = ich habe
keine Zeit, um sie zu besuchen
to spend time reading = Zeit mit Lesen
verbringen
I've been waiting for some time = ich warte
schon seit einiger Zeit
a long time ago = vor langer Zeit

• (*when talking about a specific hour or
period*)
the time is 2 o'clock = es ist zwei Uhr
what's the time? = wie spät ist es?
what time does the film start? = um wie
viel Uhr fängt der Film an?
to arrive on time = pünktlich ankommen
(**!** *sein*)
just in time = gerade rechtzeitig
in [five days' | a year's | two months' ...] time =
in [fünf Tagen | einem Jahr | zwei Monaten ...]
this time last year = heute vor einem Jahr
• (*moment, experience*)
at times = manchmal
at the right time = im richtigen Moment
at any time = jederzeit
for the time being = vorläufig
in no time = im Handumdrehen
to have a good time = sich amüsieren
• (*occasion*) = (das) Mal
this time = diesmal
three times a day = dreimal täglich
the first time I saw him = das erste Mal, als
ich ihn sah
from time to time = von Zeit zu Zeit
• (*when comparing*)
ten times quicker = zehnmal schneller

timetable *noun*
• (*for trains, buses*) = (der) Fahrplan
• (*at school*) = (der) Stundenplan
• (*at work, for events*) = (das) Programm

tin *noun*
• (*metal*) = (das) Blech
• (*British: can*) = (die) Dose

tin-opener *noun* (*British*)
= (der) Dosenöffner

tiny *adjective*
= winzig

tip *noun*
• (*point, end*) = (die) Spitze
• (*money*) = (das) Trinkgeld
• (*advice*) = (der) Rat, = (der) Tip✗

tire (*US*) ▶tyre

tired *adjective*
= müde

tiring *adjective*
= ermüdend

tissue *noun*
= (das) Papiertaschentuch

to *preposition*
• (*in the direction of*) = zu (+ *dative*)
to come to someone = zu jemandem
kommen (**!** *sein*)
he gave the parcel to me = er hat mir das
Paket gegeben
(*to a country, town*) = nach (+ *dative*)
we went to Munich = wir sind nach
München gefahren

Time of day

For days of the week, months and dates, ▶ **Dates p. 213.**

what time is it? = wie spät ist es?, = wie viel Uhr ist es?
could you tell me the time? = können Sie mir sagen, wie spät es ist?
it's 3 o'clock = es ist drei Uhr

In German timetables and official situations, the 24-hour clock is used, so *4 pm* is **sechzehn Uhr.**

00.45 = null Uhr fünfundvierzig

8 o'clock = acht Uhr
8 o'clock in the morning = acht Uhr morgens *or* früh
4 o'clock in the afternoon = vier Uhr nachmittags, = sechzehn Uhr
8 o'clock in the evening = acht Uhr abends, = zwanzig Uhr

1.00 = ein Uhr, *(p.m.)* = dreizehn Uhr
1.05 = ein Uhr fünf, = fünf (Minuten) nach eins
1.15 = ein Uhr fünfzehn, = Viertel nach eins
1.25 = ein Uhr fünfundzwanzig, = fünf (Minuten) vor halb zwei
1.30 = ein Uhr dreißig, = halb zwei
1.35 = ein Uhr fünfunddreißig, = fünf (Minuten) nach halb zwei
1.45 = ein Uhr fünfundvierzig, = Viertel vor zwei
1.55 = ein Uhr fünfundfünfzig, = fünf (Minuten) vor zwei

Note that in German, *1.30 (half past one)* is translated by **halb zwei**; the half-hour is 'half way to' the next hour.

at 9 o'clock tomorrow = morgen um neun Uhr
at about eight = gegen acht Uhr
from ten o'clock onwards = ab zehn Uhr

(to the cinema, theatre, school, office) = in (+ *accusative*)
we went to the cinema = wir sind ins Kino gegangen
❗ *Note that* ins *is a shortened form of* in das.

(to a wedding, party, university) = auf (+ *accusative*)
to go to the toilet = auf die Toilette gehen (❗ *sein*)
• *(as far as, until)* = bis (+ *accusative*)
she counted up to 3 = sie hat bis drei gezählt
• *(indicating position)*
with my back to the wall = mit dem Rücken zur Wand
to the left/right = nach links/nach rechts
• *(send, address, fasten to)* = an (+ *accusative*)
I'm sending the letter to my mother = ich schicke den Brief an meine Mutter
• *(indicating a reaction, showing an attitude)*
to his surprise = zu seiner Überraschung
to the best of my knowledge – nach meinem besten Wissen
there's nothing to it = es ist nichts dabei
• *(in expressions of time)* = vor (+ *dative*)
5 minutes to 8 = fünf Minuten vor acht
• *(in verbal expressions with the infinitive)* = zu
the question is difficult to answer = die Frage ist schwer zu beantworten

❗ *Note that with separable verbs* zu *is put between the prefix and the verb.*
she tried to ring = sie versuchte anzurufen

❗ *Note that* zu *is not needed before the infinitive after the verbs* dürfen, können, mögen, müssen, sollen *or* wollen.
he had to go = er musste gehen
(showing purpose, and after too) = um ... zu
she went home to visit her mother = sie fuhr nach Hause, um ihre Mutter zu besuchen
too young to marry = zu jung, um zu heiraten
(following another verb)
to want to do something = etwas tun wollen
I forgot to tell you = ich habe vergessen, es dir zu sagen
(following an adjective) = zu
to be polite to someone = höflich zu jemandem sein

❗ *Note that* to *is often used with adjectives* (be grateful to someone, be nice to someone, *etc.) and with verbs* (to apologize to someone, to write to someone, *etc.). You will find translations for these under the entries* apologize, grateful, nice, write, *etc.*

toast *noun*
= (der) Toast

toaster *noun*
= (der) Toaster

today *adverb*
= heute

toe *noun*
= (der) Zeh

together adverb
= zusammen
(at the same time) = gleichzeitig

toilet noun
= (die) Toilette

toilet paper noun
= (das) Toilettenpapier

tomato noun
= (die) Tomate

tomorrow adverb
= morgen

tongue noun
= (die) Zunge

tonight adverb
(this evening) = heute Abend
(during the night) = heute Nacht

too adverb
• (also) = auch
• (more than necessary) = zu
  it's too big = es ist zu groß
  I ate too much = ich habe zu viel gegessen
• (very)
  he's not too happy = er ist nicht besonders
  glücklich

tool noun
= (das) Werkzeug

tooth noun
= (der) Zahn

toothache noun
= Zahnschmerzen (plural)
  ! The translation for an **ache** is the plural
  Schmerzen.

toothbrush noun
= (die) Zahnbürste

toothpaste noun
= (die) Zahnpasta

top
1 noun
• (highest part) = (die) Spitze
  at the top of = oben auf (+ dative)
  at the top of the stairs = oben auf der
  Treppe
• (cover, lid)
  (on a bottle, jar) = (der) Deckel
  (on a pen, tube) = (die) Kappe
  (of a table) = (die) Platte
• (highest level)
  to be top of the class = der Erste/die Erste
  der Klasse sein
  to get to the top = Erfolg haben
2 adjective
• (highest) = oberster/oberste/oberstes
• (best) = bester/beste/bestes

torch noun
= (die) Taschenlampe

tortoise noun
= (die) Schildkröte

total
1 noun
  (number) = (die) Gesamtzahl
  (sum) = (die) Gesamtsumme
2 adjective
  (comprising the whole) = gesamt
  (complete) = völlig
  to have total freedom = völlige Freiheit
  haben

touch
1 verb
  (with one's hand) = berühren
  (get hold of) = anfassen
  don't touch that! = fass das nicht an!
2 noun
  to keep in touch with someone = mit
  jemandem in Verbindung bleiben (**!** sein)
  to get in touch with someone = sich mit
  jemandem in Verbindung setzen

tough adjective
• (not soft or sensitive) = hart
• (difficult) = schwierig
• (rough) = rau
• (resistant) = widerstandsfähig

tour
1 noun
• (journey) = (die) Tour
• (by a band, team) = (die) Tournee
• (inspection of a building, city) =
    (die) Besichtigung
  to go on a tour of the castle = das Schloss
  besichtigen
2 verb
  to go touring = herumreisen (**!** sein)

tourism noun
= (der) Tourismus

tourist noun
= (der) Tourist/(die) Touristin

tourist office noun
= (das) Fremdenverkehrsbüro

toward, towards preposition
• (in the direction of) = zu (+ dative)
  (facing) = nach (+ dative)
  towards the east = nach Osten
• (with time) = gegen (+ accusative)
  towards evening = gegen Abend
• (when talking about attitudes) = gegenüber
  (+ dative)
  ! Note that **gegenüber** always follows a
  pronoun or noun.
  towards you = dir gegenüber
  I'm fair towards him = ich bin ihm
  gegenüber fair

towel noun
= (das) Handtuch

tower noun
= (der) Turm

tower block noun (British)
= (das) Hochhaus

town noun
= (die) Stadt
to go to town = in die Stadt gehen (**!** sein)

town hall
= (das) Rathaus

toy noun
= (das) Spielzeug

track noun
• (path) = (der) Weg
• (for sports) = (die) Bahn
• (rails) = (das) Gleis
• (left by a person, animal or vehicle)
tracks = Spuren (plural)

tracksuit noun
= (der) Trainingsanzug

trade noun
• (business) = (der) Handel
• (craft) = (das) Handwerk

traffic noun
= (der) Verkehr

traffic jam noun
= (der) Stau

traffic lights noun
= (die) Ampel

train
1 noun = (der) Zug
by train = mit dem Zug
2 verb
• (teach) = ausbilden
to train someone as a teacher = jemanden
zum Lehrer ausbilden
• (in sport) = trainieren

trainer noun (British)
• = (der) Trainer
• trainers (shoes) = Trainingsschuhe (plural)

translate verb
= übersetzen

translation noun
= (die) Übersetzung

translator noun
= (der) Übersetzer/(die) Übersetzerin

transport (British), **transportation**
(US) noun
= (der) Transport

trap noun
= (die) Falle
to set a trap for someone = jemandem eine
Falle stellen

trash noun (US)
= (der) Müll, = (der) Abfall

trash can noun (US)
= (der) Mülleimer

travel verb
= reisen (**!** sein)

travel agency noun
= (das) Reisebüro

traveler (US), **traveller** (British) noun
= (der/die) Reisende

traveler's check (US), **traveller's
cheque** (British) noun
= (der) Reisescheck

tray noun
= (das) Tablett

treat verb
• (deal with) = behandeln
• (pay for)
to treat someone to an ice cream =
jemandem ein Eis spendieren

treatment noun
= (die) Behandlung

tree noun
= (der) Baum

tremble verb
= zittern

trendy adjective
= modern

trial noun
= (der) Prozess
to be on trial for theft = wegen Diebstahls
angeklagt sein

triangle noun
= (das) Dreieck

trick
1 noun
• (joke) = (der) Streich
• (to deceive, entertain) = (der) Trick
2 verb = täuschen, = hereinlegen*

trip
1 noun
(journey) = (die) Reise
(day out) = (der) Ausflug
to make a trip to London = nach London
fahren (**!** sein)
2 verb
• = stolpern (**!** sein)
• to trip someone up = jemandem ein Bein
stellen

trouble noun
• (difficulties) = Schwierigkeiten (plural)
to get someone into trouble = jemanden in
Schwierigkeiten bringen
• (effort) = (die) Mühe
to take the trouble = sich (dative) die Mühe
machen
to go to a lot of trouble = sich (dative) viel
Mühe geben

trousers noun
= (die) Hose

trout noun
= (die) Forelle

T

truck noun
= (der) Lastwagen

true adjective
= wahr
to come true = in Erfüllung gehen (**!** sein)

trunk noun
• (of a tree) = (der) Stamm
• (large case) = (der) Koffer
• (for storage) = (die) Truhe
• (of an elephant) = (der) Rüssel
• (US: in a car) = (der) Kofferraum

trust verb
• (believe) = trauen (+ dative)
• (rely on)
  you can't trust him = man kann sich nicht
  auf ihn verlassen

truth noun
= (die) Wahrheit

try
1 verb
• = versuchen
  to try to [come | ring | relax …] = versuchen [zu
    kommen | anzurufen | zu entspannen …]
  try again = versuche es noch einmal
• (test)
  to try a recipe = ein Rezept ausprobieren
  to try on a pair of jeans = Jeans
    anprobieren
• (taste) = probieren
• (in court) = vor Gericht stellen
2 noun = (der) Versuch

T-shirt noun
= (das) T-Shirt

tube noun
• (container) = (die) Tube
• (pipe) = (das) Rohr
  inner tube = (der) Schlauch
• (British: underground) = (die) U-Bahn

Tuesday noun
= (der) Dienstag ▶ **Dates p. 213**

tuna noun
= (der) Thunfisch

tunnel noun
= (der) Tunnel

turkey noun
= (die) Pute

Turkey noun
= die Türkei ▶ **Countries p. 208**

turn
1 verb
• (twist) = drehen
  to turn the handle to the right = den Griff
    nach rechts drehen
• (turn around) = sich umdrehen
  she turned and waved = sie drehte sich um
    und winkte

• (change direction)
  to turn right = nach rechts abbiegen (**!** sein)
  to turn the corner = um die Ecke biegen
    (**!** sein)
• (become) = werden (**!** sein)
  to turn red = rot werden
2 noun
• (bend) = (die) Kurve
• (in games)
  whose turn is it? = wer ist an der Reihe?
  in turn = der Reihe nach
• (rotation) = (die) Drehung
• at the turn of the century = um die
    Jahrhundertwende

turn around
• (face the other way) = sich umdrehen
• (rotate) = sich drehen

turn away
= sich abwenden

turn back
= umkehren (**!** sein)

turn down
• to turn the radio down = das Radio leiser
    stellen
• (reject) = ablehnen

turn off
= ausschalten
  to turn the lights off = das Licht ausschalten
  to turn the tap off = den Hahn zudrehen
  to turn off the oven = den Backofen
    ausmachen

turn on
= einschalten
  to turn the lights on = das Licht einschalten
  to turn the tap on = den Hahn aufdrehen
  to turn on the oven = den Backofen
    anschalten

turn over
• (roll over) = sich umdrehen
• to turn over the page = umblättern

turn up
• to turn up the heating = die Heizung
    aufdrehen
  to turn the music up = die Musik lauter
    machen
• (show up) = auftauchen (**!** sein)

turtle noun
= (die) Schildkröte

twelve adjective
= zwölf ▶ **Numbers p. 282**

twenty adjective
= zwanzig ▶ **Numbers p. 282**

twice adverb
= zweimal
  twice a year = zweimal im Jahr

twin
1 noun = (der) Zwilling
2 adjective
  his twin brother = sein Zwillingsbruder

twist verb
• (bend out of shape) = verbiegen
• to twist one's ankle = sich (dative) den
    Knöchel verrenken

✗ in informal situations

- (*of a road, river*) = sich winden

two *adjective*
= zwei ▶**Numbers p. 282**

type
1 *noun*
(*kind*) = (die) Art
(*person*) = (der) Typ
2 *verb*
= mit der Maschine schreiben, = tippen✱

typewriter *noun*
= (die) Schreibmaschine

typical *adjective*
= typisch

typist *noun*
= (die) Schreibkraft

tyre *noun* (*British*)
= (der) Reifen

Uu

ugly *adjective*
= hässlich

umbrella *noun*
= (der) Regenschirm

unbearable *adjective*
= unerträglich

unbelievable *adjective*
= unglaublich

uncle *noun*
= (der) Onkel

uncomfortable *adjective*
= unbequem
I feel uncomfortable = mir ist unbehaglich
zumute

unconscious *adjective*
- (*after an accident*) = bewusstlos
- (*unaware*) = unbewusst

under *preposition*
- = unter (+ *dative or accusative*)

> ! *Note that* unter *is followed by a noun in the dative when position is described. The accusative follows when there is movement towards something.*

to hide under the bed = sich unter dem
Bett verstecken
to push the chair under the table = den
Stuhl unter den Tisch schieben
- (*less than*) = unter (+ *dative*)
(*in price*) = weniger als
children under 5 = Kinder unter fünf
Jahren

- (*other uses*)
under German law = nach deutschem
Recht
under construction = im Bau

underground
1 *adjective* = unterirdisch
2 *noun* (*British*) = (die) U-Bahn

underline *verb*
= unterstreichen

underneath
1 *adverb* = darunter
2 *preposition* = unter (+ *dative or accusative*)

> ! *Note that* unter *is followed by a noun in the dative when position is described. The accusative follows when there is movement towards something.*

the dog lay underneath the table = der
Hund lag unter dem Tisch
the baby crawled underneath the chair =
das Baby kroch unter den Stuhl
underneath it = darunter

underpants *noun*
= (die) Unterhose

understand *verb*
= verstehen
I can understand her doing it = ich kann
verstehen, warum sie es tut
to make onself understood = sich
verständlich machen

understanding *adjective*
= verständnisvoll

underwear *noun*
= (die) Unterwäsche

undo *verb*
= aufmachen

undress *verb*
= sich ausziehen

uneasy *adjective*
= unbehaglich

unemployed *adjective*
= arbeitslos

unfair *adjective*
= unfair, = ungerecht

unfortunately *adverb*
= leider

unfriendly *adjective*
= unfreundlich

ungrateful *adjective*
= undankbar

unhappy *adjective*
- (*sad*) = unglücklich
- (*not satisfied*) = unzufrieden

unhealthy *adjective*
= ungesund

U

uniform noun
= (die) Uniform

union noun
• = (die) Union
• (trade union) = (die) Gewerkschaft

United Kingdom noun
= das Vereinigte Königreich

United States of America noun
= die Vereinigten Staaten von Amerika

universe noun
= (das) Weltall

university noun
= (die) Universität

unkind adjective
(of a person) = unfreundlich
(of a remark) = hässlich

unknown adjective
= unbekannt

unless conjunction
= es sei denn

unlock verb
= aufschließen

unlucky adjective
• to be unlucky = Pech haben
• (bringing bad luck) = Unglücks-
  an unlucky number = eine Unglückszahl
  it's unlucky to walk under a ladder = es
  bringt Unglück, wenn man unter einer
  Leiter durchgeht

unpack verb
= auspacken

unsuccessful adjective
= erfolglos

unsuitable adjective
= unpassend

untidy adjective
(of a person, room) = unordentlich
(of a person's looks) = ungepflegt

until
1 preposition = bis (+ accusative)
I'm staying until Thursday = ich bleibe bis
Donnerstag

  ! Note that until followed by a noun is
usually translated as bis zu, which takes
the dative.

until the evening = bis zum Abend

  ! Note that not until is translated by erst.

not until next week = erst nächste Woche
2 conjunction = bis
I'll wait until you get back home = ich
warte, bis du wieder nach Hause kommst
not until = erst wenn

✗ in informal situations

unusual adjective
= ungewöhnlich

up

  ! Note that up is often used with
verbs—blow up, give up, own up, etc. You
will find translations for these under the
entries blow, give, own, etc.

1 preposition
to be up on something = oben auf etwas
  (dative) sein
to go up the stairs = die Treppe
  hinaufgehen (**!** sein)
to go up the street = die Straße
  entlanggehen (**!** sein)
2 adverb
• = oben
  it's up on the wardrobe = es liegt oben auf
  dem Schrank
  up there = da oben
• (with movement) = nach oben
  to go up = nach oben gehen (**!** sein)
3 adjective
• (out of bed) = auf
  to be up all night = die ganze Nacht auf
  sein
• (higher in amount) = gestiegen
  to be up by 10% = um zehn Prozent
  gestiegen sein
  prices are up = die Preise sind gestiegen
• (wrong)
  what's up? = was ist los?✗
up to
• (well enough)
  I'm not up to it = ich fühle mich nicht wohl
  genug dazu
• (when talking about who is responsible)
  it's up to [me | you | them …] to help = [ich
    sollte | ihr solltet | sie sollten …] helfen
  the decision isn't up to me = die
  Entscheidung hängt nicht von mir ab
• (until) = bis
  up to now = bis jetzt
• (as many as) = bis zu (+ dative)
  to work up to 8 hours a day = bis zu acht
  Stunden täglich arbeiten

upset
1 adjective
  to be upset (annoyed) = ärgerlich sein,
  (distressed) = bestürzt sein
  to get upset about something = sich über
  etwas (accusative) aufregen
2 verb
• (make unhappy) = erschüttern
• (mess up plans) = ducheinander bringen
• (annoy) = ärgern
• (knock over) = umstoßen, (spill) =
  verschütten

upstairs adverb
= oben

  ! If movement is involved, upstairs is
translated by nach oben.

to go upstairs = nach oben gehen (**!** sein)

urgent *adjective*
= dringend

us *pronoun*
= uns
they know us = sie kennen uns
it's us = wir sinds
| **!** sinds *is short for* sind es.

they are older than us = sie sind älter als wir

USA *noun*
= die USA (*plural*) ▶ **Countries p. 208**

USB port *noun*
= (der) USB-Anschluss

use
1 *verb*
• (*make use of*) = benutzen
  he uses this room as an office = er benutzt dieses Zimmer als Büro
  what is it used for? = wofür wird das benutzt?
  to use a different word = ein anderes Wort gebrauchen
• (*take advantage of*) = ausnutzen
  to use someone = jemanden ausnutzen
  to use the opportunity to speak German = die Gelegenheit ausnutzen, Deutsch zu sprechen
• (*use up*) = verbrauchen
  (*on food*) **use before . . .** = mindestens haltbar bis . . .
2 *noun*
• = (der) Gebrauch
  to be in use = in Gebrauch sein
  to make use of a room = von einem Zimmer Gebrauch machen
• (*using*) = (die) Benutzung
  to have the use of a car = ein Auto benutzen können
• (*purpose*) = (die) Verwendung
• **to be of use to someone** = jemandem nützlich sein
  it's no use complaining = es hat keinen Zweck, sich zu beschweren
use up
  to use up all the money = das ganze Geld verbrauchen
  to use up the milk = die Milch aufbrauchen

used
1 *verb*
  I used to read a lot = ich habe früher viel gelesen
2 *adjective*
  to be used to [animals | noise | the cold ...] = an [Tiere | Lärm | die Kälte ...] gewöhnt sein
  to get used to a new job = sich an eine neue Stelle gewöhnen

useful *adjective*
= nützlich

useless *adjective*
• (*not usable*) = unbrauchbar
• (*having no point*) = zwecklos
• (*having no purpose*) = nutzlos

• (*lacking ability*)
  to be useless at chemistry = Chemie überhaupt nicht können
  he's useless = er ist zu nichts zu gebrauchen

usually *adverb*
= normalerweise

Vv

vacant *adjective*
= frei

vacation (*US*) ▶ **holiday**

vacuum *verb*
= saugen

vacuum cleaner *noun*
= (der) Staubsauger

valid *adjective*
= gültig

valley *noun*
= (das) Tal

valuable *adjective*
= wertvoll

value *noun*
• (*financial worth*) = (der) Wert
• (*usefulness*) = (der) Nutzen

van *noun*
= (der) Lieferwagen

vanilla *noun*
= (die) Vanille

various *adjective*
= verschieden
  there are various ways of saying it = man kann es auf verschiedene Weise sagen

vary *verb*
• (*become different*) = sich ändern
• (*be different*) = verschieden sein

vase *noun*
= (die) Vase

value added tax *noun*
= (die) Mehrwertsteuer

veal *noun*
= (das) Kalbfleisch

vegetable *noun*
= (das) Gemüse
  fresh vegetables = frisches Gemüse

vegetarian *noun*
= (der) Vegetarier/(die) Vegetarierin

V

vein *noun*
= (die) Vene

velvet *noun*
= (der) Samt

versus *preposition*
= gegen (+ *accusative*)

very
1 *adverb* = sehr
to eat very little = sehr wenig essen
2 *adjective*
on the very day = genau am selben Tag
the very thing = genau das Richtige
at the very beginning = ganz am Anfang
the very first person = der Allererste/die
Allererste

vest *noun*
• (*British: underwear*) = (das) Unterhemd
• (*US: waistcoat*) = (die) Weste

vet *noun*
= (der) Tierarzt/(die) Tierärztin

via *preposition*
= über (+ *accusative*)

vicious *adjective*
• (*violent*) = brutal
• (*nasty*) = boshaft

victory *noun*
= (der) Sieg

video
1 *noun*
• (*recording*) = (das) Video
• ▶video cassette, video recorder
2 *verb*
• (*record*) = aufzeichnen
• (*film*) = filmen

video camera *noun*
= (die) Videokamera

video cassette *noun*
= (die) Videokassette

video recorder *noun*
= (der) Videorekorder

video shop *noun*
= (die) Videothek

view *noun*
• (*line of sight*) = (die) Sicht
it came into view = es kam in Sicht
• (*scene*) = (die) Aussicht
• (*opinion*) = (die) Ansicht
in my view = meiner Ansicht nach

village *noun*
= (das) Dorf

vineyard *noun*
= (der) Weinberg

violent *adjective*
• (*fierce*) = heftig
• (*of behaviour*) = gewalttätig

violin *noun*
= (die) Geige

Virgo *noun*
= (die) Jungfrau

visit
1 *verb* = besuchen
to visit someone = jemanden besuchen
I'm only visiting = ich bin nur auf Besuch
da
to visit with someone (*US*) = bei jemandem
zu Besuch sein
2 *noun* = (der) Besuch

visitor *noun*
= (der) Besucher/(die) Besucherin
to have visitors = Besuch haben

vocabulary *noun*
= (der) Wortschatz

voice *noun*
= (die) Stimme
to speak in a low voice = leise sprechen

volleyball *noun*
= (der) Volleyball

vomit *verb*
= sich übergeben

vote
1 *noun* = (die) Stimme
2 *verb*
to vote for someone = jemanden wählen

Ww

wage *noun*
= (der) Lohn

waist *noun*
= (die) Taille

waistcoat *noun* (*British*)
= (die) Weste

wait *verb*
• = warten
to wait for someone = auf jemanden
warten
to wait for something = auf etwas
(*accusative*) warten
to wait for someone to ring = darauf
warten, dass jemand anruft
to wait one's turn = warten, bis man an der
Reihe ist
I can't wait to see them = ich kann es kaum
erwarten, sie zu sehen
• (*in a restaurant*)
to wait at table (*British*), to wait on table
(*US*) = servieren

wait up
= aufbleiben (**!** *sein*)

waiter *noun*
= (der) Kellner

waiting room *noun*
= (der) Warteraum
(*doctor's*) = (das) Wartezimmer

waitress *noun*
= (die) Serviererin, = (die) Bedienung

wake *verb*
to wake someone = jemanden wecken
wake up
• to wake someone up = jemanden
aufwecken
• to wake up at 10 o'clock = um zehn Uhr
aufwachen (**!** *sein*)

Wales *noun*
= (das) Wales ▶**Countries p. 208**

walk
1 *verb*
(*rather than run*) = gehen (**!** *sein*)
(*rather than drive or ride*) = laufen (**!** *sein*),
= zu Fuß gehen (**!** *sein*)
(*for pleasure*) = spazieren gehen (**!** *sein*)
to walk down the street = die Straße
entlanggehen (**!** *sein*)
the child can't walk yet = das Kind kann
noch nicht laufen
to walk the dog = mit dem Hund spazieren
gehen (**!** *sein*)
to walk someone home = jemanden nach
Hause bringen
2 *noun* = (der) Spaziergang
to go for a walk = spazieren gehen (**!** *sein*)
it's 5 minutes' walk = es ist fünf Minuten
zu Fuß
walk around
= herumlaufen (**!** *sein*)
walk away
= weggehen (**!** *sein*)
walk back
= zurücklaufen (**!** *sein*)
walk by
= vorbeigehen (**!** *sein*)
walk in
= hereinkommen (**!** *sein*)
walk out
• (*leave*) = gehen (**!** *sein*)
to walk out of the room = aus dem Zimmer
gehen
to walk out on someone = jemanden
verlassen
• (*go on strike*) = in den Streik treten (**!** *sein*)
walk up
to walk up to someone = auf jemanden
zugehen (**!** *sein*)

Walkman® *noun*
= (der) Walkman®

wall *noun*
(*inside a building*) = (die) Wand
(*outside*) = (die) Mauer

wallet *noun*
= (die) Brieftasche

wallpaper *noun*
= (die) Tapete

walnut *noun*
= (die) Walnuss

wander *verb*
to wander around town = durch die Stadt
bummeln (**!** *sein*)

want *verb*
• = wollen
he wants to [go home | play | sleep ...] = er
will [nach Hause gehen | spielen | schlafen ...]
do you want me to come? = willst du, dass
ich mitkomme?
• (*need*) = brauchen
do you want anything in town? = brauchst
du etwas aus der Stadt?
to be wanted by the police = polizeilich
gesucht werden (**!** *sein*)

war *noun*
= (der) Krieg

wardrobe *noun*
= (der) Kleiderschrank

warm
1 *adjective*
• (*not cold*) = warm
I'm very warm = mir ist sehr warm
it's nice and warm in this room = es ist
schön warm in diesem Zimmer
• (*enthusiastic*) = herzlich
a warm welcome = ein herzlicher Empfang
2 *verb*
to warm the plates = die Teller wärmen
to warm one's hands = sich (*dative*) die
Hände wärmen
warm up
• (*get warm*) = warm werden (**!** *sein*)
(*for sport*) = sich aufwärmen
• (*make warm*) = aufwärmen

warn *verb*
= warnen
to warn someone about the risks =
jemanden vor den Gefahren warnen
I warned him not to go by car = ich habe
ihn davor gewarnt, mit dem Auto zu
fahren

wash *verb*
• (*clean*) = waschen
to wash one's hands = sich (*dative*) die
Hände waschen
to wash the clothes = Wäsche waschen
to wash the dishes = abwaschen
• (*get clean*) = sich waschen
wash up
• (*British: do the dishes*) = abwaschen
• (*US: get clean*) = sich waschen

washbasin *noun*
= (das) Waschbecken

W

washing *noun*
= (die) Wäsche
to do the washing = die Wäsche waschen

washing machine *noun*
= (die) Waschmaschine

washing-up *noun* (*British*)
= (der) Abwasch
to do the washing-up = abwaschen

wasp *noun*
= (die) Wespe

waste
1 *verb* = verschwenden
to waste one's time = seine Zeit
verschwenden
2 *noun* = (die) Verschwendung
a waste of money = eine
Geldverschwendung
a waste of time = eine Zeitverschwendung

watch
1 *verb*
• (*look at*) = sich (*dative*) ansehen
to watch a film = sich (*dative*) einen Film
ansehen
to watch television = fernsehen
• (*observe*) = beobachten
we are being watched = wir werden
beobachtet
• (*be careful with*) = aufpassen auf
(+ *accusative*)
watch the children = pass auf die Kinder
auf
watch you don't fall = pass auf, dass du
nicht hinfällst
2 *noun* = (die) Uhr, = (die) Armbanduhr
watch for
= achten auf (+ *accusative*)
watch out
• (*be careful*) = aufpassen
• to watch out for someone (*look for*) = nach
jemandem Ausschau halten

water
1 *noun* = (das) Wasser
2 *verb* = gießen

waterfall *noun*
= (der) Wasserfall

water-skiing *noun*
= (das) Wasserskilaufen

wave
1 *verb*
• = winken
to wave to someone = jemandem
winken
to wave goodbye = zum Abschied
winken
to wave one's handkerchief = mit dem
Taschentuch winken
to wave flags = Fahnen schwenken

× in informal situations

• (*direct*)
to wave someone on = jemanden
weiterwinken
2 *noun* = (die) Welle

way *noun*
• (*manner*) = (die) Art
(*method*) = (die) Art und Weise
that's not the way to learn French = auf
diese Art und Weise kann man nicht
Französisch lernen
he does it the wrong way = er macht es
falsch
I like the way they live = mir gefällt ihre
Art zu leben
you can do it this way or that way = man
kann es so oder so machen
in a way = in gewisser Weise
• (*route, road*) = (der) Weg
I met him on the way to the station = ich
habe ihn auf dem Weg zum Bahnhof
getroffen
which is the way to the station? = wie
kommt man zum Bahnhof?
we can eat it on the way = wir können es
unterwegs essen
on the way back = auf dem Rückweg
to lose one's way = sich verlaufen, (*in a
car*) = sich verfahren
• way in = (der) Eingang
way out = (der) Ausgang
• (*direction*) = (die) Richtung
that's the wrong way = das ist die falsche
Richtung
this way = hier entlang, = in diese
Richtung
• to be in someone's way = jemandem im
Weg sein
to get out of the way = aus dem Weg gehen
(**!** *sein*)
• (*distance*) = (das) Stück
you still have a little way to go = du musst
noch ein kleines Stück gehen
it's a long way from here = es ist weit weg
von hier
• (*what one wants*)
if I had my own way, I'd stay = wenn es
nach mir ginge, bliebe ich hier
to get one's way = seinen Kopf durchsetzen
• by the way = übrigens

we *pronoun*
= wir

weak *adjective*
• = schwach
• (*watery*) = dünn

wealthy *adjective*
= reich

wear *verb*
• (*be dressed in*) = tragen
to wear jeans = Jeans tragen *or* anhaben**×**
to wear black = Schwarz tragen
• (*put on*) = anziehen
I've got nothing to wear = ich habe nichts
anzuziehen

wear out
= abnutzen
he wears his shoes out quickly = er trägt
die Schuhe schnell ab
to wear oneself out = sich kaputtmachen✶

weather *noun*
= (das) Wetter
what's the weather like? = wie ist das
Wetter?
in [cold | bad | nice…] weather = bei [kaltem |
schlechtem | schönem…] Wetter
in wet weather = wenn es regnet

weather forecast *noun*
= (die) Wettervorhersage

Web *noun*
= (das) Web

website *noun*
= (die) Website

wedding *noun*
= (die) Hochzeit

Wednesday *noun*
= (der) Mittwoch ▶Dates p. 213

week *noun*
= (die) Woche
in two weeks' time = in zwei Wochen

weekend *noun*
= (das) Wochenende

weigh *verb*
= wiegen
what do you weigh? = wie viel wiegst du?
to weigh oneself = sich wiegen

weight *noun*
= (das) Gewicht
to lose weight = abnehmen

weird *adjective*
= bizarr

welcome
1 *verb* = begrüßen
to welcome someone = jemanden
begrüßen
2 *adjective*
• = willkommen
to be welcome = wilkommen sein
welcome to Germany = willkommen in
Deutschland
• (*acknowledging thanks*)
you're welcome = bitte, = gern geschehen

well
1 *adverb*
• = gut
the work is well paid = die Arbeit wird gut
bezahlt
she is well able to look after herself = sie
kann sich gut selbst versorgen
• (*other uses*)
you might as well go = du kannst ruhig
gehen
I can't very well say no = ich kann kaum
nein sagen

2 *adjective*
• = gesund
she is not well = es geht ihr nicht gut
get well soon! = gute Besserung!
• as well = auch
she can sing as well as dance = sie kann
singen und auch tanzen

well-known *adjective*
= bekannt

Welsh
1 *noun*
• (*people*) the Welsh = die Waliser
• (*language*) = (das) Walisisch
2 *adjective* = walisisch ▶Countries p. 208

west
1 *noun* = (der) Westen
to the west of London = westlich von
London
2 *adjective* = westlich, = West-
the west coast = die Westküste
3 *adverb* = nach Westen

West Indies *noun*
= die Westindischen Inseln (*plural*)

wet *adjective*
• (*damp*) = nass
to get wet = nass werden (❗ sein)
• (*when talking about the weather*) =
regnerisch
a wet day = ein regnerischer Tag

what
1 *pronoun*
• (*in questions*) = was
what's in that box? = was ist in der
Schachtel?
what is your address? = wie ist Ihre
Adresse?
what's your name? = wie heißt du?
what for? = wozu?
• (*that which*) = was
you can do what you want = du kannst
machen, was du willst
2 *adjective*
• = welcher/welche/welches
what book did you choose? = welches
Buch hast du dir ausgesucht?
• (*asking for an amount*) = wie viel, (*with
plural*) = wie viele
what weight is it? = wie viel wiegt es?
at what time? = um wie viel Uhr?
• (*in exclamations*) = was für
what a lovely day = was für ein schöner
Tag
• (*other uses*)
what if? = was ist, wenn?
what about tennis? = wie wärs mit Tennis?

❗ Note that **wärs** *is a shortened form of*
wäre es, *used in conversational German.*

W

whatever *pronoun*
= was ... auch
whatever they do, they'll still lose = was sie
  auch machen, sie verlieren trotzdem
whatever happens = was auch geschieht
take whatever you want = nimm, was du
  willst

wheat *noun*
= (der) Weizen

wheel *noun*
= (das) Rad

wheelchair *noun*
= (der) Rollstuhl

when
1 *conjunction*
  (*with the present or future*) = wenn, (*with
    the past*) = als
  when he comes we'll go for a walk = wenn
    er kommt, gehen wir spazieren
  I was still asleep when the bell rang = ich
    schlief noch, als es klingelte
2 *adverb* = wann
  I don't know when the film starts = ich
    weiß nicht, wann der Film anfängt
3 *pronoun*
  by when/till when? = bis wann?
  from when? = ab wann?
  since when? = seit wann?

where
1 *adverb* = wo
  where are you going? = wo gehst du hin?
  do you know where he comes from? =
    weißt du, woher er kommt?
2 *conjunction* = wo
  I'll leave the key where you can see it = ich
    lasse den Schlüssel, wo du ihn sehen
    kannst

whether *conjunction*
= ob
can you check whether it's correct? =
  können Sie nachprüfen, ob es richtig ist?

which
1 *adjective* = welcher/welche/welches

  ! *Note that* welcher, welche *and* welches
  change their endings in the same way as
  der/die/das.

  which book do you want? = welches Buch
    willst du?
2 *pronoun*
• = welcher/welche/welches

  ! *Note that* welcher (*masculine*), welche
  (*feminine*) *and* welches (*neuter*) *agree in
  gender with the noun they stand for.*

  which (one) do you want? =
    welchen/welche/welches willst du?

• (*as a relative pronoun*) = der/die/das
  the film which is on at the moment = der
    Film, der gerade läuft
  the blue book, the title of which I've
    forgotten = das blaue Buch, dessen Titel
    ich vergessen habe
  (*when referring back*) = was
  he's always late, which I can't stand = er
    kommt immer zu spät, was ich nicht
    leiden kann

while
1 *conjunction* = während
  while I was writing a letter he watched TV
    = während ich einen Brief schrieb, sah er
    fern
  she fell asleep while watching TV = sie
    schlief beim Fernsehen ein
2 *noun*
  a while = eine Weile
  a while ago = vor kurzem

whisper *verb*
= flüstern

whistle
1 *verb* = pfeifen
2 *noun* = (die) Pfeife

white *adjective*
= weiß ▶Colours p. 204

who *pronoun*
• (*in questions*) = wer
  who told you? = wer hat dir das erzählt?
  (*in the accusative*) = wen
  who did you invite? = wen hast du
    eingeladen?
  (*in the dative*) = wem
  who did you go to the cinema with? = mit
    wem bist du ins Kino gegangen?
• (*as a relative pronoun*) = der/die/das

  ! *A relative pronoun must agree in gender
  and number with the noun to which it
  refers.*

  my friend who lives in London = meine
    Freundin, die in London wohnt

whole
1 *noun*
  the whole = das Ganze
  the whole of [the country | London | August ...]
    = [das ganze Land | ganz London | den ganzen
    August ...]
  on the whole = im Großen und Ganzen
2 *adjective* = ganz
  three whole weeks = drei ganze Wochen

whose *pronoun*
• (*in questions*) = wessen
  whose dog is that? = wessen Hund ist das?
  whose is this? = wem gehört das?
• (*as a relative pronoun*) = dessen/deren/
    dessen

> **!** *The pronoun agrees in gender and number with the noun to which it refers. In this example,* **whose** *is* **deren** *because* die Frau *is feminine.*

the woman whose house I am buying = die Frau, deren Haus ich kaufe

why *adverb*
= warum
why not? = warum nicht?
that's why I can't stand him = darum kann ich ihn nicht ausstehen

wide
1 *adjective*
* (*broad*) = breit
the room is 5 metres wide = das Zimmer ist fünf Meter breit
* (*large*) = groß
a wide range of games = eine große Auswahl an Spielen
* (*extensive*) = weit
2 *adverb* = weit
to open the window wide = das Fenster weit aufmachen

wife *noun*
= (die) Ehefrau

wild *adjective*
* (*not tame*) = wild
* (*out of control*) = verrückt
* (*furious*) = wütend, = wild✗
to go wild = wild werden✗ (**!** *sein*)

wildlife *noun*
(*animals*) = (die) Tierwelt
(*animals and plants*) = (die) Tier- und Pflanzenwelt

> **!** *A hyphen is used to represent the second part of the compound noun* Tierwelt *and avoid repetition.*

will *verb*

> **!** *In German the future tense is formed by* werden *and the infinitive of the main verb. However, the present tense and verbs implying the future, such as* können (= can)*,* sollen (= should) *and* müssen (= must)*, are often used to express the future tense.*

* it will be sunny tomorrow = morgen wird die Sonne scheinen
what will we do? = was machen wir?

> **!** werden *is used when some doubt is expressed about the future.*

they will probably leave tomorrow = sie werden wahrscheinlich morgen abfahren
* (*expressing intentions, making assumptions*)
she'll be there by now = sie wird jetzt schon da sein

> **!** *Note the use of the present tense below.*

we won't stay long = wir bleiben nicht lange

I'll wait for you at the airport = ich warte am Flughafen auf dich
* (*expressing willingness*) = wollen
he won't help me = er will mir nicht helfen
* (*in invitations, requests, short questions etc*)
will you have some more coffee? = möchten Sie noch Kaffee?
he will be there, won't he? = er wird doch da sein?
will you please be quiet! = sei bitte ruhig!
he won't be ready yet—yes he will = er wird noch nicht fertig sein—doch

win *verb*
= gewinnen

wind *noun*
= (der) Wind

window *noun*
= (das) Fenster

windscreen *noun*
= (die) Windschutzscheibe

windscreen wiper *noun*
(der) Scheibenwischer

windsurfing *noun*
= (das) Windsurfen

windy *adjective*
= windig

wine *noun*
= (der) Wein

wing *noun*
= (der) Flügel

winter *noun*
= (der) Winter
in winter = im Winter

wipe *verb*
= abwischen
to wipe one's mouth = sich (*dative*) den Mund abwischen
to wipe one's feet = sich (*dative*) die Schuhe abtreten
to wipe the floor = den Boden aufwischen
wipe up
= aufwischen
(*dry dishes*) = abtrocknen

wire *noun*
= (der) Draht

wireless *adjective*
drahtlos

wise *adjective*
= weise
(*of a decision*) = klug

wish
1 *noun* = (der) Wunsch
best wishes = alles Gute, (*in a letter*) = mit freundlichen Grüßen ▶**Letter-writing p. 262**

W

2 *verb*
= wünschen
to **wish** for something = sich (*dative*) etwas wünschen
to **wish** someone a happy birthday = jemandem alles Gute zum Geburtstag wünschen

with *preposition*
- = mit (+ *dative*)
  to go away **with** friends = mit Freunden wegfahren (**!** *sein*)
- (*at the house of*) = bei (+ *dative*)
  I stayed the night **with** friends = ich habe bei Freunden übernachtet
- (*showing emotion*) = vor (+ *dative*)
  to tremble **with** fear = vor Angst zittern

  ! *Note that* with *is often used after adjectives*—to be angry *or* happy with someone, *etc. You will find translations for these under the entries* angry, happy, *etc.*

without *preposition*
= ohne (+ *accusative*)

wolf *noun*
= (der) Wolf

woman *noun*
= (die) Frau

wonder
1 *verb*
- (*ask oneself*) = sich fragen
  I **wonder** if I should do it? = ich frage mich, ob ich es tun soll?
  I **wonder** [who | why | what ...]? = [wer | warum | was ...] wohl?
- (*in polite requests*)
  I **wonder** if you could help me? = könntest du mir vielleicht helfen?
  I **wonder** if I could ask you a favour? = könnte ich Sie vielleicht um einen Gefallen bitten?
2 *noun* = (das) Wunder

wonderful *adjective*
= wunderbar

wood *noun*
- (*timber*) = (das) Holz
  made of **wood** = aus Holz
- (*forest*) = (der) Wald

wool *noun*
= (die) Wolle

word *noun*
= (das) Wort
I didn't say a **word** = ich habe kein Wort gesagt
to have a **word** with someone = mit jemandem sprechen

× in informal situations

! *Note that* Wort *has two plurals:* Worte *is used when the words are connected in a text or conversation, and* Wörter *when the words are unrelated.*

in other **words** = mit anderen Worten
words in the dictionary = Wörter im Wörterbuch

word processor *noun*
= (das) Textverarbeitungssystem

work
1 *verb*
- = arbeiten
  to **work** at home = zu Hause arbeiten
  to **work** as a doctor = Arzt/Ärztin sein
  ▶ Professions p. 298
- (*function*) = funktionieren
  the TV isn't **working** = der Fernseher funktioniert nicht
  it's not **working** = es funktioniert nicht, = es geht nicht×
- (*to be successful*)
  (*of an idea*) = klappen
  (*of medicine*) = wirken
- (*use, operate*) = bedienen
  to **work** the brake = die Bremse betätigen
2 *noun*
- = (die) Arbeit
  to be out of **work** = arbeitslos sein
  to be off **work** = nicht arbeiten
  it's hard **work** learning German = Deutsch zu lernen ist schwer
- (*for building, repairs*)
  work(s) = Arbeiten (*plural*)
- (*by an artist*) = (das) Werk
work out
- (*solve*) = lösen
  to **work** out the answer = die Antwort herausfinden
- (*understand*) = verstehen
- (*with figures*) = ausrechnen
- (*go well*) = klappen
- (*take exercise*) = trainieren
work up
to get **worked** up = sich aufregen

worker *noun*
(*in a factory*) = (der) Arbeiter/(die) Arbeiterin
(*in an office*) = (der/die) Angestellte

working-class *adjective*
= der Arbeiterklasse
a **working-class** family = eine Familie der Arbeiterklasse
to be **working-class** = zur Arbeiterklasse gehören

world *noun*
= (die) Welt
the biggest city in the **world** = die größte Stadt auf der Welt
all over the **world** = in der ganzen Welt

worm *noun*
= (der) Wurm

worried *adjective*
= besorgt

worry verb
- (be worried) = sich (dative) Sorgen machen
 don't worry about it = mach dir darum keine Sorgen
- (make worried) = beunruhigen

worse adjective
- = schlechter
 he's getting worse (in health) = es geht ihm schlechter
- (more serious) = schlimmer
 there's nothing worse = es gibt nichts Schlimmeres

worst
1 noun
 the worst = das Schlimmste
 that's the worst of all = das ist das Allerschlimmste
 he/she is the worst at French = er ist der Schlechteste/sie ist die Schlechteste in Französisch
2 adjective = schlechtester/schlechteste/ schlechtestes
 (most serious) = schlimmster/ schlimmste/schlimmstes
 the worst film I've ever seen = der schlechteste Film, den ich je gesehen habe
 his worst enemy = sein schlimmster Feind

worth adjective
 to be worth £100 = hundert Pfund wert sein
 it isn't worth it = es lohnt sich nicht

would verb

> **!** Note that would is usually translated by the imperfect subjunctive of **werden**, to form the conditional tense.

 I would do it = ich würde es tun
 I would pay, but I haven't got any money on me = ich würde zahlen, aber ich habe kein Geld dabei
 he wouldn't talk to me = er wollte nicht mit mir sprechen

> **!** The imperfect subjunctive, especially of **haben** or **sein**, can be used instead of the conditional tense.

 we would have missed the train if we had left later = wir hätten den Zug verpasst, wenn wir später weggegangen wären
- (in reported speech)
 he said he'd come = er sagte, er würde kommen
- (when talking about one's wishes, asking)
 what would you like? = was möchten Sie?
 we would like to stay another night = wir möchten noch eine Nacht bleiben

wrap verb
 = einwickeln

wreck
1 verb = zerstören
2 noun = (das) Wrack

wrestling noun
 = (das) Ringen

wrist noun
 = (das) Handgelenk

write verb
 = schreiben
 to write to someone, (US) **to write someone** = jemandem schreiben
 to write to a company = an eine Firma schreiben
 to write a letter = einen Brief schreiben
 to write a cheque = einen Scheck ausschreiben

write back
 = zurückschreiben
write down
 = aufschreiben
write out
 to write out a list = eine Liste aufstellen
 to write out a cheque = einen Scheck ausstellen

writing pad noun
 = (der) Schreibblock

wrong
1 adjective
- (not correct) = falsch
 that's wrong = das ist falsch
 to say the wrong thing = das Falsche sagen
 to be wrong (make a mistake) = sich irren
- (not as it should be)
 to be wrong = nicht stimmen
 there's something wrong = etwas stimmt nicht
 what's wrong? = was ist los?
 what's wrong with you? (if ill) = was fehlt dir?, (if behaving oddly) = was hast du?
- (dishonest) = unrecht
 it's wrong to steal = es ist unrecht zu stehlen
 she hasn't done anything wrong = sie hat nichts Unrechtes getan
2 adverb
 to get something wrong = etwas falsch machen
 the radio has gone wrong = das Radio ist kaputtgegangen✗

X-ray
1 noun = (das) Röntgenbild
 to have an X-ray = sich röntgen lassen
2 verb = röntgen

Y y

yacht *noun*
= (die) Jacht

yard *noun*
* (*of a building*) = (der) Hof
  (*for storage*) = (das) Lager
* (*measure*) = (das) Yard
* (*US: garden*) = (der) Garten

yawn *verb*
= gähnen

year *noun*
* = (das) Jahr
  last year = voriges Jahr
  he's lived there for years = er wohnt seit
  Jahren da
  18 years old = achtzehn Jahre alt
  a 4-year-old = ein Vierjähriger/eine
  Vierjährige
  to work all year round = das ganze Jahr
  über arbeiten
  that'll take years = das dauert ewig
* (*group of students, vintage*) =
  (der) Jahrgang
  which year are you in? (*at school*) = in
  welche Klasse gehst du?
  a first-year student = ein Student/eine
  Studentin im ersten Jahr

yell
1 *verb* = schreien
2 *noun* = (der) Schrei

yellow
  adjective = gelb ▶ **Colours p. 204**

yes *adverb*
* = ja
  are you coming with us?—yes I am =
  kommst du mit?—ja
* (*when contradicting*) = doch
  they don't know each other—yes they do
  = sie kennen sich nicht—doch

yesterday *adverb*
= gestern

yet
1 *adverb*
* = noch
  it's not ready yet = es ist noch nicht fertig
* (*in questions*) = schon
  have they arrived yet? = sind sie schon
  angekommen?
2 *conjunction* = doch
  and yet = und doch

yoghurt *noun*
= (der) *or* (das) Joghurt

✖ in informal situations

you *pronoun*

> ❗ *In German* **you** *has two forms,* **du** *and*
> **Sie**. *Note that* **du** *is less formal and is
> used when speaking to someone you
> know well, a child or a family member.
> Young people always address each other
> as* **du**. *When speaking to a person or a
> group of people you do not know very
> well, use the polite form,* **Sie**.

* (*as the subject of a sentence, in the
    nominative*)
  (*informal*) = du, (*plural*) = ihr
  (*polite*) = Sie
  it was you = du warst es/ihr wart es/Sie
  waren es
  you two are annoying me = ihr zwei ärgert
  mich/Sie zwei ärgert mich
* (*as the object of a sentence, in the
    accusative*)
  (*informal*) = dich, (*plural*) = euch
  (*polite*) = Sie
  he knows you = er kennt dich/euch/Sie
* (*as an indirect object, in the dative*)
  (*informal*) = dir, (*plural*) = euch
  (*polite*) = Ihnen
  I'll give you my address = ich gebe
  dir/euch/Ihnen meine Adresse
* (*indefinite use*) = man

> ❗ *Note that* **man** *can only be used as the
> subject of a sentence. The direct-object
> form in the accusative is* **einen**. *The dative
> is* **einem**.

  you never know = man kann nie wissen
  he can make you angry = er kann einen
  ärgern
  she helps you if she can = sie hilft einem,
  wenn sie kann
  smoking is bad for you = Rauchen ist
  ungesund

young
1 *adjective* = jung
  young people = junge Leute
2 *noun*
* (*young animal*) = (das) Junge
* **the young** (*young people*) = die Jugend

your *adjective*
* (*informal*) = dein, (*plural*) = euer
  (*polite*) = Ihr

> ❗ *Note that* **dein**, **euer** *and* **Ihr** *change their
> endings in the same way as* **ein**. *The
> informal and polite forms follow the same
> rules as for* **you**.

  I hate your dog = ich hasse
  deinen/euren/Ihren Hund

> ❗ *Note that the second e is dropped in*
> **euren**.

* (*indefinite use*) = sein

> ❗ *Note that* **sein** *is used when* **you** *would
> be translated by* **man**.

  you buy your ticket at the door = man
  kauft seine Karte an der Tür
  smoking is bad for your health = Rauchen
  ist schlecht für die Gesundheit

yours *pronoun*
- (*informal*) = deiner/deine/deins, (*plural*) = eurer/eure/eures

> ! Note that the pronoun agrees in number and gender with the noun it stands for: yours (*meaning the pencil*) is red = deiner (*der Bleistift*) ist rot; yours (*meaning the shoes*) are new = deine (*die Schuhe*) sind neu.

a friend of yours = ein Freund von dir/euch
these books are yours = diese Bücher gehören dir/euch

> ! This pronoun has informal and polite forms that follow the same rules as for you.

- (*polite*) = Ihrer/Ihre/Ihrs
my garden is bigger than yours = mein Garten ist größer als Ihrer
she is a friend of yours = sie ist eine Freundin von Ihnen

yourself *pronoun*

> ! This pronoun has informal and polite forms that follow the same rules as for you.

- (*when translated by a reflexive verb in German*)
(*informal*) = dich, (*polite*) = sich
calm yourself = beruhige dich/beruhigen Sie sich
(*reflexive dative pronoun*) = dir, (*polite*) = sich
did you hurt yourself? = hast du dir wehgetan?/haben Sie sich wehgetan?
- (*used for emphasis*) = selbst
you said it yourself = du hast es selbst gesagt/Sie haben es selbst gesagt
- by yourself = allein

yourselves *pronoun*

> ! This pronoun has informal and polite forms that follow the same rules as for you.

- (*when translated by a reflexive verb in German*)
(*informal*) = euch, (*polite*) = sich
calm yourselves = beruhigt euch/beruhigen Sie sich

- (*reflexive dative pronoun*) = euch, (*polite*) = sich
did you hurt yourselves? = habt ihr euch wehgetan?/haben Sie sich wehgetan?
- (*used for emphasis*) = selbst
are you going to organize it yourselves? = organisiert ihr das selbst?/organisieren Sie das selbst?
- by yourselves = allein

youth *noun*
- (die) Jugend
- (*young man*) = (der) Jugendliche

youth hostel *noun*
= (die) Jugendherberge

Zz

---

zap *verb*
- (*kill*) = abknallen✶
- (*switch channels*) = umschalten
- (*remove from a computer screen*) = löschen

zapper *noun*
= (die) Fernbedienung

zebra *noun*
= (das) Zebra

zebra crossing *noun* (*British*)
= (der) Zebrastreifen

zero *noun*
= (die) Null

zip *noun* (*British*)
= (der) Reißverschluss
to undo the zip = den Reißverschluss aufmachen

Zip code *noun* (*US*)
= (die) Postleitzahl

zipper *noun* (*US*) ▶zip

zodiac *noun*
= (der) Tierkreis

zone *noun*
= (die) Zone

zoo *noun*
= (der) Zoo

Contents

Contents

German in use

Regular verbs

Most German verbs are regular and add the same endings to their stem. You find the stem by taking away the **-en** (or sometimes just **-n**) from the end of the infinitive. The infinitive of the verb, for example **machen**, is the form you look up in the dictionary. The stem of **machen** is **mach-**. There are six endings for each tense, to go with the different pronouns:

ich = *I*   du = *you*   er/sie/es = *he/she/it*
wir = *we*   ihr = *you*   sie/Sie = *they/you (polite form)*.

Present tense
For example, *I make, I am making* or *I do make*:

infinitive	ich	du	er/sie/es	wir	ihr	sie/Sie
machen	mache	machst	macht	machen	macht	machen

Imperfect tense
For example, *I made, I was making* or *I used to make*:

infinitive	ich	du	er/sie/es	wir	ihr	sie/Sie
machen	machte	machtest	machte	machten	machtet	machten

Future tense
For example, *I will make* or *I shall make*. This is formed by using the present tense of **werden**, which is the equivalent of *will* or *shall*, with the infinitive verb: **ich werde machen**.

infinitive	ich	du	er/sie/es	wir	ihr	sie/Sie
werden	werde	wirst	wird	werden	werdet	werden

Perfect tense
For example, *I made* or *I have made*. For most German verbs the perfect is formed by using the present tense of **haben**, which is the equivalent of *have*, with the past participle: **ich habe gemacht**. Some verbs take **sein** instead of **haben**, and these are all marked (**! sein**) in the dictionary. They are mainly verbs expressing motion and involving a change of place:

he drove to Berlin today = er ist heute nach Berlin gefahren

Or they express a change of state, and this includes verbs meaning to happen (**geschehen**, **passieren**, **vorkommen**):

he woke up = er ist aufgewacht

infinitive	ich	du	er/sie/es	wir	ihr	sie/Sie
haben	habe	hast	hat	haben	habt	haben
sein	bin	bist	ist	sind	seid	sind

Irregular verbs and other forms

Some German verbs are irregular and change their stem or add different endings. All the irregular verbs that appear in the dictionary are given in the *List of irregular verbs* on page 361.

The subjunctive
This is a form of the verb that is used to express speculation, doubt or unlikelihood. It is rarely used in English (*if I were you* instead of *if I was you* is an exceptional example), but is still used in both written and spoken German.

Present tense

infinitive	ich	du	er/sie/es	wir	ihr	sie/Sie
machen	mache	machest	mache	machen	machet	machen
sein	sei	sei(e)st	sei	seien	seid	seien

Imperfect tense
For regular verbs this is the same as the normal imperfect forms, but irregular verbs vary.

infinitive	ich	du	er/sie/es	wir	ihr	sie/Sie
machen	machte	machtest	machte	machten	machtet	machten
werden	würde	würdest	würde	würden	würdet	würden
sein	wäre	wär(e)st	wäre	wären	wär(e)t	wären

The imperfect subjunctive of werden is used with an infinitive to form the conditional tense. This tense expresses what might happen if something else occurred.

he would go = er würde gehen
I wouldn't do that = das würde ich nicht machen

Reflexive verbs

The object of a reflexive verb is the same as its subject. In German, the object is a reflexive pronoun. This is usually in the accusative (I wash = **ich wasche mich**). The reflexive pronouns of some verbs are in the dative (I imagine = **ich stelle mir vor**), and these are marked in the English–German part of the dictionary with (*dative*).

infinitive	ich	du	er/sie/es	wir	ihr	sie/Sie
sich	wasche	wäschst	wäscht	waschen	wascht	waschen
waschen	mich	dich	sich	uns	euch	sich
sich	stelle	stellst	stellt	stellen	stellt	stellen
vorstellen	mir vor	dir vor	sich vor	uns vor	euch vor	sich vor

The passive

In the passive form, the subject of the verb experiences the action rather than performs it: he was asked = **er wurde gefragt**. In German, the passive is formed using parts of **werden** with the past participle:

present passive	*it is done*	es wird gemacht
imperfect passive	*it was done*	es wurde gemacht
future passive	*it will be done*	es wird gemacht werden
perfect passive	*it has been done*	es ist gemacht worden

When forming the perfect passive, note that the past participle of **werden** becomes **worden** rather than **geworden**.

Separable verbs

Separable verbs are marked in the German–English part of the dictionary, with a vertical bar after the prefix: **an|fangen**. In the perfect tense, the **ge-** of the past participle comes between the prefix and the verb, for example **er/sie/es hat an*ge*fangen**.

Articles

There are two articles in English, the definite article *the* and the indefinite article *a/an*. The way these are translated into German depends on the gender, number and case of the noun with which the article goes.

There are three genders of nouns in German: masculine (**der Mann** = the man), feminine (**die Frau** = the woman) and neuter (**das Buch** = the book). There are two forms of number: singular (**der Baum** = the tree) and plural (**die Bäume** = the trees). And there are four cases, which show the part a noun plays in a sentence: nominative, accusative, genitive and dative.

Definite article

the = der/die/das, (*plural*) = die

	SINGULAR masculine	feminine	neuter	PLURAL all genders
nominative	**der** Mann	**die** Frau	**das** Buch	**die** Bäume
accusative	**den** Mann	**die** Frau	**das** Buch	**die** Bäume
genitive	**des** Mannes	**der** Frau	**des** Buches	**der** Bäume
dative	**dem** Mann	**der** Frau	**dem** Buch	**den** Bäumen

Indefinite article

a/an = ein/eine/ein. This article can only be singular.

	masculine	feminine	neuter
nominative	**ein** Mann	**eine** Frau	**ein** Buch
accusative	**einen** Mann	**eine** Frau	**ein** Buch
genitive	**eines** Mannes	**einer** Frau	**eines** Buches
dative	**einem** Mann	**einer** Frau	**einem** Buch

Nouns

In German, all nouns start with a capital letter: **das Buch** = the book.

Gender

There are three genders of nouns in German: masculine (**der Mann** = the man), feminine (**die Frau** = the woman) and neuter (**das Buch** = the book). These three examples are logical, with masculine for a male person, feminine for a female person and neuter for an object. But it is not always like this with German nouns. Gender is sometimes determined by a noun's ending. For example, **das Mädchen** (= the girl) is neuter rather than feminine, simply because the ending **-chen** is always neuter.

The gender of German nouns is given in the dictionary. There are some general rules regarding the gender of groups of nouns, but individual genders must be checked by looking them up.

Masculine nouns

- male persons and animals: **der Arbeiter** = worker; **der Bär** = bear
- 'doers' and 'doing' instruments ending in **-er** in German: **der Gärtner** = gardener; **der Computer** = computer
- days, months and seasons: (**der**) **Montag** = Monday
- words ending in **-ich**, **-ig** and **-ling**: **der Honig** = honey; **der Lehrling** = apprentice
- words ending in **-ismus**, **-ist** and **-ant**.

Feminine nouns

- female persons and animals: **die Schauspielerin** = actress; **die Henne** = hen; the feminine form of professions and animals is made by adding **-in** to the masculine (**der Schauspieler/die Schauspielerin** = actor/actress)
- nouns ending in **-ei**, **-ie**, **-ik**, **-in**, **-ion**, **-heit**, **-keit**, **-schaft**, **-tät**, **-ung**, **-ur**: **die Gärtnerei** = gardening; **die Energie** = energy
- most nouns ending in **-e**: **die Blume** = flower; note that there are many exceptions, including **der Name** = name, **der Käse** = cheese, **das Ende** = end.

Neuter nouns

- names of continents, most countries and towns (see page 208): (**das**) **Deutschland** = Germany; (**das**) **Köln** = Cologne
- nouns ending in **-chen** and **-lein** (indicating *small*): **das Mädchen**, **das Fräulein** = girl.
- most (but not all!) nouns beginning with **Ge-** or ending in **-nis**, **-tel** or **-um**: **das Geheimnis** = secret; **das Zentrum** = centre
- infinitives of verbs used as nouns: **das Lachen** = laughter; **das Essen** = food

Compound nouns

When two nouns are put together to make one compound noun, it takes the gender of the second noun:

    der Brief + die Marke = die Briefmarke.

Plural

There are no absolutely definitive rules for the plural forms of German nouns. Plurals generally add an ending (**der Freund**, **die Freunde**), and change a vowel to an umlaut (**der Gast**, **die Gäste**; **das Haus**, **die Häuser**). Feminine words ending in **-heit**, **-keit** and **-ung** add **-en** to make the plural (**die Abbildung**, **die Abbildungen**).

The plurals of all nouns are given in the German–English part of the dictionary.

Case

There are four cases, which show the part a noun plays in a sentence: nominative, accusative, genitive and dative. The noun's article changes according to the case, and the ending of the noun changes in some cases:

SINGULAR		
masculine	feminine	neuter
nominative der Mann	die Frau	das Buch
accusative den Mann	die Frau	das Buch
genitive des **Mannes**	der Frau	des **Buches**
dative dem Mann	der Frau	dem Buch

PLURAL		
masculine	feminine	neuter
nominative die Männer	die Frauen	die Bücher
accusative die Männer	die Frauen	die Bücher
genitive der Männer	der Frauen	der Bücher
dative den **Männern**	den Frauen	den **Büchern**

The nominative is used for the subject of a sentence; in sentences with **sein** (to be) and **werden** (to become), the noun after the verb is in the nominative.

the dog barked = der Hund bellte
that is my car = das ist mein Wagen

The accusative is used for the direct object and after some prepositions:

she has a son = sie hat einen Sohn

The genitive shows possession, and is also used after some prepositions:

my husband's dog = der Hund meines Mannes

The dative is used for the indirect object. Some German verbs, such as **helfen**, take only the dative. They are marked (+ *dative*) in the English–German part of the dictionary. The dative is also used after some prepositions:

she gave the books to the children = sie gab den Kindern die Bücher

The following sentence combines all four cases:

der Mann gibt der Frau den Bleistift des Mädchens = *the man gives the woman the girl's pencil*
der Mann *is the subject* (*in the nominative*)
gibt *is the verb*
der Frau *is the indirect object* (*in the dative*)
den Bleistift *is the direct object* (*in the accusative*)
des Mädchens *is in the genitive* (*showing possession*).

Adjectives

An adjective is a word describing a noun. In German, an adjective in front of a noun adds endings that vary with the noun's gender, number and case. Adjectives that come after a noun do not add endings.

With the definite article
Adjectives following **der/die/das** take these endings:

	SINGULAR masculine	feminine	neuter	PLURAL all genders
nominative	der rote Hut	die rote Lampe	das rote Buch	die roten Autos
accusative	den roten Hut	die rote Lampe	das rote Buch	die roten Autos
genitive	des roten Hutes	der roten Lampe	des roten Buches	der roten Autos
dative	dem roten Hut	der roten Lampe	dem roten Buch	den roten Autos

Some German adjectives follow the pattern of the definite article, and adjectives after them change their endings in the same way as after **der/die/das**. For example, **dieser/diese/dieses** (= this):

	SINGULAR masculine	feminine	neuter	PLURAL all genders
nominative	dieser	diese	dieses	diese
accusative	diesen	diese	dieses	diese
genitive	dieses	dieser	dieses	dieser
dative	diesem	dieser	diesem	diesen

Other common examples are:

jeder/jede/jedes = *every, each*
jener/jene/jenes = *that*
mancher/manche/manches = *many a, some*

solcher/solche/solches = *such*
welcher/welche/welches = *which*

These adjectives appear in this way, with their masculine/feminine/neuter forms throughout the dictionary.

With the indefinite article

Adjectives following **ein/eine/ein** take these endings:

	SINGULAR masculine	feminine	neuter
nominative	ein roter Hut	eine rote Lampe	ein rotes Buch
accusative	einen roten Hut	eine rote Lampe	ein rotes Buch
genitive	eines roten Hutes	einer roten Lampe	eines roten Buches
dative	einem roten Hut	einer roten Lampe	einem roten Buch

Some German adjectives follow the pattern of the indefinite article, and adjectives after them change their endings in the same way as after **ein/eine/ein**. They are:

dein = *your*   kein = *no*
euer = *your*   mein = *my*
lhr = *your*   sein = *his/its*
ihr = *her/their*   unser = *our*

These adjectives can also go with plural nouns: no cars = **keine Autos**. All genders take the same endings in the plural:

	PLURAL all genders
nominative	keine roten Autos
accusative	keine roten Autos
genitive	keiner roten Autos
dative	keinen roten Autos

Without an article

Adjectives in front of a noun on their own, without an article, take the following endings:

	SINGULAR masculine	feminine	neuter	PLURAL all genders
nominative	guter Wein	frische Milch	kaltes Bier	alte Leute
accusative	guten Wein	frische Milch	kaltes Bier	alte Leute
genitive	guten Weins	frischer Milch	kalten Biers	alter Leute
dative	gutem Wein	frischer Milch	kaltem Bier	alten Leuten

Adjectives as nouns

In German, adjectives can be used as nouns, spelt with a capital letter: **alt** = old, **ein Alter** = an old man, **eine Alte** = an old woman.

With the definite article (**der/die/das**), these nouns take the following endings:

	SINGULAR masculine	feminine	PLURAL both genders
nominative	der Fremde	die Fremde	die Fremden
accusative	den Fremden	die Fremde	die Fremden
genitive	des Fremden	der Fremden	der Fremden
dative	dem Fremden	der Fremden	den Fremden

The feminine noun refers to a female stranger or foreigner. In the dictionary, this noun appears as:

der/die **Fremde**, *plural* **Fremden**.

With the indefinite article (**ein/eine/ein**), these nouns take the following endings:

	SINGULAR masculine	feminine	PLURAL both genders, without an article
nominative	ein Fremder	eine Fremde	Fremde
accusative	einen Fremden	eine Fremde	Fremde
genitive	eines Fremden	einer Fremden	Fremder
dative	einem Fremden	einer Fremden	Fremden

Comparative and superlative

In English, the comparative of the adjective *small* is *smaller*, and of *difficult* is *more difficult*. The superlatives are *smallest* and *most difficult*. In German, there is just one way to form the comparative and superlative: by adding the endings **-er** and **-(e)st**:

small, smaller, smallest   = klein, kleiner, der/die/das kleinste

Many adjectives change their vowel to an umlaut in the comparative and superlative:

cold, colder, coldest   = kalt, kälter, der/die/das kälteste

Some important adjectives are irregular:

big, bigger, biggest	= groß, größer, der/die/das größte
good, better, best	= gut, besser, der/die/das beste
high, higher, highest	= hoch, höher, der/die/das höchste
much, more, most	= viel, mehr, der/die/das meiste
near, nearer, nearest	= nah, näher, der/die/das nächste

Comparative and superlative adjectives take the same endings as basic adjectives:

a smaller child	= ein kleineres Kind
the coldest month	= der kälteste Monat

Adverbs

In German almost all adjectives can also be used as adverbs, describing a verb, an adjective or another adverb.

she sings beautifully = sie singt schön

In the dictionary, most adjectives are not listed as adverbs as well. The adverb is only given if it has special importance, a different meaning, or if it is formed differently in German.

Some words, such as **auch** (= also), **fast** (= almost), **immer** (= always) and **leider** (= unfortunately) are used only as adverbs:

she is very clever = sie ist sehr klug

Comparative and superlative

The comparative is formed by adding **-er** to the basic adverb, and the superlative by putting **am** in front of the basic adverb and adding the ending **-(e)sten**:

clearly, more clearly, most clearly   = klar, klarer, am klarsten

Some important adverbs are irregular:

soon, earlier, at the earliest	= bald, früher, am frühesten
well, better, best	= gut, besser, am besten
willingly, more willingly, most willingly	= gern, lieber, am liebsten

Pronouns

Pronouns are words—such as *he*, *which* and *mine* in English—that stand instead of a noun.

Personal pronouns

These pronouns, such as he/she/it = **er/sie/es**, refer to people or things.

	I	you	he/it	she/it	it	we	you	they	you
nominative	ich	du	er	sie	es	wir	ihr	sie	Sie
accusative	mich	dich	ihn	sie	es	uns	euch	sie	Sie
dative	mir	dir	ihm	ihr	ihm	uns	euch	ihnen	Ihnen
	me	*you*	*him/it*	*her/it*	*it*	*us*	*you*	*them*	*you*

The genitive form is not given, because it is so rarely used.

In German there are two forms for you, **du** and **Sie**. **Du** is less formal and is used when speaking to someone you know well, a child or a family member. When speaking to a person or a group of people you do not know very well, use the polite form, **Sie**.

German pronouns agree in gender with the noun they refer to. In the nominative case, *it* might be translated by **er** or **sie**, as well as **es**:

it (the pencil) is red = er (der Bleistift) ist rot
it (the rose) is beautiful = sie (die Rose) ist schön
it (the car) is expensive = es (das Auto) ist teuer

Possessive pronouns

The possessive pronouns are:

mine = meiner/meine/mein(e)s
yours (informal singular) = deiner/deine/dein(e)s
his = seiner/seine/sein(e)s
hers = ihrer/ihre/ihr(e)s
its = seiner/seine/sein(e)s

ours = unserer/unsere/unser(e)s
yours (informal plural) = eurer/eure/eures
theirs = ihrer/ihre/ihr(e)s
yours (polite) = Ihrer, Ihre, Ihr(e)s

They all take endings like **meiner/meine/mein(e)s**, as follows:

	SINGULAR masculine	feminine	neuter	PLURAL all genders
nominative	meiner	meine	mein(e)s	meine
accusative	meinen	meine	mein(e)s	meine
genitive	meines	meiner	meines	meiner
dative	meinem	meiner	meinem	meinen

Throughout the dictionary, these pronouns are given in their three nominative singular forms, in the order masculine/feminine/neuter: **meiner/meine/meins**. As can be seen in the table, in the neuter form an **-e-** can be added (making **meines**). This applies to all the possessive pronouns, but the extra **-e-** is rare.

Relative pronouns

These pronouns are used to introduce and link a new clause. In English they are *who*, *which*, *that* and *what*. In German they are **der**, **die** or **das**, depending on the noun referred to:

	SINGULAR masculine	feminine	neuter	PLURAL all genders
nominative	der	die	das	die
accusative	den	die	das	die
genitive	dessen	deren	dessen	deren
dative	dem	der	dem	denen

Relative pronouns can be left out in English, but never in German:

the book (that) I'm reading = das Buch, das ich lese

They agree in gender and number with the noun they refer back to:

the man who visited us = der Mann, der uns besucht hat (**der** is masculine singular)

But the case of the pronoun depends on its function in the clause it introduces:

the pencil I bought yesterday = der Bleistift, den ich gestern gekauft habe

(**den** is masculine singular, but accusative because it is the object of the clause it introduces)

Interrogative pronouns

These pronouns are used to ask questions:

who? = wer?
what? = was?
which? = welcher/welche/welches?

Wer changes as follows:

nominative	wer?
accusative	wen?
genitive	wessen?
dative	wem?

Reflexive pronouns

The object of a reflexive verb is the same as its subject. In German, the object is a reflexive pronoun. This is usually in the accusative (I wash = **ich wasche *mich***). The reflexive pronouns of some verbs are in the dative (I imagine = **ich stelle *mir* vor**).

Indefinite pronouns

These pronouns do not refer to identifiable people or objects. In German, many indefinite pronouns, such as **etwas** (= something) and **nichts** (= nothing) never change. But some do take endings:

	someone	no one
nominative	jemand	niemand
accusative	jemanden	niemanden
dative	jemandem	niemandem

The genitive case is rarely used.

Prepositions

Prepositions are small words like *in*, that stand in front of a noun or pronoun. In German, the noun following a preposition always has to be in one of three cases—dative, accusative or genitive.

Prepositions can be prefixes and form separable verbs:

to walk along the street = die Straße entlanggehen
he is walking along the street = er geht die Straße entlang

In the dictionary, the case governed by a preposition is given:

mit (+ *dative*) *means* mit *always takes the dative case.*

The most common case used after prepositions is the dative. The following prepositions always take the dative:

aus	nach
außer	seit
bei	von
mit	zu

Some prepositions always take the accusative:

bis	gegen
durch	ohne
entlang	um
für	

Some prepositions always take the genitive:

anstatt
trotz
während
wegen

There is a group of prepositions that can take the dative or the accusative, depending on the sentence. They are:

an	über
auf	unter
hinter	vor
in	zwischen
neben	

If the phrase containing one of these prepositions describes position—where something is happening—the dative case is used:

she sat in the kitchen = sie saß in der Küche

But if the phrase containing the preposition describes movement—motion towards something—the accusative follows:

she went into the kitchen = sie ging in die Küche

Some forms of the definite article are usually shortened when used with prepositions:

am (an dem); **ans** (an das); **aufs** (auf das); **beim** (bei dem); **durchs** (durch das); **fürs** (für das); **im** (in dem); **ins** (in das); **ums** (um das); **vom** (von dem); **zum** (zu dem); **zur** (zu der).

Conjunctions

Conjunctions are small words, such as *and* = **und**, which join clauses together in a sentence. These common conjunctions link clauses together:

aber = *but*
denn = *for*
oder = *or*
sondern = *but (on the contrary)*
und = *and*

The conjunctions do not change normal word order in the two clauses:

ich gehe, und er kommt auch = *I am going, and he is coming too*

But there are many other conjunctions that send the verb to the end of the second clause:

als = *when*, = *as*   ob = *whether*
bevor = *before*   während = *while*
bis = *until*   wenn = *when*, = *if*
da = *since*   weil = *because*
dass = *that*

er konnte nicht in die Schule gehen, *weil* er krank *war* = *he couldn't go to school, because he was ill*

Word order

The basic rule for German word order is that the verb comes second in a sentence. The subject of the sentence usually comes before the verb:

meine Mutter fährt am Freitag nach Köln = *my mother is going to Cologne on Friday*

When the verb is made up of two parts, such as in the perfect and the future tenses, the auxiliary verb comes second in the sentence, while the past participle (in the perfect) or infinitive (in the future tense) goes to the end:

wir haben sehr lang gewartet = *we waited a very long time*
sie wird sicher bald kommen = *she is sure to turn up soon*

Past participles and infinitives go to the end in other sentences too:

ich kann dieses Lied nicht leiden = *I can't stand this song*
du musst hier bleiben = *you must stay here*

When a sentence starts with a clause, the verb stays in second place:

da ich kein Geld hatte, blieb ich zu Hause = *since I had no money, I stayed at home*

In the clause itself, the verb goes to the end:

er konnte nicht in die Schule gehen, weil er krank war

The relative pronouns **der**, **die** and **das**, as well as a number of conjunctions, send the verb to the end of the clause:

der Junge, der hier wohnt = *the boy who lives here*

When separable verbs separate, the prefix goes to the end:

der Film fängt um acht Uhr an = *the film starts at 8 o'clock*

In questions and commands, the verb is usually first in the sentence:

kommst du heute Abend? = *are you coming this evening?*
komm schnell rein! = *come in quickly!*

When there are a number of phrases in a sentence, the usual order for the different elements is 1 time, 2 manner, 3 place:

wir fahren heute mit dem Auto nach München = *we are driving to Munich today*
(*time* = heute; *manner* = mit dem Auto; *place* = nach München)

Glossary of grammatical terms

Abbreviation A shortened form of a word or phrase: etc. = usw.

Accusative The case of a direct object; some prepositions take the accusative.

Adjective A word describing a noun: a *red* pencil = ein *roter* Bleistift.

Adverb A word that describes or changes the meaning of a verb, an adjective or another adverb: she sings *beautifully* = sie singt *schön*.

Article The definite article, the = der/die/das, and indefinite article, a/an = ein/eine/ein, used in front of a noun.

Auxiliary verb One of the verbs—haben, sein, werden—used to form the perfect or future tense: I will help = ich *werde* helfen.

Case The form of a noun, pronoun, adjective or article that shows the part it plays in a sentence; there are four cases—nominative, accusative, genitive and dative.

Clause A self-contained section of a sentence that contains a subject and a verb.

Comparative The form of an adjective or adverb that makes it 'more': smaller = kleiner, more clearly = klarer.

Compound noun A noun formed from two or more separate words: der Flughafen = airport.

Compound verb A verb formed by adding a prefix to a simple verb; in German, some compound verbs are separable (anfangen), and some are inseparable (verlassen).

Conditional tense A verb tense that expresses what might happen if something else occurred: he would go = er würde gehen.

Conjunction A word used to join clauses together: and = und, because = weil.

Consonant A letter representing a sound that can only be used together with a vowel, such as b, c, d; see vowel.

Dative The case of an indirect object; many prepositions take the dative.

Definite article the = der/die/das.

Direct object The noun or pronoun directly affected by the verb: he caught *the ball* = er fing *den Ball*.

Ending Letters added to the stem of verbs, as well as to nouns and adjectives, according to tense, case, etc.

Feminine One of the three noun genders: die Frau = the woman.

Future tense The tense of a verb that refers to something that will happen in the future: I will go = ich werde gehen.

Gender One of the three groups of nouns: masculine, feminine or neuter.

Genitive The case that shows possession; some prepositions take the genitive.

Imperfect tense The tense of a verb that refers to something that happened in the past: I went = ich ging.

Indefinite article a/an = ein/eine/ein.

Indefinite pronoun A pronoun that does not identify a specific person or object: one = man, something = etwas.

Indirect object The noun or pronoun indirectly affected by the verb, at which the direct object is aimed: I gave *him* the book = ich gab *ihm* das Buch.

Infinitive The basic part of a verb: to play = spielen.

Informal Informal language is used in everyday conversation. Informal German is marked with a ✱ in the dictionary.

Inseparable verb A verb with a prefix that can never be separated from it: verstehen, ich verstehe.

Interjection A sound, word or remark expressing a strong feeling such as anger, fear or joy: oh! = ach!

Interrogative pronoun A pronoun that asks a question: who? = wer?

Intonation The pattern of sounds made in a sentence as the speaker's voice rises and falls.

Inverted commas The quotation marks put around direct speech: "Yes," he said = "Ja," sagte er.

Irregular verb A verb that does not follow one of the set patterns and has its own individual forms; see pages 361 to 364 for a list.

Masculine One of the three noun genders: der Mann = the man.

Neuter One of the three noun genders: das Buch = the book.

Nominative The case of the subject of a sentence; in sentences with sein and

werden the noun after the verb is in the nominative: that is my car = **das ist mein Wagen**.

Noun A word that names a person or thing: apple = **Apfel**.

Number The state of being either singular or plural.

Part of speech A grammatical term for the function of a word; noun, verb, adjective, etc., are parts of speech.

Passive In the passive form the subject of the verb experiences the action rather than performs it: he was asked = **er wurde gefragt**.

Past participle The part of a verb used to form past tenses: made = **gemacht**.

Perfect tense The tense of a verb that refers to something that happened in the past: I have said = **ich habe gesagt**.

Personal pronoun A pronoun that refers to a person or thing: he/she/it = **er/sie/es**.

Phrasal verb A verb combined with a preposition or an adverb to have a particular meaning: to run away = **weglaufen**.

Phrase A self-contained section of a sentence that does not contain a full verb.

Plural Of nouns, etc., referring to more than one: the trees = **die Bäume**.

Possessive pronoun A pronoun that shows possession, belonging to someone or something: mine = **meiner/meine/meins**.

Prefix A syllable or word added to the beginning of another word; in German, the prefix can move from separable verbs (**anfangen**), but stay fixed to inseparable verbs (**verlassen**).

Preposition A word that stands in front of a noun or pronoun, relating it to the rest of the sentence; with = **mit**, for = **für**.

Present participle The part of a verb that in English ends in -ing, and in German adds -d to the infinitive: asking = **fragend**.

Present tense The tense of a verb that refers to something happening now: I make = **ich mache**.

Pronoun A word that stands instead of a noun: he = **er**, she = **sie**, mine = **meiner/meine/meins**, etc.

Pronunciation The way of pronouncing, or speaking, words.

Reflexive pronoun A pronoun that goes with a reflexive verb: **mich, dich, sich, uns, euch, sich**. The reflexive pronouns of some verbs are in the dative.

Reflexive verb A verb whose object is the same as its subject; in German, it is used with a reflexive pronoun, for example **sich waschen**.

Regular verb A verb that follows a set pattern in its different forms.

Relative pronoun A pronoun that introduces a subordinate clause, relating to a person or thing mentioned in the main clause: the man *who* visited us = **der Mann, *der* uns besucht hat**.

Sentence A sequence of words, with a subject and a verb, that can stand on their own to make a statement, as a question or to give a command.

Separable verb A verb with a prefix that can be separated from it in some tenses: **anfangen, ich fange an**.

Singular Of nouns, etc., referring to just one: the tree = **der Baum**.

Stem The part of a verb to which endings are added; **fahr-** is the stem of **fahren**.

Subject In a clause or sentence, the noun or pronoun that causes the action of the verb: *he* caught the ball = **er fing den Ball**.

Subjunctive A verb form that is used to express doubt or unlikelihood: it could be true = **es könnte wahr sein**.

Superlative The form of an adjective or adverb that makes it 'most': the *smallest* house = **das *kleinste* Haus**, most clearly = **am klarsten**.

Syllable Part of a word that forms a spoken unit, usually a vowel sound with consonants before or after: **an-ge-ben**.

Tense The form of a verb that tells when the action takes place: present, future, perfect.

Umlaut Two dots over a vowel—ä, ö, ü—to show a change in pronunciation.

Verb A word or group of words that describes an action: the children *are playing* = **die Kinder *spielen***.

Vowel A letter representing a sound that can be spoken by itself; in German a, ä, e, i, o, ö, u, ü, y.

German irregular verbs

Present tense

In the present tense, the stem often changes in the **du** and **er/sie/es** forms. For example, **befehl**-becomes **befiehl**- and **fahr**- becomes **fähr**-. The other forms add regular endings to the stem.
Some examples:

infinitive	ich	du	er/sie/es	wir	ihr	sie/Sie
befehlen	befehle	befiehlst	befiehlt	befehlen	befehlt	befehlen
fahren	fahre	fährst	fährt	fahren	fahrt	fahren

Imperfect tense

In the imperfect tense, the stem usually changes. The same endings are added to the changed stem in many cases. Some examples:

infinitive	ich	du	er/sie/es	wir	ihr	sie/Sie
befehlen	befahl	befahlst	befahl	befahlen	befahlt	befahlen
fahren	fuhr	fuhrst	fuhr	fuhren	fuhrt	fuhren

Future tense

This is formed using **werden** and the infinitive, as with regular verbs: **ich werde fahren**.

Perfect tense

The stem often changes in the perfect tense, making an irregular past participle:

> befehlen—ich habe befohlen;
> gehen—ich bin gegangen.

Auxiliary verbs

There are three verbs in German that help to make a compound tense, such as the future and imperfect. They are also used as verbs in their own right: to have = **haben**; to be = **sein**; to become = **werden**. Their present tenses are given on page 351.

haben	ich	du	er/sie/es	wir	ihr	sie/Sie
imperfect	hatte	hattest	hatte	hatten	hattet	hatten
perfect	habe gehabt	hast gehabt	hat gehabt	haben gehabt	habt gehabt	haben gehabt

sein	ich	du	er/sie/es	wir	ihr	sie/Sie
imperfect	war	warst	war	waren	wart	waren
perfect	bin gewesen	bist gewesen	ist gewesen	sind gewesen	seid gewesen	sind gewesen

werden	ich	du	er/sie/es	wir	ihr	sie/Sie
imperfect	wurde	wurdest	wurde	wurden	wurdet	wurden
perfect	bin geworden	bist geworden	ist geworden	sind geworden	seid geworden	sind geworden

List of irregular verbs

In this list of irregular verbs, the 1st, 2nd and 3rd persons singular of the present tense (**ich, du, er/sie/es**) are given.

The 1st and 3rd persons singular of the imperfect are always identical:

> ich backte, er/sie/es backte

The other forms add regular endings to the stem.

Separable verbs, such as **anfangen**, are not listed. You can look them up in the table under the simple verb without the prefix, such as **fangen**.

infinitive	present tense ich, du, er/sie/es	imperfect tense er/sie/es	perfect tense er/sie/es
backen	backe, bäckst, bäckt	backte	hat gebacken
befehlen	befehle, befiehlst, befiehlt	befahl	hat befohlen
beginnen	beginne, beginnst, beginnt	begann	hat begonnen
beißen	beiße, beißt, beißt	biss	hat gebissen

infinitive	present tense ich, du, er/sie/es	imperfect tense er/sie/es	perfect tense er/sie/es
bekommen	bekomme, bekommst, bekommt	bekam	hat bekommen
bergen	berge, birgst, birgt	barg	hat geborgen
besitzen	besitze, besitzt, besitzt	besaß	hat besessen
betrügen	betrüge, betrügst, betrügt	betrog	hat betrogen
biegen	biege, biegst, biegt	bog	hat or ist gebogen
bieten	biete, bietest, bietet	bot	hat geboten
binden	binde, bindest, bindet	band	hat gebunden
bitten	bitte, bittest, bittet	bat	hat gebeten
blasen	blase, bläst, bläst	blies	hat geblasen
bleiben	bleibe, bleibst, bleibt	blieb	ist geblieben
braten	brate, brätst, brät	briet	hat gebraten
brechen	breche, brichst, bricht	brach	hat gebrochen
brennen	brenne, brennst, brennt	brannte	hat gebrannt
bringen	bringe, bringst, bringt	brachte	hat gebracht
denken	denke, denkst, denkt	dachte	hat gedacht
dürfen	darf, darfst, darf	durfte	hat gedurft
einladen	lade ein, lädst ein, lädt ein	lud ein	hat eingeladen
einweisen	weise ein, weist ein, weist ein	wies ein	hat eingewiesen
empfangen	empfange, empfängst, empfängt	empfing	hat empfangen
empfehlen	empfehle, empfiehlst, empfiehlt	empfahl	hat empfohlen
entscheiden	entscheide, entscheidest, entscheidet	entschied	hat entschieden
erfahren	erfahre, erfährst, erfährt	erfuhr	hat erfahren
erfinden	erfinde, erfindest, erfindet	erfand	hat erfunden
erschrecken	erschrecke, erschrickst, erschrickt	erschrak	ist erschrocken
ertrinken	ertrinke, ertrinkst, ertrinkt	ertrank	ist ertrunken
essen	esse, isst, isst	aß	hat gegessen
fahren	fahre, fährst, fährt	fuhr	ist gefahren
fallen	falle, fällst, fällt	fiel	ist gefallen
fangen	fange, fängst, fängt	fing	hat gefangen
fechten	fechte, fichtst, ficht	focht	hat gefochten
finden	finde, findest, findet	fand	hat gefunden
flechten	flechte, flichtst, flicht	flocht	hat geflochten
fliegen	fliege, fliegst, fliegt	flog	ist geflogen
fliehen	fliehe, fliehst, flieht	floh	ist geflohen
fließen	fließe, fließt, fließt	floss	ist geflossen
fressen	fresse, frisst, frisst	fraß	hat gefressen
frieren	friere, frierst, friert	fror	hat or ist gefroren
geben	gebe, gibst, gibt	gab	hat gegeben
gefallen	gefalle, gefällst, gefällt	gefiel	hat gefallen
gehen	gehe, gehst, geht	ging	ist gegangen
gelingen	es gelingt mir/dir/ihm/ihr/ihm	gelang	ist gelungen
gelten	gelte, giltst, gilt	galt	hat gegolten
genießen	genieße, genießt, genießt	genoss	hat genossen
geraten	gerate, gerätst, gerät	geriet	ist geraten
geschehen	es geschieht	geschah	ist geschehen
gewinnen	gewinne, gewinnst, gewinnt	gewann	hat gewonnen
gießen	gieße, gießt, gießt	goss	hat gegossen
gleichen	gleiche, gleichst, gleicht	glich	hat geglichen
graben	grabe, gräbst, gräbt	grub	hat gegraben
greifen	greife, greifst, greift	griff	hat gegriffen
haben	habe, hast, hat	hatte	hat gehabt
halten	halte, hältst, hält	hielt	hat gehalten

infinitive	present tense ich, du, er/sie/es	imperfect tense er/sie/es	perfect tense er/sie/es
hängen	hänge, hängst, hängt	hing	hat gehangen
heben	hebe, hebst, hebt	hob	hat gehoben
heißen	heiße, heißt, heißt	hieß	hat geheißen
helfen	helfe, hilfst, hilft	half	hat geholfen
hinweisen	weise hin, weist hin, weist hin	wies hin	hat hingewiesen
kennen	kenne, kennst, kennt	kannte	hat gekannt
klingen	klinge, klingst, klingt	klang	hat geklungen
kneifen	kneife, kneifst, kneift	kniff	hat gekniffen
kommen	komme, kommst, kommt	kam	ist gekommen
können	kann, kannst, kann	konnte	hat gekonnt
kriechen	krieche, kriechst, kriecht	kroch	ist gekrochen
lassen	lasse, lässt, lässt	ließ	hat gelassen
laufen	laufe, läufst, läuft	lief	ist gelaufen
leiden	leide, leidest, leidet	litt	hat gelitten
leihen	leihe, leihst, leiht	lieh	hat geliehen
lesen	lese, liest, liest	las	hat gelesen
liegen	liege, liegst, liegt	lag	hat gelegen
lügen	lüge, lügst, lügt	log	hat gelogen
mahlen	mahle, mahlst, mahlt	mahlte	hat gemahlen
meiden	meide, meidest, meidet	mied	hat gemieden
melken	melke, melkst, melkt	melkte	hat gemolken
messen	messe, misst, misst	maß	hat gemessen
misslingen	misslinge, misslingst, misslingt	misslang	ist misslungen
mögen	mag, magst, mag	mochte	hat gemocht
müssen	muss, musst, muss	musste	hat gemusst
nehmen	nehme, nimmst, nimmt	nahm	hat genommen
nennen	nenne, nennst, nennt	nannte	hat genannt
pfeifen	pfeife, pfeifst, pfeift	pfiff	hat gepfiffen
quellen	quelle, quillst, quillt	quoll	ist gequollen
raten	rate, rätst, rät	riet	hat geraten
reiben	reibe, reibst, reibt	rieb	hat gerieben
reißen	reiße, reißt, reißt	riss	hat gerissen
reiten	reite, reitest, reitet	ritt	ist geritten
rennen	renne, rennst, rennt	rannte	ist gerannt
riechen	rieche, riechst, riecht	roch	hat gerochen
rufen	rufe, rufst, ruft	rief	hat gerufen
saufen	saufe, säufst, säuft	soff	hat gesoffen
schaffen	schaffe, schaffst, schafft	schuf	hat geschaffen
scheiden	scheide, scheidest, scheidet	schied	hat or ist geschieden
scheinen	scheine, scheinst, scheint	schien	hat geschienen
schieben	schiebe, schiebst, schiebt	schob	hat geschoben
schießen	schieße, schießt, schießt	schoss	hat geschossen
schlafen	schlafe, schläfst, schläft	schlief	hat geschlafen
schlagen	schlage, schlägst, schlägt	schlug	hat geschlagen
schleichen	schleiche, schleichst, schleicht	schlich	ist geschlichen
schleifen	schleife, schleifst, schleift	schliff	hat geschliffen
schließen	schließe, schließt, schließt	schloss	hat geschlossen
schmeißen	schmeiße, schmeißt, schmeißt	schmiss	hat geschmissen
schmelzen	schmelze, schmilzt, schmilzt	schmolz	ist geschmolzen
schneiden	schneide, schneidest, schneidet	schnitt	hat geschnitten
schreiben	schreibe, schreibst, schreibt	schrieb	hat geschrieben

infinitive	present tense ich, du, er/sie/es	imperfect tense er/sie/es	perfect tense er/sie/es
schreien	schreie, schreist, schreit	schrie	hat geschrien
schweigen	schweige, schweigst, schweigt	schwieg	hat geschwiegen
schwimmen	schwimme, schwimmst, schwimmt	schwamm	ist geschwommen
schwören	schwöre, schwörst, schwört	schwor	hat geschworen
sehen	sehe, siehst, sieht	sah	hat gesehen
sein	bin, bist, ist	war	ist gewesen
singen	singe, singst, singt	sang	hat gesungen
sinken	sinke, sinkst, sinkt	sank	ist gesunken
sitzen	sitze, sitzt, sitzt	saß	hat gesessen
sollen	soll, sollst, soll	sollte	hat gesollt
spinnen	spinne, spinnst, spinnt	spann	hat gesponnen
sprechen	spreche, sprichst, spricht	sprach	hat gesprochen
springen	springe, springst, springt	sprang	ist gesprungen
stechen	steche, stichst, sticht	stach	hat gestochen
stehen	stehe, stehst, steht	stand	hat gestanden
stehlen	stehle, stiehlst, stiehlt	stahl	hat gestohlen
steigen	steige, steigst, steigt	stieg	ist gestiegen
sterben	sterbe, stirbst, stirbt	starb	ist gestorben
stinken	stinke, stinkst, stinkt	stank	hat gestunken
stoßen	stoße, stößt, stößt	stieß	hat gestoßen
streichen	streiche, streichst, streicht	strich	hat gestrichen
streiten	streite, streitest, streitet	stritt	hat gestritten
tragen	trage, trägst, trägt	trug	hat getragen
treffen	treffe, triffst, trifft	traf	hat getroffen
treiben	treibe, treibst, treibt	trieb	hat getrieben
treten	trete, trittst, tritt	trat	ist getreten
trinken	trinke, trinkst, trinkt	trank	hat getrunken
tun	tue, tust, tut	tat	hat getan
überweisen	überweise, überweist, überweist	überwies	hat überwiesen
umziehen	ziehe um, ziehst um, zieht um	zog um	ist or hat umgezogen
verbieten	verbiete, verbietest, verbietet	verbot	hat verboten
verderben	verderbe, verdirbst, verdirbt	verdarb	hat or ist verdorben
vergessen	vergesse, vergisst, vergisst	vergaß	hat vergessen
verlieren	verliere, verlierst, verliert	verlor	hat verloren
verschwinden	verschwinde, verschwindest, verschwindet	verschwand	ist verschwunden
verstehen	verstehe, verstehst, versteht	verstand	hat verstanden
verzeihen	verzeihe, verzeihst, verzeiht	verzieh	hat verziehen
wachsen	wachse, wächst, wächst	wuchs	ist gewachsen
waschen	wasche, wäschst, wäscht	wusch	hat gewaschen
wenden	wende, wendest, wendet	wandte or wendete	hat gewandt or gewendet
werben	werbe, wirbst, wirbt	warb	hat geworben
werden	werde, wirst, wird	wurde	ist geworden
werfen	werfe, wirfst, wirft	warf	hat geworfen
wiegen	wiege, wiegst, wiegt	wog	hat gewogen
wissen	weiß, weißt, weiß	wusste	hat gewusst
wollen	will, willst, will	wollte	hat gewollt
ziehen	ziehe, ziehst, zieht	zog	hat gezogen
zwingen	zwinge, zwingst, zwingt	zwang	hat gezwungen

Pronunciation guide

The following are general guidelines to the way in which German is pronounced. Some of the German sounds can be imitated quite well by using English equivalents, but remember that these are close rather than exact imitations. You will need to listen to native German speakers, perhaps on tape or on the radio, and then imitate their pronunciation, particularly of the vowels a, o and u.

Listening and imitating will also help you with German intonation, the pattern of sounds made in a sentence as the speaker's voice rises and falls.

Vowel sounds

Here there is a major difference between German and English. German vowels are pure sounds, whereas in English vowels usually have one sound quickly followed by another.

In German, each vowel has a long and a short form: for example, an a can be long, as in **Bahn**, or short, as in **hat**. These are given separately in the following list, along with the nearest English equivalent. As a general rule, vowels are long when followed by h (**Bahn**) or by one consonant (**bar**) and short when followed by two consonants (**lassen**).

When they follow consonants, vowels are not normally run on as they are in English. For example, **ein Apfel** is pronounced as two separate words, whereas *an apple* might be run together as if it were one word, *'anapple'*.

Particular care must be taken with the umlaut sounds—ä, ö and ü—which do not exist in English.

German vowel	long or short	German example	nearest English equivalent
a	short	hat	vowel sound between hat and hut
a	long	Bahn	barn
ä	short	Geschäft	left
ä	long	Käse	between pair and pace
ai	long	Kaiser	fine
au	long	aus	cow
äu	long	Häuser	boy
e	short	essen	lesson
e	long	geben	gate
e	short, in unstressed syllables	Nase	ago
ei	long	weit	right
eu	long	Heu	boy
ey	long	Meyer	fire
i	short	billig	bit
i	long	ihn	ease
ie	long	viel	feel
o	short	Post	lost
o	long	Monat	bone (pronounced without moving tongue or lips)
ö	short	können	fur (with short u)
ö	long	böse	burn (with long u)
u	short	Nuss	put
u	long	Hut	moon
ü	short, like the French tu	Müll	round your lips and try to say ee
ü	long, like the French tu	über	round your lips and try to say longer ee
y	long, like the French tu	typisch	round your lips and try to say longer ee

Consonants

Some German consonants change pronunciation according to their position in a word. For example, at the end of a word or syllable, b, d and g are pronounced p, t and k respectively.

German consonant	notes	German example	nearest English equivalent
b	at the beginning of a word	**Ball**	ball
b	at the end of a word or syllable	**ab**	up
c	hard, before a, o, u	**Comic**	café
c	soft, before e, i	**Celsius**	bits
ch	after a, o, u	**Loch**	loch, pronounced in the Scottish way
ch	after e, i	**ich**	similar to the first sound in huge
ch	hard	**Charakter**	car
chs		**sechs**	six
d	at the beginning of a word	**dann**	done
d	at the end of a word or syllable	**Bad**	dart
dt		**Stadt**	rat
f		**Fuß**	fat
g	at the beginning of a word	**Gast**	guest
g	at the end of a word	**Tag**	park
g	-ig, at the end of a word	**billig**	similar to the first sound in huge
h		**hat**	hat
h	at the end of a syllable	**sah, sehen**	not pronounced, and makes the previous vowel long
j		**ja**	yet
k		**kalt**	kit
l		**Last**	lот
m		**Mast**	mast
n		**Name**	name
p		**Person**	person
qu		**Quatsch**	pronounced kv (to make 'kvatsch')
r	rolled, usually at the back of the mouth	**rasten**	rest
s	hissing ss sound	**es**	set
s	before a vowel, z sound	**Hase**	zoo
s	before p or t at the beginning of a syllable, sh sound	**Stunde**	ship
sch	like English sh	**Schule**	shut
ß	same as ss	**heiß**	press
t		**Tal**	tip
tsch	like English ch	**deutsch**	chin
v	like English f	**vier**	fat
v	in most foreign words	**Vene**	vase
w	like English v	**was**	van
x		**Taxi**	taxi
z	like English ts	**Zahl**	hits

The German words you must know

A
Abend der
aber
Abfahrt die
Achtung
Adresse die
all
allein
alles
als
also
alt
Amerikaner der
Ampel die
an
anbieten
Anfang der
Angebot das
angenehm
Ankunft die
annehmen
anrufen
Antwort die
Apfel der
Apotheke die
April
Arbeit die
arm
Arm der
Arzt der
auch
auf
aufstehen
Auge das
August
aus
Ausgang der
Auskunft die
aussehen
außen
Austausch der
Ausweis der
Autobahn die

B
Bäckerei die
Badezimmer das
Bahnhof der
bald
Bank die
bauen
Bauer der
Baum der
beginnen
bei
Bein das
bekommen
benützen
Berg der
berühmt
besetzt
besonders
bestellen
Besuch der
Bett das
bezahlen
Bier das
Bild das
billig
bis

bitte
blau
bleiben
Blick der
brauchen
braun
brechen
breit
Brief der
Brille die
Brot das
Brötchen das
Bruder der
Buch das
Burg die

C
Campingplatz der
Chef der
Computer der

D
da
danken
dann
das
dass
decken
deutsch
Deutsch
Deutsche der
Deutschland
Dezember
dick
Dienstag
dieser
doch
Donnerstag
Dorf das
dort
drehen
dritte
Drogerie die
drücken
dünn
durch
dürfen
durstig
Dusche die

E
Ei das
eigen
ein/eine/ein
einfach
Einfahrt die
einige
einsteigen
Eintritt der
einverstanden
Einwohner der
Eis das
Ende das
eng
Engländer der
englisch
entlang
Entschuldigung die
Erbse die
Erdbeere die

Erfolg der
erlauben
erst
essen
etwas
Euro der

F
Fabrik die
fahren
Fahrer der
Fahrkarte die
Fahrrad das
Fahrt die
fallen
falsch
Familie die
Familienname der
Farbe die
fast
Februar
fehlen
Fehler der
Feld das
Fenster das
Ferien die
fest
finden
Finger der
Fisch der
flach
Flasche die
Fleisch das
Flughafen der
Flugzeug das
Fluss der
Frage die
Frau die
Fräulein das
frei
Freitag
freitags
Fremde der
Freund der
froh
früh
Frühling der
Frühstück das
für
furchtbar
Fuß der

G
ganz
Gang der
Garten der
Gast der
geben
geboren
gefallen
gefährlich
gegen
gegenüber
gehen
gelb
Geld das
genau
genug
gerade
gern

Geschäft das
geschehen
Geschenk das
geschieden
geschlossen
gestern
Gesundheit die
gewinnen
Gewitter das
gewöhnlich
Glas das
glauben
gleich
Gleis das
glücklich
Grad der
grau
groß
Größe die
grün
Gruppe die
gut

H
Haar das
haben
halb
Hallo
Haltestelle die
halten
Hand die
Handy das
hart
Haus das
Heft das
heiß
heißen
Hemd das
Herbst der
Herr der
heute
hier
Hilfe die
hinter
hinunter
hoch
Hof der
hoffen
holen
hören
Hotel das
hübsch
Hund der
hungrig

I
Idee die
immer
in
Industrie die
Informatik die
innen

J
ja
Jahr das
Januar
jeder
jemand
jener

jetzt
Juli
jung
Junge der
Juni

K
Kaffee der
kalt
Kamera die
Karte die
Käse der
Kasse die
Katze die
kaufen
Kaufhaus das
kein
Kellner der
kennen
Kind das
Kino das
Kirche die
Klasse die
Kleid das
klein
Knie das
Kohl der
komisch
kommen
Konditorei die
können
Kopf der
kostenlos
krank
Krankheit die
Kreis der
kriegen
Kuchen der
Küche die
kühl
Kunst die
kurz

L
lachen
Laden der
Land das
lang
langsam
lassen
laufen
laut
Lebensmittel die
leer
Lehrer der
leicht
Leid tun
leider
lernen
lesen
Leute die
Liebe die
liegen
Linie die
links
Liste die
Lohn der
los
Luft die
Lust haben

M
machen
Mädchen das
Mahlzeit die
Mai
Mal das
man
Mann der
Mappe die
Markt der
Meer das
mehr
Menge die
Mensch der
Menü das
Messer das
Metzgerei die
mieten
Milch die
Minute die
mit
Mittag der
Mittagessen das
Mittwoch
Möbel das
mögen
möglich
Monat der
Montag
morgen
Morgen der
müde
Musik die
müssen
Mutter die

N
nach
Nachmittag der
Nachrichten die
nächst
Nacht die
Name der
Nase die
nass
natürlich
neben
nehmen
nein
neu
nicht
nichts
nie
niemand
noch
Norden der
nötig
November
null
nur
nützlich

O
Obst das
oder
offen
öffnen
ohne
Ohr das
Oktober

Onkel der
Osten der
Österreich
Österreicher der

P
Papier das
Park der
Parkplatz der
Partner der
passieren
Pause die
Person die
Pferd das
Pflanze die
Plan der
Platz der
plötzlich
Polizei die
Polizist der
Post die
Postkarte die
Preis der
prima
probieren
Prüfung die
putzen

Q
Quadrat das

R
Rad das
rauchen
Rechnung die
rechts
Regel die
regnen
reich
reichen
Reise die
Reisende der
reisen
reiten
reservieren
Rettung die
richtig
Richtung die
Rock der
rot
Rücken der
ruhig

S
Saft der
sagen
Salz das
Samstag
satt
sauber
S-Bahn die
Schachtel die
schaden
Schaf das
Scheibe die
Schein der
schicken
schieben
Schinken der
schlafen

schlecht
schließen
schlimm
Schloss das
schmecken
Schmerzen die
schmutzig
Schnee der
schnell
Schokolade die
schon
schön
schrecklich
schreiben
Schuh der
Schule die
schwach
schwarz
Schweinefleisch das
Schweiz die
schweizerisch
schwer
Schwester die
schwierig
Schwimmbad das
See der
See die
sehen
sehr
sein
seit
Selbstbedienung die
selten
Serie die
Sessel der
sich setzen
sicher
singen
Sitz der
Ski fahren
so
Socke die
sofort
Sohn der
sollen
Sommer der
Sonne die
Sonntag
Spaß
spät
Speisekarte die
Spiel das
sportlich
Sprache die
sprechen
Stadt die
Stadtplan der
stark
stehen
steigen
Stelle die
sterben
Stimme die
Strand der
Straße die
Straßenbahn die
streng
Stück das
Student der
Stuhl der

Stunde die
Sturm der
suchen
Süden der
Suppe die
süß

T
Tafel die
Tag der
täglich
Tankstelle die
Tanz der
Tasche die
Tasse die
Tee der
Telefon das
Teller der
teuer
Tier das
Tisch der
Tochter die
toll
Torte die
Tourist der
tragen
treffen
Treppe die
trinken
trocken
tun
Tür die
Tüte die

U
U-Bahn die
über
Uhr die
um
umsteigen
und
ungefähr
unmöglich
unter
Unterkunft die
Unterschied der
Urlaub der

V
Vater der
sich verabschieden
verboten
verbringen
verdienen
Verein der
vergessen
vergleichen
verkaufen
Verkehr der
verlassen
verlieren
verschieden
verstehen
Verzeihung die
viel
vielleicht
Vogel der
voll
von
vor

Vormittag der
Vorname der
Vorsicht
vorziehen

W
Wagen der
wählen
während
wahrscheinlich
Wand die
wandern
wann
warm
warum
was
Wasser das
wechseln
Wecker der
wegen
weil
Wein der
weiß
weit
welcher
Welt die
wenig
wenn
wer
werden
wert
Westen der
Wetter das
wichtig
wie
wieder
willkommen
Winter der
wirklich
wissen
wo
Woche die
wohnen
Wohnung die
wollen
Wort das
wunderbar
Wurst die

Z
zahlen
Zahn der
zeigen
Zeit die
Zeitung die
Zentrum das
ziehen
Zigarette die
Zimmer das
zu
Zucker der
Zug der
zurückgehen
zurückkommen
zweite
zwischen

Phrasefinder

Contents

Key phrases	Nützliche Redewendungen
yes, please	ja bitte
no, thank you	nein danke
sorry!	Entschuldigung!
you're welcome	nichts zu danken
I don't understand	ich verstehe das nicht
Meeting people	**Wir lernen uns kennen**
hello/goodbye	hallo!/auf Wiedersehen!
how are you?	wie geht es Ihnen?/wie geht's?
fine, thank you	danke, gut
see you later!	bis nachher!
Asking questions	**Fragen**
do you speak English/German?	sprechen Sie/sprichst du Englisch/Deutsch?
what's your name?	wie heißen Sie?/wie heißt du?
where are you from?	woher kommen Sie?/woher kommst du?
how much is it?	wie viel kostet das?
how far is it?	wie weit ist es?
Statements about yourself	**Alles über mich**
my name is...	ich heiße...
I'm English	ich bin Engländer/Engländerin
I don't speak German/English very well	ich kann nicht gut Deutsch/Englisch sprechen
I'm here on holiday	ich bin im Urlaub hier
I live near Manchester/Hamburg	ich wohne in der Nähe von Manchester/Hamburg
Emergencies	**Im Notfall**
can you help me, please?	können Sie mir bitte helfen?
I'm lost	ich habe mich verlaufen
call an ambulance	rufen Sie einen Krankenwagen
get the police/a doctor	holen Sie die Polizei/einen Arzt
watch out!	Vorsicht!, Achtung!

❶ Going Places

Unterwegs ❶

On the road

where's the nearest garage (for repairs)/petrol station (*Amer* filling station)?

what's the best way to get there?

I've got a puncture

I'd like to hire a bike/car

where can I park around here?

there's been an accident

my car's broken down

the car won't start

Auf der Straße

wo ist die nächste Werkstatt/Tankstelle?

wie komme ich am besten dorthin?

ich habe eine Reifenpanne

ich möchte ein Rad/Auto mieten

wo kann man hier parken?

es ist ein Unfall passiert

mein Auto hat eine Panne

der Wagen springt nicht an

By rail

where can I buy a ticket?

what time is the next train to York/Berlin?

do I have to change?

can I take my bike on the train?

which platform for the train to Bath/Cologne?

the train is arriving on platform 2

there's a train to London at 10 o'clock

a single/return to Birmingham/Frankfurt, please

I'd like a cheap day return/an all-day ticket

I'd like to reserve a seat

Mit der Bahn

wo kann ich eine Fahrkarte kaufen?

wann geht der nächste Zug nach York/Berlin?

muss ich umsteigen?

kann ich mein Rad im Zug mitnehmen?

von welchem Bahnsteig fährt der Zug nach Bath/Köln ab?

der Zug fährt auf Gleis 2 ein

es gibt einen Zug nach London um zehn Uhr

einmal einfach/eine Rückfahrkarte nach Birmingham/Frankfurt, bitte

ich möchte eine Tagesrückfahrkarte/Tageskarte

ich möchte einen Platz reservieren

At the airport

when's the next flight to Paris/Rome?

what time do I have to check in?

where do I check in?

I'd like to confirm/cancel my flight

can I change my booking?

I'd like a window seat/an aisle seat

Am Flughafen

wann geht der nächste Flug nach Paris/Rom?

um wie viel Uhr muss ich einchecken?

wo checkt man ein?

ich möchte meinen Flug bestätigen/stornieren

kann ich umbuchen?

ich möchte einen Fensterplatz/Platz am Gang

Asking how to get there

could you tell me the way to the castle?

how long will it take me to walk there?

how far is it from here?

which bus do I take for the cathedral?

where does this bus go?

where do I get the bus for...?

does this bus/train go to...?

which bus goes to...?

where do I get off?

how much is the fare to the town centre (*Amer* center)?

what time is the last bus?

how do I get to the airport?

where's the nearest underground (*Amer* subway) station?

is this the turning for...?

take the first turning right

Nach dem Weg fragen

können Sie mir bitte sagen, wie ich zum Schloss komme?

wie lange braucht man zu Fuß?

wie weit ist das von hier?

mit welchem Bus komme ich zum Dom?

wohin fährt dieser Bus?

wo fährt der Bus nach... ab?

fährt dieser Bus/Zug nach...?

welcher Bus fährt nach...?

wo muss ich aussteigen?

was kostet es ins Stadtzentrum?

wann fährt der letzte Bus?

wie komme ich zum Flughafen?

wo ist die nächste U-Bahn-Station?

ist das die Abzweigung nach...?

nehmen Sie die erste Straße rechts

❷ Keeping in touch

In Verbindung bleiben ❷

On the phone

where can I buy a phone card?

do you have a mobile (*Amer* cell phone)?

what is the code for Leipzig/Sheffield?

I'd like to make a phone call

I'd like to reverse the charges (*Amer* call collect)

the line's engaged/busy

there's no answer

hello, this is Natalie

can I speak to Simon, please?

who's calling?

sorry, I must have the wrong number

just a moment, please

please hold the line

please tell him/her I called

can I leave a message for Eva?

I'll try again later

please tell her that Danielle called

can he/she ring me back?

my home number is...

my office number is...

we were cut off

Am Telefon

wo kann man Telefonkarten kaufen?

haben Sie ein Handy?

wie ist die Vorwahl von Leipzig/Sheffield?

ich möchte gern telefonieren

ich möchte ein R-Gespräch anmelden

es ist besetzt

es meldet sich niemand

hallo, hier spricht Natalie

kann ich bitte Simon sprechen?

wer ist am Apparat?

Entschuldigung, ich habe mich verwählt

einen Augenblick bitte

bleiben sie bitte am Apparat

richten Sie ihm/ihr bitte aus, dass ich angerufen habe

kann ich eine Nachricht für Eva hinterlassen?

Ich versuche es später noch einmal

sagen Sie ihr bitte, dass Danielle angerufen hat

kann er/sie mich zurückrufen?

meine Privatnummer ist...

meine Nummer im Büro ist...

wir sind unterbrochen worden

Writing

can you give me your address?

where is the nearest post office?

two one-euro stamps

I'd like a stamp for a letter to Germany/Italy

can I have stamps for two postcards to England/the USA, please?

I'd like to send a parcel/a telegram

Schreiben

können Sie mir Ihre/kannst du mir deine Adresse geben?

wo ist die nächste Post?

zwei Briefmarken zu einem Euro

ich hätte gern eine Briefmarke für einen Brief nach Deutschland/Italien

kann ich bitte Briefmarken für zwei Postkarten nach England/in die USA haben?

ich möchte ein Paket abschicken/ein Telegramm aufgeben

On line

are you on the Internet?

what's your e-mail address?

we could send it by e-mail

I'll e-mail it to you on Thursday

I've looked for it on the Internet

he found the information surfing the net

Online

hast du Zugang zum Internet?

was ist deine E-Mail-Adresse?

wir könnten es per E-Mail schicken

ich schicke es Ihnen am Donnerstag per E-Mail

ich habe es im Internet gesucht

er hat die Information beim Surfen im Internet gefunden

Meeting up

what shall we do this evening?

where shall we meet?

see you outside the cinema at 6 o'clock

do you fancy joining in?

I can't today, I'm busy

Verabredungen

was machen wir heute Abend?

wo treffen wir uns?

ich treffe dich um sechs Uhr vor dem Kino

hast du Lust mitzumachen?

ich kann heute nicht, ich habe keine Zeit

❸ Food and Drink

Essen und trinken ❸

Booking a table in a restaurant

can you recommend a good restaurant?

I'd like to reserve a table for four

I booked a table for two

Vorbestellungen

können Sie uns/mir ein gutes Restaurant empfehlen?

ich möchte einen Tisch für vier Personen bestellen

ich habe einen Tisch für zwei Personen bestellt

Ordering

could we see the menu/wine list, please?

do you have a vegetarian/children's menu?

could we have some more bread?

what would you recommend?

I'd like a white/black coffee

... an espresso
... a decaffeinated coffee
... a liqueur
could I have the bill, (*Amer*) check, please?

Wir möchten bestellen

können wir bitte die Speisekarte/Weinkarte haben?

haben Sie vegetarische Gerichte/Kinderportionen?

noch etwas Brot, bitte

was würden Sie mir/uns empfehlen?

ich möchte einen Kaffee mit Milch/einen Kaffee ohne Milch
... einen Espresso
... einen entkoffeinierten Kaffee
... einen Likör
... die Rechnung, bitte

You will hear

hätten Sie gern einen Aperitif?

haben Sie schon bestellt?

möchten Sie eine Vorspeise?

was nehmen Sie als Hauptgericht?

möchten Sie eine Nachspeise?

möchten Sie einen Kaffee?/einen Likör?

haben Sie noch einen Wunsch?

guten Appetit!

die Bedienung ist (nicht) inbegriffen

Sie hören

would you like an aperitif?

are you ready to order?

would you like a starter?

what will you have for the main course?

would you like a dessert?

would you like some coffee?/a liqueur?

anything else?

enjoy your meal!

service is (not) included

The menu

starters	**Vorspeisen**
canapés	Häppchen
hors d'oeuvres	Horsd'oeuvres, Vorspeisen
omelette	Omelett
soup	Suppe

fish	**Fisch**
bass	Barsch
cod	Kabeljau
eel	Aal
haddock	Schellfisch
hake	Seehecht
herring	Hering
monkfish	Anglerfisch
mullet	Meeräsche
mussels	Muscheln
oysters	Austern
plaice	Scholle
prawns	Garnelen
red mullet	Meerbarbe
salmon	Lachs
sardines	Sardinen

Die Speisekarte

Vorspeisen	**starters**
Häppchen	canapés
Horsd'oeuvres, Vorspeisen	hors d'oeuvres
Omelett	omelette
Suppe	soup

Fisch	**fish**
Aal	eel
Austern	oysters
Barsch	bass
Calamares	squid
Forelle	trout
Garnelen	prawns
Hering	herring
Kabeljau	cod
Krabben	shrimps
Lachs	salmon
Meeräsche	mullet
Muscheln	mussels
Sardinen	sardines
Schellfisch	haddock
Scholle	plaice

shrimps	Krabben	Seehecht	hake
sole	Seezunge	Seezunge	sole
squid	Calamares	Steinbutt	turbot
trout	Forelle	Thunfisch	tuna
tuna	Thunfisch		
turbot	Steinbutt		

meat	**Fleisch**	**Fleisch**	**meat**
chicken	Hühnchen	Ente	duck
duck	Ente	Gans	goose
goose	Gans	Hase	hare
guinea fowl	Perlhuhn	Hühnchen	chicken
hare	Hase	Kalbfleisch	veal
kidneys	Nieren	Kaninchen	rabbit
lamb	Lammfleisch	Lammfleisch	lamb
liver	Leber	Leber	liver
pork	Schweinefleisch	Nieren	kidneys
rabbit	Kaninchen	Sauerbraten	braised beef
steak	Steak	Schweinefleisch	pork
veal	Kalbfleisch	Steak	steak
wild boar	Wildschwein	Wiener Schnitzel	breaded escalope
		Wildschwein	wild boar

vegetables	**Gemüse**	**Gemüse**	**vegetables**
artichokes	Artischocken	Artischocken	artichokes
asparagus	Spargel	Aubergine	aubergine
aubergine	Aubergine	Blaukraut (*Aust.*)	red cabbage
beans	Bohnen	Blumenkohl	cauliflower
cabbage	Kohl	Bohnen	beans
carrots	Möhren, Karotten	Endivie	endive
cauliflower	Blumenkohl	Erbsen	peas
celery	Sellerie	Kartoffeln	potatoes
endive	Endivie	Kohl	cabbage
mushrooms	Pilze	Möhren, Karotten	carrots
onions	Zwiebeln	Paprikaschoten	peppers
peas	Erbsen	Pilze	mushrooms
peppers	Paprikaschoten	Rotkohl	red cabbage
potatoes	Kartoffeln	Sellerie	celeriac
red cabbage	Rotkohl, Blaukraut (*Aust.*)	Spargel	asparagus
		Zwiebeln	onions

the way it's cooked/	**wie es zubereitet wird**	**wie es zubereitet wird/**	**the way it's cooked**
boiled	gekocht	englisch gebraten	rare
fried	gebraten, in der Pfanne gebraten	gebraten, geröstet	roast
		gebraten, in der Pfanne gebraten	fried
grilled	gegrillt	gegrillt	grilled
medium	halb durchgebraten	geschmort	stewed
puréed	püriert	durch	well done
rare	englisch gebraten, schwach gebraten	halb durchgebraten	medium
roast	gebraten, geröstet	püriert	puréed

stewed	geschmort	schwach gebraten	rare
well done	durch		

desserts	**Nachspeisen**	**Nachspeisen**	**desserts**
cheese	Käse	Eis	ice cream
cheeseboard	Käseplatte	Käse	cheese
chocolate gateau	Schokoladentorte	Käseplatte	cheeseboard
fruit	Obst	Kaiserschmarren (*Aust.*)	pancake strips sprinkled with sugar and raisins
fruit tart	Obsttorte		
ice cream	Eis	Kompott	stewed fruit
pie	Obstkuchen	Kuchen	cake
		Nockerln (*Aust.*)	sweet dumplings
		rote Grütze	red-berry compote

side dishes/condiments	**Beilagen/Gewürze**	**Beilagen/Gewürze**	**side dishes/condiments**
bread	Brot	Brot	bread
butter	Butter	Brötchen	rolls
herbs	Gewürzkräuter	Butter	butter
mayonnaise	Majonäse	Essig	vinegar
mustard	Senf	Gewürze	seasoning
olive oil	Olivenöl	Gewürzkräuter	herbs
pepper	Pfeffer	Majonäse	mayonnaise
rolls	Brötchen, Semmeln (*Aust.*)	Olivenöl	olive oil
salt	Salz	Pfeffer	pepper
sauce	Soße	Salz	salt
seasoning	Gewürze	Semmeln (*Aust.*)	rolls
vinegar	Essig	Senf	mustard
		Soße	sauce

drinks	**Getränke**	**Getränke**	**drinks**
beer	Bier	alkoholfreies Getränk	soft drink
bottle	Flasche	Bier	beer
carbonated	mit Kohlensäure	Bier vom Fass	draught beer
draught beer	Bier vom Fass	Flasche	bottle
half-bottle	eine halbe Flasche	Likör	liqueur
liqueur	Likör	mit Kohlensäure	carbonated
red wine	Rotwein	ohne Kohlensäure	still
rosé	Rosé	Rosé	rosé
soft drink	alkoholfreies Getränk	Rotwein	red wine
spritzer	Schorle	Schoppenwein	wine by the glass
still	ohne Kohlensäure	Schorle	spritzer
table wine	Tafelwein	Tafelwein	table wine
white wine	Weißwein	Wein	wine
wine	Wein	Weißwein	white wine

❹ Places to stay Übernachtungsmöglichkeiten ❹

Camping

we're looking for a campsite

this is a list of local campsites

can we pitch our tent here?

can we park our caravan here?

do you have space for a caravan/tent?

are there shopping facilities?

how much is it per night?

we go on a camping holiday every year

Camping

wir suchen einen Campingplatz

in diesem Campingführer stehen alle hiesigen Campingplätze

können wir hier zelten?

können wir unseren Wohnwagen hier parken?

haben Sie Platz für einen Wohnwagen/ein Zelt?

gibt es Einkaufsmöglichkeiten?

was kostet es pro Nacht?

wir machen jedes Jahr Campingurlaub

At the hotel

I'd like a double/single room with bath

we have a reservation in the name of Milnes

I reserved two rooms

for three nights, from Friday to Sunday

how much does the room cost?

I'd like to see the room first, please

what time is breakfast?

can I leave this in the safe?

bed and breakfast

we'd like to stay another night

please call me at 7:30

are there any messages for me?

Im Hotel

ich möchte ein Doppelzimmer/Einzelzimmer mit Bad

wir haben auf den Namen Milnes reservieren lassen

ich habe zwei Zimmer reservieren lassen

für drei Nächte, von Freitag bis Sonntag

was kostet das Zimmer?

ich möchte das Zimmer erst sehen, bitte

wann gibt es Frühstück?

kann ich das im Safe lassen?

Zimmer mit Frühstück

wir möchten noch eine Nacht bleiben

bitte wecken Sie mich um 7:30

hat jemand eine Nachricht für mich hinterlassen?

Hostels

could you tell me where the youth hostel is?

what time does the hostel close?

I spent the night in a youth hostel

the hostel we're staying in is great value

I'm staying in a youth hostel

I know a really good youth hostel in Dublin

I'd like to go backpacking in Australia

Heime und Jugendherbergen

können Sie mir sagen, wo die Jugendherberge ist?

um wie viel Uhr macht das Heim zu?

ich habe in einer Jugendherberge übernachtet

unsere Herberge ist sehr preiswert

ich wohne in einer Jugendherberge

ich kenne eine sehr gute Jugendherberge in Dublin

ich würde gern in Australien mit dem Rucksack herum reisen

Rooms to let

I'm looking for a room with a reasonable rent

I'd like to rent an apartment for three weeks

where do I find out about rooms to let?

what's the weekly rent for the apartment?

I'm staying with friends at the moment

I rent an apartment on the outskirts of town

the room's fine—I'll take it

Zimmer zu vermieten

ich suche ein preiswertes Zimmer

ich möchte eine Wohnung für drei Wochen mieten

wo kann man sich nach Fremdenzimmern erkundigen?

was kostet die Wohnung pro Woche?

ich wohne zur Zeit bei Freunden

ich habe eine Wohnung am Stadtrand gemietet

das Zimmer ist gut—ich nehme es

❺ Shopping and money Einkaufen und Geld ❺

At the bank

I'd like to change some money

I want to change 100 euros into pounds

do you take Eurocheques?

what's the exchange rate today?

I prefer traveller's cheques (*Amer* traveler's checks) to cash

I'd like to transfer some money from my account

I'll get some money from the cash machine/ATM

a £50 cheque (*Amer* check)

can I cash this cheque (*Amer* check) here?

can I get some cash with my credit card?

Finding the right shop

where's the main shopping district?

is the shopping centre (*Amer* mall) far from here?

where's a good place to buy sunglasses/shoes?

where can I buy batteries/postcards?

where's the nearest pharmacy (*Amer* drugstore)?

what time do the shops open/close?

where did you get those?

I'm looking for a present for my mother

Are you being served?

how much does that cost?

can I try it on?

can you keep it for me?

could you gift-wrap it for me, please?

please wrap it up well

can I pay by credit card/cheque (*Amer* check)?

do you have this in another colour?

I'm just looking

a receipt, please

I need a bigger size

I take a size...

it doesn't suit me

Changing things

can I have a refund?

can you mend it for me?

can I speak to the manager?

it doesn't work

I'd like to change the dress

I bought this here yesterday

In der Bank

ich möchte gern Geld wechseln

ich möchte 100 Euro[s] in Pfund wechseln

nehmen Sie Euroschecks?

wie steht der Wechselkurs heute?

mir sind Reiseschecks lieber als Bargeld

ich möchte Geld von meinem Konto überweisen

ich hole mir Geld vom Automaten

ein Scheck über 50 Pfund

kann ich diesen Scheck hier einlösen?

kann ich auf meine Kreditkarte Bargeld bekommen?

Das richtige Geschäft finden

wo ist das Haupteinkaufsviertel?

ist das Einkaufszentrum weit von hier?

wo kauft man am besten Schuhe/eine Sonnenbrille?

wo kann ich Batterien/Postkarten kaufen?

wo ist die nächste Drogerie?

um wie viel Uhr machen die Läden auf/zu?

wo hast du die her?

ich suche ein Geschenk für meine Mutter

Werden Sie schon bedient?

was kostet das?

kann ich es anprobieren?

können Sie es mir zurücklegen?

können Sie es bitte als Geschenk einpacken?

verpacken Sie es bitte gut

kann ich mit Kreditkarte/Scheck zahlen?

haben Sie das in einer anderen Farbe?

ich sehe mich nur um

eine Quittung bitte

ich brauche die nächste Größe

ich habe Größe...

das steht mir nicht

Umtauschen

kann ich mein Geld zurückbekommen?

können Sie es mir reparieren?

kann ich den Geschäftsführer/die Geschäftsführerin sprechen?

es funktioniert nicht

ich möchte das Kleid umtauschen

ich habe das gestern hier gekauft

⑥ Sport and leisure

Freizeit und Sport ⑥

Keeping fit

where can we play football/squash?

is there a local sports centre (*Amer* center)?

what's the charge per day?

is there a reduction for children/a student discount?

where can we go swimming/play tennis?

do you have to be a member?

I play tennis on Mondays

I would like to go fishing/riding

I want to do aerobics

I love swimming/playing baseball

we want to hire skis/snowboards

Wir halten uns fit

wo kann man Fußball/Squash spielen?

gibt es hier ein Sportzentrum?

was kostet das pro Tag?

gibt es eine Ermäßigung für Kinder/Studenten?

wo kann man schwimmen gehen/Tennis spielen?

muss man Mitglied sein?

ich spiele jeden Montag Tennis

ich würde gern angeln gehen/reiten

ich möchte Aerobic machen

ich schwimme gern/spiele gern Baseball

wir möchten Skier/Snowboards mieten

Watching sport

is there a football match on Saturday?

who's playing?

which teams are playing?

where can I get tickets?

can you get me a ticket?

I'd like to see a rugby/football match

my favourite (*Amer* favorite) team is Bayern

let's watch the match on TV

Zuschauen

gibt es am Samstag ein Fußballspiel?

wer spielt?

welche Mannschaften spielen?

wo kann man Karten bekommen?

kannst du mir eine Karte besorgen?

ich würde gern ein Rugbyspiel/Fußballspiel sehen

ich bin ein Bayern-Fan

sehen wir uns das Spiel im Fernsehen an

Going to the cinema/theatre/club

what's on at the cinema/at the movies?

what's on at the theatre?

how long is the performance?

when does the box office open/close?

what time does the performance start?

when does the film/movie finish?

are there any tickets left?

how much are the tickets?

where can I get a programme (*Amer* program)?

I want to book tickets for tonight

I'd rather have seats in the stalls

we'd like to go to a club

I go clubbing every weekend

Wir gehen ins Kino/Theater/in einen Club

was läuft im Kino?

was wird im Theater gespielt?

wie lange dauert die Vorstellung?

wann macht die Kasse auf/zu?

um wie viel Uhr fängt die Aufführung an?

wann ist der Film zu Ende?

gibt es noch Karten?

was kosten die Karten?

wo kann man ein Programm kaufen?

ich möchte für heute Abend Karten bestellen

Plätze im Parkett wären mir lieber

wir wollen in einen Club gehen

ich gehe am Wochenende immer in Clubs

Hobbies

do you have any hobbies?

what do you do at the weekend?

I like yoga/listening to music

I spend a lot of time surfing the Net

I read a lot

I collect comics

Hobbys

hast du irgendwelche Hobbys?

was macht ihr am Wochenende?

ich mache gern Yoga/höre gern Musik

ich surfe viel im Internet

ich lese viel

ich sammle Comichefte/Comics

❼ Weights & measures   Maße und Gewichte ❼

Length/Längenmaße

inches/Zoll	0.39	3.9	7.8	11.7	15.6	19.7	39
cm/Zentimeter	1	10	20	30	40	50	100

Distance/Entfernungen

miles/Meilen	0.62	6.2	12.4	18.6	24.9	31	62
km/Kilometer	1	10	20	30	40	50	100

Weight/Gewichte

pounds/Pfund	2.2	22	44	66	88	110	220
kg/Kilogramm	1	10	20	30	40	50	100

Capacity/Hohlmaße

gallons/Gallonen	0.22	2.2	4.4	6.6	8.8	11	22
litres/Liter	1	10	20	30	40	50	100

Temperature/Temperatur

°C	0	5	10	15	20	25	30	37	38	40
°F	32	41	50	59	68	77	86	98.4	100	104

Clothing and shoe sizes/Kleider- und Schuhgrößen

Women's clothing sizes/Damengrößen

UK	8	10	12	14	16	18
US	6	8	10	12	14	16
Continent	36	38	40	42	44	46

Men's clothing sizes/Herrengrößen

UK/US	36	38	40	42	44	46
Continent	46	48	50	52	54	56

Men's and women's shoes/Schuhgrößen

UK women	4	5	6	7	7.5	8			
UK men				6	7	8	9	10	11
US		6.5	7.5	8.5	9.5	10.5	11.5	12.5	13.5	14.5
Continent	37	38	39	40	41	42	43	44	45

❽ Street signs and information notices

Abfahrt	departure(s)
Achtung	caution, danger; (*announcement*) attention please
Ankunft	arrival(s)
Aufzug	lift
Ausfahrt	exit (motorway)

Ausgang	exit
Auskunft	information
Bahnsteig	platform
besetzt	engaged
bitte eintreten	please enter
Damen	ladies
drücken	push
Erdgeschoss	ground floor
Fahrkarten	tickets

frei	vacant; free
Gefahr	danger
geöffnet	open
geschlossen	closed
Gleis	platform
heiß	hot
kalt	cold
kein Zutritt	no admittance

nicht berühren	do not touch
Notausgang	emergency exit
Öffnungszeiten	opening hours
Rauchen verboten	no smoking
verboten	forbidden
Vorsicht!	caution
ziehen	pull
Zimmer frei	vacancies, rooms

Dates for your diary

January
⟨1⟩ 8 15 22 29
2 9 16 23 30
3 10 17 24 31
4 11 18 25
5 12 19 26
⟨6⟩ 13 20 27
7 14 21 28

February
1 8 15 22
⟨2⟩ 9 16 23
3 10 17 24
4 11 18 25
5 12 19 26
6 13 20 27
7 14 21 28

March
1 8 15 22 29
2 9 16 23 30
3 10 17 24 31
4 11 18 25
5 12 19 26
6 13 20 27
7 14 21 28

April
⟨1⟩ 8 15 22 29
2 9 16 23 30
3 10 17 24
4 11 18 25
5 12 19 26
6 13 20 27
7 14 21 28

May
⟨1⟩ 8 15 22 29
2 9 16 23 30
3 10 17 24 31
4 11 18 25
5 12 19 26
6 13 20 27
7 14 21 28

June
1 8 15 22 29
2 9 16 23 30
3 10 17 24
4 11 18 25
5 12 19 26
6 13 20 27
7 14 21 28

July
1 8 15 22 29
2 9 16 23 30
3 10 17 24 31
4 11 18 25
5 12 19 26
6 13 20 27
7 14 21 28

August
1 8 15 22 29
2 9 16 23 30
3 10 17 24 31
4 11 18 25
5 12 19 26
6 13 20 27
7 14 21 28

September
1 8 15 22 29
2 9 16 23 30
3 10 17 24
4 11 18 25
5 12 19 26
6 13 20 27
7 14 21 28

October
1 8 15 22 29
2 9 16 23 30
⟨3⟩ 10 17 24 ⟨31⟩
4 11 18 25
5 12 19 ⟨26⟩
6 13 20 27
7 14 21 28

November
⟨1⟩ 8 15 22 29
⟨2⟩ 9 16 23 30
3 10 17 24
4 ⟨11⟩ 18 25
5 12 19 26
6 13 20 27
7 14 21 28

December
1 8 15 22 29
2 9 16 23 30
3 10 17 ⟨24⟩ ⟨31⟩
4 11 18 ⟨25⟩
5 12 19 ⟨26⟩
⟨6⟩ 13 20 27
7 14 21 28

◇ Celebrated in German-speaking countries / In deutschsprachigen Ländern begangene Tage

1 January Neujahr New Year's Day is always a public holiday and tends to be a quiet day when people are recovering from the *Silvester* celebrations.

6 January Heilige Drei Könige Epiphany or Twelfth Night is a public holiday in Austria and some parts of southern Germany. In some areas, children dressed up as the Three Kings go from house to house to bless the homes for the coming year and collect money for charity. This is also traditionally the day when the Christmas tree is taken down.

2 February Mariä Lichtmess Candlemas is celebrated in the Catholic church but is not a public holiday.

1 April Erster April April Fool's Day is the time to make an April fool of your family and friends (*jdn. in den April schicken*) or to play an April fool trick (*Aprilscherz*).

1 May Erster Mai May Day is a public holiday in Germany, Austria and Switzerland. It is celebrated by trade unions as *Labour Day*, often with rallies and demonstrations. Many people simply use the day for a family outing or picnic, and in rural areas maypoles are put up in the villages.

3 October Tag der deutschen Einheit Germany's national holiday, the *Day of German Unity* commemorates German reunification on 3 October 1990.

26 October Nationalfeiertag Austria's national holiday.

31 October Reformationstag Reformation Day is a public holiday in some mainly Protestant parts of Germany and commemorates the Reformation.

1 November Allerheiligen All Saints' Day is a public holiday in Catholic parts of Germany and Austria.

2 November Allerseelen All Souls' Day is the day when Catholics remember their dead by visiting the cemeteries to pray and place wreaths, flowers and lighted candles on the graves. This is often done on 1 November as *Allerseelen* is not a public holiday.

11 November Martinstag St Martin's day is not a public holiday, but in Catholic areas the charitable Saint is commemorated with processions where children carry lanterns and sing songs. Traditional food includes the *Martinsgans* (roast goose) and *Martinsbrezel* (a kind of soft pretzel).

6 December Nikolaustag On the eve of St. Nicholas' Day, children put out their boots in the hope of finding presents and fruit, nuts and sweets in the morning. The Saint may also turn up in person, looking much like Santa Claus or Father Christmas.

24 December Heiligabend Christmas Eve is not a public holiday but many firms and shops close early for the Christmas period. This is the day when traditionally the Christmas tree is put up and decorated. Christmas presents are given in the evening, and many people attend midnight mass.

25 December Erster Weihnachtstag Christmas Day is a public holiday in Germany, Austria and Switzerland. It tends to be a quiet day for family get-togethers, often with a traditional lunch of goose or carp.

26 December Zweiter Weihnachtstag Boxing Day is a public holiday in Germany, Austria and Switzerland. In Austria and Switzerland it is called *Stephanstag* (St Stephen's day).

31 December Silvester New Year's Eve is not a bank holiday, but firms and shops tend to close early.

New Year's Eve New Year's Eve is usually celebrated with parties, champagne and fireworks. "Bleigießen" is also popular, that is melting leaden figures on a spoon, then tossing the liquid into a bowl of cold water and trying to interpret what the figure that is then created means for the new year. If you are speaking to someone before midnight wish them "einen guten Rutsch" (literally: a good slide). At midnight Germans toast each other saying "Prost Neujahr" (cheers New Year). At midnight, the new year is toasted in Sekt (German sparkling wine), and everybody goes outside to admire the fireworks.

Movable feasts and holidays

Rosenmontag The day before Shrove Tuesday is not an official public holiday but many people, especially in the Rhineland, get the day off work or school to take part in the *Karneval* celebrations, which involve masked balls, fancy-dress parties and parades. The street parades in Düsseldorf, Cologne, Mainz and other cities are attended by thousands of revellers and shown live on television.

Faschingsdienstag Shrove Tuesday is the final day of *Fasching* (Carnival) in Southern Germany, with processions and fancy dress parties similar to Rosenmontag in the

Northwest. In the far south, ancient customs to drive out the winter with bells and drums survive. The pre-Lent carnival in and around the Rhineland is called Karneval. Almost every town has its own carnival prince and princess, and organizes a street parade with decorated floats, which is watched by thousands of revellers in fancy dress.

Aschermittwoch Ash Wednesday marks the end of the carnival season and the beginning of Lent. This day is celebrated in the Catholic church but is not a public holiday.

Karfreitag Good Friday is a public holiday and generally a very quiet day. Catholics traditionally eat fish on this day.

Ostern Easter traditions include hiding Easter eggs (often dyed hardboiled eggs, or the chocolate variety) in the garden for the children. The *Osterhase* (Easter bunny) is supposed to have brought them. Ostermontag (Easter Monday) is also a public holiday.

Weißer Sonntag (Sunday after Easter) In the Catholic Church, first communion is traditionally taken on this Sunday.

Muttertag (second Sunday in May) On Mothers' day, children of all ages give their mothers small gifts, cards or flowers.

Christi Himmelfahrt (40 days after Easter) Ascension day is a public holiday in Germany, Austria and Switzerland. This day is also Fathers' day when fathers traditionally go out on daytrips or pub crawls.

Pfingsten (seventh Sunday after Easter) As *Pfingstmontag* (Whit Monday) is also a public holiday in Germany, Austria and Switzerland, Whitsun is a popular time to have a long weekend away.

Fronleichnam (second Thursday after Whitsun) Corpus Christi is a public holiday in Austria and in parts of Germany and Switzerland. In Catholic areas, processions and open-air masses are held.

Buß- und Bettag (third Wednesday in November, 11 days before the first Advent Sunday) This 'day of repentance and prayer' is a public holiday only in some parts of Germany.

Volkstrauertag (second Sunday before the beginning of Advent) In Germany, this is a national day of mourning to commemorate the dead of both world wars, and the victims of the Nazis.

Totensonntag (last Sunday before the beginning of Advent) Protestants remember their dead on this day.

Advent The four weeks leading up to Christmas, beginning with the 1. Adventssonntag (first Sunday in Advent) in late November or early December, still have a special significance in Germany, even for non-religious people. An Advent wreath with four candles is present in almost every German household during this time, and on each Sunday of Advent one more candle is lit.

Quick reference guide to life and culture

Arbeitsagentur The local employment office to be found in every German town (formerly called *Arbeitsamt*). It provides career guidance, helps the unemployed find new jobs, and processes all claims for benefits.

Archiv der Jugendkulturen Since 1998 the Archive of Youth Culture in Berlin has been collecting and cataloguing books, magazines, CDs, and other materials of special interest to young people.

AStA — Allgemeiner Studentenausschuss A students' union which consists of twelve student boards elected by a student parliament that is voted in annually. AStA deals with all student issues, including financial, cultural, and social concerns, offering advice and support.

Bachfest This ten-day music festival is held annually in honour of the great German composer Johann Sebastian Bach (1685–1750), and takes place in Leipzig, where Bach spent many years of his life.

Bauhaus A school of architecture and the applied arts founded in 1919 in Weimar and later housed at Dessau. Under the leadership of Walter Gropius (1883–1969) and Ludwig Mies van der Rohe (1886–1969), it became the centre of modern design in the 1920s.

Bayreuth The Franconian city of Bayreuth in Bavaria is a magnet for opera fans. The German composer Richard Wagner (1813–83) lived there from 1872. Since 1876 the Richard Wagner Festival has been staged annually in the Festspielhaus.

Berlin After WIEDERVEREINIGUNG, Berlin became the capital of Germany. This vibrant city has about 3.5 million inhabitants and is a major cultural and commercial centre.

Besenwirtschaft An inn set up temporarily by a local winegrower for a few weeks after the new wine has been made. They are mainly found in southern Germany.

Betriebsrat The staff in any German company with at least five employees are entitled to have a *Betriebsrat*. This is a committee elected by the workers to represent their interests, as opposed to those of management.

Bier Germany and Austria rank among the world's top beer producers and consumers, with a vast range of beer varieties (Bock, Alt, Dunkel, Export, Hell, Kölsch, Lager, Malzbier, Pils, Märzen, Weizenbier or Weißbier, and Berliner Weiße) to choose from. Germans brew more than 5,000 varieties, and each beer tastes different depending on the ratio of ingredients, brewing temperature and technique, alcoholic content, ageing time, and colour.

Blauer Engel The Blue Angel label on goods for sale shows consumers that the product is environmentally friendly.

Bodensee This is the German name for Lake Constance, Germany's biggest lake, bordered by Germany, Switzerland, and Austria.

Brandenburger Tor Once a symbol of divided Berlin, the Brandenburg Gate triumphal arch has become a symbol of reunited Germany. It is the entrance to the boulevard Unter den Linden.

Bund This term refers to the federal state as the top level of government, as opposed to the individual LÄNDER which make up the BUNDESREPUBLIK.

Bundesbank Properly called the Deutsche Bundesbank, Germany's central bank is an autonomous non-governmental institution located in Frankfurt am Main.

Bundeskanzler The chancellor is the head of government in Germany and Austria. The German chancellor is normally elected for four years by the ministers in the *Bundestag* after being proposed by the *Bundespräsident*. The *Bundeskanzler* chooses the ministers and decides on government policies.

Bundesliga The German national soccer league is split into two divisions of eighteen teams: *Bundesliga* and *2nd Bundesliga*.

Bundesrepublik Deutschland, or Bundesrepublik for short, is the official name of the German state (the Federal Republic of Germany, or FRG). Established on 23 May 1949, the republic became fully independent from British, French, and US control in May 1955. In October 1990 the Federal Republic merged with the DDR to form a single, unified Germany.

Bundeswappen The federal coat of arms is the eagle. This heraldic bird – emblem of the Roman emperors – was adopted by Charlemagne and became the coat of arms of the German Empire when it was founded in 1871.

Bundeswehr This is the name for the Federal Armed Forces, which come under the control of the defence minister. The *Bundeswehr* consists of professional soldiers and conscripts on national service.

CDU – Christlich-Demokratische Union One of the main German political parties, it was founded in 1945 and is committed to Christian and conservative values.

CSU – Christlich-Soziale Union The Bavarian sister party of the CDU was founded in 1946 and has enjoyed an absolute majority in Bavaria for over 30 years. It now forms part of the governing Grand Coalition in Germany.

DAAD – Deutscher Akademischer Austauschdienst The German Academic Exchange Service is a joint organization of universities and other institutions of higher education for the promotion of academic exchanges in Germany and abroad.

DBJR – Deutscher Bundesjugendring The German Federal Youth Association, based in Berlin, is made up of twenty-four national youth organizations and sixteen regional youth councils. The Bundesjugendring aims to represent young people in their everyday lives.

DDR – German Democratic Republic The communist state, established in the Soviet-occupied zone of Germany after the Second World War. It lasted from 1949 to 1990.

Deutscher Kulturrat The German Arts Council was founded in 1982 as a non-governmental commission representing cultural associations and institutions. The function of the Kulturrat is to coordinate, advise, and inform on cultural matters, make recommendations on cultural policy, and further international cultural relations.

Deutsche Welle Aimed at listeners abroad, this radio station is controlled by the government and broadcasts programmes on German politics, business, arts, and culture.

Deutschlandlied This has been the German national anthem since 1922. The song, entitled *Lied der Deutschen*, was written by Hoffmann von Fallersleben in 1841 and set to music by Joseph Haydn (1732–1809).

Diplomprüfung Final (degree) examination at a university or equivalent higher education institution in a technical or scientific subject.

Eigenheim Germany and Switzerland have the lowest levels of home ownership in Europe, while Austria has the highest. In Germany, many people live in rented flats or houses, but most dream of buying or building their *Eigenheim* (own home) one day. First-time buyers are usually middle-aged and expect to stay in their home for the rest of their lives.

Einwohnermeldeamt (residents' registration office) Anybody who moves to Germany or relocates within Germany is legally obliged to register their address with the *Einwohnermeldeamt* within a week.

Elternzeit A German mother or father who looks after a child at home is entitled to up to three years' extended maternity or paternity leave. At the end of this *Elternzeit* they are entitled to return to their old job. Around 95 per cent of German mothers take time out of work for at least a year after the birth.

Entwerter In many German cities, *Entwerter* (ticket-cancelling machines) are located on U-Bahn and S-Bahn platforms, or on trains, trams, or buses. When travelling on public transport in Germany, cancel (*entwerten*) the ticket in one of the machines.

Fasching, Fastnachtszeit This is the carnival season, which begins in November and ends on Aschermittwoch for Lent. Depending on the region it is called *Karneval*, *Fastnacht*, *Fasnet*, or *Fasching*, and is celebrated in Germany, Austria, and Switzerland.

FDP – Freie Demokratische Partei The German Liberal party, founded in 1948. This relatively small party supports a free-market economy and the freedom of the individual.

Flohmarkt There is a *Flohmarkt* (flea market) on Sundays in most big cities.

Frankfurter Allgemeine Zeitung (FAZ) One of Germany's most serious and widely respected daily newspapers. It tends to have a centre-left to liberal outlook.

Frankfurter Buchmesse is the most important annual publishing trade fair in the world. Leipzig also stages an important annual book fair.

Gastarbeiter The term used for workers from foreign countries, who came to Germany in the 1960s and 1970s. Despite the fact that they have lived in Germany and the fact that their children have grown up there, the issue of integration is still widely discussed.

Gemeinde The lowest level of local government, run by a local council chaired by the *Bürgermeister* (mayor).

Goethe-Institut An organization promoting German language and culture abroad. It is based in Munich and runs about

140 branches offering German language classes, cultural events and a library.

Grundgesetz The written German constitution which came into force in May 1949. It lays down the basic rights of German citizens, the relationship between BUND and LÄNDER, and the legal framework of the German state.

Grüner Punkt A symbol used to mark packaging materials that can be recycled. Any packaging carrying this logo is collected separately under the Duales System recycling scheme.

Hansestadt Hansestädte (Hanseatic cities), such as Bremen and Hamburg, were once part of an association of trading cities along the North Sea and Baltic coasts. The Hanse (Hanseatic League) remained a powerful force until the late sixteenth century, after which it declined.

Hausordnung These 'house rules' are what a tenant has to adhere to in order to maintain a harmonious relationship with neighbours. They might cover the maintenance of common areas and the appearance of the house or apartment block; for example, forbidding a tenant from hanging washing from a front window. But usually the *Hausordnung*, whether written or unwritten, refer to restrictions on noise, possibly even including running a late-night bath.

Heurige This is an Austrian term for both a new wine and an inn with new wine on tap, especially an inn with its own vineyard in the environs of Vienna. On warm, late summer evenings Viennese wine devotees sit on wooden benches and sample the new wine of the year.

Hochdeutsch There are many regional variations and dialects in Germany, Austria, and Switzerland. Hochdeutsch is the standard German that can be understood by all German speakers. Newspapers and other publications are generally printed in Hochdeutsch, which is regarded as 'proper' German.

Hochschule Anybody who has passed the *Abitur* is entitled to go to university (except for some subjects which have a restriction on numbers, or NUMERUS CLAUSUS). They tend to be very large and impersonal institutions. Students may receive a *Bafög* grant and often take more than the minimum eight semesters (four years) to complete their course.

Hochzeit Church weddings are not legally recognized in Germany, Austria, or Switzerland, and all couples must be married in a civil ceremony. The civil ceremony is held in a *Standesamt* (registry office, called a *Zivilstandsamt* in Switzerland). The civil marriage tends to be a private family affair; if the couple also has a church ceremony afterwards, that is usually a more public event. The bachelor party is known as *Junggesellenabschied*, and there is often also an informal party held before the wedding known as *Polterabend*. Since 2001, same-sex couples have been able to register a civil union called a *Lebenspartnerschaft*.

Kfz-Kennzeichen This is the number plate on German motor vehicles, which have to be licensed by the *Zulassungsstelle* (vehicle registration office) for the owner's registered place of residence. The first letter, or first two or three letters, on the *Kfz-Kennzeichen* indicate where the car comes from.

Kinder- und Hausmärchen Jakob Grimm (1785–1863) and his brother Wilhelm (1786–1859) collected fairy tales for their book of *Kinder- und Hausmärchen* (Household and Nursery Tales).

Kirchensteuer Any taxpayer who is a member of one of the established churches in Germany (mainly Catholic and Protestant) has to pay *Kirchensteuer* (church tax). It is calculated as a proportion of income tax and is collected at source by the tax office, which then passes on the money to the relevant church.

Kriminalpolizei – Kripo The criminal investigation department deals with serious offences, including murder, terrorism, and organized crime.

Kulturstadt Weimar This thousand-year-old city has played an important role in Germany's cultural history. The composer Johann Sebastian Bach (1685–1750) and the artist Lucas Cranach (1472–1553) lived and worked here. Other important writers and poets such as Johann Wolfgang von Goethe (1749–1832), Johann Gottfried von Herder (1744–1803) and Christoph Martin Wieland (1733–1813) made the city their home. Friedrich von Schiller (1759–1805) wrote many of his plays in Weimar, while the composer Franz Liszt (1811–86) composed and gave concerts here. In 1919 the Bauhaus was founded in Weimar; in the same year, the constitution of the Weimar Republic – was drafted in the city.

Ladenschlusszeit Shops are allowed to stay open until 8 p.m. on weekdays and 4 p.m. on Saturdays, and bakeries may open for three hours on Sundays.

Länder Germany is a federal republic consisting of sixteen member states called *Länder* or *Bundesländer*. Austria is a federal state consisting of nine *Länder*. The Swiss equivalent of a German or Austrian *Land* is a *Kanton*.

Loveparade A techno music and dance festival which takes place in Berlin every summer, with hundreds of thousands of mainly young people attending.

Markt Weekly markets are still held in most German cities and towns, usually laid out very attractively in the picturesque market squares. Many Germans still buy most of their provisions '*auf dem Markt*'.

Mauer *Die Mauer*, or the Berlin Wall, a 42-km (26-mile) structure of concrete blocks, was built overnight in 1961. It was designed to halt the exodus of inhabitants from the Communist-controlled East of the city to the West and lasted until 1989. A few sections remain as a memorial and tourist attraction.

Meldepflicht An 'obligation to register' that applies to all German residents, regardless of nationality. Residents must inform the EINWOHNERMELDEAMT every time they change their address. The system means that every resident can quickly be traced.

Numerus clausus The *Numerus clausus* system is used to limit the number of students studying certain oversubscribed subjects such as medicine at German universities.

Oktoberfest Germany's most famous beer festival (the Munich October Festival) actually starts each year in September. Over 5 million litres of beer are drunk over a period of sixteen days. The first *Oktoberfest* was in 1810.

Ossi A colloquial and sometimes derogatory term for someone from the former East Germany (DDR), as opposed to a WESSI (someone from the former West Germany).

Personalausweis The standard German identity card, with the holder's photograph and particulars, should in theory be carried at all times. If you are stopped by the police without any ID, you might be taken to a police station and kept there for up to six hours.

Pinakothek der Moderne This gallery of modern art, design, graphics, and architecture opened in Munich in 2002. Its collections concentrate on 20th- and 21st-century art, complementing the nearby Neue Pinakothek (exhibiting 19th-century art) and Alte Pinakothek (14th–18th century art).

Prater Vienna's largest and most popular amusement park. The Prater has old-fashioned swings, skittle alleys, and merry-go-rounds. A *Riesenrad* (big wheel) with a diameter of 67 m (200 ft) is a famous Viennese landmark.

Rechtschreibreform After much controversy, a reform aiming to simplify the rules governing German spelling was implemented in 1998. The new spellings are still controversial and are only binding for schools and public authorities.

Reichstag This historic building in the centre of Berlin became the seat of the *Bundestag* in 1999.

Religion In Germany, the Christian community is divided almost equally between Roman Catholics (26.6 million people) and Protestants (mostly Lutheran, 26.3 million). There are also more than 3 million Muslims. Eighty-eight per cent of Austrians are Catholic, while in Switzerland there are slightly more Catholics than Protestants, with Muslims making up just over 4 per cent of the population.

Ruhezeit This is the accepted 'quiet time', usually between one and three o'clock in the afternoon, late evening, and on Sundays. *Ruhezeit* prohibits loud music and any noisy work, including drilling and vacuuming. However, many young Germans no longer adhere to the letter of the *Ruhezeit*.

Salzburger Festspiele Since 1920, this annual festival has been held in Salzburg, the home of Wolfgang Amadeus Mozart (1756–91).

Schule German children have to attend school from the ages of 6 to 18. Full-time schooling is compulsory for nine or ten years, until pupils are at least 15. All children go to a *Grundschule* for four years (six in Berlin) and move on to a *Hauptschule*, *Realschule*, *Gymnasium*, or *Gesamtschule*, depending on their ability. From the age of 15, some pupils attend a *Berufsschule*, a part-time vocational school.

Schwarzwald The Black Forest, a mountainous area in Baden Württemberg in southwestern Germany, is a popular holiday destination for Germans and foreign tourists alike. The name refers to the large coniferous forests in the region.

Schweizerische Eidgenossenschaft The Swiss Confederation is the official name for Switzerland. The confederation was established in 1291 and today comprises twenty-six self-governing cantons.

siezen/duzen German has two forms for 'you', the formal *Sie* and the familiar *du*. *Du* is used when speaking to a friend, a child, or a family member. Young people always address each other as *du*. When speaking to a person you do not know very well, the polite form *Sie* is used, especially in work situations and when you would use Mrs or Mr in English.

SPD — Sozialdemokratische Partei Deutschlands One of the main German political parties. Reformed after the war in 1945, it is a workers' party supporting social-democratic values.

Stammtisch A large table reserved for regulars in most German pubs. The word is also used to refer to the group of people who meet around the table for a drink and lively discussion.

Straußwirtschaft An inn set up temporarily by a local winegrower for a few weeks after the new wine has been made.

Verein There are over 300,000 officially registered *Vereine* (clubs or associations) with their own constitution and by-laws. Millions of Germans belong to a club; nearly one in four is a member of a sports club, and there are around 15 million hiking-club members. Membership fees are usually low, and everybody is encouraged to socialize at club level.

Weihnachtsmarkt During the weeks of Advent, Christmas markets take place in most German towns, selling Christmas decorations, handmade toys and crib figures, traditional Christmas biscuits, and mulled wine to sustain the shoppers.

Social survival tips

Talking to people

Addressing people, saying 'you' If you make someone's acquaintance or talk to a bank or shop assistant make sure that you always use the polite form "Sie". Once you get to know someone better then he or she might offer you to change to the familiar "du". It's best to let the German person suggest this first. If you are a teenager or student and are talking to others of your own age group then it is quite safe to use "du" from the start.

It is not that common for Germans to call each other by their Christian names, the exceptions being among friends or teachers to schoolchildren. You'll also find that work colleagues in more traditional environment won't use Christian names. It is safer to stick to Herr or Frau until you become friends or get to know each other better.

How are you? If you ask a German how he or she is they will take it much more literally than just a polite greeting. They may go into detail and mistake your empty question for genuine interest. So if you are short of time just stick to a greeting like "Guten Tag" (literally: 'good day') or "Hallo".

Shaking hands If you visit a German in their home, or if you meet someone you know on the street, they will automatically stretch out their hand to shake yours. They will find it awkward or rude if you do not do the same.

Going out

Invitations If you are invited to someone's house for a meal take flowers, chocolates, or a bottle of wine. If you take flowers, remember to unwrap them first.

Tipping Tipping works differently in Germany. A tip of ten to fifteen percent is normally already included in the bill. You should however round a bill up by a euro or so if you were pleased with the service you received.

Mealtimes

Meals The main mealtime in a German home is lunchtime. In the evening Germans usually have 'Abendessen', which usually consists of bread with cold meat or cheese, gherkins and tomatoes.

Abendbrot, Abendessen For most Germans, *Mittagessen* is still the main meal of the day. *Abendbrot* or *Abendessen* normally consists of bread, cheese, meats, perhaps a salad, and a hot drink. It is eaten by the whole family at about 6 or 7 p.m. *Abendessen* can also refer to a cooked meal, especially for people who are out at work all day.

Frühstück Breakfast in Germany typically consists of strong coffee, slices of bread or fresh rolls with butter, jam, honey, sliced cheese and meat, and maybe a boiled egg. For working people and schoolchildren, who have little time for breakfast first thing in the morning, a *zweites Frühstück* is common at around 10 a.m.

Kaffee This refers not only to coffee as a drink but also to the small meal taken at about four in the afternoon, consisting of coffee and cakes or biscuits. It is often a social occasion, as it is common to invite family or friends for *Kaffee und Kuchen* (rather than for tea or dinner), especially on birthdays and other family occasions.

Mittagessen This is a cooked meal eaten in the middle of the day and is the main meal of the day for most Germans. Schoolchildren come home from school in time for *Mittagessen*, and most large companies have canteens where hot meals are served at lunchtime. On a Sunday, *Mittagessen* might consist of a starter such as clear broth, followed by a roast with gravy, boiled potatoes and vegetables, and a dessert.

Schnellimbiss Usually a *Schnellimbiss* is just a stand, selling different kinds of *Würstchen* (sausages), rissoles, *Döner* (doner kebab) or *Leberkäse* (meat loaf), depending on which region you are in. You can eat there or take the snack away. *Currywurst* – sausages served with ketchup (or a tomato-based sauce) mixed with curry powder – is a *Schnellimbiss* favourite.

Wein Germany, Switzerland, and Austria are wine-producing countries, best known for their white wines. Germany's main wine regions are Franconia, the Rhineland-Palatinate, the Moselle area, and Baden-Württemberg. Rhine wine (or hock) is sold in tall brown bottles and wine from the Moselle in green bottles; Franconian Bocksbeutel comes in wide, bulbous bottles. There are two categories of German wine, the cheap *Tafelwein* (table wine) and the superior *Qualitätswein* (quality wine). The best wines are designated *Qualitätswein mit Prädikat*. Sekt is a champagne-like sparkling wine. Austria grows red and white wines, mainly in the Burgenland, in Styria, and around the Neusiedler See where the *Heurige* is celebrated. More than a third of the total area of grape cultivation in Austria is devoted to Grüner Veltliner, a full-bodied, fruity white wine. Swiss wines are mostly drunk locally and are produced in the Thurgau region.

Weinstube A cosy wine bar which offers a wide choice of wines and usually also serves a few dishes that are considered to go well with wine. A *Weinstube* can be more upmarket than an ordinary pub, or else fairly rustic, especially in wine-growing areas.

Recycling

All *Hausmüll* (domestic waste) in Germany is collected in at least three bins, and waste materials are recycled and reused. The *Biotonne* is for biodegradable kitchen waste (vegetable and fruit peel, meat, cheese, nutshells, tea leaves, and coffee filters, etc.). The *Wertstofftonne* can be used for plastic containers, metal objects, cans, aluminium, textiles, etc., and anything with a *grüner punkt* (a symbol used to mark packaging materials that can be recycled). A separate *Papiertonne* is used for paper and cardboard, although most wrapping is discarded at source or reused – German supermarkets don't hand out a free supply of plastic bags. The *Restmüll* is for sweepings and general household rubbish. Bottles and glass are taken to the *Glascontainer* (bottle bank). A deposit on drinks bottles encourages returning empties to the shop. There are also collection points for fridges, freezers, and bulky items.

Transport

Autobahn Germany's motorway network is very extensive and not subject to a general speed limit, other than a recommended limit of about 80 mph (130 km/h). But increasingly speed limits are in force on long stretches of the *Autobahn*. Many motorways have only two lanes. To ease congestion, lorries are not allowed to use the *Autobahn* on Sundays. German motorways are free for passenger traffic. Lorries over twelve tonnes pay a toll known as *Autobahngebühren*. On Austrian and Swiss motorways, all vehicles must display a *Vignette*.

BahnCard A rail pass for frequent rail travellers within Germany. *Bahncard 25/Bahncard 50/Bahncard 100* entitle the holder to 25 per cent, 50 per cent, or 100 per cent discount respectively. There are a number of other passes and saver tickets offering reductions throughout Germany, Austria, Switzerland, and neighbouring countries.

Parkscheibe In Germany, some areas only allow limited parking time; here you have to display a *Parkscheibe* (parking disc) on your windscreen, with the hands of its clock set to your arrival time. These blue cardboard or plastic discs are available at newsagents and department stores.

Schutzpolizei (Schupo) Colloquially referred to as the Schupo, the Schutzpolizei is the general police force dealing with public security, order, and traffic offences. Most people know the Schupo only as traffic police.

Tempolimit Speed limits are either compulsory – 50 km/h (30 mph) in towns, 100 km/h (60 mph) on other roads – or recommended when driving in bad weather conditions, on dangerous stretches, and in urban areas. On the *Autobahn* the *Richtgeschwindigkeit* (recommended maximum speed) is 130 km/h (80 mph). In residential areas the limit can be as low as 30 km/h (20 mph); the 30-Zone was introduced to protect children and pedestrians.

U-Bahn Most large cities have a *U-Bahn* (*Untergrundbahn*) (underground railway network) that connects with an *S-Bahn* (*Schnellbahn* or *Stadtbahn*) (city and suburban railway). The same ticket can normally be used for both services.

Vignette In order to be able to use Austrian and Swiss motorways, all vehicles must display a sticker on the windscreen called a *Vignette*. These stickers are usually valid for one year, but foreign tourists in Austria can buy stickers for a period of ten days or two months.